PEOPLE, POLITICS, AND GOVERNMENT

A CANADIAN PERSPECTIVE SEVENTH EDITION

JAMES JOHN GUY

D1328106

Pearson Canada
Toronto

This edition is dedicated to my two grandsons, Nicholas James and Thomas Matthew.

Library and Archives Canada Cataloguing in Publication

Guy, James John, 1943–
    People, politics and government : a Canadian perspective / James John Guy.—7th ed.

Includes index.
ISBN 978-0-13-206443-9

    1. Political science—Textbooks.   2. Canada—Politics and government—Textbooks.   I. Title.

JA66.G89 2010   320   C2009-901385-1

ISBN-13: 978-0-13-206443-9
ISBN-10: 0-13-206443-X

Vice-President, Editorial Director: Gary Bennett
Editor-in-Chief: Ky Pruesse
Senior Acquisitions Editor: Laura Forbes
Sponsoring Editor: Carolin Sweig
Executive Marketing Manager: Judith Allen
Associate Editor: Megan Burns
Production Editor: Claire Horsnell
Copy Editor: Anne Borden

Proofreaders: Rob Gianetto, Trish O'Reilly
Production Coordinator: Avinash Chandra
Compositor: Integra
Permissions Research: Dayle Furlong
Art Director: Julia Hall
Cover Designer: Anthony Leung
Cover Image: Getty Images

Photo Credits: page 31, Heather Hiscox, CBC News: Morning; page 136, PMO Photo by Deb Ransom; page 142, Sgt Eric Jolin, September 27, 2005, Rideau Hall. Reproduced with the permission of the Office of the Secretary to the Governor General; page 201, courtesy of Ian Bennett; page 236, ©Philippe L. Andreville, 2008; page 270, Gilles Duceppe, MP for Laurier/Sainte-Marie and Leader of the Bloc Québécois; page 313, Don Newman, CBC News: Politics. Cartoons on pages 18, 154, 238, 295, 325, 355, 370, 387, 393, 432 courtesy of Sean Leslie Casey, Cape Breton Post.

Statistics Canada information is used with the permission of Statistics Canada. Users are forbidden to copy the data and redisseminate them, in an original or modified form, for commercial purposes, without permission from Statistics Canada. Information on the availability of the wide range of data from Statistics Canada can be obtained from Statistics Canada's Regional Offices, its World Wide Web site at http://www.statcan.ca, and its toll-free access number 1-800-263-1136.

3 4 5   13 12 11 10

Printed and bound in the United States of America.

BRIEF CONTENTS

CONTENTS

2 Understanding Political Thinking 39

3 Nations, States, Rank, and Power 74

8   Law and the Courts   216

9   Understanding Constitutions   244

List of Tables

List of Figures

List of Boxes

Focus On

Perspectives

Crosscurrents

Preface

Welcome to the seventh edition of *People, Politics, and Government*. Launching yet another new edition of an established volume has been a wonderful experience for this author. Each new edition has taught me so much more about how students learn about politics and government. I know how much of a personal experience learning is: I know that this generation of students wants to use texts that allow them to apply their individual learning abilities to understand a complex, changing world. This edition was revised with this reality in mind. So I have tried to design this new text as a teaching framework that can enrich the individual learning styles of the students using it.

But the seventh edition of *People, Politics, and Government: A Canadian Perspective* is also a tribute to all the professors who have adopted it and have remained so loyal to its pedagogy over the years. Their allegiance to the text as a teaching tool, along with their helpful suggestions, has encouraged me to write this new edition. I hope readers will find it much improved for understanding our exciting world of politics and government.

Good texts provide "coloration" for material that may not always present itself as exciting and relevant. The examples I use show the relevance of political science to the everyday life of students. Among others, they include confronting issues of the environment, poverty, racism and sexual diversity. I also draw examples that help students understand politics and government from the research of other fields, such as anthropology, economics, law, philosophy and sociology. In all of this I have tried to introduce the idea that politics and government have something to do with our personal survival, our national survival, and ultimately our global survival.

To this end, I have revised every chapter, drawing on new scholarship and examples of recent events, including:

- The worldwide economic crisis (first examined in Chapter 1);

- The prorogation of Canada's Parliament in December 2008 (discussed at length in a feature on *Canada's Governor General* in Chapter 5);

- The 2008 Canadian federal election (key details to be found in Chapter 10);

- The election of the first African-American President of the United States (discussed at length in Chapter 11); and

- Developing issues such as the rise of terrorism, and the threat of climate change (both discussed in Chapter 15).

Adopters can teach their courses knowing that the materials in my text are not only current, but also that they carry the basic concepts of introductory political science. Tables and charts have been updated, new boxed presentations and factfiles are included, many chapter segments have been rewritten, and special effort has been made to clarify both the content and writing style for students.

A first course in the field of political science should be comprehensive, informative, and relevant. But above all it should be fun for the students to experience. I love what I do as a professor of political science. I want the same passion that I feel for what I do to be felt by the students who read this new edition. Students need to know that the study of politics and government is exciting and worthwhile. They should come to realize that knowledge of political science can help them in whatever profession or vocation they choose.

This text will enable students to relate personally to the role of politics in their lives. It will encourage them to compare Canadian government institutions and the politics we experience with those of other states in the global community. For this reason, the comparative nature of the text is a vital teaching and learning tool in this world of rapid change.

My goal has been to create a teaching package that is as enjoyable to teach as it is to study. As much as possible I have tried to present useful learning aids, such as

- *Crosscurrents:* These box features raise issues that are at once timely and provocative. They also provide a forum to engage students in controversial issues that are introduced in the chapter.
- *Factfiles:* These are thumbnail sketches presenting interesting and compelling facts that are related to the information presented in each chapter.
- *Perspectives:* This edition continues to include the Perspectives feature established in earlier editions. Designed to engage students and to challenge them to critically analyze what they have read, they provide varying viewpoints on the issues raised in each chapter.
- *Focus On:* These boxes are designed to draw students into the substance of the text by putting a spotlight on personalities and events of special significance to the theme of the chapter. The profiles of personalities are designed to personalize politics for students with first-hand introductions to important institutions and the people who hold jobs within these organizations, such as ambassadors, judges, lobbyists, and political scientists. These thought-provoking boxes give students anecdotal accounts of people and events in politics.

- *Chapter Summaries:* At the end of each chapter is a review of the main points presented.
- *Discussion Questions:* Thought-provoking questions at the end of each chapter are designed to stimulate class discussions and to help students review the topics introduced.

In addition, the *Chapter Objectives* and *Endnotes* (found at the end of the book) are all continued features that have been updated.

The *Weblinks, Suggested Readings*, and the *Glossary* have also been updated and can be found on the Text Enrichment Site that has been developed especially for this text.

SUPPLEMENTS

A **Text Enrichment Site** has been developed for the seventh edition of *People, Politics, and Government*, and includes resources such as weblinks, suggested readings, and a glossary. You can access the site at the following URL: **www.pearsoned.ca/text/guy**.

MyTest from Pearson Education Canada is a powerful assessment generation program that helps instructors easily create and print quizzes, tests, and exams, as well as homework or practice handouts. Questions and tests can all be authored online, allowing instructors ultimate flexibility and the ability to efficiently manage assessments at anytime, from anywhere. MyTest for *People, Politics, and Government*, seventh edition, includes multiple choice, fill-in-the-blank, and true/false questions. These questions are also available in Microsoft Word format in the online catalogue (see Test Item File below).

The following instructor supplements are available for downloading from a password-protected section of Pearson Education Canada's online catalogue (www.pearsoned.ca/highered). Navigate to your book's catalogue page to view a list of supplements that are available. See your local sales representative for details and access.

- An **Instructor's Manual** contains lecture outlines and chapter outlines. All information has been thoroughly updated to reflect the new information in the text.

- A **Test Item File** in Microsoft Word format. This test bank includes all the questions in the MyTest as detailed above.

Technology Specialists. Pearson's Technology Specialists work with faculty and campus course designers to ensure that Pearson technology products, assessment tools, and online course materials are tailored to meet your specific needs. This highly qualified team is dedicated to helping schools take full advantage of a wide range of educational resources by assisting in the integration of a variety of instructional materials and media formats. Your local Pearson Education sales representative can provide you with more details on this service program.

CourseSmart is a new way for instructors and students to access textbooks online anytime from anywhere. With thousands of titles across hundreds of courses, CourseSmart helps instructors choose the best textbook for their class and give their students a new option for buying the assigned textbook as a lower cost eTextbook. For more information, visit www.coursesmart.com.

ACKNOWLEDGMENTS

Even though there is only one author's name on the cover of this book, so many other people made it possible for me to research and made it a pleasure for me to write. Without a single exception, many of my students were so perceptive in pointing out improvements I could make to this edition. Over the years, my students have not only inspired me to revise the text this many times, but also they have been especially skilled at making suggestions for improving its content.

In addition to those here, students at many other colleges and universities where the text is adopted have sent me letters and emailed their reactions and evaluations (jim_guy@capebretonu.ca). I read and answered each one personally with the intent to revise the book based on their input.

Many heartfelt thanks and deep appreciation also go out to each and every critical reviewer who enabled me to put more life into this seventh rendering of political science and thereby teach thousands more about a subject I love. Authors usually do not know who their reviewers are until after the edition of their book is published. My secret wish has been to be able to call on them while writing. Their suggestions have been so helpful and so informed. Reviewers from some of Canada's most prestigious colleges and universities made valuable suggestions for this seventh edition. They are: Gilbert Gagné, Bishop's University; Paul Hamilton, Brock University; Carolyn Johns, Ryerson University; Christian Leuprecht, Royal Military College; Leo Y. Liu, Brandon University; Shauna Longmuir, Fleming College; Alex Marland, Memorial University of Newfoundland; Richard Nimijean, Carleton University; Filippo Sabetti, McGill University; Julie Simmons, University of Guelph; Lori Turnbull, Dalhousie University; and Nelson Wiseman, University of Toronto.

One of the joys of writing this book through seven editions has been the ongoing support of many of my colleagues at Cape Breton University. Special thanks must go to my political science colleagues, especially to Lee-Anne Broadhead, who allowed me to do a profile of her in this edition but who also became my trusted friend. I am fortunate to have learned from her high professional standards and personal energy. Another of my departmental colleagues to thank sincerely is Dr. Tom Urbaniak, who is so knowledgeable and approachable. Dr. David Johnson also writes texts and has been both a source of information and encouragement. Dr. Terry Gibbs and her partner, professor Garry Leech, have valuable expertise in international affairs and terrorism. Dr. Brian Howe, whom I had the pleasure of hiring, has been a wonderful addition to our department and an advisory colleague. Special mention and gratitude must be given to Dr. Edwin MacLellan, professor of Engineering, who gave me the idea of comparing the energy footprint of Canadians with other nation-states in Chapter 15. He also provided the data and the confidence to use it. I also want to thank Dr. Sharon Beckford at Saint Mary's University Department of English who has inspired me to write beyond political science.

Without a doubt, an exclusive pledge of thanks must go to some of the professional staff who run our university library. Research and reference librarian Anne Fisher can track down information on anything, anywhere, anytime. Another brilliant library researcher who was so helpful with this edition is Cathy Chisholm. Two other librarians, Mary Dobson and Debbie MacInnis, made sure interlibrary loans were negotiated, delivered, and returned. I am also grateful to the librarians who assisted me on my regular research visits to Acadia University, Dalhousie University, St. Mary's University, St. Francis Xavier University and McGill University in Montreal. The special collections at these universities have been very helpful to this project.

Two Cape Breton University administrators, Jennifer Pino and Marilyn O'Neil, have offered valuable insights on behalf of the many students who use this textbook in our Distance Education Program. Their advice for adapting my book to an ever-expanding e-learning market is much appreciated.

A special thanks must go to Kirk MacRae, who sits on the board of the Royal Canadian Mint and who helped connect me with some of the important interviews I did in Ottawa for this book. To Ambassador Michael Wilson and his cooperative staff in Washington, thank you for your insights on diplomacy and the opportunity to write a profile about you. To Supreme Court Justice Rosalie Abella, thank you for sharing your wisdom about justice in Canada and for permitting my profile of you.

The editorial staff assigned to me has shown remarkable professional skill and good humour throughout this project. Pearson Education has attracted some of the most creative people I know in Canadian publishing, who were assigned to this edition. I benefited from the advice and encouragement of Carolin Sweig, my sponsoring editor. Megan Burns, my developmental editor, has been unfailingly encouraging and responsive. She made the revisions seem so effortless. The splendid cover is the creation of Miriam Blier. Claire Horsnell, as the production editor, commanded the final product for you to enjoy.

Finally, it takes an entire family for an author to write a book. My wife Patti is ever so encouraging and supportive. Katha, Scott, Carolyn, and Trevor are part of the entourage of love that surrounds my life here in Cape Breton. And thanks again must go to Puccina, my trusted standard poodle, who barks sense into me from time to time. She's very smart!

About the Author

James J. Guy was born in Montreal and studied political science at Concordia University (Loyola), Fordham University, and Saint Louis University where he received his Ph.D in political science and international law in 1975.

A professor of political science at Cape Breton University, James Guy established and chaired the new Department of Political Science in 1994. In addition to CBU, Professor Guy has taught at the University of Kentucky, Saint Louis University, Indiana University, Bellarmine College (Louisville), Mansfield University, and the University of Prince Edward Island.

In addition to contributing to the *Encyclopaedia of Public Policy and Administration* and the *Encyclopaedia of Politics: The Left and Right* as well as numerous academic journals in Canada, the United States, Europe, and South America, Professor Guy has written a number of well-received books. These include *How We Are Governed*, *Expanding Our Political Horizons*, and seven editions of *People, Politics, and Government*. His hobbies include boating, arboriculture, and birdwatching, and he performs as a percussionist and bassist with the Cape Breton Orchestra and a 28-piece swing band called The Right Stuff.

CHAPTER 1

What Is Politics?

After reading this chapter, you will be able to:

- define *politics* and apply this term to government and other organizations

- think about politics as behaviour that has personal as well as public significance

- understand politics as a product of culture, values, human conflict, co-operation, and the need to survive

- recognize how politics is different in every part of the world

- identify the roles politics play in community-building and nation-building

- understand how we learn about politics, as children, adolescents, and adults

- recognize that the agents of political learning in society differentiate how we learn politics from how we express our political opinions

- list the properties of political opinions and learn how they can be measured

- think about whether our political opinions really influence governments and other groups in the political system

• • • •

WHAT IS POLITICS?

Extraordinary things occur every day in the world of politics. Headlines capture our attention about political events and personalities around the world: "*Two More Canadian Soldiers Killed in Afghanistan*"; "*United Nations Calls on Israel and Hamas to Enact an Immediate Ceasefire*"; "*Finance Minister Warns Canadians of Impending Deficit*"; "*Barack Obama May Be the First Global President.*" Today's headlines also tell of complex political relationships taking place in and among all societies. Every society generates its own politics in order to survive in a complex world. Politics help us resolve social conflict, build nation-states and protect citizens from external threat. It is at the political level that we debate and decide the best ways to maintain a successful social order.

> **FACTFILE** The Greek word *politikos* means politics and pertains to civic affairs. It was eventually incorporated into everyday English language as *political* in 1529.

Over the years students of politics have attempted to define *politics* in order to understand the political world. David Easton sees politics as a "process by which values are authoritatively allocated in society."[1] Note Easton's use of the words "authoritative" and "values." He believed when certain values are important in a society the public will debate them and the state will enforce them.

American political scientist Harold Lasswell referred to politics simply as "who gets what, when and how."[2] Vladimir Lenin, the great Bolshevik revolutionary, saw politics as "who does what to whom,"[3] and Mao Tse Tung, China's greatest communist leader, defined it as "bloodless war."[4] Chancellor Otto von Bismarck of Prussia asserted that politics was the art of getting things done. He defined politics as "the doctrine of the possible, the attainable."[5]

In all of this there is much room for disagreement. The world does not consist of a political reality that everyone sees in the same way. This is because politics is highly complex social behaviour driven by different ways of thinking, living, and governing. Many political scientists try to understand politics using Aristotle's premise that we are basically political animals—we are political because we need to survive. Ultimately, our survival is *political* because it is linked to how we as humans relate to each other and how we adapt to the world around us.

There are four main levels of political influence (see Figure 1.1). The *social level* includes the most fundamental and enduring forces that influence the political and governmental system: the family structure, how we conduct ourselves, what goods and services we produce, and the social and cultural movements that influence our lives. The *political level* embraces the political culture, political opinion, our leaders, political parties, interest

Figure 1.1   Four levels of political influence

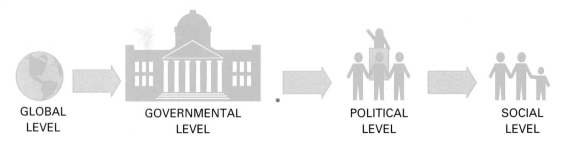

GLOBAL LEVEL → GOVERNMENTAL LEVEL → POLITICAL LEVEL → SOCIAL LEVEL

and pressure groups, and the mass media. The *governmental level* involves the constitutional rules of the game, the institutions we use to make our decisions, and the officials who make and implement public policy. The *global level* carries the influence of worldwide events on the domestic political and social environment. This level encourages nation-states to depend more and more on each other for their economic and political well-being. This level makes us aware that everything we do as nation-states and governments affects the planet and its limited resources.

Perspectives   Globalization Is Changing the World of Politics

The terms "global community" and "global awareness" are now everyday expressions in our vocabulary. Marshall McLuhan used the word *global* in a new way when he said that everything now takes place in the "global village." As an expert in communications, he noted that global politics enters the national and local levels as if borders no longer matter. Everything global has become local.

Some see globalization as a positive force that benefits humanity. Others see it as a threat that thwarts social progress in a world already filled with inequality.

The integration of the economies of the world into a global organic system through trade and financial flows took place gradually throughout the twentieth century. For example, in 1913 world trade amounted to a mere $20 billion. In 2008, globalization produced $12.3 trillion in the global exchange of goods, services and cash flows. That means that every society and its government must develop effective policies to meet world standards of finance, trade, and investment.

The same market forces that took place within national economies 50 years ago are now operating globally, 24 hours a day. Human economic activity taking place in village markets can connect electronically with urban industries and financial centres. Nothing demonstrated this more than the way Canadian governments were forced to respond to the rapid market meltdown which was called the global economic crisis in the fall of 2008. The most accelerating force of globalization has been the invention of the microchip and the consequent spread of instantaneous electronic communications.

All of the political influences that affect Canada as a member of the world community are derived from the global environment. Our political leaders and the institutions in which they work must respond to these events when they happen outside their decision-making jurisdictions. Canada's political system must now be able to relate to the world as a whole rather than just responding to some individual states or preferred regions.

Canadian politics changed significantly after the United States was attacked by terrorists on September 11, 2001. Canada's Parliament and our provincial legislatures passed many new laws affecting national security, defence, and immigration. We sent our soldiers to Afghanistan to defend the interests not only of non-terrorist Afghanistan but also of the US, Europe, and Latin America. We responded to a global event, the "war on terror," as if the events of 9/11 had happened directly to us.

Globalization leaves no level of politics untouched. Some have called it the process that makes the world a single place (the "global village"). Never before have Canadian decision makers been so involved with matters of global importance. Thus economic policies, the environment, human rights, animal rights, medical research, space research, and peace are not addressed as solely Canadian problems. They are part of our own politics and are just as intimately connected to world politics on a daily basis.

Canadians live in a world of great political change and, for many, these times are both a curse and a blessing. On the one hand, the curse: the challenge of national unity, labour unrest, unemployment, toxic waste, asserting our sovereignty in the North, and crumbling government infrastructures; on the other hand, the blessing: natural and material abundance, new opportunities in a global economy, technological breakthroughs, economic growth,

and, thus far, a history of successful national unity. Canadians seem to have concluded that changing political and social conditions are here to stay and that, under present circumstances, our governments are hard-pressed to make things better. Do Canadians have adequate government organizations to handle the social changes we face in the twenty-first century? Is Parliament ready with an elected House of Commons and an appointed Senate? Are provincial and territorial governments capable of meeting global challenges under the rules of our federal system? Do Canadians understand that their world is not just Canada but rather the whole world?

POLITICS IS ALL ABOUT US

In Canada, politics is seen as both an **institutional phenomenon** and a **behavioural phenomenon**. For example, Professor John Redekop defines it this way:

> Politics, then, refers to all activity whose main purpose is one or more of the following: to reshape or influence governmental structures or processes; to influence or replace governmental office holders; to influence the formation of public policies; to influence the implementation of public policies; to generate public awareness of, and response to, governmental institutions, processes, personnel and policies; or to gain a place of influence or power within government.[6]

Institutions are excellent places to discover politics, but we should also be prepared to observe political elements at other levels of human interaction. Politics is a recognizable characteristic of people acting toward, responding to, and influencing one another in the public milieu. It may

manifest itself as group demands for more money, order, or justice in a society. One person may feel that voting for a particular party or candidate in an election will bring job security and a higher standard of living. Another will complain that there is too much government intervention in society and will support a party that advocates reducing bureaucratic regulation. A women's organization might pressure a provincial government to improve parental leave and child care, and organized labour may lobby cabinet ministers to create more jobs.

These actions are examples of traditional political behaviour. But less traditional activities are just as political in their social effect as are voting, supporting a party, or lobbying. These could include protesting higher university tuition fees, crossing or not crossing picket lines, or joining a group of citizens that takes legal action against a company using dangerous chemicals to spray forests near populated areas. All of these activities involve people engaging with the political structures of their society. These kinds of political activities are linked to the pursuit and balance of private and social interests.

POLITICS AS NATURAL BEHAVIOUR

Some social scientists have pointed out that politics is a natural result of people interacting with their environment.[7] A number of important theoretical studies have identified the two primary dimensions of political behaviour as the psychological and the social.

Psychological Basis

From the psychological perspective, political behaviour appears as thought, perception, judgment, attitudes, and beliefs. The psychological basis of politics is also seen in the constructs of personality, expectations, and motivations that explain individual and group responses to environmental stimuli. For example, some studies point out that leaders are more likely to possess certain personality characteristics to a higher degree than do followers.[8] Leaders are found to demonstrate a higher rate of energy output, alertness, originality, personal motivation, self-confidence, decisiveness, knowledge, and fluency of speech than do followers.

The psychological dimension of politics underlies how we package and sell issues and candidates. In most states, modern election-campaign strategies apply advanced propaganda and entertainment techniques to gather crowds for rallies and to influence voter behaviour. Images and issues can be carefully crafted to appeal to the widest possible range of voters. The psychological manipulation of voter preferences today is built into the campaign strategies of most candidates for public office.

Social Basis

The social basis of politics is found in actions such as voting, protesting, campaigning, lobbying, and caucusing. In the broadest social sense, behaviour with political consequence may be observed in any institutional setting—public or private. It is often revealed as aggression, co-operation, compromise, negotiation, posturing, decisiveness, assertiveness, dominance, and virtually any human strategy that leads to decisions that have social impact.

What better place to witness these two dimensions of political behaviour than at leadership conventions? Not only are the candidates for the leadership of political parties presenting their ideas in formal speeches to the delegates who attend, but also many other examples of political behaviour are evident. At leadership conventions, enthusiasm is high and the opening ceremonies become contests to see which camp has the strongest lungs. There are not only vocal battles for attention: posters, banners, and placards bounce up and down in eager hands, balloons float through the arena, and hats and T-shirts sporting different alliances weave through the convention hall. Laptops, BlackBerries, and cellphones are everywhere. Candidates now use online social networking sites, such as Facebook, to promote themselves.

Much of the wheeling and dealing for the delegates' votes goes on during the convention festivities. Some of the best political sideshows take place around the activities of these conventions. When the delegates arrive, the candidates are waiting with all of the paraphernalia that has become so much a part of selecting political leaders in Canada. Hotel lobbies are filled with booths that are plastered with pictures of the candidates. Campaign buttons appear everywhere and there seems to be an endless flow of food, beer, and liquor. Bars open early and close late. Methods may vary in every political party but the candidates' goals remain the same: to get and keep the delegates' support. Candidates woo delegates with food, fireworks, music, and giant movie screens flashing well-known faces. In some instances, teary-eyed orators, lavishing praise, introduce their candidates with appeals to the emotions of the delegates.

Campaign strategists make sure that support for their candidates appears on placards at every corner of the convention floor. Whom candidates talk to, look at, and walk toward all become psychologically dynamic gestures in the process of selecting a political leader.

For the candidates themselves, image, winability, and what pundits call "the sizzle factor" supersede the issues raised and the policies debated by the party intelligentsia. The ultimate test that demonstrates the leadership qualities of a candidate is his or her individual character. Character shows itself as the respect candidates display toward the delegates, and the coolness and grace they display under fire, when events take a difficult turn.

For candidates, the pressures of politics are enormous. They have just completed exhausting campaign tours around the country. They have invested themselves, their time, and their money. As tension builds on the floor of the convention hall, their emotions become quite raw. Party conventions are ideal places to witness the psychological and social determinants of political behaviour. Here, politics cuts across many levels of social conduct: imitation, frivolity, fads, mimicry, and emotion are as fundamental to political behaviour as are decision making, elections, authority, and **consensus**.

These are the dynamics that went into the selection of Steven Harper, Stéphane Dion, and Jack Layton as national party leaders. Michael Ignatieff, however, was not first chosen as the leader of the Liberal Party of Canada by a convention of delegates. He was appointed Leader by the Liberal caucus and National Party Executive in December 2008, an appointment that would be ratified by the Liberal Convention scheduled for April/May 2009.

POLITICS AS CULTURE
We Share a Political Culture

In politics, culture is as culture does. A **political culture** is an overall set of values shared within society. Over time, a political culture becomes an accumulation of beliefs, customs, expectations, attitudes, traditions, skills, symbols, and values that are shared in a given political system (see Figure 1.2). All these components indicate how society *does* politics and are a product of its political experience from the remote and recent past. They are inputs into the political environment of a society in its quest to survive and maintain social order. Because every society has a unique past, every political culture is unique and many nation-states (such as Canada and the United States) even experience different political subcultures flourishing within them.

> **FACTFILE**   According to its 2007 survey, the Dominion Institute (www.dominion.ca) found that Canadians are increasingly identifying more with their region or province than with the country as a whole and this affects the character of Canada's political culture.

Although a great variety of political cultures exist throughout the international system, each reflecting distinctive qualities, certain components are found in all of the ways of conducting politics:

- *Political customs* are accepted practices that may be recognized as a working part of the political and governing system. They are sometimes reinforced through the legal actions of the state: as when a cabinet minister resigns because of inappropriate behaviour or because he or she cannot subscribe to the policies of the government.

- *Political beliefs* are deeply held convictions about political reality that are based on one

Figure 1.2   Components of political culture

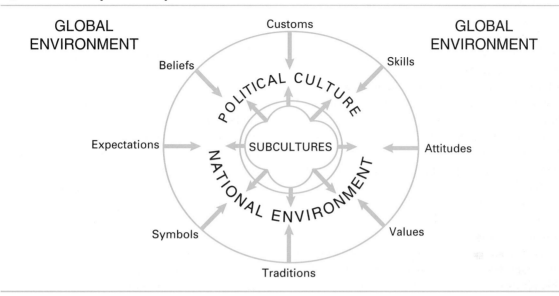

or more fundamental assumptions about human behaviour: e.g., that humans are basically selfish and governments should legislate and enforce the sharing of resources in a complex society.

- *Political expectations* are assertions about what people believe ought to happen in the political world: e.g., that governments should not engage in patronage.

- *Political symbols* are entities that represent something else, but have special meaning because they unify people: e.g., the maple leaf is a symbol of Canada.

- *Political attitudes* are learned predispositions that relate to political issues, events, personalities, and institutions in either a favourable or unfavourable manner, and usually in a consistent or characteristic way.

- *Political values* are attitudes and standards of judgment about what things are important, desirable, and right: e.g., Canadians consider it desirable and proper for people to pursue their own goals and interests as individuals under the law.

- *Political traditions* are customs made legitimate by long and continued practice: e.g., the tradition of appointing Canadians as governors general began in 1952, when another tradition began—that of alternating English-speaking and French-speaking Canadians in that office.

- *Political skills* consist of how we use our knowledge, procedures, strategies, and tactics to achieve desired social goals: e.g., lobbying, negotiating.

Political Cultures Differ

There are many different political cultures. In each one, people share a similar language, as well as ideals, procedures of government, and patterns of political behaviour that are learned and passed on from generation to generation. We are all very much part of our own political culture and we identify with it to distinguish ourselves from other political cultures.

Gabriel Almond was the first political scientist to bring to our attention the link between political behaviour and the wider phenomenon of transmitting political knowledge from the past into the present. For Almond, "every political system is embedded in a particular pattern of orientations to political action."[9] Once established, a political system tends to generate informally its own support mechanisms within a society. These usually take the form of certain norms and values that are regarded as virtues and recognized by succeeding generations of political actors. For example, candidates to Canada's Parliament have learned that legislators must display **party loyalty** because the survival of the parliamentary system requires it. But in the United States, the expectation is that representatives will usually act more independently and will advance the interests of their constituency before those of the party.

Samuel Beer and Adam Ulam theorized that a political culture transmits to people "how government ought to be conducted and what it should try to do."[10] This all-encompassing nature of culture is what prompts people to expect certain qualities and values in political behaviour and to behave politically the way they do. For example, in Canada and in the United States most people believe that their constitution, as the basic law of the land, will last indefinitely and be amended only from time to time. This is in line with what Sidney Verba contends about political culture: that it is a "system of beliefs about patterns of political interaction and political institutions."[11]

The Qualities of Political Culture

We can identify three general qualities of political culture. First, there is widespread awareness of the rules and structures of the political system. Canadians are generally conscious of the presence of Parliament and that it operates as a political and law-making institution. They understand the formal and informal political relationships of politicians, which centre on Parliament most of the time. Second, politics and the political system are widely accepted. Not only are people committed to the roles and functions of political institutions, but also they usually comply with the laws and regulations the system produces. **Compliance** is the invisible glue of any political system; without it, the political and social fabric of nation-states would fall apart. In Canada, most people believe that Parliament is a legitimate government institution: People respect its procedures and generally comply with the laws it passes.

Finally, the third element of a political culture is the expectation of certain behaviour within the **political system**. People are sensitive to the growth and size of government as an encroachment on their lives. They hold government accountable for its actions and judge the appropriateness of political conduct, such as whether ministers engage in patronage.

Because of size and ethnic composition, many nation-states contain more than one political culture. In Canada, there are distinctive regional political cultures or political subcultures that constitute the political system. A regional political culture has been defined as "a set of values, beliefs, and attitudes that residents of a region share and that, to a great or lesser extent, differentiate them from the residents of other regions."[12]

Many Political Cultures

Political scientist Steven Ullman observes that while a homogeneous political culture is detectable across a wide range of Canadian political behaviour, regional political cultures can also be identified. In some instances political cultures appear along provincial and territorial boundaries, as well as in regions that may consist of one or more provinces. One soon discovers that a Cape Breton coal miner, a Montreal taxi driver, a Saskatchewan wheat farmer, an Alberta oil executive, and a student at the University of Victoria do not share the same political values and beliefs about Canada's political destiny.

In Canadian political culture, a majority of people holds in common certain fundamental attitudes and beliefs about the role of Parliament, the ethical behaviour of politicians and bureaucrats, and the legitimacy of national legislation and certain government programs. But one would also find basic differences in attitudes and values of Albertans and Maritimers over the extent to which provincial and federal governments should be actively engaged in the economy. Simeon and Elkins have explained the presence of regional subcultures in Canada by pointing to the many differences in the historical and economic development of various parts of Canada.[13]

All political cultures, whether national or regional, nurture symbols with which people identify. A *political symbol* is a meaningful object that represents some shared value or goal of a community of people. Thus the Canadian flag, which is a rectangular, multi-coloured piece of cloth, represents "the true North strong and free," democracy, justice, and other values. Canadians have come to make a psychological association between the flag as an object and the values it represents. The significance of the flag is much greater than its physical appearance. All Canadians make the association between our political symbols and these symbols' meaning; Canadians share the symbols as part of our political culture. Symbols bind us as a group and unite our loyalties.

But the situation in the United Kingdom is different from that in Canada. The Canadian flag, with its prominent and symbolic maple leaf is seen everywhere in Canada—and not just on July 1. Flags are flown prominently at Canadian schools, universities, post offices, and other public buildings. Car dealerships fly them and many private homes fly them 365 days a year. In Great Britain, however, the Union Jack is not widely seen as a prominent symbol of the country and is rarely seen on display: post offices do not fly the Union Jack, and it is not present at Whitehall, the seat of the British government's administration.

Another aspect of political culture is the *political style* of a society. Every political system develops its own characteristic style of politics that reflects its people's historical experiences, traditions, and values. Canadians have a highly competitive, open political system that invites voluntary participation of people who want practical solutions to social problems. Canada has achieved a high degree of bargaining, compromise, and negotiation in the area of inter-provincial and federal politics.[14] This has made politics in Canada a healthy, competitive exercise for both the citizen and the professional politician.

Viewing politics as culture is an important way of understanding the uniqueness of each political system. Our political culture is a looking glass through which Canadians observe and judge other political cultures. We must constantly be aware of how our own political values affect our evaluations of the many other people who make up the international system.

POLITICS AS VALUES
The Power of Strong Beliefs

Sociologists tell us that all societies are made up of groups that share certain values. Within groups, values are widely believed to be desirable for their own sake and are used as standards to judge the behaviour of others. Values reveal themselves as human preferences and priorities, as beliefs about duty, about right and wrong, and about what ought to be done in certain situations. Seymour Lipset found that Canadians tend to value authority more than do Americans.[15] For him, Canadians are more law-abiding and more inclined to recognize the authority of the police than are Americans. By comparison, Americans value personal freedom so highly that they tend to resist regulations and are more likely to feel hostile to authority figures. Lipset noted in his comparison of political cultures that Canadians value diversity more than **homogeneity** and are more collectively oriented than Americans who are more individualistic and suspicious of government.

Canadian and American political values are similar but are achieved and protected differently in each political system. Canadians would agree with Americans that "life, liberty and the pursuit of happiness" are important values. But Canadians differ with their neighbour on the role of government in protecting these values. They differ significantly on what kind of healthcare system is best, who should be allowed to own handguns, and whether the pursuit of happiness should be primarily an individual's right as compared with a community's right.

Political values are shared beliefs that provide standards for judging human thought and action. They may be viewed as pressures that motivate social behaviour within a political culture. Politics results from the interplay of values among individuals and groups pursuing different goals for their own benefit. Within every society

or among societies, politics is the **process** of competition and co-operation by which values gain priority.

These priority values are authoritatively allocated by the political system in order to legitimize their binding effect on the lives of the majority of people. One value that has become an integral part of the fabric of Canadian society is political equality. Because of this, various groups have fought for the **authoritative** allocation of equal treatment in Canada. For example, Canadian women are celebrating some 90 years as "persons" recognized under the *British North America Act*. In 1920, Judge Emily Murphy, Nellie McClung, and three other women from Alberta successfully took legal action that affirmed that Canadian women should not be classed with "lunatics" and "children" as people who were not responsible for their actions. Similarly, the federal government granted Canadian Indians full citizenship only in 1960. It was 1967 before a Supreme Court order struck down the prohibition that Canadian Indians were not legally entitled to drink alcohol. And, in 2008, the Canadian Human Rights Tribunal found that the Treasury Board of Canada had discriminated against women, contrary to the *Canadian Human Rights Act*, by excluding maternal and parental leave for certain time-frames of employment. The point is that a belief in equality held by a majority of Canadians does not mean that this standard has applied in practice to all groups in Canada.

Politics and the Pursuit of Power

Lord Acton made the now famous remark that "Power tends to corrupt, and absolute power corrupts absolutely." Power is the currency of all political behaviour and it weaves its way into every area of human interaction. People want to experience power and are fascinated by those who appear to be in positions of influence. They have a natural curiosity about the political impact of people like K.C. Irving and the late Ken Thomson, two of Canada's best-known billionaires, or about the methods and tactics used by cabinet ministers in managing the Canadian government.

In Canada, power and political institutions are intimately related. As a value, however, Canadians prefer to think of power not in coercive terms but rather as authority that is granted by consent and achievement. In other words, rulers must be recognized as having earned, by following recognized legal procedures, the right to control the behaviour of other people.

In many countries power is expressed coercively by the state. Illegitimate power—coercion—is power that most people do not accept as rightly exercised over them. In dictatorships, the military is often visible in civilian areas as a deterrent against democratic expression. Many times, demonstrators are arrested and treated harshly, as was the case in China during the 2008 Olympics.

Power may also be expressed by means of influence and political position. The prime minister, because of his or her position in government, will almost inevitably be influential in and out of cabinet and party circles. Stephen Harper used his influence as prime minister in 2008 to persuade Canadians directly on his strategy to avoid his government's certain defeat by asking the Governor General to prorogue (end a session of) Parliament. Influence as power plays a major part in the Canadian and American governing systems.

Power and authority do not come from personal characteristics but are often vested in persons whom Canadians have traditionally considered rightful leaders. Authority is power that people accept as legitimate rather than coercive. As such, the real basis of institutional power in Canada is derived from legal and procedural authority. This authority is granted by the position; it is not in the person. The rights, privileges, obligations, and power come with the office. When an individual leaves that office, the next person to occupy it is granted the same rights and obligations.

When in an office of power, a person is expected to behave in accordance with certain values and standards of conduct. The federal and provincial governments have established rigorous new standards for public officeholders and cabinet officials. These include disclosing personal investments to prevent conflicts of interest while serving in public office and strict guidelines as to the use of government property for private purposes. In 2002, the federal government launched special guidelines for ministers who raise funds to become party leaders. And Stephen Harper's minority government passed the *Accountability Act* to counter the dynamic of corruption on the use of program money that was disclosed during the Gomery Inquiry on the Sponsorship Scandal. This large document touched upon most aspects of government performance, even making deputy ministers accountable for the operation of their department. Protections were also extended to "whistle-blowers" who inform their employers or the media of questionable government behaviour.

Power is more properly understood as a relationship among individuals, groups, and societies. In this regard, Robert Dahl sees power as "the capacity to change the probability of outcomes,"[16] and Karl Deutsch sees it as the "ability to make things happen that would not have happened otherwise."[17]

Politics and the Pursuit of Wealth

Wealth has been a political issue since the dawn of time. It enables people to satisfy their material needs, individually and collectively. But, invariably, wealth can lead to the exercise of political power. The political nature of wealth has always revolved around its possession, use, and distribution in a society. All political systems are sharply affected by the internal divisions of income and wealth. Wealthy economies like Canada's and those of Europe have more equitable income distributions than poorer countries such as Mali and Mexico. The association of **industrialization** and wealth has been significant historically, but comparisons of wealth between and among economies are seen through the lenses of a post-industrial economy. The global inequalities of wealth seen in most pre-industrial societies are the primary causes of the political instability in many developing states. It is a reason often used to explain the susceptibility of poorer societies to embracing radical ideologies and egalitarian political movements.

By 2007, Canada's net worth was more than $7 trillion—about $220 000 for each Canadian if the country was liquidated and the wealth divided equally among its 32 million people. This national balance sheet calculated by Statistics Canada includes tangible assets—houses, durable consumer goods, business and government buildings, and equipment, land, and money owed to individuals, businesses, and governments—totalling $10 trillion. When financial liabilities amounting to $3 trillion are subtracted from tangible assets, our net worth is just over $7 trillion. Collectively, Canadians may be very wealthy; however, many individuals never share in the affluence of the economy.

In Canada, wealth is a widely valued commodity but is usually accompanied by attendant poverty. One out of every 12 Canadians lives on welfare and one in six children grows up in a poor family. The rate of poverty among children was reported at 24 percent in 2006. Yet the levels of welfare payments paid to families with children designated as "poor" that have been established in all provinces are below the **poverty line** (low income cut-off line). The National Anti-Poverty Association (NAPO) estimates that more than 5 million Canadians are living below the federal government's low-income cut-off line. In 2006, poverty was defined in terms of an income less

than $22 852 for a family of four. The average "poor" family in Canada has an annual income of $19 962, compared with an average income of $63 001 for all Canadian families with children in 2006. Canada provides the least generous basic child benefit to median-income families among all major industrialized states.

> FACTFILE As of 2006, if a Canadian family spends more than 63 percent of its gross income on clothing, food and shelter it will fall below the low-income cut-off point and likely experience poverty.

In Canada, the distribution of poverty is not random but tends to be concentrated among certain racial minorities, Aboriginal peoples, female-headed households, and children. The proportion of Canadian families living in poverty and suffering homelessness has increased significantly since 1980. Among the richest economies in the world, Australia and the United States are the only two states reporting higher levels of poverty than Canada. Germany, Sweden, and Norway have been much more successful in reducing the incidence of poverty in their general populations.

The Politics of Health

Some of Canada's great wealth is used to purchase health and well-being for Canadian citizens. Even though most of the health and welfare services are within the constitutional jurisdiction of the provinces, the largest department of the federal government is Health Canada, which spends approximately 40 percent of the annual government budget. Canadians, through their federal government, have made considerable efforts to improve public health. In 2007, a newborn Canadian female had about an 84-year life expectancy and a male about a 78-year life expectancy. This contrasts with states such as Nepal and Afghanistan, where life expectancy is well below the age of 50 for both males and females. The gap in life expectancy between First Nations and

Crosscurrents   Pay the Rent or Feed the Kids

Mel Hurtig's book entitled *Pay the Rent or Feed the Kids*[18] captures the contradictions in the politics of poverty and wealth in Canada. The title has particular significance for many, especially single-parent nuclear families and the so-called working poor. Every month many Canadians must choose whether to pay the rent or feed their kids—the kind of distasteful decision we would likely ascribe to the poor who live far away in developing countries.

Social scientists debate the causes of child poverty, some blaming the individual parents involved and others pointing to flaws in the wider society. Proponents of the former blame the victim, holding that the poor are primarily responsible for their own poverty, are lazy, and do not take advantage of the opportunities in the economy. Support for this notion is strongest among people who are well off and is usually found among those who are conservative-minded in social and economic matters.

Those who blame society hold that poverty is a result of the unequal distribution of income within society. They call for the creation of a national income program, usually referred to as a "guaranteed annual income," provided by the government whether people are working or not. It is unlikely that any government in Canada will adopt such a policy in the near future, given the recent **public sector** attention to deficit and debt reduction, coupled with major tax reductions implemented by the federal government and promised by the provincial governments.

other Canadians is significant: First Nations' expectancies are 66.9 years for men and 74 years for women.

FACTFILE   While all Canadians have access to a universal healthcare system, an estimated 45 million out of 307 million Americans have no medical insurance whatsoever.

Canadians take their health care very seriously, as is evident by the role the federal government has played in health services since the passage of the *Federal Medical Care Act* in 1966. By 2007, nearly 10 percent of Canada's GDP was being spent on healthcare services. This is primarily the result of political decisions. There is a widely held value that access to good health care is in the national interest and that individuals should not be left vulnerable to the high costs of medical services.

Canada ranks with Sweden, Switzerland, the Netherlands, Germany, and Britain for its exceptionally well-developed arrangements for health care, including care of the elderly and the handicapped. Canada's aging **baby boomers** (one-third of the population) have already placed upward pressures on healthcare costs, forcing politicians to consider new policy directions to care for the aged. According to Statistics Canada, the number of Canadians 65 and older is likely to double in the next 50 years (2060) and the very old—those over 85—will increase twice as fast.

Politics and the Need to Learn

In most states, governments assume a major role in education, especially of their young people. That said, many states now also have special programs for adult education. Because education requires great social investment to pay for teachers, professors, researchers, administrators, libraries, schools, colleges, and universities, there is a politics of education. What budget priorities should governments assign to education? Who should assume most of the costs?

In industrial societies, education is one of the main means of upward mobility. While there are still great differences between rich and poor economies, education stands out as a primary value in all societies. Levels of **literacy** among people 15 years of age and older range from 14 percent in Niger to 97 percent in Canada and the United States.[19] Similar contrasts are found with respect to university and college students. The number of university students per 1000 population ranges from 0.2 in Ethiopia and Malawi to 43 and 46 for Canada and the United States, respectively.

Despite the popular expectation that there is equality of educational opportunity in Canada, wealth and social class are still significant factors in determining access to university. Education opportunities vary provincially. A person from Alberta, British Columbia, or Ontario is more likely to acquire a university education than someone from the Atlantic provinces or Quebec. This ensures continued social differences across the country. Aboriginal Canadians in particular tend not to acquire a university education. Less than 1 percent of Aboriginal people attend university, compared with 17.7 percent of the general population aged 18 to 24.

FACTFILE   Based on Canada's 2006 Census, about 22.7 percent of all Canadians have no high school education with an almost equal percentage (22.6 percent) having completed a university degree.

Education is a global political value because it is closely related to what people can learn and what they produce in their societies. It is an important political resource because those who possess it improve their own welfare and make demands on the political system. Yet, despite its importance, poor national economies have great difficulty making strides in education. This is because it is difficult for a developing economy to spend more of its GDP on education.

Politics and Employment

Work and employment are the basis of all cultures. It is no wonder that work should be so highly prized as a political value in society. Employment links a person to a network of socially rewarding interactions. People gain self-worth from what they do. Without work, people feel disenfranchised from their social and political systems. In short, they become alienated from society.

FACTFILE   According to Canada's 2006 Census, the largest number of jobs flows to workers from international trade, followed by manufacturing and health care.

At the peak of **recession** unemployment levels in 1993, 1 586 000 Canadians, or about 13 percent of the labour force, could not find jobs—the highest rate since World War II (Figure 1.3). By 2007, the national unemployment levels had fallen to 6.3 percent. But the actual numbers remain over one million because many Canadians have given up looking for jobs. Because of general public concern, unemployment is recognized by the federal government as the major socio-economic problem in Canada, ranking higher than inflation and interest rates as a national priority. As the Canadin economy faced another recession, following two successive quarters of decline by 2009, the unemployment rate began to climb steadily higher toward 7 per cent.

Work and skills have been seriously affected by national policy in Canada since 1966. At that time, the Canadian government consolidated its manpower policy to co-ordinate labour market developments and immigration. Canada Manpower Centres were first established to provide services to individuals seeking jobs. Today, each Human Resource Centre of Canada tries to match workers to jobs by funnelling information from employers to prospective employees. Occupational mobility and the maintenance of skills in the marketplace have necessarily been elevated to the highest level

Figure 1.3   **Rate of unemployment in Canada since World War II**

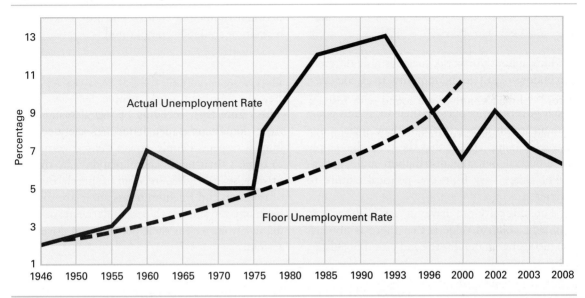

Sources: Statistics Canada, *The Labour Force (Ottawa, 1999), and* Historical Labour Force Statistics *(Ottawa, 1998)*; Statistics Canada, *"Rate of Unemployment in Canada since World War II," adapted from* Labour Force Information *(catalogue 71-001, August 9, 2002)*.

of political concern in a country as large and as complex as Canada. Because government policies are now blamed and credited for the job market, employment issues will continue to be regarded as an important political value.

The Politics of Justice

Justice and righteousness are passionately and universally pursued in the international community. General principles of international law focus on justice and equity in global affairs. Since World War II, the idea that individuals and states can commit "crimes against humanity" demonstrates the need to apply principles of justice everywhere in the world. All legal and court

systems, in their own ways, attempt to portray "justice." However, all justice and legal systems are imperfect; some fail completely by the standards of other systems. In Canada, the Marshall Inquiry painfully deliberated the circumstances that led to the wrongful conviction of a young Mi'kmaq Indian, Donald Marshall, who served 11 years in prison for a murder he did not commit. Other individuals, such as David Milgaard, Guy Paul Morin, and Steven Truscott have also challenged the standards in our justice system. In 2007 Steven Truscott was acquitted by the Ontario Court of Appeal of the murder and rape of 12-year-old Lynne Harper some 50 years before, and his wrongful conviction was declared a miscarriage of justice by the court.

Throughout the world, societies hold different perceptions of justice and morality. In all societies, there is a politics of justice, because the means by which governments operate their legal and court systems are an integral part of their social value system. It might appear that the rules they apply are universal, but the distribution and application of justice vary from one political culture to another.

The difficulty we have in establishing this dominant political value is that there is not just one justice but many. Justice and morality cluster, compete, and conflict. Most debates about justice are not debates between right and wrong but between rights and rights—and this makes their resolution endlessly complicated.

Politics and Human Respect

The rights and freedoms people demand from their communities are based on the need for human respect. People expect their governments to respect their needs and demands. The right to privacy, sexual rights, freedom of speech, freedom of religion, and freedom of assembly are some of the many ways in which people derive respect and dignity from within their political and governing system.

Crosscurrents   Why Does Sexuality Have to Be a Political Issue at All?

Political scientists know that everything humans do can at some point become a political issue. Being gay, lesbian, bisexual, or transgendered (GLBT) is no exception. The issue of GLBT rights is a significant political topic in democratic countries such as Canada. The power of the debate is twofold: first, it is a part of *popular culture* (because sexuality attracts attention in a way many other topics do not) and second, it concerns human rights, a fundamental of our *political culture* in Canada.

The **politicization** of GLBT rights in Canada can be traced to the 1960s, as part of a greater movement for sexual freedom. Until 1969, homosexuals in Canada could be jailed under Section 149 of the Criminal Code—simply for being who they were. For example, in 1967 the Supreme Court of Canada upheld the conviction of Everett Klippert to life imprisonment for being homosexual. In effect, he was put behind bars just for who he *was*.

This and other incidents inspired activists and lawmakers alike to call for reform.

As Minister of Justice in 1969, Pierre Elliott Trudeau declared: "the state has no place in the bedrooms of the nation." He knew that Canada enforced the most draconian laws against homosexuals among advanced industrialized states, and he introduced sweeping reforms to the Criminal Code to soften Canada's harsh laws. These reforms, influenced by earlier legal reforms in the United States and Europe, paved the way for more enlightened political views of GLBT rights.

Today, protection of gays and lesbians is enshrined in Canada's law in the *Charter of Rights and Freedoms*, and GLBTs are often viewed by the courts as a minority much like ethnic or language minorities, deserving of protection against discrimination. In 2005, Canada became the fourth country in the world to legalize same-sex marriage.

In contrast, the United States has had a more difficult time integrating GLBT rights into its political life. Only a handful of US states have legalized same-sex marriage or "civil unions," and bitter court battles continue in those states. Laws vary dramatically across the US; some states offer protection against discrimination in their Constitutions, while others have yet to overturn outdated laws against "sodomy."

It is often said that "the personal is political," and this is especially true in the case of GLBTs. When a gay, lesbian, bisexual or transgendered person "comes out" by telling friends and family he or she is GLBT, it can be both a personal and a political act. A number of well-known individuals have come out as openly GLBT: examples of politicians include US Congressional Representatives Tammy Baldwin and Barney Frank and Canadian Members of Parliament Scott Brison and Libby Davis.

In Canada, colleges and universities have played a major role in supporting the GLBT rights movement. Many provide discussion forums, clubs, newsletters, and social events for GLBT students. As well, university researchers in sociology, law, and public policy have all contributed to the broader cultural and political understanding of the issues.

While discrimination remains a reality for GLBTs in Canada, much progress has been made in the last 50 years. Indeed, Canada may be moving toward a day when being GLBT will no longer be such a political issue.

Some of the highest honours bestowed on individuals are conferred by governments in respect of their accomplishments and qualities. In Canada, the governor general bestows orders, declarations, and medals as the highest marks of merit achieved by Canadians. For example, the Order of Canada recognizes excellence in many important fields.

The need for respect surfaces in areas of international relations as well. Debtor militancy among the economies of the Third World is a message to the banking systems of the wealthy economies that they should respect the impoverished economies of the developing world. At the Olympics, where respect is literally put to the test, politics transcends the spirit of the games when states count their medals as tallies of national strength. And in Quebec, the separatist and independence movement is in large part a demand for respect of its sovereign national aspirations to become an independent French-speaking republic.

Respect for the territorial integrity of states and the principle of non-intervention have become most important in the international law of the twenty-first century. The charters of the United Nations, the Organization of American States, and the African Union make frequent references to these norms of international behaviour.

The need for respect may often appear hidden behind rhetoric and human aggression. Terrorist groups, unions, interest groups, and governments are all social and political manifestations of this powerful value in politics.

Politics and Human Security

As a political value, security is usually defined in military terms, whereby the power of armed forces is regarded as a deterrent to external and internal attack, and thus we feel secure. The spectre of "superterrorism" in the wake of the attacks of 9/11 stimulated the belief in the United States that the use of military force was needed in order to guarantee domestic and international security. *Superterrorism* is defined as the use of nuclear devices or chemical and biological weapons by terrorists.

However, many states also recognize that real security is not just military strength but also the ability of society to satisfy basic human needs. While these needs may include the prevention of war, they also include adequate food, health care, shelter, a healthy and safe community environment, and respect for human rights.

Increasingly, people in all parts of the world are asking if they can be "secure" when poverty is widespread and permanent, when economic prosperity results in the destruction of the environment, when criminal violence is so widespread, and when racism and discrimination are commonplace and, in many states, embedded in government institutions.

The problems that threaten security are both military and non-military, global and domestic. Real security cannot be ensured by military means alone. Yet, in most nation-states, including Canada, defence policy still tends to dominate security policy. Most governments exaggerate the military element in matters of security, thus causing other security needs to be shortchanged.

Canada spends more than $17 billion annually on its Department of National Defence and Armed Forces. In 2007, it spent over eight times more on the military than on the environment and over four times more on the military than on external assistance to developing economies.

However, on the domestic front, Canada is one of a minority of states in the world that spends more on social programs than on its military as a percentage of gross national product. But critics ask to what extent military spending cuts into resources available for matters of domestic security, such as health and education, crime prevention, justice administration, legal aid, and police.

Increasingly, people and governments are coming to realize that security may be much more than a military issue. Many citizens now feel that none among us is secure while injustice, oppression, and deprivation exist. None among us is secure while the global environment is at risk.

None among us is secure while states arm themselves in the name of security.

Politics and Affection

At first glance, love and affection seem distant from politics. But upon closer examination, we can see how the need for human affection touches every level of society, including the political system. For Plato and Aristotle, people and politics are part of a cosmic order built for the perfection of human beings as they relate to one another within and among societies. Politics must establish the framework within which affection can be demonstrated.

Although it can always be shown that politics does much to destroy goodwill among human beings, there is also much evidence that political behaviour fosters friendship and co-operation. Each day, governments extend courtesies to one another through cultural, diplomatic, and scientific exchanges. For example, at certain times Canada has given immature bald eagles from Cape Breton to the United States Fish and Wildlife Service to re-establish its population of eagles, the American national symbol. And as an act of gratitude toward the City of Boston, which was the first community to come to the rescue of the citizens of Halifax after the Halifax explosion in December 1917, the province of Nova Scotia each year gives Bostonians a large spruce Christmas tree, ceremoniously lit by the province's premier. As well, the United Nations sponsors national and international programs aimed at improving cultural co-operation and international friendship among states.

> **FACTFILE** As of 2008, the United Nations listed more than 2000 treaties of friendship worldwide.

Hundreds of treaties of friendship and mutual aid are signed by governments each year. In fact, the vast majority of interactions and transactions conducted each day among the states of our international system are amicable. Never before in history have so many international organizations been established for peaceful and friendly purposes. If we look closely, we can see that politics often does succeed in fostering the growth of affection among people.

POLITICS AS CONFLICTING INTERESTS

Politics inevitably involves conflict. In Canadian society, many interests compete for access to the resources of the country as well as for protection by and representation in government policies.

Conflict theorists point to the perception of inequalities as a prime source of political competition. Some groups feel that they do not share equally in the prosperity of the country or are denied equal opportunities because of power imbalances and exploitation. The Métis in Alberta, for example, claim that they are owed over $60 million in unpaid royalties from hundreds of oil and gas wells that are situated on their land.

Most of the present-day conflicts between Aboriginal people and the various levels of government in Canada originated in the past misuse of power by government officials. Many of the land claims disputes are over a century old,

dating to a period when government officials could take Indian reserve land and sell it to white interests. The Canadian government and private business have derived tremendous economic benefits from the unequal treatment of Aboriginals and their land.

POLITICS AS NATION-BUILDING

Modern societies are not born; they are built. Politics plays a major role in their construction. The economic and social base of any society requires political direction. At various levels, politics provides the building blocks for national development—the **infrastructure** of a community. In the broadest sense, the infrastructure of a society consists of systems of transportation, communication, education, and power grids; the industrial and technological base; and the political system itself. These all form the structural components of a society.

In the same way that a house is constructed from various building materials—in different patterns and designs, rapidly or slowly, according to the will and power of its builders—so too does a nation-state develop from its resources, according to different plans, quickly or gradually. At its heart is the will and skills of its citizens.

The political and governing system organizes, plans, and directs policies toward its developmental goals. Canada's federal system gives two levels of government—federal and provincial—primary responsibilities for making public policies. While it is true that municipal governments make public policies, they do so only because provincial governments supervise their structures and services.

Public policies are intimately related to nation-building at all levels of government. Public policies can make us richer or poorer, happy or angry, even alive or dead. Public policy is what a government *does* as well as what public officials sometimes choose *not* to do. In the most fundamental ways, societies survive and change on the basis of whatever governments choose to do or not to do. Government policies on municipal services, education, health, welfare, agriculture, business, defence, and international relations are all part of the nation-building process.

Local Governments and National Development

Political science research has only recently begun to discover the important role that cities and towns play in national development. The political decisions and actions of local governments transform the landscape of a country. They plan and regulate local construction and land use, and provide important services like utilities and transportation.

By 2007, most people of the world lived in cities. At that time, the gradual shift of political and economic power to urban centres was irreversible, making cities the primary centres of human development and important decision-making units of most political systems. In 1950, there were 76 cities in the world with a population over one million; the United Nations projected that at the end of the twenty-first century there would be 440 such cities, 284 of them in the developing world. Already the physical expansion of the corporate limits of cities

has created overwhelming human problems and added many jurisdictional questions to the national and subnational legislatures of most states. As cities and towns have grown, so have public demands for increased responsibilities and services. In some cities, such as Mexico City and São Paulo, the demands are in response to unmanageable and ungovernable social conditions.

FACTFILE   According to Census 2006, half of all Canadians now live in Ontario's Golden Horseshoe (Toronto, Hamilton, Oshawa, Kitchner-Waterloo, and Barrie), Montreal and Vancouver, giving Canada one of the most concentrated urban populations in the western hemisphere.

The result: the **division of powers** and responsibilities between national governments and local governments now carries great significance for the politics of national development. Usually, the costs of administering public services go beyond the financial capacities of cities, so other levels of government share costs or completely finance the administration of services (Table 1.1).

National governments are increasingly dependent on cities as economic and social centres of national development. Municipal problems have become national problems and municipal successes have become national successes.

The Fathers of Confederation could not predict where most Canadians would live by the end

Table 1.1   General municipal services

Locally financed	*Cost-shared*
Fire protection	Public education
Planning and maintenance	Transportation
Refuse collection and disposal	Health
Municipal libraries	Public housing
Police	Hospitals and medical care
Water supply	Public welfare
Parks and recreation	Pollution control

of the twentieth century. The federal system they designed did not give municipal governments a constitutional role and concentrated the exercise of government in the hands of the federal government and the provinces.

In Canada, more than 4000 municipalities and countless boards, commissions, and other local bodies contribute to the growth and development of Canadian society. But their contributions have had their share of recurring financial problems, and have also met with a general public attitude that local government should be concerned primarily with administration and efficient service delivery, but not with politics.[20]

> **FACTFILE** According to its 2006 Census survey, Prince Edward Island and Nunavut are the only two jurisdictions in Canada where the majority of people are living in a rural setting.

Under section 92 of the *Constitution Act, 1867*, the provinces were granted full responsibility for municipal institutions. Thus, local governments have remained what a federation of Canadian municipalities calls "puppets on a shoestring."[21]

In spite of the fact that over 80 percent of all Canadians currently live and work in cities and receive most personal essential services from their municipal governments, local administrations remain the most neglected and least regarded of all three levels of government. In the years ahead, public opinion may reverse its sentiments about the role of local governments in Canada's national development and draw closer to Sir Ernest Simon's view that "the City Council's services mean the difference between savagery and civilization."[22]

Subnational Governments and National Development

In geographically large states, nation-building requires the co-operation of two or more levels of government, each with its own special jurisdictions, political institutions, and popular support. This is the substance of Canada's federal system. The provinces have special powers reserved for them in the *Constitution Act, 1867*, listed under section 92.

In addition to 10 provincial political systems, Canada has 3 large territories that together make up 40 percent of the entire area of the country and yet hold only 0.2 percent of Canada's population. The Yukon Territory is governed by a Cabinet (Executive Council) appointed from the majority party in the 18-member elected Legislative Assembly. A federally appointed commissioner serves as the head of government in a capacity similar to that of a provincial lieutenant governor. The Northwest Territories—the largest region within Canada—is governed by a premier with a Cabinet (Executive Council) and a 19-member Legislative Assembly. A federally appointed commissioner acts as would a provincial lieutenant governor.

Canada's newest territory is Nunavut (Our Land), situated in the eastern Arctic and comprising the regions of Kitikmeot, Keewatin, and Baffin. What the new territory lacks in population, it makes up for in sheer size: it is larger than Quebec, the largest province. Because of its small tax base and shared royalties from oil, gas, and mineral resources, Nunavut must rely on federal government transfers to build its society as an Aboriginal nation within the Canadian federation. At present, about 90 percent of its annual government budget is transferred from Ottawa.

The *Constitution Act, 1867*, enumerated 15 classes of subjects that have given provinces exclusive and substantive law-making powers and elevated them to economic instruments of nation-building. The provinces have responsibility for local governments and jurisdiction over education, as well as control of provincial Crown lands, natural resources, and the provincial administration of justice. They also have concurrent powers with the federal government in agriculture and immigration. Historically, the politics of federal and provincial relations have transferred additional spending powers to the provinces, particularly under successive Liberal governments since 1968. The federal government spends billions annually in the areas of health, welfare, and post-secondary education. However, it allows provinces to administer and influence the policy direction of these programs.

Each province of Canada generates a gross provincial product that is a constituent part of the gross domestic product, which is the total value of all goods and services produced within national boundaries. For example, British Columbia offers a primary product and resource economy to Canada. Its main exports are fish, pulp and paper, primary metals, and manufactured goods. Table 1.2 shows that British Columbia contributed $179 701 billion to Canada's gross domestic product of $1 439 291 billion in 2006.

All of Canada's provinces are key political and governing units within a federal system, and con-tribute to Canada's economic development as an independent nation-state in the international community. How provincial governments manage their economies, their deficits, and their cumulative debts affects the economic integrity of the country. No one province can divorce itself from the overall economic viability of the Canadian economy.

Together, the provinces constitute just 60 per-cent of the area of Canada. But sprawling across the top of the western hemisphere are the Northwest Territories, Nunavut, and the Yukon. They encom-pass an area nearly one-and-a-quarter times the size of India, with a population of only about 70 000 peo-ple. These territories are just beginning to attract Canada's business pioneers in the areas of mining, hydrocarbon exploration, and oil exploration and refining. In 2007, the territories contributed more than $7.6 billion to Canada's gross domestic product.

National Governments

The ultimate instruments of nation-building are held by national governments. They are the final arbiters of politics and legitimate decision making

Table 1.2	Provincial gross domestic product, 2007

	$Billions
British Columbia	190 214
Alberta	259 941
Saskatchewan	51 166
Manitoba	48 586
Ontario	582 019
Quebec	298 157
New Brunswick	26 410
Nova Scotia	33 296
Prince Edward Island	4 538
Newfoundland and Labrador	29 034
Yukon Territory	1 687
Northwest Territories	4 580
Nunavut	1 371
Canada	1 531 427

Source: Data from Statistics Canada, Gross Domestic Product, Expenditure-based, by Province and Territory. *www.40.statcan.ca/l01.cst01/econ15.htm. Catalogue No. 13-213-PPB, 2007.*

in most states. National governments control the overall capacity of a political and economic system to affect every level of society.

From the perspective of public policy, nation-building in Canada has had an important **regional** dimension that is far-reaching for all three levels of government, but particularly affects the federal government. Canada's federal system sustains the regional character of the country. It enables provincial governments to provide services that cater to local needs and demands. Federalism has allowed Canadians to develop local and regional loyalties but also to contribute to the wider Canadian political culture.

Since the 1950s, billions of dollars have shifted from the national treasury—through federal transfer payments—to adjust and diminish regional economic differences in Canada. From 1993 to 2004, transfer payments to the provinces were reduced, thereby reducing provincial revenues used for welfare programs, education, and health care. In 2004, however, the Martin Liberal **minority government** increased the transfers to the provinces, giving them greater spending options. Transfers were also buttressed by the minority government of Stephen Harper.

Ever since it was elevated to the level of public policy in Canada, regional development has been politically driven. Indeed, the federal structure of Canada's governing system tends to reinforce the focus of public policy on regionalism, and on regional solutions to economic development. Yet the concept has never been adequately defined by governments, either in economic or political terms. Some economists even reject the idea that "region" is a valid concept for economic policy analysis. They hold that economic development can be directed only at people, as opposed to places or regions.

Lucian Pye has noted the centrality and importance of politics to the process of nation-building.[23] His position is that without a developed political and governing system, national development will falter. National governments often establish a complex set of political and

economic structures in order to achieve desired national goals—such as energy self-sufficiency, economic independence, universal medical services, or economic prosperity. For example, Canadian governments have created Crown corporations to facilitate the process of nation-building and province-building in areas of the economy where the private sector cannot or will not assume the cost and risks of development such as oil, gas, forestry, and ferry services.

In Canada, the job of nation-building has always been initiated, controlled, and directed by the federal government. The *Constitution Act, 1867* granted the federal government the nation-building powers it needed to expand the role of the state directly and indirectly in the lives of individuals and groups, and in the jurisdictions of other levels of government. It is important to note that the division of powers outlined in our Constitution clearly gives most powers to the federal Parliament, establishing it as the dominant decision-making authority in Canada. The "peace, order and good government" clause of the 1867 Constitution grants **residual power** to the federal Parliament, giving it the necessary legal basis to involve itself in areas of jurisdiction not specifically assigned to the provinces. Historically, this constitutional legitimacy, when combined with federal spending and taxing power, has provided the federal government with the means for expanding the national state apparatus to build Canada.

The size of the government sector has grown steadily since Confederation and rapidly since World War II. Total government spending as a percentage of gross national expenditures (the total output of the economy) grew from 23.7 percent in 1947 to over 39 percent in 2007. The number of federal government portfolios grew sporadically from 19 in 1947 to 40 in 1984 and 33 in 2006.

Debt and Nation-Building

During the latter half of the twentieth century, the politics of nation-building was conditioned by the debts federal and provincial governments incurred to administer public affairs. Whether governments administer their affairs efficiently determines overall economic performance and their ability to overcome **national debt**. The way governments borrow and how they spend, raise revenues, and deliver their services substantially contributes to their nation-building ability. All of this may be complicated by corruption in government, inefficiency and mismanagement, and how governments tax their populations. Most national economies incurred severe national debt and recurring **budget deficits** during the final decades of the twentieth century. By 2009 the global economic meltdown caused all developed economies, including Canada's, to incur national deficits, creating more national debt. Such circumstances restrict the ability of governments to develop their societies. Uncontrolled national deficits reduce or eliminate a government's spending on education, on systems of transportation and communication, health care, and research and development.

FACTFILE   In 2008, the U.S. Congressional Budget Office estimated the national deficit to be $1.18 trillion for that year, and predicted that deficits for 2010 and 2011 could also reach $1 trillion.

By the turn of the twenty-first century, many nation-states had amassed national debts almost equal to or greater than their gross domestic products (Table 1.3). The public-sector debt ratio includes the sum total of national, provincial, municipal, and government agency debt.[24] The indebtedness of Ottawa and all the provinces amounts to about 88 percent of Canada's gross domestic product in the early years of this decade.

The impact of an unfavourable debt-to-GDP ratio endangers national economic growth. In order to pay off loans, governments have to use funds that could otherwise be reinvested in the national economy.[25] Canada's total federal and provincial debt equals almost all of the economic activity going on in the country, as measured by

Table 1.3   Ratio of debt to gross domestic product in selected economies

National Economy	Debt/GDP ratio
Burundi	90%
Ethiopia	94%
Canada (federal = 49%) (federal + provincial = 81%)	81%
Guyana	791%
Italy	82%
Morocco	81%
Mozambique	420%
Poland	79%
United States	97%
Democratic Republic of the Congo	120%

Sources: World Bank, World Development Indicators Report 2006: *http://www.web.worldbank.org/WBSITE/ EXTERNAL/EXTABOUTUS/0contentMDK:20041066~menuPK:34582~pagePI & Public Sector Statistics, 2007/2008". The information can be found in Table 3.1: Balance sheets and net financial debt—Federal, provincial and territorial general governments and local government. Adapted from Statistics Canada, "Public Sector Statistics" Cat.#68-213-XWE. www.statcan.gc.ca/bsolc/olc-cel/olc-cel?catno=68-213-X&lang=eng.*

the GDP during one year. Economies that are heavily indebted this way experience a huge loss of financial resources that they desperately need for social and economic development.

From Government Deficits to Surpluses and Back Again

Just as the deficit and debt have permeated almost every federal budget since the 1970s, so have large surpluses defined Canada's fiscal policies. In 2007, the annual federal surplus was $13.2 billion, and surpluses totaling $41 billion were forecast to accrue to the year 2011. That would all change in the fall of 2008, as the government of Stephen Harper faced a turbulent global recession.

A generation of Canadians grew up under the shadow of federal and provincial deficits and a persistently increasing national debt. By the start of 2009, they were confronting a return to deficit spending and increasing debt. All governments in Canada had to abandon their fiscal policies of surplus budgeting and return to managing economies exposed to new deficits and an increasing debt. At the beginning of the global recession in 2008, Canada's ratio of debt to gross domestic product was about 81 per cent (federal plus provincial debts). The expectation was that this could be reduced to about 20 per cent by 2025, if the economy continued to produce surpluses (Table 1.3). Until the global economy, and Canada's economy, produce growth again, it is unlikely the exposure to debt will meet these expectations.

The most significant difference between this new fiscal world and the old one is the government's freedom to choose the direction nation-building will take in Canada. But what should the federal and provincial governments do to address the current situation? Should they lower taxes, increase spending on infrastructure, keep borrowing, or just ride the economic storm with the economy as it is, facing high unemployment and widespread business and personal bankruptcies?

Federal and provincial surpluses have enabled Canada to reduce its debt until the world's economic crisis emerged. Spending on decaying infrastructures was already taking place in budgets with surpluses. Now this same dynamic is taking place using borrowed money, as a stimulus to the economy. The federal government has already increased transfer payments to refurbish municipal infrastructures and to restore confidence in healthcare and secondary education. Whether Canada is running a surplus or a deficit, these areas of Canadian society continue to demand attention and stimulation.

LEARNING ABOUT POLITICS
Political Socialization

Political socialization is how we learn about politics and government. It is the master concept used by political scientists to account for the ways that the content of a political culture or a group of political cultures is transmitted to new generations. In various ways, every society teaches its members the political values, traditions, norms, and duties that it deems desirable and acceptable for its survival.

All individuals experience the subtle pressures that entice them to **internalize** and adopt their society's norms. Even though individuals in democracies may be dissatisfied with political leadership, they have learned to accept elections—rather than riots or **insurgencies**—as the best route to political change. In totalitarian societies, individuals learn that only one political party has the undisputed right to interpret and implement political goals, without dissent or competition from individuals or groups.

In societies undergoing violent change—such as the current situations in Israel, Palestine, Iraq, and Afghanistan—people internalize the use of violence as a necessary and acceptable means of political and governmental change.

Political scientists see political socialization as both a process and a goal. As a process, political socialization has been defined by Easton and Dennis as "those developmental processes through which persons acquire political orientations."[26] For Roberta Sigel, "political socialization refers to the learning process by which the political norms and behaviours acceptable to an ongoing political system are transmitted from generation to generation."[27]

In some political cultures, the goal and effect of political socialization is to mould a child or adult to a prescribed set of conventions organized and engineered by the state. Following the successful Cuban revolution, children were housed, socialized, and educated by state organizations. Adult political values were shaped by organizations like the Committees for the Defense of the Revolution (CDRs), which still induct people into Cuba's revolutionary political culture.

Political socialization may be incidental to other life experiences, or it may be as deliberate as a state-monitored program of **indoctrination**. As a general rule, democratic political systems provide a subtle environment in which political information is transmitted in a casual manner.

Profile of the Political Self

Much more research, by political scientists and social psychologists, is anticipated on what psychological processes are involved in early political socialization because little is still known about it. It is very difficult to get into the heads of children as they acquire the initial political stimuli in their lives. Many political scientists who have specialized in this area have based their theories of observation on their own children or on relatively small numbers of randomly selected children. However, their work has been extremely important in helping us to understand how children first learn about politics.

At the outset, we should avoid making the false assumption that early socialization is a predictor of how we think at later stages of life, especially our political values. Adult character is highly changeable and continues to be that way well into old age. Nevertheless, it is useful for us to focus on early or primary political socialization as an attribute of the child's development of "self." Each person's self-development is unique and may not follow the stages of expected chronological human growth from child to adult. Some children may be more politically aware than their parents, though the opposite is normally true. Research observations can be made about political learning in children, adolescents, and adults. However, understanding the political "person" in all of us requires knowledge of our "self" and its general learning experiences.

The American sociologist Charles Horton Cooley saw the self as a looking glass in the process of socialization, political or otherwise.[28] Our political behaviour is a reflection of how we see ourselves in a complex world. Self-image determines our general interest in politics and affects our political identities. As we pass through various levels of human development, we learn political behaviour that satisfies the needs of our self.

Political socialization is a lifelong process intimately tied to our self-definition. The foundations of political behaviour are laid in childhood. Political socialization begins as children interact first with parents and later with peers, teachers, and other adults. It also occurs as we are exposed to messages from radio, television, and other mass media. Each political system tries to teach new members, especially children, what the accepted behaviours, norms, and values are. The goal is to condition the self-defining individual to accept the means society uses to achieve social order. If political socialization is effective, new members (children and immigrants) adopt supportive attitudes toward officeholders, political procedures, institutions, and the ways policy decisions distribute rewards and punishments.

How Children Learn about Politics

David Easton and Robert Hess found that even though children do not develop a political vocabulary until the age of 11 or 12, many basic political attitudes and values have been firmly established by the time the child begins elementary school. James Chowning Davies discovered that before schooling starts, a child's familiarity with power is well at work within the framework of the family.[29] Later, in school, children learn that there are *public* forces at work in their lives. Government policy dictates that they be in school, that they get immunized against disease, and that public property does not belong to them. They learn that there are many rules and regulations that should be respected in the outside world.

In spite of the apparent regulatory nature of the political world, Easton and Dennis point out that the North American child "learns to like the government before [he/she] really knows what it is."[30] Early in their lives, children naturally develop favourable feelings toward the symbolic and ceremonial character of the state and government. The flag, the national anthem, emblems, the military, and the head of state are all presented as special representations of the majesty of the state and country.

This is particularly true for most Canadian youth. One study of 6000 Canadian children found that students from grades 4 to 8 held high levels of affection for the Queen, the governor general, and the prime minister.[31] **Party identification** also tended to increase from grades 4 to 8, with some changes in affection noted toward the prime minister. Ronald Landes discovered that Canadian children possess more knowledge about leaders than about institutions and processes.[32] Formal politics, its institutions, and its actors are not central factors in a child's personal development. However, the underlying currents of political behaviour—such as competition, co-operation, compromise, power, and manipulation—are learned during childhood.

These experiences are linked to later adolescent and adult political behaviour.

Teens and Political Learning

Adolescents learn political lessons more explicitly. Social science, history, and political science classes deal with the structure of Canadian government, bringing issues of democracy, freedom, and equality to the attention of students.

> **FACTFILE** An Ipsos Reid poll in 2001 found that only half of Canadians (51 percent) could identify John A. Macdonald as Canada's first prime minister, 49 percent knew that Trudeau invoked the *War Measures Act*, and 19.5 percent knew Laurier was Canada's first Francophone prime minister.

During adolescence, people become increasingly aware of the existence of authority outside the family and school. Adolescents become familiar with institutions of authority such as the courts, Parliament, and municipal government. At this stage of maturation and change, the individual begins to express independent political views and to distinguish parental influences from general social ones.

Politicization may become highly personalized during adolescence. It may reveal itself as **political cynicism**, **political efficacy**, **political apathy**, or **political participation**. During adolescence, individuals demonstrate different capacities for learning political information and reflect different levels of maturity with respect to opinion formation and expression.

By the time they reach their twenties, most Canadians have a reasonably well-formed set of basic values, a sense of belonging to a political party, some policy preferences, and some evaluations of government performance.

Learning about Politics as an Adult

Adult socialization refers to changes in learning and attitudes that take place after the adolescent years. Because adult political socialization is a continuous experience, we should avoid the assumption that young people are usually more liberal and that aging leads to political conservatism. Roberta Sigel and Marilyn Hoskin noted that adults change political attitudes regularly throughout their lives in response to issues that affect self-interest.[33] A person who at 35 holds politically conservative views on social and economic assistance may at age 65 show strong support for government-sponsored programs.

FACTFILE   Only 8 percent of Canadians name the Queen as the head of state; 57 percent incorrectly believe the prime minister fulfills that role.

Adults quickly learn that their political and economic freedoms are only relative. As people establish homes and families, they begin to worry about property, taxes, school for their children, protection against crime, and such things as garbage collection. Most importantly, they learn that there is still much to learn politically at all stages of adulthood. The values and beliefs learned in childhood may no longer be adequate or relevant to us as adults who experience role change.

Under some government regimes, adults may experience a political re-socialization. The term **brainwashing** is used to describe an attempt to change attitudes or ideologies against a person's will. Brainwashing is a Chinese expression for purifying the mind of any political beliefs in the old order that existed before the Revolution. The old "mistaken" ideas are washed away and the "right" political values are put in place.

What are the environmental agents of socialization? How do they influence the way we learn about politics?

Focus On   Studying Political Science in Canada

Political science is now an accessible area of study for most Canadians. As a social science, it currently appears in the high school curriculum of all the provinces. Because studying political science is a career in its own right, it is now offered at most colleges and universities across the country. Currently, there are more than 1200 full-time political scientists employed by over 65 departments in Canada.

Colleges and universities provide the necessary environment for teachers and professors to conduct their research in an atmosphere of academic freedom. They are free to investigate any area of study related to politics, government, and public policy. They can choose to work alone or with other colleagues in the profession to complete their research goals.

As a field of study, political science is very diversified. Many approaches are available to practitioners who might choose to use historical, legal, and statistical methods to study what interests them. Because political science is such a large field of study, universities have recognized certain subfields and specializations. These fields are represented in the Canadian Political Science Association and other such provincial associations. They also form the core presentations in the American Political Science Association and its affiliates across the United States. The following categories are recognized at most Canadian colleges and universities as general areas of study in political science*:

American Politics and Government examines the political and governmental institutions of the United States as well as its role as a super-power in international affairs.

Canadian Politics and Government focuses on all aspects of federal, provincial, and municipal public affairs in Canada. It is a study of Parliamentary and other political institutions such as political parties and interest groups in Canada.

Comparative Government and Politics compares and analyses political institutions from a cross-national perspective in two or more countries.

Gender Politics studies the role of women in public affairs, sometimes comparing the different approaches of men and women to public affairs.

International Politics looks at the relations between and among states from a global perspective. It examines the presence of international organizations, such as the United Nations and non-governmental organizations, such as the Red Cross. Issues include war and peace, the environment, globalization, terrorism, and development.

International Law traces the history of the binding rules of the international and global system. It examines the instruments of lawmaking, compliance, and enforcement as they relate to treaties, courts, and international bodies.

Municipal Politics and Government studies local and urban politics, how councils make decisions, and how municipal administrations carry out the services most people depend upon.

Political Economy considers the relationship between the economy and political decisions. It examines how public policies are shaped by the forces of the economy.

Political Theory and Ideology examines the great ideas of our time and times gone by. It considers the major issues of democracy and justice as well as the relationship of the individual to the state.

Provincial and Territorial Politics studies the relationship of federal and provincial governments and the institutions of decision making in the provinces and territories.

Public Administration focuses on the branch of government that implements the laws passed by legislatures. It studies the dynamics of bureaucratic politics in the public sector.

* It is important to note that the division of some of these areas may be contested by political science practitioners. An analysis of the direction political science is taking can be found on the Text Enrichment Site for this book.

AGENTS OF POLITICAL LEARNING

The agents of political socialization most frequently identified by political scientists have been the family, school, peers, the media, and the political system. By "agents" we mean those social institutions and experiences that condition, indirectly influence, or directly determine the development of a person's political views and actions.

Accordingly, a person whose parents have little interest in politics is less likely to acquire political knowledge than one whose parents are highly active and motivated politically. The greater the exposure a person has to politically charged agents of socialization, the greater the likelihood that the values will be assimilated and internalized.

Figure 1.4 shows the approximate exposure to five of the most familiar agents of socialization. In Canada, as in most other places, people learn the norms and expectations of their community from their parents, teachers at school, friends and associates, TV, radio, and the print media, as well as political parties and government agencies. These

Figure 1.4 Estimated exposure to significant agents of political socialization

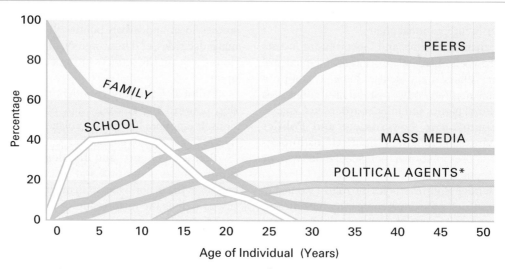

*Government, political parties, pressure groups

are the primary sources of political information for most people. They help to shape our attitudes, values, and political behaviour throughout our lives. In Figure 1.4, the age of a person is represented on the horizontal line from birth to age 50. The vertical line shows exposure as the percentage of interactions people have that lead to a significant socializing effect on them.

The Family

Most children get their first ideas about government and politics from their parents and siblings.

Families share their opinions directly with children, who may adopt these opinions. In effect, parents say or do things that children imitate. The family as a social institution places its members in a network of social and economic relationships that influence how children see the world and also how the world sees them.

Even though the family is neither instituted nor designed as an agent for transmitting politi-

cal values, it is considered by many scholars to be the most important source of political learning. A child's exposure to family influences remains high until late adolescence. Then, other agents of socialization begin to attract as much or more attention. But the family may influence a person's predispositions toward authority, party identification, and general political norms and behaviour throughout his or her life. Because most of our early personal development takes place at home, we can understand why the family contributes so much to the profile of our political self.

The School

Canadian children spend a substantial portion of their working hours in a school setting. For many, attendance at a university prolongs this exposure into early adulthood. Because of their constant influence in the formative years of life, schools rival parents as agents of teaching important values and norms in a community.

Because most schools in Canada are tax-supported public institutions that determine teaching standards and follow standardized curriculum guidelines, they inadvertently serve to transmit socially and politically approved values. Schools usually promote positive orientations toward the political and economic system and introduce students to the rituals and symbols of the political process. Teachers, whose credentials are normally determined by provincial governments, also transmit political skills and values over and above those in the curriculum.

Peer Groups

Figure 1.4 shows that as the family influence diminishes, there is increased contact with peers. **Peer groups** are normally formed among individuals who share common backgrounds, outlooks, and values. In Canadian society, peer groups occupy an important position for influencing adult socialization in all matters—including politics. For most of us, peers affect us before we enter school. With peers, we are first introduced to the value of equality—being equal among equals. We learn to share, compete, co-operate, compromise, and manipulate those in equal standing to ourselves. We also learn about leadership and the unwritten rules of being recruited and accepted by a group. In adult life, peer groups become the most significant agents of political socialization, particularly when

Heather Hiscox, CBC News: Morning

politics is important to the group itself. Because of the personal nature of most peer-group relationships, they apply subtle pressure on individuals by communicating political values and encouraging certain standards of political conduct.

The Mass Media

Another source of political socialization cannot be ignored: the mass media. The impact of the media on children and adults has been the focus of increased government and scholarly attention in recent years. In Canada, the mass media have played a major role in politicizing the population. Most newspapers and magazines are highly political in content and coverage. Radio and television are a shared media that link Canada's 10 million square kilometres of area with coverage of politics, economics, and cultural happenings across the country. The internet brings world politics to computers in every home.

> **FACTFILE** In Canada, the media are generally biased toward bad-news stories, which vastly outnumber good-news stories. Generally, the media tend to over-report violence, conflict, scandal, corruption, sex, and political incompetence.

The mass media enlighten us about public policy, how well policies are working, who are the best political leaders, what alternative leaders and policies might be considered, and what effects they have. The media also act as a vehicle for the government, political parties, and interest groups that want to communicate their positions to the people, educating and persuading, or even manipulating their opinions.

The media are expected to act as independent agents of political socialization, bypassing parents, the education system, and peers. Canadians spend 50 percent more time (about 25 hours per week) watching television than in any other leisure activity. The electronic media (television and computers, followed by radio) are considered the most influential and believable of all media sources. Non-electronic media such as newspapers and magazines are also highly influential. Television, especially, plays a central role in the formation and change of political orientations among Canadians. It does so by structuring their attitudes about politics and by influencing the information on which these attitudes are based.

Political Agents: Government, Parties, and Pressure Groups

The political system is filled with numerous competing groups—the government, political parties, and interest groups—that have a vested interest in educating the public. Political events do not always speak for themselves; often they are explained to the public by interest groups or political parties that have political axes to grind. As such, they bring particular biases or points of view to bear in transmitting information about politics to the general public. Political leaders' interpretations of what is going on can also have significant effects on public perception.

Governments spend millions of dollars each year trying to tell Canadians about the positive consequences of what they do. Governments want us to know that they are improving the economy, creating jobs, and managing public affairs competently. In this way, they are teaching us about politics and government from their perspective. Today, they play a major role in the general process of political socialization.

Political parties can greatly simplify matters for the voter. Often people will choose a political party as a shortcut or substitute for interpreting issues and events they may not comprehend. Competition among political parties can also increase public awareness of, and interest in, candidates and issues. Party competition attracts attention and gets people involved.

Although interest groups differ in size, goals, budgets, and scope of interest, they are intensely involved in educating the public about their concerns. Interest groups perform certain functions in Canada's political system that cannot be performed as well through the conventional structures of government.

WHY POLITICAL OPINIONS MATTER

Expressing Public Opinions

When we express our attitudes about politics and government, we are participating in an important form of political behaviour. We are influencing others by what we say, and we are being influenced by what they say. Every **political opinion** is learned and acts as an indication of how much we have learned about politics. Usually, political opinions express our political values in day-to-day terms. They indicate how people feel about their representatives, their institutions, and their national goals. Political opinions reflect our ideology, our values, our conduct, and our expectations. To be sure, many opinions lead to no action, but most political opinions imply that political behaviour will follow. It is because of this expected link between opinion and action that democratic theorists lay such great emphasis on the role played by **public opinion** in political affairs.

We can trace the high regard for public opinion from the earliest writings of political philosophers to the present day. Although Greek and Roman philosophers described it as "mass opinion," they quickly identified its importance to the world of politics. Among modern political theorists, Jean-Jacques Rousseau was the first to make use of its present meaning by employing the phrase "l'opinion publique" in regard to his notion of "general will." Since the eighteenth century, public opinion has been courted by politicians, condemned by philosophers, catered to by business and governments, feared by military leaders, and analyzed by statisticians.

Political scientists are interested in the formation and expression of opinions to the extent that they influence and change public policy. By observing the role of public opinion in the formation of public decisions, we heighten our understanding of how our political system works.

What Is a Political Opinion?

All opinions amount to an expression of attitudes and beliefs. In our society, opinions constitute an expression of personal and group power. We build and destroy governments with opinions. In our legal system, opinions judge the behaviour of individuals and corporations. They operate as forceful and dynamic *social messages* representing any collection of vocalized individual opinions.

In everyday discourse, public opinion refers to general public attitudes toward everything from athletics to the zodiac. But *political opinions* are specific and relate to all matters of government and political affairs. So, as students of politics, we should consider V.O. Key's definition of public opinion as "those opinions held by private persons which governments find it prudent to heed." For purposes of political analysis, public opinions become significant when they link the opinions of people to political action and government attention.

Is There Only One Public?

Often, when referring to political opinion, people make the incorrect assumption that there is only one "public." This interpretation of public opinion is often misleading. Very few issues in a society concern an entire public. We assume that "the people" really is *one* enormous individual with a single opinion, quite probably one that agrees with our own. For analytic purposes, however, it is important to be careful with aggregate references to "Canadians" or "Americans," keeping in mind the actual diversity of views that individual members of a given segment of the public may hold on most questions.

It is true that for issues of widespread impact—such as war, inflation, unemployment, capital punishment, and universal medicare—the general public will voice related opinions that are measurable as a national response. But only on a relatively small number of issues does a public respond organically as one voice. It is much more accurate to hold that there are many publics with special interests in issues of a local nature. For example, most Manitobans may not be concerned about the state of the fishery in British Columbia because it is a distant reality for them. Analysts have concluded therefore that only *special publics* that are immediately affected by a particular event will likely hold informed opinions on the matter. In fact, all across Canada there are many special publics holding intense and directed opinions, as distinct from the *general public* that holds opinions on everything.

PROPERTIES OF POLITICAL OPINIONS

Political opinions have several distinctive characteristics. First, they have *content*. They are about something with political consequence—candidates, issues, economic and social conditions. Second, they have *direction*, i.e., an opinion is not a simple statement about an alleged fact: it indicates or implies a value preference. A Canadian's opinion about the Organization of American States (OAS), for example, will express approval or disapproval of the organization, as well as his or her understanding of what the OAS is and does. The direction of an opinion informs us whether the public response is positive, negative, or indifferent. Third, opinions have *intensity*—an emotional characteristic of public opinion that tells us how committed people are to the position they have taken. Intense clusters of Quebec opinion have polarized in about a 50/49 percent distribution of divided expressions of self-determination. Intensity involves not only the "extremeness" of an opinion but also the extent to which the issue is *salient* to a person, i.e., how much he or she really cares about it.

The intensity of opinions is of great importance to government decision makers. If people hold opinions of low intensity on an issue, governments may decide to proceed with a particular policy direction that is not very popular. Or intensity may reflect a strong consensus, compelling a government to act or not to act in a particular policy direction. In Canada, governments spend millions of dollars each year on public-opinion surveys to test how people will react to policy initiatives.

The *stability* of public opinion is another characteristic of particular interest to governments. Stability is the degree to which the direction and intensity of an opinion remain the same over time. Some people may adhere to a particular viewpoint for decades, while others shift positions frequently. People also vary greatly in the consistency of their opinions. A Canadian may believe that government spending should be increased, but if he or she also wants taxes reduced, we would regard the opinion as inconsistent. Changes in opinion may require a modification of policies and programs by governments. The stability and volatility of public opinion are important measures for government decision makers and a constant challenge to political leadership.

Measuring Political Opinion

Before the 1930s, governments, historians, and political observers had to guess at public opinion by analyzing the contents of newspaper stories, political speeches, voting returns, and diaries. The founding fathers in both Canada and the United States felt that they could tap into public opinion by implementing representation by population in the legislative structures of each country. They thought that attitudes and actions in the legislatures would reflect public opinion on a wide variety of issues. However, after much experience

with these legislative structures of government, it became evident that bills passed by a majority of elected representatives do not necessarily reflect the opinions of a majority of citizens.

Random Sampling

In the nineteenth century, newspapers and magazines often enlivened their coverage of politics by conducting straw polls or mail surveys of their readers. The difficulty in relying on the results of these polls was that the method of **sampling** was not random. Not until the 1930s were efficient new scientific surveys and sampling techniques pioneered by George Gallup, Elmo Roper, and Archibald Crossley, all of whom had developed modern polling methods in advertising and marketing research.

The first scientifically measured public opinion poll in Canada was conducted during World War II. The "little" Gallup poll was based on the theory that a sample of individuals selected by chance from a population will be "representative" of the entire population. A few thousand interviews, representative of the total population, would thus be far more effective in tapping public opinion than millions of ballots collected in a biased or haphazard fashion. This means that the traits of individuals in a sample—their attitudes, beliefs, political characteristics, and so on—will reflect the traits of the *entire* population. Sampling theory does not posit that the sample will exactly match the population, only that it will reflect the population within some predictable degree of accuracy.

FACTFILE Professional pollsters watch for the "halo effect," which is the tendency of survey respondents to provide socially acceptable replies instead of their honest views; because of this tendency, a survey may understate the true extent of prejudice, hatred, and bigotry.

Three factors condition the degree of accuracy for the sample. One is that the sample must be taken *randomly*, such that each individual in the population has the same chance of being selected. In Canada, direct random sampling is complicated, given the size and dispersion of the population. Instead, pollsters first divide the country into geographical areas, then randomly choose areas and eventually sample individuals who live in those areas. The second factor that affects the accuracy of sampling is the amount of *variation in the population*. It is important to stratify the sample so that the same variations in the population, i.e., linguistic, racial, and gender differences, are reflected in the sample. Finally, the *size of the sample* also affect the accuracy of the survey. The larger the sample, the more accurately it will reflect the population. For example, a sample of 400 individuals will predict accurately to a population within 6 percentage points (plus or minus) 95 percent of the time. Most national samples, such as the Ipsos-Reid, Gallup Canada, Pollara, and Environics Research polls, are accurate within 2.5 to 4 percentage points 19 times out of 20.

Patterns of Political Opinion

The results of public opinion polls are often displayed in charts like those in Figure 1.5, which depicts three idealized patterns of distribution— normal, skewed, and bimodal. Two basic elements that contribute to the shape of the opinion distribution are the percentage of the population that holds the opinion (vertical axis) and the direction and intensity of the opinion (– – to ++ on the horizontal axis). Different patterns of public opinion affect the options open to policy makers.

FACTFILE When asked by Globe-Environics, Decima Research, and Gallup Canada, usually over 80 percent of Canadian respondents state that they are not influenced at all by polls.

Opinions that are normally distributed permit government policies to range on either side of the centrist position (note the portion of the population with no opinion or weak opinion that clusters around the centre). Thus the pattern in (a) is *permissive* because leaders may act freely without fear of much public reaction. The patterns in (b) are skewed to the pro side or the con side of an issue and represent the *consensus* pattern of opinion. In these patterns, the options open to leaders are more limited because most people have made up their minds and hold an opinion on one side of the issue. It would be politically perilous for government to ignore such a consensus of opinion, pro or con. The pattern of public opinion in (c) is conflictive and *divisive*. In such a bimodal distribution, opinions divide almost evenly over an issue. Bimodal distributions of opinion have the greatest potential to generate political conflict, especially if people on both sides feel intensely about the issue.

The Reliability of Opinion Polls

Former Prime Minister John Diefenbaker made the following comment about polls: "Every morning when I take my little dog, Happy, for a walk, I watch with great interest what he does to the poles." Mr. Diefenbaker may have had a strong dislike for political opinions polls because in the late 1950s and early 1960s the media and the general public were not very well versed in interpreting them.

The first Gallup polls appeared in the 1940s. The public was very slowly educated about the scientific theory behind them. Often, the public's spin on the content of a political poll was wrong, and too much information was inferred from the poll results. The current practice of tracking polls was uncommon. Today, **poll tracking** (conducting the same poll numerous times over a period of time) is a common practice.

Anyone who bases decisions on the results of polls should be aware of their limitations. In addition to the possibility of incorrect assumptions, sampling error, or being outdated, polls may present an inaccurate picture because of the way questions are worded, the way surveys are conducted, or the way the responses are interpreted.

Figure 1.5   **Patterns of political opinion**

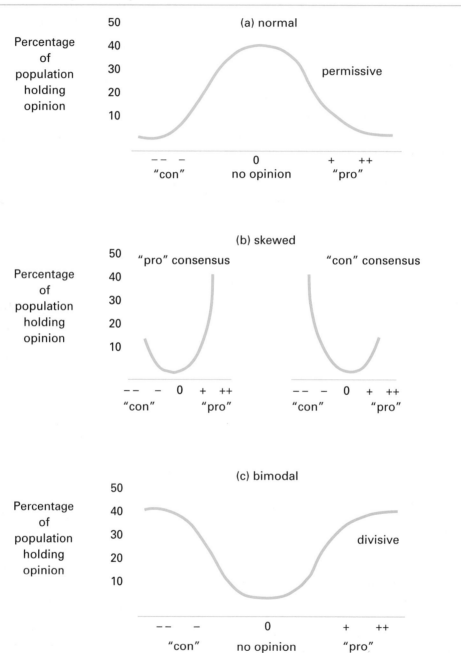

Many media and political party organizations have developed in-house expertise in conducting their own polls, independent of professional polling companies. The media have learned that their polls can themselves be persuasive tools. Sometimes poll findings are selectively publicized by the media in order to add substance to the content of a story or to put a spin on a commentary or documentary.

Political scientists keep certain guidelines in mind when interpreting poll results. First, they want to know whether the sample represented in the poll was random. Only random samples permit the analyst to accurately infer information about the total population under study. Second, political scientists want to know what the sample margin of error is. Most political polls claim between a 3 and 5 percent margin of error. When an election is close among competing leaders and their parties, the margin of error is crucial. For example, if the random sampling error is ±4 percent and if party A leads party B by 2 percent (say, 51 to 49), the election is too close to call. Third, political scientists want to determine whether the group sponsoring the poll has a vested interest in the results. They will treat skeptically any findings disclosed by candidates, their party organizations, and supporters. Fourth, political scientists examine the survey questions. The wording of the questions, their placement in the survey, and the responses permitted can all affect the results. The use of any positively or negatively valued buzzwords, symbols, goals, or names of individuals that may influence responses are noted. Wording surveys impartially is very important.

Finally, political scientists check the time frame during which the poll was conducted. They want to know whether any intervening events changed respondents' opinions between the time the poll was taken and the day the results were published.

Most political scientists believe that political opinion polls are here to stay as a valuable aid to discover what the people want their government to do so that the governing system can respond to the popular will in a democracy.

Chapter Summary

Politics covers a large area of public and private social activity. The use of the term *politics* includes many of the activities of private life—from "office politics" and "university politics" to the struggles over the control of corporations or other private groups. But politics is usually observed as a public activity, being a natural outgrowth of living together with limited resources in a competitive social system. As a public phenomenon, politics can enable us to build a united and prosperous society or it can divide us to the point of social conflict. In order to make sense of the political world, many political scientists portray politics as a multi-dimensional characteristic of human experience—something that can be studied as behaviour, as culture, as values, or as competing or conflicting interests. In all societies, politics can be the powerful force behind social construction, yet it may also facilitate social destruction: we can survive because of it or die from it.

We need to think about politics as an intrinsic part of our personal behaviour that ultimately has social consequences. Being selfish has social consequences as does being altruistic. We learn about politics and express opinions about it every day. We negotiate, co-operate, compromise, and bargain in almost all of our interactions with others. Politics frequently, and indeed usually, involves questions about what we expect our governments to do, how we want our politicians to meet our needs, and who are the most influential individuals and groups that get things done in society.

How can we understand the scope of politics as a national and international reality in our lives? The answer lies in taking a wide perspective on what the components of politics are and on applying them as a framework to analyze political and governmental systems.

Looking at politics as a *behavioural* phenomenon gives us insight into the ordinary and extraordinary activities carried out by groups and individuals in the political world. Political behaviour has a psychological dimension because it manifests itself as attitudes, beliefs, judgments, ideas, and powerful ideologies that change society. Political behaviour also has a social dimension because it involves collective activity, such as voting, protesting, campaigning, lobbying, and violence.

Politics is also *cultural*, because it gives us a shared means of surviving in a world of scarcity and competition. It provides the lens through which we see and judge the world around us, and ultimately affects every aspect of who and what we are. Political culture is the way we orient ourselves to issues of politics and government and manifests itself as the way or ways we "do" politics and operate our governments. A political culture reflects the totality of a society's political experience—its symbols, values, beliefs, skills, customs, traditions, expectations, and attitudes.

Politics is the means by which we debate, choose, and legislate the most important values in our society. Our political values are socially shared ideas about what is "good," "right," and "desirable." Politics and government reflect values that are demanded by people who hold them with great conviction and work toward achieving them with great energy.

Politics is conflictive. Because society is so diverse, politics will inevitably attempt to harmonize the many individual and group interests that pressure our governments to make public policy. Issues such as abortion, gun control, language rights, and sovereignty drive the political system to reconcile conflicting demands on the desired course of action for society to take.

Politics is the means by which we form our governments, and by which we build our cities, towns, provinces, and nation-states. Political decisions are required to produce the infrastructures that enable our communities to develop. These comprise implementing systems of communication, education, transportation, and power grids; technological innovation; and the political system itself. Nation-building is a political accomplishment, requiring governments to attract competent decision makers, make progressive public policies, and manage public administration efficiently.

Politics is learned behaviour. Political socialization is the process by which citizens absorb the values and skills of the political culture. Through political socialization, we internalize and incorporate into our thinking the beliefs, values, judgments, and ideologies that form the backbone of the political world in which we live. Most of what we learn about our political culture comes to us through the agents of socialization in society—the family, schools, peer groups, the media, interest groups, parties, and governments. What we learn about politics from one generation to another may be occasionally predictable, though not always. Generations do change, but each new generation will, in most cases, reflect the political values of the old.

Political behaviour is measurable. Political scientists, journalists, and governments use scientific methods to measure and track our political opinions on the major issues confronting society. They observe the characteristics of our opinions and other forms of political behaviour, measuring the content, direction, intensity, and stability of what Canadians and other nationals think about government and politics.

Discussion Questions

1. Why is it so difficult for us to define politics? How would a Canadian definition of politics differ from an American one? Do First Nations people see politics differently? Design your own definition of politics based on five values you believe are essential for a just society.

2. Is there a different political culture in each Canadian province? Why or why not? Outline the main components of Canada's national political culture. How does Quebec's political culture differ from those of other provinces?

3. Distinguish the roles of the federal government, the provinces, the territories, and the municipalities in the politics of nation-building in Canada. How do rural areas contribute to nation-building? How are cities contributing to national prosperity? Does Canada need to be a federal state? Can Canada be built as a country without building its cities?

4. Do political opinion polls strengthen or weaken democracy? Why must we know what others think about political issues before we make up our minds?

5. Do you trust the science behind polling? If not, why not? What question about politics or government would you like to ask Canadians or people in your local area? What do you think the results would be?

Understanding Political Thinking

2 CHAPTER

After reading this chapter, you will be able to:

- understand what roles political ideologies play in our lives

- identify and describe ideologies by type

- ponder how we learn our political ideologies and how they affect our behaviour

- unpack the components of ideologies and describe each of them carefully, with an eye to comparing what they mean in each ideology

- examine the goals of ideologies in various political and governing systems

- describe the outstanding features of democratic ideologies

- analyze the qualities of non-democratic ideologies, with a focus on Marxism

- examine the content of other ideologies such as nationalism, anarchism, fascism, and feminism

- consider how movements and ideologies are connected

- discuss the relevance of ideologies in Canada and other political systems

WHAT IS AN IDEOLOGY?

During the Enlightenment, the French philosopher Antoine Destutt de Tracy (1754–1836) coined the word *ideologie* to mean the "science of ideas": the study of the origins, evolution, and nature of ideas. Many philosophers of the time (the *philosophes*) believed that the application of human reason to society could reveal new belief systems, setting ideals and common purposes for communities to pursue.[1] Until the Enlightenment, ideologies were primarily religious—the world was perceived and explained in terms that linked political and economic beliefs with religious ones—for example, those of Buddhism, Calvinism, Catholicism, Islam, and Shintoism. The writers and critics who forged the "enlightened" ideas of the eighteenth century felt that the future of humankind lay not so much in the blind adherence to divine commandments but rather in the application of **human reason** to economic, social, and political challenges.

The term *ideology* enjoyed good standing until the nineteenth century, when Napoleon began to call his political enemies "ideologues" because they advocated liberal ideals and held **utopian** and antireligious views. A negative connotation was attached to the word and continues to this day in some countries of the world, depending on how the term is used.

To many Americans and Canadians, ideology is to politics what superstition is to religion. In societies founded on philosophical **pragmatism** and freedom, where individual choices determine leadership, programs of action, and reforms, people distrust the intellectual and emotional commitment required to sustain what in their minds is an ideology. They see ideologies as abstract, utopian systems of ideas that demand a blind and uncritical allegiance of believers to fixed ways of thinking.

To view *ideology* as such serves no useful purpose to scholarship or understanding because, to varying degrees, all societies are ideological. An ideology is a value system through which we perceive, explain, and accept or reject the world. Ideologies give us a total view of things and claim to supply answers to all questions. Karl Deutsch holds that ideologies are like maps in that they outline "a simplified image of the real world."[2] To some degree, consciously or unconsciously, all people are **ideologues** in that they map out their interpretation of the real world and its significance to their world. Robert Dahl emphasized this fact when he said, "Prior to politics, beneath it, enveloping it, restricting it, conditioning it . . . is ideology."[3]

> **FACTFILE** Much of the history of the twentieth century was the struggle between two powerful ideologies: democratic capitalism and communism.

Contemporary ideologies, such as anarchism, capitalism, conservatism, communism, and socialism, contain mainly socio-economic elements that dominate the beliefs people adopt and the biases they reflect. Ultimately, these systems condition people's political behaviour. *Political ideology* may be defined as a "belief system that explains and justifies a preferred political order for society, either existing or proposed, and offers a strategy (processes, institutional arrangements, programs) for its attainment."[4] Robert E. Lane classified a number of important functions of political ideologies.[5] They are summarized as follows:

- Ideologies present a simplified "cause and effect" interpretation of a complex world.

- Ideologies integrate a theory of **human nature** with life's basic economic, social, and political values.

- Ideologies appear normative and moral in tone and content and aspire to perfect our behaviour.

- Ideologies draw their philosophical premises from constitutions, declarations, manifestos, and writings.

- Ideologies constitute a broad belief system and advocate reforms in the basic fabric and structures of society.

- Ideologies address fundamental questions about leadership, recruitment, political succession, and electoral behaviour.

- Ideologies persuade and **propagandize** people, who learn not to be influenced by opposing views.

Because ideologies are value-laden belief systems, they often come into conflict and competition: thus, conservatism vs. liberalism, capitalism vs. socialism, and nationalism vs. internationalism. Some political cultures appear more ideologically based than others. But whether an ideology is prominent, as in China or Cuba, or subtle, as in Canada or Australia, there is an ideological base to all political cultures.

Ideas Matter in Politics

We should distinguish political ideology from other forms of political thought, such as *political philosophy* and *political theory*. Political philosophy is a detached and often solitary "search for the principles of the good state and the good society."[6] The political philosopher asks fundamental questions about human nature and the nature of political society, and often prescribes moral and ethical solutions for what "ought" to be a better polity. Political theory attempts to formulate testable and verifiable generalizations drawn from relatable variables that explain a particular political phenomenon. Where the political philosopher is **rational** and deductive, the theorist is empirical and descriptive of "what is" rather than "what ought" to be. The words of Carl Friedrich help us to further clarify the distinctions we have just made: "Ideologies are action-related systems of ideas. . . . [They] are sets of ideas related to the existing political and social order and intended either to change it or defend it."[7]

Focus On   Great Ideas of Our Time

All of the great ideologies of our time are taken from the ideas of political philosophers. Throughout the ages, many political thinkers contributed their ideas to such monumental ideologies as anarchism, communism, democracy, nationalism, and socialism. The thoughts of people such as Plato, Aristotle, Machiavelli, Hobbes, Locke, Rousseau, Marx, and John Rawls were used to build the ideologies of the present day. With their concerns about the proper role of citizens, the state, the nature of justice, and what sort of constitution produces a great society, political philosophers laid the foundation for all of the ideologies in our civilization.

Taken together, through the centuries, philosophers have been the architects of our contemporary political wisdom and sometimes folly, telling us what political beliefs we ought to adopt, what values are desirable and moral, and what goals we should pursue in our society.

Today, the great ideas of our time are both generated and debated in the modern discipline called "analytic political philosophy." Students of politics ask: Is the nation-state still the best way to organize political society? What is the future of the nation-state? Are we at the point in the evolution of human political development where a world government is desirable and feasible? Can we successfully address the global issues of human survival and climate change as nation-states that govern their limited national interests?

Perspectives Five Dimensions of Political Thinking

The labels *radical*, *liberal*, *moderate*, *conservative*, and *reactionary* are frequently used in the literature on ideologies and in the media in Canada. It is important for students of political ideas to give these terms special consideration. Political scientists sometimes place these ideas on a continuum to better understand the logic of political thinking.

Five Dimensions of Political Thinking

Radical   Liberal   Moderate   Conservative   Reactionary

- The *radical* perspective tends to press its views toward the extreme and to challenge established ways of thinking about social and political matters.
- *Liberal* thinking is generally open to change, and embraces critical views of accepted ideas and practices, while adhering to the dictum that society is evolutionary.
- *Moderate* positions take the middle ground, attempting to balance and conciliate by permitting the existence of opposing views and seeking to find a consensus of political opinion.

- The *conservative* state of mind relies upon common sense, tradition, and convention in order to maintain the established social and political order.
- The *reactionary* thinker is not merely resistant to change but wants to put the clock back and return to some earlier order of society that is perceived to have possessed more positive characteristics, such as honesty, discipline, productivity, and predictability.

The action-related character of ideologies to which Friedrich refers is significant. History confirms that ideologies energize people, capture their imaginations, and motivate them to dismantle old orders or construct new ones. Ideologies tend to inspire people to organize themselves, which reflects itself at the political level. The ideological message is mobilized and carried by political **elites**, political parties, insurgent groups, pressure groups, education systems, and the media. Once in place, an ideology is culturally transmitted through families, peer groups, the media, and other agents of political socialization.

Types of Ideologies

Political ideologies can be distinguished broadly as *dominant ideologies* and *counter-ideologies*. Dominant ideologies generally prescribe and support existing social and political arrangements, while counter-ideologies rally the forces of change in society.

> **FACTFILE** Liberal political ideas were not originally seen in Canada as a distinct belief system of only one class—an entrepreneurial or business class—but rather as the common property of all Canadians.

Dominant ideologies

Dominant ideologies are the prevailing mindsets that assert themselves in the social and governing system. For example, the institution of private property and capitalism dominate Canada's economy and its political organization. In the context of a socialist state, however, public ownership and the collective means of production prevail in the economy and are protected by the political system.

Crosscurrents   Politically Correct (PC) Thinking

One ideological dynamic that has spread throughout Canadian institutions is what is commonly called *politically correct (PC) thinking*. In places of work, such as government, business, and universities, PC activists seek to suppress opinions and expressions they consider racist, sexist, and homophobic. They demand that nothing should be said or written that causes discomfort to "protected" groups. Political correctness asserts that our language and its use of expressions reflect systematic oppression of certain groups, such as women, people of colour, gays, and others. Examples might include a male student making remarks in class such as "women just aren't as good in this field as men," or an individual commenting in a derogatory way about another individual's sexual orientation or religious beliefs.

Universities are particularly affected by PC because they have a special responsibility to protect the freedom of expression. Many people working at universities consider PC a counter-ideology because it intervenes in the free and unfettered exchange of views that is regarded as essential to the advancement of knowledge—in fact, the very purpose for which universities are established.

As Canadian university researcher Philippe Rushton learned, anyone who may publish or voice unpopular positions, however scientifically supported, may be pilloried, bullied, criticized, punished, or even "re-educated." Based on his and others' research, Rushton argued that "East Asians, blacks, and whites are three distinct races that reveal significant behavioural and intellectual differences." His research, however specious, led him to conclude quite incredibly that blacks are the least "evolved," while East Asians are the most "evolved." He also concluded that blacks are the least intelligent, least altruistic, most licentious, and most criminal of the three groups. Other data led him to disclose that blacks have the most children and are the least nurturing of these three races. His claims—not surprisingly—elicited outrage from other researchers, the media, and representative groups.

Often in Canada, students and faculty must seek the protection of the courts from attempts by universities to limit their speech or their research findings. Is PC really a counter-ideology? Does it repress free speech and freedom of expression? Or is it the best way to rinse racist and sexist language out of our vocabularies?

Ideologies have power and can be dominant in a society in two ways. First, they are dominant when most people accept and articulate them. Second, they can be dominant because the most powerful people in society support them, but the majority or significant numbers of people may not accept the ideology. Many believe that Aboriginal peoples lost their title and rights to territorial sovereignty when large migrations of Europeans settled in North America. They hold that Aboriginal peoples should assimilate into the Euro-Canadian culture, accepting Canadian laws and other social prescriptions as their own. The dominant characteristics of this ideology are embedded in the ***Indian Act***, and in the treatment of Native peoples by Canadian authorities when they made their claims on Canada's governing system.

FACTFILE The "right" generally refers to conservative, capitalist, and nationalist ideologies with the extremes of fascism and forms of anarchism included: The "left" includes welfarists, socialists, and communists with some representation in anarchism as well.

Other prevailing ideas include sexism and **ageism**, which justify the unequal treatment of people based on their gender and age. The Supreme

Court of Canada ruled that mandatory retirement at age 65 is discriminatory but that it constitutes a reasonable limit. It also ruled that women cannot claim child-care costs as business expenses. These ideas can circulate within the context of democratic thought, even though it preaches the lofty values of equality and justice for all. The same ideas may also circulate within the ideologies of communism and socialism.

The dominant ideology enables a society to control subordinate groups, such as women, young and old people, and those who adhere to competing ideologies if they constitute a minority in society.

Counter-ideologies

Counter-ideologies advance reforms and radical change in society. Sometimes the dominant ideologies in one society can be the counter-ideologies in another. They are a response to perceived inequality that, for one reason or another, is a product of how a society thinks and behaves. Counter-ideologies challenge the status quo and threaten to discredit it so that it loses credibility among adherents. Feminism is a counter-ideology that challenges the practices and assumptions of such dominant patriarchal ideologies as capitalism, socialism, and democracy. Feminists ask whether there is gender equality in any society, however it may be organized. Feminism politicizes human relations, making equality and human freedom fundamental ideological prescriptions.

The competitive interaction among groups that hold dominant and counter-ideologies is a reason why political change takes place in society. For years, leftist counter-ideology in Canada proclaimed that public enterprise should be a tool of public policy to control the ruthless marketplace and to offer services that the private sector failed to provide. Now, most political parties in Canada support the need for the presence of certain public enterprises in the Canadian economy. And the "green" counter-ideology—with its calls for concern for the environment, zero-population growth, and recycling of waste products—has become permanently ingrained in the platforms of political parties across the country.

THE COMPONENTS OF IDEOLOGIES

Ideologies address fundamental questions about the nature of society and its political character. We can identify some of the most common themes found in modern political ideologies:

1. the disposition of human nature;

2. the role of the individual in society;

3. the role of the state;

4. the sources and limits of political authority;

5. a preferred economic and social order.

These are some of the important elements analysts look for when examining the contents of ideologies.

What Is Human Nature?

One theme found in many ideologies addresses the question of human nature. Are human beings born basically good or bad, or does social conditioning determine their character? Is it possible to perfect human nature, or is it fundamentally unalterable? Modern attempts to scientifically answer these questions have been inconclusive. Convincing evidence falls on all sides and ultimately conclusions tend to be based on our own value preferences. But choosing from the many ideologies open to societies automatically implies a view of human nature.

> **FACTFILE**   In the eighteenth century, some philosophers (Rousseau, Locke, and Montesquieu) developed the idea that only free will governs human behaviour, such that the fate of the human race is not predetermined by God or by some divine plan but by our free choices.

Whatever view is expressed in the ideology has immediate implications for the economic, political, and social preferences that flow from its belief system. The conservative view generally asserts that human nature is unchangeable and that the purpose of social and political institutions is to control the undesirable tendencies in human behaviour. The liberal view posits the inherent goodness of human nature, which thus should not be too closely controlled and directed by government. At the same time, the belief that people are perfectible can lead to ideological prescriptions of radical social and institutional change, as exemplified in Marxism.

The Role of the Individual

Through the centuries, political thinkers have asked where the individual fits in the social scheme of things. Does the state and its government serve the interests of individuals, or are individuals subservient to the goals of the state? Where do we draw the line on the role of the individual in the political and social system? Many ideologies take into account the social obligations of individuals. They hold that people living in a society are not isolated individuals. Invariably, the ways in which people act as individuals affect the opportunities for the self-development of others.

FACTFILE   Democratic ideologies advocate that the rights of individuals should be entrenched in their constitutions in order to protect those individuals from any legislation or executive orders that might remove those rights or diminish them in any way.

To the doctrinaire socialists who adhere closely to the ideology of Marxism, the individual's welfare is subordinate to the welfare of the whole society. Even modern liberals concede that the greater liberty of one person can cause the lesser liberty of another. To liberals, the government is the necessary instrument for refereeing, equalizing, and thus maximizing individual freedom. A fundamental tenet of liberalism is the obligation to respect and

protect all individuals' rights and to safeguard them from deprivation by other individuals or groups.

The Role of the State

Ever since political ideas were debated, the state has been the focus of much ideological controversy. In times past, the state was believed to have derived from the will of God, the fall of man, the **social contract**, the process of natural evolution, the family, and the institution of private property. The controversy continues well beyond the notion of how the state originated because ideologies also differ sharply on the state's role in the political and social system. In some ideologies, the state appears as a necessary evil or as a target for destruction. Some anarchists, libertarians, and ultra-conservatives see the state as a set of institutions that attracts uncontrollable corruption, impedes economic and social progress, and threatens human liberty. In other ideologies, the state represents the highest of human endeavours. Its purpose is viewed as raising civilized standards; its hallmark as justice; and its essence as law, founded on right reason and popular consent.

FACTFILE   Jean-Jacques Rousseau (1712–1778), in his famous book *The Social Contract*, defined the doctrine of popular sovereignty. As a citizen of Geneva, he watched his city revolt against the Holy Roman Empire—in his view, precisely an act of popular sovereignty.

Most modern ideologies, with the exception of some strains of anarchism, believe that humans need a state apparatus of some kind to unite a country and to cope with the many problems of surviving in a competitive international community. In some ideologies, the concept of **sovereignty** denotes the supreme and final power of the state above and beyond which no other power exists. Others concede that actually there is no such thing as absolute, utterly unqualified state power, and hence no absolute sovereignty. Where does sovereignty reside, in the people or in the state? Is sovereignty divisible or indivisible? Who may express sovereignty?

Political Authority

One predictable component of most modern ideologies is the consideration of the source and scope of political authority. Political authority is usually portrayed as a form of power based upon the recognition it receives from those over whom it is exercised. In essence, political authority is a communication between leaders and those who are led, enabling them to relate to each other in such a way that the political system survives, be it a democracy or a dictatorship.

For some, political authority is derived from the consent of the governed, while others, such as fascists and Marxist-Leninists, point to the source of political authority as the coercive will of the state or of dictators. For them, state authority must be in the commanding position whereupon a **consensus** on the right policy choices is moulded and controlled by government. In contrast, democrats hold the essence of authority to be subjective, psychological, and moral. Authority is an influence that is intimately related to legitimacy, the belief held by the citizenry that a government has the right to rule and that a citizen ought to obey the rules of that government.

FACTFILE In Islamic fundamentalist countries such as Iran, the authority of religious rulers and the state governs both government institutions and the political rights of individuals.

Political authority has relevant meanings common to all ideologies. First is the *credibility* of the political communication itself—be it a law, regulation, decree, or succession of power. It is believed, almost regardless of its content, because it is derived from a source that has the power of force or procedure. A second shared meaning is that political authority is to be obeyed because compliance ensures the legitimate performance of the political system.

The Economic and Social Order

Ideologies usually address the economic and social conditions that prevail in society. How should society organize, protect, and distribute the products of human labour and ingenuity? What social and political institutions are needed to facilitate the required economic and social order? Who should reap the benefits of economic productivity and wealth?

Aristotle perceptively noted the economic and social basis of politics. Since his analysis, most modern ideologies have reflected the close relationship between the economy and the system of government. Changes in the ways we behave and produce goods and services in society will inevitably induce sweeping changes elsewhere in society. In this regard, ideologies try to reconcile a society's values with its political and economic structures.

The Marxists have searched for a more equitable way of organizing society and of ensuring that the satisfaction of individual economic needs does not contradict the fulfillment of social needs. Anarchists, insofar as they are willing to entertain the concept of order at all, insist on the free and spontaneous association of citizens in the economic and social life of society. For capitalists, the economic and social system works best, and the competitive ideal is most likely to be achieved, when people are free to decide for themselves what they want and what they are willing to pay.

THE GOALS OF IDEOLOGIES

Although ideologies differ a great deal in scope and content, they perform similar functions. Most of the time, people are not even aware that ideologies influence and condition their social behaviour. But ideological assumptions do consciously or unconsciously justify many of our thoughts and actions. Ideologies make us feel comfortable or uncomfortable about the institutions, leaders, and expectations of the political society we have created. They can divide or unite us. They can move us to act to change the world around us.

Doing It Right

The process whereby ideology gains acceptance for itself in the eyes of those who are influenced by it is *legitimation*. For some Marxists, legitimation is the major function of ideology because it represents the prescribed political institutions and processes in such a way that political obligation seems natural and right.[8]

From an ideological perspective, legitimation is a relative term. What is deemed legitimate by one ideology may not be regarded as legitimate by another. But generally an ideology will advance the belief that a political system is valid and justified, and will be recognized as such by those over whom its authority is exercised.

In capitalist societies, **stratification** tends to be widely accepted and even defended—not just by people identified as privileged but often by those in the lower stratum as well. Sociologists sometimes refer to this form of ideological legitimation as *false consciousness* because members of the lower stratum of society often accept the ideology that justifies the very system that oppresses them. Instead of blaming the system, they attribute their low status to "luck," "fate," "nature," or the "will of God"— factors usually beyond their control. However, when an ideology facilitates *class consciousness*—an objective awareness of the lower stratum's common plight as an oppressed group—political sociologists begin to question the legitimacy of the system or the ideology that sustains the system. The lower stratum may then be attracted to a different ideology, one that justifies its own class interests and consequently may seem revolutionary to the dominant stratum.

Focus On **Our Political Self**

We know that individuals are not born with a developed set of political beliefs—i.e., as liberals, conservatives, or anarchists. Men, women, and children acquire their political beliefs and their ideologies after developing a "political self" as they mature through their life experiences.

The concept of *political self* is rather vague as a tool of analysis. But we certainly experience it as real: all of us have some fairly definite notions of how we feel about politics. Probably the first political thought to blossom in the mind of a Canadian child is a psychological attachment or identification with a province or region or with Canada itself. This is by no means a sense of what Canada or, say, Quebec *is*—just a feeling of belonging to it.

But whatever our self as "political" consists of, it is a social product, created and modified throughout life by interaction with other people. The political self in all of us is molded and shaped by the attitudes and values of, and experiences with, our families; by our friends, workmates, and schoolmates; by the media, our communities, and our education; and by the major political events that affect our lives.

At the core of this political self are strong feelings toward the nation-state, its governmental institutions, and certain learned and deeply rooted conceptions about freedom, equality, and rights. Over time, the political self senses how government works; develops impressions and knowledge of politics; and cultivates preferences regarding public policies, political parties, and leaders.

Some analysts note that all governments legitimately operate on some kind of "make-believe."[9] The make-believe involves accepting the idea that those who govern are the servants of the people or that the people have a voice in government or that everyone is treated equally in society by governments. As they are consumed by the public, these kinds of fictions produce the basis of legitimacy for the governing regime. The fictions are often the basis for a governing system's defence, and are the underlying assumptions of the dominant ideology.

Leadership

One goal almost always articulated in ideologies is leadership. With the exception of anarchism, which is an ideology founded upon the absence of leadership, all ideologies address this phenomenon on the social and political level. Who may lead us? What qualifications should leaders have? How should we choose our leaders? When and how should leadership change? Ideologies often contain specific references to the nature of leadership and how it should shape the collective patterns of society. But, while ideologies may prescribe certain desirable leadership characteristics, the personal qualities of a single, highly placed decision maker may themselves become a factor of power or revolutionary historical change: e.g., Castro in Cuba, de Gaulle in France, Tito in the former Yugoslavia, Nehru in India.

From the ideological perspective, leadership is closely related to authority, power, influence, and political succession. Leadership was a central feature of Fascist and Nazi ideologies, as expressed in the concepts of *Il Duce* and the *Fuhrerprinzip*, whereby the leader embodied the state and for this reason had to be obeyed.

FACTFILE   Sociologist Irving Janis coined the term *group-think* to refer to the narrowing of individuals' thought to meet the will of a group, leading the members of the group to believe that they are right and that even to suggest alternative ideas is a sign of disloyalty.

With Marxism, leadership was intrinsic to the "dictatorship of the proletariat," which would bring under state control all the means of production, communications, transportation, and commerce. Lenin instituted the leadership of an elite revolutionary party in order to develop revolutionary consciousness among the masses. However, these patterns of leadership are not compatible with democratic thought. Democracy requires that the system of leadership recruitment be open and that the right and opportunity to seek leadership not be arbitrarily denied to any individual or category of persons.

Great Ideas Have Goals

One common attribute shared by the major ideologies is an end, goal, or purpose. Most of these ideologies focus on material abundance as the leading goal or purpose of the political system. Liberalism was the first ideology to articulate this end clearly and to develop the institutions designed to promote material rewards. Conservatism also keeps a watchful eye on national unity and the preservation of wealth. Communism, born much later, focuses on the possibility of overcoming scarcity, showing a passion for accelerating the pace of economic superabundance.

Ideological conceptions of purpose also focus on what governments are expected to do. The democratic idea of "constitutional government" posits that government cannot do everything and should be limited to certain specific social functions.

The classical form of liberalism assigned these to the preservation of order and property. But modern liberalism has added the concept of "welfare" to the proper role of government, and places limitations on individual freedoms. Quite to the contrary, Nazism fused the role of government to the state, based on the idea of the *Volkstadt*, in which there was no distinction between the will of the state and the will of the people. Nazis openly admit to the role of government and party as "totalitarian."

FACTFILE With the exception of fascism and radical Islam, all ideologies now argue that democracy is the most desirable form of government—an ideal toward which all societies should strive, however successful they may be in achieving it.

Critique of Other Ways of Thinking

One important psychodynamic of many ideologies is *criticism*. Karl Mannheim, best known for his development of the sociology of knowledge, saw the significance of differing and opposed positions in ideologies.[10] Mannheim identified two kinds of ideological thinking. One is utopian, which is the thinking of reformers who are unhappy with the status quo and want to change it in order to build new institutions and values. The other is in defence of the status quo, which is under attack.

Democrats, who strongly believe that criticism is necessary for political systems to function, are themselves the target of severe attacks from opposing ideologies. The very nobility of democracy's goals invites an especially caustic flow of criticism regarding the gap between theory and practice. The heaviest attacks are concentrated on the practice, rather than the ideals, of democracy. Virtually every democratic government in history has permitted, and sometimes generated, elements of **aristocracy** and **oligarchy**.

Maurice Duverger defined democracy as government *of* the people by an elite sprung *from* the people.[11] Many democratic legislatures (particularly upper houses) give added weight to age, wealth, conservatism, and social status, resulting in an unacknowledged fusion of democracy with oligarchy and privilege. According to Marx, capitalist ideology justified the use of the democratic law-making institutions of the state to consolidate

and perpetuate the socio-economic domination of one class—the **bourgeoisie**.

FACTFILE The historian Richard Hofstadter referred to critique in ideology as "paranoid politics," whereby competing ideologies are intolerant of each others' opinions and are willing to attack, disrupt, and intimidate those with whom they disagree.

Prescribing the Best Ideas

Many ideologies are concerned with the way the state and society should be organized and the way citizens should relate to these prescribed structures and social values. Ideologies make certain assumptions about human behaviour, followed by prescriptions as to which political order best protects or challenges these assumptions. Each ideology, by means of its own logic and evidence, claims to possess the right path to progress, and directs its followers to implement its goals.

Anarchists prefer little or no government and reject state intervention in private lives, contending that individuals must have maximum choice to achieve the highest levels of morality, fulfillment, and perfectibility. Therefore, they prescribe a free society of individuals, with few social constraints. Nationalists, on the other hand, prescribe a strong government, with a state apparatus organized to unify the national ambitions of a preferred group. Nationalists believe in the moral corporate personality of the *nation*, which should be protected against the whims of individualism or the cultural encroachment of other nations. In its extreme, as with national socialism (Nazism), the nation is seen as superior to the individual as well as to all other foreign nations.

What ideologies instruct us to do can stir us to act, arousing our commitments to achieve the goals the ideology puts forward. These ideological instructions often include an interpretation of the past, an evaluation of the present, and a vision of the future.

DEMOCRATIC IDEOLOGIES

Democratic thought is usually traced to the Greeks, although many aboriginal and Indo-American cultures produced democratic governing institutions that predate those in Greece. During the fifth century, the Athenians, in particular, used the term *democracy* to refer to government by the many, as contrasted to government by the few (oligarchy) or by one person (monarchy). In his famous "Funeral Oration," Pericles (495–429 BC) declared that "our [Athens'] constitution is named a democracy, because it is in the hands, not of the few, but of the many."[12] The idea that the ultimate political authority lies with, and should flow from, the general public remains central to all modern conceptions of democracy.

> **FACTFILE**   Athenian democracy required that every significant policy issue be considered, debated, and decided by the public: there had to be a quorum of at least 6000 citizens (out of a total of approximately 22 000), who met on the Pynx, a hill west of the Acropolis.

The first great European political theorist to consider democracy as a coherent system of thought was Aristotle, the Macedonian philosopher who lived from 384 to 322 BC. Aristotle saw democracy as direct *popular government*, which he thought would degenerate into mob rule because it lacked institutions capable of ensuring individual liberty and of controlling self-seeking interests. Direct democracy was too unrestrained and unstable, so Aristotle enlarged the concept by combining other elements: popular sovereignty, majority rule, and minority rights, which formed what he called constitutional government or polity. Aristotle's assessment of democracy in the *Politics* had remarkable range, even calling for a huge middle class: "It is clear therefore that the political community administered by the middle class is the best . . . in which the middle class is numerous . . . it sways the balance and prevents the opposite extremes from coming into existence."[13]

> **FACTFILE**   Despite the deep attachment of Americans to the ideals of democracy, the United States was not a full participatory democracy until the 1960s, when black Americans were at last guaranteed the right to vote in the *Voting Rights Act* of 1965.

The earliest Greek democracies were city states. They emphasized the equality of all who qualified as citizens in their right to participate in the life of the community. Participation was widespread, with decisions based on oratory and face-to-face discussion. Citizens took part in such processes as jury trials and lawmaking, but more important than any other political rights was a broad notion of civic spirit. We are indebted to antiquity for the earliest examples of democracy in theory and practice.

Since Aristotle, many philosophers have contributed to the development of democracy. But the foundations of modern European democratic ideology were fashioned in the seventeenth, eighteenth, and nineteenth centuries. The great thinkers of the time, John Locke, Jean-Jacques Rousseau, Thomas Jefferson, Thomas Paine, Jeremy Bentham, James Mill, John Stuart Mill, and Alexis de Tocqueville all contributed to the present composition of modern democratic ideologies. The great debates over the creation of the best institutional framework for democracy resulted in three fundamentally distinctive ideologies: liberalism, conservatism, and socialism.

Liberalism

Liberalism became a discernible ideology in the eighteenth and nineteenth centuries. It was an outgrowth of an earlier revolt against oligarchic government, one that culminated in the "Glorious Revolution" of 1688 in England. Led by the **Whigs**, the bloodless "glorious" revolution saw the downfall of King James II, established the sovereignty of Parliament over the monarchy, and blocked the royal family from suspending acts of Parliament or interfering with the decisions of the courts.

The **Industrial Revolution** stimulated a demand to free the taxpayer from arbitrary and restrictive government action. This demand for freedom of action came primarily from the rising industrial and trading classes, whose enterprises were frequently restricted by arbitrary government interests, through legislation, common law, and judicial decisions.

Liberals derived their political ideas from the writers of the Enlightenment, and from the so-called principles of 1789, as embodied in the French Declaration of the Rights of Man and Citizen. The leading thinkers of the eighteenth century believed that human-made laws and institutions were the modern answer to progress. Liberal politicians in Europe wanted to establish a political framework that would permit legal equality, religious tolera-tion, and freedom of the press. They believed that the legitimacy of government was not inherited, but rather emanated from the freely given consent of the governed. The popular basis of this kind of gov-ernment should be expressed through elections and representative parliamentary bodies. For liberals, free government required that the political execu-tive must be "responsible" to the legislature rather than to the monarch.

The British philosopher Leonard Hobhouse listed the key liberal principles that became prominent throughout the evolution of modern liberalism:[14]

- **Rule of law**: Liberals fought to limit govern-ment power by proclaiming the supremacy of law, promoting the legal equality of all individuals, and protecting the rights of peo-ple from arbitrary interference by officials.

- **Responsible government**: The democratic principle that all public officials are accountable to the people and can be ruled only by their consent.

- **Civil liberties**: These represent the freedoms of thought, expression, association, religion, and the press.

- **Constitutionalism**: By means of a fundamen-tal charter, social contract, or convention, a people can outline, define, and limit the exer-cise of government power by establishing the constitution as the first law of the land.

- **Individualism**: The principle that the chief function of government is to foster the well-being of each person and to permit each one to reach self-fulfillment.

- **Majority rule**: The principle that public decisions are weighted in favour of the greater number of citizens.

- **Popular sovereignty**: The source of all government and public authority flows from the people.

- **International co-operation**: Liberals called for the reduction or elimination of all trade barriers, tariffs, quotas, and other instruments of economic protection in order to expand national economies and foster international interaction.

These ideological prescriptions may seem quite ordinary to us today. But, none of the major European states enjoyed such democratic guaran-tees in the late seventeenth and eighteenth centuries. The people who espoused these changes in govern-ments tended to be those groups who were excluded from the existing political world.

In the chaotic years of nineteenth-century Europe, these groups organized and, stressing the values of liberty, human dignity, and individualism, sought to establish a constitutional order that would protect civil liberties, limit government, permit political competition, and separate church and state.

The twentieth century witnessed a further transformation of democratic liberal thought, from its earlier forms to an ideology that postulates the "best" society is rooted in individual freedom, social concern, and human dignity. Liberalism abandoned its eighteenth-century advocacy of the economic freedoms of laissez-faire capitalism, and by the twentieth century postulated new roles for democratic government: to manage the economic and social maladjustments of industrialization, to redistribute wealth, and to develop a policy framework for the health, education, and welfare of all citizens.

One outstanding intellectual who helped to develop the rationale to support a greater government role in modern society was John Dewey (1859–1952).[15] This popular American philosopher noted the intimate connection between political democracy and economic well-being in society. For him, the political system should guarantee a dignified life for all citizens, and the role of the state should be expanded to achieve that goal.

Currently, liberalism is a loosely knit mosaic of beliefs, practices, theories, and differing pragmatic approaches to solving economic, political, and social problems. Liberals believe that a strong central government is necessary to protect individuals from the inequities of a rapidly changing technological society. For liberals, the growth of government has enhanced, not diminished, individual freedom. They see the role of the state as correcting the injustices of the marketplace, but not suppressing its potential to generate economic prosperity.

Focus On   Liberal-Minded and Conservative-Minded Views

Not everyone who holds liberal-minded positions in the world of politics supports a party with that name or parties of the left. The same may be said of those who express a conservative approach to life and politics but do not support parties of the right. Liberal-minded people are likely to agree with certain statements about the world of politics and government. Conservative-minded people are inclined to hold similar views about human nature and the role of government in society.

You are liberal-minded if you agree that:	You are conservative-minded if you agree that:
Governments should regulate the economy to protect the public interest.	Free-market competition will protect the public interest better than government regulation.
Tax increases are essential to support public services for all.	Tax cuts stimulate the economy: Taxation should be kept as low as possible.
Governments should spend more on social welfare programs to benefit the less fortunate.	Government bureaucracy is too big and too powerful.
Governments should spend more to alleviate social conditions such as poverty, crime, homelessness, and drug abuse.	Government-funded social programs reduce the incentive to work.
Governments should do more to protect the rights of women, minorities, and First Nations.	More police, more prisons, and longer court sentences will increase public safety.
Same-sex couples should have all the legal rights of heterosexual couples.	Government should restrict abortion: Taxpayer money should not pay for abortions.

Governments should invest more in post-secondary education.

Affirmative action is necessary to improve healthcare, educational opportunity, and employment equity.

Governments should convert more human rights into legal and constitutional rights.

Government should meet current international standards for giving aid to developing states (1 percent of GDP) and for meeting global standards to combat climate change.

Government should not legislate social and economic opportunity based on race or sex.

Government should not legitimize same-sex marriage.

Government should pursue the national interest first before giving aid to poorer economies.

Global climate change can be addressed by national policy goals related to economic capability.

Conservatism

The term *conservatism* was coined from the French word *conservateur*, the label given to French writers and statesmen who demanded a return to pre-revolutionary conditions after the fall of Napoleon. The birth of conservatism is usually associated with the publication of Edmund Burke's *Reflections on the Revolution in France* (1790), which excoriated the French revolutionaries for the arrogance with which they assumed they could alter the natural continuity of history.[16] The defeat of Napoleon and the diplomatic settlement of the Congress of Vienna re-established the conservative social and political order in Europe.

Monarchies, aristocracies, and the established churches made up the main pillars of **Tory** conservatism. These institutions were ancient, but the conscious allegiance among the throne, wealth, and altar was new and made them reluctant allies. Conservatives knew they could be toppled by liberal political groups who hated them. They regarded themselves as surrounded by well-organized enemies; they felt permanently on the defensive against the forces of liberalism, nationalism, and the unforeseeable consequences of popular sovereignty. A sense of alarm felt by European aristocrats, families of long-established wealth, and the clergy encouraged them to organize their own political groups.

Classical Conservatives

Classical conservatism combined the ideological perspectives of Burke and those of other thinkers such as Thomas Hobbes and David Hume. Hobbes had asserted that human nature was essentially selfish, requiring the restraint of coercive government power to tame the natural tendencies of people to satisfy their needs at the expense of others in society. Conservatives saw this selfishness expressed as social whim, demands for rapid or radical change, and license for unfettered individual freedoms. David Hume, in his *Treatise of Human Nature* (1740), argued that, given the tendency of human reason to reach selfish conclusions, it was necessary for people to be controlled by laws, conventions, and institutions that had proved their social wisdom over time.

FACTFILE   Winston Churchill once said, "If you are not a liberal at 20, you have no heart, and if you are not a conservative at 40, you have no head."

Burke presented his conservative views of the world with power and conviction. He held that *humankind* was wise, but that the *individual* was not. Burke confirmed the fundamental conservative distrust of human nature. As individuals, people were basically weak, given to passion and instinct, and generally untrustworthy. Such characteristics required institutional restrictions on human behaviour by law, government authority, and other social constraints on individual freedoms. The role of the state was seen as essentially to control people for their own good.

Burke also stressed the *organic* nature of society—the idea that society is an organism to which all people in a community belong. The institutions that have evolved within this organic social system cannot be cut away without endangering the life of that organism, just as removing the internal organs of any living being would destroy that organism. Thus, society is not merely a social contract, as the liberals assert, but an indissoluble and perpetual convention that assigns duties and responsibilities to be carried out from one generation to the next. Individuals are temporary and perishable. But society as an organic expression is a partnership between those who are dead, those who are living, and those yet to be born. Therefore, the interests of society must transcend individual interests.

In the early part of the twentieth century, the British political writer F.J.C. Hearnshaw set forth a classic statement of the principles of conservatism:

- **Reverence for the past**: Societies accumulate wisdom from their customs and traditions, and must respect and retain the accomplishments of their ancestors.

- **Organic conception of society**: Societies are greater than the sum of their parts and take on a corporate or communal identity and unity.

- **Constitutional continuity**: Constitutions are indissoluble conventions that carry the proven political norms and practices of the past into the present.

- **Opposition to revolution**: Conservatives reject radical change because it destroys proven customs and institutions.

- **Cautious reform**: Change should be evolutionary and carefully deliberated.

- **The religious basis of the state**: The state has a moral, religious, and sacred character beyond its political and legal personality.

- **The divine source of legitimate authority**: Political and legal authority is divine in its origin.

- **The priority of duties over rights**: Conservatives recognize that individuals have civic duties as well as personal rights and are obligated to fulfill them in the interests of the body politic.

- **Loyalty**: Conservatives demonstrate loyalty to church, family, school, party, institutions, and country.

- **Common sense and pragmatism**: Conservatives are people of practical action rather than theory, and are devoted to sound administration rather than abundant legislation.[17]

Modern conservatism is much less a body of coherent beliefs (as outlined by Hearnshaw) than a modern attitude or a state of mind. Conservatives usually want to preserve the *status quo* or return to a preferred previous state of affairs. In the current decade, conservatism aspires to trim the size of government, reduce public spending, reform taxation laws to encourage investments, deregulate business to promote economic growth, and manage the fiscal and monetary sides of the economy.

FACTFILE In Canada, a "red Tory" is a conservative who values tradition and advocates an active welfare role for the state to ensure community cohesion, dignity, stability, and a sense of place and belonging.

In other economic matters, conservatives draw upon many of the ideas of nineteenth-century liberalism. Conservatism essentially has become a defence of economic individualism against the growth of the **welfare state**. In their earlier manifestations, conservatives were the supporters of strong central government. They believed that only a government of the talented and propertied elite could preserve the sacred rights of humans. As the voting franchise extended to more people during the twentieth century, conservatives lost faith in central government and focused on the rights of property, and the rights of individuals to be free of government interference. Thus, contemporary conservatives, now called **neo-conservatives**, tend to oppose any increase in the role of the state in the economy, and contend that a vibrant and unfettered *private sector* can best create jobs for the poor, immigrants, and minorities. For them, welfare programs create a permanent class who are dependent on the state, and who have little impetus to enter the workforce.

On social and cultural issues, conservatives come close to Burke's ideals. They believe that the state should promote virtue and social responsibility, thus improving the moral climate of society. They interpret this as opposition to abortion, pornography, and often affirmative rights for groups such as gays and lesbians. Conservatives challenge the idea of quotas and other affirmative-action policies: they argue that human rights guarantee equality of treatment, not equality of social results.

Democratic Socialism

Socialism is articulated by democratic as well as non-democratic ideologies.[18] Unlike other systems of thought, it has enjoyed political prominence throughout recorded history. It has been adopted in both pre-industrial and modern societies as a rationale for societal planning and social equality. The prominence of socialist thought and practice over time, in most parts of the world, may have resulted from the very nature of society: men, women, and children surviving together as families, tribes, villages, cities, and nation-states. The early socialists lacked any strong following: their doctrines lacked focus and were viewed as outlandish by their contemporaries.

The utopians

FACTFILE   The word *utopia* is taken from Sir Thomas More's philosophical romance, *Utopia* (1516). More's work featured an ideal state wherein private property was abolished.

Among the first to articulate this social bias was a group of writers called **utopian socialists** by their later critics. Thomas More (1478–1535), Francis Bacon (1561–1621), and Tommaso Campanella (1568–1639) were considered utopians because they were idealists whose ideas were visionary. These utopians looked nostalgically at earlier societies as though they were without selfishness and social antagonisms. They were called socialists because they criticized existing economic systems. One such early socialist pioneer was the French aristocrat Claude Henri, Count of Saint-Simon (1760–1825), who believed that private wealth, property, and enterprise should be socially administered by experts at arm's length from these assets to alleviate poverty. He came to be regarded as the father of the modern welfare state.

The major British contributor to early socialist thought was Robert Owen (1771–1858), a successful cotton manufacturer. Owen held a partnership in a large British cotton factory at New Lanark, Scotland, where he put socialist ideas in practice, organizing the industry so that workers and managers lived together and produced their goods in co-operation. Although his experiment failed in New Harmony, Indiana, Owen contributed to socialist thought his belief that co-operative production under humane working conditions was possible. Charles Fourier (1772–1837), a contemporary of Owen, advocated the construction of morally liberated agrarian communities called *phalanxes*, which would permit individuals to perform different tasks to avoid boredom and dullness. Fourier believed that societies would be more productive if social classes and labour specialization were eliminated.

In the later part of the nineteenth century, the democratic socialists who exerted the most influence were associated with the Fabian Society. Founded in 1884, in England, the society took its name from Q. Fabius Maximus, the Roman general who defeated Hannibal by waiting a very long time before attacking. By acting out this strategy, the society advocated a gradual approach to major social reform. Some of its notable members were Sidney (1859–1947) and Beatrice (1858–1943) Webb, H.G. Wells (1866–1946), Graham Wallas (1858–1932), and George Bernard Shaw (1856–1950). They believed that, through democracy, the great social questions of the day could be addressed. In their view, the goals of socialism could be achieved without revolution.

This belief was echoed in the work of the German socialist revisionist Eduard Bernstein (1850–1932), who questioned whether Marx had been "correct" in his pessimistic appraisal of capitalism and the necessity of revolution. In his *Evolutionary Socialism* (1899), Bernstein pointed to the rising standard of living in Europe and the failure of Marx's predictions to materialize. As a revisionist, he wanted socialist parties to gain control of governments to implement a moderate brand of socialism.

Contemporary socialism

In the twenty-first century, democratic socialism is a political and economic ideology. Also known as **neo-socialism**, it aims to preserve individual freedom in the context of social equality achieved through a centrally planned economy. While a private sector continues to exist under socialism, major industries and corporations, in the national interest, are owned by the state, and thus the government is responsible for planning and directing the economy. The state may take ownership of only strategic industries and services, such as railways, airlines, mines, banks, radio, TV, telecommunications, medical services, universities, and important manufacturing enterprises.

Important decisions concerning foreign investments, wages, and prices are placed in the hands of public institutions. The tax system is designed to prevent excessive profits or an undue concentration of wealth. No democratic socialist state aspires to communism. What separates democratic from non-democratic socialists is the latter's acceptance of violent revolution. Democratic socialists advance peaceful and constitutional change and want to achieve goals.

But while socialist societies may redistribute wealth more evenly than capitalist ones, they are less efficient at creating wealth in the first place. In socialist economies, decisions are more centralized. Public administrators often determine what goods and services will be produced, the prices, and who will receive them. This is why socialist societies are more bureaucratic and less productive than capitalist ones.

The contemporary descendants of evolutionary socialism are the social democratic and labour parties of North America, Western Europe, and Latin America. They have often abandoned the more radical elements of their ideology (for example, nationalization of industry and opposition to capitalism). When in power, they have pursued policies aimed at creating a welfare state and winning votes—all within the capitalist framework.

The Global Appeal of Environmentalism

Perhaps no other idea is as democratic as knowing that all humans are equally part of nature and that we are universally obligated to take care of the natural world. Getting along with nature is the first democratic law of human survival.

The idea that the earth is a precious and delicate environment that must be protected can be traced to ancient times. Long before the so-called green revolution and the idea of a global commons, aboriginal cultures in the Americas and elsewhere believed that how we live has a profound effect on the places where we live. It was this logic that, surviving some 3000 years of "civilization," nurtured a modern ideology of environmentalism based on these ancient beliefs. This ideology has found expression around the contemporary world.

Environmental issues vividly demonstrate the reality of global interdependence. Globalization has increased international interdependence through economic integration and transnational communication. Global threats to the natural environment are a major cause of interdependence, as governments co-operate to address issues of air pollution, water pollution, deforestation, and many other related problems. These issues cannot be resolved by any single nation-state but require an international, if not a global, effort.

FACTFILE In 2007, the American Meteorological Society claimed that the whole Arctic is warmer today than it has been in the last thousand years, threatening ecological life systems everywhere on the planet but also reflecting some of the early assertions of environmentalists that humans are responsible for it.

Environmentalism is an ideology that has been adopted in systems of political thought such as liberalism, conservatism, and socialism. But many political systems have seen the formation of independent "green" parties that carry the main attributes of environmental ideology. The ideology of environmentalism focuses on the growth of population, industry, energy use, and the extraction of natural resources. What is the carrying capacity of the planet? How much can we take from it without incurring a collapse of our and other animal populations, causing a depletion of the earth's non-renewable resources, or making the planet uninhabitable?

The destruction of forests and lakes by acid rain; the depletion of the earth's protective ozone layer; radioactive waste from nuclear power plants; the destruction of tropical rainforests; the death of birds, fish, and mammals from oil spills

and pesticides; the rapid extinction of hundreds of species—these are all problems being addressed by the ideology of environmentalism.

Our politics are connected with how we view and treat the planet. For example, the idea that humans are superior to other species—what some call *speciesism*—has enabled us to rationalize ecological destruction to satisfy political and economic desires. Environmentalists argue, however, that this rationalization is flawed, pointing out that ecological destruction is now threatening human populations as well as animals and the environment.

FACTFILE The World Wildlife Federation (WWF) argues that trade has a destructive impact on the environment because trade contributes to the over-consumption of natural resources.

Environmentalism warns us that to the degree we are selfish, to the extent we are ignorant and heedless of our proper place in nature, we will endanger the delicate ecology of the earth.

NON-DEMOCRATIC IDEOLOGIES
Communist Ideologies

The idea that there should be no private property and that all things should be held in common is an ancient one. In the biblical book of Genesis, everything comes from God and no one has inherent rights of possession. In Deuteronomy, all debts are automatically cancelled every seven years in the "year of release," according to the ancient Hebrew beliefs of egalitarianism, welfare, and communist norms. In Leviticus, the "year of Jubilee" is described as the time, every 50 years, when all the accumulated inequalities of land distribution are eliminated and the land is redistributed equally among Hebrew tribes.

Much later, in the sixth century, some Christian monastics criticized private ownership and called for a return to the ancient principle of equality believed to have been prominent in a "golden age" of communal life. The utopian socialists wrote of societies organized according to communist principles founded among the earliest human communities.

Marxism

Karl Marx's (1818–1883) socialist philosophy eventually triumphed over most alternative versions of socialism in Europe and elsewhere.[19] Marx immersed himself in Hegelian philosophy, which introduced him to the idea that all phases of human history are the inevitable product of class and ideological conflict. French utopian socialists gave Marx his focus on the ideals of communal life. And the view that the condition of the working class could not be improved, shared by the British economists, notably Adam Smith, David Ricardo, and Thomas Malthus, gave him a pessimistic focus.

In 1844, Marx met Friedrich Engels, another young middle-class German, whose friendship with Marx led to an intellectual collaboration of enormous ideological consequences. In 1847, they wrote *The Communist Manifesto* for a newly organized secret Communist League. They had adopted the name "communist" because the word was much more emphatically radical than "socialist." Communism called for the outright abolition of private property and required the extensive re-organization of society. A work of less than 50 pages, the *Manifesto* would become the most influential document in modern European history. By the time *Das Kapital* (Vol. 1, 1867) was published, predicting the disintegration of capitalism, Marxism had emerged as the single most important strand of socialism in Europe.[20]

Marx and Engels contended that the main lesson from history is that the organization of the means of production generates conflict between classes. History is driven and unfolds through this necessary conflict. Marxian analysis therefore assumed that the path to socialism was through *revolution* rather than reform of present institutions. The era of the utopian community had ended.

The materialist conception of history

Marxism begins with the "materialist conception of history," which asserts the human necessity to produce and acquire what we need to live. That is, the material lives of people determine their ideology and their supporting institutions. Thus, changes in material conditions bring about predictable changes in the social and political infrastructures of society.

Historical inevitability

Marx borrowed another idea from Hegel and others—that history moves in predictable directions. Marx and Engels developed a theory about the movement of history that purports to explain why one economic system (mode of production) would give way to another and why it is possible to predict to the final historical stage of human development: communism (Figure 2.1). They devoted much of their work to plotting the development of human history from pre-industrial communism through slavery and feudalism to capitalism and socialism.

Much of their work, however, focused on capitalism and its inevitable collapse, not on the future of societies. Capitalism marked a transient stage of historical development, destined to disintegrate because its antagonistic classes—capitalist and **proletariat**—will inevitably clash, resulting in a victorious workers' revolution.

Class struggle

Marx recognized that many social classes have emerged at different times under different modes of production. For example, in pre-industrial Europe, the aristocracy, who owned the land, was the ruling class, and the peasants, who tilled it, were the workers. During the industrial period, two classes alone—the bourgeoisie and the proletariat—were

Figure 2.1   **Class struggle and the predictability of history**

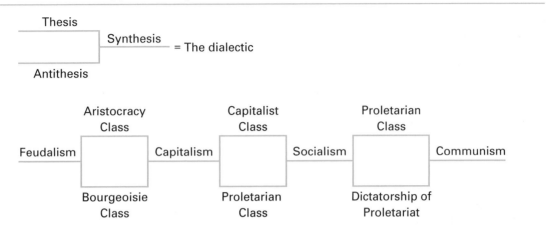

the forces that shaped the economic destiny of the period. For Marx, social classes arise from the "relations of production" that occur in the economy. Accordingly, the major classes of the modern era were the landowners and capitalists and the class of wage earners.

In the course of time, classes become self-aware. Because the state reflects the ideology of the ruling class, its coercive power is applied against the disadvantaged proletarian class. The **superstructure** consists of the laws, the political and social institutions, and the economic organizations that enforce, produce, and consolidate human relations in society. Almost always the superstructure is controlled by the most powerful classes who manipulate the institutions of government to protect their interests over those of other classes.

Out of this situation, revolutions are born. Marx saw history as a **dialectic** of revolutionary change (Figure 2.1). For him, the dialectic is a process of class conflict and struggle, involving social contradictions as thesis and antithesis. This struggle produces a conflict, out of which a new and higher social-order synthesis emerges. Marx and Engels asserted that class conflict would be resolved in the final proletarian revolution, resulting in the final historical synthesis, *communism*.

Alienation

The Marxian theory of alienation seeks to explain how individuals living in a capitalist society lose their understanding and control of the world around them. This makes them become something less than full human beings. Under capitalism, workers feel dissociated from what they produce. They are alienated because they compete with other workers, receive only a small portion of the value of what they produce, and do not own the means of production or have much say in how they are used.

Marx believed that the capacity to work is a distinctive human characteristic, but workers in a capitalist system have diminished responsibilities and are reduced to a lesser part of the work process. They perceive themselves as mere cogs in the production of the economy. Work becomes an enforced activity, not a creative or satisfying one, because the profit produced by the labour of the worker goes to someone else.

Labour theory of value

Marx witnessed some of the worst manifestations of capitalism while he lived in England. He saw abusive child labour, the vicious competition of workers for low-paying jobs, dangerous and unhealthy working conditions, and ruthless employers who cared very little about the fate of those who worked for them. From his experience, he concluded that the majority of men, women, and children suffered poverty and need. The few who did not do manual labour enjoyed most of the wealth produced by labourers. Thus, from his perspective, the capitalist mode of production extracts *surplus value* from wage-labour to the benefit of the capitalist class.

As Marx saw it, the true value of any commodity is derived by computing the labour that was necessary to produce it (labour theory of value). He believed that because capitalists are not labourers, they do not produce value. However, workers are not compensated for the total value of the goods they produce, and what the capitalist withholds from the worker is surplus value. The surplus value is used to expand capital, a process conditioned by competition. In Marx's view, surplus value is a waste of social energy because the amount of effort workers invest in generating wealth for individual capitalists could be used to benefit society as a whole.

Dictatorship of the proletariat

For Marx, the *dictatorship of the proletariat* is the state under the control of the proletarians: those who defend the gains made during the revolution and guide society through the inequalities and deprivations occurring during the transformation to communism. By means of its political dominance, the proletariat is able to bring under its control all the means of production, industry, land, business, communications, transportation, and commerce.

The term *dictatorship* was never fully explained by Marx. In the dictatorship of the proletariat, the state is a committee of proletarians making decisions, drafting laws, and taking action on behalf of the proletarian class. For this brief period, the proletariat is the ruling class that prepares the way for a classless society.

Marxism-Leninism

The vanguard party

V.I. Lenin (1870–1924) was a determined, relentless **Bolshevik** revolutionary who studied the strengths and weaknesses of pure Marxist theory, as it could be applied to a revolution occurring in a backward country such as Russia. He brought his own ideas to Marxist thought, producing what came to be known as *Marxism-Leninism*. In his work *What Is to Be Done?* (1922), Lenin explained why the autocratic conditions of Russia demanded a unique kind of organization to guide the revolution to fruition. For him, only a small elite made up "of people who make revolutionary activity their profession"—the vanguard party—could lead the masses with any disciplined determination.

Imperialism

In 1916, Lenin published *Imperialism: The Highest Stage of Capitalism*, thereby adding another ideological element to Marxism-Leninism. Lenin observed that advanced capitalist economies had temporarily postponed social and economic chaos by entering new markets in the developing economies of the world. He saw imperialism and colonialism as a consequence of monopoly capitalism. Lenin's observations altered Marxism by linking colonialism with the spread of capitalism in the developing world, and by advancing the possibility that revolutions need not necessarily occur only in the most advanced industrialized economies.

Leninism

Lenin's main theoretical contribution to Marxism was the idea that revolution was not necessarily spontaneous or historically inevitable; rather it could be planned, calculated, and orchestrated by a disciplined, militant party organization.[21]

Another important principle developed by Lenin in his theory of party organization was **democratic centralism**. According to this principle, democratic participation by means of free discussion is permitted for all party members *until* a decision is taken, at which time no further debate or dissent is tolerated and party members are expected to fully support the decision.

A corollary to Lenin's idea of engineered revolutions was his "theory of the weakest link." In it, Lenin held that the greatest possibilities of revolution are not found in capitalist economies but in the weakest links of the capitalist chain, where the proletariat and/or the peasantry was more susceptible to revolutionary rhetoric and mobilization. Russia was portrayed as the weakest link in the chain of European capitalism prior to 1917. Lenin expressed confidence in the ability of Russia to attain socialism.

OTHER IDEOLOGIES

Nationalism

The roots of nationalism can be traced deep into the past, appearing when England, France, and Spain were transformed from feudal principalities into national monarchies and when their people regarded themselves as "English," "French," and "Spanish" nationals rather than as Yorkshiremen, Gascons, and Andalusians. Somewhat later, during the Hundred Years' War (1337–1453), England and France drew upon strong feelings of national sentiment to centralize their governments, to build their economies, and to wage war. Much later, in the seventeenth century, the Treaty of Westphalia (1648) nurtured distinctive nation-states, each with its own political, cultural, and religious identity. The emergence of the nation-state unleashed the forces of competitive nationalism in the modern world

With the crumbling of the Holy Roman Empire came the need for a new type of political organization in Europe. Nationalism proved to be one of the strongest motivating forces of the nineteenth and twentieth centuries, demonstrating its powerful tendency to unite millions of people on the one hand, yet, when desirable, to destroy millions on the other.

German **Romantic** writers portrayed nationalism as the glorification of individual cultures. Johann Fichte (1762–1814) challenged the younger generation of Germans to recognize their national duty, which historical circumstances had placed on their shoulders. Johann Herder (1744–1803) saw human beings and societies as developing organically, like plants, over time. He urged the collection and preservation of distinctive German songs and sayings and seized upon the conception of the *Volksgeist* or national spirit. Perhaps the most important person to develop the ideology of nationalism during the Romantic period was G.W.F. Hegel (1770–1831), who recognized that people united as a national *cultural* unit constituted one of the few forces capable of changing world history.

These Romantic writers defined *nation* as a cultural phenomenon in terms of common language, common history, common customs, and a loyalty to a homeland. Thus, all persons of the same nationality should embody the same *nation-state*, to be preserved, perfected, and protected from foreign influence.

During the nineteenth century, the political consolidation of one or more nations under the jurisdiction and administration of a single nation-state began to flourish. Before this time, the characteristic political organizations were small states comprising fragments of a nation, such as were present in Europe. For many people in the nineteenth century, nationalism became a kind of secular faith.

Perspectives   What Is Radical Thought?

Political extremes of the left and right have more in common as radical ideologies than either side might like to admit. Although decidedly different as radical political philosophies, both members of the Canadian neo-Nazi groups and members of left-wing communist groups reject Canadian democracy and assert the supremacy of the "people" over laws, institutions, and individuals.

The radical dimension of an ideology can only be defined in the specific context in which it is used; its meaning varies from time to time and from place to place. *Radicalism* means to get down to the root of the matter, coming from the Latin word *radix*, or root. It is most frequently used to convey an extreme difference from the point of view of those who express the central versions of an ideology. Thus, radicalism can emerge as a counter-ideology of a dominant ideology. Radicals live for the future; they work to do good as they see it and to change the world in a fundamental way.

On the whole, it seems fair to say that there are very few independent radical ideologies attracting significant numbers of adherents in Canada today. There is anarchism, fascism, Nazism, as well as other radical ideologies, but they appeal only to small groups of Canadians.

People who hold "radical" views are often associated with the political left or the right because they reject the status quo and want to bring about fundamental changes to the existing governmental, political, and social order. The radical perspective takes note of the conflicting interests in society and examines the need to maintain social order. It focuses on the injustices of inequality and what must be done to reduce it. Traditionally, Canadian society has been unreceptive to radical politics. Canada's political and governmental system tends to neutralize the radical dimension of an ideology by stealing its thunder when the public is attracted to its assertions. Elements of radical thought are often absorbed by competing political parties that offer them to the public as policy preferences, such as the "greening" of the Liberal, Conservative, and New Democratic parties on environmental issues.

As an ideology in the nineteenth century, nationalism came to mean the will of a particular nationality or group of nationalities to accept the power of a state to administer its interests, such as with the creation of a new Italy, a new Germany, and a new Canada.

In the twenty-first century, nationalism continues in many ways as an extension of its nineteenth-century predecessor.[22] However, nationalist sentiment took on a more doctrinaire form throughout the twentieth century. The contemporary ideology of nationalism accepts the idea that the human species will naturally form into nations that reflect a peculiar character. This idea of a natural right to form a nation leads to the right of self-determination and self-government, whereupon other states may provide their recognition of a new independent member with equal rights and duties in the international community.

Totalitarian Nationalism

In its extreme form during the twentieth century, nationalism manifested itself as the ideologies of fascism and national socialism (Nazism). Latent in German thought in the nineteenth century, nationalism became an irrational obsession. One eminent German historian, Leopold von Ranke

(1795–1886), in his work *Latin and Teutonic Peoples*, taught that the Germans had a mission from God to develop a "pure" culture "corresponding to the genius of the nation." Friedrich Nietzsche (1844–1900) wrote about the "heroic man," the "superman," the "spineless multitude," and the "slave morality," and influenced the superiority theories of Adolf Hitler. Another German philosopher, Arthur Schopenhauer, who wrote *The World as Will and Idea*, advocated the idea of "subjective truth," which later inspired Hitler's use of propaganda to distort reality and engage in psychological warfare.

> **FACTFILE** According to the American political scientist Karl Deutsch, nationalism has killed more people than any other ideology in the intellectual history of humankind.

Even though there are important theoretical differences between Italian fascism and German national socialism, both emphasized the historical importance of building state institutions that united the common cultural identities of the people. These ideologies are not dead. Support for fascist thought has reappeared in states such as Austria, Belgium, Italy, and Switzerland. There are also fascist groups in Canada and the United States. They invariably focus on the nation rather than the individual and on the superiority of the state over the citizen. There is never the emphasis on individual rights, natural rights, or a social contract that forms the basis of liberal democracy.

In ancient Rome, the *fasces* (a bundle of rods tied to an axe) symbolized the unity of the nation served by an administrative state. In the twentieth century, governments regarded as fascist were intensely nationalistic, imperialistic, anti-democratic, anti-Marxist, and anti-Semitic. They expressed a deep pride in their past cultural achievements and proclaimed a cultural superiority over other national cultures. Benito Mussolini often referred to Italy's *sacro egoismo* as irredentism, the rationale for taking the territory of other states where Italians live. The

Nazis likewise called for the union of all Germans to form the "Great Germany." Those who did not share in the superpatriotism of the period and the resurrected glory of the past were treated as "un-German" or "aliens."

The underlying nationalist ideology of Nazism is racist. Hitler embraced the image of the "Aryan race" as a blond, blue-eyed, and uniquely gifted "master race" that had diluted its genetic heritage by intermarriage with "lesser breeds." The fear of intermarriage with the "inferior races" became linked with all kinds of sexual fears and phobias. In the Nuremberg Laws (1935) proclaimed by the Nazis, German Jews were denied their citizenship, and intermarriage between Germans and Jews was outlawed. Anti-Semitism thus became a Nazi government policy that laid the basis for the so-called Final Solution, which was the extermination of Jews in the death camps of Germany, Austria, and Poland.

Fascist ideology had rejected the political inheritance of the French Revolution and the democratic traditions of liberalism. All individuals existed to enhance the power of the state and the nation it represented. The mystical entity of the nation was viewed as an organic body headed by the leader and sustained by the enforced unity, coercion, and discipline of the state.

Canadian Fascism

The Great Depression, the prairie drought, and the popular spread of communist ideology spawned right-wing social movements in Canada during the 1930s. Fascism emerged from these economic and social conditions in Canada. In 1929, a professional journalist in Montreal, Adrien Arcand, spawned a movement in Quebec based on racial nationalism. Calling itself the "Ordre Patriotique des Goglus," and modelled after Italian Fascism, by February 1930 it claimed as many as 50 000 members. Even before Hitler came to power, Arcand was a loyal patron of fascist ideology. He shared Hitler's anti-Semitism and he organized boycotts of stores and other businesses owned by Jews. Arcand edited a weekly newspaper in which he publicized his idea that Jews should be expelled. He attacked communism and socialism, as did all fascists, but in Canada this won him support among some business owners.

FACTFILE   The legacy of Hitler and Mussolini is still a powerful political force in the presence of neo-Nazis who hold that the "white" race should dominate blacks, Jews, and aboriginal peoples wherever they live in Europe, South Africa, the Middle East, and the Americas.

Once Hitler came to power, Arcand's group became even more virulent in its anti-Semitism. His followers wore blue shirts, mimicking the fascists operating in Europe. Other fascist groups, some competing with Arcand's, sprang up as well. A brown-shirt group, the Canadian Nationalist Party, headed by William Whittaker, an ex-British soldier, was based in Manitoba. This party regularly published anti-Semitic literature. In Ontario, "Swastika Clubs" emerged, comprising gangs of youth who wore swastika insignias and harassed Jews in public places. In 1939, a national fascist convention was held at Massey Hall in Toronto, attracting about 2000 participants. Arcand, his group now publicized bilingually as "Le Parti National Social Chrétien/The National Social Christian Party of Canada," wanted to be known as the Canadian *Führer*. Eventually he outdistanced his closest rivals—the black-shirted Canadian Union of Fascists—in competition for dominance.

When the Nazis began their invasions in Europe, Arcand and other fascists were arrested and imprisoned for the duration of the war. Following his release after the war, Arcand continued to produce anti-Semitic literature until he died in 1967.

But the extreme right has never disappeared in Canada. The Ku Klux Klan and other racist groups have used terror, intimidation, and political agitation. Klan agitation has been very successful, and contributed to successful amendments to Canada's immigration laws in 1929. These established quotas for targeted, less-preferred immigrants; the Klan was a force behind the toppling of the Liberal government in Saskatchewan in the same year.

Many other groups comprise the racist right in Canada.[23] Neo-Nazi groups have formed in most Canadian cities, finding new support among frustrated and disaffected people. Groups such as Aryan Nations, the Aryan Resistance Movement, The Church of the Creator, The Heritage Front, and Final Solution portray a mixture of **xenophobia**, **white supremacy**, and nostalgia for the hegemonic power of Nazi Germany. Neo-Nazis, after years of skulking at the margins of politics in Europe and North America, suddenly feel part of a wider international movement. Most of these groups attempt to enlist young people into their movements by recruiting actively at schools, distributing hate literature by mail and on the internet, and engaging in violence against gays, Jews, African-Canadians, and Aboriginals.

FACTFILE   Anti-foreign and anti-Catholic sentiment led to the establishment of the Ku Klux Klan in Canada in 1925. The Klan was the strongest in Saskatchewan but attracted supporters in most other provinces.

Anarchism

The Greek word *anarchos* means "without a leader or chief." Like the Greek cynics who first developed the doctrines of anarchism, modern anarchists believe that government and the state apparatus are unnecessary for the meaningful arrangement and operation of society. They are essentially optimistic about human nature, believing that the inherent goodness in people alleviates the need for political and organizational constraints on their behaviour. Today, anarchists are not universally agreed on what kind of economic order is desirable.

The debate over the economic system currently splits anarchism into two schools. One school believes that only capitalism can be appropriately combined with anarchism, while the other school advocates returning to an agrarian economy based on socialist economic principles. As for social justice, all anarchists advocate that we should live in a society where there is no compulsion of any kind. For them, social justice is the chance to lead the life that best suits each individual.

Because anarchists are against the excesses of organized political power, they have tried to establish a countervailing force at the basic infrastructure of society, e.g., through tenants' associations, daycare and housing associations, and municipal organizations. Instead of forming political parties, anarchists prefer to project themselves as a movement within the organizational framework of established labour, communist, and socialist parties. In Latin American states such as Argentina, Chile, and Mexico, and in France, Germany, and Spain, *anarcho-syndicalism* has appeared in various labour parties. The central element of anarcho-syndicalism is workers' control of each industry. Once this occurs, representatives from each business come together as an association of individuals to administer the economy of the country.

In the context of communist and socialist parties, anarchists frequently identify with the theories of Peter Kropotkin, Herbert Reid, and Alexander Berkman.[24] Kropotkin argued that co-operation rather than conflict was a natural law of human nature. He and Herbert Reid believed that the ultimate level of co-operation will only be possible when people are able to do away with coercive institutions. Berkman's contribution to anarchist thought emphasized the need to develop a society without any social coercion.

In the period from the mid-1930s to the 1960s, not much was heard of anarchism in any part of the world. However, by the late 1960s, a growing number of academics began to publish manuscripts on anarchism. Students who rioted in Paris carried the anarchist banner in June 1968. By the mid-1970s, the black flag of anarchism was frequently seen in anti-war and disarmament demonstrations in Europe and North America. In spring 1982, the Montreal-based *Anarchos Institute* was established as a clearing house of information and as a vehicle of public education for the western hemisphere.

Anarchists explain the tensions of global politics in terms of the competitive interaction of states, with organized governments as both the actors and targets of human aggression. Thus, anarchists want to dismantle the sovereign state system and replace it with a global society of autonomous groups that interact for political purposes on bases other than those now subsumed under the concepts of "state" and "government."

Ideologies of Development

The political ideologies that are most popular among the developing nation-states have their roots in the great systems of nationalist, democratic, non-democratic and socialist thought.[25] Most modern ideologies of development date from the end of World War II, when a large number of European colonies in Asia and Africa began their struggle toward political independence. The republics of Latin America have had a much longer period of independence after their revolutionary insurrections of the early nineteenth century.

Pragmatism and Development

Pragmatism is now a common mode of political thought in developing countries. What works best for these countries in their unique political and economic circumstances is borrowed from more developed countries and blended with indigenous ways of conducting politics and government. Many developing countries reject the ideals of liberalism, capitalism, socialism, and communism because, in their view, the application of such ideas would not work for them. Thus, an individualist, politically competitive, capitalist, and market-oriented system might not fit easily into the political environment of some Latin American and African states. In all developing nation-states, political leaders search for a unique blend of ideological solutions to their national development goals.

The four most common ideological goals of developing states are

1. national self-determination;
2. economic development;
3. political and social modernization;
4. self-styled democracy.

The ideological component of self-determination postulates the right of a people who consider themselves separate and distinct from others to determine for themselves their economic, political, and social destiny.

Many states in Asia, Africa, and the Caribbean adopt an ideology that prescribes a strong charismatic leader, a single party, a loyal but conspicuous military, and authoritarian methods to achieve national priorities. The blended ideology calls for a quick fix to underdevelopment by means of land reform, the redistribution of wealth, nationalization of certain industries, and economic planning.

Political modernization is portrayed as an ongoing, continuous process that leads to greater citizen participation, better representative institutions, and a more efficient and egalitarian decision-making system. The evolution toward democracy is said to be "guided" or "directed" by an elite party organization or through executive government directives.

REVOLUTIONARY THOUGHT: IDEOLOGIES OR MOVEMENTS?

The meaning of *revolution* has changed considerably since it was first used as a political term in 1688 during the Glorious Revolution in England.[26] Initially a revolution was reactionary: it referred to a revolving return to some pre-established point or some pre-ordained order, i.e., the restoration of the English monarchy in 1660 was therefore a "revolution." In the eighteenth century, as enlightened philosophies flourished, revolution came to mean progress, moving forward—ideas or actions that could alter history. By the nineteenth century, revolution was equated with liberation and freedom.

In the twentieth century, the term *revolution* came to incorporate three distinct processes:

1. destruction of an old regime;
2. a period of chaotic disorder;
3. the creation of a new social order.

Revolution became identified with the most radical and far-reaching kinds of societal change— a sharp break with the past and a change in the basic patterns of life, altering institutions, traditions, and social expectations. As the twenty-first century proceeds, revolutionary thought will be expressed through many ideologies and movements. We see the powerful emergence of terrorism as an ideology that is combined with anarchism, communism, national liberation, and religious fundamentalism.

Movements are often a prelude to revolutionary change because they create or resist attitudes, behaviour, and institutions. Political, social, and religious movements depend on ideologies to establish their identities as well as to gain public visibility. A movement's ideology serves several functions: it provides direction and self-justification; it offers arguments for use in both attack and defence; and it is a source of inspiration for members. Some movements are shapeless, without leadership or clear goals. Others are more directed and fundamentally more ideological.

There are broad distinctions among contemporary movements.[27] *Value-oriented movements* concentrate on matters of general social and political concern, such as democracy, peace, and nationalism. *Norm-oriented movements* are much narrower: one example is to establish or change a particular social or political practice such as the use of alcohol, birth control, and gun control. A *power-centred movement* uses political muscle to achieve certain ends, as with the prohibition movement, movements organized around the abortion issue in Canada, and the civil rights movement in the United States. Power-centred movements sometimes use illegitimate means to meet their goals. A *persuasion-centred movement* uses education, including propaganda and legitimate political action to advance its cause, as with some feminist, pacifist, and environmental movements. These movements tend to favour gradual change and compromise. *Participation-centred movements* focus on creating a unified group of committed members, such as utopian communities and many religious sects. *Revolutionary movements* seek fundamental changes in the entire social structure, usually combined with violent social conflict to establish a new political and social order.

The nationalist (separatist) movement in Quebec falls into the revolutionary category because it seeks, at the very least, a radical restructuring of federal institutions to give Quebec more political and economic autonomy. Failing that, Quebec nationalists would argue, the need to protect their distinct society requires the establishment of an independent state and the complete re-organization of existing institutions.

One faction of the separatist movement in Quebec was the Front de Libération du Québec (FLQ), the militant wing of the independence movement. In the 1960s, it employed tactics similar to those used by other groups in various parts of the world that have struggled toward similar goals: clandestine meetings, kidnapping, bombings, and attacks on the symbols of Quebec's colonial history. In October 1970, two cells of the FLQ incited what came to be known as the October Crisis, when they kidnapped a British diplomat, James Cross, and Quebec cabinet minister Pierre Laporte. The federal government invoked the *War Measures Act*, giving the police and the armed forces powers to stop the FLQ and to arrest hundreds of peaceful separatist supporters. In all of the confusion that transpired, the FLQ published its manifesto through the media.

Canada has given birth to many movements, reflecting a social tendency to political fragmentation and lack of consensus among Canadians. Various groups—e.g., farmers, French-speaking Canadians, women—have at one time or another felt estranged from the mainstream of society. As a result, movements such as the United Farmers, the Co-operative Commonwealth Federation, the Social Credit League, the National Action Committee on the Status of Women, and the Parti Québécois have evolved.

Revolutionary Ideologies

Psychiatrist and theorist Frantz Fanon (1925–1961) advocated the creation of revolutionary movements to initiate radical political change in the developing nation-states. While in Algeria, Fanon became a supporter of the revolutionary movement that eventually led to the French withdrawal from Algeria. He became one of the most widely read anti-colonialists. Fanon's revolutionary ideology rejected the Marxist assertion that the proletariat is necessarily the revolutionary class, and opted instead to identify the African peasantry as such. He emphasized the idea of revolutionary action, *praxis*, such as acts of violence by black peasant "subjects" against white (and black middle-class) colonial "masters." Revolutionary action generates revolutionary consciousness. Fanon's advocacy of revolutionary action stimulated movements in Algeria, Kenya, Zaire, and the Portuguese colonies of Angola and Mozambique.

> FACTFILE   The Islamic faith calls all Muslims to *jihad*, the Arab word for "struggle," against selfishness and evil tendencies. But radical Islamists take it to mean war against what they see as the enemies of Islam: the values of liberalism and secularism.

Another revolutionary theorist, Herbert Marcuse (1898–1979), rejected the working class as a group that has revolutionary potential. For Marcuse, the possibility for revolutionary change can be found in the substratum of a society's outcasts and outsiders, the exploited and the persecuted, the unemployed and the unemployable. Marcuse was essentially a Marxist influenced by Freudian psychology. He developed a notion

of political and sexual liberation that he viewed as contrary to the prevailing trend toward repression and exploitation in advanced societies. Marcuse believed that there was "logic to domination"— people become conditioned to oppression usually by the infusion of carefully planned but limited affluence.

> FACTFILE   No suicide bombings took place in Iraq prior to the military occupation of that country by the United States, which has been ongoing since 2003.

Régis Debray (1941–), the French philosopher who spent considerable time in Cuba after Castro came to power, saw revolution not only as containing elements of violence or military action but also as a process by which the military within the revolution becomes the guerrilla *foco* itself, generating theory and inspiration for the masses. The guerrilla force is the party in embryo, but war

Focus On The Ideology of Violence

World war, civil war, guerrilla war, genocide, terrorism, weapons of mass destruction, conventional weapons, nuclear weapons, and *suicide bombers* are all words that describe the same human phenomenon: violence. Violence has been a conscious aspect of human existence since the dawn of civilization. In fact, humans are the only animals that rationalize, plan, organize, and execute the death blow to members of their own species. Individuals do it every day at the ground level of society through acts of murder, and societies do it as a matter of public policy by legitimizing state violence in quelling disturbances, riots, criminal behaviour, and perceived external military threats.

History confirms our conviction that— because we can think about violence—we live in a violent world. Francis Beer, in his monumental study on war and peace, estimated that since 3600 BC there have been nearly 14 000 incidents of violence in the international system resulting in 1.2 billion military deaths. In his book *Meanings of War and Peace,* Beer isolated only 597 years of peace in over 5500 years of history.[28] When one adds civilian deaths to military casualties, the total number of violent deaths worldwide is estimated at 4 billion, an amount approaching the population of the contemporary world.

is necessary to make the revolution. In fact, the conditions for a successful revolution can be engineered. Debray taught that the Cuban lesson of armed guerrilla warfare should be applied throughout the world of underdeveloped states to win revolutionary struggles. This, as Debray's book title clearly states, is a *Revolution in the Revolution*.

These iconoclasts hold that a political revolution, as opposed to any other basic transformation of society, aims to overthrow a government and destroy the power of the social groups that support it. Ideologically, this has translated into a number of fundamental precepts about revolutionary behaviour:

1. Organized armed forces are vulnerable to popular or trained guerrilla insurrections.

2. Violent action (*praxis*) can generate ideal conditions for revolution before they may naturally evolve.

3. The rural setting is better than urban areas for the organization and initiation of violent revolutionary guerrilla warfare.

4. Guerrilla warfare is not decisive in itself. Revolutionary change requires the fundamental alteration of economic, social, and political institutions.

A political revolution should be distinguished from a political revolt or *coup d'état*, which merely replaces one set of leaders with another or changes only the form of government without affecting the social order.

Feminism—Ideology or Movement?

The political struggle for sexual equality is not new in North America. In 1848, some 300 women and men met at Seneca Falls, New York, to protest the oppression of women. This first manifestation of the "women's movement" grew out of a demand for social reforms during the 1830s and 1840s, when women were denied the right to speak out publicly against slavery.[29]

By the mid-nineteenth century, the women's movement had faded from view, subsumed within the Victorian cultural ideal of feminine purity and dependency. The movement was revived during the reform-minded Progressive period in the early twentieth century.

The Canadian women's movement was influenced by developments in Britain and the United States. The political needs of working women and children were advocated by the National Council of Women, founded in 1893 by Lady Aberdeen, the British wife of Canada's governor general at that time, the Earl of Aberdeen. Other organizations, such as the Toronto Women's Literary Club and the Women's Christian Temperance Union, demanded the right to vote, and gained it in every province between 1916 and 1922 (except Quebec, where women got the vote in 1940).[30]

In North America and Europe, suffragists devoted their energies to gaining the right to vote and to establishing greater access for women to the political system. Women won voting rights first in New Zealand in 1893; Australia, Sweden, Norway, and Finland soon followed. In Russia, women participated in socialist terrorist movements before and after the Revolution, a woman led the assassination of the czar, and many women fought as soldiers for the Bolsheviks. Under totalitarian socialism, women seemed to gain greater opportunities, particularly in occupations, than in other states.

In democratic states, suffragists made the erroneous assumption that the power of the franchise would bring about changes in the workplace, university, religion, and the family. In fact, gaining the vote made very little difference in the lives of women. The high unemployment levels of the Depression sustained the widely held belief that men should get the few jobs generated in the economy.

Not until World War II was this trend reversed. World War II served as a benchmark for opening paid employment opportunities to women. During the war, government propaganda declared that it was women's duty to work in factories and offices to support the war effort. However, after the war, women were encouraged to leave the labour force to assume their traditional role of homemakers so that returning veterans would find employment. Many women liked working for pay, and wanted to continue after the war ended. But peace terminated employment opportunities for most women, closing child-care centres and discontinuing training programs. Throughout the 1950s, the women's movement entered a dormant period, lacking communication and organizational networks to facilitate the spread of its nascent ideology.

The 1960s saw most of the elements of a successful political movement come together: organization, leadership, a growing membership, and an ideology that focused on a widespread sense of protest. In Canada, women's organizations, such as the Canadian Federation of University Women and the Federation des Femmes de Québec, established a communications system among knowledgeable, politically active women. In the United States, the 1961 President's Commission on the Status of Women led to the establishment of the National Organization for Women (NOW), the chief organization in the older, reform-oriented wing of the American women's movement. Betty Friedan's *The Feminine Mystique* linked the oppression of women to cultural variables and began to articulate the ideological basis of the contemporary women's movement in North America. Friedan's book encouraged millions of women to re-examine their social roles in economic and political terms.

FACTFILE   Sweden, Norway, Finland, and Denmark show the highest levels of women participating in Parliament and government in the range of 40 percent: Canada, the United States, Greece, and France show female participation in the national legislature at below 20 percent.

By the 1970s, the women's movement had evolved through the idea of "women's rights" to the idea of "women's liberation." In Canada, the National Action Committee on the Status of Women, the umbrella organization for most other contemporary feminist groups, was established in 1972. Feminists began to identify women's inferior position in society with male supremacy in the family and other social and political structures. During this decade, feminism won wider public acceptance and gained new economic and legal advantages for women. Membership in the movement grew dramatically, attracting predominantly white, middle-class, and college-educated people who supported programs that would benefit working-class and minority-group women.

At the end of the decade, the women's movement took on the characteristics of a power-centred movement, with detectable conservative, moderate, and radical wings. It also developed an international character, as leaders and organizers in different countries became known to each other and communicated on a regular basis. Most countries now have a visible women's movement, albeit with diverse ideological, political, and strategic goals.

Just as no single organization can claim to represent the whole movement, no unified political ideology is detectable either. *Liberal* feminism, sometimes called reform or bourgeois feminism because it accepts the structure of the present society, calls upon the political and legal system to re-examine the degree to which individuals enjoy equal opportunities from the perspective of the inherited qualities of sex and race. This current of feminism wants society to remove all the barriers that actively discriminate against women. *Radical* feminism, sometimes called cultural or separatist feminism, points to biological and psychosocial differences between men and women. It advocates the development of a women-centred culture and anti-militaristic, non-hierarchical political and social structures based on co-operation. *Socialist feminism*, sometimes called Marxist feminism, identifies capitalism and its social and political superstructures as the systemic reasons for the oppression of women. This perspective posits that women are the proletarians in the gender division of labour and men are the bourgeoisie because they control the means of production.

Feminism has focused on certain ideological factors present in most contemporary societies, regardless of their economic and political organizations. One is *patriarchy*.[31] In feminist writings, patriarchy refers to the dominance of social, economic, and political institutions by men. A close correspondence is held between patriarchy and capitalism, in which both the generation and distribution of wealth reflects a male lineage. Historically, the idea that political authority is a male preserve has been the justification for the exclusion of women from access to social power.

Culture is the focus of socially mediated information about the role of women in society and male views of femininity.[32] In many cultures, women are expected to be pretty, sexually passive, emotional, understanding, cultured, child-oriented, slightly helpless, dependent, and in need of male protection. Culture conditions gender identity by creating stereotypes about men and women as reflected in children's books, the adult print media, television, and the movies. These stereotypes are reinforced by toys, games, and sports that influence the learning of gender identity in school, the workplace, and at home.

Another focus of feminism is *epistemology*, the theories and methods of perceiving and thus acquiring knowledge. Feminists recognize that all knowledge is socially constructed and our perceptions and interpretations of the world are coloured by the society in which we live, as well as by our position within that society. Many feminists believe that the dominant ideology (including law, religion, political philosophy, and so on) is essentially sexist and serves the legitimized interests of the male ruling class. In their view, all knowledge is culturally conditioned.

Feminist analysis also takes critical note of history by exposing discrimination against women in previous generations. Women have been granted invisible status within historical analysis. Having only recently been given the rights of citizens, women have suffered society's refusal, throughout history, to include them in the public sphere. Feminists call for a reconstruction of historical interpretation to trace the moral and political beliefs about women to deeper metaphysical, or even biological, sources.

Chapter Summary

Conceptualizing about society can be ideological, in that people hold a set of beliefs that are organized, logical, and offer a consistent plan of action and view of the world. *Political ideology*, as it is used interchangeably with the term *political ideas*, refers to the kind of government people think they "should" have and what it "should" do.

An ideology usually includes ideas about the economy, how we should produce and consume products and services, who can own and operate the corporate units of production, and what roles the government should play in the management of economic matters. Most ideologies hold strong positions on human nature, as well as the roles of the state and the individual in society. But beyond that, an ideology is basically a description of a preferred way of life. The prevailing political ideas have a lot to do with shaping the kind of life Canadians enjoy. A political ideology is an acquired set of political ideas about what constitutes the best form of government and the most equitable and just political order.

Political ideologies are concerned with the proper functions of government, the kinds of political institutions we have to achieve our social goals, and how we distribute economic, social, and political benefits. All of this has to do with how comfortable we feel about the scope of government activities in our lives.

Most of us are not usually conscious of the fact that ideologies affect the content of our private and social thoughts. They underlie what we think as well as what we think about. In fact, ideologies are not only outside us but "inside" us. They are not things in the objective sense but are the products of any and all relationships among people in society.

For these reasons, ideologies include everyone; no one is free from their influences. Ideologies affect how people perceive the world and what they say and do, yet for the most part, people are not always informed of them even though they are usually under their influence, and are disinclined to consider them at all critically. Canadians are predisposed to see the world in certain ways that guide their thinking and their behaviour.

Political discourse in Canada is often dominated by the terms *liberal* and *conservative*, by the analysis of "left" versus "right." But the great array of political ideas cuts into a substantial share of the history of human intellectuality: anarchism, Marxism, conservatism, liberalism, democratic socialism, and feminism are just some of those ideologies that give us our political orientations on the world. As such, they offer, with varying degrees of success, descriptions and explanations of human nature, society, government, power, justice, and equality.

Liberalism is a loosely knit mosaic of beliefs, practices, theories, and approaches to solving economic and political problems based on the rule of law, responsible government, civil liberties, constitutionalism, individualism, majority rule, and popular sovereignty.

Conservatism sees society as an organic partnership of the past, with its values and accomplishments, and the present as a continuation of the accumulated wisdom conserved in social and political institutions.

Socialism is a composite of political, economic, and social ideas equated with values of equality, justice, and the end of exploitation of the poor in society. This is achieved by establishing a planned economy and the institution of government bodies to implement social welfare policies. Socialist ideologies have evolved both as democratic and non-democratic systems of thought.

Nationalism is an ideology people have adopted when they display a strong identification with the physical attributes of a country, combined with a strong and conscious historical identification, and a common language and culture.

Anarchists are philosophically opposed to the idea that government and other forms of political organization are absolutely necessary for the operation of society.

Feminism is an ideology that asserts the equality of women with men, the historical contributions of women in public and private life, and a recognized political status of equality for women in society.

Discussion Questions

1. Evaluate the relative importance of ideas and ideologies in politics. Discuss the role political socialization plays in support of a society's formal ideology. Which values and beliefs are likely to comprise an ideology?

2. Discuss how one could go about examining a society's national ideology. Does Robert E. Lane's classification of the functions of political ideologies suggest any particular ideology? Which one and why?

3. Discuss the following statements:
   • Canadians are not highly ideological.
   • Most Canadians describe themselves as liberal or conservative, but there are not sharp differences between them.
   • Nazism could never flourish in Canada.

4. Which values and beliefs are likely to comprise an ideology? Why is it so important to address the nature of human nature in constructing an ideology? Differentiate between political philosophy and ideology. Differentiate between ordinary ideas and ideologies.

5. Discuss what ideologies do. Why do ideologies criticize other ideologies? Examine other textbooks used in related disciplines (sociology and social psychology). Are some of the observations and generalizations made about ideologies helpful to your understanding of political ideology?

6. What are your general beliefs about human nature? Are these beliefs consistent with what you observe in the world of politics?

7. In your opinion, what are the most sensible assumptions of conservatism? Of liberalism? Of socialism?

8. Describe your own political belief system. Give three of your most fundamental political beliefs as they apply to individuals in society.

9. Analyse the political beliefs of another student in your class. Are you in agreement with him or her? In what areas do you disagree?

10. What three questions would you ask a politician about her or his political beliefs to determine his or her ideological profile?

CHAPTER 3

Nations, States, Rank, and Power

After reading this chapter, you will be able to:

- differentiate between the concepts of nation, state, political system, and government
- plot the growth of nation-states in the global community
- define sovereignty and place it in the context of global problems
- define the concept of *power* and relate it to the behaviour of governments in the international system
- analyze the components of power and apply them to individual political systems
- distinguish between the concepts of *unitary* and *federal state*
- evaluate the effect of adopting a unitary or federal structure of government on performance and efficiency
- identify the various economic systems
- differentiate between the terms *First World, Second World, Third World*, etc.
- illustrate what makes a state powerful or not
- differentiate the use of power in the world community as *hard* and *soft*

• • • •

WHAT IS A NATION-STATE?

Some of the most widespread confusions in our political vocabularies concern the meaning of the terms *nation*, *state*, and *country*. People may sometimes use these terms interchangeably in casual conversation but, for professional purposes, they should be distinguished. They have somewhat different meanings and require definition for use in political science and international law.

The term *state* refers to a legal/political and administrative entity composed of a governing central authority that makes and enforces laws and is recognized as the primary subject of the international legal system. The Montevideo Convention on the Rights and Duties of States (1933) laid down four criteria that states must possess to qualify as **persons** under international law. The Convention declared that a state must have:

1. a permanent population,
2. a defined territory,
3. a government, and
4. a capacity to enter into relations with other states.

In the contemporary international system there are more than 200 such legal/political entities functioning as states and claiming international legal status. This status entitles them to sign treaties, form alliances, join international organizations, and exchange ambassadors.

FACTFILE The first peoples in North America became many nations, each with its own social and political culture, its own leaders and ways of choosing them, and its own ways of making binding decisions.

States may be the hosts of many nations: one state may govern a multinational society. In contrast to a state, a nation is a **sociocultural** entity, made up of a group of people who identify with each other ethnically, culturally, and linguistically. A nation may not have a government or a geographically delimited territory of

Table 3.1	**First Nations in Canada: Pre-Confederation**	
Abenaki	Huron	Mi'kmaq
Algonquin	Inuit (Caribou)	Montagnais
Assiniboine	Inuit (Copper)	Neutral
Beaver	Inuit (Iglulik)	Ojibwa
Bella Coola	Inuit (Mackenzie Delta)	Salish
Beothuk	Inuit (Netsilik)	Sioux
Blackfoot	Inuit (Sadlermuit)	Tahltan
Carrier	Iroquois	Tlingit
Chipewyan	Kutchen	Tsimshian
Cree	Kutenai	Tunit
Dene	Kwakiutl	
Haida	Maliseet	

Sources: Graham Reynolds, Richard MacKinnon, People in Atlantic Canada *(Sydney, NS: Folkus Atlantic, 2002); www.folkus.com and www.learnersportal.com.*

its own. But many nations may exist within the political and administrative **jurisdiction** of a state. Canada is a multinational entity, with more than 30 First Nations and millions of Québécois who identify with each other as nationals.

FACTFILE   The Mi'kmaq and the Beothuk of Atlantic Canada were among the first peoples to encounter the newcomers from Europe who would eventually impose their political institutions and culture on all Aboriginal peoples within the confines of a nation-state called Canada.

Many scholars refer to the relationship between the state and the nationalities it serves as a *nation-state*.[1] The modern nation-state weaves nationalities together according to a deliberate political design: it determines official languages, creates a uniform system of law, manages a single currency, controls the education system, builds a national bureaucracy to defend and socialize different people and classes, and fosters loyalty to an abstract entity, such as "Canada," "Brazil," or the "United States." Scholars may use the term "state" in reference to the actions of a government or its bureaucracy, and likewise, international organizations usually call their members "states." However, many scholars use the term "nation-state" when they refer to a society in its entirety, as a political, social, and governmental entity.

FACTFILE   The European Union is an example of a large-scale economic and political regrouping of nation-states with supranational structures that may become the United States of Europe.

Today, the nation-state is the most effective instrument of social and political integration as well as the primary vehicle for national economic modernization. But sometimes nation-states unravel into a multiplicity of smaller governing entities, the most dramatic being the Soviet Union, which in 1991 collapsed into 15 independent nation-states. Only 211 such nation-states make up the present international system, yet together they host more than 1400 nationalities existing in the world.[2]

The term *country* refers to the all-inclusive characteristics of a geographical entity—its physical, material, and socio-economic components. Use of the term *country* is widespread in political-science literature, but can sometimes result in confusion if it is not properly clarified. To refer to the country of Ireland requires specific reference either to the six counties of Northern Ireland under Great Britain or to the 26 counties in the south that form the Republic of Ireland. The same problem exists with other divided countries such as North Korea and The Republic of Korea (South).

The Growth in the Number of Nation-States

The modern nation-state system has existed for some 360 years—less than 10 percent of the 5500 years of recorded human history. In 1648, the Peace of Westphalia terminated the Thirty Years' War in Europe, bringing an end to the view of the world as an organized system (Holy Roman Empire) based on a Christian commonwealth governed by the Pope and the Holy Roman Emperor. We know that states such as England and France predate the Peace of Westphalia as sovereign political units. But at the time of the Peace of Westphalia, the international system, formally and legally, was transformed into a society of legally equal states, each exercising complete territorial jurisdiction over well-defined boundaries.

With the disintegration of the Holy Roman Empire into **autonomous** political organizations, the modern nation-state came to dominate the international system as a legal/political entity subject to no higher secular authority. The doctrine of **sovereignty** thus became the first general principle of international law. It asserts that the nation-state is the supreme decision-making power within a geographically delineated frontier and is subject to external authority only by its consent. A question of sovereignty has been raised for a number of decades against Canada's claim to the Northwest Passage by states such as the United States, Russia, and Denmark. These governments see the Northwest Passage as international waters, not as waters protected by Canadian sovereignty.

FACTFILE Sovereignty is at the core of the Act of State Doctrine, which requires each state to respect the public acts of other states by not passing judgment on the legality or the constitutionality of its actions within its own territory.

Out of the doctrine of sovereignty emerged the principle of the **legal equality of states**. This establishes that sovereign nation-states enjoy the same rights and duties under international law, regardless of size, population, wealth, or military power. This principle is affirmed in the legal equation of one state, one vote, which is practised and enjoyed by all nation-states in the international councils of the world.

Crosscurrents Does Sovereignty Prevent Us from Solving Urgent Global Issues?

When you woke up this morning, you probably didn't think of yourself as an *earthling*. Not very many people did, because they woke up under the sovereign authority of a nation-state somewhere on the planet. Most people think of themselves in terms of country: as American, Belgian, Canadian, Peruvian, Zambian, and so on.

But what happens in other parts of the world has an impact on your life, and what happens here in Canada impacts the people of other nations. For example, climate change in Canada's Arctic has environmental implications around the world, and air pollution from the United States can have an impact right in your own backyard.

At this juncture of history, sovereign nation-states and their international organizations rule the world. But they rule as a collection of states with specific national interests, not as a global governing system focused on all peoples. Generally speaking, nation-states only consider global issues that impact negatively on their own nation.

Sovereignty—the notion that governments are free to do what they want within their own territory—has been the organizing principle of international relations since the sixteenth century. Little has changed about the concept of sovereignty, and yet the world has transformed dramatically. In essence, we have entered the twenty-first century with a sixteenth-century value system.

Some nation-states are recognizing that we need to be globally united—to move beyond sovereignty and think about our shared interests as "citizens of the world." But the question remains as to whether nations will be willing to surrender their national sovereignty for the global good. Can we fast-forward ourselves to a global governing system that can protect the environment for all peoples? Can we create effective means of enforcement? And will we move beyond the doctrine of strict national sovereignty before it's too late?

The proliferation of nation-states was a gradual occurrence from the Peace of Westphalia through the second half of the twentieth century, when the **decolonization** of remaining European empires escalated following World War II. Since 1945, the number of nation-states has tripled from roughly 65 to more than 200, with most of these newcomers appearing in Africa, but many appearing in Eastern Europe since the Soviet Union disintegrated and its state succumbed to **extinction** (Figure 3.1). Today, less than 1 percent of the world's population and territory remain without self-government. The emergence of new nation-states is likely to continue for some time because some states continue to break up or **devolve** into two or more independent states. In some cases **state secession** may occur, whereby a state's sovereignty is transferred to another state or other states. For example, the former Czechoslovakia was partitioned in 1992, creating two independent states—the Czech Republic and Slovakia.

FACTFILE In its "failed state index," the journal *Foreign Policy* (July/August 2005) identifies the ten most endangered states that are likely to fail: Ivory Coast, Congo, Sudan, Iraq, Somalia, Sierra Leone, Chad, Yemen, Liberia, and Haiti.

Power and the Nation-State

The nation-state is an organization specifically designed to accumulate, institutionalize, and articulate power in a competitive international system. Most analysts of international relations see the power of a nation-state in terms of its capacity to influence other entities in its environment. Karl Holsti defines power as "the general capacity of a state to control the behavior of other states."[3] Karl Deutsch sees it as "the ability to prevail in conflict

Figure 3.1   Independent nation-states, 1648–2007

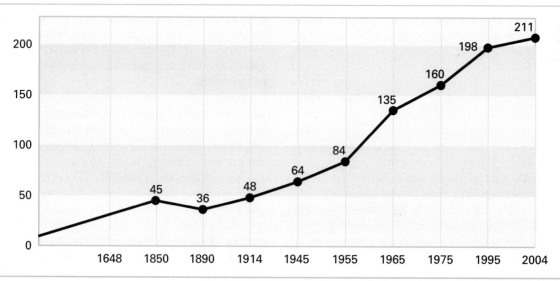

Sources: Michael Wallace & David Singer, "Intergovernmental Organization in the Global System, 1815-1964: A Quantitative Description," International Organization 24 *(Spring 1970) © MIT Press. Used by permission. Dr. Barry Turner,* Statesman's Yearbook, 2004, *Published 2003. © Palgrave Macmillan. Reproduced with permission of Palgrave Macmillan.*

and overcome obstacles."[4] For Robert Dahl, "Power is the ability to shift the probability of outcomes."[5] Dahl also sees it as a psychological relationship between those who exercise it and those over whom it is exercised. Each of these definitions is an attempt to explain a highly complex set of power components that cluster together, building the overall capacity and potential of the nation-state. Ray Cline constructed a conceptual formula to illustrate the parameters of power at the disposal of a nation-state.[6] He states it as:

$$Pp = (C + E + M) \times (S \times W), \text{ where}$$

Pp = perceived power
C = critical mass: size, location, population, and natural resources
E = economic capability
M = military capability
S = strategic purpose
W = will to pursue national strategy $\quad$ *quantifiable?*

Perceived power expresses the psychological relationship between those who use power and those over whom power is exercised. It has both a domestic as well as an international dimension: the power of a nation-state is a product not only of its externally perceived power but also of its own self-perception.

One of Prime Minister Trudeau's first foreign-policy statements in 1968 was to disclaim Canada's post-war international status as the smallest of the large powers, repositioning Canada's contemporary role as "the largest of the small powers."[7] Trudeau's perception of Canada's power was a reflection of Canada's internal aspirations to relate its international role to domestic capabilities: "We shall do more good by doing well what we know to be within our resources to do than to pretend either to ourselves or to others that we can do things clearly beyond our national capacity."[8]

The perception of the power of a nation-state can flow from the characteristics of its critical mass, its economic capability, and its military capacity. But these elements alone will not determine the power potential of a nation-state. They must be brought together by the deliberate and planned strategy of decision makers. Thus, strategic purpose and the will to pursue a strategy of power are important considerations in realistically appraising the strength of a nation-state. Let us examine each of these various components of power.

Critical Mass

The tangible elements of national power (**tangible power**) are frequently identified as size, location, population, and natural resources. These elements affect the political conduct of people and are used in association with the study of national strength. Together, they constitute the power inventory of a nation-state. They are measurable features that condition rank and status in the international system. We know that physical and human resources may serve to enhance the power status of a nation-state, but they may also function to create major obstacles to development. For example, Japan has the reputation of an economic **superpower**, but it is severely circumscribed by population pressure and the lack of raw materials. And Canada, the geographically second-largest country in the world, with a population of 33 million, a modern economy, and vast natural resources, can attain only middle ranking in the international community. Both nation-states, for opposite reasons, must overcome obstacles created by their size and the distribution of their populations.

Size

Political geography informs us that the size of a nation-state—the amount of territorial space it incorporates—presents advantages and disadvantages to a government's ability to enhance its power profile. After all, the total world land mass is limited, and larger states do have greater access to the bulk of resources from which power can be derived than do smaller states. The United States (the fourth largest) is a superpower blessed with a wide range of raw materials. The abundance of natural resources is a prime requisite for power, perhaps even more important than the capacity to exploit them. Countries such as Australia, Brazil, Canada, China, and Mexico are nation-states with great potential for increasing their influence in world affairs, based on their size and share of natural resources. While it is true that size alone does not determine national power, it is also true that the world's most powerful nation-state, the United States, happens to be very large.

With vastness in size come problems of social cohesion, economic disparities, political organization, and national control. Canada is a good example. The physical characteristics of Canada create enormous challenges for achieving political and economic integration. Canada's area is nearly 10 million square kilometres. The country spans seven time zones and possesses large natural internal barriers: the Appalachians, the Canadian Shield, the Rocky Mountains, the Great Lakes, and the Arctic desert. These features tend to divide rather than unify its population. In addition, Canada is a composite of six geographic regions: the Atlantic provinces, Quebec, Ontario, the Prairies, British Columbia, and the North, each with distinctive physical characteristics that tend to foster both economic and political regionalism.

Politically, Canada is at war with its geography. Of the world's federal states, Canada has the most decentralized federal system, with each provincial government possessing significantly wider political powers and jurisdictions in economic, social, and cultural matters than do those in other federations.[9] The Canadian constitution gives the impression that Canada would be a highly centralized state if the original government jurisdictions—which convey how the Fathers of Confederation wanted the country to work—were adhered to. Throughout Canada's federal history, the provinces have become more and more empowered to deliver some

of the most essential services to Canadians. At the extreme, some provinces have even developed a special role in international and commercial affairs, as in the case of Quebec. For Canada, sheer size has made its functioning as an independent nation-state a political miracle.

Table 3.2 lists the relative size of the 10 biggest nation-states in the world. These 10 countries control more than half the land surface of the globe. We can see from the table that size is not the most significant criterion upon which to judge the power profile of a nation-state: 6 of the 10 largest countries of the world are among the world's less-developed nation-states. And, in the case of Canada, size creates staggering political and economic problems in terms of national unity and development.

Very large states often experience internal divisions due to natural barriers caused by vastness—Australia's central desert and Canada's Rocky Mountain belt exemplify this. Both Canada and Brazil have the problem of diminishing the "empty" aspect of their sparsely populated regions by encouraging population resettlement in these areas. Brazil relocated its capital city, Brasilia, to the heart of the jungle just for the purpose of encouraging the westward migration of people. The African state of Sudan is vast, spanning Arab Africa through black Africa. The Arab population in the north, which concentrates in the capital of Khartoum, is racially and culturally distinct from the black Africans in the south.

Location

The location of a nation-state influences its power potential in strategic as well as geographic ways.

Location determines a state's neighbours, its access to the oceans, its proximity to the world's major trade routes, and its strategic importance in matters of national and international security. Therefore, location is politically important to a nation-state for purposes of trade, transportation, defence, and attack. While it is true that the

Table 3.2	**The world's 10 largest countries by area**	
Country	*Area (km²)*	*Percentage of World Total*
Russia	17 075 000	17.9
Canada	9 976 139	7.3
China	9 596 961	7.1
United States	9 363 123	6.9
Brazil	8 511 965	6.3
Australia	7 686 848	5.7
India	3 287 590	2.4
Argentina	2 766 889	2.0
Sudan	2 505 813	1.8
Algeria	2 381 741	1.8
Subtotal	**76 162 069**	**61.6**
World	**135 830 000**	**100.0**

Sources: Data for the World's 10 Largest Countries by Area (p.6) (created into table 3.2) from Oxford Atlas of he World, 13th Edition, data by Lye, Keith (2006). © Oxford University Press. Reprinted by permission of Oxford University Press, Inc. www.oup.com

location of a state is permanently fixed geographically, the political ramifications of the space it occupies constantly change as other nation-states evaluate its significance in terms of their national interest. For example, the strategic importance of Canada to the United States goes without saying. Any state or terrorist group that militarily attacked Canada would incur the retaliation of both Canada and the United States.

Access to oceans and important waterways is another critical factor in determining a state's power. These are extensions of the land-based commercial power of a nation-state. Strategically, access to oceans provides most states with the military advantages of sea power. Today, sea power is a crucial factor in both conventional- and nuclear-war deterrence. The world's foremost sea powers possess the naval capability of massive retaliation from any point on the globe in response to a first strike from an enemy state. In 2002, US and British air strikes were mounted against Iraq in its "no-fly zone" from aircraft carriers poised in the Persian Gulf.

Not having access to oceans and waterways also affects the power of the state. Because they do not have easy access to the international marketplace, the now more than 40 independent nation-states of the world that are landlocked have special economic problems. The export/import relations of such economies are dependent upon the national policies of coastal states and are always subject to higher transportation and handling costs. At best, landlocked states must negotiate with coastal states to gain permission to carry on overseas trade without interference or harassment.

In 1921 in Barcelona, a Freedom of Transit Conference was held that produced a convention to encourage signatories to assist landlocked states in the movement of goods to the nearest seaport without levying discriminatory taxes or freight charges on them. In 1965, the United Nations drafted a convention outlining concessions to landlocked states to provide them with customs exemptions, free storage, and free ports of entry.

Location has had important political implications for Canada's international role. Canada's geographical position is unusual in that it shares a vast border with only one country and that country happens to be a superpower. The presence of only one powerful land neighbour has been the single most significant factor in the history of Canada's external relations. While historically Canada has used access to the oceans to escape the influence of the United States on its cultures and economy, the pull of free trade has entrenched Canada's international interests in the western hemisphere. But geographically, Canada's location is unique because it is the only mainland country directly connected to three oceans.

The total length of Canada's coastline, bordering on the Atlantic, Pacific, and Arctic oceans, is over 36 000 kilometres, more than twice the circumference of the earth. These three ocean avenues have allowed Canada to diversify its international ties, as well as to enrich its natural resource base. The Atlantic Ocean has maintained Canada's links with Europe. The Pacific Ocean has opened ties with Asia and the economies of the Pacific Rim, especially those of Japan and the Republic of Korea. By the early 1970s, Japan had surpassed Great Britain as Canada's second most important trading partner after the United States. The Republic of Korea is Canada's third largest export destination in the Asia-Pacific region, after China and Japan. The Arctic Ocean is also vital to Canada for its vast untapped natural resources, as well as for its strategic value in protecting the western hemisphere.

Population

The nation-states of the world vary as much in population as they do in territorial size. Population ranges from the Vatican, with a population of about 1000, to China, with a population of more than one billion people, or about one-fifth of all humanity. When population is discussed as a global concern, the analysts tend to focus on those nation-states with the largest populations (Table 3.3). But it is interesting to note that more than 140 of the states of the world contain populations of fewer

Table 3.3	Leading nation-states in population, 2007	
Nation-State	**Population**	**Percentage of World Total**
China	1 321 851 888	19.7
India	1 129 866 154	16.8
United States	301 139 947	4.49
Indonesia	234 693 997	3.50
Brazil	190 010 647	2.83
Pakistan	164 741 924	2.45
Bangladesh	150 448 339	2.24
Russia	147 377 752	2.19
Nigeria	135 031 164	2.01
Japan	127 433 494	1.90

Source: © 2009 by Matt Rosenberg (http://geography.about.com/cs/worldpopulation/a/mostpopulous.htm). Used with permission of About, Inc. which can be found online at www.about.com. All rights reserved.

than 25 million people. From the perspective of a majority of these states, small population is a more central concern in terms of economic growth and development than is overpopulation.

Difficulties are often faced by large countries with small populations. For example, Canada's total population of just over 33 million inhabitants makes up less than one-half of 1 percent of the global population, yet this population has the task of developing nearly 10 percent of the world's living room. Canadian governments construct highways, railways, communication networks, and also participate in a military system that serves the western hemisphere and Europe. Canada's businesses and governments must manage vast natural resources with a population about the same as the state of California's. In the development of their capital projects, Canadians must depend heavily on foreign investment, over 80 percent of which flows from the United States. Even Russia, which has the sixth-largest population in the world, has most of its population clustered west of the Ural Mountains, leaving large expanses of territory unoccupied and undeveloped.

Like the factors of territorial size and location, the size of a nation-state's population is not necessarily an indication of its power. However, the effectiveness of the population, whatever its size, in contributing to the agricultural, industrial, and military capacities of the state in a highly competitive world is important. In addition, the size of a population must be analyzed with respect to the resources at its disposal and the political and economic organization of the state.

FACTFILE According to United Nations projections, India will surpass China as the most populous country in the world in 2025.

The growth, distribution, density, and mobility of a population are factors that must be constantly evaluated to get a clear picture of the potential in a nation-state. For Canada, a population increase can contribute to the productive strength of the economy only because the problems of food supply, welfare, education, and other factors are adequately met by the economic system. But for Bangladesh, Ethiopia, and India, population increases are too burdensome for the economies: this problem nullifies the benefits of human resources.

Natural Resources

The natural resources of a nation-state generally refer to the resources found on, above, and under the surface of the earth. A country's soil, animal life, forests, vegetation, water, sunshine, climate, and minerals are natural resources. For example, Canada is the most powerful country in the world in its capacity to generate hydroelectricity, producing over 75 percent of its electrical power consumption. For some countries, such as Australia, Canada, the United States, Russia, and the Ukraine, nature has provided an extravagant resource endowment. But for others, such as Chad, Ethiopia, and Haiti, nature's provisions have not been so generous.

Sometimes, however, the sheer will and capacity of a population to industrialize from imported raw materials can propel it to economic superiority: Japan has little locally accessible natural resources. But Japan is an exception. For most of the economies of the world, national power is directly related to the possession of and accessibility to raw materials and the capacity to use them to produce food and consumer goods. Without a solid agricultural base and access to raw materials, nation-states cannot develop into prosperous industrial and technological economies.

FACTFILE The process we refer to as the world economy, globalization, or in French mondialisation, began in the middle of the nineteenth century—when the first transatlantic telegraph cable was laid in 1858.

No national economy is completely self-sufficient in respect to foods or natural resources. **Economic interdependence** is a basic law in the modern international system, and is now commonly referred to as *globalization*. The uneven distribution of arable land and raw materials is the primary motivation for national economies to engage in international trade. Never before in human history have nation-states relied so much on each other to obtain the essentials of life. Since World War II, the growth of world trade in goods and services has greatly expanded: it is estimated that it now totals more than US $13 trillion per year (Figure 3.2). The material resources of a nation-state, derived

Figure 3.2   Growth of world trade, 1913–2006 (in billions of dollars)

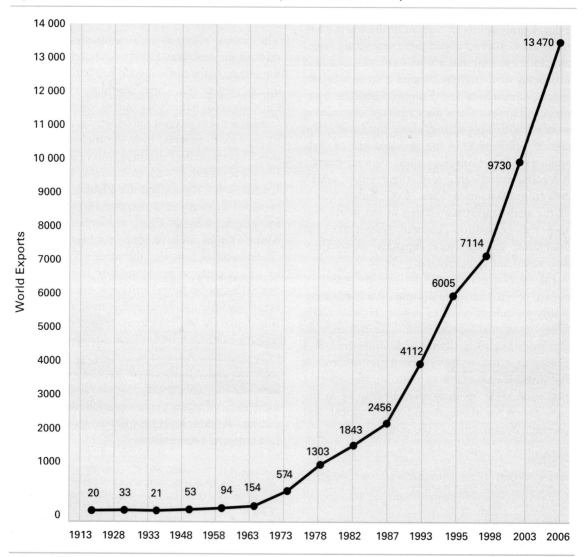

Sources: Adapted from International Monetary Fund (IMF), Direction of Trade Statistics *(Washington, DC, June 2001);* and World Trade 2006, Prospects for 2007, *World Trade Organization, 2008; and see www.wto.org/english/news/archives*

from its agricultural and industrial output, help determine its power potential.

HOW POLITICAL ORGANIZATION AFFECTS AN ECONOMY

All independent states exercise effective organization and control over their territorial boundaries. The political-territorial organization of a state is not just the organization of geographical space, but also the foundation of its economic capacity. The way a state divides or centralizes political power and the decision-making functions of government translates into economic advantage or disadvantage. Economic capacity is almost always a product of political organization.

The political system establishes the communications and transportation networks, the arrangements of the land-tenure system, and the application of an overriding structure to enhance human opportunity and exploit natural resources. For example, an efficient communications network is of vital importance for political and economic cohesiveness in a nation-state. Canada's communication system is technically the most advanced in the world. With the launching of the Anik satellite series in 1972, Canada became the first state to establish a national telecommunications system based on signals from space.

Perspectives Do We Need a New Index to Measure the Economy?

The two most commonly used measures of economic output are Gross Domestic Product (GDP) and Gross National Product (GNP). Some economists say that these should be replaced by another index called the Genuine Progress Index (GPI). They say that in the GDP every transaction in the economy is considered positive as long as money changes hands; if the GDP rises, everything added is a gain, making no distinction between costs and benefits, progress or decline.

A GPI would measure things differently, and would include activities ignored by the GDP. The GPI consists of more than 20 social, economic, and environmental variables that measure human, social, and natural capital. Included would be such things as the costs of crime, air pollution, water pollution, family breakdown, and ozone pollution. It would calculate the value of time spent on housework, parenting, and volunteer services. Thus, the GPI distinguishes between those transactions that contribute to and diminish well-being. It operates more like a business income statement that adds values and benefits and subtracts the costs.

For example, resource depletion—which takes a variety of forms—remains one of the primary factors that contribute to provincial debt and economic decline. The GPI considers losses such as reduction of stock and of farmland, wetlands, and forests, measuring each case. Resource depletion is considered a positive influence on the economy in the year the resource is consumed as a transaction in the GDP. But, in the GPI, resource depletion is calculated as a detrimental effect on the economy and people in all future years. Thus, the GPI treats resource depletion as a negative factor, pure and simple.

The advantage of the GPI is that it recognizes that true long-term prosperity and well-being are ultimately dependent on the protection and strengthening of our social and environmental assets.

The manner in which a nation-state has organized its government, economy, and defence is an important indication of its internal institutional power and its perceived external power in the political world. In this regard, the political organization of a nation-state, as distinct from its form of government, is either unitary or federal.

ORGANIZING THE DYNAMIC OF POWER WITHIN A STATE

The question is sometimes asked, Where does the power lie within a state? Some people think power is concentrated in the hands of a small group, perhaps even an anonymous one. Others believe it is widely dispersed among the people, or that various levels of government share the jurisdictions of power between or among them. Thus, the distribution of power is an important consideration when we analyze the power equation of a nation-state. Unitary states have certain advantages in exercising power, which may or may not be available in states that use the federal system of government. The exercise of power has everything to do with how a state is organized and how it distributes power within its borders. These characteristics determine to what extent states can and will radiate an expression of power towards other states and the whole international community.

Unitary States

The unitary state is the most common type of political organization, accounting for 90 percent of all independent nation-states. A unitary state is one in which all sovereign power resides in the national government: all other units of government are merely its subdivisions.[10] Any delegation of power to regions, districts, or municipalities is largely at the discretion of the national government and may be legally reduced, increased, or removed, even if only for reasons of administrative efficiency. In this type of political organization, the national government can impose its decisions on local governments, regardless of the unpopularity of those decisions. This high degree of political centralization is not always intended to foster economic efficiency: rather, it is frequently implemented to facilitate political and social control. The chief advantage of the unitary system of government lies in its simplicity: there is only one responsible government to which citizens pay taxes and from which they receive services.

As a general rule, unitary states such as Japan and France enjoy a high level of internal homogeneity and cohesiveness. But some unitary states, such as Spain and South Africa, lack social homogeneity and are geographically large enough to warrant federal systems. In Spain, the existence of four spoken languages—Spanish, Portuguese (in Galicia), Basque, and Catalan—serves to divide rather than unify the affairs of state. In 1910, the Union of South Africa joined four provinces under a unitary system that facilitated Apartheid.

The average unitary state is small and densely populated, with one **core area**. There is a direct one-level relationship between the people and their national government (Figure 3.3). People are not burdened with the complications and duplications of government services. One central agency designs school curricula, issues licenses and permits, raises taxes, and plans the economy. All

Figure 3.3   Unitary states

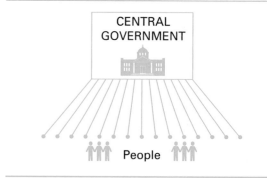

CENTRAL GOVERNMENT

People

government units are administrative subdivisions of the same government so that, under normal conditions, unitarism has cost-efficient benefits.

Many former colonial territories have embraced the unitary form of political organization. All of the former French territories adopted the unitary system of political organization. Most British-influenced states in Africa—for example, Kenya, Sierra Leone, and Ghana—are unitary. All Arab states in the Middle East are unitary, and the majority of emergent black African states also chose this form of political organization. All Central American republics are unitary states, and in South America, Colombia, Ecuador, Peru, Chile, Bolivia, and Paraguay function as unitary states. China holds the distinction of being the largest unitary state in the world. The unitary organization of the Chinese government enables the totalitarian regime to maintain direct controls on all regions of the country.

Federal States

Federalism is not a common way of organizing governments around the world. Less than 10 percent of the world's nation-states are politically organized as federal systems. No simple generalization can be made about the size of federal states. National and subnational governments are organized according to legal and constitutional prescriptions. While it is true that a federal structure is especially suitable for large states such as Canada and the United States, it is also true that many unitary states (China and Sudan) are larger than some federations, such as India and Argentina.

> FACTFILE The founding of Canada in 1867 is referred to as a confederation, but Canada was from the very beginning, and has remained, a federal state.

Geography is but one of the many divisive complications. All federal states have human as well as geographic factors that divide them. The federal structure is effective in countries occupied by people of widely different ethnic origins, languages, religions, and political cultures. India, which has the world's second-largest population and a federal system of government, has 14 main languages and more than 200 secondary ones. Canada has a complicated federal system in which social differences have regional political expression, in that some peoples see different parts of Canada as a homeland.

The word *federal* finds its origins in the Latin *foederis*, meaning "league." It implies an alliance of a state's diverse internal regions and people. K.W. Robinson says that "federation does not create unity out of diversity; rather, it enables the two to coexist."[11] Federalism organizes a system of governing in which significant government powers are divided and shared between the central government and smaller governmental units. Neither one completely controls the other; each has room for independent policy making.

The federal arrangement is a political balance of constantly shifting centrifugal and centripetal forces in a country. *Centrifugal* forces move power away from the political centre of a state to the component areas. These are many and varied: regional loyalties; different historical experiences; distinct forms of economic specialization; differences of language, culture, and population densities; as well as remoteness from the federal capital. *Centripetal* forces centralize political power and control at the federal level of government. They diminish separatist pressures by reducing the perception of internal differences, encouraging national loyalty, unifying the economy, and centralizing political decisions.

> FACTFILE Switzerland is the world's smallest federal state but its structure protects many different languages spoken throughout its cantons: German, French, Italian, Serbo-Croatian, Albanian, Portuguese, Spanish, English, and Romansch.

In every example of a federated political organization there exists a constitutional division and sharing of powers among the various levels of government. Federalism simply means

Figure 3.4   **Federal states**

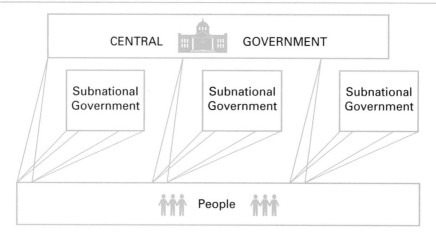

that more than one unit of government has responsibility for a citizen living in any part of the country (Figure 3.4). The subnational units are well defined geographically. They are called states in the United States and Mexico, provinces in Canada, *Länder* in Germany, cantons in Switzerland, and autonomous provinces in Russia. The 1994 South African Constitution created a new federal state with a national government and nine provinces.

There are three types of federations among the nation-states that practise federalism: mature federations, conciliatory federations, and centralized federations. A *mature federation* is one that over time has achieved national, economic, and political integration among people of diverse ethnic origins. The constituent parts share a mutual interest in the goals of the national government and have a stake in supporting the original divisions of power and jurisdiction. The component parts accept their assigned constitutional roles and are willing to yield powers to the federation in order to make viable the larger economic and political unit. Seven of the world's twenty federal nation-states fall into this category, with the United States and Australia as prime examples.

FACTFILE   A confederation is a political association formed by independent member-states that seek a form of union for purposes of defence, foreign affairs, or trade, but which retain their sovereign powers. Notable confederations that failed are the United States (1781–87), Germany (1815–66), and Switzerland (1815–74).

Conciliatory federations are characterized by a high degree of assigned constitutional centralization, but an ongoing process of compromise and negotiation between the national government and the subnational units produce a rough equality of autonomy in matters affecting jurisdictions and the divisions of power. Unlike those in mature federations, the various entities that make up conciliatory federations have retained their own identities, with their own laws, policies, customs, and languages. These federations appear inherently quarrelsome and perhaps even contradictory as a form of political organization. Jurisdictional disputes frequently arise as political issues. Constant bickering can characterize the relationship between the central government and the governments of the lower units. In this type of federalism, no level of government can effectively govern without the co-operation of the other levels. Nevertheless, conciliatory federalism is much more responsive to local and regional needs than would be a unitary state. Seven states can be labelled conciliatory, including Canada, India, Malaysia, and the states of the United Arab Emirates.

Canada's experience illustrates the nature of conciliatory federalism.[12] But the *Constitution Act, 1867*, placed in the domain of the federal government four important powers that enabled centralized government. These powers—the residual power, the declaratory power, and the powers of disallowance and reservation—gave the federal government the sovereign capacity of a unitary state cloaked in the guise of federalism. The *residual power* is enshrined in the "Peace, Order and Good Government of Canada" clause, which—in circumstances such as those that encouraged the government to invoke the *War Measures Act* in 1970 and wage-and-price controls in 1975—permits the federal government to penetrate provincial jurisdictions. The *declaratory power* allows the federal government to displace provincial powers if, in the view of Parliament, such an action is "for the general Advantage of Canada or for the Advantage of Two or more of the Provinces." *Disallowance* is a pre-emptive power of the federal government to void a provincial law within a year of its passage. *Reservation* allows all federally appointed lieutenant governors to reserve royal assent on a provincial bill, placing the final decision before the federal cabinet.

Crosscurrents   Does Canada Need a National Government?

Much has changed in Canada since the fathers of Confederation gave shape to a federal state with a strong national government. That was the time when most Canadians lived in the countryside, not in cities where most of us live today. Many of our ancestors were born in their homes, not in hospitals. In fact, they rarely went to a hospital or saw a doctor for medical treatment, except when they were dying. Going to school meant getting through grade 5 or 6, and then going out to work. It was also a time when a university education was a rare commodity, attracting only a few interested Canadians.

The authors of our constitution thought municipalities, health care, and education were not crucial to our survival in the nineteenth century. So they gave these jurisdictions to the provinces—governments that they believed would eventually disappear and dissolve under a powerful national state.

The *Constitution Act, 1867*, gave the federal government control over the main nineteenth-century concerns—trade, the post office, public works, the banks, and criminal law. The provinces received jurisdiction over what would eventually become the most significant functions of government in our lives—cities, education, social services, and health care.

In the twenty-first century, big cities are where we live, everybody wants access to a doctor or a hospital, and post-secondary education is now a goal for most students in high school across Canada. All of these concerns fall under the responsibility of our provincial governments. Thus, Canadians now regard the most important government services in their lives as those provided by their provincial government, not by the federal government.

In the eyes of many Canadians, the federal government has become a distant banker, the government with surplus money that transfers national wealth back into the provinces, but not much else—and not without a fight. The Millennium Scholarship program links the federal government directly to university students. The Canada Child Tax Benefit steps around provincial social-assistance plans and sends cheques straight to low-income families. But apart from these uncommon initiatives, the federal government does not have much direct relationship with Canadians.

What appeared in 1867 to be a tight, compartmentalized federation with designated powers among the federal government and provincial governments was transformed over the years from an **agrarian society** to a **post-industrial economy**. By 2007, Canada, with all of the requisites of a highly centralized state in its constitution, had become the most decentralized federation in the international system. Over the decades, this dramatic change of character was brought about largely by provincial challenges to federal autonomy, supported by a number of judicial decisions on the side of the provinces.

In addition, since the 1940s the federal government has been reluctant to use its four autonomous powers against the provinces. Another major cause of decentralization lies in the changing priorities of Canadian society since the nineteenth century. When the *Constitution Act, 1867*, was adopted, provincial powers in the areas of education, health, municipalities, and welfare were of minor importance. Today, Canadians no longer consider the role provincial governments play in their lives as secondary to that of the federal government.

Focus On The Changing Nature of Canadian Federalism

At the outset of Canadian federalism in 1867, the character of the system was "quasi-federal" because the national government assumed major administrative responsibilities for the bulk of public services. In the period from 1896 to 1914, provinces demanded more power and consultation from the federal government. "Emergency federalism" characterized the war period, when Parliament delegated sweeping authority to Ottawa to levy personal and corporate income taxes, to apply wage-and-price controls, and to prohibit strikes in wartime.

This quality of federalism would return just before and after the Depression (1929–1937) until the end of World War II. But during the 1920s, provincial autonomy grew as a result of revenues drawn from licensing automobiles and taxing gasoline and liquor. The 1940s saw the forces of centralism return to Canadian federalism. What has been called "father knows best" federalism resulted from the enormous post-war

taxing powers of the federal government and its ability to penetrate the administrative purview of the provinces by funding certain shared-cost programs.

"Co-operative federalism" is said to characterize the decade from about 1950 to the mid-1960s, as provincial governments experienced unprecedented demands for expanded services in health, education, welfare, and resource development. Co-operative federalism made use of federal–provincial conferences, involving first ministers, departmental ministers, and deputy ministers.

The next phase of intergovernmental affairs has been labelled "confrontational federalism" and it lasted from the 1960s to the 1980s. The rise of nationalism and separatism in Quebec spawned confrontations with Ottawa and spread the dynamic of provincial autonomy to other provinces. Divisive politics also underscored relations among western provinces and the federal government.

Since 1984, analysts have observed a "disengaging federalism," characterized by the federal government's disengagement from many of the policy areas traditionally under its watch. Ottawa has largely withdrawn from the areas of energy, forestry, health care, and mining. Federal and provincial governments work closer together in matters of immigration and tourism. There has been a downloading of fiscal responsibility by the federal government to the provinces for the implementation of most of the public policies Canadians regard as essential.

The 1990s saw a growing acceptance of conciliation and collaboration between the federal government and Quebec. The idea that Canada could survive as a country along asymmetrical lines by recognizing the special political status and autonomy of Quebec is labeled "asymmetrical federalism." Favourable to Quebec has been the federal government's recognition of it as a nation with a unique societal culture, which permits that province to develop its societal culture as a political unit that administers its affairs independently when necessary in the areas of pensions, health care, immigration, human resources, and diplomacy. To counter the asymmetrical perception in the rest of the country, the government under Stephen Harper promised a more "open federalism" to resolve the "fiscal imbalance" among the provinces.

Centralized federations include nation-states that have federal constitutions on paper, but which in practice are run as highly centralized unitary states. Argentina, Brazil, Venezuela, Nigeria, Tanzania, and Russia are centralized federations. In these states, the federal structure really serves the interests of the national government while giving the appearances of decentralized decision making. There is usually no actual division of powers between the national and subnational governments. Any attempts on the part of the subnational governments to govern autonomously are controlled or prevented entirely by the powers of the national government.

ECONOMIC ORGANIZATION

Political organization is as essential for the economic structure and strength of a nation-state as it is for the administration of political power. A national economy is the organized process of developing markets for natural resources, industrial production, agricultural output, and technological innovations. All nation-states must choose not only how their natural resources should be exploited to meet social needs, but also how to distribute the goods and services produced from them. Essentially, these political decisions constitute **monetary policies**, which distribute the wealth in the economy and determine the economic organization of a nation-state. The economic institutions established within states to solve the problems of what commodities to produce, how to produce them, and how to distribute output and income constitute the economic system.

The kinds of production and distribution systems nation-states adopt contribute to their capacity to generate wealth or poverty within their economies. Thus, the world is divided into rich economies and poor economies, some with such extreme internal contrasts that their citizens live fundamentally different kinds of lives. While the average Canadian enjoys a comfortable home, a car, two television sets, and so on, the average citizen of Bangladesh or Somalia struggles for a living and may at any time face a sudden national disaster or economic failure in his or her life

Perspectives   What Is Monetary Policy?

Of all the economic policies a government can draft to produce a stable economy, monetary policy is the most influential. Monetary policy refers to the control of the Bank of Canada over short-term interest rates and the money supply. The Bank of Canada is the lender of last resort to the chartered banks.

There is a direct relation between the amount of money in circulation and consumer and business activity. If the Bank of Canada wants to provide a boost to the economy, one way to do this is to influence the direction of short-term interest rates. By pushing short-term interest rates down, the Bank of Canada will induce more people to borrow money to either spend or invest. For example, as interest rates fall, more people may decide to buy houses. This results in more work for builders, painters, furniture retailers, and so on. If the Bank wants to control inflation, it will raise interest rates to slow economic growth, creating less demand and hence reducing inflationary pressures.

The actions of the Bank of Canada are closely watched by many observers. The setting of the bank rate is especially important. An increase in the bank rate tells us the Bank of Canada wants to "tighten" the money supply (making borrowing more costly in order to curtail spending and business investment). A rate decrease indicates an intention to increase the money supply (by making borrowing less costly in order to stimulate spending and business investment). In determining monetary policy, the Bank monitors the performance of the economy, looking at such indicators as employment, inflation, and exchange rates. The Bank of Canada will play a pivotal role, using its monetary powers first to stabilize the Canadian economy and then to point it in the direction of growth. The difficult transitions in the world economy since 2009 will keep the Bank's focus on the size and persistence of government deficits in Canada. Unlike previous deficits before the mid-1990s, which became a symbol of economic mismanagement, the current use of deficit spending is a tool to cure an ailing economy facing a global crisis.

(Figure 3.5). In rich economies, a high proportion of citizens are able to afford feeding themselves and to provide for decent shelter, education, and transportation needs. The wealthy economies have achieved a technological sophistication in their communications capabilities, such that people are able to share information in business, education, finance, and government with great ease, efficiency, and speed.

In the world today, three main types of economic systems are distinguishable among nation-states: the *capitalist system*, the *socialist system*, and the *mixed economic system*. The capitalist system is characterized by the widespread practice of private enterprise, by the private ownership of resources, and by a limited amount of government intervention in the economy. Theoretically, in this type of economic organization, the production, pricing, and distribution of goods and services are determined by millions of individuals, each attempting to maximize personal gain. Of course, in the real world these factors are also determined by large domestic corporations,

Figure 3.5   Rich economies and poor economies: Per capita GNP, 2007

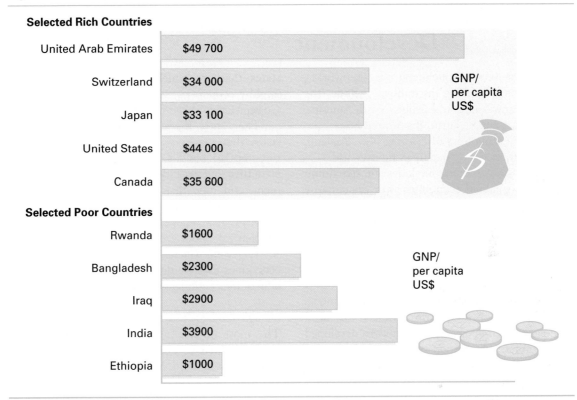

Selected Rich Countries

United Arab Emirates — $49 700

Switzerland — $34 000

Japan — $33 100

United States — $44 000

Canada — $35 600

GNP/per capita US$

Selected Poor Countries

Rwanda — $1600

Bangladesh — $2300

Iraq — $2900

India — $3900

Ethiopia — $1000

GNP/per capita US$

Source: Adapted from CIA's World Factbook *(Reader's Digest, 2009)*

multinational corporations, and the political actions of other states.

A pure capitalist economy does not exist in the international community. Capitalist economies are more or less organized as "free enterprise" environments. In a socialist system, all resources are theoretically owned and controlled by the state for social purposes. In a politically directed economic system, the supply, demand, and prices of goods and services are determined by government policies. In many economies, the two systems have merged into a hybrid organization called a *mixed economy*. In this system, control of the economy is shared by public and private institutions.

Economic power is both a means and an end to the status of national power. At all times, economic considerations influence the power equation of a nation-state. Economic power serves as both a goal and a tool of national power. The use of economic instruments by states for their political ends is called economic statecraft.[13] The goal of economic statecraft is sovereignty, whereby states want to keep control of their economies as a fundamental aspect of their international power status.

Focus On   The Five Worlds of Economic Development

The *First World*, which controls the world's financial and banking institutions, includes the richest nation-states of Europe, North America, and Asia. Canada, Japan, the United States, the developed economies of Europe, New Zealand, and Australia clearly qualify as First World.

The *Second World* includes all remaining centrally planned economies after the collapse of the Soviet Empire in the late 1980s and early 1990s. Their numbers quickly dwindled to only a few, as their economies had relied heavily on the presence of other communist economies for preferential trade, investment, and development assistance.[14]

The *Third World* is made up of large numbers of "less-developed countries" (LDCs) that need time and technology to build modern developed economies. The nation-states in this category include the oil-rich states and other resource-rich states that are widely viewed as potentially wealthy economies, such as Brazil, India, Ivory Coast, Mexico, Nigeria, and Venezuela.

The *Fourth World* consists of those nation-states that may possess enough raw material resources to build a modern economic **infrastructure** but lack the capital, foreign investment, and time that it takes to develop their economies. This category includes Benin, Kenya, and Sri Lanka. They show low per capita savings and generally poor economic performance.

The *Fifth World* comprises those national economies that are doomed to remain on some kind of international dole. They possess very few easily exploited resources and are unable to grow enough food to feed their starving populations. The most notable in this disparate group of poverty-ridden economies are Chad, Ethiopia, Guinea-Bissau, Mali, Mozambique, and Nepal.

MILITARY POWER

Force and usually the threat of force play a prominent role in international relations. Many of the states of the world use their military as an expression of national power. The ability to project military prowess beyond national boundaries is viewed by some analysts as a key indication of power among states.

> FACTFILE   There are about a dozen nation-states that have no standing armies at all, either because they have non-threatening neighbours or because they do not fear an arms-led coup.

It is tempting to assume that the possession of nuclear or conventional weapons is the most significant factor in the power equation of a nation-state. But a paradox emerges in a world of militarily credible states. Those states that have vast military strength cannot always exercise it as an effective instrument of national policy. Modern international law rejects inter-state violence as a means of settling disputes, except in cases of self-defence or collective international peacekeeping operations.[15] With increasing frequency, the international community engages the military power of a coalition of states to force the compliance of recalcitrant states, their leaders, or states that experience civil war. For example, failing to mobilize a coalition against Iraq in the United Nations, former US president George W. Bush constructed a "coalition of the willing" to legitimize his determination to wage war against Saddam Hussein.

Crosscurrents

Will *Soft* Power Trump *Hard* Power in the Twenty-First Century?

After centuries of using military force to establish power positions in a competitive international system, the citizens and leaders of many nation-states are changing their views about what is *legitimate power*. Because of the widespread destructive capability of modern warfare, we may be at a turning point in human history.

Hard power is military power. It is almost always lethal, and it kills civilians as well as military personnel. Hard power is coercive and aggressive, based on the logic of fear and terror. It is destructive to the environment and a drain to national economies. With modern warfare technologies, hard power can be dangerous to the survival of humankind.

Soft power repudiates the military pathway to global security. Greater legitimacy is assigned to power as *influence* rather than power as the use of *military force*. Soft power translates national interests more readily into global interests. It is diplomatic and conciliatory, communicative and collaborative.

The history of war reveals that most casualties have occurred from the actions and policies of only a few states that rely upon hard power to implement their national interests. Some 90 percent of all war deaths happened in great power conflicts.

Paul Kennedy, in *The Rise and Fall of the Great Powers*, describes a pattern, since 1500, of great powers eventually losing their grip on the international pecking order because of their over-commitment to military strategies and the massive expenditures associated with them.

Given this history and the contemporary factors of modern war, it is possible that soft power may trump hard power on the global stage in our lifetime.

The use of multilateral military power in Iraq (1991, 2003), Afghanistan (2002), Somalia (1992), and Haiti (1993, 2004), and the threat of its use in Bosnia-Herzegovina and Croatia (1994) and Yugoslavia (1999) reflects a growing international consensus that military action by a group of states can defend nation-states and ethnic minorities or force nation-states to comply with international law.

Although force continues to be used by some states **unilaterally**, such acts are now legally indefensible in the eyes of the international community unless they are conducted in self-defence. Most states believe that nuclear technology will not be used against them.

Some analysts have noted that military power is more a result than a cause of international tensions. The underlying causes of military competition for power among states are widely regarded as economic and social. Historian Paul Kennedy, in his widely acclaimed book *The Rise and Fall of the Great Powers*, suggests that the military power of a state tends to be based on its relative economic standing in the world.[16] If Kennedy is correct, the rise of the United States as a world military power in the twentieth century is entirely logical, given the growth and dominance of its economy.

FACTFILE The US government spends more to train one soldier than Russia spends to train an entire battalion of its troops.

The Persian Gulf War in 1991 and the recent war in Iraq confirm the fact that the United States is the world's most capable military power. Its ability to send hundreds of thousands of troops to the Persian Gulf region on short notice reflects the status of the United States as a military "superpower"—that is, a state armed with the necessary military technologies to project its power into any area of the world. Likewise, in 2001, Afghanistan experienced the awesome power of the US military in coalition with the Australian, British, Canadian, and German forces.

It may be an oversimplification to argue that military capabilities and the power of a state are synonymous. Power is also expressed in terms of trade, aid, economic productivity, and scientific and technological advancement. The extent to which military capability enhances the power of a state is still open to debate. Argentina, Brazil, Iraq, Iran, the Republic of Korea, and Taiwan are among the states expected to join the expanding nuclear-powers club. Would Argentina have been a more successful combatant against Great Britain over the Falkland Islands by possessing nuclear weapons? Does Pakistan graduate from the Fourth World to the Third World with a nuclear arsenal? Would nuclear weapons promote Canada from the rank of middle power to superpower? The proliferation of sophisticated military technology may make states more dangerous, but not necessarily more powerful.

NATIONAL WILL AND STRATEGIC PURPOSE

The tangible elements of power, i.e., population, geography, and natural resources, remain stagnant without national will and strategic purpose, the intangible elements of power. Together, they enable a state to influence and control the behaviour of others. Although *national will* is difficult to measure, some analysts rank it as the most important determinant of power.[17] Hans Morgenthau sees it as "the degree of determination with which a nation

supports the foreign policies of its government in peace and war."[18] Support may be enthusiastic toward a particular strategy, or it may be sluggish and apathetic.

The will of a population and its leadership will often compensate for the lack of some economic and military resources within a nation-state. Recent history abounds with examples of powerful states deferring to or losing influence against seemingly less powerful states. National will is the force that enabled North Vietnam and the Vietcong to repel the United States, even though the US held superior economic and military strength. Sheer determination may have been the momentum behind Saddam Hussein's defiance of near global condemnation for his adventurism in Kuwait and his defiance of many United Nations resolutions.

However, national will can also temper leadership to refrain from exercising the full economic and military powers at its disposal. The power of national will has also been a pivotal dynamic in the war between Israel and Palestine in the 2000s.

In Canada, a conservative public on the use of military power has kept a watchful eye on the development and direction of Canadian foreign policy and on the aggressive use of its military; a particular example is Canada's refusal to wage war with the US in Iraq in 2003. Canada's participation in the war in Afghanistan since 2003 has been controversial and divisive. Many Canadians believe that Canada, with its peacekeeping experience, should have maintained its distance from the US-dominated sortie. They questioned why Canada was so quick to join US troops, and the long-term wisdom of the decision. Many Canadians want Canada to remain solely a peacekeeper. But since 9/11, a groundswell of opinion in Canada has emerged, demanding that the government spend more on the military and that it supply Canadian forces with better equipment.

Given its respected role in the global system, Canada is part of an informal international economic directorate (**Group of Eight, G-8**), made up of eight of the most economically powerful nation-states—Canada, France, Germany, Great Britain, Italy, Japan, Russia, and the United States. The strategic issues that directly affect Canada as one of the G-8 are jobs, trade, international investment, and the regulation of currencies in the global economy.

International analysts such as political scientist Ray Cline have placed Canada as high as fourth, and seldom below tenth, on a scale of the most powerful nation-states in the world. Yet Canadians have consistently rejected the military road to power, favouring economic strength and diplomatic skills as the most desirable indicators of rank and status. In the twenty-first century, the meteoric rise in the importance of resources, especially food, fuel, and water, will provide Canada with the opportunity of becoming a principal player in continental and world politics.

Sometimes the assumptions about power are confusing. For example, the Vatican, an independent state of 104 acres, with fewer than 1000 people and no military or natural resources, exercises powerful influence in every corner of the world. This example shows that size, location, population, resources, and military preparedness are significant in some situations and meaningless in others.

In Cline's equation for measuring national power, the elements of strategic purpose and the will to pursue national strategy are often immeasurable. But his analytical design is flexible enough to incorporate the intangible elements of power as variables that can change the power formula. It enables the researcher to challenge the classical assumptions that size and military capability are decisive determinants of national power in the twenty-first century.

Chapter Summary

However it is defined, power remains a central theme among both political analysts who observe it and national leaders who perceive and use it in international relations. This chapter distinguishes among the concepts of nation, state, and government, and weaves the phenomenon of power into the fabric of the global community. Power is introduced as a multidimensional dynamic in both the national and international systems. Political scientists examine the various components of power, such as critical mass, population, natural resources, economic and military capability, strategic purposes, and national will. Cline states that power is a psychological as well as a political phenomenon that is perceived by individuals and states as flowing from the characteristics of states, their location, population size, natural resources, and economic and military capabilities.

Political scientists study the evasive character of national power and are sensitive to those variables that may intervene in the power equation of nation-states. Power is also associated with the political organization of a state as either unitary or federal. These concepts are distinguished in this chapter so as to relate them to national power in a relevant way. The political organization of a state can facilitate or dampen its perceived strength within the international community. Is there a shift in the perception of how power should be used to satisfy the national interest? Are we entering an era in human history that will abandon the age-old reliance on military (hard) power to embrace the attributes of power-as-influence, or soft power?

The concept of *power* is generally defined as an ability to make things happen that otherwise would not happen. The exercise of power in the global system is identified with certain properties possessed by nation-states, such as size, population, government organization, economic capacity, and military credibility.

Federal states, which divide and share powers of government among the subnational units and the national government, have advantages and disadvantages. They usually can accommodate more social and regional diversity than can unitary states. But their government systems are complex and expensive to operate.

Unitary states, which have only one level of government, are usually smaller states, and are more efficient in the implementation of public policy than are the large federal states. Most of the nation-states of the world are unitary states.

The international system is made up of rich economies, relatively wealthy economies, and poor economies. Gross National Product (GNP), which is the value of all goods and services produced by a national economy within a fiscal year, can be used to compare the relative wealth and poverty within states. When GNP is divided by the population of a state, the GNP per capita shows the approximate amount of national currency individuals have to spend on the essentials of living. Some argue that a Genuine Progress Index (GPI) would be a much better measure of real prosperity.

The degree of economic interdependence nation-states enjoy by trading among themselves has grown steadily since the early twentieth century, and has produced a global economy of substantial and increasing size in the twenty-first century. All nation-states must participate in the global system if they are to sustain their national economies.

Discussion Questions

1. Discuss the differences among the concepts of nation, country, state, government, and nation-state. Examine the growth in the number of nation-states in the international community since 1648. Discuss the proliferation of states since World War II. Consider the large number of nations in relation to the relatively small number of nation-states. Consider how nation-states are evolving. Are they likely to become large regions or associations of states, or to devolve along linguistic and ethnic lines?

2. Discuss the difficulties of measuring power among the nation-states of the international system. Is Cline's conceptual formula a realistic one in a world of nuclear proliferation and militarized states? What components of Cline's formula are most relevant in the power equation of a nation-state? What is a superpower? What is a middle power?

3. Discuss how the basic political organization of a nation-state can enhance or complicate its economic potential. What advantages do unitary states have over federal states? Discuss the various types of federal systems introduced in the chapter. Which one most clearly resembles the unitary system and why?

4. Discuss the advantages and disadvantages of the various types of economic systems employed among the world's states. Suggest some of the ways that urbanization, industrialization, and communications alter political institutions. Is the GNP the best measure we can use to plot prosperity or economic decline? Discuss the political problems encountered by the trade-off between economic growth and sustainable environmental quality.

5. Is the military capacity of a state an accurate indicator of its ability to influence other states? What can be said about military power (hard power) vis-à-vis the totality of a state's perceived strength? Identify the problems inherent in comparing national power on the basis of military indicators. Prepare a list of soft power strengths a state can cultivate to move from hard power towards peaceful strategies for resolving conflict.

Thinking about Government

4

After reading this chapter, you will be able to:

- define and classify governments in the global environment

- realize how much government affects our daily lives

- profile the parliamentary form of government

- outline the characteristics of the presidential form of government

- compare the similarities and differences in both forms of government

- discuss the significance of an emerging United States of Europe

- describe the components of supranational government as they are represented in the European Union

- understand the fundamental elements of dictatorship

- distinguish between authoritarian and totalitarian dictatorship

- evaluate the advantages and disadvantages of different forms of government

WHAT IS GOVERNMENT?

Anthropologists tell us that about 30 000 years ago human beings began to organize into societies. These first human communities attempted to regulate human behaviour with respect to food gathering, family life, and protection from predatory animals. The social system may have been informal, folk-sustained, non-centralized, and non-institutional—but it did contain a *social government*. *Political government*, the centralized system that maintains an institutionalized system of order within a society large or small, first appeared only about 10 000 years ago when the first civilizations developed in Asia Minor and northern Mesopotamia. As people gradually concentrated in cities, social controls were needed to maintain order in a more complex organizational system. Government by political elites and by detailed **legal codes** was developed to maintain control over these populations.

The word *govern* is derived from Middle English *governen* and the Old French *governor*. The Latin *gubernare* (to direct, steer) is taken from the Greek *Kubernan* (to steer, govern). The Greeks combined the notions of steering and government in the concept of *kubernetes*, the word for "steersman" or "helmsman" of a ship (a person who governs a ship by operating the rudder). The image of "the ship of state" appears in the writings of many political writers, especially in those of Plato and Aristotle.

The American political scientist Karl Deutsch adapted the modern concept of *cybernetics* (the

science of communication and control) to the study of government. For Deutsch, "steering depends on a country's *intake* of information through its 'receptors' (such as embassies abroad or statistical offices at home) from the outside world, the recall of other information from *memory* (including memories about past goals and decisions), the transmission of commands for action to 'effectors,' and the *feedback* of information from the outside world about the results of the action just taken."[1]

Modern governments have elaborate networks for transmitting and receiving information. Governments gather and store information on attitudes and events occurring in their domestic and external environments. In Canada, all three levels of government process information on every aspect of Canadian life. Municipal governments monitor where we build and renovate our homes for tax purposes. Health Canada informs us that "most Canadians don't smoke" from research it conducts on drug addiction across the country. The Canada Revenue Agency tells us that in terms of income assessed, West Vancouver, BC, is the wealthiest city, while the Cape Breton Regional Municipality (CBRM) is the poorest in Canada. The Department of Foreign Affairs and International Trade knows that the United States is Canada's largest trading partner. Such knowledge can be the basis for creating or changing public policy. It is also the basis for surviving as a society.

The idea of government as steerer affords us the opportunity to distinguish it from the concepts of *state* and *politics*. Many people erroneously consider the state synonymous with government and politics. The *state*, the most formal of political organizations, is one of the hallmarks of civilization. Inherent in the concept of the state is the idea of a sovereign and permanent bureaucracy that functions to administer

Perspectives   Should Canadians Know More about Their Governments?

Ignorance is not bliss in a democracy. A democratic political system can fail because citizens are ignorant about how their governments work. Having basic political information helps citizens identify the best ways they can act in their interests. We need political knowledge so that we can discern which level of government has which responsibilities. Political knowledge enables us to participate in the very system that governs us and facilitates our survival as individuals and communities. People active in politics have a high sense of their efficacy—they believe they can make a difference. Most people can't be politically active every day of their lives, but it is essential to our democratic ideals that citizens be informed and able to act when their needs are not being met by governments.

Numerous surveys (www.ipsos.ca) indicate that the majority of Canadians know very little about their political system. Most Canadians do not understand the rules in place to elect their governments and oppositions. They cannot distinguish between a majority and a plurality election result, and they do not understand the basic rules of our electoral system. Ask Canadians the difference between a majority and a minority government and you may not get a very clear answer. Most do not know how many MLAs their provincial government has or

how many members of parliament go to Ottawa from their province. Even knowing provincial and territorial capitals can stump many Canadians.

In 2007:

- 4% of Canadians could name the requirements a person must meet in order to vote in federal elections.
- 8% could identify Queen Elizabeth II as Canada's Head of State. (51 % said it was the current Prime Minister).
- 12% knew that the Governor General represented Canada's Head of State and could name her.
- 38% could name the four political parties represented in the federal House of Commons (down from 72 % in 1997).
- 32 % could correctly identify the number of Canadian provinces and territories (only 15% of Quebecers could do so).
- 18% could not state the name of the current Prime Minister, Stephen Harper.
- 42% could not recite the first two lines of Canada's national anthem "O Canada" and over 50 % got the rest of it wrong.

Source: Dominion Institute (www.dominion.ca) and Ipsos Reid Survey (June 5 and 7, 2007) accurate to within 3.1 percentage points, 19 times out of 20 (www.ipsos-na.com/news/results).

the public affairs of its citizens as well as relations with other states. States are also the primary legal units in the international community, recognized as such (**state recognition**) because they have a population, occupy a defined territory, and have an effective government capable of entering into binding agreements with other states.

The international rights and obligations of a state are not affected by a change of government.

New governments are bound by the provisions of treaties signed by previous governments, unless they can negotiate different terms with the other signing parties. However, a *government* is an organized group of people who—for a time—constitute the political executive and administrative machinery of a state. Governments make authoritative decisions and steer the political system in the direction of their policy goals.

Governments are *political*; they rise and fall, while states are *bureaucratic* and more enduring. *Politics* is influential behaviour that leads to the making of public decisions, either within or outside the institutional frameworks of government. All political behaviour has an impact on the community. Thus, the activities of a group of women to start a community crisis centre for sexual assault victims are as political as the decisions of politicians to fund the project at various levels of government. While there is a tendency for us to identify politics with government, we should be aware that many, if not most, political decisions are made outside government. *Politics* is the articulation and, when possible, the harmonization of conflicting values and preferences, while *government* is the institutionalized process of allocating and distributing values as binding decisions on people.

FACTFILE   The Inuit of northern Canada and Russia do not view crime as an offence against the state or government but rather consider all offences as disputes between individuals, to be settled among the disputants themselves.

Politics is an inescapable process that serves to harmonize, and sometimes cause, conflict in human affairs. Government is the set of organizations within which much of that process takes place. But why government? What is its purpose? For political philosophers such as John Locke and

Perspectives   Governments Are Everywhere in Our Lives

7:00 A.M. You wake up to Standard Time or Daylight Saving Time, which is set by the Provincial Government.

7:15 A.M. You wash, bathe, or shower with water supplied or regulated by a municipal or regional government.

7:30 A.M. You have a bowl of cereal with milk for breakfast. The "Nutrition Facts" on the cereal box are a federal requirement, the milk is pasteurized by provincial law, the "best before date" is a federal standard, and the recycling of the cereal box is a municipal government requirement.

8:30 A.M. The public transportation you take to the campus is a municipally regulated service and is subsidized by all levels of government. If you drive, the air bags in your car are a federal requirement, and most of the roads and bridges are a provincial responsibility.

9:00 A.M. The campus you attend is funded by provincial and federal grants. Labs and building codes come under municipal regulation.

Noon Some of the food you buy at the university cafeteria is taxed by the federal and provincial government.

2:00 P.M. You have a part-time job at the university library. The minimum wage is set by your province, and working conditions are governed by federal and provincial labour laws.

6:00 P.M. You eat dinner at a fast food restaurant where the meat is inspected by the federal and provincial governments

10:00 P.M. You walk home. The street lighting is provided by taxes paid to a municipal government.

10:15 P.M. You watch TV. The networks are regulated by the federal government.

Midnight Just before going to bed you put out the garbage, which is collected by a municipal sanitation department.

Jean-Jacques Rousseau, government is essential to civilization. To government falls the task of ensuring human protection, decency, and restraint. "Taxes," wrote the American justice Oliver Wendell Holmes (1902–1932), "are what we pay for civilized society." The English philosopher Thomas Hobbes wrote that in the absence of government, life among individuals would be "solitary, poor, nasty, brutish, and short."

Throughout history, philosophers have posited that government in varying degrees is essential to protect people from one another, by force if necessary. If people kill or assault one another or steal from each other, government must intervene to protect society. If it does not, civilization is simply not possible. People could not enjoy the fundamental pleasures of life—a walk in the park, a hockey game, a concert—if their physical well-being were constantly threatened by others whose violent acts went unhindered or unpunished. Government is essential to human liberty.

Every political science student quickly learns that governments differ in many ways: in size, ideology, degree of **centralization**, openness, **legitimacy**, effectiveness, and the degree and kind of political participation by individuals and groups outside the centre of authority. Correspondingly, there are various ways in which governments may be classified: by structure and character, from democratic to authoritarian and totalitarian, open to closed, leftist to rightist.

Traditional Classifications of Government

Greek students of government designed typologies. These classifications, although rudimentary by today's research standards, were the first serious attempts to build a systematic body of knowledge about existing government structures and institutions. The Greek historian Herodotus grouped all governments into monarchies (government by one), aristocracies (government by elites), and democracies (government by all).

FACTFILE In 335 BC, Aristotle returned to Athens from Macedon to establish his own school, the Lyceum. Because he used such rigour to study government and politics, he may properly be identified as the first known political scientist.

Nearly a century later, Aristotle revised the typology to include six types of government (Table 4.1). He made the distinction between genuine forms of government (where the ruling authority governs according to the common good) and the degenerate forms (where the ruling authority uses the powers of government for selfish gain). Thus, as rulers depart from the substantive meaning of the good, kings become tyrants, aristocrats become cliquish oligarchs, and democrats become selfish **demagogues**. An oligarchy, for example, which is oriented around wealth, is not directed to achieve the common good. This is one reason why it is a degenerate form of government for Aristotle.

Table 4.1	Aristotle's typology of government	
Ideal Form	**Number of Rulers**	**Degenerate Form**
Kingship	Rule of one	Tyranny
Aristocracy	Rule of the few	Oligarchy
Polity	Rule of the majority	Democracy

Throughout history, many political theorists have constructed typologies for classifying various systems of government. Classical comparisons were essentially normative in that they pertained to value judgments on how to perfect human behaviour, and prescriptive in that they asserted the preferred means of achieving desired social goals. Plato and Aristotle compared and described governments in order to discover their ideal form. On the one hand, Plato was primarily interested in studying the "ideal forms" of government. His typology was designed to prescribe the best form of government without necessarily referring to a real situation. Aristotle, on the other hand, rejected Plato's forms and described forms of government that actually existed, while passing normative and **prescriptive judgments** on them.

In the fifteenth century, Machiavelli saw advantages in the republican form of government and urged **political expediency** for governing executives (princes) to unify states. Later, Thomas Hobbes, in his *Leviathan*, recommended an absolute monarchy as the preferred form of government to contain the destructive tendencies of people in society. In contrast to Hobbes, John Locke concluded that the sovereign trust can safely reside in the people, and is revocable from government if its leaders and institutions should become absolutist and arbitrary. His comparative choice strongly favoured a constitutional democracy, constantly upholding governments to popular scrutiny.

By the eighteenth century, theorists focused on reforming political institutions rather than advancing hypothetical forms of government. Montesquieu compared monarchical and parliamentary institutions, advocating a separation of powers among the executive, legislative, and judicial branches of government. James Madison and others in the *Federalist Papers* incorporated this experimental model of government in the United States Constitution of 1787.

FACTFILE   By means of what is referred to as "devolution," the highly centralized United Kingdom has decentralized some legislative and administrative functions of government in Wales, Scotland, and Northern Ireland.

The comparative study of political institutions grew steadily during the nineteenth century. Theorists assumed that the British and American models of government were the best, although many theorists were highly critical of the continuing presence of slavery under a government seemingly dedicated to freedom and equality. But in the **empires** of Europe, the political order seemed to stand still.

One of the most renowned critics of the old government systems in Europe was Karl Marx. For him, various types of government were the products of class struggle, through which the dominant class came to control the political institutions by virtue of its economic strength. But Marx's influence as a political analyst was posthumous.

Other critics of the traditional typologies identified with Marx's elitist assumptions about class and group power. Some seriously challenged the principle of majority rule in democratic governments and posited the hypothesis that minorities hold the reins of government.[2] From their viewpoint, the important analytical focus was not the formal processes of government institutions but the sociology of government, i.e., how an elite is recruited and over whom it exercises its power.

Comparing Governments Today

The field of comparative government is based on the assumption that students of government can better understand how societies are ruled if they compare political cultures and institutions across national boundaries. Analysts learn by making comparisons, by distinguishing similarities and differences between and among states, by measuring government performances, and by contrasting the succession and durability of political systems. In taking a comparative perspective, we learn that government institutions are the products of those behavioural patterns by which people seek order and stability. No government can be understood without giving principal consideration to that fact.

The comparative study of government has undergone many changes. The emergence of political science as an academic discipline influenced the nature and scope of political inquiry into the dynamics of government. Comparative studies were broadened to include all regions of the world, not just western governments, and focused on the gap between the rich and poor economies.

Analysts began to construct a political sociology of government. David Truman advanced the proposition that governments were an outgrowth of group competition and interaction.[3] Truman's group theory encouraged political researchers to look behind the institutional facade of government to discover the social variables of political power. In emphasizing the sociological basis of government, group theorists had penetrated a vital area of political knowledge, laying the foundations for the more sophisticated concepts of political culture and **political modernization**.

The concept of *political culture* (a term developed by political scientists Gabriel Almond and Sidney Verba) opened new vistas for learning about the evolution of modern governments.[4] Political culture can be defined simply as the way citizens orient themselves to politics and government. Drawing heavily on the insights of psychology and sociology, political scientists can isolate the particular actions, attitudes, values, and skills that culturally determine the persistence and maintenance of certain types of governmental systems. They call attention to the fact that the cultural environments of governments differ in countries of different historical experience, even though their political systems are described as democratic, authoritarian, or totalitarian.

A range of similarity may exist among political cultures that generate similar types of government, even though the political and governing institutions appear to be quite different. Canada and the United States are two similar political cultures that have produced markedly different democratic institutions.

In many ways, Canadians are more like Americans than any other people one might select for comparison. Both countries span a continent with all of the diversity of territory, settlement, and development that this implies. Both are sociologically similar, occupied by Aboriginal peoples and settled by immigrants from abroad, with histories deeply rooted in Anglo-Saxon, European, Asian, and African traditions. Many other national attributes that underscore their likeness would lead one to expect very similar systems of government. Yet Canadians borrowed heavily from the British system of parliamentary and cabinet government, whereas Americans chose a different path in 1787 and adopted a republican form of government with a novel presidential/congressional scheme.

Political scientist Allan Kornberg's work focuses on the comparison of political practices in Canada and the United States.[5] His analysis has led him to the conclusion that while there are striking similarities in the political cultures and folkways in each country, divergent political practices can be explained as a different response to the different forms of democratic institutions. Canada and the United States both achieve democracy, but through uniquely different institutional forms.

Classifying Governments

The basic message derived from the analysis of political culture has been that every government is different. This has made it difficult for political scientists to assemble typologies that can neatly classify governments into "either/or" categories. For example, to say that Canada and Mexico are democracies is as much an oversimplification as to say that El Salvador and Lebanon are authoritarian. Their political cultures have constructed political systems of varying degrees of democracy and authoritarianism. Canadians enjoy more elections, more party competition, and a greater amount of government accountability than do Mexicans. But Mexicans enjoy greater constitutional protections for their Indo-American peoples than do Canada's First Nations. Some governments are more democratic than others, just as some are more coercive than others.

Instead of thinking of governments in a compartmentalized fashion, we should consider a continuum of governments running from democracy to totalitarianism, as represented in Figure 4.1. The continuum is analytically more sophisticated than a typology because it permits the analyst to distribute governments according to a range of perceived criteria detected in the political culture. Thus, if due process of law or party competitiveness were found to be stronger in one democratic state than in another, the former would appear closer to the generic type. Each observer may choose to scatter states along the continuum somewhat differently. But the figure presented here will serve to magnify the variations within and between forms of government.

In a world of more than 200 nation-states, it is not surprising that significantly different ways of governing exist. It is important to realize that while it is possible to classify governments under general categories, every political system is unique.

Figure 4.1   Continuum of selected states with democratic, authoritarian, and totalitarian characteristics: A hypothetical dispersion

Democracy	Authoritarianism	Totalitarianism
• accountability	• dictatorial decision making	• official ideology
• constitutionalism	• restricted pluralism	• a single elite-directed
• human rights, civil liberties	• personalistic ideology	mass party
• majority rule, minority rights	• controlled political competition	• secret police
• individualism	• militarism	• state-controlled media
• political competition	• directed economy	• state control of weapons
• rule of law	• limited political participation	• command economy
• popular sovereignty		• restricted pluralism

strong ◄——► weak	weak ◄——► strong	weak ◄——► strong
Canada Mexico	Argentina Rwanda	Cuba China

 Where would you place the following nation-states along this continuum?

Australia, Albania, Brazil, Costa Rica, Croatia, El Salvador, France, Germany, Great Britain, Guatemala, Honduras, Hungary, India, Israel, Kenya, Latvia, Pakistan, Paraguay, Poland, Russia, Switzerland, Turkey, Ukraine, United States, Venezuela, Zambia.

Focus On The World's Top Ten Democracies

Less than 30 of the world's 200 nation-states can be classified as full democracies. Almost every state in the world claims to be a democratic government with a constitution, elections, and the appearance of political party competition. Yet only a few can meet the standards of modern democracy. Even Canada operates a Parliament wherein two of its primary institutions are undemocratic: the Monarch and the Senate.

1. Sweden
2. Iceland
3. Netherlands
4. Norway
5. Denmark
6. Finland
7. Luxembourg
8. Australia
9. Canada
10. Switzerland

Source: www.aftenposten.no/english/local/article1543571.ece.

DEMOCRATIC FORMS OF GOVERNMENT

The word *democracy* comes to us from the Greek *democratia*: *demos* for people and *kratia* for government. Throughout the history of governments, democracies were not always viewed in such high regard. Even the ancient Greeks who invented it believed that democracy could work only in small communities where all of the citizens could participate directly in the making of public decisions. They feared that democracies would eventually degenerate into mob rule.

Until the nineteenth century, there was continuing distrust in the ability of ordinary people to make rational decisions about complex social matters by means of **initiatives**, **referendums**, **recalls**, and **plebiscites**. In fact, the Athenian model of direct democracy has been a rare occurrence in history (examples include the Athenian general assembly, the North American town meeting, and the Israeli **kibbutz**). An eloquent Winston Churchill said that "democracy is the worst form of government . . . except for all the others." This remark captures the mixed feelings prevalent about democracy.

FACTFILE Canadians have only had three referendums at the national level: for the prohibition of liquor (1898), for conscription during World War II (1942), and on the Charlottetown Accord (1992).

Despite widespread skepticism, democracy is what Bernard Crick describes as "the most promiscuous word in the world of public affairs."[6] Even Libya's Moamer al-Khaddhafi applied the term in a unique adaptation to his country: "Democracy—it has been construed to be a Greek word, but originally it is an Arabic word from two parts—*demo*, which in Arabic means the continuation, and *cracy*, the chair. And, therefore, the continuation of the people on the chairs of power is democracy."[7]

Even though many states in Asia, Africa, Europe, and Latin America appear to be moving in the direction of democratic government, there are many non-democratic governments still operating in these regions of the world.

Because credible liberal democratic systems are not universal, it is necessary to examine the basic characteristics of this form of government. All democratic systems exhibit the following attributes, although the institutions and procedures for their implementation tend to vary in each state:

- *accountability* of all public officials directly and indirectly by constitutional limitations, fair elections, and public opinion;

- *constitutionalism*, whereby the scope of government authority is limited in a written or unwritten constitution that can be tested in an independent judiciary;

- *human rights* and *civil liberties* protected by a constitution or government legislation to guarantee freedoms and safeguards against the arbitrary abuse of legitimate power;

- *a doctrine of individualism* that relegates government to the service and protection of each person, so that individuals can realize their full capabilities;

- *majority rule and minority rights* that govern the decision-making apparatus in the political system, permitting consensus to override dissent but giving the minority the right to challenge the majority;

- *political competition* flowing from the principle of pluralism, which allows individuals and groups to compete for political power;

- *popular sovereignty* demonstrating the basic democratic principle that people directly or indirectly are the ultimate source of political authority; and

- *rule of law*, which proclaims the legal equality of all individuals and the supremacy of law over unlimited personal and bureaucratic power.

Two types of democratic government have evolved in the Western world and are prevalent today. One is the *parliamentary form* of government (also referred to as cabinet government), modelled after the British system. The other is the *presidential form* of government, modelled after the

Crosscurrents   Is Democracy Contagious?

Democracy spread in varying degrees throughout the twentieth century. The first notable wave of democratization happened after World War I, with the collapse of the Austrian and German empires. Many of these European states threw off their old dictatorial systems and embraced the constructs of democratic government. At this time, some Latin American states sought to nurture democratic governance. But many of the new democracies in Europe, such as Germany in 1918, failed to survive under the economic pressures of the Great Depression and in the turmoil that led to World War II.

After that war, a second wave of democratization led to democratic regimes in Germany, Italy, and Japan, and a large number of former European colonies in Africa, Asia, and Latin America began to democratize. A third wave commenced in the 1970s in southern Europe when Greece, Portugal, and Spain adopted democratic institutions of government. A similar wave swept Latin America, in Ecuador and Peru in 1978,

Bolivia in 1982, Argentina in 1983, Uruguay in 1984, Brazil in 1985, and Chile in 1989.

The fall of the Berlin Wall and the demise of the Soviet Union in 1989 unleashed a larger wave of democratization around the world. Many former communist states in Eastern Europe made democratic advancements: East Germany (re-united with West Germany), Poland, Russia, Czechoslovakia (devolving into the Czech Republic and Slovakia), Hungary, Bulgaria, Romania, and, temporarily, Yugoslavia. Algeria moved closer to democracy between 1989 and 1991, as did Egypt, Jordan, and Tunisia. These states were in the company of the Philippines (1986), the Republic of Korea (1987), Pakistan (1988), Haiti (1990), Nepal (1990), and Nicaragua (1990). As the European Union continued to expand—ten states joined in 2004 and Bulgaria and Romania joined in 2007 —countries adopted modern democratic governing procedures according to European standards.

The African continent is host to a large number of states undergoing democratization. South Africa, Botswana, Tanzania, Kenya, and Ethiopia, to name a few, have adopted democratic institutions. Other states, such as Mali, Madagascar, Namibia, Niger, and Zambia, are in transition but are committed to democracy.

Why has democracy spread so steadily? One explanation is that many dictatorial governments have lost their internal popular support, or powerful dictators died without successors. Another reason given is the strong international pressures for democracy, through sanctions that are applied against governments that violate the rights of their citizens. Still another reason is the presence of democratic technologies, such as radio, television, computers, cell phones, and iPods, which spread the expectations of democracy. The global media instantaneously reports on the activities of dictatorial governments and informs the international community when some of its members defy international norms. Finally, dictatorial governments tend to produce uncompetitive economies, resulting in lower standards of living, extreme poverty, and government corruption.

American system. Both are general political frameworks into which power, authority, and democratic values are allocated by different institutions. Some states, such as France, Finland, and Portugal, combine some of the characteristics of a presidential system with those of a parliamentary system. In practice, the institutions that make democracies what they are include an executive and legislative branch of government, an independent judiciary, a bureaucracy, and competitive political parties.

Parliamentary Government

Among the democratic states, the most widely practised form of government is the parliamentary system, which places sovereignty (the legitimate right to govern) in a parliament. A parliament is a legislative body usually comprised of two houses of assembly. The Canadian Parliament consists of the Queen and her Canadian representative, the Senate and the House of Commons (as shown in Figure 4.2). The parliamentary form of government also appears in states where monarchies have become constitutional democracies, e.g., some members of the Commonwealth and Scandinavia, and in other countries such as France, Germany, and Italy.

The parliamentary executive

The parliamentary executive comprises a *head of state* (monarch or president) and a *head of government*, usually called a prime minister (*chancellor* in

Figure 4.2   Basic institutions of Canadian government

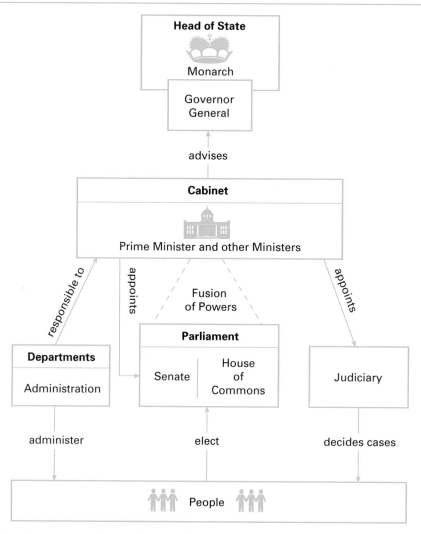

Germany), who is nominally selected and sworn into office by the head of state. The prime minister or head of government in turn chooses the cabinet, which is collectively responsible to the parliament. The cabinet is the most visible and central executive committee of government in the whole parliamentary system. It guides, directs, and virtually drives the process of parliamentary government. In terms of policy and lawmaking, the cabinet *is* the government. The supremacy of Parliament is premised on the assumption that a government should be formed from among members of parliament (MPs). The political executive is thus *fused* to the legislative branch of government that collectively embodies the sovereignty of the people. Unlike other forms of government, the executive in the parliamentary system is dependent for both its authority and tenure in office on maintaining the confidence of the parliament.

Thus, in Canada the word *government* has two basic meanings. In a narrow legal sense, the government is essentially the prime minister and cabinet, who have been appointed by the governor general to administer or govern the country. The cabinet determines priorities and policies, ensures their implementation, and presents government legislation to Parliament for approval. This narrow sense of government also includes the federal government departments that assist in developing, complementing, and administering the government's policies. The word *government* is also used to describe the range of institutions and even the philosophies that make up our "system of government." Canada's system of government is a constitutional monarchy and a parliamentary democracy.

Fusion of powers

In Canada, the essential fusion of the executive and legislative branches of government is accompanied by the belief that Parliament is supreme. Canadian political culture dictates that sovereignty resides in Parliament; laws cannot be made or amended, taxes cannot be raised or monies borrowed unless formal parliamentary approval is granted. But in Canada as well as in some other parliamentary systems, the government has differentiated itself more and more from Parliament, placing itself in a strong position to control policy and legislation. Both the prime minister and the Cabinet, known collectively as the government, usually enjoy majority support in the House of Commons, the only popularly elected house in the Canadian Parliament. The continuous support of the majority party assures the legislative confidence of Parliament and is regularly demonstrated when the government submits its programs and policies for approval.

FACTFILE   From 1921 to 2008 in Canada, there have been 11 federal minority governments, most of which fell at the will of the Prime Minister, not the opposition.

However, *majority governments* are not always formed. Occasionally, minority governments are formed in the House of Commons and the provincial legislatures. Such was the case in June 1979, when Prime Minister Joe Clark's new government captured only 136 seats (6 short of a majority), becoming Canada's ninth minority government in 60 years. The defeat of the Clark government came, after only six months in office, on a **non-confidence motion** that fatally attacked the Tory budget. Minority governments are vulnerable to the whims of partisan politics in the House of Commons. In these circumstances, the Cabinet tends to be much more responsible to Parliament in order to maintain the necessary support to sustain the government. In the period from 1972 to 1974, a minority Trudeau government successfully wooed the support of the New Democratic Party by adjusting its legislation and by being more consultative with the opposition. Since 1998, Nova Scotia has had a succession of Liberal and Progressive Conservative minority governments.

The opposition

Because majority governments have so much control over the direction and passage of legislation, the continuing supremacy of Parliament falls squarely on the shoulders of the opposition. Given the desired tendency of the Canadian parliamentary system to develop strong executive authority based on a cohesive party majority, it follows that the opposition has a crucial role to play in the democratic process. The role of the **opposition** is to criticize government, its behaviour, the administration of its policies, and to offer alternatives to government policies. This became particularly evident in 2008 when the three opposition parties in Parliament formed a

Coalition against the newly elected minority government of Stephen Harper. Faced with what they saw as a failure of the Harper government to address the economic crisis, Stephane Dion, Jack Layton, and Gilles Duceppe formed the Liberal–NDP Coalition, supported by the Bloc Quebecois, which agreed to topple the Conservative government and replace it with the new Coalition government.

On rare occasions, Canadian elections have produced no *elected* opposition. In the election of 1987, a rejuvenated Liberal Party in New Brunswick, led by Frank McKenna, won all of the 58 seats in the provincial legislature—an electoral accomplishment seen only once before in Canadian history when, in 1935, the Liberals of Prince Edward Island took all 30 seats under Premier Walter Lea.

Single-party legislatures challenge the assumptions of parliamentary democracy, which rest upon the presence of an elected opposition to provide legitimate checks on the actions of government. When this occurs, the role of the opposition can fall upon backbenchers who may use legislative rules and procedures to critically question ministers. In addition, many expect the media to play a key role in scrutinizing government as an extra-legislative opposition. Some rely on the vigorous opposition of defeated parties and interest groups outside the legislature to raise the dust generally and keep a close watch on government business.

Inside legislatures, opposition parties will tailgate governments by forming **shadow cabinets**. Most opposition parties try to assign one of their members to each government cabinet post. The shadow cabinet is expected to recommend new policies or changes to existing policies, as well as working vigorously to criticize the government.

Many of the strengths and weaknesses of the parliamentary system are determined by the quality of the opposition. An obstructionist opposition prevents the government from getting on with the business of running the country in an efficient way, thus interfering with the spirit of parliamentary government. Sometimes, in the collective mind of the opposition, delaying the passage of a **bill** is a patriotic act.

FACTFILE   The fate of minority governments in Canada tends to be short-lived, lasting on average 18 months compared with majority governments, which endure on average for over three years.

In Canada, the rules and procedures of the House of Commons permit the opposition to "oppose" the government by the technique of **filibuster**, by which every member of the opposition speaks as long as the rules allow during each stage of the debate. Such a strategy can effectively delay, if not prevent, both the division and passage of government legislation. The opposition frequently uses the threat of filibuster to gain concessions from the government on the content of legislation before the House. The rules give the government an ace-in-hand by providing for **closure**, whereby the government, by means of the Speaker's ruling, limits the tenure of debate to not more than 10 sitting days of Parliament.

Since 1969, a change in the **Standing Orders** of the House of Commons has substantially strengthened the ability of a government to control the length of debate. For example, Standing Order (SO) 75(c) allows the government to unilaterally limit debate at each stage in the passage of a bill. The severe competition for time in Parliament usually leads to deals between the government and the opposition parties. Hence, resorting to the extreme tactics of filibuster and closure by parliamentarians is rare these days because it tends to turn public opinion against those who use these devices too often.

General audit function

In the Canadian parliamentary system, accountability is facilitated by what Van Loon and Whittington call the "general audit function."[8]

These are rules and procedures that allow members of Parliament to scrutinize and criticize the government record publicly. Party cohesion and discipline guarantee that most of the watchdog functions of Parliament are conducted by opposition parties. But government **backbenchers** may also avail themselves of the same procedures to question and criticize their government's performance. Sometimes government backbenchers will publicly question and criticize their government's policies.

The process of general auditing is witnessed in a number of parliamentary debates and procedures. Standing Order 38(1) of the House of Commons requires a debate on the "Address in Reply to the **Speech from the Throne**." The Throne Speech Debate continues for eight days and usually elicits expressions of undaunted support from the government of the House to pessimistic appraisals of government intentions from the members of the opposition. The Throne Speech Debate gives backbenchers the opportunity to bring to public attention the most salient issues in their constituencies, as well as to criticize or applaud the government.

Another important general audit function of the Canadian Parliament is seen in the 25 supply days allocated to the opposition (5 days in the fall, 7 days before March 31, and 13 days before the end of June). These "opposition days" are intended to give members of parliament time to criticize the spending policy of the government. The opposition chooses the topics for debate and their motions enjoy precedence over government business. Each speaker is recognized for 20 minutes, during which time government business (ways and means) is discussed. The opposition always uses its allocated days to expose cases of wasteful government spending, mismanagement, and wrongdoing.

The most widely observed parliamentary debate is the *Budget Debate*, which follows the **Budget Speech**. Parliamentary accountability is at its height preceded, however, by another sacred

tradition of British cabinet government—*pre-budget secrecy*. In order to prevent anyone from profiting from inside knowledge, the budget is traditionally kept top secret until the finance minister reads the speech in the House of Commons. The premature release of information contained in a budget would pre-empt the privilege of Parliament as the only legitimate forum to hear firsthand the financial and monetary direction the country will take over a designated period of time.

According to the customs of parliamentary accountability, a minister of finance resigns when there is a serious breach of budget secrecy. Normally, the country watches attentively as the minister of finance brings down the budget by tabling the government's **ways and means motions**. The Budget Debate begins with the minister's speech and lasts for six days, during which time members of parliament speak to the ways and means proposals contained in the budget. The debate is an occasion for the opposition parties to raise issues of national significance, such as economic policy, unemployment, and tax policy.

FACTFILE   The liveliest event on the daily agenda of the House of Commons is perhaps the 40-minute Question Period. Ministers are not given notice of questions from the opposition, although most questions are anticipated.

Another important dimension of parliamentary accountability in Canada is the **Question Period**.[9] Standing Order 39(5) sets aside 40 minutes a day, while the House is sitting, for MPs to ask the government "questions on matters of urgency." Opposition members seize the opportunity to embarrass ministers by confronting them with intrusive questions about their actions, words, and policies. If not satisfied with the minister's reply, a member will call for a supplementary question in order to clarify an evasive answer. These televised exchanges are often quite humorous as members banter and heckle each other across the floor of the House.

Sometimes MPs simply require information from the government. Such questions are written and placed on the **Order Paper**. The answers to both the written and oral questions are printed verbatim in **Hansard**.

As a final recourse of action for a member who feels a question was not fully answered, a member can serve notice that the matter will again be raised "on the adjournment" of the House. Questions raised on the adjournment are debated at the end of the daily sitting period, when a member with a question can speak for seven minutes and other members have three minutes in which to make comments. These adjournment debates are yet another example of parliamentary accountability.

Presidential Government

Presidentialism and *presidential democracy* are two terms frequently used by political scientists to describe a form of government in which the executive is institutionally separated from the legislature. The oldest working presidential form of government is the **republic** of the United States.[10] **Republicanism** may be contrasted with constitutional monarchy in that the rule of the monarch as head of state is hereditary, whereas most republican heads of states are elected representatives.

FACTFILE   Because many Americans were uncomfortable with the term "democracy" in the 1780s, the term "republic" was used to mean a system of government in which the interests of citizens were represented by more educated and wealthier leaders.

American government has played a model role for many other political systems, especially those operating in Latin America, where varieties of this model are more common than in Europe or Asia (see Figure 4.3). However, fidelity to the constitutional dictates of presidential democracy is another question. In many states of Central and South America, presidentialism is the facade of authoritarian dictatorship. In these systems, the president dominates all institutions of government and is above the law.

In all presidential democracies, however, the unique feature of government is the strict adherence to the constitutional proclamation of the **separation of powers**, first implemented by the United States.

Separation of powers

According to the Constitution of the United States, "all legislative powers herein granted shall be vested in a **Congress**" (article I), "the executive Power shall be vested in a President" (article II), and the "judicial power . . . shall be vested in one Supreme Court, and in such inferior Courts as the Congress may from time to time ordain and establish" (article III).

FACTFILE   James Madison, collaborator in *The Federalist Papers*, a Congressman, founder of the Democratic-Republic Party, secretary of state, and president, advocated the "separation of powers" as the main dynamic of the United States government.

The principle of separation of powers has two functional dimensions. First is the **separation of personnel**, whereby no person may hold office in more than one of the three branches of government at the same time. Thus, unlike the practice in the parliamentary form of government, the executive cannot simultaneously hold a seat in the legislature. If a US senator is elected president or is appointed to the Supreme Court, he or she must resign the Senate seat. Second is the system of **checks and balances**. Under this system, powers are shared by the three branches of government so that no one branch comes to dominate the governmental apparatus. In effect, all three branches share executive power.

The executive power of the president to **veto** a bill by returning it to Congress can be overridden by a two-thirds vote in the House of Representatives and the Senate. Article I, section 7, of the US Constitution also provides for a "**pocket veto**." If a president neither signs nor vetoes a bill within 10 days of its passage by Congress, the bill becomes

Figure 4.3   Basic institutions of American government

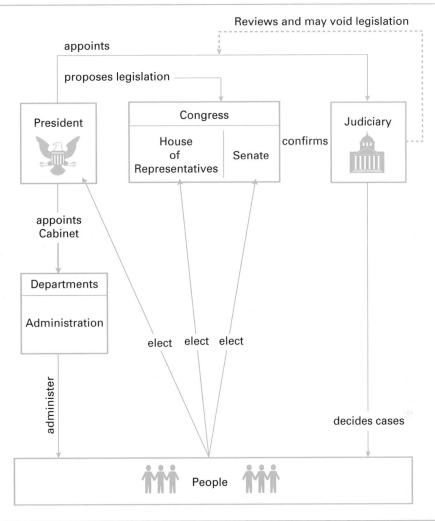

law without his signature unless Congress adjourns within 10 days. The Supreme Court can declare an Act of Congress unconstitutional and block the actions of the executive branch. Thus, executing, lawmaking, and judging are divided and shared by all three branches of government.

FACTFILE   US President Franklin D. Roosevelt holds the record for the most vetoes, at 625, of which 263 were pocket vetoes and 9 were overridden.

The president

To understand the distinguishing characteristics of presidential democracy, it is necessary to identify the principal features of the presidential type of government. In political systems such as the United States, Mexico, and Venezuela, the president represents the majesty and pageantry of the state. The president is both the *ceremonial* head of state as well as the *political* head of government.

As the ceremonial or titular head of state, the president is analogous to a monarch. He or she is the only symbolic representative of all of the people. As the political head of government, the president is responsible for supervising the national bureaucracy, executing legislative decisions, and enforcing court orders.

In presidential systems, the constitution specifies a fixed term for the president, who is usually elected directly. In the United States, as a matter of form, the president is indirectly elected by an electoral college. But, in fact, the election of the president is the result of a popular vote, and most voters so perceive it. In France, the president is directly elected for a seven-year term and is eligible for a second term. In the US, the fixed term of an independently elected executive means that the president cannot dissolve the legislature and call a general election as in the parliamentary system of government. But in France, where the constitution is a presidential and parliamentary blend, the president can dissolve the legislature at any time and call for an election. The US president cannot be legally removed from office during the fixed four-year term except through the legal process of **impeachment** and conviction. In France, no impeachment procedures exist, but the president can be tried by a special tribunal for acts of treason or for acts contrary to the Criminal Code.

FACTFILE   Woodrow Wilson is the only American political scientist thus far to become president of the United States (1912–1920).

The presidential form of government seems to focus primarily on the executive branch. But, in actual fact, it is a multidimensional form of government based on balancing the competitive forces among executive, legislative, and judicial institutions. Under this arrangement, the executive institutions carry out the decisions of the two other branches of government; the legislative institutions deliberate and decide on making general laws; and the judicial institutions apply these laws to particular cases.

In the presidential system, the general audit function is a product of political competition among legislative and executive institutions. The elaborate machinery of lawmaking is meant to ensure that laws are formulated carefully and that the bulk of the population—as well as major interest groups—perceive the laws passed as legitimate.

SUPRANATIONAL GOVERNMENT
The United States of Europe

Few people would have imagined at the close of World War II that by the 1990s a United States of Europe would be forming as a **supranational** political system—what many see as the new superpower of the twenty-first century.[11] It is a community of nation-states, seeking to eliminate borders and trade barriers and uniting its members by the use of one currency and a common foreign and defence policy. As a government it uniquely combines elements of parliamentary and presidential organization with a powerful bureaucracy.

The genesis of a United States of Europe originated in 1951 with the formation of the European Coal and Steel Community (ECSC). The concept was that European wars had their origin in economic rivalry. To substitute peace for war it was necessary to substitute economic co-operation for economic rivalry. The European Community (EC) started this way simply because coal and steel were the sinews of war and because former enemies found more and more interests to share. The six founding nation-states forming the ECSC—Belgium, France, Germany, Italy, Luxembourg, and the Netherlands—were the major powers in Western Europe that agreed to gradually eliminate duties, quotas, and price discriminations in coal and steel. From that simple idea, the ECSC deepened economic integration by creating the European Economic Community (EEC) in 1957. By 1967, the European Community emerged. By 1973, the six founding members were joined by Ireland, Britain, and Denmark. In 1981, Greece joined the EC, and in 1986, the membership reached 12, with the entry of Portugal and Spain. In 1995, Austria, Finland, and Sweden joined the European Union, increasing its membership to 15. In 2003, Poland joined Malta, Slovenia, Hungary, Lithuania, and Slovenia for EU entry. The Czech Republic, Estonia, and Latvia held referendums in 2004 and subsequently joined, while Cyprus joined without a referendum. Bulgaria and Romania joined in 2007. With the entry into force of the Maastricht Treaty in November 1993, "European Union" (EU) became the umbrella term for the institutions of the EC.

> **FACTFILE**   On January 1, 2007, with the addition of Bulgaria and Romania, the EU expanded to 27 member-states, representing 18 languages. This expansion created an economic powerhouse of the first world's largest single market, totalling more than 500 million people.

The dream that began with Charlemagne—shared by Kant, Rousseau, Victor Hugo, and Garibaldi, among others—the dream of a United Europe, is close to being fulfilled. The new Europe of the twenty-first century is a multinational, multicultural, multilinguistic community, sharing a new flag, a government in Brussels, a court in Luxembourg, and a parliament in Strasbourg. It is a Europe that aspires to be a world power, filling the vacuum of the collapse of the Soviet empire, being whole as its manifest destiny. But for now, the road to Europe's manifest destiny takes the more pedestrian route of the single market.

Europe's governing institutions

It was inevitable that the visionaries of a new supranational governing system for Europe would collide with the advocates of nationalism and national sovereignty. How could a United States of Europe spring from the traditional forces of national pride and patriotism? The signing of the Single European Act (SEA) of 1987 reflected a determination to deepen European integration by unifying the economic and monetary policies of the EU's member states and weakening the remaining forces of nationalism. The treaty included a central bank and a single currency, the *euro*.

The major governing institutions of the EU are the Council of the European Union, the European Council, the European Commission, the European Parliament, and the European Court of Justice (Figure 4.4). All of these bodies derive their financial resources directly from a levy on the yield of each member state's value-added tax (VAT), the major indirect tax, as well as from customs duties, agricultural levies, and duties on industrial imports.

Council of the European Union

Based in Brussels, with meetings also held in Luxembourg, the Council of the European Union is the autonomous decision-making body of the EU. The presidency of the Council rotates among the member states every six months. The Council is composed of ministers of each member state and represents *national* as opposed to *community* interests. It acts on proposals made by the European Commission after these proposals have been examined by the European Parliament. It has the power to amend or reject proposals made by the Commission. In effect, all of the decisions of the "eurocrats" have to be approved by the Council. Certain decisions require the unanimous support of the Council—for example, whether to admit new member states. On most other matters, voting is by qualified majority, by which a measure must obtain 70 percent of the Council's support to pass.

In practice, much of the day-to-day work of the Council is carried out by civil servants

Figure 4.4   EU: Decision-making process

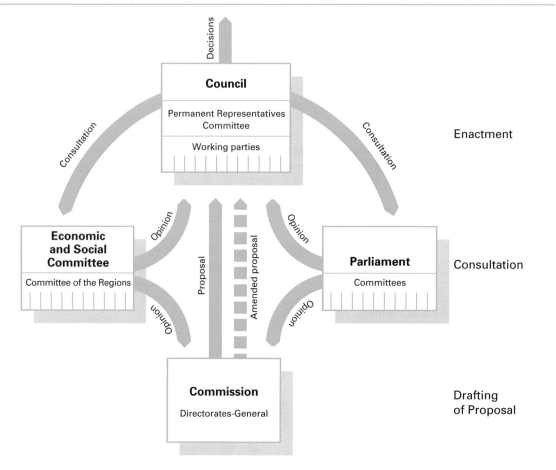

Decisions

Council

Permanent Representatives Committee

Working parties

Consultation

Consultation

Enactment

Opinion

Opinion

Economic and Social Committee

Committee of the Regions

Opinion

Proposal

Amended proposal

Parliament

Committees

Opinion

Consultation

Commission

Directorates-General

Drafting of Proposal

Source: The process of codecision from http://ec.europa.eu/codecision/stepbystep/diagram_en.htm © European Communities, 1995-2009.

appointed by member states and by working groups organized by the Council. Since the adoption of the SEA, specialized councils (e.g., the Agriculture Council) meet to discuss problems related to their interests.

European Council

The European Council or Summit is composed of the heads of member governments, usually the prime minister for most nation-states and the president for France. The European Council meets at least once every six months and is presided over by the Commission president. The Council does not legislate, but its written conclusions lay down the guidelines and provide impetus for the Union. The purpose of the European Council is to provide the highest-level forum to reconcile policy differences. The European Council has launched key initiatives such as the European Monetary System (EMS) in the late

1970s and the principle of political union in 1990. The European Council is the arena of last resort in which these policy conflicts are addressed, and influential advice (with no formal constitutional status with the EU) offered.

European Commission

The European Commission is a special embodiment of the EU, with an existence distinct from the member states and governments. Located in Brussels, it consists of 27 commissioners, appointed by the member states for four-year terms, two each from Germany, Italy, Britain, France, Spain, and Great Britain, and one each from the remaining nine member states. The Commission serves as the executive of the EU, overseeing and implementing policy. It manages a large bureaucracy, with more than 19 000 Eurocrats, divided among more than 25 directorates-general and agencies, who are employed by the Commission in Belgium, Luxembourg, and other EU locations. As the nerve centre of the new Europe, the Commission functions independently of any member state in the interests of the European Union as a whole and implements the treaties they ratify. It has the authority to initiate EU policies, and generally has the sole right to propose legislation to the European Parliament.

It is here in the International Congress Centre in Brussels that the Eurocrats draw the blueprints for further integration and make rules affecting everything from taxes to making beer to making sure that German toasters work when they are plugged in in France. All of this bureaucracy is intended to serve the interests of a new Europe where trade barriers have come down and the free flow of people, goods, and capital is routine. In all, thousands of industrial and manufacturing standards are implemented among member states. This means Eurocrats must work overtime, deciding everything from the length of condoms to the maximum noise level of lawnmowers.

The Eurocrats are the elite, the clergy of the new Europe, who spend much time with the many lobbyists who approach them for political favours. The drive toward the single market has produced another kind of competition—competition for the Eurocrat's ear. EU officials are the ones who are drafting the rules for this new single market, so it is not surprising that most of the lobbying associated with the European Union is centred in Brussels. Over a thousand multinational companies now have an office in Brussels—that is twice the number of companies in Washington, DC. In all, there is about one lobbyist for every five bureaucrats.

The Commission issues directives that aspire to achieve the objectives of the policies decided on by the Council of the European Union. These directives address an endless array of matters. They can prohibit member governments from subsidizing their own farmers, veto mergers of companies on the grounds that they will reduce competition in Europe, and ban the sale of food and drugs because they are unsafe.

The Commission sees its mandate as accelerating the pace of European integration, sometimes against the expressed national interests of member states. It can take members of the European Communities to the European Court of Justice should they breach treaties or renege on their responsibilities to the supranational organization.

European Parliament

The European Parliament (EP) has both a legislative and an advisory role. The Parliament is the only directly elected EU institution, and is located in Strasbourg, France. As of 2007, there were 785 members of the European Parliament (MEPs), elected to fixed five-year terms by elections held on the same date in each member state. They are grouped by political affiliation, not national affiliation. Party representation in the European

Parliament consists of Socialist Group, European People's Party and European Democrats (Christian Democratic Groups), Alliance of Liberals and Democrats for Europe, European People's Party, Union for Europe of the Nations Group, Group of Greens European Free Alliance, Confederal Group of the European United Left, Nordic Green Left and Independent Democracy Group.

The EP's main functions are to debate, question, and formally register advisory opinions on proposals made by the Commission. The European Commission and the Council of the European Union are not bound by these opinions, but no legislation can be enacted without the EP's first officially issuing one. The EP has the power to dismiss the entire Commission but not individual commissioners.

The Parliament may consider a wide range of legislative matters, from the marketing of plums and bananas to the tariff barriers placed on nonmembers. It has the right to reject the budget of the EU as a whole, and it has the last word on amendments to the budget. The EP is the watchdog over the workings of treaties, such as the Lome Convention, signed between the EU and other states including Canada (see *Focus On* box), as well as treaties signed among members, such as the Maastricht Treaty and the Treaty of Rome.

European Court of Justice

Created in 1958, the European Court of Justice (ECJ) hears legal disputes arising under the Treaty of Rome. The Court sits in Luxembourg with 27 justices and 8 advocates-general appointed by agreement of the member states for six-year terms. It should not be confused with the European Court of Justice on Human Rights (ECJHR) at Strasbourg, France. In the widest sense, the ECJ is an international court empowered to interpret EU treaties and to settle disputes that arise among the institutions of the EU, between individuals, enterprises, and member states. About one-third of its cases are requests for preliminary rulings submitted

by national courts. Its decisions are binding on member states, national courts and parliaments, all EU institutions, and enterprises and individuals. The rulings of the European Court have empowered EU law, granting it precedence over national law when the two are in conflict.

Any member state, EU institution, corporation, or individual may appeal to the court for the enforcement of EU laws or treaty rights. What makes this court different from other international courts is that individuals can use the court as well as governments. Basically the ECJ may declare an act or behaviour of any member state illegal if it violates the EC or subsequent European law.

AUTHORITARIAN DICTATORSHIP

Authoritarian regimes are familiar phenomena to political scientists.[12] The similarities of authoritarian and totalitarian dictatorship are well known but, as we shall see, the two systems of government are quite different from each other.

While dictatorship is declining in some parts of the world, especially in Latin America, the Islamic fundamentalist presence in the Middle East sustains dictatorial government institutions.

FACTFILE In the Middle East, Islamic revolutionary movements are increasingly active in Algeria, Tunisia, Jordan, and Tajikistan, reinforcing the culture of authoritarianism.

Authoritarianism is a system of government principally characterized by **autocratic** decision making, restricted pluralism, and limited public participation. Just as democracy is an outgrowth of a society attached to values of open government, pluralism, and political party competition, so is authoritarianism a product of unique historical variants within a political culture. That pattern reveals itself historically as a tendency to concentrate all political power in the hands of a few, to distrust

Focus On   **Canada and the European Union**

The formation of the European Community added a new dimension to the traditional relationship that had existed between Canada and the individual member states of the EU. In recognition of the importance of the EC, in 1959 Canada accredited its ambassador to Belgium also to serve as ambassador to the European Community. Since 1973, a separate Canadian ambassador has been appointed to Brussels to maintain and strengthen Canada–EU bilateral relations.

In some sectors, however, problems have arisen, such as discriminatory provincial liquor board practices, or the EU restrictions on certain types of untreated softwood lumber. Despite these problems, Canada–EU trade remains buoyant.

Trade and Investment

Next to the United States, the European Union is Canada's most important trading partner and source of foreign investment capital. Trade between the EU and Canada is non-preferential in nature, but is based on a **most-favoured-nation clause**. In 2007, Canada's trade with the EU was $91 billion. Canadian companies such as Alcan, Bombardier, Magna, Nortel, and Quebecor World rely in no small measure on their sales in Europe.

The main Canadian exports to the EU are wood pulp, aircraft engines and parts, aluminum, newsprint, and softwood lumber. Imports from the EU comprise mainly organic chemicals, aircraft engines and parts, alcoholic beverages and mineral water, computers, cars, and engines and parts.

For many years, Canada maintained a trade surplus with the EU. Since 1984, however, it has been the EU that has enjoyed a trade surplus with Canada. European Union investment in Canada in 2007 showed dramatic increase amounting to $119.4 billion, while Canada's investment in the EU totalled $118.8 billion. The EU ranks second to the United States as a source of direct foreign investment for Canada.

democratic institutions, and to expect **political succession** as a violent and unstable event.

Four types of authoritarian governments manifest themselves in the international system. *Tyrannies* are governments dominated by an absolute civilian or military rulership that arbitrarily exercises political power in a highly repressive and often **personalistic** fashion. Governments in contemporary Uganda, Somalia, and Sudan are some examples. *Dynastic regimes* are monarchies wherein members of the royal family exercise absolute political powers ascribed by religious law, custom, and inheritance. Examples of these are Saudi Arabia and the Sultanate of Brunei. *Military regimes* are governments in which the executive, legislative, judicial, and administrative institutions are controlled by members of the armed forces. A multitude of African examples exist in states such as Guinea-Bissau and Sierra Leone. *Single-party regimes* are governments instituted with the support of only one political party or a coalition of parties that dominates the electoral system exclusively but sometimes tolerates weak opposition parties. States such as Kenya, Iraq, Syria, and Tanzania have provided examples of this type of regime.

Focus On Dictatorships to Watch

Dictatorial Islamic Regimes

Iran is ruled by Seyed Ali Khamenei and not so much by the media-focused Mahmoud Ahmadinejad. Iran is governed by a 12-man Guardian Council of mullahs, headed by Ayatollah Khamenei.

Turkmenistan's dictator is Saparmurat Niyazov, who rules his country in the fashion of Joseph Stalin. His cult of personality dominates a government that has recently banned car radios, lip-synching, and playing recorded music on TV and at weddings. The month of January was named after him and April is named after his mother.

Libya is led by Muammar al-Qaddafi, infamous for his former challenges to the United States and other western governments. He has made peace with them but continues to run a brutal dictatorship with extensive control over all aspects of life in Libya.

Pakistan: Asif Ali Zardari, elected in 2008 as Presidential successor to Pervez Musharraf, has promised a tougher fight against members of the Taliban and other extremist groups who have sought haven in rural Pakistan. It remains to be seen how much will change under the new government.

Saudi Arabia is dominated by King Abdulla, who enforces Islamic law as state law and whose citizens are required to be Muslim. This government executes people for witchcraft and beats them for being alone with someone of the opposite sex who is not related to them.

Sudan has one of the most ruthless dictatorships under Omar al-Bashir, who has been in power since 1989. Hundreds of thousands have been massacred by his soldiers. The genocide of over 200 000 and the displacement of 2 million in Darfur is all under his direction.

Syria: Bashar al-Assad inherited his rule from his father, Hafiz al Assad in 2000. He balances the internal power of the military, the intelligence service, the ruling political party, and the bureaucracy. This is the government that tortured Canadian Maher Arar.

Uzbekistan is led by Islam Karimov, former president of this Soviet Republic, who uses torture to terrorize his people. Thousands have been massacred and many are likely to die under this dictatorial regime.

Other Noteworthy Dictatorships

China has become such a major part of the global economy that most governments ignore its abysmal human rights record. While capitalism dominates the market place, communism rules most aspects of citizens' lives. Hu Jintao heads a government that practises rampant corruption, forced labor, control of media, and restrictions on fundamental freedoms of speech, religion, and mobility.

Cuba: Its leader for 50 years, Fidel Castro, is facing serious health challenges. His brother Raul Castro is trying to consolidate his power and is preparing for full political succession. But Raul is 75 years old and not in the best of health himself. Castro's sons, Antonio and Fidel, could eventually take the reins of power. But they are professional men, one a doctor and one an engineer, with no previous political ambitions or experience.

Zimbabwe: At age 80, Robert Mugabe has been in power since 1980. After leading a successful war of liberation for independence, it was hoped that Mugabe would guide Africa to a new era of democracy. His government instead became one of the most dictatorial and abusive on the continent, violating the rights of his citizens and bringing the economy to near ruin.

The chief characteristics of the authoritarian type of government are the following:

- Dictators are often **charismatic**, elitist, and personalistic. They exercise political power in personal and subjective ways rather than according to the rules of democratic governing institutions in which the rule of law supersedes the rule of the rulers.

- **Personalism** is an effective means of attracting mass support and centralizing government power. People are encouraged to identify with the leader rather than with institutions or the ideals of a formal government system.

- Authoritarian dictators do not promote an official, undisputed ideology that prescribes a national or international mission for their government. If an ideology does exist, it reflects their personal world view and frequently reflects short-range pragmatic considerations.

- A plurality of interest groups may exist with the permission or tolerance of the dictator, but these groups are licensed or closely monitored by the government. If they support the regime their activities go unhindered, but if they oppose the government they are usually harassed or repressed.

- The political-party system may appear to be competitive, but it is always dominated by one political party, the government party. Opposition-party competition is sometimes legal, provided it remains weak and divided.

- A pretense of constitutional law based on liberal democratic norms masks authoritarian operating structures. Authoritarian regimes practise a type of legalism that embraces law and regulation, but its purpose is to control people, not to limit government.

- The economy is "directed" toward the problem of securing economic development and modernization. But authoritarian governments generally do not attempt to control every aspect of human economic activity. Free enterprise, free markets, and other components of laissez-faire principles are permitted in the economy.

- Authoritarian regimes usually have a strong military component that from time to time intervenes in the political process. The presence of the military in an authoritarian state ranges from holding a veto over the actions of a civilian government, to direct intervention in the political process, to instituting a military regime.

- The government limits and controls popular participation in the system. Political mobilization is encouraged by the government only for support of its economic and political policies.

Civilian Dictatorships

Dictatorship may manifest itself in a number of different civilian and military forms. *Caesarism* is the kind of dictatorship in which the leader enjoys absolute power by virtue of control over the military. The military is the coercive arm of the civilian dictator. It can be summoned to neutralize political enemies, as well as to repress dissidents in the population. Thus, most civilian dictators court the loyalty of the military by catering to its materialistic needs, such as regular pay raises, fringe benefits, overseas travel, and access to state-of-the-art equipment and hardware.

The caesaristic dictator often has the support of the masses, a modern political machine, and a program combining personal charisma with a socio-economic plan of action for modernization. Many people, including the dictator, regard the dictatorship as the only salvation for the country.

Caudillismo—from the Spanish word *caudillo* meaning "man on horseback"—is a type of dictatorship that has been a principal feature of Latin American politics since the nineteenth century. The strong-arm style of rule is based on the force of personality of the *caudillo*, not on an ideology as a program of action. The caudillo comes to power on the back of personal mystique, using charm and effective oratory to capture the support of the people. By appealing to the forces of nationalism and high ideals, the caudillo gains mass appeal.

However, behind this popular facade is almost always a repressive dictatorship that uses the loyalty and physical power of the military to maximize personal gain and effectively control opposition. Political rights and liberties are often suspended: restrictions are placed on the activities of political parties and interest groups; and newspapers are monitored or bridled. Elections become an event of the past or the future, and the authority of the judiciary is curtailed.

Military Dictatorships

Militarism—the intrusion of the armed forces into the political life of a country—is a salient feature of authoritarian governments all over the world. Since 1945, over two-thirds of the states of Africa, Asia, the Middle East, and Latin America have experienced varying degrees of military government.[13] Cycles of military intervention alternating with civilian rule are a typical pattern within authoritarian states, especially in Haiti, El Salvador, and Guatemala.

Usually, during periods of political and economic crisis, the armed forces are likely to step in. In many cases, any circumstance that threatens the status quo is enough to bring the military running from the barracks. In the post-war period, the armed forces in Latin American states attribute their political intrusions to the threat of revolutionary regimes. But often, the rationale for military intervention is civilian corruption or government mismanagement. One reason that is openly admitted to by military officers is adventurism. Soldiers have guns, tanks, and planes—the most persuasive tools for acquiring the ultimate power of the state. Sometimes a **cuartelazo**, a military **coup d'état** against a military government, is conducted to sustain military government.

By definition, military regimes are those in which the armed forces have seized power by a coup d'état, and have taken command of the highest positions of government. A military council or **junta** is usually formed to control all executive and legislative functions. Many military governments create mixed military/civilian executives to enhance the legitimacy of the regime. Civilians are almost always included in the cabinet and hold high bureaucratic positions as advisers in the formation of government policies. But their presence and influence is largely on the sufferance of the military governors.

From the beginning of their tenure in power, the military portray themselves as responsible and patriotic officers who are temporarily forced to take the reins of government away from incompetent civilians or a previously inept military regime. Ostensibly, their goals include altering the system of government to rid it of excessive, corrupt, and inefficient partisan politics.

Initially, the military are concerned with economic problems they claim result from civilian rule: high inflation and unemployment, wasteful government spending, and balance-of-payments deficits. Viewing themselves as "iron surgeons," they often employ drastic economic measures to correct the malaise in the economy. They restrict the supply of money to address inflation and invite foreign investment to reduce unemployment. Cutbacks in social security, medical, and education programs are implemented to reduce public spending. But progressive measures to redistribute wealth and institute land reforms are usually avoided in the military's approach to reconstruct the economy. The basic contours of the social system are preserved or only mildly altered. Military governments will usually eliminate or limit the political rights of the civilian population. Some political parties, newspapers, and trade unions are permitted to operate under the close scrutiny of government authorities. Almost always, the existing leadership of political organizations and labour unions is purged and replaced by people acceptable to the regime.

FACTFILE   Canada and Holland are constitutional monarchies because the monarch is subject to the law, but Saudi Arabia is an absolute monarchy because the monarch is above the law and has unlimited power to rule.

The immediate reasons for limiting political competition and muzzling the media are quite apparent. The military take power to prevent certain changes. They will not provide former rulers and their supporters with the means to challenge them. Because the justification for taking power is to prevent failures in civilian government performance, the military are determined to neutralize the power potential of those responsible for these failures.

If the significance of a particular form of government depends on the frequency with which it occurs, then the study of military government is paramount. Given the frequency of military interventions in *authoritarian* systems, military governments must be viewed as a global political

phenomenon. Research confirms that the most likely aftermath of military government is military government.

TOTALITARIAN DICTATORSHIP
Totalistic Controls

Totalitarianism is a uniquely novel product of the twentieth century, quite distinct from modern authoritarianism and far removed from the autocracies of the past. The essential trait of totalitarianism in contrast to authoritarian dictatorship is its claim upon most aspects of a citizen's life in the service of national goals, as determined and interpreted by the rulers. In the totalitarian state, the regime's presence is "totalistic" in that no realm of private and social life is completely immune from its control.

The emergence of totalitarianism (since World War I) can be attributed to breakthroughs in mass-communication technologies as well as in techniques of social control and manipulation discovered from experimental research in social psychology. By means of these devices, totalitarian states are characterized by a system of government in which one party enjoys a monopoly of political, economic, judicial, and military power. The party has the capacity to penetrate all levels of society, to determine its values, and to direct the lives of individuals towards the achievement of its prescribed ideology.

Big Brother

In 1948, George Orwell alarmed the democratic world with his nightmarish novel *1984*, an icy satire of life under totalitarian government. Orwell's vision of totalitarian government portrayed a society with the political and technological capacity to remold and transform people according to an official plan. With modern electronic devices, the government spies on its citizens: television cameras scan the streets, listening devices monitor private conversations, and even private thoughts and actions can be learned by the state. Watched by an ever-present "Big Brother," people are highly controlled by the government. They are subjected to constant censorship and surveillance and indoctrinated in daily "two-minute hate" sessions, directed against a phantom enemy with whom they are endlessly at war. In the end, the hero becomes a mindless robot, believing everything the government tells him to believe, fearing what he is told to fear and hating what he is told to hate.

In hindsight, Orwell's novel was an exaggeration of the menacing and horrific features of totalitarianism. But all totalitarian governments have the institutional and technological capacity to achieve the most repressive forms of social control. In China, the government has ensured the compliance of its citizens by means of torture, harassment, and fear. Often, recalcitrant citizens have been subjected to threats, attacks, questioning, searches, eviction, firing, and imprisonment. And in Cuba, the 6000 Committees for the Defence of the Revolution (CDRs) have kept close watch on the social and political behaviour of Cubans. But it is important to note that all of the technologies of population control enabling totalitarian governments to emerge are also present in democratic societies.

Elements of Totalitarian Dictatorship

One of the most comprehensive analyses of totalitarianism was conducted by Carl Friedrich and Zbigniew Brzezinski.[14] They identify six essential characteristics of this twentieth-century government phenomenon:

- An official undisputed ideology that encompasses all aspects of human life: history, the economy, and all social and political

institutions, as well as one that prescribes an international mission of global conversion or domination.

- A single, elite-directed mass party, led by a dictator and a core of militants dedicated to realizing the goals of the ideology. Recruitment of party membership is controlled, usually about 15 percent of the population. The organization of the party is linked to the formal institutions of government and touches every level of society.

- A secret policy apparatus that uses modern communications technology and psychological methods to ensure mass allegiance to party ideology.

- The monopolized control of the mass media in order to indoctrinate the masses in the official ideology. The media function as organs of mass propaganda to educate citizens about the goals of the state.

- The monopoly of weapons control to prevent the possible armed resistance of dissidents.

- A centrally controlled "command economy" in which most means of production and consumption are owned and planned by the state according to ideological prescriptions.

Models of Totalitarian Dictatorship

Two models of totalitarianism appeared in the twentieth century: right-wing totalitarianism and left-wing totalitarianism. Italian Fascism and German National Socialism are the two generic examples of right-wing totalitarianism. But fascism and Nazism were not uniquely Italian and German experiences.[15] Both were parts of an ideological movement that swept Europe in the period between the two world wars. Right-wing totalitarianism first appeared in Italy, where by 1922 Mussolini had gained complete control of the

Chamber of Deputies. By 1933, in Germany, the National Socialists were the only legal party under the iron grip of Adolf Hitler. Germany and Italy aided Francisco Franco and his *Falangist* Party in Spain and inspired Juan Perón in his successful quest for power in Argentina.

FACTFILE   In 1915, Benito Mussolini organized the first *fasci di combattimento* (combat troops), known as *fascisti*. This term spawned the name for the fascist movement, which terrorized Europe and other parts of the world in the 1930s.

Fascism proclaimed a romantic ideology of mythic consensus and social unity in conforming to political roles. Human dignity was to be achieved by the integration of individuals into an all-encompassing corporate moral order, represented by the fascist state. But none of the fascist regimes revolutionized their societies; rather, they built a powerful government apparatus for social control and expected individuals to glorify the goals of the state.

The remaining totalitarian socialist states have nationalized the means of production in their industrial and commercial sectors. This has usually extended to individual entrepreneurs, artisans, street vendors, taxi drivers, and other small commercial services. But some governments are encouraging economic innovation by permitting the spread of private enterprise in these sectors. Today in China, it is possible to purchase a computer or other technologies from private businesses all over the country.

In all societies that try to regulate almost everything, **black economies** and **black markets** (second economies) have come to play a large part in the economic structure of the country. In the past, many people under communist regimes have resorted to illegal sources to procure goods and services that are not available in a centrally planned economy. Black market capitalism grew spontaneously in all totalitarian socialist states, at least in part because of the absence of privately motivated market mechanisms based on profit.

The overall evaluation of the performance of the three types of regimes discussed in this chapter—democratic, authoritarian, and totalitarian—can be made by answering the following questions: To what extent is human well-being enhanced by the presence of the regime? Do people feel they can participate in the decisions of the system? Are the rights of individuals upheld by the government and its officials? Does the government respond to the most necessary demands of its citizens? Does it use its capacity to generate good for all of its citizens most of the time?

In the following chapters, we will learn that governments are multidimensional, usually comprising four branches: the executive, legislative, bureaucratic, and judicial. Each can be compared as a separate part of a political system, and each must be understood as a constituent element of the whole political system.

Chapter Summary

Ours is a world of many governments. When we compare them, we need to designate some general concepts, such as democratic, authoritarian, and totalitarian regimes, to help understand the fundamental similarities and differences among states. This chapter introduces us to the historical presence of "government" in all societies since the dawn of time. One of the tasks of political scientists in the field of comparative politics and government is to contrast the conduct of leaders and the efficiency of the decision-making institutions of governments.

What we learn from this is that every government is unique. Even when institutions carry the same label, such as parliamentary or congressional, we discover great variations in their roles and performance. Institutional structures, for instance, play different roles in different regimes. A democratic congress serves a very different function from one in an authoritarian regime. By comparing governments, we learn that each government evolves from different historical, cultural, economic, social, and international determinants that all shape its particular character and quality. Comparative analysis permits political scientists to understand the stability of governments, how supported they are, how developed their institutions are, who can participate in decision making, and their performance in relation to economic growth and bureaucratic efficiency.

Political scientists evaluate democratic governments by how accountable they are to the people, by their adherence to constitutional law and the rule of law, by the civil liberties individuals enjoy, by the rights of minorities, and by the amount of political competition in the political system.

Parliamentary governments *fuse* executive and legislative powers, and require governments to resign if defeated and to regularly call elections based on the tenure of the parliament, usually five years. The judiciary is independent and appointed by the political executive.

Presidential or congressional government is another form of democratic system. It *separates* the powers of government so that the executive branch operates independently outside the legislature, each branch with its own personnel and a system of *checks and balances* to control the powers of government. The judicial branch of government is independent and is empowered to act as a check on the other branches of government.

Authoritarian governments are civilian or military dictatorships characterized by unelected elites, personalistic styles in decision making, controlled political competition, government-directed economic planning, and limited constitutional guarantees.

Totalitarian dictatorship appeared twice in the twentieth century: the right-wing Nazi and fascist regimes of Germany and Italy, and the left-wing communist regimes still in existence. They operate with an official ideology, a single elite-directed mass party, unaccountable secret police, state control of the media and weapons, and a command-driven economy.

Discussion Questions

1. Distinguish between *politics* and *government*. Define the following terms in relation to both definitions:
   (a) accountability
   (b) constitutionalism
   (c) popular sovereignty
   (d) rule of law

2. Discuss the most salient attributes of democratic, authoritarian, and totalitarian governments. Why is Canada thought to be a democratic state? What makes China a totalitarian regime? Name an African and a South American state that would represent the model of authoritarianism described in this chapter.

3. Contrast the main characteristics of parliamentary and presidential governments. Explain and compare the governments of Canada and the United States from the perspective of fusion of powers, separation of powers, and checks and balances.

4. Is Nazism likely to resurface as a model of government? If so, what kind of political environment will produce it and what modern-day technologies will aid it?

5. What about the future of communism? Are communist regimes likely to disappear entirely? Or do you think there will always be communist governments in the international system?

Executives

CHAPTER 5

After reading this chapter, you will be able to:

- identify and describe the executive branch of government
- list the resources available to executives in the exercise of their official duties and functions
- describe the general functions of executives
- classify executives
- differentiate and explain the qualities of the parliamentary executive
- outline and describe the components of Canada's ceremonial and political executive
- outline and describe the components of the executive branch of government in the United States
- compare the parliamentary and presidential executives
- profile the executive elements of dictatorship
- describe the characteristics of the executive branch of government in totalitarian regimes

THE POWERFUL RESOURCES OF EXECUTIVES

Of all the branches of government, the executive is the oldest and the most widely adopted institution. Archaeological evidence in the Middle East indicates that the institution of **kingship** was already well established over 5000 years ago.[1] The executive branch of government has been the focal point of political power and effective decision making since groups began to organize governments in society. Even today, in the mind of the public, the executive is synonymous with government. Every political system has an executive in which leadership is concentrated in the hands of a single individual or a small elite group. Whether in democracies or **autocracies**, executive power is inevitable. This can be explained by the fact that all political executives have access to a wide range of available political resources that are usually not accessible to other branches of government.

The Power of Information

One important political resource available to executives is information. Because executives are primary decision makers, they are privy to classified information flowing from within the country, and internationally to **intelligence** from other governments. They know how good things are and how bad things are before most of us do. For this reason, executives tend to know much more than either assemblies or judiciaries about what is going on in government. Executives can control, to a great extent, what other participants in government get to know because they generate considerable information themselves and can act in secrecy.

FACTFILE   Canada belongs to a global intelligence network that gathers information through virtually every type of communications system, from long-distance phone calls, e-mail, listening devices, and electronic monitoring technologies used logistically within Canada's military alliances.

In Canada, the **Cabinet** exercises extensive control of government information with the assistance of the **Prime Minister's Office** (PMO), the **Privy Council Office** (PCO), and the **Treasury Board**. Sometimes called the "gatekeepers," these three bodies advise the prime minister and the Cabinet on the advisability and financial feasibility of pursuing a given policy.[2] All administrative and security information is filtered through these offices to the prime minister and the Cabinet. At this level, information is carefully guarded; even backbenchers on the government side of the House must wait for access to information in secret caucus and remain silent according to the written and unwritten rules of party discipline. Such is the case for matters related to Canada–US border security strategies and the negotiations between both states on the implementation of a ballistic missile-defence system in the western hemisphere.

In the United States, the president and his appointed cabinet draw and control vital information from four sources: the **Executive Office of the President** (EOP), the **National Security Council** (NSC), the **Office of Management and Budget** (OMB), and the **Council of Economic Advisors** (CEA). The doctrine of *executive privilege* allows a president to guard secrets in matters of national security, internal bureaucratic discipline, and individual privacy. Even executive decisions can be made within the bounds of secrecy and are accountable only through the works of congressional investigation, journalism, and judicial testimony.

In non-democratic states, executives enjoy a vast amount of information control because they usually are not accountable to a legislature, the media, or the people. They participate in the formation of policy, where information may be deliberately kept scarce. In many non-democratic states, executives acquire direct or indirect control of the communication facilities in the country and have the coercive powers to destroy all rival centres of information and communication. Usually, *military intelligence* is the major clearing house for political information in a non-democratic state although it may also be this way in democratic states.

FACTFILE   The intelligence-gathering arsenal against terrorism includes satellite surveillance, monitoring telephone lines, reports from embassies, the media, and spy agencies.

The Power of Organization

A second political resource readily available to the executive branch of government is organization. All executives are surrounded by some form of professional civil or military bureaucracy, as well as a political party organization capable of serving the highest levels of government.

In Canada, the prime minister and the Cabinet enjoy a virtual monopoly of power over the organization of government. Canada's political executive has instant access to an army of bureaucratic expertise from which to draft and legislate policy. Not only do the PMO and PCO provide essential expertise for executive decision making, but the entire public service is also at the disposal of the prime minister and the Cabinet. The political executive can draw from ministerial staffs, the party structure, and the government caucus to provide information and advice on policy initiatives.

FACTFILE   In Canada, the Privy Council Office (PCO), formally established as a secretariat to the Cabinet in 1940, is headed by the Clerk of the Privy Council and Secretary to the Cabinet.

In the United States, the White House staff is only a small part of the presidential establishment, but it links the president with the vast organizational machinery of American government.[3] Under the numerous agencies of the EOP, NSC, OMB, and CEA, more than three million executive-branch employees serve the president. Every year, those executive agencies bring forward their

new proposals for legislation, both to improve the handling of existing programs and to innovate with new ones.

Unlike the Canadian executive, which is fused to the legislative process and thus to the entire bureaucracy of government, the US Congress is a genuinely independent government body, with a separate bureaucracy of its own to serve it. Because the American executive leadership and the Congressional bureaucracy do not necessarily work in concert, there is always a tension between the president and the other organizations of government.

In autocratic states, executives have much more direct control over the various organizations of government. The ministries and bureaucracies simply function as agencies that implement policies after the decisions have already been reached by the executive.

The Power of Rightful Authority

Another important political resource available to executives is legitimacy—the exercise of political authority in a way that is perceived as rightful and is accepted by the members of the political community. One test of legitimacy is the degree of coercion the executive must use against people to achieve acceptance and obedience. As a general rule, the more coercion, the less legitimacy.

FACTFILE   In Canada, all cabinet ministers must have a seat in Parliament, i.e., the House of Commons or the Senate.

No executive can claim to rule on the basis of force alone, because that would allow equal legitimacy to any dissenting groups or opposing movements. In democratic political systems, executives have legitimacy because they adhere to constitutional principles and follow standard procedures when establishing policy. Judgments about the wisdom or morality of a particular executive decision may vary, but legitimacy goes unquestioned. For example, Canadians usually accept Cabinet decisions as legitimate, even if they do not always agree with them.

Even in dictatorial regimes, executive institutions are protected from the adverse consequences of unpopularity by the appearance of legitimacy.

In these types of political systems, legitimacy attaches to executive institutions because people sense that they are firmly established and here to stay. The legitimacy of the executive is not based merely on coercion but is instilled in the civilian population through political indoctrination and socialization. Especially in totalitarian regimes, children are taught from early years to trust and respect political authority, often symbolized by executives.

In authoritarian regimes, dictatorial executives have decisive control over government but choose not to control a wide range of social and private behaviour. Thus, executive legitimacy is frequently based on the personal charisma of the leader who usually rules without an official ideology to legitimize executive power. Popular support enables a dictator to decree laws, often bypassing the legislative and judicial branches of government entirely.

Economic Power

Economic power is another major resource often favouring the executive branch of government. Because of their dominance in the structure of government, executives appropriate to themselves a vast share of the economic resources of their country. These resources are available to them through their position in government, the powers of taxation and confiscation, and may also be derived from the profits of state enterprises. Canada's federal and provincial government ministers tend to grant the lion's share of government contracts to the constituencies they represent, spending millions that often ensure their re-election.

In Canada's political executive, the Cabinet wields enormous economic power.[4] It is through the Cabinet that revenues are raised, finances are managed, and policies are planned and legislated within the confines of the budgetary process of government. The Financial Administration Act is the legislation that gives the Cabinet full control of the budgetary process. The Treasury Board, a statutory committee of Cabinet, oversees the economic power of the Canadian government. It advises the Cabinet about the financial feasibility of government goals. Finance Canada is the revenue-raising organ of the Canadian executive. Its authority extends over all aspects of the taxation system, and it co-ordinates its efforts with the Cabinet committees directly responsible for the making of public-revenue policy.

In the United States, the economic policy of the national government receives its most overt expression in the executive budget. Every year, the president makes thousands of decisions to spend or not to spend money on particular projects. These include dams, environmental programs, urban-renewal projects, highways, airports, university facilities, and numerous other public works. Increasingly, presidential discretion has played a greater role in deciding where and when a particular project will be implemented. Different presidents have different attitudes about the extent to which political considerations should dictate decisions concerning federal expenditures. Because members of the House of Representatives and the Senate are always eager to obtain federal projects for their constituents, the White House can use this executive economic power—which in some cases is at the sole discretion of the executive branch—to lure favourable votes in Congress.

In authoritarian states, the economic powers of the executive are often corrupted. It is not uncommon to find the highest public officials with their hands deep in the national till, taking public property, including land, money, and lucrative concessions in criminal as well as legal activities. In 1999, the International Monetary Fund revealed that Russian president Boris

Yeltsin was allowing members of his family to use IMF accounts to pay personal expenses from foreign banks. When Yeltsin resigned on December 31, 1999, the deal he made with his successor Vladimir Putin was that he would be granted immunity from prosecution on all financial matters that arose during his presidency.

In communist regimes, the single most powerful individual is not a government official but rather the general secretary of the Communist Party. The ideological priorities of the highest party officials determine the direction of economic planning and investment in the economy. In political systems such as these, the executive can mobilize the entire resources of the country to achieve its economic goals and improve the general standard of living.

WHAT EXECUTIVES DO

Even though political styles and organizational structures differ remarkably across the international system, what executive leaders do enables us to make generalizations. In all cases, executive conduct is a product of the political culture; the roles and functions of modern executives are determined by the ways people think about and do politics.

The Role of Symbol and Ceremony

All of the symbolism and ceremony in the executive branch of government is centred on the head of state. In Canada, the pomp and circumstance surrounding the formal delivery of the Speech from the Throne rivals the regal splendour of British imperial majesty. The appearance of the president of the United States before a joint session of Congress to deliver the State of the Union Address has the magnificence of a Hollywood spectacle. In most systems of government, there is a separation of personnel within the executive (see Table 5.1).

There are a number of advantages to the separation of the head of state and the head of government. For many states, it is important to have some office (and the person who occupies it) independent of the deeply enmeshed political battles of government. The head of state transcends the brush fires of partisan politics and can foster both unity and historical continuity within the nation-state (Table 5.2). In Canada and Great Britain, the reigning monarch or the official representative of the reigning monarch is the living symbol of the state and acts independently in the interests of the whole community. The head of state opens Parliament and attends public

Table 5.1 Types of executives

State	Head of State	Head of Government
Canada	Monarch	Prime Minister
France	President	Prime Minister
United Kingdom	Monarch	Prime Minister
United States	President	President
Federal Republic of Germany	President	Chancellor
Russia	President	President

Table 5.2	Sovereign reign over Canadian territory since Confederation
1837–1901	Victoria
1901–1910	Edward VII
1910–1936	George V
1936	Edward VIII
1936–1952	George VI
1952–	Elizabeth II

functions at which the majesty of the state is to be given symbolic or ceremonial representation. When there is an election, or when a government falls, the head of state formally appoints the political executive to proclaim its right to govern. In this way, the head of state is the transmitter of legitimacy and the personification of the state.

Heads of state, like those in Britain, Canada, the Netherlands, and Norway, who appear to be only figureheads subject to overriding powers of the political executive, often exercise considerable *de facto* executive power and influence. For example, when there is doubt about who leads a majority party or when no party commands a majority, the head of state can decide who should be prime minister designate. In Canada, this power ensures that Canadians always have a prime minister, even if it is used to deny a request to dissolve Parliament and call an election. This situation occurred in 1926, when Canada's governor general, Lord Byng, refused to grant Prime Minister Mackenzie King a dissolution of Parliament. Instead, he called upon the Leader of the Opposition, Arthur Meighen, to form a new government, because Meighen's Conservatives had enough support from former King supporters to permit him to appoint a Cabinet.

FACTFILE   Andrew Bonar Law is the only Canadian to have served as the leader of another country, becoming a Conservative Prime Minister of Great Britain in October 1922.

In political systems where the ceremonial and political executive are the same person, as in the United States, there is always the risk that the president will use symbolic authority to enhance political power or that involvement in politics will hamper the unifying and ceremonial functions of the executive. In the United States, this dual role of the president in the affairs of state and government has given the presidency almost continuous media exposure and thus pre-eminent power among competing political institutions.[5] However, this power can be checked and/or balanced by Congress by means of its abilities to override the president on matters of legislation and to scrutinize the initiatives of the president in matters of foreign policy and judicial appointments.

Providing Leadership

The executive has evolved to become the locus of leadership in all modern political systems. It is where political power gravitates, concentrates, and disseminates through the various levels of government. The leadership qualities of those entrusted with the destiny of a state can activate every factor of power and extract inordinate advantages from limited resources. There is no question that a society's success or failure, indeed its very survival, depends in large part on the quality and competence of the executive leadership it is able to attract.

In fact, the ability of a single highly placed decision maker to mobilize other human resources is itself a factor of power. No political leader can do the job alone. Thousands of other people must be included in the process of leadership if the resources of a state are to be used to maximum capacity. The role of the political executive in recruiting other human talent is therefore paramount. Presidents and prime ministers have extensive appointive powers, not just to fill a cabinet, politburo, or judiciary, but also to place key personnel in the bureaucratic machinery of the state.

In times of peace or war, the political executive must effectively lead the people and the institutions that make up a state. Executives in states that possess nuclear weapons hold the fate of all of humankind in their hands: they have the final responsibility for using weapons of global destruction. Ultimately, their decisions reach far beyond their national constituencies.

Even in the realm of domestic economic problems, political leadership has global implications. Executives who do not manage their economies well threaten the stability of the international economy.

Making Policy

Executives are the nerve centres of modern government decision making. Ever since the beginning of organized government, making and enforcing binding rules has been the preserve of the executive branch of government. For centuries, executive political structures functioned without legislatures for making laws.[6]

Not surprisingly, the modern executive is the most important structure of policy making in all governments around the world. Public policy may be defined in a variety of ways, but it is generally the result of whatever executives choose to do or not to do with the resources available to them. Financing AIDS research, reducing or raising taxes, increasing defence spending, or launching a bill to establish a centre on substance abuse are all examples of public policies. Nowadays, the executive initiates new policies and programs and, depending on the division of powers between the executive and the legislature, has a substantial role in their adoption. Under any system—democratic or non-democratic—the executive oversees the implementation of its policies with the assistance of an army of professional administrators.

Often it is only the political executive that can adequately communicate with the general public on questions of policy. By means of press conferences, statements, and speeches in parliament, and frequent exposure on radio and television, the political executive has many opportunities to communicate important information to the public about domestic and foreign policy issues.

Supervising the Bureaucrats

Every executive is responsible for implementing legislative decisions and enforcing court orders. To fulfill this role, political leaders must supervise the bureaucratic machinery at the national level. In many states, the national bureaucracy is an immense, complicated organization. In the US political system, the national bureaucracy is a multi-layered system of organizations, crisscrossed by the executive and legislative branches of government. The presidency of the United States has its own administration, separate from Congress, which itself controls a vast bureaucratic machine. In Canada, the federal bureaucracy comes under the supervision of the Cabinet, which manages the various departments of government, boards,

Perspectives   The Symbolic Role of the Prime Minister

No one in Canada—including public officials—is able to command as much public attention as the prime minister. He or she monopolizes the media. This level of visibility reflects the fact that the prime minister is both the head of government and the symbolic leader of the country.

The symbolic nature of the office can cause the Canadian public to turn rapidly on the prime minister when events do not turn out the way they think they should. While in power, most prime ministers fail to live up to the expectations elections produce in the minds of the electorate. Whether they make their decisions on the economy or about a war in a distant land they will alienate support, somewhere, among certain groups.

The prime minister so dominates public perceptions at the federal level that he or she can do little to avoid the critical scrutiny of the media and the informed public. Because of the symbolic image of the prime minister, Canadians have come to expect much more from this person. Higher public expectations induce prime ministers to make more promises than they can keep, and to assume more power than is intended by the parliamentary system that keeps them accountable.

What Canadians expect from their prime minister is often paradoxical: They want a prime minister to be both tough and gentle—to stand up to foreign challenges by other leaders but to be gentle enough to show concern for the less-fortunate in Canada and around the world. They want a prime minister to have strong convictions on issues but to be flexible enough to make compromises for the public good. They expect the prime minister to both lead and listen—to initiate new ideas and new ways of doing government and politics, and to also pay attention to the opinions of ordinary Canadians.

Canadians also want the prime minister to be able to inspire the country with high ideals and personal example. They expect the prime minister to be above politics but to be political enough to convince parliamentary colleagues that his or her vision of the country is correct and worthy of support.

Canadians expect the prime minister to be "one of us," yet extraordinary enough to be distinctive among world leaders. They want a prime minister to project confidence in the presence of other prime ministers and presidents of the most powerful governments of the world.

commissions, and Crown corporations. This administration of government is a *fusion* of executive and legislative functions, unlike the *separate* administrations operating in the United States.

FACTFILE   Prime Minister Alexander Mackenzie created the Office of the Auditor General in 1878, to allow for greater supervision of public accounts managed by Canadian politicians and bureaucrats.

In the final analysis, the role of the executive and its administrative bureaucracy is to apply laws, make sure that the programs of government are put into action, and enforce statutes. Of course, the executive also initiates programs, as when the minister of finance announces a tax reform or when the prime minister and the minister of foreign affairs embark on new foreign-policy directions for Canada.

Diplomatic and Military Functions

Diplomacy and defence have remained primary responsibilities of the executive branch of government throughout history. Both diplomatic and military matters have always been intrinsically tied to the security of the state, thus requiring the decisiveness and secrecy of executive decision making.

Diplomats are appointed representatives of the head of state and are, by custom and convention, personifications of the sovereign authority of the executive wherever they are accredited. All diplomats take their directives from, and are responsible to, the political executive. The principal executive powers in the area of diplomacy are:

- sending and receiving diplomats;

- recognizing new governments and establishing or withdrawing diplomatic relations;

- determining and implementing foreign policy; and

- negotiating treaties and agreements through normal diplomatic channels and at the summit level.

In fact, in most states, tradition has established the head of government as the sovereign power in foreign affairs, making this person the chief diplomat. In Canada, depending on the importance of a particular foreign-policy matter, either the prime minister or the minister of state for foreign affairs and international trade fulfills such a role.

In all states where there is a military, the control of the armed forces is an exclusive function of the executive. In some states, the military accepts a distinctly subordinate position to the civilian chief executive, whether president, prime minister, party chairman, or monarch. In other states, there is virtually no distinction between the highest-ranking members of the military and the executive branch of government. On matters of internal security or foreign involvements, the executive can summon the legitimate physical force of the military to protect the interests of the state.

The Canadian Forces are under civilian control. At the top of the organizational scheme of the Canadian Forces is the minister of defence, who is chairperson of the Defence Council, which meets once a week with its mixed staff of civilian and military advisers. The minister must answer to Parliament for everything involved in the operation of Canada's defence and peacekeeping forces. In the United States, the president acts as Commander-in-Chief of the US Armed Forces. As witnessed after the 9/11 attacks on the United States, the president has extensive military powers for preserving internal order and defending the country against external aggression. To these ends, the president may decree partial or total mobilization of the armed forces to cope with a serious internal or external threat.

Judicial Functions

In the judicial realm, many political executives have assumed or have had extensive authority conferred on them. Usually in accordance with the constitution, the executive is required to oversee the general administration of justice and to guarantee its impartiality and fairness to all citizens. That is why one of the most important judicial functions of the executive is the power to appoint judges. The chief executive is charged with enforcing the law by ensuring that judicial decisions are carried out. Executives are responsible for the operation of the courts and must make sure that judges comport themselves with dignity in their official conduct within their official national responsibilities.

Among the important judicial powers, an executive is usually authorized to grant **pardons** and **reprieves**, both as a means of preventing possible judicial malpractice and in the spirit of justice and mercy. Another executive judicial power is the granting of **amnesty**—a blanket pardon extended to large groups, usually political offenders and conscientious objectors. Less than 24 hours after taking the oath of office, President Jimmy Carter granted an amnesty to the US military deserters of the Vietnam War, nearly 50 000 of whom had come to seek refuge in Canada.

In some states, a blanket executive amnesty for illegal immigrants has been a useful tool. It allows governments to grant a large number of people a swift change of status, thus avoiding costly and lengthy proceedings, and addresses the problem of illegal entrants filtering into the economy. Since World War II, Canada has offered nine partial immigration amnesties, allowing more than 160 000 people, who would not have qualified as refugees, to in effect jump to the head of the immigration lines.

CLASSIFYING EXECUTIVES

We will focus on the classifications of the executive branch as the most salient aspect of modern government. Executives in the principal modern states may be classified under these types, corresponding to the governmental systems discussed in the last chapter: parliamentary and presidential executives as they appear in democratic, authoritarian, and totalitarian systems of government. Within these classifications, the methods of selection, tenure in office, and public accountability of executives vary enormously.

Crosscurrents   Are US Presidents More Powerful Than Canadian Prime Ministers?

North America provides political science students with a laboratory for comparing the power exercised by political executives.

Throughout the years, US presidents and Canadian prime ministers have stated publicly that they wished they had the powers exercised by each other as executives in government.

Is the president of the United States more powerful than the prime minister of Canada? Which political executive has access to more levers of power?

In some ways, each has powers and advantages the other does not. The US president has constitutional legitimacy, and is elected in a national election for a fixed term to a national office. The Canadian prime minister is not mentioned in the constitution and is elected, as are other members of parliament, to represent a federal constituency. The prime minister holds such a title not because all Canadians elect him or her in a separate election campaign, but because he or she leads a political party capable of forming a government.

Presidents are difficult to remove from office. Impeachment proceedings require the president to have committed "high crimes and misdemeanours." A prime minister may be charged for any crime committed and may see his or her government defeated by a vote of non-confidence. But the prime minister can survive this type of political challenge, whereas a president's executive career is terminated by a successful impeachment.

The principle of *separation of powers* requires a president to work with, and sometimes against, the Congress and the US Supreme Court. A president's agenda may not be effectively adopted by a Congress. Therefore, the president can sit in office as a "lame duck" because of the powerful checks and balances built into the American legislative system of government.

In contrast, the *fusion of powers* principle used in Canada enables a prime minister to introduce a bill in the House of Commons and to simultaneously have all of his or her party supporters vote favourably on the legislation until it becomes law. The prime minister's legislative agenda is effectively guaranteed because the Cabinet can usually attract a majority of members' support in Parliament. It is important to note that the majority support may not always come entirely from their party, but from members of opposition parties who do not want the government to fall. Prime ministers normally carry the confidence of the legislature and use it to enhance their decision-making powers.

Fixed terms restrict the power of a president because his or her tenure as an executive leader is firmly limited. Usually, a president has two years of a four-year term to govern and the next two years to campaign for re-election. Prime ministers are not limited by the number of terms of Parliaments they can direct.

The enormous wealth of the United States provides a president with economic abilities not readily available to a Canadian prime minister. This difference is reflected in both the foreign and domestic policy choices available to each leader. The president appoints thousands of people in the executive branch and judiciary, many more people than the prime minister appoints. Presidents have larger staffs than prime ministers, providing a significant information-gathering resource. The president can appoint to Cabinet anyone in America who isn't elected, while the Canadian prime minister must choose his or her Cabinet from the pool of elected people in Parliament. The ability of the president to find the best-qualified person for a cabinet post is therefore much greater than that of a prime minister.

If Canada enjoyed the superabundant resources present in the American economy, the prime minister would be the most powerful executive in the world.

FACTFILE US presidents have asserted that their constitutional power to execute the laws, command the armed forces, and determine foreign policy gives them the authority to make agreements with other nations and heads of state without obtaining approval of the US Senate.

THE PARLIAMENTARY EXECUTIVE

The parliamentary executive is the most widely adopted form of democratic leadership. It is used by most of the world's political democracies: Australia, Austria, Belgium, Canada, Denmark, Finland, Germany, Iceland, India, Ireland, Israel, Italy, Japan, Luxembourg, the Netherlands, New Zealand, Norway, Sweden, and the United Kingdom.

In these states, the executive is divided into two parts: a head of state and a head of government. The main political function of the head of state is to appoint the head of government, usually the party leader who wins a national election. The powers of the head of state are essentially formal, although many governments entrust this person with the authority to protect and defend the political system.

Focus On

The Queen: Is the Role of the Monarchy Eroding?

Constitutionally, Elizabeth II is the Queen of Canada, our sovereign and head of state. Yet the air of crisis surrounding the House of Windsor in Great Britain—the break-up of three royal marriages, the constant exposure of the Royal Family in the tabloid press, and the renewed call for a republic—may have eroded the legitimacy of the monarchy in its position of head of state in the Commonwealth. In recent years, in matters concerning the public relations of the Royal Firm, as her father George VI liked to call it, the Queen stands in sharp relief from her children.

When King George VI arrived in Canada in 1939 on the first royal tour in Canadian history, enraptured crowds greeted him at every stop. But his daughter, Queen Elizabeth II, has rarely been received so enthusiastically. She has been openly snubbed by Quebec nationalists and embarrassed by high-profile political remarks supporting the adoption of a republic in Canada. The Queen is regarded by many Canadians as a foreign monarch whose family troubles make for interesting gossip but little else. Though many still feel great affection and admiration for the monarch, she is no longer perceived as part of us.

Queen Elizabeth has set foot on Canadian soil 30 times and her husband, Prince Philip, an even more frequent visitor, has been to Canada more than 60 times since 1952. Royal tours, such as the Queen's Golden Jubilee in 2002, are more common in Canada, in part because the Queen has fewer places to visit as head of state than in the past. At the start of her reign, the Queen was sovereign of 50 states, but today that number has dwindled to only 14, many of them small islands such as Barbados.

There are other, more subtle signs of the erosion of the Queen's traditional role in Canada. Since 1978, "letters of credence," by which foreign envoys serving in Canada introduce themselves to the Canadian head of state, give greater prominence to the governor general and less to the Queen. All Canadian ambassadors and high commissioners bring letters of credence signed by the governor general to their host states.

But Canadian historian John Saywell believes that the Queen's role in Canada should not be carelessly discounted. For Saywell, Canadians have so few distinguishing qualities that they should keep the ones they have, even if they are largely mythical and traditional. And in Canada, the Royals—however diminished by the media—still have greater drawing power than any hometown head of state.

FACTFILE Although the prime minister is prominent in Canada's national governing system, the office is not defined in federal statutes or constitutional documents.

The head of government is the more important politically. Whether called the prime minister, premier, or chancellor, he or she is the leader of the majority party in the Parliament or a person able to form a coalition that will sustain the *confidence of the House*. The political executive chooses the Cabinet, which is a collective body politically responsible to Parliament. Theoretically, Parliament is supreme over the executive. But no matter what constitutional documents may say about their fusion of powers or legislative supremacy, the executive is *de facto* the essence of government and the embodiment of authority. The legislature may have critical functions, but its position is always defined by its relation to the executive.

THE EXECUTIVE IN CANADA

The Constitution Act, 1867 (section 9), affirms that executive authority is vested in the Queen and exercised by her appointed representatives, the governor general and the lieutenant governors. In 1947, the legitimizing authority of the Queen was delegated to the governor general, but it was not effective until 1977. However, in practice the governor general usually plays only a passive executive role by following the advice of the prime minister and the Cabinet. In actual fact, the governor general is submitting to the will of the Canadian electorate when he or she gives one party a majority of seats in the House of Commons.

Governor General

Under the Canadian Constitution, the governor general has the right to be consulted, to advise, and even to warn the political executive if they abuse their powers. Considerable differences of opinion may be found concerning the advantages of the Crown as a formal appendage to executive government in Canada. But a brief summary of the duties of the governor general indicates the significance of the office as both a formal and effective part of Parliament. The governor general:

- summons, **prorogues**, and **dissolves** Parliament;
- appoints the prime minister and the Cabinet and swears them into office;
- signs all bills, conferring **royal assent** before they become law;
- must be advised of and sign all **orders in council** issued by the Cabinet;

- signs letters of credence of Canadian ambassadors and accepts similar credentials of ambassadors and high commissioners appointed to Canada.

As the personification of the Crown, the governor general is above all political affiliations and is in a position to represent and speak for Canada at home and abroad.

Notwithstanding the legal supremacy of the formal executive over the political executive in Canada's Constitution, the office of governor general has essentially become symbolic and ceremonial by custom and convention. Although the monarch may do so from time to time, the governor general usually delivers the **Speech from the Throne** at the opening of each session of Parliament. As the representative of the head of state, the governor general accepts the credentials of diplomats, entertains other heads of state and political executives, bestows honours and awards on Canadians, and generally embodies the majesty of the Canadian state. Hence, this person is a symbol of the unity and continuity of Canadians.

FACTFILE   John Buchan, Canada's fifteenth governor general, was also a famous author, having published over 70 books, including a commercially successful thriller, *The Thirty-Nine Steps* (1915).

The **Letters Patent** of 1947 provide for the replacement of the governor general should this person die, become incapacitated, or be absent from the country for a period of more than one month. The replacement is the Chief Justice of the Supreme Court of Canada and, if that post is vacant, it is the senior *puisne* (lower rank) justice who is appointed as the Administrator of Canada and who assumes all of the formal executive powers and serves until the governor general can return to the office.

While the position of governor general is the oldest continuous institution in Canada, reflecting Canada's evolution from colony to independent nation-state, Canadians have been appointed to the office only since 1952. Up to the present, of the 27 governors general, only 10 have been Canadians. History has shown that the importance of the office depends a lot on the personal dynamism and esteem of the incumbent.

The office of governor general has never had the full support of Canadians.[7] One reason for this is a lack of public awareness of the significance and role of the **Crown** as a functional institution in the Canadian political system. One poll conducted by Data Laboratories Research Consultants found that 42.5 percent of Canadians identified the prime minister as head of state.[8] Some 14.3 percent named the governor general as head of state, and 36.7 percent recognized the

Focus On Canada's Governor General

The Right Honourable Michaëlle Jean was installed as Canada's 27th Governor General in September 2005. Born in Port au Prince, Haiti, she was forced to leave her country with her family in 1968 to seek refuge in Canada.

In Montreal, she earned a Bachelor of Arts in Italian and Hispanic languages and literature and pursued a Master of Arts degree at the Université de Montreal. From 1984 to 1986 she taught in the university's Faculty of Italian Studies. During the 1980s she also studied linguistics and literature at the University of Perugia, the University of Florence, and the Catholic University of Milan. Her studies developed her fluency in five languages: Creole, English, French, Italian, and Spanish.

In Quebec, Michaëlle Jean worked with shelters and transition houses for abused women. Her work experience also includes aid organizations for immigrant women, Employment and Immigration Canada, and the Conseil des Communautés culturelles du Quebec.

For 18 years Michaëlle Jean was employed as a journalist and anchor of news programs. She

worked as a news and public affairs reporter for Radio-Canada, contributing to programs such as *Actuel*, *Montreal ce soir*, *Virages* and *Le Point*. She also contributed to the *Passionate Eye* and *Rough Cuts* on the CBC's English network.

By 2001, Michaëlle Jean was anchoring the news broadcast *Le Téléjournal*. In 2003, she became the anchor of *Le Téléjournal*'s daily edition, *Le Midi*. The year before she was installed as Governor General, Michaëlle Jean hosted her own show, *Michaëlle*, broadcast on both French-language public television networks.

Her first major challenge came at the end of 2008 when Prime Minister Stephen Harper asked her to prorogue Parliament—temporarily terminate its activities—to give him time to prepare a budget and mount a counter-offensive to the Liberal-NDP Coalition. Using prorogation to avoid a confidence vote was unprecedented. She could have denied it, provided a qualified prorogation and placed limits on the government, or provided an unqualified prorogation to Stephen Harper. She chose to grant his request without qualification.

Queen as head of state. Another reason is the reluctance of many French-speaking people in Quebec and other parts of Canada to identify with the symbol of the British Crown.

Queen's Privy Council

Another feature of Canada's formal executive is the Queen's Privy Council (section 11, *Constitution Act, 1867*). Originally a private advisory body to royalty and privy to secrets of the Crown, the Privy Council evolved to become the legal precursor of the modern-day Cabinet.

The Cabinet is not mentioned in the Constitution and thus has no legal existence whatsoever apart from the fact that it forms a committee of the Privy Council. In order to transfer constitutional legality from the formal executive to the political executive in Canada, members of the Cabinet are sworn into office as members of the Privy Council. Accordingly, Cabinet decisions are issued as "orders in council." The Privy Council has survived as the formal machinery through which the prerogative powers of the sovereign are exercised.

The Privy Council is made up of all present and former Cabinet members, regardless of party affiliation, and other persons appointed by the governor general on the recommendation of the prime minister. People appointed to the Queen's Privy Council in Canada serve for life. Members include people of distinction such as the Duke of Edinburgh, the Prince of Wales, and even a British prime minister. Hence, we find that currently there are more than 100 members of the Privy Council, yet the Cabinet can range in size from 20 to 40 people. By constitutional custom, the Privy Council may not advise the government of the day. The full Privy Council meets rarely, usually to honour a visit by the Queen or other members of the Royal Family in the Privy Council Chamber in the East Block of the Parliamentary Buildings.

CANADA'S POLITICAL EXECUTIVE

The political executive in Canada consists of both parliamentary and bureaucratic components. Within the framework of Parliament, the executive is the prime minister and the Cabinet who are elected to govern the country, and are responsible and accountable to Parliament and the Canadian public. They are assisted by the Prime Minister's Office (PMO) and the Privy Council Office (PCO), which serve both to advise and administer the affairs of government at the highest levels.

The Prime Minister

The focus of leadership and political power in Canada culminates in the prime minister and the Cabinet. The prime minister is uniquely powerful because of his or her **prerogative** to call an election, to gain public visibility, to instruct the formal executive, to lead a political party, to form a government, and to build a federal consensus among the premiers.[9]

The authority to advise the dissolution of the House of Commons at any time is an important strategic power enjoyed by the prime minister. The political careers of all members of parliament are challenged by an election. Consequently, the timing of an election is crucial. Usually, the prime minister will go to the polls when the government party enjoys a safe margin of popularity over the opposition parties. Sometimes what appears to be a smart decision to call an election turns against the prime minister, and members of the prime minister's party bear the brunt of bad judgement.

Such was the fate of the Liberals in Canada, for example, when John Turner decided to call a snap election in 1984 and earned the dubious distinction of serving the second-shortest term in office as prime minister after Sir Charles Tupper, who governed for only 69 days in 1896. At other times, a prime minister has very little option concerning when to call the election, either because the government has been defeated or because the five-year limit on Parliament has been reached. But Stephen Harper's fixed election law reduced that limit by one year. In spite of his own law, Prime Minister Harper called for an election before the fixed election dated of October 19, 2009. He mistakenly believed he could attain a majority government by having an election a year before it would have occurred under his fixed-election date. But perhaps the greatest disappointment for calling an election went to Conservative Prime Minister Kim Campbell when she called the election that led to the dramatic defeat of her government in October of 1993 as the five-year Parliament was ending.

Another dimension of executive power flows from the fact that the prime minister tends to dominate public perceptions of national politics. In Canada, everything about a prime minister seems to be a source of fascination to the mass media—what the PM has for breakfast and dinner, how the PM spends leisure time, if married what the spouse does, the PM's tastes in decorating 24 Sussex Drive, what pets the PM keeps. This extremely high level of visibility can be an important and powerful political resource. But it also means that the prime minister is held accountable when things go wrong, regardless of any actual responsibility for them.

Usually, however, the prestige of the office can be used by the prime minister in a highly personalized way to gain political advantage. Standing at the centre of Canadian politics, the prime minister can steal the show from most political opponents by capturing the lion's share of news and other media coverage.

One of the most distinguishing features of prime ministerial power is the unique relationship this person has with the formal executive. The prime minister is the sole link between the formal and political executives. Only the prime minister can advise and instruct the governor general to prorogue and dissolve Parliament. It is the prime minister who formally recommends those who are appointed to the Privy Council and the Senate. It is also the prime minister who connects the Cabinet and, indeed, Parliament, with the governor general.

FACTFILE Two Canadian prime ministers, John Abbott (1891–1892) and Mackenzie Bowell (1894–1896), led the country from the Senate, although it is now accepted that the prime minister must have, or quickly obtain, a seat in the House of Commons.

The power of the prime minister is also enhanced by the fact of leading a political party, usually one with a majority of seats in the House of Commons. Because the prime minister is seen by the governing party as the architect of electoral victory, i.e., the person who won the reins of political power in Canada for the party, the PM is usually in an impregnable position within the party. As a rule, the rank and file are highly supportive of a successful leader.

The party caucus can be a much more critical body because it consists of some of the prime minister's rivals for office. But the prime minister, by virtue of having powers to appoint party faithful to rewarding positions in the public and diplomatic service, as well as to the bench, is able to command the loyalty of the caucus. In addition to the Cabinet, the heads of Crown corporations, deputy ministers, and other key mandarins in the public service are among more than 4000 Canadians appointed under the authority of the prime minister. The people surrounding the prime minister are among the most influential on Parliament Hill, and their ranks always include friends and advisers who helped during the election campaign.

Party discipline places the prime minister at the apex of the apparatus of government. As government leader, the prime minister has control over the political futures of the party's elected members. The prime minister can fire recalcitrant members who are serving as parliamentary secretaries or refuse to assign them to committees. Others who oppose the prime minister or violate the norms and expectations of the party face the possibility that their nomination papers will not be signed in the next federal election.

The possibility of transforming **backbenchers** into ministers and vice versa is a continuing asset of the prime minister in the process of encouraging undisputed party loyalty and support. In addition, the Senate has long been treated by the prime minister as a place to put political workhorses out to pasture. The great majority of Canadian senators have their posts because—and only because—of prior loyalty to the prime minister.

Cabinet Making

We have yet to account in full measure for the conventional prerogatives of the prime minister. Nothing demonstrates the strength in the office of the chief political executive so forcefully as the power to form a government by appointing a Cabinet. As an organization in its own right, the Cabinet is the executive council of the Canadian government, the key decision-making forum for initiating laws and policies, raising and spending public monies, and a source of advice to a prime minister pondering major decisions.

The prime minister chooses who will enter the Cabinet, how large a body it will be, and the extent to which individual cabinet ministers exert influence on the direction of public policy in Canada. It has been said that the prime minister is the first among equals (*primus inter pares*) in relations with his Cabinet colleagues. But no Canadian Cabinet has ever operated as a body of individuals equal in power.

Many factors affect the prime minister in determining the size and composition of the Cabinet. One is the mood—of the country and in the PM's party—about whether the government,

as currently constituted, is too big or too small. Since John A. Macdonald's first 14-member Cabinet in 1867, Canada has evolved one of the largest cabinets among the democratic states of the world.

Since the 1970s, the wholesale growth of government responsibilities prompted the enlargement of Canadian cabinets. Trudeau's largest Cabinet had 37 ministers, 9 more than the largest convened under Lester Pearson. Under John Turner the size of the Cabinet shrank to 29, the same number of ministers as in the short-lived Joe Clark government in 1979. But the largest Cabinet in Canadian history was assembled by Brian Mulroney in 1984; it totalled 40 people, including the prime minister, selected from 210 Tory MPs. Mulroney's successor, Kim Campbell, reduced the size of her Cabinet to 25 ministers. Jean Chrétien formed his first Cabinet of 23 ministers following the federal election of October 1993. But Chrétien's Cabinet grew to 38 after his 1997 election and remained that size after 2000. Paul Martin's first Cabinet in 2004 had 39 ministers. His minority government in 2004 also had 39 ministers. Martin's second Cabinet had 30 full ministers. In January 2006, Stephen Harper's first minority government Cabinet had only 25 ministers, but his second minority government Cabinet was much larger at 38 members. Compared with other parliamentary democracies, Canada's cabinet is the largest.

Another factor of major importance for the prime minister when forming the Cabinet is the principle of *representation*. Today, the general political parameters a prime minister must follow in striking a Cabinet roster cut across economic, geographic, gender, linguistic, political, and social criteria. In some cases, the choices for representation with major portfolios are well signalled. But there is always the difficulty of forming a truly national government. This means that, to the extent it is possible, every province or region should be allocated at least one Cabinet minister. When this is not possible because representatives have not been elected to the governing party's caucus from every province, the prime minister sometimes appoints senators to the Cabinet to represent these provinces, or gives a minister from a neighbouring province special ministerial assignments in a province that has no government representation.

To complicate the job of making a representative government along provincial and regional lines, every effort must be made by the prime minister to include people who represent the business community, Aboriginals, women, Catholics, Protestants, Jews, and those of French and other non-English origins. John A. Macdonald once said, "Like any cabinet maker, I do the best I can with the lumber you furnish me."

FACTFILE   Canada's first woman federal Cabinet minister was Ellen Louks Fairclough, who entered the Cabinet on June 21, 1957, appointed as Secretary of State and later as Minister of Citizenship and Immigration by John Diefenbaker.

The Cabinet must be representative of women, who make up over 50 percent of Canada's population. In 1984, Mulroney named a record six women to his first Cabinet from the 28 elected nationwide, doubling the previous record of three. However, these six women comprised only 15 per cent of the Cabinet. Prior to the appointment of the six women ministers by Mulroney, only eight women had ever sat around a Canadian Cabinet table. Women were given some tough portfolios—External Relations, Energy, Mines and Resources, and the Environment—a signal that when women are elected with the right credentials, they do not have to sit as backbenchers. In 1989, Mulroney's first Cabinet shuffle again included six women, selected from 39 elected to a larger House of Commons. His successor, Kim Campbell, including herself, had five women in the Cabinet. Jean Chrétien appointed four women to his first Cabinet in 1993 and eight women were included in the federal Cabinet by 2000. Paul Martin brought that number up to 11

in his first Cabinet as Canada's twenty-first prime minister, but appointed only 9 women out of 33 female MPs in his minority government of 2004. Stephen Harper appointed 7 women to his first Conservative minority government in 2006. In 2008, his Cabinet had 11 women members chosen from among 23 women MPs.

There is also an obvious political or partisan dimension to Cabinet making. The prime minister may place heavy emphasis on loyalty in each selection, drawing on personal memory of early campaign and convention supporters. Leadership candidates at party conventions are often able to win Cabinet appointments because of the politics at the party convention where their supporters and delegates may have been helpful to the victory of the prime minister.

Having appointed the ministers to the Cabinet, as well as to its standing committees, the PM retains a large amount of authority and power over their political destinies. By means of the Cabinet shuffle, the PM can promote the most loyal and promising ministers or demote those whose performance is less than satisfactory. Sometimes a prime minister will appoint an *interim Cabinet* to finish old parliamentary business before making more permanent appointments. The principle of *cabinet solidarity* ensures that collectively the Cabinet is one with the prime minister and that recalcitrant ministers will either acquiesce to the corporate will of the government or resign.

Traditionally, ministers appointed to the Cabinet were assigned **portfolios** to head major government departments. In fact, only the prime minister and the government leader in the Senate were appointed without portfolios and did not and still do not carry any departmental responsibilities. Today, the only other administrative responsibility of the prime minister is the Privy Council Office.

The *Ministries and Ministers of State Act, 1970* (revised, 1985), places the present designation of cabinet ministers into five categories.[10] The first are the ministers of regular government departments, such as the minister of finance. The second designation is for ministers who are assigned parliamentary responsibilities without heading a department or ministry, such as House Leader. The third category may include ministers of state who are assigned junior portfolios, such as a junior minister of finance. The fourth category is for ministers of state appointed to assist regular ministers, such as the minister of state for science and technology. The fifth category consists of ministers without a portfolio appointed as undesignated ministers of state who are assigned to assist ministers with a portfolio.

Even among the various ministries, a pecking order exists beneath the prime minister. Historically, the departments of Finance, Justice, and Foreign Affairs wield much more influence in the inner circles of Cabinet than do Communications or Fisheries and Oceans.

The prime minister chairs the plenary Cabinet. This powerful co-ordinating position keeps the prime minister as the political nerve centre of government. He or she can expand or reduce the size and number of Cabinet committees.

The Prime Minister's Office (PMO)

In Ottawa, the initials PMO are a synonym for power.[11] They refer to the Prime Minister's Office, the partisan political staff that advises, schedules, briefs, represents, and runs errands for the Prime Minister of Canada. Located in the Langevin Block near the Parliament Buildings, this executive support agency protects and promotes the personal and professional interests of the prime minister. The prime minister appoints his or her most loyal and trusted advisers to this executive body. On the personal level, they boost the prime minister's ego, and shield the PM

from enemies and the incursions of the media. Correspondence to the prime minister can reach as much as 300 000 pieces per week. The correspondence unit of the PMO is kept busy receiving, answering, and filing mail. On matters involving the prime minister's professional role, they assist in everything from drafting the Speech from the Throne and other speeches to guiding the prime minister through the maze of political and bureaucratic hurdles confronting executive leadership in Canada. The PMO collaborates with the Privy Council Office to develop a national policy framework, including a public relations strategy for the government. The PMO is therefore a practical policy think-tank charged with an advisory capacity on the political fortunes of the prime minister and his or her Cabinet. On a daily basis, the PMO answers the prime minister's mail, schedules his or her appointments and invitations, and keeps a close watch over the patterns of popularity and unpopularity that affect the political executive.

The Privy Council Office (PCO)

One executive body formally attached to the Privy Council is the Privy Council Office (PCO).[12] The role of the PCO has evolved from that of a body responsible for dealing with the occasional formalities of the Privy Council to a major policy-advising **central agency** of the federal government. It is a department of government that provides public service support to the prime minister and the Cabinet. Under the direction of the Clerk of the Privy Council and Secretary to the Cabinet, the PCO helps the Cabinet facilitate the smooth and effective operation of the Government of Canada.

> FACTFILE   There are five central agencies in Canada's federal public administration: the PMO, the PCO, the Department of Finance, the Treasury Board, and the Federal–Provincial Relations Office.

The Privy Council Office is staffed by career public servants. These are people who are recruited from other government departments and serve in the PCO for a limited period, after which they leave for positions in other departments. This policy of rotating personnel brings new expertise into the PCO on a regular basis and enables its staff to effectively advise the prime minister, the plenary Cabinet, and its subcommittees on the activities of the government and matters of national policy.

As the Cabinet secretariat, the PCO sets Cabinet agendas, takes minutes at Cabinet meetings, and transmits Cabinet decisions to the bureaucracy: the PCO arranges the meetings, circulates agendas, distributes documents, provides advice to each chairperson on committees, and records Cabinet decisions. It works with departments of government to prepare ministerial proposals for the Cabinet to consider and keeps government departments informed about what the Cabinet has decided. The PCO also ensures that orders in council and other statutory instruments are announced throughout the government.

The Treasury Board

The Treasury Board, like the Cabinet, is formally a committee of the Privy Council, headed by a Cabinet minister who is called the President of the Treasury Board. Until 1966, its original function, under the jurisdiction of the Department of Finance, was as an overseer of the budgetary process of government, to ensure that public funds were being spent only on authorized government projects. Today, as a separate government department and central agency, the Treasury Board keeps track of current and projected expenditures. Its large secretariat operates as a board of management for the government, providing highly influential advice in both financial management and the overall personnel management of the public service.

The financial management of contemporary government priorities would be chaotic were it not for a central monitoring agency like the Treasury Board. The Treasury Board can apply controls on the spending demands of federal departments as each ministry tries to gain a greater share of the government budget.

THE PRESIDENTIAL EXECUTIVE

The modern presidential type of chief executive began with the US Constitution of 1787. In spite of its great success in the United States, it has not been as widely embraced as the parliamentary type of executive. The presidential executive is most commonly found in Latin American states because of their historical links with the American experience. It has also been installed by Liberia and the Philippines, as well as in some of the African states like Burundi, Mali, and Nigeria.

> **FACTFILE**   When Warren Harding, one of America's most indulgent presidents, was in office (1920–1924), attorney Clarence Darrow remarked, "When I was a boy, I was told that anybody could become president. Now I'm beginning to believe it."

While a growing number of states have adopted this type of executive, many of its advantages have not been widely recognized. The presidential executive establishes a solid and stable centre of power in the executive branch, an advantage particularly appropriate to newer states requiring a strong democratic central government. The presidential system provides that the head of state, who is also the head of government, is elected for a definite term of office. The president has the entire country as a constituency and is independent of the legislative branch of government. The president acts as the official ceremonial head and as leader of the government that proposes, directs, and enforces the state's public policies.

The US President

In the United States, the president is indirectly elected by an electoral college for a fixed term of four years. In the electoral college, each state has a number of electoral votes equal to the size of its *congressional delegation*, the number of House representatives and Senators, e.g., California, 55; New York, 31 (Figure 5.1). The state parties select slates of electors, positions they use as a reward for faithful service to the party. In 48 of the 50 states, if a presidential candidate wins a *plurality* of votes (although a majority of popular votes sometimes occurs) in a particular state, he or she also wins all of the electoral votes for that state. Electors vote as

a bloc for the winner, whether the winner gets 30 percent or 99 percent of the popular vote. Only two states, Maine and Nebraska, do not follow this "winner-takes-all" formula.

Of a total of 538 electoral votes, 270 are required to elect a president.[13] The largest states are hotly contested during a presidential election because they yield the greatest number of electoral votes. Thus, a minimum winning coalition of states needed to secure 270 electoral votes and win the presidency could be California, New York, Pennsylvania, Illinois, Texas, Ohio, Michigan, Florida, New Jersey, Massachusetts, and Wisconsin.

In 1984, Ronald Reagan won 525 electoral votes and his opponent, Walter Mondale, won

Figure 5.1   Electoral college: State and district delegations

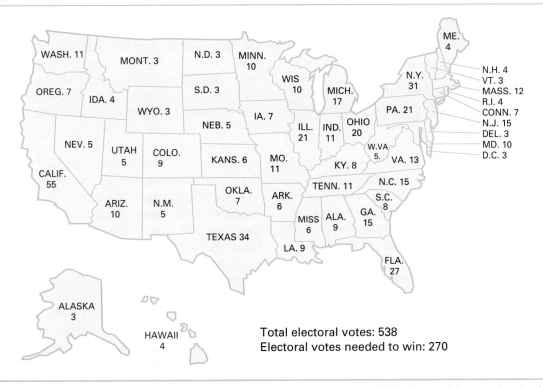

Total electoral votes: 538
Electoral votes needed to win: 270

Source: From Politics in America, *7th Edition, by Thomas R. Dye. Copyright © 2007 by Pearson Education. Reprinted by permission.*

only the District of Columbia and the state of Minnesota, giving him 13 electoral college votes. In the 1988 presidential election, George H.W. Bush Sr. did not match the enormous landslide of his predecessor, but he did take 40 states for 426 electoral votes against Michael Dukakis, who won only 10 states and the District of Columbia for 112 electoral college votes. In 1992, Bill Clinton defeated Bush by winning 370 electoral votes, leaving Bush a total of 168 electoral votes. Ross Perot, who ran as a third presidential candidate, won no electoral votes. In 1996, President Clinton was re-elected, winning 379 electoral votes and outdistancing Bob Dole, who won 159 electoral votes, and Reform Party candidate Ross Perot, who won no electoral votes. In 2000, George W. Bush was declared winner of the electoral college vote for president by the narrowest of margins: 271 to 267 for Al Gore. His electoral college margin was wider in 2004: 286 to 252 for John Kerry. Barack Obama's electoral college victory gave him 365 to 173 for John McCain.

FACTFILE   In the controversial 2000 US election, for the first time in American history, a presidential election was decided by a decision of the Supreme Court of the United States.

According to the twenty-second amendment of the US Constitution, adopted in 1951, "no person shall be elected to the office of President more than twice." The only legal way a president can be removed from office is through the process of impeachment. As in the case of Bill Clinton in 1999, by a simple majority vote the House of Representatives can vote to **impeach** the president (as well as other members of the executive). Once this happens, the Senate convenes as a court, chaired by the chief justice of the Supreme Court, to weigh the evidence for and against the president. It takes a two-thirds majority of the Senate to convict the accused. The only two presidents in US history to stand trial before the Senate were Andrew Johnson in 1868 and Bill Clinton in 1999.

However, the Senate failed to convict either president—Johnson by only one vote, and the vote on Clinton was tied at 50–50, leaving him with a tarnished reputation but still in office.

FACTFILE   In 1974, US President Richard Nixon resigned after the House Judiciary Committee recommended impeachment but before a vote was taken by the full House of Representatives.

To qualify for holding the office, a presidential candidate must be a "**natural born**" citizen, at least thirty-five years of age, and have held residency in the United States for 14 years. If a president is impeached and convicted, dies, resigns, or is incapable of performing duties of the office, the presidency goes to the vice-president, then, in order of succession, to the Speaker of the House of Representatives, the president *pro tempore* of the Senate, and then to Cabinet members.

The US Constitution briefly enumerates the executive authority of the president in general terms: that he or she "shall take care that the laws be faithfully executed" and shall "take an oath to preserve, protect and defend the Constitution." Provision is also made in the Constitution for the president's relations with the other branches of government. From time to time, the president must give Congress a report called the "**State of the Union Address**" and may recommend policies and programs for its consideration. The president is authorized to call special sessions of Congress, and most bills and joint resolutions passed by Congress must be signed by the president. Some exceptions are joint resolutions, which are rarely signed; a president may decide not to sign a bill, and it might well die unless the veto can be overridden by a two-thirds vote in each house.

In the United States, the work of the federal executive is conducted by 15 departments and a host of non-cabinet agencies such as the Central Intelligence Agency (CIA) and the Federal Trade Commission (FTC). Each department is headed by a *secretary*, appointed by the president and confirmed by the Senate. Thus, there is a Secretary of State, of Commerce, of Treasury, and so forth. The president, the vice-president, and the secretaries make up the *cabinet* in American government. From election day in November to Inauguration Day on January 20, a president or president elect has about 11 weeks to select a Cabinet and form the next administration. As in Canada, the term "Cabinet" does not appear in the Constitution, but any comparisons with the Canadian Cabinet, which plays a major leadership role in Canada's political life, would be totally misleading.

FACTFILE   In 1861, Abraham Lincoln, who knew that as president he did not have to take his cabinet's advice, asked them to vote on an issue, and all voted against the president. But he announced the results of the vote as "seven nays and one aye . . . the ayes have it."

Nevertheless, all presidents since George Washington have had one. The American Cabinet is *not* the executive council of government as in Canada. Its meetings are infrequent, brief, and often superficial. Most presidents use Cabinet meetings to inform their secretaries of new directions in the strategies of the executive and to inform one department what other departments are doing. For actual consultation on policy matters, presidents use hand-chosen advisers. Traditionally, only one or two members of the president's Cabinet have a significant advisory function. For the most part, the Cabinet is chosen to satisfy different factions in the president's party; i.e., the Secretary of Labor is usually someone associated with organized labour and the Secretary of Commerce is a prominent business person.

One expert on the American presidency, Richard Neustadt, has written that "a President is many men or one man wearing many hats."[14] There are several major roles that any president must carry out: head of state, head of government, party leader, chief legislator, commander-in-chief, and chief diplomat.

As the *head of state*, the president is the central figure in the elaborate ceremonial life of the country. The president speaks and acts on behalf of all of the people and is the foremost symbol of the political community. It is the president who greets foreign dignitaries in the name of the United States, makes the annual State of the Union Address, opens a national arts center, and proclaims national holidays. In so doing, the president is the personal embodiment of the United States of America.

In sharp contrast with the ceremonial role as head of state, the president is also *head of government*. As chief of the executive branch of government, the president controls a vast portion of the federal bureaucracy. Because of the separation of powers, the president does not have full control of the permanent public service but does have considerable influence over it. In the United States, the federal civil service consists of more than 3 million people.

In addition to appointing the cabinet, the president appoints approximately 8000 people, and through them supervises and directs federal policies in the complicated network of the federal government. These "president's people" link the executive with the other branches of the federal bureaucracy and are crucial appointments for the success of any administration. So important are these appointments to the executive control of government that modern-day presidents establish special personnel-selection teams to search for loyal and qualified individuals. The president guides the operation of government by means of advice from the cabinet, the White House advisers (also known as the domestic council), the executive office of the president, and the office of management and budget. The National Security Council plays a similar role with respect to foreign policy.

The tensions between the ceremonial and political functions of the president are especially evident in the role of *party leader*. As partisan leader, the president leads one political faction of the country against all others, yet as the head of state, the president must represent and unify all factions. Because the president has such vast powers of appointment and is the leader of a successful political party, it is not surprising that top-level policy-making positions will be offered to members of the president's own party. Party patronage is used to reward those who have been loyal to the president, a loyalty expressed in the form of campaign contributions or other influential support that enabled an individual to win the party's presidential nomination, and then the presidency itself.

In addition to job patronage, the party expects its leader to spearhead the raising of campaign funds and to endorse and campaign on behalf of party candidates at the national, state, and local levels. Hence, it is always difficult for the American chief executive to appear above politics as the embodiment of the lofty aspirations of the state, yet at the same time be politically responsible to the party.

Closely associated with the president's role as party leader is that of *chief legislator*—proposing a legislative program and urging Congress to pass it. What is distinctive about the US political system, unlike most parliamentary democratic governments, is that the executive leadership and the legislature do not necessarily work in concert. Often, the policy views and the political interests of these two independent institutions are not identical. Each year, numerous executive agencies come forward with the president's proposals for legislation, both to improve the administration of existing programs and to create new ones. Not all members of the president's party will automatically vote for what is proposed, but the executive program will definitely be a partisan focus for the party's congressional membership.

The president will make use of every available power to influence and gain the support of Congress. All Congresspersons are interested in directing the highly desirable patronage appointments of the president to their own political supporters. They know that the **pork barrel** in Washington will contain lucrative federal projects for their constituents. In addition, Congress does take note of the popularity of the president when considering executive requests, although it often ignores such requests. But by appearing on television, a president can gain the support of millions of Americans in a single speech. And when all else fails, the president can exercise the executive **veto**. Sometimes, this alone is enough to persuade Congress to frame its legislation to the president's liking.

The Military and Diplomatic Power of the President

One constitutional power of the president that has great significance far beyond the national boundaries of the United States is that of *Commander-in-Chief*. Since 1776, presidents of the United States have involved their country in six "undeclared wars," and in 129 instances (including the Persian Gulf in 1988 and 1992, Somalia in 1993, Afghanistan in 2002, and Iraq in 2004), US presidents have ordered the armed forces to take military actions abroad without obtaining prior congressional authorization.

FACTFILE   As president, Washington personally led troops to crush the Whiskey Rebellion in 1794; Abraham Lincoln wrote the orders to his generals in the Civil War; and Lyndon Johnson personally chose bombing targets in Vietnam.

However, the president can only act alone for a limited time when (as commander-in-chief) military action is initiated. In order to continue military actions abroad, the president requires congressional co-operation to engage the armed forces and use public funds. The Vietnam experience demonstrated that once a president commits US troops to combat, Congress is expected to support the executive decision by providing manpower and funds for the continuation of the military operation.

The War Powers Act of 1973 requires that if a president commits armed forces anywhere without a declaration of war, a written report must be submitted to Congress within 48 hours of any such commitment. Under these circumstances, the armed forces must terminate their mission within 60 days after the president reports to Congress unless Congress

1. declares war;

2. authorizes a continuation of the use of armed forces; or

3. cannot convene because of an armed attack against the United States.

Both tradition and constitutional prescription have established the president as the *chief diplomat*. The constitution outlines the foreign policy responsibilities of the president to "make treaties," to "receive ambassadors and other public ministers," and to exercise "the Executive power." But the Constitution requires that treaties need the support of two-thirds of the Senate and that the appointment of diplomats needs the advice and consent of the Senate.

More importantly, the power to declare war is a joint legislative and executive responsibility. The executive power allows a president to enter into an agreement with a foreign executive and to bypass treaty procedures that require Senate approval. Executive agreements have been routinely formulated by presidents since World War II in Europe, Asia, and Latin America.

Unlike the Congress, the president is in "continuous session" and international events happen quickly, requiring an immediate executive response, as in the case of 9/11. The president is always poised to act, aided by intelligence operations and instant contact with a network of embassies and consulates spread throughout the world.

Much of the history of the United States—its highest and lowest points—has been written largely as a result of the political and personal behaviour of its presidents. More than other executives, the president of the United States can alter world history. In the words of William Young, "The President of the United States of America is, without question, the most powerful elected executive in the world."[15]

THE AUTHORITARIAN EXECUTIVE

The formal constitutional framework for most authoritarian executives today fictitiously appears as "democratic," "parliamentary," or "presidential" systems.[16] What the constitutions may prescribe is one thing, but the practice of executive power is sometimes quite another. In all authoritarian states, instead of being constitutionally limited and responsible, the executive so far overshadows the other branches of government that for all practical purposes the president or prime minister *is* the government. "L'état c'est moi," boasted Louis XIV of France; in all authoritarian states, the executive comes close to being a twenty-first-century version of that monarch's boast.

One of the key characteristics of the authoritarian executive is the dominance of the individual person, often a charismatic leader, in the political and government system. Political power is highly *personalized* (in the interests of the leader) rather than *institutionalized* (in the interests of the state), usually despite constitutional guarantees to the contrary. Other centres of power exist beside the ruler, sometimes acting as a check on the extensive powers of the political executive. Such institutions as the church, the military, economic organizations, the bureaucracy, and political parties are often sources of restraint on arbitrary government. However, the power relations among these groups are manipulated or controlled by the

MUGABE

ruler, so that none of them is able to establish an independent position of power or threaten the dominant position of the executive.

FACTFILE Authoritarian dictatorships number about 100 states or about half of the total number of states in the world. They are located mostly in Central and South America, Africa, and parts of Asia.

The most common form of authoritarian executive today is military rule. In this type of executive, a military **junta** (or council) collectively exercises executive powers. Juntas are usually made up of three ranking officers of the army, navy, or air force, who preside over the executive branch of government following a successful coup d'état.

Regardless of whether the executive appears in the civilian or military mode, the powers of the authoritarian president or prime minister are great—far greater than in most democratic states. In many cases, the executive exercises a broad collection of legislative, administrative, and judicial powers. Included among these many powers is the authority to issue decrees, form a Cabinet, make administrative and judicial appointments, declare a state of siege, suspend the constitution, command

the military, control finance and public revenues, grant pardons, and intervene in local government.

One very important power of the authoritarian executive is the authority to issue *decrees*. Decrees are laws issued by the executive rather than passed by the legislature. The decree power gives the executive supraconstitutional legislative authority because decree laws have the same legal standing as congressional laws, and are recognized with the option to bypass the legislature or to neutralize the electoral process.

Often, dictators will change the composition of their cabinets as a housecleaning strategy aimed at restoring public confidence and asserting the legitimacy of the government.

Easily one of the most important powers of the authoritarian executive is the authority to proclaim a *state of siege*, also known as the suspension of constitutional guarantees. This emergency power is used when the state is threatened by a foreign invasion or by serious internal disorder. Military governments declare a state of martial law, which is similar to the state of siege, the main difference being that under the latter the civilian police and regular organs of civilian government continue to function; while under the former, civilian control is replaced by the military. This special emergency power grants extraordinary powers to the president or prime minister and authorizes the executive to take drastic steps that affect all aspects of national life. In recent years, martial law has been declared in Algeria, Myanmar (formerly Burma), Guyana, Haiti, Rwanda, Somalia, and Yugoslavia in order to crush democratic uprisings in each country.

Yet another area in which authoritarian executives enjoy unique powers is internal intervention. This is the coercive action undertaken by the national government in the affairs of subnational units, particularly in federal states, as well as in the financial institutions, the judicial system, and the media. The practice among federal states varies, but intervention can be extensive, such as the replacement of state and provincial governors, legislators, and other officials whom the president deems a challenge to national executive authority and national autonomy.

Authoritarian executives also have very broad powers over the financial institutions of the state. A president or prime minister can authorize a new monetary system, re-organize the structure of financial institutions, and modify the banking system. Often dictators will try to appease foreign bankers and international lending institutions, such as the International Monetary Fund. It is not uncommon in authoritarian states to see the executive interrupt the process of justice, pack the courts with supportive judges, or simply ignore the judicial branch of government. Dictatorship almost invariably plays havoc with judicial independence. And, in almost all cases, authoritarian executives strongly resist the critical scrutiny of a free press. Restrictions on the freedom of the press are usually imposed by decree, ostensibly under the authority of the constitution.

THE TOTALITARIAN EXECUTIVE

The models of the totalitarian executive have been produced historically in fascist and so-called communist states.[17] In today's international system, the fascist model no longer exists and there is a much closer correspondence between dictatorial, or "communist," states and totalitarianism, although these states have been dramatically reduced in numbers since the disintegration of the Soviet Empire.

Still, executive power in those remaining communist states is exercised mainly through party channels. The executive authority of the party, which is the distinguishing trait of communist regimes, initiates and co-ordinates the major decision making and policy directions of the state. The state's bureaucracy is subordinate to the party executive. It is the instrument the political executive uses to enforce and administer party policy through the government ministries.

Communist states are *usually* headed by a collective executive, called a *politburo* or *presidium* as in Cuba. Some are headed by a *council of state*, as in China. These collective bodies are made up of high-ranking state officials headed by a chairman who sometimes also serves as head of state.

Whatever the degree of executive power, the Communist Party in all communist societies controls and co-ordinates government activities; it exercises "sovereign" authority. Thus, the executive organ of the Party dominates the executive structure of government and the policy process. However, the formulation of policy, normally the preserve of the cabinet in Western democratic systems, is really the province of the Party elite in communist states.

In many communist states, it is *only* the Party and *not* the government that issues directives and administrative orders that have the weight of law. Thus the basic executive functions of the top Party leadership is to control a complex and interlocking network of bureaucratic and governmental structures, enabling a small group of people to control society.

There is a tendency in communist political systems to concentrate executive power in the hands of one or a very few dictators. The leader or leaders then often become the embodiment of the state apparatus and the continuing revolution, as has been demonstrated in such executives as Fidel Castro in Cuba, Mao Tse-tung in China, Kim Il-sung in North Korea, Enver Hoxha in Albania, Ho Chi Minh in Vietnam, Tito in Yugoslavia, and Robert Mugabe in Zimbabwe.

One of the important differences between totalitarian and authoritarian dictators is that the totalitarian leaders are less inclined to subvert the aims of the party for personal reasons and ambitions. While the "cult of personality" does surface in communist states, political power still tends to be institutionalized more than it is personalized.

Chapter Summary

The executive branch of government comprises numerous officials, both elected and appointed, organized into numerous agencies that have the powers to make decisions and implement them simultaneously. In many parliamentary systems of government, as in Canada's, the executive is made of a ceremonial head of state and a political head of state. The executive branch of government is the oldest, the most decisive, and the most powerful. Executives enjoy privileged and exclusive access to information and economic resources; they formulate and administer laws; control the bureaucracy; execute their own orders, rules, and regulations; send armies abroad and use force at home; and tax and spend money.

In Canada, the ceremonial executive comprises the Queen and her representative, the governor general. The political executive is the prime minister and the Cabinet. They are assisted by special bureaucracies, the Prime Minister's Office (PMO) and the Privy Council Office (PCO), which advise and administer the affairs of the Cabinet. In the United States, the ceremonial and political executive functions are combined and served by the president.

Under authoritarian regimes, ceremonial and political executives often give the appearance of operating within democratic institutions. But they are dictatorial, frequently using the military to govern internally, controlling the media, and using repressive decision-making measures.

In totalitarian regimes, the Communist Party exercises executive powers, initiating and co-ordinating the major decision-making and policy directions of the state. The government bureaucracy is subordinate to the Communist Party executive.

The executive branch of government possesses the most powerful resources available to government: the control of information, the control of bureaucracy, the perception of rightful authority, and vast economic powers.

Executives play significant roles in government: They are symbolic and ceremonial, lead their governments in the legislature and in the public domain, make public policy, supervise large bureaucracies, influence foreign policy, act as the commander and chief of the military, and perform certain judicial functions.

Executives are normally classified under two general forms: the parliamentary executive, formed by constitutional procedure and by the elective representation of political parties in a parliamentary legislature; and the presidential executive, formed according to constitutional directives and elected directly or indirectly by the national electorate.

Many variations of the parliamentary and presidential executives exist in dictatorial systems. In authoritarian regimes, they appear as formal presidential institutions occupied by civilian or military dictators. In totalitarian regimes, they appear within the confines of politburos or presidia.

Discussion Questions

1. Many argue that the executive branch is the most capable of formulating public policy. To what extent is this true in light of the resources available to the executive? In Canada, the resources of the Cabinet are many, but what are the constraints on executive power? Are there signs that Parliament may be reasserting its powers? What are they?

2. Discuss the advantages and disadvantages of separating the head of state from the head of government and party in the parliamentary system. Under the US presidential system, is it really possible for the same person to carry out partisan duties and represent the public interest for the nation-state as a whole? As head of state, the US president spends a tremendous amount of time at ceremonial functions. Should these duties be assigned to someone else, freeing the president for political work?

3. List, compare, and discuss the functions of the executive branch of government in the United States and Canada. From what you surmise, which state is more democratic? Which executive is potentially more powerful, the Canadian or the American? Why?

4. Discuss why in both authoritarian and totalitarian regimes the executive tends not to be subject to the limitations and checks that confront democratic executives.

5. How do the Prime Minister's Office (PMO), Privy Council Office (PCO), and the Treasury Board enable the Cabinet to govern more effectively?

CHAPTER 6

Understanding the Legislative Process

After reading this chapter, you will be able to:

- distinguish between the legislative and executive branches of government

- explain the various features of legislative assemblies, such as size and tenure

- understand the concepts fusion of powers and separation of powers

- distinguish and explain unicameralism, bicameralism, and tricameralism

- outline and compare the functions of democratic and non-democratic legislatures

- describe the features of Canada's legislative assemblies

- identify and describe the functions of the chief legislative officers of the House of Commons

- discuss the role of committees in the legislative process

- distinguish between the legislative functions of the Canadian Senate and the House of Commons

- recount the process of how a bill becomes law in Canada

- outline the federal legislative process in the United States

- compare how bills are passed into law in Canada and the United States

- describe the functions of legislatures in dictatorships

• • • •

ASSEMBLIES

Compared with the executive branch of government, legislatures are relatively new creations among political institutions. The only legislature to survive to the present without changing its earliest forms is the British Parliament. Dating back to the eleventh century, the English legislative structure has become the prototype of the modern legislature, inspiring many variations on the parliamentary model, even among authoritarian and totalitarian regimes. When William of Normandy conquered England in 1066, he imposed Norman feudal institutions on his new subjects. These included the *Curia Regis*, an assembly of nobles to advise the king, and the *Curia Regis Magnae*, a large assembly of lesser nobility that met three times annually to counsel and present petitions to the king.

FACTFILE   Canada's Parliament has three elements: the Queen, the Senate, and the House of Commons, in that order.

Over time, English kings and queens summoned this Great Council with increased frequency. Made up of knights, burgesses, and members of the clergy, the council met separately from the barons to advise the monarch and approve taxes for projects that affected their constituencies. Eventually, this body of advisers came to be the House of Commons, and the assembly of nobles became the House of Lords. Originally, neither institution was intended to be democratic and autonomous. But by the nineteenth century, the British Parliament came to symbolize modern democracy.

Most modern states have developed a legislative branch of government consisting of bodies of elected or appointed individuals called parliaments, congresses, assemblies, diets, or chambers. A small number of absolute monarchies, such as Oman and Saudi Arabia, do not have a legislative assembly. In all other states, the role and function of the legislature are determined by the type of political system, i.e., whether that system is democratic, authoritarian, or totalitarian. It is significant that regardless of the character of a regime, nearly all modern nation-states find it necessary to maintain some form of representative assembly, either as an effective law-making body or as a symbol of government legitimacy. Even in the most repressive regimes, the legislature contributes to the formal proclamation of the law by lending popular endorsement to the law-making initiatives of the executive.

Focus On   250 Years of Parliamentary Democracy in Nova Scotia

The year 2008 marked the 250th anniversary for Nova Scotia as the birthplace of parliamentary democracy, where the first sitting of a democratically elected legislature took place on October 2, 1758. First situated in a small wooden building at the corner of Argyle and Buckingham streets in Halifax, this first Parliament, called the General Assembly, comprised just 22 members.

It was the first of what would be copied in the other North American colonies: Prince Edward Island, 1773; New Brunswick, 1784; and Upper and Lower Canada (later Quebec and Ontario) in 1791.

When the colonists came to the new world, their general approval of Britain's parliamentary system led them to adopt similar two-house legislative bodies in the individual colonies, both in

Canada and the United States. One house was to be directly elected by the people; the other would be a crown-appointed council that worked under the authority of the colonial government. Today all of Canada's legislative assemblies at the federal, provincial, and territorial levels are Parliaments in the tradition of British parliamentary democracy.

These colonial assemblies were originally established as advisory bodies to the royal governors who were appointed by the monarch. Gradually they assumed more power and authority in each colony. Nova Scotia was the first colony, in what is now Canada, to win representative government from Britain. Settlers here set the stage for future struggles in other parts of British North America. Colonial reformers wanted their legislative assemblies to enjoy the same powers exercised in the House of Commons in Britain.

In the aftermath of the American Revolution in 1776, the British government was concerned about the possibility of unrest in the remaining colonies with growing populations, such as Nova Scotia. This fear was confirmed during the Louis-Joseph Papineau rebellion in Lower Canada in 1837 and the William Lyon MacKenzie rebellion in Upper Canada from 1837 to 1839.

Aware of these and other possibilities that might rise up against Britain, Lord Durham in his famous report recommended that the remaining colonies be granted "responsible government." In Nova Scotia, Joseph Howe would lead the application of this new democratic idea in 1848, making it the first in the British Empire.

"Responsible government" makes the cabinet *responsible* to Parliament. If the cabinet loses the confidence of the House of Commons through a defeat on an important piece of legislation, it loses the right to govern and should stand for an election.

As democracy evolved to form a new Canada in the 1860s, *responsible government* became a fundamental constitutional principle entrenched in our *Constitution Act*. Today, all of our governments in Canada have obligations to their legislatures, which are made up of people elected by us. If government fails to meet these obligations they must resign and defend their seats in an election.

But it should be remembered that while Nova Scotia spearheaded responsible government, it was also the province where anti-confederates led by Joseph Howe set out to repeal the union called Confederation. The anti-confederates won 18 of 19 seats in the House of Commons and virtually all of those in the Nova Scotia Assembly. They even sent Howe to London, demanding repeal of the Union. But the imperial government did not agree and the movement lost its momentum in 1868.

Unlike in the US, which separates the executive and legislative branches, in Canada the executive branch of government was merged with the legislative branch in an accountable relationship that political scientists call the *fusion of power*. By this principle, members of the cabinet must hold seats in Parliament. They are "responsible" to it in the bills they present and the policies they make. If they cannot keep the confidence of elected members, the cabinet must resign or ask the governor general to dissolve Parliament in preparation for an election.

Democracy in Canada has come a long way since these ideas were first planted by Nova Scotians some 250 years ago. Canadians have great respect for our written constitution; we believe in the supremacy of Parliament and of its laws; we allow many groups (parties and interest) to compete for power; we have greatly expanded the voting franchise; we have ombudsmen in the provinces and at the federal level, auditors general, a Charter of Rights and

Freedoms, privacy legislation, and freedom of information legislation.

We are, some would say, hyper-democratic. We obsessively demand accountability, transparency, fairness, and honesty from those we elect, and even from bureaucrats.

But we still have a way to go to be able to call ourselves a "modern democratic society." Two of the components of Canada's Parliament are still undemocratic, meaning Canadians do not choose them. Yet they perform a significant role in our governing system. They are: the Monarch and the Senate.

Canadians do not choose our head of state or our ceremonial executives at the provincial level (lieutenant-governors). We also do not choose our Senators. Yet they play an important role in passing legislation from the House of Commons, and both these institutions cost Canadians significant amounts of money. Some citizens are calling for reforming these institutions in order to completely democratize our system of government.

The *Democracy 250* initiative recognized Nova Scotia's pioneering role in shaping democracy in the western hemisphere. But it also gives us an opportunity this year to pause and consider how democratic we have become and how much more democratic we may become in the future.

Number of Legislative Chambers

Parliamentary bodies can be *unicameral* (one chamber), *bicameral* (two chambers), or *tricameral* (three chambers). Today, unicameral national assemblies outnumber bicameral assemblies by a ratio of three to two.[1] On the eve of World War I, most of the world's political systems had bicameral national assemblies. But as new nation-states emerged, more and more political systems adopted the unicameral form of legislature. The largest number of unicameral legislatures is found in Africa, Asia, Central America, and the Middle East. One-house assemblies can also be found in homogenous nation-states with democratic traditions, such as Denmark, Finland, and New Zealand. Even in those states with bicameral national assemblies, many of the subnational legislative bodies are unicameral: for example, the Diets (*Ländtage*) of the *Länder* in Germany, Canada's provincial legislatures, those of the states of India, and that of the state of Nebraska in the United States.

Democracies and Bicameralism

Approximately two-thirds of all *democratic* governments have bicameral legislatures.[2] The centre of political power is always located in the "lower house," which tends to have a larger elected membership and shorter terms of office. Examples of such houses are the Canadian *House of Commons*, the *Assemblée Nationale* of France, the Swiss *Nationalrat*, and the US *House of Representatives*. The second chamber, customarily called the "upper house," usually has the smaller membership, longer tenure, and is selected in different ways. For example, the members of the Canadian Senate are *appointed* by the governor general on the advice of the prime minister. Senators must retire at age 75. In the United States, 100 senators are elected in 50 statewide dual-member constituencies for six-year terms. In contrast, members of the Austrian *Bundesrat* are elected by the legislatures of the various *Länder* (lands).

One justification for bicameralism in democratic federal states is that it permits a system of dual representation for the constituent parts of the union. This certainly applies in democracies such as Australia, Germany, Switzerland, and the United States. But in Canada, the legislative role of the appointed Senate to the House of Commons has diminished its ability to effectively represent regional and provincial interests, as originally intended. This is because the composition of the Senate favours provinces with large populations, where most Canadians have decided to live. Its regional role is sacrificed in that the representation it provides to the larger provinces of Ontario and Quebec undermines its representation of Atlantic Canada and most of the Western provinces. The demand to allow the Senate equal representation of all provinces would change the dynamic of representation in that body, giving the regions more political clout.

> FACTFILE Provinces are not represented in the Canadian Senate the same way American states are in the US Senate, which gives equal representation per state. In Canada, the Senate was designed to represent geographical regions equally, such as the Maritimes and the West, not individual provinces.

Another noted advantage of bicameral legislatures is that they prevent legislative power from concentrating in one assembly. They provide a second forum for further deliberating legislation. Sometimes, they act as a check on executive power. In some democracies, a second chamber is considered a necessary conservative influence, a place for sober second thought, to reduce hasty or impulsive decision making that may originate in a lower house. In the United States, the Senate performs this conservative function with respect to the House of Representatives. But as a deliberative body it also has important checks on the initiatives of the US president, with its powers to confirm or reject presidential appointments and ratify or deny ratification of the treaties the president signs.

In some states, the second chamber is particularly well suited for advising the lower house, as does Germany's *Bundesrat* (upper house). Its members are state government members who advise the *Bundestag* (lower house) of the desirable or undesirable consequences national legislation might have in the *Länder* (German provinces).

The Canadian Senate has considerable legislative powers on paper, although it is limited in the use of these powers because its members are not elected. But even so, the Senate has delayed and even killed legislation originating in the House of Commons. Generally, however, the Canadian Senate, as currently mandated, functions as a house of formal reward for party stalwarts who have paid their political dues. Accordingly, as Canada's Senate demonstrates, the mere presence of a second chamber provides no guarantee that bicameralism will function to fulfill the representative needs of Canadians.

> FACTFILE In the Canadian Senate, the distribution of seats respects the principle of regional representation, such that the people who live in the less-populated areas of the country actually hold a majority of 54 percent of the seats.

But two chambers can be particularly adaptive to multi-ethnic and multinational states because the legislatures provide political representation of these special groups. Sometimes an upper chamber is a power concession made to special groups in order to reduce political tensions. Bicameralism can provide actual and symbolic concessions to special groups. For example, in Switzerland the Council of States provides representation to four linguistic groups: German, French, Italian, and Romansch.

Why States Choose Unicameralism or Bicameralism

There are no hard-and-fast rules to explain why a particular state adopts a unicameral, bicameral, or tricameral legislature (such as Croatia's *Sobor*). Legislative structure depends on the traditions, needs, and goals of a political system or regime. Some states, such as Vietnam, have adopted unicameral legislatures for ideological reasons, one being that "the will of the people must be one" under communism. In communist states, a second chamber is associated with the privilege of the bourgeois capitalist state.

In authoritarian regimes, such as Paraguay, the unicameral legislature enables centralized political control and functions as a rubber stamp for the actions and policies of the dictator.

But there can be any number of other reasons why it is an advantage for a political system to adopt single or multiple chambers in order to make law. For reasons of efficiency and the centralization of decision making, Sweden reduced its bicameral parliament to a single chamber in 1971. But Pakistan reverted to bicameralism in 1973, as did Spain in 1977, when its new bicameral parliament, the *Cortes*, was constituted.

Size and Tenure of Assemblies

FACTFILE   On February 17, 2008, the Parliament of Kosovo unilaterally declared its independence from Serbia, evoking strong objections from the parliaments of Serbia and Russia, which requested that the UN Security Council declare the move to be legally invalid because Serbia never agreed to cede Kosovo as a provision of the 1999 ceasefire.

The size of most legislatures is determined by **constituency** representation as it relates to total population. Some legislatures use a system of *functional representation*, whereby people are represented according to occupation rather than according to where they live. For example, in Ecuador's upper house, senators represent occupational groups in agriculture, commerce, industry, journalism, and labour. Similarly, the 60-member Irish Senate (*Seanad Eireann*) employs functional representation: 11 are nominated by the prime minister (*Taoiseach*), 6 are elected by universities, and 43 are elected from special panels of candidates representing the public services and other interests, such as the arts, languages, literature, agriculture, banking, labour, and

industry. In Indonesia, the 400-member House of Representatives has 300 elected representatives and a functional group composed of 100 representatives who gain their seats from the support of professions and occupations.

FACTFILE   Using data from its national census, Canada's House of Commons increased its number of representatives from 301 to 308 in 2004.

But most legislatures follow the principle of **representation by population**. As a general rule, as population varies, so does the representative size of the legislature. In Canada, under federal law, independent three-member commissions in each province redraw constituency boundaries approximately every 10 years. Within the provinces, the boundaries of many constituencies were redrawn to adapt to population swings while producing ridings with roughly the same number of electors.

Many less-populated states in Africa, Asia, and Latin America have lower houses with fewer than 100 members; for example, Botswana's has 47 members, Gambia's has 50 members, and Gibraltar's has 18 members (Table 6.1). Another large group of states, including Austria, Colombia, Mexico, and Venezuela, have legislatures with between 100 and 200 members. Canada, with its 308-member House of Commons, falls into a group of states with relatively larger lower houses. The more populous states tend to have lower houses ranging in size from 400 to 3000 members: Germany's *Bundestag* varies in size but has around 670 members; China's National People's Congress has 2979 members who meet once a year for two or three weeks; Great Britain's House of Commons has 652 members; Japan's House of Representatives has 500 members; and the United States House of Representatives has 435 members.

As a general rule, most upper chambers have fewer members than lower houses. Paraguay's Senate has 45 members, Canada's Senate has 105 members, and the Senate of France has

Table 6.1	Size and tenure of national assemblies: Selected nation-states		
Nation-State	*Legislature(s)*	*Size*	*Term*
Botswana	National Assembly	47	5 years
	House of Chiefs	8	appointed
Canada	House of Commons	308	5 years
	Senate	105	appointments to age 75
China	National People's Congress	2979	5 years
France	Assemblée Nationale	577	5 years
	Senate	321	9 years
Indonesia	House of People's Representatives	400	5 years
Japan	House of Representatives	500	4 years
	House of Councillors	252	6 years
United States	House of Representatives	435	2 years
	Senate	100	6 years

Note: The fixed election date passed by the Harper government in 2007 reduces the tenure of the House of Commons to four years from five.

Source: Data extracted from Canadian Global Almanac, 2004 *(Toronto: John Wiley and Sons Canada, 2004).*

321 members. This is usually because most upper houses exercise regional representation and represent larger constituencies than lower houses. There are some notable exceptions to the upper house having fewer members than the lower house. One is the case of the non-elective British House of Lords, which has nearly twice the number of members of the House of Commons. The size of the membership of the British upper House of Lords is based on peerages (duke, marquis, earl, viscount, or baron) created by the sovereign, without limit to number. Peerages are held for life and may or may not be hereditary.

FACTFILE In 2007, the Harper government moved to readjust how seats are determined based on population increases. As a result, three provinces will have their number of seats increased after the 2011 census: Ontario to 110, British Columbia to 38, and Alberta to 29, bringing the total number of seats in the House of Commons to 315.

Like size, the length of legislative terms in lower houses varies considerably. The United States House of Representatives has a two-year term; Australia, Mexico, New Zealand, and Western Samoa have legislatures with three-year terms; Canada, Great Britain, France, the Republic of Ireland, Italy, and South Africa all have five-year legislative terms; and a term of six years is found in India, the Philippines, and Sri Lanka.

Legislatures across Canada, including Parliament, are meeting less now than they did in the late 1970s. The average number of sittings in Canada's Parliaments since 1977 has declined from 19 weeks to 13. Assembly records for New Brunswick show that the number of sittings in that province has been cut in half, from 64 in 1977 to 30 in 2001. New Brunswick sits less than any other province, followed by Alberta and Nova Scotia. In comparison during the same period, Prince Edward Island, the smallest province, held 69 sittings, while Ontario had 135.

Many upper chambers differ in tenure from their legislative counterparts because of the divergent systems of representation and the sometimes different ways of selecting representatives for upper houses and lower houses. Members of upper chambers are selected by appointment, indirect election, or popular election. In the United Kingdom and Luxembourg, they are appointed for life. In some other states, members are appointed by the head of state on the advice of the head of government for limited terms, as in the Bahamas, Canada (to age 75), and Jamaica. Indirect election is conducted in Austria, France, and the Netherlands, for fixed terms. Directly elected upper chambers are found in Australia, Colombia, Italy, the United States, and Mexico.

Problems with Large Legislatures

It is normally more difficult for large legislatures, like those in China, Great Britain, Japan, and the United States, to deliberate complicated issues and to reach a collective decision easily. In most democratic states, even if all other commitments (servicing constituents, ceremonial functions, studying community problems, electioneering, and political party work) allowed time enough for legislators to meet and deliberate, not one of them could be reasonably informed about the variety of matters that require legislative action. How, for instance, can a Canadian MP become sufficiently knowledgeable so that he or she can deal in quick succession with legislation on air safety, tariff policy on textiles, immigration quotas, and a fishing treaty with the United States? Most legislative leaders are aware that the larger the legislature and the more complicated the issues, the less likely the legislature as a body can deal effectively with them.

Large legislatures can be very expensive to operate, although Canada's does not fall into this category. They require vast sums of taxpayers' money to meet the expenses of building maintenance, individual members' pensions, expenses for travel to and from their constituencies, paying for staff and research, renting offices, buying computers, advertising costs, and other housekeeping expenses involved in the legislative process.

Crosscurrents   Europe's Largest Parliament

In the spring of 2004, Europe elected its largest parliament in the history of the European Union. The European Parliament (EP) is the only directly elected EU body. It took nearly a week for electoral bureaucrats to tally the votes of some 492 million eligible voters, who elected 785 Members of the European Parliament (MEPs).

This parliament attempts to represent voter interests in 27 EU states. It is a legislature charged with the almost impossible task of making laws for what is now the largest democratic society outside India.

The election of 2004 produced a fragmented parliament, with more than its share of political unknowns and retreads of national politics from across the European continent. The new parliament is an unpredictable mixture of those who believe in a united Europe and "Eurosceptics" who see the continental government institutions of Europe as destined to fail.

The largest party controls the centre-right on the political spectrum. A significant swath of seats is occupied by socialists, with other segments of support going to Liberals, the far left, Greens, regionalists, nationalists, independents, Gaullists, and Eurosceptics. Thus, the new parliament is very divided and is composed of a range of opposing political parties that will attempt to address continent-wide issues flowing out of a complex single-market European economy. It is expected to decide on a budget and to make laws for a multilingual, multinational society.

With more than a half a million constituents for each seat, it is difficult for the MEPs to become widely known among those they represent. It is also difficult for them to get to know and co-operate with each other.

The European Parliament has a big influence on the lives of citizens in EU member states, whether they realize it or not. EU laws apply in all member states, and most laws passed by national parliaments must meet the standards of the EP. It has the power to amend or reject EU legislation and its MEPs have more real power than the members of national parliaments.

FUNCTIONS OF DEMOCRATIC LEGISLATURES

Because each nation-state has a unique political culture, legislatures differ in organization, power, and structure. The US Congress competes and co-operates with the president to make law. Some legislatures are weaker than others, such as in Great Britain and Canada, where Parliament is dominated by majority parties that control all cabinet posts, and thus control the legislative agenda. As they have evolved in most democratic states, legislatures represent people; formulate, initiate, and enact laws; control public finances; check the executive; adjudicate on executive behaviour; and amend constitutions.

Sometimes the forces of emergent nationalism result in the creation of new legislative assemblies. In 1999, Great Britain devolved limited legislative powers from Westminister to Scotland, Wales, and Northern Ireland. Scotland celebrated the opening of its first parliament in nearly 300 years, as did Wales. London will keep control over defence, and foreign and economic policy. But the new legislatures will assume powers from London on a range of domestic issues such as law and order, health, environment, housing, agriculture, and sport. And in 1999 in Canada, the Territory of Nunavut opened its first legislative assembly in its capital, Iqaluit.

Representation

FACTFILE   According to a 2007 report of the Inter-Parliamentary Union, Canada ranks thirtieth among democratic states for representing women in its national Parliament, with about 20 percent of its legislators being women.

Hanna Pitkin defines representation as "re-presentation—that is, making present of something absent, but not making it literally present. It must be made present indirectly, through an intermediary; it must be made present in some sense, while nevertheless remaining literally absent."[3] That is precisely what a legislature does. It makes present an authorized sample of the population

Focus On   The National Assembly for Wales

Throughout history, the government of Great Britain has remained a unitary state. But in the late twentieth century, the British government devolved power and governing authority to local and regional legislative bodies, thus departing from a strict definition of a unitary state.

In 1997, the British Labour government moved quickly to fulfill its promise of devolution—to establish regional government decision making in Northern Ireland, Scotland, and Wales.

Based in Cardiff, the National Assembly for Wales was established by the *Government of Wales Act* of July 31, 1998. Under this act, the National Assembly for Wales can make laws called "subordinate legislation," as distinguished from primary legislation, passed by Parliament in Westminster. Subordinate legislation refers to orders-in-council, orders, rules, regulations, bylaws, and other legislative instruments made under the authority of the new government of Wales.

The first representatives of the sixty-member Assembly were chosen in regional elections held on May 6, 1999. The Assembly for Wales can make subordinate legislation that shapes the policies of Wales. The Assembly has the power to develop policies in the areas of agriculture, forestry, fisheries and food, industry, culture, local government, economic development, social services, education, sports, the environment, tourism, health services, town planning, highways, transport, housing, and the Welsh language.

The Whitehall government retains primary legislative powers for overall economic policy, defence, armed forces, foreign policy, and the justice system. The Assembly does not have taxing powers. The head of government in Wales is called the "first secretary," and the cabinet is composed of "secretaries."

---

representing all the rest who must remain absent from the decision-making process of society. In Canada, the average number of constituents each Member of Parliament represents is about 95 000.

> FACTFILE   In Greece in the sixth century BC, the Assembly, situated near the Acropolis, held direct democratic sessions about 40 times each year. Any citizen could add his or her own items to these legislative meetings. All could vote directly on motions put before the Assembly.

Legislatures are a political compromise between the principles of "perfect" democracy (direct popular participation in the law-making process) and the realities of indirect representation in modern complex nation-states. Because there is no way yet devised for any entire modern society to assemble, debate, and decide on public policies, we compromise our commitment to these principles by selecting a group of people who deliberate the issues of the day, and who are ever conscious of the interests and preferences of those who sent them to the legislature.

> FACTFILE   Democrat Nancy Pelosi is the first female Speaker of the US House of Representatives. The person in that position is second in line to the presidency after the vice-president.

Many variables come into play as influences on those who represent us (Table 6.2). Such characteristics as the size of the legislature affect members'

Table 6.2	Some influences on the behaviour of representatives

- Size and tenure of the legislative assembly
- Type of electoral system used in elections
- Member's own values and beliefs about representation
- Values and beliefs of constituency voters about representation
- Party discipline
- How legislative committees and subcommittees operate
- The competence of a member's staff to communicate with voters
- How the executive branch of government is organized
- How effectively interest groups lobby representatives
- The role and prominence of national and subnational party leaders
- How the media report on representation

ability to speak on behalf of constituents. Party discipline can cause a representative to vote as a loyal party member, sometimes at the expense of constituents. One important influence on the quality of representation is the electoral system that elects or appoints representatives. Proportional representation permits legislatures to represent on the basis of the percentage of popular support. Thus, a party that earns 25 percent of the popular vote can expect to hold approximately 25 percent of the seats in the legislature. In Canada's electoral system, which is based on the principle of plurality, a candidate wins a seat in the legislature by simply gaining one or more votes than the closest opponent. If this occurs in many ridings, it is possible for our representatives to win a majority of parliamentary seats with less than a majority of popular support.

FACTFILE   Louis Riel was the first Aboriginal person elected to the House of Commons. He was elected three times in the 1870s, but never took his seat in the chamber. In commemoration of this passionate Métis leader, Manitoba began celebrating Louis Riel Day on February 18, 2008.

In all democratic legislatures, representation is based on three principles: *authorization*, *accountability*, and *responsibility*. Authorization means that a representative acts on our behalf. Representatives are accountable to the people by means of elections, **initiatives**, **referendums**, **petitions**, **recall**, public opinion polls, and **roll-call voting** in legislatures. How representatives act reflects their sense of responsibility. Some argue that true responsibility is acting in the best interests of the constituency, regardless of whether **constituents** agree with the actions of the representative. Others argue that true responsibility means that representatives should act as their constituents want them to act.

Making Laws

In most democratic legislatures, policy is both introduced and formulated by the executive branch of government.[4] Australia, Canada, Great Britain, and other parliamentary systems operate legislatures that fuse executive and legislative powers according to the majority principle: the political party or coalition that enjoys the support of a majority of seats in the legislature forms an executive that drafts and initiates legislation. These "government" bills are introduced by a minister. Then, as a body, the legislature debates and enacts government bills into law.

As a general rule in parliamentary democracies, any member—whether on the government or opposition side—may introduce a bill. But the success rate of **private-members' bills** is extremely low because of the urgency of government bills and the power of the executive to mobilize disciplined party support to push *its* program through the legislature. In fact, for this reason, some states do not permit individual legislators to introduce bills of their own. For example, in the German *Bundestag* (lower house), individual members who want to initiate a bill must form a *fraktion* (a group of at least 15 members) before the bill can be introduced. This guarantees that there is a group of legislators who are supportive of the bill and that there is the possibility of others' being converted to support the proposition.

FACTFILE   In Canada, a bill can be introduced in the House of Commons (C-bills) or the Senate (S-bills), but most bills get their start in the Commons. Either house can do four things with a bill: pass it, amend it, delay it, or defeat it.

Increasingly, in the United States, the initiation of new laws originates in the executive branch, where one of many agencies drafts a proposal and finds a sympathetic legislator to introduce the bill in Congress. But even in the US political system, unless there is widespread support for a proposed bill, the legislation will die 80 to 90 percent of the time.

In the world's two major types of democratic political systems, the parliamentary and the presidential, the support and leadership of the executive must accompany the role of the legislature in the enactment of law. The parliamentary system is particularly well suited to executive leadership in the legislature through the prime minister and the cabinet, as the Canadian experience has shown. The presidential system is much more complicated because the president and the cabinet are not present in the Congress. But in both systems, the increasing complexities of government have made the legislature dependent on the executive for

the initiation and proclamation of the laws. Essentially, the function of the modern legislature is to criticize, examine, amend, adopt, and, from time to time, reject legislation and bring down governments.

The Role of Legislative Committees

Most legislatures delegate the drafting of legislation to small groups of legislative experts who form committees. All parliaments must have committees because of the large number of bills introduced; there is simply not time for each member of a parliament to do a careful job on all bills that come down each year. Out of the necessity to cope with the law-making process, many legislatures have established **committee systems**, sets of **standing committees** and **ad hoc committees**, to give consideration to the content of proposed legislation. In Canada, committees of the House of Commons have been in place since Confederation but did not function in an efficient way until the 1960s; in the United States, a much longer history of standing committees and **subcommittees** has been the response to complex congressional matters.

FACTFILE   There are six types of parliamentary committees at the federal level in Canada: standing committees, standing joint committees, special committees, legislative committees, special joint committees, and the Committee of the Whole, which is the full House sitting as a committee.

Today in Canada and the United States, committees and subcommittees conduct a vast amount of legislative work. Policies are shaped, interest groups heard, and legislation hammered out. Standing committees are the permanent committees that consider bills and conduct hearings and investigations. They perform the valuable function of dividing labour and specialization of expertise among members of parliament on both the government and opposition sides. No legislator can hope to know the details of hundreds, and sometimes thousands, of bills introduced in a Parliament or Congress. They must rely on the expert knowledge that members of the committees gather in their consideration of the bills before them. Once a committee has reviewed the contents of a bill, other members of the legislature generally assume that the committee has considered the legislation carefully, applied its expertise, and made the right decision after all is considered.

As a result of using committees to consider bills, legislators specialize in various fields, such as transportation, gun control, the media, health, or education. Sometimes they become more knowledgeable in their areas than the public servants who administer the laws. Although committees usually process legislation, they perform other tasks, such as educating the public on important issues by means of hearings and investigations. Many scholars argue that a legislative body should have some forum where members of competing political parties can provide their input and attempt to resolve their differences with the government. In effect, committees serve this purpose; they are natural arenas for political bargaining and legislative compromise.

Control of Public Finances

The power to scrutinize and control public finances varies widely among legislatures. In Canada and the United States, executive budgets are drawn up and submitted to the legislature for approval. In states with an elected cabinet, such as Canada and Switzerland, the budget is approved or rejected in its entirety by the legislature. If it is rejected, the government is defeated, the cabinet must resign, Parliament is dissolved, and an election follows. If the budget is approved in Canada, the House of Commons has an important *audit function* that guarantees a measure of financial control over the ways the government raises taxes and spends money.[5]

The Canadian **auditor general** reports directly to the House of Commons and conducts audits of government spending to assure the legislature that the provisions approved in the budget are implemented faithfully. Unlike other executive officers, the auditor general is an employee of Parliament, not of the Cabinet. In France and Germany, the executive has greater power of the purse than does the legislature. The French president, in consultation with the prime minister, can overrule legislative disapproval of the budget by executive order. The German chancellor may also bypass the legislature and authorize expenditures by **executive prerogative**. In the United States, the president can only veto the entire budget or accept the entire budget. But the president may also refuse to spend the money.

Perhaps the oldest and most enduring function of the legislature is the power to *levy taxes*. But as with so many other legislative functions, the raising and spending of revenues have shifted primarily from legislative to executive control. Most democratic legislatures now retain only the power to scrutinize and revise budgets proposed by the executive branch. The legislature is always in a tricky political position—caught between the public's desire for increased government spending on favoured programs and the public's resistance to paying the increasing costs of programs through higher taxes.

Checks on the Executive

In democratic parliamentary systems like Canada's, Parliament can place checks on the political executive during **Question Period**, in committees, and simply by voting against government bills. The government is fused to the legislature and must sit before it to defend its policies: ministers must be members of the legislative body and are responsible to it, as in Australia, Canada, Great Britain, and Ireland. In other states, cabinet ministers are not members of either house, but the legislature has the power of approving executive appointments, as in France, the Netherlands, and Norway. In the United States, the Senate must approve executive appointments for ambassadors, the cabinet, and federal judges and other officers.

FACTFILE   Question Period attracts more media and public attention than any other part of the daily sitting in Canada's House of Commons.

Many other executive acts may be subject to legislative approval, such as the ratification of treaties, issuance of decrees, and declarations of national emergency. In Canada, there is no constitutional requirement for the parliamentary ratification of treaties. The decision to accede and ratify a treaty is an executive act legitimized by the royal prerogative. Most treaties are simply tabled in the House of Commons. But major multilateral treaties are by tradition submitted to Parliament before ratification.

One of the most effective means of controlling the executive is to keep it under the watchful eye of the legislature. In Canada, Great Britain, and many other Commonwealth states, the parliamentary Question Period is an effective device for gaining information about government actions. In some parliamentary systems, the process of **interpellation** is a more pointed method of legislative scrutiny of the executive. In Japan, opposition parties can question or "interpellate" government ministers and their assistants in the various committees drafting legislation before it goes to a full or plenary session of the Japanese Diet. The opposition wants to embarrass, delay, and even shape government-sponsored legislation. In Belgium, Italy, Netherlands, and Switzerland, interpellation forces specific questions that are unsatisfactorily answered to debate and formal vote, sometimes resulting in a motion of censure against the government.

Judicial Role

Some democratic legislatures have the power to adjudicate the behaviour of executive officials. The Constitution of the United States gives Congress the power to **impeach** any civil officer of the national government: the House hears the evidence and decides whether to impeach; the Senate sits as the court, with the power to convict on a two-thirds vote of its members. In France, the Assemblée nationale and the Sénat can decide to impeach the president and the ministers of state, but the accused must be tried by the High Court of Justice.

In Canada and Great Britain, Parliament does not *impeach* members of the executive because the House of Commons has the power to defeat a government whose members have acted illegally or unethically. Most parliamentary systems permit a prime minister to remove from the cabinet a minister who has been found guilty of a crime. But usually a person removed retains a seat in the legislature unless by a unanimous vote he or she is deprived of members' parliamentary privileges.

In Canada, the House of Commons has investigated the activities of MPs to determine if they could hold their seats. For example, in 1890 the House reviewed a previous conviction for forgery and the allegation that an MP's conduct was corrupt on a matter involving the granting of timber permits. And on two occasions Louis Riel was expelled, once because he failed to obey a House order to appear in his seat, and then for having been judged an outlaw for committing a felony. The House demonstrated its right to expel an MP when, in 1946, Fred Rose was convicted and sentenced to six years' imprisonment for conspiring to commit offences under the *Official Secrets Act*. Since then, a number of MPs who have been convicted in the courts have resigned before the House could exercise its right to expel them.

FACTFILE   The Mulroney-Schreiber controversy was investigated by the House of Commons Ethics Committee in 2007 to gather evidence as to whether a former prime minister received inappropriate payments while still in office for work as a lobbyist in Canada and abroad.

CANADA'S LEGISLATIVE ASSEMBLIES

FACTFILE   In 1867, the total number of seats in the House of Commons was 181, representing a national population of 3 230 000.

Amending Constitutions

Because many constitutions were originally drafted by national legislatures, it is appropriate that legislatures are authorized to exercise some role in the process of constitutional reform. In some states, such as Great Britain and New Zealand, constitutional change is primarily a function of the national legislature. In other states, such as Australia, France, and Switzerland, constitutional amendments are proposed by the national legislature, and then ratified by voters in a nationwide referendum.

In the United States, Congress has the power to propose a constitutional amendment by a two-thirds vote, and the proposed amendment must then be ratified by three-quarters of the states in order to be adopted. In Canada, constitutional reform is a lengthy and complicated process involving five different methods, depending on the nature of the amendment. In three of the methods, the legislative assembly of each province, or of those provinces to which the amendment applies, or the federal Parliament, must approve the proposed constitutional amendment.

In general, legislatures are involved in three methods of amending constitutions. One is by the action of the legislature alone, with requirements that might vary from unanimous approval (as in Ecuador) to certain specific legislative majorities, as in Canada and the United States. Another method of amendment involves a proposal by the legislature followed by a constitutional convention to ratify the amendment, as employed in Argentina. A third method, practised in most federal states, gives a distinctive role in the amending process to the subnational units, such as to Canada's provinces.

Canada's bicameral Parliament consists of two houses: the *House of Commons* and the *Senate*. Elected members of the House of Commons are called members of parliament (MPs); members of the Senate are called senators, although technically they are members of parliament. The Canadian House of Commons is modelled after the British lower house. The country is divided into political constituencies that are roughly equal in population, each sending a representative to Ottawa. Originally, the Senate was modelled after the British House of Lords. But in Britain there is no limit on the membership of the House of Lords: new appointments may be made from any constituency. However, Canada's *Constitution Act, 1867*, limits the size of the Senate by the principle of equal regional representation. The Constitution also stipulates that there must be a session of the Parliament of Canada at least once each year and that the maximum life of a Parliament between elections is five years. Under certain emergency conditions, such as war, this normal tenure can be and has been extended.

The House of Commons

If Parliament is the symbol of political authority in Canada, the House of Commons is where the actualities of this legislative authority are centred. The House of Commons consists of 308 members and is responsible for most of the legislation introduced in Parliament. The House of Commons is a rectangular room divided by a central aisle. The government sits on the Speaker's right and the opposition on the left (Figure 6.1). On the

Figure 6.1   **House of Commons Chamber**

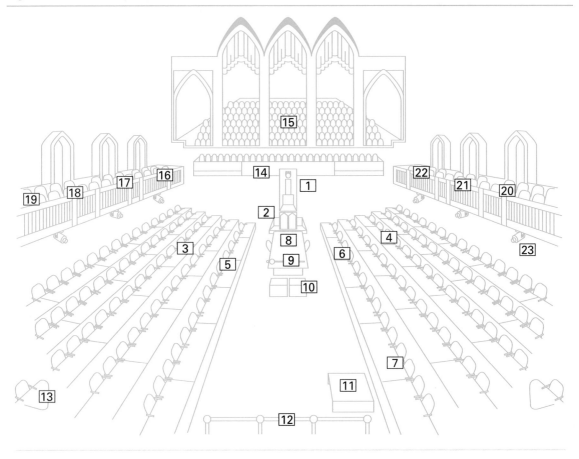

1. Speaker	8. Clerk and Table Officers	17. Leader of the Official
2. Pages	9. The Mace	Opposition's Gallery
3. Government Members	10. Hansard Reporters	18. Members' Gallery
4. Opposition Members	11. Sergeant-at-arms	19. Members' Gallery
5. Prime Minister	12. The Bar	20. Members' Gallery
6. Leader of the Official	13. Interpreters	21. Speaker's Gallery
Opposition	14. Press Gallery	22. Senate Gallery
7. Leader of the second	15. Public Gallery	23. Television Cameras
largest party in Opposition	16. Officials' Gallery	

Source: Library of Parliament

government side, about halfway down the aisle, the prime minister sits in the front row, and the Cabinet ministers sit in the centre seats of the first two rows. The leader of the Official Opposition sits directly opposite the prime minister, surrounded by the senior members of his or her party. Leaders of smaller opposition parties sit farther away from the Speaker. The principal divisions of legislative power do not run between Parliament and Cabinet, but within the House of Commons between the majority party (which controls the Commons and Cabinet) and the opposition.

> **FACTFILE** Canada's Constitution does not fix the size of the House of Commons, which can be re-adjusted every ten years after a census.

The Speaker

These divisions are reflected in the structural composition of the House of Commons, between the government and the members of the opposition, with the Speaker as the presiding officer of the House. On the Speaker's right sits the government, and on the left sits the opposition, an adversarial positioning of political opponents in the legislative framework.

By presiding over the debates and acting as the administrative head of the House of Commons, the Speaker plays a central role in the legislative process. The Speaker is a bilingual member of the House who is elected by that body for the duration of Parliament. Any MP who has not crossed his or her name off the list of candidates for Speaker is deemed a candidate for the job and the voting takes place by secret ballot. As the presiding officer of the House of Commons, the Speaker is expected to be **non-partisan** and impartial in applying the rules and procedures and in recognizing members who want to debate. During each sitting of the House, the Speaker

rules on time limits for debate, on parliamentary privileges when they are violated, and on motions of adjournment and closure. In the case of a tie, the Speaker casts the deciding vote. As the administrative head of the House of Commons, the Speaker is responsible for preparing and defending the internal estimates, which are the costs of staffing and operating the lower house.

Concurrent with the election of the Speaker is the election of a *deputy speaker*. The deputy speaker replaces the Speaker when he or she is absent, and acts as the chairperson of the Committee of the Whole. Like the Speaker, the deputy speaker can be selected from either the government or opposition sides of the House, although the conventional practice is for the government to select both people. When both the Speaker and the deputy speaker are absent, the House of Commons temporarily appoints the *deputy chairperson of committees* from the government side of the House to the Speaker's chair.

> **FACTFILE** The Mace represents the authority of the Speaker and thus of Parliament itself. It dates back to the medieval period, when bishops carried it into battle instead of a sword.

The Clerk of the House

The House of Commons staff is headed by a permanent civil servant, the **Clerk of the House**, who advises the Speaker and members of the House on parliamentary procedure. The Clerk sits at a table in front of the Speaker in the House of Commons. Some of the most important responsibilities of this officer are to keep the official record of the proceedings and to prepare Commons documents. Much like a deputy minister in charge of a government department, the Clerk supervises all the permanent staff of the

Focus On **The Tradition of Parliamentary Privilege**

Parliamentary privilege grew out of the disputes between Stuart kings and the British Parliament in the seventeenth century. These privileges were claimed by members of parliament to protect them from the power and influence of the monarch and the House of Lords. Following the expulsion of James II in 1688, the *Bill of Rights* was passed, which guaranteed that members of parliament could speak freely and could no longer be arrested for their critical views.

Parliamentary privileges were formally assigned to Canada's Parliament in the *Constitution Act, 1867* and are now represented in the *Parliament of Canada Act*. The most prominent privilege is freedom of speech. Members may say anything they want about anyone without fear of being sued for libel or slander, provided they say it during the proceedings of Parliament.

There are some restrictions about what they can say about each other, however. Calling another MP a liar is considered "unparliamentary language" and may result in the name-caller being suspended from the House or the Senate for a period of time. Members who engage in disgraceful conduct, such as hitting another member or making offensive non-verbal signals across the floor, may be expelled. Provincial parliamentarians also enjoy privilege and may even make disparaging remarks about federal members without penalty. It is argued that, without privilege, members of parliament could not perform their public duties.

House of Commons. As the chief parliamentary administrator, the Clerk prepares and delivers the daily order paper to the Speaker. The Clerk provides the minister of justice with two copies of every bill tabled in the House.

Party whips

Party whips are important in the organization and structure of the House of Commons.[6] A whip seeks to assure that all party members are present for important votes. The authority of the whip is accepted because MPs recognize that only by voting as a bloc can their party continue to be effective in the House of Commons, as government or opposition. To defy the whip by abstaining or even voting for the other side is to seriously challenge party discipline. Such actions may result in MPs' losing the support and respect of their party colleagues. So, in addition to ensuring party discipline, the party whip must educate party members about the ramifications of party policies so that these are as acceptable to as many members as possible. Whips are the party negotiators who decide among themselves what items on the agenda are subject to political compromise and how much debate will be expended on them.

Working alongside the whips are the *House leaders* of the various parties. The House leaders guide the flow of business through the House of Commons. On the government side, the House leader is a Cabinet member responsible for the organization of government business and, if possible, its quick passage through the House of Commons. Like the party whips, House leaders negotiate the apportionment of time to be spent on legislation and other matters of procedural business.

Perspectives   Canada's Parliamentary Whip System

A former Chief Government Whip sarcastically remarked: "Once you get beyond the taxicab radius of Ottawa, nobody seems to have heard of a whip. For that matter, nobody in Ottawa, three blocks from the Hill, has ever heard of a whip either!"

The origin of the term "whip" comes from the British hunting phrase "whipper-in," referring to a hunter's assistant who keeps the hounds from straying off scent and staying on the trail of the fox. Edmund Burke first used the phrase in 1769 when he complained that the government of the day had "whipped-in" its supporters on a matter to push it though the House. When political parties emerged in the nineteenth century, each party appointed a member of its caucus to maintain the loyalty of its members, to make sure they were present for important votes, and to vote as a block either as the governing party or as an opposition party.

Today, whips are stealthy party officials. They operate below public visibility as a matter of strategy so that they can encourage party discipline and cohesiveness. Whips also work quietly to get an insider's understanding of opposition demands in order to get their party's legislative agenda through the House.

The whip system helps maintain party unity in Parliament, but it is particularly important in the House of Commons because of the large numbers of party members whose positions must be considered before a party's voting strategy is made.

The authority of the whip is also strengthened by some special administrative services that each member sees as essential. Whips allocate members' offices and can give the better offices to those who demonstrate party loyalty. They also select members to serve on certain parliamentary committees and delegations that are prestigious. Whips constantly monitor the attendance of members on committees in the House and approve travel requests. Who gets to speak and ask questions during debates is also facilitated by the whip.

At first glance, the role of the whip appears to be routine and mundane. But on closer examination, whips have the power to discipline party members, give them advantages and evaluate their loyalty to the party. Ultimately the party whip can influence a member's relationship with organizers in his or her constituency. This is a very powerful dynamic.

FACTFILE Canada's longest-serving party whip was Stanley Knowles, who performed that job for the CCF/NDP for twenty-five years. Most serve in that post from three to five years.

The importance of committees

The structure and functions of the House of Commons are also determined by its committee system. The basic challenge to the House of Commons is how to organize its 308 diverse members in order to get things done. One major response to the challenge since the mid-1960s is the specialization of parliamentary business in numerous legislative committees. Currently, there are 19 standing committees of the House of Commons, 16 standing committees in the Senate, and 3 standing joint committees made up of members of the House and the Senate. The selection committee (sometimes called a "striking committee") decides on the membership of the standing committees. Each party caucus provides the **striking committee** with the names of qualified committee candidates. This prevents the government from assigning the least experienced and least able opposition members to important standing committees (Table 6.3).

Under the **Standing Orders** of the House of Commons, adopted in June 1978, these committees are permanent and are struck at the commencement of each session of Parliament to consider all subjects

Table 6.3	Standing committees of Parliament: Fortieth Parliament 2008

House of Commons

- Aboriginal Affairs and Northern Development (AANO)
- Access to Information, Privacy, and Ethics (ETHI)
- Agriculture and Agri-food (AGRI)
- Canadian Heritage (CHPC)
- Citizenship and Immigration (CIMM)
- Environment and Sustainable Development (ENVI)
- Finance (FINA)
- Fisheries and Oceans (FOPO)
- Foreign Affairs and International Trade (FAAE)
- Government Operations and Estimates (OGGO)
- Health (HESA)
- Human Resources Development and the Status of Persons with Disabilities (HUMA)
- Industry, Natural Resources, Science and Technology (INDU)
- Justice, Human Rights, Public Safety, and Emergency Preparedness (JUST)
- Liaison (LIAI)
- National Defence and Veterans Affairs (NDDN)
- Official Languages (LANG)
- Procedure and House Affairs (PROC)
- Public Accounts (PACP)
- Status of Women (FEWO)
- Transport (TRAN)

Senate

- Aboriginal Peoples
- Agriculture and Forestry
- Anti-terrorism Act (Special)
- Banking, Trade, and Commerce
- Energy, the Environment, and Natural Resources
- Fisheries and Oceans
- Foreign Affairs
- Human Rights
- Internal Economy, Budgets, and Administration
- Legal and Constitutional Affairs
- National Finance
- National Security and Defence
- Official Languages
- Rules, Procedures, and the Rights of Parliament
- Selection Committee
- Social Affairs, Science, and Technology
- Transport and Communications

Source: www.parl.gc.ca: Committee Business: House of Commons List and Senate List.

arising from the process of national lawmaking in Canada. Committee assignments are party-based and reflect the percentage of seats a party commands in the Commons. For example, if the government party won 60 percent of the seats in the House of Commons, it would occupy approximately the same proportion of positions on each committee. So if there were 10 positions on a committee, the members of the governing party would occupy six. Committee power is more closely concentrated in the House when there is strong majority government. But opposition parties can be more influential in committees in a minority-government situation.

A number of factors influence MPs' requests for committee assignments. One of these is the desire to be where the action is. They also want to serve on committees that handle the broadest central concerns of government—like the Public Accounts Committee. Another major motive of House members in requesting committee assignments is being in a position to influence public policy. Some committees are attractive to members because they play important roles in the key areas of government decision making, like taxing and spending, the economy, and social welfare policy.

Making Laws

The main function of the House of Commons is the passage of legislation from a bill to law. Bills may be proposed and introduced to the House of Commons as a private-members' bill or as a government bill. A private-member's bill can be introduced by any member of parliament, on either the government or opposition side of the House. Usually, at the time they are introduced, these kinds of bills do not have the support of the government and almost never become law. Opposition members who introduce private-members' bills recognize these facts, using the opportunity to generate public opinion that will influence the direction of a particular government policy.

A government bill is a policy proposal or a **money bill** requiring legislation that is introduced in the House by a cabinet minister (Figure 6.2). The minister responsible calls for the drafting of legislation by the Department of Justice. The draft is then approved by the responsible minister before it is presented to the Cabinet Committee on Legislation and House Planning. Once this committee has approved the draft bill, it is then signed by the prime minister and introduced in the House of Commons in its *first reading* by the responsible minister. During this stage, the title of the bill is read, followed by a short explanation of its contents. At the *second reading*, the bill is debated and a vote is taken on principle to approve or reject it in total. If it is "approved in principle," and it usually is, the bill is then considered by the appropriate standing committee, where it is given a clause-by-clause examination. At the *committee stage*, the bill is debated and witnesses may be called to testify about their positions, pro or con. All standing committees are empowered to make amendments to the original draft. It should be noted that money bills, unlike other bills, are not considered by standing committees; rather, they go before the **Committee of the Whole**.

FACTFILE The House of Commons went on air live on October 17, 1977, making Canada the first country in the world to broadcast the complete proceedings of its national legislature.

When the committee has completely examined the bill to its satisfaction, it reports the bill with any recommended amendments back to the House of Commons. In this *report stage*, the opposition will vigorously debate the bill and try to reintroduce the amendments it made at the committee stage. Any final changes the government wishes to make must also be made at this time, before the bill goes to its *third reading*. In almost all instances, a bill passes quickly through its third reading.

Figure 6.2   **How a Canadian bill becomes a law**

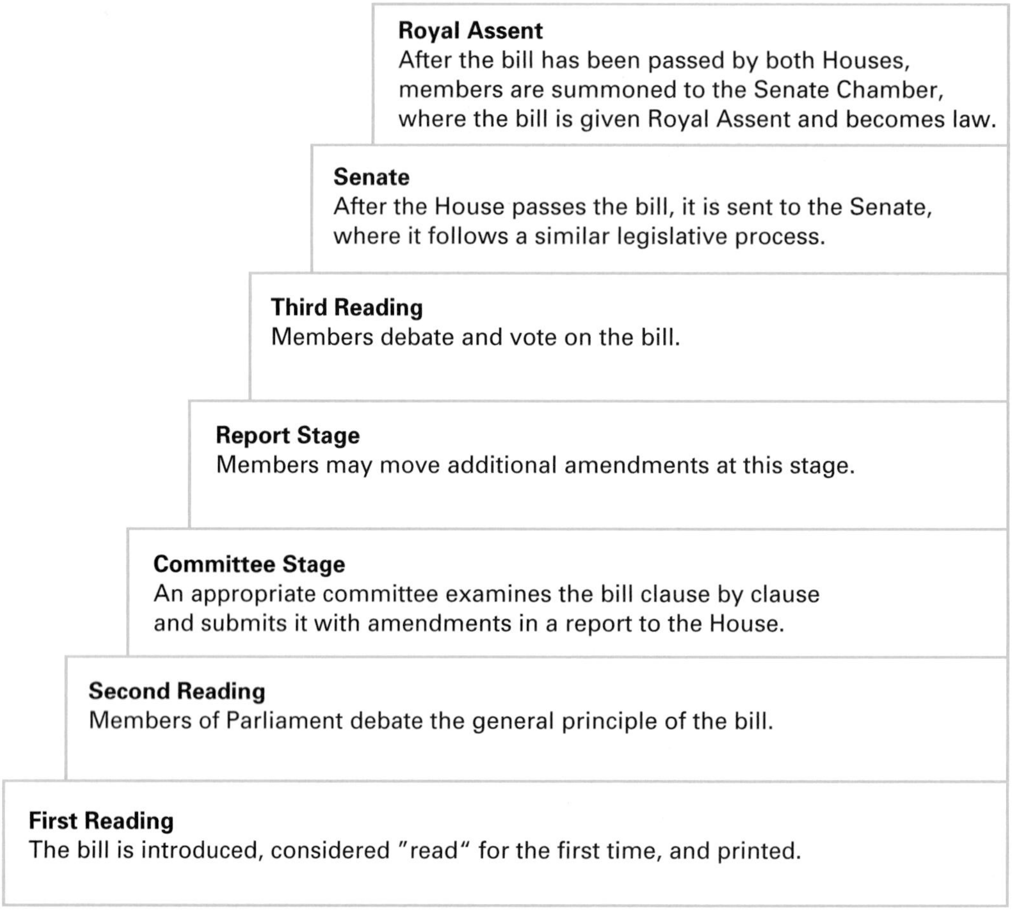

Royal Assent
After the bill has been passed by both Houses,
members are summoned to the Senate Chamber,
where the bill is given Royal Assent and becomes law.

Senate
After the House passes the bill, it is sent to the Senate,
where it follows a similar legislative process.

Third Reading
Members debate and vote on the bill.

Report Stage
Members may move additional amendments at this stage.

Committee Stage
An appropriate committee examines the bill clause by clause
and submits it with amendments in a report to the House.

Second Reading
Members of Parliament debate the general principle of the bill.

First Reading
The bill is introduced, considered "read" for the first time, and printed.

However, if revisions made during the committee stage are unacceptable to the full House, the bill can be rejected. After a bill is finally passed through the House of Commons at this third reading, it is then introduced in the Senate, where it receives a *pro forma* repetition of the legislative process of the House. Once a bill is passed by both houses of Parliament, it is presented to the governor general, who confers *royal assent* by signing it into law. *Proclamation*, which can be delayed, follows royal assent, and a new Canadian law has finally been enacted.

The Senate

Anyone reading the *Constitution Act, 1867*, would have to conclude that the Senate and the House of Commons are about equal in power. But because the Senate is an appointed body, it has usually avoided the exercise of its constitutional powers in a manner that would challenge the popular legitimacy of the House of Commons. In recent years, the Senate has struggled to promote itself as a useful institution, facing severe criticism for the lack of attendance on the part of some senators, and because the Red Chamber has a light work week—only between two and four hours a day from Tuesday to Thursday. Extensive legislative breaks are taken at Christmas and Easter, and sometimes the Senate will recess its sittings for weeks. The $50 million-a-year Senate sits for only about 65 days a year, while the House of Commons sits five days a week and an average of 150 days a year.

Originally, the Fathers of Confederation expected the Senate to do two things: first, to play a legislative-review role by acting as a check against the majority in the elected House of Commons and, second, to represent the various regions of the country. The Senate has usually not been able to do either effectively. As a legislative-review body, the Senate lacks the authority to exercise its substantial powers because the public does not think it has the legitimacy to use them. In fact, the Cabinet has assumed the Senate's legitimate role as a forum for regional representation. So have first ministers' conferences, which give provincial governments a special voice to provide their own views on national issues and policies. This has been referred to as "executive federalism"—the direct result of frequent federal/provincial negotiations for settling questions of regional concerns. Finally, political parties have displaced the role of the Senate; especially, their elected representatives have assumed the responsibility for the expression of regional viewpoints. Thus, regional representation at the national level is carried out by a variety of other political institutions.

FACTFILE In 1975, the Yukon and the Northwest Territories were given one senator each, as was Nunavut in 1999, so that the total number of seats in the Senate is currently 105.

Nevertheless, the Senate remains an integral part of Canada's Parliament. All senators are formally summoned by the governor general, who appoints them on the advice of the prime minister. Currently, the Senate has 105 seats, allocated on the basis of four representative divisions: Ontario and Quebec each have 24 seats; the three Maritime provinces share 24 seats (10 each for New Brunswick and Nova Scotia, and 4 for Prince Edward Island); the four western provinces share 24 seats equally; Newfoundland has 6 seats; and the Yukon, Northwest Territories, and Nunavut have 1 each.

Controversies sometime flare up about the conduct of the Senate, often resulting in calls for its abolition as a parliamentary institution in Canada. When the Senate stalls a supply (money) bill, or calls on a government to justify its use of **governor general's special warrants**, or defeats a piece of Commons legislation such as the abortion bill, controversy flares. Such actions usually create a new round of demands for reform, even outright abolition.

On paper, the Senate can amend or reject a bill passed by the House of Commons; this is as important a part of the law-making process as are royal assent and proclamation. From 1960 to 2008, 21 bills sent from the Commons to the Senate failed to receive royal assent. Although the Senate powers of *delay*, *rejection*, and *amendment* have been rarely exercised, the formal role of the Senate in the passage of legislation remains mandatory.

FACTFILE Liberal Prime Minister Mackenzie King—Canada's longest serving head of government—is on record for having made the largest number of appointments (103) to the Senate during his 21-year career.

Senate Reform

Interest in changing the Senate is demonstrated by a wide range of publications and proposals.[7] Senate reform was an important provision in the constitutional proposals made by Quebec in its submission to the Constitutional Conference of 1968. The Government of Canada drafted white papers on Senate reform in 1969 and 1978. A Special Joint Committee of the Senate and the

House of Commons on the Constitution published its report in 1972. But in 1978, the Supreme Court of Canada struck down an attempt by the Trudeau government to replace the Senate with a House of the Federation because the provinces had not given their consent. And in 1985, Brian Mulroney's government moved to draft a Constitutional amendment that would prevent the Senate, as presently constituted, from ever repeating its stalling action on important government business. This could prove to be a daunting task. Under the Constitution, the Senate's powers could be curtailed only with the consent of at least seven provinces representing 50 percent of the Canadian population—and even after that, the Senate could itself delay changes in its powers for 180 days.

Reports on reforming the Senate were also prepared by the governments of British Columbia (1978) and Alberta (1982 and 1985); the Ontario Advisory Committee on Confederation (1978); the Progressive Conservative Party of Canada (1978); the Canada West Foundation (1978, 1981); the Canadian Bar Association (1978); the Pépin–Roberts Task Force on Canadian Unity (1979); La Fédération des francophones hors Québec (1979); the Goldenberg–Lamontagne report of 1980; and the Royal Commission on the Economic Union and Development Prospects for Canada (1985), known as the Macdonald Commission. The future role of the Senate was also a major part of the deliberations of the Federal–Provincial Continuing Committee of Ministers on the Constitution in the years 1978 through summer 1980. In its "beige paper" entitled "A New Canadian Federation," the Quebec Liberal Party recommended an intergovernmental council that would operate independently of Parliament but would perform some of the functions proposed for a reformed Senate.

In 1985, a Special Select Committee on Senate Reform, established by the Government of Alberta, recommended a *"Triple E"* Senate: a Senate where members are directly *elected* based on *equal* representation from each province, and a Senate with *effective* powers. Since 1985, important progress has been made towards Senate reform. In 1986, all Premiers agreed at the Annual Premiers' Conference in Edmonton that Senate reform is a priority for constitutional change. In the same year, the federal government pledged to address Senate reform in a new constitutional amendment.

The 1987 Constitutional Accord contained a provision for Annual Conferences of First Ministers to address Senate reform. This was the first time that both the federal and provincial governments had agreed to concrete measures to reform the Senate. The Accord promised that Senate reform would be the next priority in building national reconciliation. The 1992 Charlottetown Accord would have changed the Senate by representing provinces equally, with six elected Senators each, no matter what the population, and the Territories would elect one Senator each.

The architects of a new Canadian Senate have many options from which to choose. They can reconstruct the second chamber in such a way that its present legislative-review and legislative-support functions are effectively enhanced by means of new methods of appointing or electing senators. To give senators more representative legitimacy in the eyes of Canadians, the federal government and the provincial governments could share a method of appointment. This would give people of all regions in the country a feeling of being effectively represented. Another recommended method of appointment would remove the federal government entirely from the process and give the power of appointment solely to the provinces. This would institutionalize provincial and regional input into the national legislative process. It would also give the provinces additional powers beyond those already delegated to them in the Constitution.

Focus On Senate Truancy

One senator single-handedly spawned widespread calls for Senate reform with his chronic truancy and laissez-faire attitude toward his professional duties as a parliamentarian. Senator Andrew Thompson, whose name appeared on the Senate Honour List, was among the honourable, but the honourable senator was nowhere to be seen. In December of 1997, Thompson was stripped of his office, secretary, telephone, and most of his travel privileges because he had earned the dubious distinction of being the most absent member of what has come to be called "the other place" in Parliament. Senator Colin Kenny attempted to have Thompson declared "in contempt" of the Senate.

For about 30 years, Thompson has been drawing a Senate income—now about $75, 000 a year—while spending the bulk of his time in his palatial Mexican home. No one knows how poor his attendance was for the first 16 years of his appointment to the Senate, but this second-longest serving member of the upper house attended only a dozen times in 459 sittings since 1990—at best a 2.5 percent attendance record on full salary.

Although there are penalties for missed sittings (a senator who misses 21 sitting days in a session is docked $120 per day of absence), Thompson claimed illness to exempt himself from being fined and professed to be doing humanitarian work in Mexico, even comparing his efforts to those of the late Princess Diana.

When Thompson was confronted by the Canadian media in Mexico, in his own defence he called for Senate reform, criticizing the place as a "morgue."

Under the Constitution, a senator's place automatically becomes vacant when he or she fails to attend two parliamentary sessions in a row (sessions last roughly one year each). This provision would have to be strengthened by adding an amendment to raise the minimum attendance requirement substantially and by adding strict language requiring senators to fulfill their parliamentary duties. Such an amendment could be accomplished by the federal Parliament acting alone.

As an immediate attempt to reform the situation of chronic truancy among a substantial minority of senators, a Senate committee stripped Thompson of his Ottawa office, secretary, telephone, and travel privileges until the senator showed up for work on Parliament Hill.

The Thompson affair is just one in a long line of attempts to reform Parliament. Most of the ideas to transform the institutions of Parliament have been aimed at the Senate. In spite of the proliferation of blueprints for change, nothing concrete has been accomplished since 1965, when the age limit of 75 was introduced.

Senate reform remains what it has been for more than 100 years—a continuing subject for political debate.

Another possible way of choosing senators is by indirect election—a Senate elected by the provincial legislatures. In 1978, the federal government proposed a Senate selected by means of proportional indirect election. Under the terms

of the proposal, the Senate would reflect the proportional popular performance of political parties in the most recent federal election. This was criticized because it would not guarantee the representation of important regions in the country if political parties were unsuccessful in gaining seats nationally.

In the reports by the Fédération des francophones hors Québec (1979), the Canada West Foundation (1981), and the Macdonald Commission (1985), direct election of the Senate was proposed. In these and other reports, it has been argued that direct election would give Canadians a feeling that the regions of the country have national as well as provincial representation. An elected Senate would be a direct voice of the people from various regions, rather than of political parties or governments. In this regard, the Senate might also be designated to reflect the existence of certain minorities, especially Canada's Aboriginal peoples. In 1989, Brian Mulroney asked for a list of provincial nominees to the Senate in the spirit of the Meech Lake Accord. The Reform Party candidate, Stan Waters, won the province-wide contest in Alberta, and his name was forwarded to the prime minister, who reluctantly appointed Waters to the Senate.

FACTFILE   In 2007, Prime Minister Stephen Harper appointed Bert Brown to the Senate, after Brown had won the 2004 Alberta Senate nominee election, making him the second elected Senator in Canadian history.

What is certain is that the present means of legislative review and regional representation, as they involve the Senate, are inadequate and perceived as such. Because of this, many Canadians continue to ask whether they should follow the example of other federations that assign a more functional use to the second chamber.

FACTFILE   Prime Minister Stephen Harper, one of the leading advocates of Senate reform, did an about-turn on his repudiation of patronage appointments to the Senate by appointing 18 people in December 2008—among them provincial Conservative politicians, Conservative Party fundraisers, and current and former journalists—to fill vacant Red Chamber seats, in order to bring the balance of Conservative and Liberals closer.

THE UNITED STATES LEGISLATURE

The United States has a bicameral national legislature called the Congress. Congress is divided into the *House of Representatives* and the *Senate*. Members of the House of Representatives are called representatives, as well as congressmen, congresswomen, or congresspersons. Members of the Senate are called senators. This structure was the result of a compromise that resolved a most important conflict of the Constitutional Convention (1787). The least-populated states feared that representation by population would favour the most-populated states of the union. Therefore, they insisted that one House—the Senate—should represent each state equally and that the approval of both Houses should be required to pass a law.

FACTFILE   The US Constitution specifies that the presiding officer of the Senate is the vice-president of the United States, who votes only in case of a tie.

The Senate has 100 members: two from each of the 50 states, elected for six-year terms that are staggered so that one-third of the senators are elected every two years. There are 435 members of the House of Representatives. This number, fixed by legislation, is divided among the 50 states in proportion to population. When states gain or lose population (taken by census every 10 years), they also may gain or lose representatives. No matter how small the population of a state is, it is entitled to at least one representative.

FACTFILE   Senators must be residents of the state they represent, must be at least thirty years old, and must have been US citizens for at least nine years.

Despite the outward appearance of the separation of powers, the Congress of the United States shares its powers with the president and the Supreme Court.[8] Although the Constitution designates the Congress as the legislative branch, the president is very much a part of the law-making process. If the president opposes legislation passed by Congress, he or she can refuse to sign it and can return it to Congress, giving reasons for so doing. This is called a **veto**. The fate of such a bill would then be up to Congress. If, after the veto, Congress passes the bill by a two-thirds vote of each house, it overrides the veto and the bill becomes law without the signature of the president.

Legislative Leaders and Committees

As with all legislatures, Congress has its legislative leaders who organize the law-making process. Each House of Congress has two sets of leaders: those who achieve strong positions (mostly committee chairpersons) usually by virtue of their seniority rule, and those who are elected to the positions of congressional leadership.

The House of Representatives, controlled by the majority party, elects the *Speaker*. The Speaker is more than a party figure; this person presides over the House and is next in line of presidential succession after the vice-president. The **minority party** in the House has no officer comparable to the Speaker. Otherwise, the leadership organizations of the two parties are similar. Each party has a **floor leader**, a whip, and a number of assistant whips in charge of floor business. On the majority side of the House, the Speaker joins these officers, acting as a party spokesman, and representing House Democrats or Republicans to the president and the general public.

Party organization in the Senate takes a similar form. The US vice-president is the presiding officer of the Senate. This person, usually not in attendance, has relatively little influence there except to cast the deciding vote in case of a tie or to issue a decision on a congressional ruling.

What role do party leaders play in the legislative process of Congress? The majority leadership in both Houses manages legislation after it comes out of committee. **Majority leaders** schedule and delegate the workload on a bill as it passes through each stage of legislation. They are at the centre of a network of information about legislation and must be consulted on every bill and kept informed on its progress. Although US congressional leaders have a great deal of influence, they do not enjoy the same degree of influence over their fellow lawmakers as do their Canadian counterparts. They cannot tell their party members how to vote or expect them to follow orders. Party discipline is much weaker in the US Congress than in Canada's Parliament. Because they only have marginal influence in keeping their party members in office, party leaders exercise only marginal power over them in Congress.

The congressional committee system is by far the most important element in the legislative organization of Congress.[9] Members of the House and the Senate establish their reputation from the committee work they do. The Congress is much too large for all its members collectively to make important public decisions. No congressperson can possibly learn about every issue before the legislatures. Only through the committee system can the work of Congress be achieved. Each bill must go through the hands of at least one, and often more than one, committee in each House. The vast majority of bills flow through standing committees for their scrutiny and approval or disapproval. There are 17 standing (permanent) committees in the Senate and 22 in the House (Table 6.4).

These standing committees are divided into subcommittees that do specialized work within the overall jurisdiction of the full committees. The party composition of standing committees is roughly equivalent to the relative party strength in each House, and the chair of the committee and subcommittee is usually held by a ranking member of the majority party.

Table 6.4   Standing Committees of Congress

House of Representatives	Senate
• Agriculture	• Agriculture, Nutrition, and Forestry
• Appropriations	• Appropriations
• Armed Services	• Armed Services
• Budget	• Banking, Housing, and Urban Affairs
• District of Columbia	• Budget
• Education and Labor	• Commerce, Science, and Transportation
• Energy and Commerce	• Energy and Natural Resources
• Financial Affairs	• Environment and Public Works
• Government Reform	• Finance
• Homeland Security	• Foreign Relations
• House Administration	• Government Affairs
• International Relations	• Health, Education, Labor, and Unions
• Judiciary	• Judiciary
• Resources	• Rules and Administration
• Rules	• Select Intelligence
• Science and Technology	• Small Business and Entrepreneurship
• Select Intelligence	• Veterans' Affairs
• Small Business	
• Standards of Official Conduct	
• Transportation and Infrastructure	
• Veterans' Affairs	
• Ways and Means	

Source: From We the People: An Introduction to American Politics, *Sixth Edition by Benjamin Ginsberg, Theodore J. Lowi & Margaret Weir. Copyright © 2007, 2005, 2003, 2001, 1999, 1997 by W.W. Norton & Company, Inc. Used by permission of W.W. Norton & Company, Inc.*

The US Congress also conducts **select committees**. Ordinarily, select committees do not play a significant role in the process of passing a bill. But there are times when select committees capture a prominent role in the legislative process, as did the Senate select committee that investigated Watergate.

Finally, two other kinds of congressional committees deserve attention. **Joint committees** are those made up of an equal number of senators and representatives. The chairs of these committees alternate between both Houses, from Congress to Congress. Joint committees rarely have anything to do with initiating legislation but conduct long-term studies on important questions like taxation. **Joint conference committees** are also composed of equal membership from both Houses, and they iron out any technical difficulties a bill encounters because of the procedural differences between the Houses. They try to reconcile major policy differences in Congress.

The committee system has earned a great deal of respect among US legislators. Congresspersons will rely on expert opinion and intelligence gathering before deciding the direction of their votes. For them, the committee has done all the credible groundwork, held hearings, studied the issues, and consulted with experts and interested parties. Consequently, committee opinion is usually respected.

How Bills Are Passed

The US legislative process follows an often slow and formidable path, although political will in the Congress can speed a bill through a labyrinth of hurdles (Figure 6.3). A bill may be formally introduced by any member of either House. Sometimes a companion bill is introduced in the other House simultaneously in order to speed up the process of legislation. In addition, any number of Congress members may *sponsor* a bill. Presidential bills are introduced by a member of the president's party who has seniority on the standing committee that will hold hearings on the bill.

When the bill is introduced on the floor, it is read and immediately assigned by the presiding officer to the appropriate standing committee handling such matters. The subcommittees of the parent committees are then assigned the job of investigating the purposes of the bill, determining its value, and amending it in accordance with the wishes of the subcommittee, and, finally, re-submitting it to the parent committee. Sometimes the full standing committee will specifically investigate certain provisions of the bill. This is generally followed by hearings of the parent committees and subcommittees. These hearings perform several broad functions. One is to assist congresspersons in collecting information and opinion from the interested parties. Within this process, special-interest groups will have their say. As the bill passes through the hands of these committees, it may come to bear only a slight resemblance to the original draft or even the intent of it.

Many riders or amendments may be added along the way. Once the House of Representatives' committee reports a bill out by returning it to the legislature, it is scheduled by the Rules Committee for the second reading, debate, and voting on the floor of the House. If a bill survives the second reading, it is **engrossed** by printing the amendments in final form and given a third reading. This reading is by title only, unless a member requests that the bill be read again in full. The speaker asks for a vote after the title is read and the bill is either defeated or passed. As in Canada, the third reading is merely *pro forma*, because the sentiments of the House have been expressed in the Committee of the Whole, where the entire legislative body sits as one large committee.

All *revenue* bills are required by the Constitution to originate in the House of Representatives. Once passed in the House, they are taken up by the Senate. But all other bills may originate in either the House or the Senate. If one House passes the bill first, it then goes to the other House, where it goes through the same process. Bills must eventually pass both Houses in exactly the same form before being sent to the president for signing. Even after a bill authorizing a new government program becomes law, the new program must still get an appropriation of money if it is actually to get under way. **Appropriations bills** go to the House and Senate appropriations committees. These committees regard themselves as having a special role to play in protecting taxpayers from unnecessary federal expenditures.

The primary concern of Congress is the thousands of bills and resolutions that are introduced each year. The number of bills and resolutions introduced in one Congress has been as high as 44 770, but between 15 000 and 20 000 is more usual. The odds are that over 90 percent of these legislative proposals will be killed or permitted to die in committee.

Although the US Congress was born in an age of great legislative activity, much has changed

Figure 6.3   How US bills pass into law: The law-making process

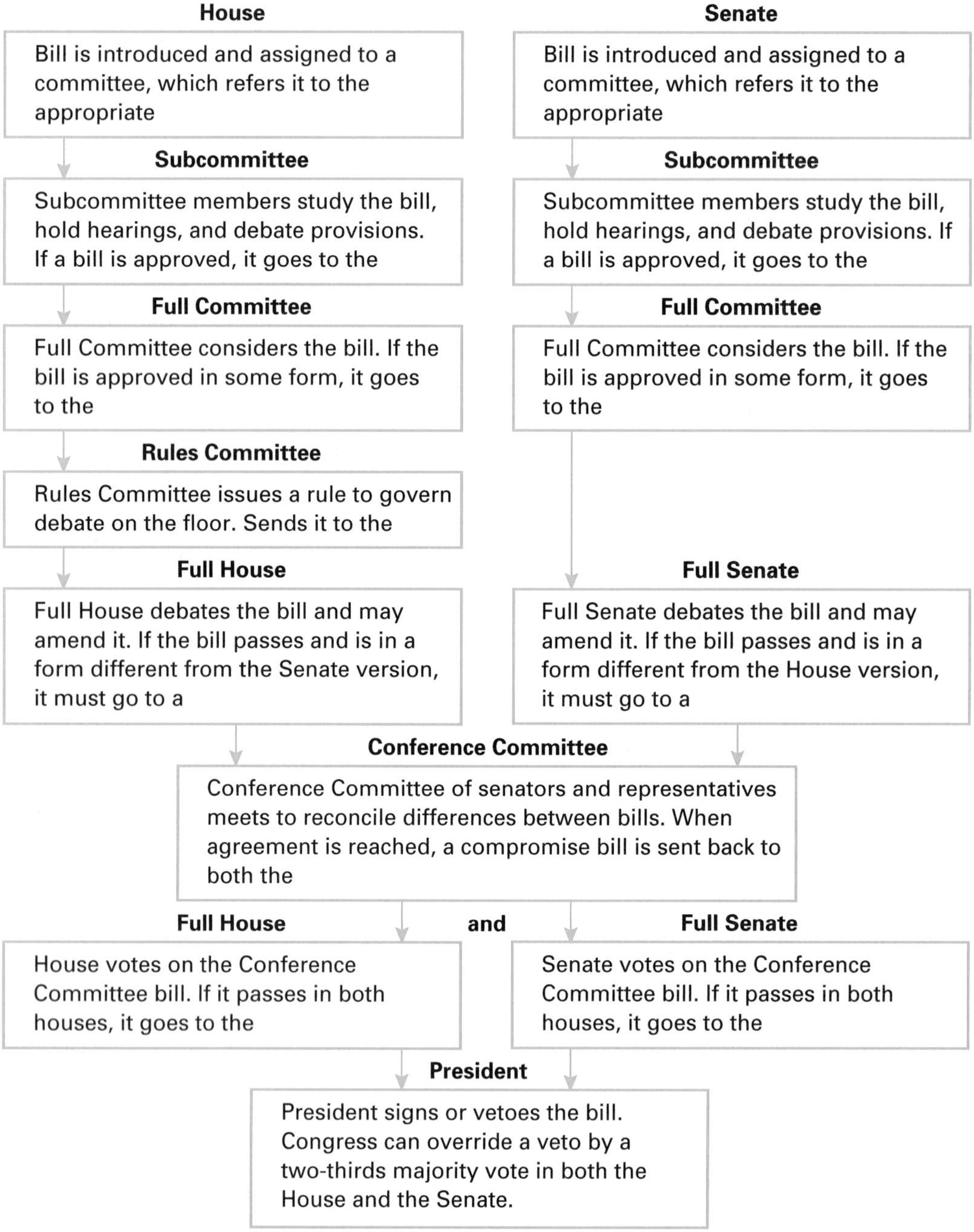

House	**Senate**
Bill is introduced and assigned to a committee, which refers it to the appropriate	Bill is introduced and assigned to a committee, which refers it to the appropriate

Subcommittee	**Subcommittee**
Subcommittee members study the bill, hold hearings, and debate provisions. If a bill is approved, it goes to the	Subcommittee members study the bill, hold hearings, and debate provisions. If a bill is approved, it goes to the

Full Committee	**Full Committee**
Full Committee considers the bill. If the bill is approved in some form, it goes to the	Full Committee considers the bill. If the bill is approved in some form, it goes to the

Rules Committee

Rules Committee issues a rule to govern debate on the floor. Sends it to the

Full House	**Full Senate**
Full House debates the bill and may amend it. If the bill passes and is in a form different from the Senate version, it must go to a	Full Senate debates the bill and may amend it. If the bill passes and is in a form different from the House version, it must go to a

Conference Committee

Conference Committee of senators and representatives meets to reconcile differences between bills. When agreement is reached, a compromise bill is sent back to both the

Full House	**and**	**Full Senate**
House votes on the Conference Committee bill. If it passes in both houses, it goes to the		Senate votes on the Conference Committee bill. If it passes in both houses, it goes to the

President

President signs or vetoes the bill. Congress can override a veto by a two-thirds majority vote in both the House and the Senate.

over the past 200 years. Today, most observers agree that the branch of government first mentioned in the Constitution has been greatly surpassed in power by the executive branch. A frequently advanced reason for the decline in the power of Congress has been its inability to organize rapidly and legislate on the ever-changing social exigencies of American society.

FUNCTIONS OF NON-DEMOCRATIC LEGISLATURES

Authoritarian Assemblies

At first glance, legislatures in authoritarian and totalitarian states resemble democratic law-making institutions. In most cases, their members are elected, and they elect or appoint presiding officers, meet regularly, make speeches, vote on proposed legislation, and formally enact laws and constitutional amendments. But on closer examination, we see that the roles they play in their respective political systems are quite different from those of democratic legislatures.

In authoritarian states, the character of the policy-making process is strongly influenced by the concentration of power in the hands of the civilian political executive or the military.[10] The very personal way in which power is exercised means that the legislature has little actual autonomy and cannot play an independent role in the policy-making process. In all authoritarian states, the vital centre of government power is the executive itself; political parties, legislatures, and courts are usually not important challenges. Any institutional constraint on these powerful executives remains extremely weak.

In many African states, legislatures are commanded by a single party or a dominant party under the influence of the military that tolerates no—or only marginal—opposition. In these authoritarian political systems, the legislature functions to uphold the government rule of the incumbent regime. As a result, the vitality of democratic accountability is virtually non-existent. The legislatures serve merely ceremonial and decorative functions. In some states, such as Kenya, the national assembly provides an arena through which members can successfully represent the claims of their constituents to gain minor amenities like a paved road or a new school. But legislators cannot effectively challenge the executive leadership in areas of general policy.

There are many reasons for the predominance of authoritarian executives and the minor supportive role of the legislatures. One is that, in many states, the legislature is a hand-picked body of the executive. This has occurred in Mali, Mozambique, Rwanda, and Uganda, where presidents have personally selected loyal legislators. Another is the role of the bureaucracy as supportive agencies of executive decrees.

Legislators in authoritarian systems are well aware that in a contest of power among the branches of government the executive holds most of the trumps, especially the high ones, such as the support of the armed forces and the national police. In a showdown of political power, executives will even use these trumps against members of the legislature.[11]

Many other factors contribute to the hindered role of legislatures in authoritarian states. At the social level, widespread illiteracy, poverty, and lack of political experience have contributed substantially to the weakness of legislatures. Low levels of education and media information curtail the formation of a participant political culture. In states such as Brazil and Ecuador, many people are denied the privilege of voting because of illiteracy. Even when suffrage is extended to a wider range of the population, the great majority of citizens in authoritarian states hardly knows what is going on in government and is uninterested in the legislature's work, its problems, or its degree of independence.

The net result is that legislatures tend to function as "rubber stamps." In authoritarian states, open debate is mainly window dressing for the international community. Usually, the legislative order of business, even the outcome of the proceedings, is a foregone conclusion. Most of the important bills considered by the legislature have already been formulated or decreed by the executive. Often, the bureaucratic machinery of the state is well under way, implementing the policies as they are being considered by the legislature.

Totalitarian Assemblies

Legislatures in totalitarian socialist states, modelled after democratic parliamentary assemblies, function quite differently. They have functioned to legitimize the policies and rules of the executive levels of government, which in this case is the party leadership. For this reason, assemblies in these states have tended to remain subordinate to the Communist Party. The impact of *democratization*, however, has altered the relationship between the party and the legislative branch of government. Some observers view the totalitarian model of government as transitional in all remaining communist regimes.[12]

The two enduring communist states, China and Cuba, have unicameral legislatures. According to the Chinese Constitution of 1982 (with amendments in 1987 and 1993), "the highest organ of state power" resides in the National People's Congress (NPC).[13] The NPC has about 3000 members and is the largest legislative assembly in the world. Its delegates are elected every five years, but its awesome size prevents it from being an effective decision-making body. The meetings of the NPC are short and mostly ceremonial because its deputies ratify the major reports presented to them by the Chinese Communist Party.

The three levels of Chinese government include national, provincial, and county or municipal.[14] Each level has a legislature called a people's congress, defined constitutionally as the "local organ of state power." Like the NPC, these local congresses meet irregularly and briefly. The standing committees of the people's congresses have the role of supervising the government organizations and of keeping the goals of the party well entrenched in the administrative structure of government. Congresses at the national and provincial levels are indirectly elected for five-year terms by lower-level congresses. But congresses at the county, district, and municipal levels have three-year terms and are elected directly by the voters. The district and township congresses are directly elected and administer government programs at the grassroots level.

The Chinese Constitution now gives formal and legal approval to several new developments in Chinese politics. It increased the legislative powers of the congresses and clearly specified the roles of the party, state, and government in the political system. The effort to give the legislative structures of government a greater role in the political process indicates the willingness of the Chinese Communist Party to institutionalize the decision-making process.

In totalitarian states, legislative power is seldom separate from executive power. Where legislatures merely function to formalize decisions made elsewhere about the laws that govern people, it is important to find out where the laws are really being made and exactly what procedures are being followed.

Chapter Summary

Most modern nation-states have legislatures. In today's democracies, at least one legislature is viewed as representative and pre-eminent, a lower house freely and openly elected, and consisting of men and women who make the laws. The prototype of the modern legislature dates back to the earliest forms of the British Parliament in the eleventh century. Most modern legislatures are *unicameral*, having only one chamber. But many states have *bicameral* legislatures, that is, parliaments or congresses with two chambers.

Democratic legislatures share similar functions: representation, lawmaking, control of public finance, checks and balances with the executive branch of government, a judicial role, and amending constitutions. In authoritarian and totalitarian states, legislatures may perform a representative and law-making function, but often they are incapable of holding executive officials and their decisions accountable to the people. Authoritarian and totalitarian regimes strive to institutionalize and legitimize executive decisions by using legislatures as a rubber stamp. In these regimes, governance is often in the hands of a single individual or of elite committees that concentrate power and decisions and are not accountable to legislatures of the general public.

Canada's Constitution established a Parliament consisting of two houses: the elected *House of Commons* and the appointed *Senate*. According to the Constitution, there must be a session of Parliament at least once each year and the maximum life of a Parliament between elections is five years.

The *Speaker*'s non-partisan role is crucial to the successful operation of the House of Commons. He or she is a bilingual member of the House who is elected by that body for the duration of Parliament on the nomination of the prime minister. The Speaker of the Senate presides over the Senate and is appointed by the governor general on the advice of the prime minister. The Senate Speaker, unlike in the House, may participate in debates.

The *Clerk of the House* is a permanent civil servant who advises the Speaker and other Members of the House on parliamentary procedures.

Party whips ensure that their party members are present and act according to the proper legislative rules and procedures in debating and voting on laws. *House leaders* guide the flow of business through the House of Commons.

Legislative committees deliberate on bills before the House and the Senate.

Discussion Questions

1. Compare the functions of legislatures in democratic, authoritarian, and totalitarian regimes. In those regimes that reflect executive dictatorship, why is it so important for their leaders to have a legislative assembly approve their initiatives?

2. It has been argued that *representative* democracy is desirable for a number of practical and normative reasons. Are there any circumstances in politics and government under which a system of *direct* democracy would be desirable? What are these? Would it be possible to initiate practices of direct democracy in any areas of Canadian society? What would these be? What would be the probable consequences of such procedures?

3. Has Parliament failed the Canadian public in its law-making function? Why or why not? What improvements, if any, might be suggested to make Parliament a more representative body? Should Canada consider designating some seats to guarantee a greater degree of social representation, e.g., designated seats for First Nations, the homeless, and the disabled?

4. In what ways can it be argued that Parliament is an *unrepresentative* institution of Canadians? Are these valid criticisms? Why or why not? Discuss whether Senate reform would benefit the implementation of public policy in Canada.

5. The US Congress was structured and empowered by the framers of the Constitution as two institutions that could check excessive presidential power. Has Congress fulfilled its mandate? Is Congress representative of today's America, for example, immigrants, the homeless, Hispanics, Native Americans? Compare the powers of the US House of Representatives with those of the Senate. Which House is more powerful? More prestigious? Why?

7

The Administration of Government

After reading this chapter, you will be able to:

- note the widespread presence of public and private bureaucracy in our lives
- describe the characteristics of public bureaucracy and relate them to Canadian government
- describe what governments do when they administer public policy
- explain the advantages and disadvantages of widespread government bureaucracies in modern political systems
- examine the role of bureaucracy in the emerging United States of Europe
- discuss the consequences of powerful public bureaucracies in a democratic system of government
- define the concept of *administocracy*
- explain how bureaucracy and bureaucrats can be controlled
- outline the instruments available in Canada for regulating the bureaucrats
- explain the relationship of ministers and deputy ministers
- compare public administrations in Canada and the United States

● ● ● ●

THE FIRST BUREAUCRACIES

Many traditional societies compiled and stored information on tilling, hunting, fishing, animal husbandry, and human population for the purposes of social **administration** and survival.[1] Egypt, China, and India produced highly developed bureaucratic mechanisms before Europe had emerged from barbarism. The so-called **bureaucratization** of human behaviour became evident as governments became involved in agriculture, commerce, fisheries, justice, military, and municipal affairs.

The casual and informal practices of governing in traditional societies, where rulers relied on family members to help them govern, would prove inadequate. As societies grew, special skills were necessary to gather and store information and to implement the laws of the executive.

For these early societies, as the problems of administration multiplied, new kinds of government positions were created, and a governmental bureaucracy began to take shape with the creation of officials who administered specific areas. Each official had a staff of scribes and lesser officials to assist with compiling written records about the civic affairs of each community. Because of the political importance of their skills and the limited number of people who could write and keep records, most scribes were regarded as members of a special class of governors whose work was vital to the survival of society.

As traditional agrarian societies evolved into industrial economies, the range of activities and diversity of officials grew enormously. The original functions of government were to preserve law and order and to defend the society from external threat. But as societies grew in population, many new services were demanded from government: to educate, to regulate, to license, to provide health care, and to manage and referee the economy. Systems of transportation and communication became essential government services. Urban communities, where people live closer together, needed fire, police, health, and other government services. Only governments, and not private individuals, could command the resources, **expertise**, and authority to deal with such problems by means of central administrations.

The full-blown model of the modern **administrative state** was Prussia. Frederick William I (1713–1740) organized an administrative corps of public servants, now generally recognized as a professional civil service.[2] He was also the first to establish universities to train government bureaucrats. Recruitment and selection of government employees were by competitive examination, after the completion of specialized training. **Career tenure** became a normal expectation in the public service.

> **FACTFILE**   In 1867, the federal budget for the government of John A. Macdonald was $8 million. The budget for Canada's federal government in 2007 was $204.4 billion.

The Prussian model was copied by many other continental states, most notably by eighteenth-century France. Under the centralizing leadership of Napoleon, France developed a professionalized civil service, with a **hierarchical** structure of offices and officials—uniform throughout the country—following elaborate patterns of law and administering rules established by the executive, legislative, and judicial branches of government. The term *bureaucracy* is derived from the French "bureaus," which were the desks of government officials that came to symbolize the authority and administration of the public service.

In Britain, the painful struggle for **parliamentary supremacy** was as much pursued to control the bureaucracies of successive kings and queens as it was to control the monarchs themselves. Monarchs could rule only through their loyal bureaucrats in the administrative structure: control of the one could not be asserted without control of the other.

The development of administrative government in both Canada and the United States owes much to Great Britain; thus, **public administration** in North America is more like that of our English cousins than the continental model. Canada in the year 1867, with its simple economy, relatively sparse population, wealth of resources, and remoteness from the broils of the Old World, in fact needed but a minimum of government of any kind. The problem of administrative development in Canada and the United States was one of overcoming a tradition hostile to bureaucracy, and deeply rooted values that stressed egalitarianism, equal opportunity, and a reluctance to staff the government system at public expense.

In the late nineteenth century, Canadians were not prepared to assign more than a rudimentary role to government involvement in their lives. There were no personal or corporate income taxes, no family allowance, no Canada Pension Plan, and no healthcare plan. CBC radio and television did not exist, nor did the Canada Council, Investment Canada, the Canadian International Development Agency (CIDA), or Atomic Energy Canada Ltd.

Government consisted of Parliament, a postal service, customs and immigration, a system of courts, and public works. The public service of the day was largely unprofessional by current standards, made up of people whose only expertise amounted to reading, writing, and perhaps some bookkeeping.

Until the early twentieth century, administrators were selected and obtained job security through an elaborate system of **patronage**: a professionalized bureaucratic service based on the European model was conspicuously absent. During the 1920s, under Mackenzie King, the Canadian civil service was upgraded from an essentially clerical force into a highly qualified group of professional policy advisers. When Conservative R.B. Bennett was elected in 1930, he retained most of the senior civil servants who were appointed by Liberal Mackenzie King. The tradition of a non-partisan civil service was firmly established. Deputy ministers were, and still are, the most powerful civil servants in Ottawa.

Today, about 560 000 people work directly for the federal government in its departments, Crown corporations, agency corporations, and other federal bodies. The Canadian system, because of its federal structure, is much less centralized than the British or French systems. Never before have so many Canadians been so involved with bureaucracy or so affected by it. If provincial and municipal administrations are added to the federal total, government administration currently employs over 12 percent of the total labour force in Canada.

Because the bureaucracy is the largest branch of government in all states, administrators spend most of a government's budget implementing policies and programs. There is a great deal of variation in size of government administrations because every state has a different set of public policy goals to administer within its geographical setting.

Table 7.1	The size of government as a percentage of gross domestic product: Selected states
Country	**Percentage of GDP**
Sweden	66
Finland	59
Netherlands	58
Germany	56
France	55
Italy	53
Greece	46
Canada	46
United Kingdom	44
Japan	37
United States	30

Source: Adapted from Thomas Dye, Politics in America *(NJ: Pearson Education, 2007), 418.*

How does the size of the public sector in Canada compare with other economically advanced, democratic states? Government spending accounts for about two-thirds of the total output in Sweden, and exceeds one-half of the total output in Finland, the Netherlands, Germany, France and Italy. Canada, Greece, and the United Kingdom spend about the same percentage of their GDPs on the provision of government services and regulation. Much of the cost of government in Canada is the result of funding Canada Pension and Old Age Pension, healthcare, transfer payments to the provinces, and infrastructure development. The high level of government spending in some countries primarily reflects greater public-sector involvement in matters of public policy and nation-building.

CHARACTERISTICS OF BUREAUCRACY

The first systematic study of bureaucracy was conducted by the German sociologist **Max Weber** (1864–1920). His classic studies formulated an ideal set of features for any public bureaucracy. Weber himself always emphasized the exaggerations and simplifications of his model in the real world of bureaucracy. The elements of what he observed are present to varying degrees in such diverse organizations as the Secretariat of the United Nations, the Vatican's Curia (which has handled the business of the worldwide Catholic Church over the past 1800 years), and Canada Customs and Revenue Agency. Weber argued that every bureaucracy—whether its purpose is to run a daycare centre, a family business, or an army—shares five basic characteristics (see Table 7.2).

In Canada, a bureaucrat goes through a process of promotion based on the merit principle provided in the civil service acts of the federal and provincial governments, and not because he or she did favours for a political party or the government. The bureaucracy is expected to value technical and professional competence, which is essential in the day-to-day functioning of a complex government.

Table 7.2	Weber's five characteristics of bureaucracy
Characteristic	**Description**
Division of Labour	Specialized experts are employed in each position to perform specific tasks in order to achieve efficiencies of outcomes for the government organization. By working at a specific task, people are more likely to become highly skilled and carry out jobs with maximum efficiency. This emphasis on **specialization** is a basic strategy in all government bureaucracies.
Hierarchy of Authority	Bureaucracies follow the principle of hierarchy, with each position under the supervision of a higher authority. For example, the Canadian Armed Forces are ultimately responsible to the command of the minister of defence. Within the armed forces, generals outrank colonels, colonels outrank majors, majors outrank captains, and the hierarchy extends downward to sergeants and privates.
Written Rules and Regulations	Through written rules and regulations, bureaucracies offer employees standards for adequate or exceptional performance. Written procedures provide a valuable sense of continuity. Government workers will come and go, but the structure and records give the organization a life of its own that outlives the services of any one bureaucrat.
Impersonality	Max Weber wrote that in a bureaucracy, work is carried out *sine ira et studio* (without hatred or passion). Bureaucratic norms dictate that officials perform their duties without the personal consideration of people as individuals. This is intended to achieve equal treatment for each person. We typically think of governments as impersonal bureaucracies.
Job Security	In a government bureaucracy, hiring is based on technical/academic qualifications and merit rather than partisanship. Performance is measured by specific standards. This is intended to protect bureaucrats against arbitrary dismissal. Promotions are dictated by written personnel policies, and individuals have a right to appeal if they believe that particular rules have been violated. Such procedures give civil servants a sense of security and encourage loyalty to the organization.

FACTFILE The federal government hired up to 12 000 full-time workers each year from 2000 to 2010, as waves of baby-boomer administrators sought to retire.

Weber introduced the concept of *bureaucracy* but tended to emphasize its positive aspects. More recently, social scientists have described the negative consequences (or dysfunctions) of bureaucracy for the individual within the organization, for the bureaucracy itself, and for the clients it serves.

Administrators point out that Weber's bureaucratic ideal has drawbacks in its application to all kinds of modern governments, democratic and non-democratic. For Weber, the bureaucracy is politically neutral, carrying out public policies regardless of which party or government faction is in power. But the bureaucracies of modern democratic and non-democratic governments do more than merely implement decisions authorized by law or by executive fiat.

Today, a bureaucracy's functions include the provision of policy information and advice to elected officials—and therein lies a source of potent influence over the shaping of policy decisions. Public policy in many states reflects the power of modern administrators over elected or

Focus On Bureaucracy and Globalization

The twentieth century witnessed the most extensive bureaucratization of human activity, with most societies adopting bureaucratic principles in the interests of efficiency. Never before have so many organizations been established to get things done within the confines of each nation-state and at the global level.

The prospect of bureaucratic activity encompassing the whole planet has now become a reality—what Arnold Toynbee has called "the universal state." This means that the infrastructure of world government has first evolved as bureaucratic activity and will ultimately acquire a legislative and executive character at some later date, most likely in this century.

The twentieth century saw the rapid growth in the number of states and an even faster percentage growth of all types of international organizations. There was a 400 percent expansion in the number of new states during the last century. According to the United Nations Department of Public Information, there has been an 853 percent growth in international organizations (IGOs) and a 6706 percent growth in the number of non-governmental organizations (NGOs) since the beginning of the twentieth century (www.undpi.org).

Over the course of the twentieth century, numerous Canadian government departments and agencies were organized to regulate and provide services to Canadians. Examples are the Canadian Wheat Board and the Canadian Food Inspection Agency. As new social and global problems have arisen, such as BSE ("mad cow" disease) SARS, and climate change, the government has created new bureaucracies, further expanding the scope of public services into the global community. Today, many Canadian government services are accessible on the internet as e-government.

The idea of a universal global government bureaucracy will be a reality in the twenty-first century. Our global society, so concentrated and interconnected, simply cannot exist indefinitely without a sovereign government for the whole.

appointed representatives. The permanent official, able to spend a career accumulating expertise in policy areas, has an enormous advantage over the elected politician whose job security depends on the electorate. Today's bureaucracies are human institutions and are not as impersonal or predictable (nor are they always as efficient) as the Weberian ideal would have them.

WHAT GOVERNMENT BUREAUCRACIES DO

We noted that modern states, regardless of their philosophical persuasion, require vast amounts of governing. All modern governments must perform a variety of administrative functions, which include implementing and formulating policies, providing services, and gathering information.

> FACTFILE   The *Constitution Act, 1867*, guarantees the rights of all to request use of both the French and English languages in the law courts and in Parliament. These rights were reaffirmed in the *Official Languages Act*, 1969, and extended to those Canadians dealing with the public service.

Implementation of Policy

The primary function of all government administrations is the execution and enforcement of the laws and regulations passed by the executive and legislative branches of government and sometimes ruled on by the courts. In this regard, bureaucratic activity often affects everybody, every day. In the process of implementing government policies, bureaucrats assess our property values, issue our driver's licenses, collect our taxes, pay us our pensions, execute court orders, and send us our employment-insurance cheques. Many people earn their living in bureaucratic jobs. Government bureaucracy determines whether we can build a house, add to the one we own, or pave our driveways. It follows us through

life, recording our marriages, the birth of our children, and finally our deaths.

Public administration can affect the quality of life of people beyond our borders. In Ottawa, the Department of Foreign Affairs and International Trade administers Canada's foreign policies, not only through a worldwide network of embassies and consulates, but also through the international divisions of other domestic departments such as Agriculture, Communications, and Fisheries and Oceans. Its policies towards other states—vis-à-vis trade, investment, and aid—create jobs for Canadians, as well as provide benefits to the people of other states where these policies apply.

Two Patterns of Government Administration

The patterns of administration vary from state to state with respect to arrangements, structures, and techniques. In the Western world, two general patterns of administration have evolved: the *Anglo-American* type and the *continental European* type.

The Anglo-American pattern grew out of a basic distrust of centralized authority and encouraged the accountability of administrators through legislative and executive controls of their activities. The federal systems of larger states like Australia, Canada, the United States, and India have intermediate levels of administration under the separate jurisdictions of provinces and states. Because of their federal structures, the administrations of these states are much less centralized and more accountable than in Great Britain, which is a unitary state.

The continental type maintains a tradition established under previous monarchical rule of administrative control from the centre. Local levels of administration are organized as appendages of the central government. In France, the ministries of the national government dominate local administration through *tutelle administrative* (administrative tutelage). One deviation from the continental model is Germany, where the *Länder* (states) conduct most administrative functions, enforce federal laws, and supply federal services. But the public funds allocated to these programs originate at the federal level.

Dictatorial governments at various levels of economic development reflect an affinity to the continental European administrative model. Their administrative structures—for reasons associated with political control—appear to allow only very limited autonomy in local bureaucratic initiatives. The national administrative organizations of authoritarian states tend to be elitist. This results in the top-down application of national policies. Many African and Latin American states have these kinds of bureaucracies. Authoritarian states in these regions of the world are characterized by centralized bureaucracies that include the usual ministries, departments, and bureaus organized under the direct control of the dictator.

Today, many authoritarian government administrations are a confusing jumble of "departments," "agencies," "sections," "offices," and "centres." Authoritarian executives have developed two control strategies over their administrations. The first is to staff as many key positions as possible with political followers, friends, and family, e.g., Saudi Arabia's ruling family. The second is to create a political and financial dependency on the executive branch of government. Patronage and corruption build an especially dependent relationship between the executive and administrative branches of government.

> FACTFILE In their book, *Reinventing Government*, David Osborne and Ted Gaebler challenged government bureaucracies to become more innovative by partnering with the private sector to contract work out, to compete among themselves, and to regard citizens as consumers of government policies and programs.

Two major effects of these formal control systems characterized by executive decision-making procedures are **red tape** and corruption. It is frequently observed that officials at all levels of public administration delay decisions for weeks and sometimes years, and accept bribes for special favours or even for the routine performance of their regularly constituted duties.

Totalitarian states create enormous administrative machines to achieve their ultimate goals of communism. Communist theorists regard the primary functions of the state apparatus as the implementation of party discipline. Because of the vastness of these administrations, the management of totalitarian government has usually been inefficient and characterized by apathy, corruption, delay, and confusion. China, the biggest and oldest of the world's bureaucracies, is also a communist administrative system. Not only does the bureaucracy in China implement the policies of government, but it is also charged with exercising political and economic control of society through the Communist Party.

Formulation of Policy

In modern democracies, the vast house of bureaucracy has come to have an immense impact on the creation of public policy. Today, public administrators have assumed the important task of initiating many policy proposals based on the changing needs of their departments and the people they serve. The fact that civil servants often *formulate* policy proposals—that are then passed by a congress or parliament—is a source of concern to the public and their elected officials because it means that politicians may be colonized by administrators.[3] In a democracy, it is one thing for administrators to exert influence on the law-making process, but quite another for them to draft the laws.

However, access to information, expertise, and the organizational wisdom of government departments makes many administrators much more than just advisers to their political bosses. In Canada's Department of Foreign Affairs and

International Trade, for example, civil servants enjoy a virtual monopoly over information on foreign policy matters. Senior civil servants take the lead in recommending changes to the minister in the complicated aspects of Canadian foreign policy. Because politicians rarely have alternative sources for analyzing Canada's external relations, they tend to accept the advice of bureaucrats in developing foreign policy.

FACTFILE   In Canada, calls for a "New Public Management" (NPM) challenge government bureaucracies to become more flexible, to measure their work in terms of productivity and outcomes, to regard citizens as clients, and to be more open and transparent.

Much of the legislation passed by democratic legislatures is broadly framed. This allows government agencies a great deal of **bureaucratic discretion** in the implementation of programs and policies. Government departments and agencies need loosely outlined rules so that they are able to meet new situations as they arise. But often the details of a program are left to the discretion of administrators out of political necessity. The end result is that administrators have broad powers of interpretation to fill in the specific details of a policy. In this process, they have much to say about how a policy is applied. Thus, the administrators are often in the business of making policy.

The Eurocrats

One of the best examples of a government bureaucracy that extensively formulates policies is the European Commission. The Commission's chief role is to initiate and propose new policies and regulations for the European Union (EU). By comparison with other democratic government bureaucracies, the European Commission overtly prepares and formulates legislation for approval by the Council of Ministers and the European Parliament.

At their massive headquarters in Brussels, *Eurocrats* make polices on everything from the elasticity of athletic shorts to the digestive quality of zucchini. They decide what regulations should be imposed on the items people manufacture and consume. So powerful are the Eurocrats in the New Europe that they can dismantle state-owned monopolies without the formal approval of the member-states. The commission also has the power to act on its own in the formulation of competition policy, farming, trade policy, and customs duties.

There are 24 000 bureaucrats, most of whom work at the International Congress Centre, the nerve centre of an expanded EU, now with 27 members. At its present stage of political evolution, the Eurocrats are the self-appointed high priests of bureaucracy, accountable to no one but themselves. The supranational government developing in Europe is an excellent example of an **administocracy** because these are the people who are making the policies that will unite the member-states and enable the governance of this new political system.

Regulating Our Behaviour

Many of us meet bureaucracy head-on when it applies the many **regulations** that governments generate and update each year. Things seem to be done to us or for us according to stringent regulations that demand our acquiescence and, always, the completion of forms. Encounters with bureaucracy are very often shaped by books of rules, manuals of procedure, and forms to fill out.

In Canada, numerous regulations flow from all the departments of the provincial and federal governments. Virtually every aspect of private, corporate, and governmental behaviour is regulated: airlines, atomic energy, customs and immigration, consumer and corporate affairs, labour, radio, television, and sports are some of the most visible areas of regulatory activity. In recent decades, the

Perspectives   What Is an Administocracy?

Administocracy is a term coined by Guy S. Claire (1934), meaning a type of government that is created when bureaucrats exercise more governing and decision-making powers than elected officials.

In an administocracy, bureaucrats make decisions that permit them to simultaneously formulate and implement public policy without having to account to those who are governed by running in elections. An administocracy results when the powers and responsibility of governance are primarily in the hands of people who are hired and appointed to government positions, not elected by the people to fill their positions.

The early theorists of bureaucracy believed that professional bureaucrats would never make policy, but that they would merely execute the will of the elected officials by implementing their policies in an impartial and efficient way. The idea of a non-partisan, neutral, and compliant administration was the original motivation behind the development of a merit-oriented public service.

An administocracy can emerge in any public administration, whether it is a government or a university. It is a distortion of the goals in any organization when the interests of its administration supersede those it is expected to serve.

An administocracy creates an aristocracy of administrators whose personnel are not publicly accountable, but who nevertheless make public policy and exercise the most powerful discretions of government in the implementation of policy.

federal government has passed more statutes regulating the economy than had been passed during the first 100 years since Confederation.[4]

Along with the dramatic increase in the number of regulatory statutes has been the proliferation of regulatory agencies by which governments seek to influence, direct, and control economic and social behaviour. For example, in three areas of fundamental importance to government in Canada—telecommunications, transportation, and energy—regulatory agencies make decisions that have enormous impact on the allocation of Canadian resources, the organization of production and consumption, and the distribution of income. The Canadian Radio-television and Telecommunications Commission (CRTC), the Canadian Transport Commission (CTC), and the National Energy Board actually make and interpret regulations in their respective fields that have the effect of law and directly affect citizens every day.

There is an extensive relationship between regulative bureaucratic agencies and the individual in contemporary Canada. In periods of high unemployment, the application of regulations of the Employment Insurance Commission and provincial welfare agencies affect the quality of life for millions of people. In recent years, regulations in Canada have extended to include the prohibition of discrimination against minorities and women in employment, the control of pollution, and the commercial uses of metric and imperial weights and measures.

FACTFILE   There are more than 200 Canadian federal and provincial regulatory tribunals that make binding decisions for resolving disputes in every conceivable facet of public policy.

Industrialization and urbanization have produced problems in transportation, health, and the public order in all countries. Growth in industry and technology has created problems of monopolies,

Crosscurrents   Do We Have Too Many Government Regulations?

Increasingly, complaints about federal and provincial governments focus on whether there are too many rules, too many forms to fill out, and too many strictures on activities that should be unrestricted or at least less restricted. Despite some moves in the 1990s to reduce certain forms of regulation, government departments and regulatory agencies still oversee a wide variety of our activities.

In Canada, governments have acquired many regulatory mandates, affecting such areas as airlines, business competition, communications, consumer protection and information, culture, energy, financial markets and institutions, food, health and safety, human rights, labour, liquor, professional licensing, transportation, rent control, and wildlife.

Critics argue that too much regulating occurs and that the effects of regulation are far from efficient. They say the problem with regulation is that it raises prices, distorts market forces and—worst of all—does not work. Critics estimate that government regulation costs the country tens of millions of dollars each year—although it is rarely estimated how much is saved through regulation. And, we must also recognize that frequently the participants in the regulatory debate are not disinterested observers.

What about *deregulation*? Arguments supporting deregulation—the drive to eliminate many regulations currently on the books and to cut back on the power of regulatory agencies—centre on the premise that the heavy hand of government has been suppressing competition and thereby discouraging both innovation and the provision of better service to customers.

Following are some of the specific accusations against the regulatory system:

- It raises prices. When producers are faced with expensive regulations on their products, for instance, gasoline and heating oil, these costs are inevitably passed on to the consumer in the form of higher prices.
- It hurts Canada's position abroad. Other states may have fewer regulations on pollution, worker safety, and other business practices than Canada. When this occurs, Canadian products cost more in the international marketplace, hurting sales of our products and services in other economies because they are less competitive.
- It does not always work well. Tales of failed regulatory policies are numerous because many regulations may be difficult to enforce. Critics charge that regulations sometimes do not achieve the results that Parliament intended, and they simply lead to more bureaucracy and less incentive.

industrial safety, the ethical applications of modern technologies, and labour exploitation. At the same time, the growth of science and the widespread attitude that people should control their environment have led to the popular acceptance that social control can be accomplished only through administrative action.

Providing Services to Us

Many administrative agencies are created to provide government services of various kinds to individuals and groups in society. Environment Canada is one of the best examples of an important service agency administered by the federal government. Its inland and marine forecasts are vital to all modes of transportation, as well as to businesses, farmers, and fishers. Canada's Department of Agriculture and its provincial counterparts conduct research on pest control, land management, livestock improvement, and the marketing and distribution of agricultural products. Human Resources Development Canada runs an extensive job-finding service in all notable Canadian towns and cities. Health Canada funds and co-ordinates Canada's health-care program with the departments of health in the provinces. And the Royal Canadian Mint, headed by a Master of the Mint, is a Crown corporation responsible for minting coins for Canada and some 30 other states.

The efforts made by governments in different administrative service areas are a percentage of the gross domestic product (GDP) and a reflection of their political values; thus, they vary from one state to the next. In 2006, Israel spent 43 percent of its GDP on defence and only 4.9 percent on health and other welfare services, whereas Germany spent 4.0 percent of its GDP on defence and 31 percent on health and other welfare services.[5]

Education, social security, and health are administrative services provided by most governments, but they are affected by the level of national wealth or the general health of an economy. It is difficult for poor economies to allocate their financial resources to services like these when their budgets are limited. The wealthier states can afford to choose how and for what purposes to provide government services to their citizens.

Licensing Our Activities

As an administrative function, licensing is both a means of control and a source of government revenue. It enables governments to set standards and

Focus On A Public Servant

Ian E. Bennett was appointed President and CEO of the Royal Canadian Mint on June 12, 2006. A distinguished federal public servant, Mr. Bennett has held several positions within the Department of Finance, including Deputy Minister from October 2004 to June 2006. Previously, he served as Executive Director of the International Monetary Fund representing Canada, Ireland, and the Caribbean countries from September 2001 to October 2004.

Mr. Bennett has also held other senior positions within the federal government, including Associate Deputy Minister of Finance and G-7 Deputy for Canada from 1996 to 2001, Associate Deputy Minister of Revenue Canada, and Deputy Secretary to the Cabinet (Operations). Born in Nelson, British Columbia, he holds a Bachelor of Arts degree (First Class Honours in Economics and Commerce) from Simon Fraser University and a Masters of Arts degree in Economics from the University of Toronto.

qualifications on activities having public conse-quences. Driving a car, hunting, fishing, practis-ing medicine or law, selling real estate, teaching in public schools, and owning and operating a radio or television station are just some of the areas in which governments impose licensing require-ments. In Canada and other federal states, most of these standards are set by the provinces; however, some licences are issued by the federal govern-ment. But in unitary states, such as France, Great Britain, and Israel, the national government is the sole licensing authority.

In one sense, licensing involves the provision of a service, but in another sense it also involves a considerable amount of regulation. The Canadian Radio-television and Telecommunications Com-mission (CRTC) is an agency that was created in 1968 to protect the Canadian broadcasting sys-tem. Its objectives are to monitor and regulate programs so that they are of high quality for public consumption. Similarly, the regulatory functions of any government agency are involved in the power to grant or withhold licenses to permit certain activities.

Gathering Information

All bureaucracies gather and store vast amounts of information from the outside world. The gathering of information is a major function of all government administrations. Eventually, information results in an output of policy or action by the political system. Governments want to know everything about you: who you are, when you were born, how much edu-cation you have, what your occupation is, when you die, and what you die from. Governments gather information by means of administrative research, questionnaires, polls, public hearings, commissions, task forces, committees, and licensing.

FACTFILE   By 2007, the number of French-Canadians in the federal bureaucracy reflected their proportion of the total population of the country at 28 percent.

In Canada, all government departments and administrative agencies generate and consume massive quantities of data about the private and corporate behaviour of Canadians, as well as about Canada's foreign relations with the international community. Canada's health ministry conducts research into the diseases that afflict Canadians. Industry Canada co-ordinates information on busi-nesses and corporations in Canada. And the Department of Foreign Affairs and International Trade receives vital information from its embassies and consulates around the world.

Many departments of government, in order to carry out their programs, gather information on the private lives of individuals. The Department of Justice has, among other responsibilities, the role of gathering statistics on crime and subver-sion. Its files hold information on even the most intimate aspects of the lives of certain individual citizens.

Most of the information collected by govern-ments is not controversial. In Canada, the census gathers information about the population in order to help government make policy choices that fit the needs of the people. Canada's sixteenth census, taken in 2006, contains millions of pages of data on Canadians. Canadians willingly told more than 30 000 enumerators whether they were athletes—more than two million said they were—and how many flush toilets they had—87 000 had none. (www.12.statcan.ca/english/census06/release/index.cfm).

But there is always a potential danger in the collection of such data. Bureaucratic agencies know about our life histories, our financial affairs, our credit ratings, our reputations for loyalty, our politics, and our places of residence. Even without our knowledge, police investigations may detail and hold on file whatever stories a neighbour or even a stranger has told about us.

In these days of computerized data retrieval, this information can be pulled together and disseminated with frightening speed. Only such human factors as the good will and decent motives of most bureaucrats may save us from the worst invasions of our privacy. But people do lose jobs and suffer other hardships because of unsubstantiated rumours that are registered in their files. The private lives, opinions, and morals of individuals are becoming increasingly vulnerable to bureaucratic scrutiny. The sheer volume of personal information in data banks, both public and private, is a threat not only to our credit ratings but also to our freedom to live as we choose.

> **FACTFILE** Since 2000, Canadians have been able to access information on government via e-government, an online government service that allows citizens greater opportunity to interact directly with their government.

In most states, the public has no right of access to the vast store of information in reports, records, files, and statistics gathered by governments through their administrative agencies. But a growing number of democratic states have decided that this practice is wrong and should be reversed: all unclassified administrative documents ought to be accessible to the public, except for information classified as secret by law. Usually called freedom-of-information acts, access acts, or privacy acts, these constitutional and legislative provisions are now operative in a growing number of states.

> **FACTFILE** Over 70 countries in the world have laws that implement some form of freedom of information for their citizens. Canada's *Freedom of Information Act*, 2000, is one such piece of legislation.

Sweden was the first state to grant the right of public access to government documents in its constitutional law in 1766. Other states have proclaimed access laws in more recent times: Australia (1982), Canada (*Privacy Act*, 1982, and *Access to Information Act*, 1983, *Freedom of Information Act*, 2000), Denmark (1970), Finland (1951), France (1978), the Netherlands (1978), Norway (1970), and the United States (1966,

revised 1974). In Canada, two provinces, Nova Scotia (1977) and New Brunswick (1978), passed access-to-information legislation applicable to provincial administrative documents and government files. By 2007, all provinces had similar legislation.

At the federal level, the *Privacy Act* gives citizens and residents access to information about them held by the government, protects their privacy by preventing others from gaining access to it, and gives them some control over its collection and use. The *Freedom of Information Act* gives the same people the right to examine or obtain copies of the records of a federal government institution, except in limited and specific circumstances. The *Access Register* and *Access Request Forms* are located in public libraries, in government information offices, and in postal stations in rural areas. However, in 2008 the minority Harper government discontinued access to the information registry, the Coordination of Access to Information Request System (CAIRS). This electronic list was used by journalists, academics, and the public to track requests and government responses to requests between government agencies.

> **FACTFILE** In Canada, when individual citizens or groups apply to the federal government for information, they are supposed to receive it within 30 days; if denied, they can appeal to the Information Commissioner, who can overrule the department.

Redistribution of wealth and income

Governments intervene in the social system for reasons other than efficiency and regulation. When governments administer what are called *redistributive policies*, then they may, in effect, take suits from wealthy tailors and give them to those who have no clothes and nothing to trade. Policies of this sort redistribute the pieces of the economic pie among certain individuals and groups in society. They are aimed at changing the existing patterns of wealth and income in the economy. In short, they aspire to widen the range of those who receive a share of the national wealth. They produce benefits to segments of society at a cost to others.

A progressive income tax is a redistributive measure because it is designed to take more tax money from the rich than the poor and thus reduce the traditional disparities of wealth and income across the population. In Canada, minimum-wage laws have a redistributive effect because they result in higher expenditures by employers on wages for unskilled workers. Welfare laws designed to help the needy are also redistributive. Each year, the federal government provides billions of dollars in the form of transfer payments to the provinces as a national strategy to redistribute wealth and, as

much as possible, to standardize the delivery of government services to Canadians.

CONTROLLING THE BUREAUCRATS

Executive Controls

All states have developed a variety of formal and informal controls on bureaucratic behaviour (Table 7.3). One obvious major government control that takes place outside the administration of government is the political executive. Prime ministers, presidents, and ministers formally control the bureaucracy through their powers of appointment

Table 7.3	Controls on bureaucratic behaviour	
	Formal	*Informal*
E	Political executives:	Public opinion
X	presidents, prime ministers,	Media
T	premiers, governors	Pressure groups
E	Elected assemblies:	Electorate
R	parliaments, congresses,	University public-
N	city councils	administration programs
A	Courts	
L	Ombuds officer	
I	Public hearings	Professional standards
N	Inquiries	Upgrading
T	Royal commissions	Accountability
E	Decentralization and	
R	deregulation	
N		
A		
L		

Sources: Donald Kettl, Civil Service Reform *(Washington, DC: Brookings Institution, 1996); David Johnson,* Thinking Government: Public Sector Management in Canada, *2nd ed. (Toronto: University of Toronto Press, 2006).*

and removal. They also have the power of the purse, from which bureaucracies are funded and programs are planned. While it is true that political executives cannot get along without the services of bureaucracies, it is also true that bureaucrats are controlled by them in a variety of ways. The executive can tame an administration by threatening to reduce government spending for a particular department, or by cutting back the size of the civil service.

Legislative Controls

Legislatures are another branch of government that can exercise significant external controls on a bureaucracy. Through questioning and criticism of the government in Parliament, public administrators are held accountable to the ministers who run the departments. The public expects legislators, both as opposition and as backbenchers, to monitor official waste of public funds and to deal with those who violate the law or violate citizens' rights in the conduct of their jobs. Legislative committees can scrutinize departmental administration and are empowered to investigate abuses of administrative authority. Public inquiries, auditors' reports, questions of parliamentarians, hearings, commissions, and court decisions all have an effect on bureaucratic performance. These formal controls work to secure a responsive, effective, and honest civil service.

> FACTFILE The attacks of 9/11 led the US government to add 40 000 federal employees, who were hired as airport security and other border security employees.

Legislatures can compel a bureaucracy to change administrative policy by creating a new law or revoking a department's or agency's powers. In all parliamentary systems of government, bureaucracies must defend their budgetary requests before an appropriate legislative committee or cabinet minister. In Canada, legislative committees have, among other functions, the power to scrutinize how government departments manage their budgets. The Public Accounts Committee and the Standing Joint Committee of the Senate and the House of Commons are chaired by a member of the opposition, whose independence from Cabinet control forces a greater accountability in the administration of government departments.

In many states, especially the United States, the **power of the purse** is as much a legislative as an executive power. The mere threat of withholding funds can force an administrative change in policy. In Canada and Great Britain, individual members of parliament indirectly exercise restraints by becoming experts on particular subjects. An MP can ask a question of any minister concerning the administrative policies and practices of his or her ministry. Asking questions is the principal method by which backbenchers can review and criticize the action of the civil service.

In Canada, another legislative control instrument that scrutinizes bureaucratic behaviour is the Office of the Auditor General (OAG) and provincial auditors in the provinces. The **auditor general** reports annually to Parliament on its verification of the government's financial records and whether departments have wisely spent the monies appropriated to them. The auditor general operates independently of executive controls, and the Auditor General's Report keeps bureaucrats accountable to their departmental budgets. In the United States, the General Accounting Office, the Congressional Research Service, the Office of Technology Assessment, and the Congressional Budget Office give Congress information about bureaucratic conduct independently from the executive branch of government.

Courts

Then there are the courts. They have the final authority to interpret the law and to rule on the proper administration and enforcement of laws in society. When private citizens or corporations feel that an administrative practice is unfair or that an administrator has stepped outside his or her jurisdiction, they can seek a legal remedy through the courts. In Canada, the courts can review administrative discretion when there have been breaches of natural justice, when the Constitution is violated by bureaucratic behaviour, and when there are errors of law made in the interpretation and implementation of public policy.

In 1991, the Supreme Court of Canada ruled that ministers cannot be held criminally responsible for what goes on in their departments unless they have special knowledge of an illegal act. But the Court also noted that ministers cannot seek refuge behind an entourage of government lawyers when bureaucrats in their departments abuse their powers without their

Focus On The Auditor General

Canadians hold their governments accountable by means of a parliamentary official called the auditor general. The Office of Auditor General (OAG) is a special independent administrative agency that prepares the annually published report to Parliament called the Auditor General's Report. This report is submitted to Parliament through the Speaker of the House of Commons and not to the government.

There was a time when these reports were limited to detailing all instances of waste and dishonesty that were uncovered by the auditor general. The office was relatively small and certainly frugal, and its work was strictly rooted in principles of accounting. It would hold the media's attention for a day or two—hence the references to the report as a "one-day wonder."

Things have changed dramatically in recent years. Since the *Auditor General Act, 1977*, the Auditor General and staff have had the power to carry out "value for money audits"—to assess policy and the substance of spending decisions. The auditor general now reports more than once a year. The so-called one-day wonder repeats itself throughout the government's fiscal year, as did the report of February 10, 2004, that disclosed the "sponsorship scandal." The auditor general may also make special reports, separate from its annual report.

The Cabinet appoints the auditor general at the rank of a deputy minister for a 10-year renewable term (until age 65). The auditor general can be removed within that term only by a resolution of both houses of Parliament. The OAG has sweeping powers to randomly audit the accounts of federal departments and agencies, and to verify whether decisions made by government politicians and administrators are being made honestly, realistically, efficiently, and effectively. This means that the financial affairs of most agencies of the federal government—including their accounting practices and how they manage and report their activities—are audited and verified by the auditor general's office. The Cabinet may deny access to material it deems confidential, opening the possibility for a court challenge from the auditor general's office and a visible controversy in Parliament.

The Auditor General's Report is widely considered an important yardstick of government performance. The report is analyzed by the Public Accounts Committee, which is the only legislative committee of the House of Commons chaired by a member of the Official Opposition. The committee then recommends changes for future budget expenditures and for improving the financial operations and control of government spending.

direct knowledge. Nor can they pretend to be blind (willful blindness) to what their departments do when these actions are held judicially accountable.

In Canada and the United States, courts can initiate remedies of bureaucratic indiscretions that may take the form of writs instructing administrators to conduct themselves in appropriate ways: a *writ of mandamus* (a court order requiring a public official to do his or her duty as the law dictates), a *writ of injunction* (a court order prohibiting an official or a private citizen from performing a particular action), or a court decision resulting in the payment of damages or the determination of responsibility for the abuse of administrative powers. A *writ of certiorari* is a superior court order that—in addition to other purposes—may be issued against bureaucracies when they violate the doctrine of fairness. *Habeas corpus* is a writ issued by a court requiring that a person who has been detained be brought before a court to determine whether that detention is legal. In administrative law this writ is rarely used except in immigration cases involving orders of custody or deportation. *Quo warranto* is a court order inquiring whether an appointment to public office is legal. *Damages* are court remedies that require a certain amount of money be paid to compensate for an injury or wrong done to an individual by a government bureaucracy. But courts are not always successful in keeping a close check on bureaucratic activities because they are primarily concerned with making and adjudicating laws, not watching over the administration of them.

Constitutional protections

The Canadian Charter of Rights and Freedoms provides constitutional protections of administrative law. This branch of law is concerned with the use and abuse of government powers and with the structures and operations of government bodies. The conduct of bureaucrats is subject to the rigour of Charter rights guarantees and makes the public service subject to the scope of constitutional protections affecting an individual's human and civil rights. Many of the statutes and regulations that existed prior to 1982 have been harmonized under the Charter.

In the United States, a basic principle of the Constitution is limited government. There are certain things that bureaucrats cannot do and should not do under the US *Bill of Rights*. Bureaucratic powers were very important to the Founders of the American republic. They expected Congress to make policy and a representative president to administer it. The US Constitution postulates a "government of laws." No one should stand above the law, especially those involved in the administration of the law.

The office of ombuds

Recognizing the limitations of legislative and judicial controls that leave the initiatives to elected officials or to the aggrieved, an increasing number of states have created a special office of *ombuds* (parliamentary commissioner) to advocate, investigate, and publicly criticize on behalf of citizens who complain about unfair bureaucratic treatment. Sweden was the first country to create a *Justitieombudsmannen* (representative of justice) in 1809. The Swedish *Riksdag* (Parliament) appoints the "ombudsman," who is empowered to hear and investigate citizen complaints of official **arbitrariness**, **negligence**, or discrimination. The ombuds has comprehensive **jurisdiction**, which includes the supervision of the courts and the military.

The office of ombuds has been adopted in about 25 democratic states, including Canada, Denmark, Fiji, Finland, France, Great Britain, Israel, New Zealand, and Germany. Not all states have offices at the national level. Canada and the United States have no general ombuds at the federal level. However, both have ombuds at the provincial and state levels, respectively. In Canada, all provinces except PEI have ombuds offices to remedy complaints against provincial administrations. In the United States, only Alaska, Iowa, Hawaii, and Nebraska have ombuds officers, but the office has been established in a number of US cities as well, such as in Atlanta and Seattle.

As an investigator and mediator appointed to protect the rights of individuals and groups in dealing with government, the ombuds office hears many complaints. When regular government agencies do not resolve problems satisfactorily, the ombuds officer is asked to investigate grievances. In general, these involve:

1. claims for social assistance benefits or workers' compensation;

2. property affected by work on highways;

3. employment or consumer services regulated by the province;

4. difficulties in obtaining licenses or permits; and

5. any other matter regulated by provincial or municipal laws.

In Canada, provincial ombuds do not have the authority to investigate grievances arising from decisions of the Cabinet, the law courts or judges, the federal government, private companies, or individuals.

In April 1978, the Trudeau government introduced a bill to create a federal ombuds office, but it died on the order paper and the government was defeated in May 1979. The Clark government left it off their legislative agenda and the new Trudeau government, elected in February 1980, did not revive the bill. The Mulroney governments (1984 and 1988) did not move on a bill for a general ombuds office to cover all aspects of federal administration. Leadership candidate Kim Campbell promised to establish such an office at the federal level, but she was defeated in 1993. Jean Chrétien's successive governments did not move on the issue. Nor did the government of Paul Martin.

FACTFILE In 2007, Canada's federal Conservative minority government announced the establishment of a Federal Ombuds for Victims of Crime to assist those who may need court-based services to present impact statements, to support victimized children, to travel to National Parole Board hearings, and for all those who may be underserved by existing programs.

It is important to note that Canada has created ombuds-like offices for special matters under federal jurisdiction. For example, a Commissioner of Official Languages reviews complaints from the public if they are treated unfairly in their own language by federal agencies. There is a Correctional Investigator who receives complaints from inmates about injustices in the penal system. Under the *Access to Information Act*, the government has established the office of Information Commissioner to deal with complaints about the wrongful denial of access to information. And, under the *Privacy Act*, the government empowers a Privacy Commissioner to investigate complaints about personal information retained by government agencies and to make recommendations to the institution involved if there is a denial of access. But all of these offices are highly specialized and in no way perform the comprehensive functions of a general ombuds officer.

Among the extra-governmental forces and agencies that attempt to control bureaucracies are pressure groups and the mass media. Pressure groups attempt to reform the bureaucracy by using their own investigative staffs to challenge the efficacy of many types of social programs and to bring pressure to bear upon the government to change the programs. In Canada, the Canadian Federation of Independent Business (CFIB) has prompted many other organizations to use public opinion and the media as ways to trigger reforms of the tax collection methods of the Canada Revenue Agency.

Bureaucratic accountability is also affected by internal controls, such as professional standards and upgrading, as well as advisory committees made up of people representing political parties and interest groups. The variety and kinds of controls vary from state to state. The term *administocracy*, coined by Guy S. Claire in the 1930s, refers to tensions between the ideals of popular sovereignty and the growth of an aristocracy of administrators within a democratic state.[6] In a democracy, people pay great attention to the values of elected officials but very little to the values of the people who administer government programs. This is all the more important to recognize because career civil servants are neither elected nor removable by the electoral process. But a multiplicity of formal and informal controls function to keep democratic bureaucracies accountable.

These controls are lacking in dictatorial states. Political executives and legislators are usually not accountable, and courts do not function as an independent branch of government. The mass media and pressure groups are strictly controlled by dictatorial governments, and bureaucracies are affiliated with the goals of the government apparatus and subordinate to it.

CANADA'S PUBLIC SERVICE

Broadly speaking, the Canadian bureaucracy consists of the personnel in federal government departments (e.g., the Department of Finance), federal government agencies (e.g., the Bank of Canada and the Canadian Wheat Board), central control agencies (e.g., the Treasury Board and the Privy Council Office), and Crown corporations (e.g., Air Canada and the Canadian Broadcasting Corporation). The great bulk of federal government employees are recruited by the **Public Service Commission**, itself a central control agency serving Parliament that performs its wide staffing functions by means of competitive examinations and interviews in which merit, not patronage, is the determining factor.

FACTFILE By 2003, employment equity programs in Canada's federal public service revealed some successes in creating a more diverse bureaucracy: 52 percent of government employees are women; 33.8 percent of executive government positions are held by women; 3.9 percent of government jobs are held by Aboriginal peoples; 5.6 percent are held by persons who are disabled, and 7.4 percent are held by people in visible minorities.

Legally, Canada's public employees are not appointed or removed from their positions for political reasons. Civil servants are directly responsible, through a definite chain of command, to their administrative superiors. It cannot be denied that political favouritism sometimes plays a part in the choice of job assignments and the speed or delay in promotions, even though in theory the public service rules out politics. In 1988, a ruling by the Federal Court of Appeal struck down part of the law (*The Public Service Employment Act*) that restricted the political rights of federal public servants on the grounds that it infringed on their freedoms of expression and association.

The key political actor in both federal and provincial levels of government is the cabinet minister, who functions as the formal department head and who is responsible for the administration of the government's policies through the public service. The success of a minister in leading a department often depends solely on the qualities of his or her personal leadership and communication skills.[7] But usually the energies of a minister are focused and directed on the politics of Cabinet decision-making. The minister tends not to tamper with the administrative functions of the department itself. Instead, the minister must learn to deal with what Flora MacDonald called the "civil service policy" and try to accommodate the political demands of the Cabinet and those from the constituency with the routines of the department's administration.[8]

The Deputy Minister (DM)

The person second in the line of authority within a department is the deputy minister (DM), who is appointed by the prime minister. Unlike other civil servants, the deputy minister retains an administrative position "at the pleasure" of the government. He or she does not enjoy permanent tenure and may be shuffled, demoted, or fired at the will of the prime minister. Although deputy ministers are held accountable for the policies they helped to devise and for the loyalties they may have demonstrated toward the government that appointed them, most of the time they seem to be able to overcome their associations with out-of-favour governments. They are usually kept on by succeeding governments as a source of valuable advice. The two most important skills of a deputy minister—that of advising and departmental management—are indispensable to

political ministers who need to take command of an administrative machine that was in operation long before they rose to power and will function quite well after they have gone.[9]

In terms of the policy process itself, the deputy minister is a senior policy adviser not only to the minister, but also to the entire government. The segmented process of federal decision making requires deputy ministers to advise other ministers and deputy ministers in order to co-ordinate Cabinet policies and programs. In particular, all deputy ministers must represent and co-ordinate their departments' affairs with three central agencies: The Prime Minister's Office, the Privy Council Office, and the Treasury Board Secretariat.

Crosscurrents Myths and Realities about Canada's Federal Bureaucracy

Myth: Canadians dislike bureaucrats.
Fact: Despite the rhetoric about bureaucracies, Canadians are generally satisfied with bureaucrats and the treatment they get from them. Even though there have been some outstanding examples of recent bureaucratic incompetence and corruption, such as the sponsorship scandal, the Radwanski affair, and the federal gun registry boondoggle, Canadians remain positive about their relationship with individual bureaucrats. In general, they are described by Canadians as helpful, efficient, fair, courteous, and working to serve the interests of the country.

Myth: Bureaucracies are growing bigger and bigger each year.
Fact: The number of public servants has been growing across the country—but not the number of federal employees. Almost all the growth in the number of public employees has occurred at the provincial and municipal levels.

Myth: Most federal bureaucrats work in Ottawa.
Fact: Only about 33 percent of federal civilian employees in the bureaucracy work in Ottawa. The rest work in other communities across Canada, and thousands work in foreign countries. You can see where federal government employees work by looking in your local phone book under the "Government of Canada."

Myth: Bureaucracies are ineffective, inefficient, and always mired in red tape.
Fact: Modern bureaucracy is simply a way of organizing people to perform work in a corporate or public setting. When bureaucracies work well, no one gives them much credit. But when they work poorly, everyone calls them unfair, incompetent, corrupt, or inefficient. Bureaucracies may be inefficient at times, but no one has found a substitute for them. And no one has determined whether government bureaucracies are any more or less inefficient than private bureaucracies.

Over many years of gaining administrative experience, the deputy minister builds an important network of personal and professional contacts that is invaluable to the operation of the government. As administrative head of a department, the deputy minister is like the managing executive of a large corporation. On a daily basis, the deputy minister is an interdepartmental diplomat, a policy coordinator, and a negotiator.

Deputy ministers advise their political bosses on policy matters, plan and control expenditures in the department, scrutinize the organization and structure of the department, and assume the wider responsibilities of coordinating departmental activities with those of other government departments. In this regard, deputy ministers are at the top of a hierarchical chain of command within the structure of the department. They must work within the framework of universal bureaucratic traits that impact on the efficiency of their employees:

1. *Specialization* or **division of labour**—individual jobs have specific tasks assigned to them irrespective of the individual who holds the job.

2. *Hierarchy* or *fixed lines of control*—each civil servant knows who the boss is, and whom, if anyone, he or she may supervise.

3. *Incentives* to attract people to work for the department and be loyal to its purposes. By far the most important incentive is the assurance that once someone has a job, he or she will keep it unless unacceptable conduct is committed.

Sometimes, deputy ministers who are the permanent heads of the department will have administrative interests that may differ from those of the minister and the prime minister they serve. Usually, deputy ministers are fiercely dedicated to the programs they administer. They expect that the minister who heads their department will take their advice and avoid the many transient political pressures that cause cabinet ministers to alter the administration of government programs. They

want the minister to represent the interests of the department to the prime minister. Sometimes, these interests are not necessarily public interests.

Ministers

Ministers are not totally without ways of dealing with central control tendencies of the bureaucracy. Cabinet ministers enjoy a **span of control** and are accompanied by an entourage of aides, executive assistants, and parliamentary secretaries who are directly responsible to them. *Parliamentary secretaries* are members of parliament who are designated by the minister to assist in the political operation of the department. In today's bureaucracy, ministerial aides, executive assistants, and parliamentary secretaries have occupied an increasingly important place in the functioning of the Cabinet. A minister's staff acts as a buffer to the power of the civil service, which can often challenge the minister's ability to control his or her department.

One major function of the minister's staff is to protect and advance the political interests of the department and the Cabinet. This includes liaising with Parliament, press relations, control of the minister's schedule, travel, and relations with major interest groups and party figures. Ministers also have assistants to perform such inevitable but disagreeable tasks as refusing access to the minister, discharging employees and officials, and denying requests for special consideration.

Parliamentary secretaries have some input into the development of new programs and legislation. They also serve to take the heat off the minister from time to time in the House of Commons by standing in to answer sensitive questions directed at the department by members of the opposition. Sometimes, as well, when the minister has accepted an engagement to speak in a politically hostile area of the country, the parliamentary secretary is sent instead to vicariously deflect the political flak away from the minister.

Despite such stratagems, all cabinet ministers are aware of the many difficulties involved in gaining control of the very bureaucracy that is one of the bases of their power.

Crown Corporations

Crown corporations are another important aspect of public administration in Canada.[10] Since World War II, public enterprises have rapidly expanded in the Canadian economy. Crown corporations have been used to meet national or local needs in the interests of the public where private enterprise and investors have not been ready or willing to take the risk to promote economic growth. The development of a national or provincial infrastructure has been costly and risky, culminating in the incorporation of such public enterprises as the St. Lawrence Seaway Authority and the Canadian Broadcasting Corporation. **Private sector** corporate behaviour is profit-motivated; government-owned corporations consider factors such as unemployment, welfare, market failures, and national standards when operating in a community.

There are a number of different ways of defining Crown corporations.[11] The characteristic of government ownership is considered the most important legal criterion. However, there is some disagreement as to what amount of government ownership determines the status of Crown corporations. *Mixed enterprises* are companies, such as the Canada Development Corporation, in which ownership is shared by the government (in the name of the Crown) with the private sector. *Joint enterprises* are public companies, such as the Newfoundland and Labrador Development Corporation, in which ownership is shared between governments, usually a provincial and the federal government.

FACTFILE   Between 1984 and 2000, the largest number of privatizations of Crown corporations took place, including Air Canada, Canadair, de Havilland, Eldorado Nuclear, Teleglobe Canada, Petro-Canada, and Canadian National (CN).

From a functional perspective, Crown corporations reflect common criteria, whether they are provincially, federally, or jointly owned:

- Majority ownership is held by a government.

- There is an arm's-length management strategy, independent from government.

- Corporate goods and services are directed at the private sector, not the government.

- Prices for goods and services provided by Crown corporations must be fair and competitive.

Federal Crown corporations are accountable to Parliament under the *Financial Administration Act* (FAA). The Canadian Broadcasting Corporation, the Canada Council, and the National Arts Centre perform special cultural functions and are distanced from the political controls applied to other corporations. Some Crown corporations, such as the Bank of Canada and the Canada Wheat Board, have been established by special legislation. They perform many diverse functions that require independence from political and ministerial control. For example, the Bank of Canada sets the prime lending rate on Canadian currency in order to keep the interest rate differential between Canada and the United States from becoming too great or too small.

FACTFILE   The Bank of Canada was formed in 1935 as the central bank to play a major role in managing the Canadian economy and in regulating many chartered bank operations.

The governor of the Bank of Canada frequently finds him- or herself at the centre of momentous struggles—involving the federal government, the provinces, and lenders and borrowers—over the bank's monetary policy on such questions as "tight money" or the most desirable political and economic means of combatting inflation or recession.

Crown corporations have a working arrangement with the Public Service Commission that allows them almost complete discretion in hiring and promotion at all levels, particularly at management levels. The labour standards of the Public Service Commission are a model aimed at preventing arbitrary and unfair decisions and equalizing promotion and pay policies for employees among the various Crown corporations.

PUBLIC ADMINISTRATION IN THE UNITED STATES

Beginning with the federal administrative establishment, the primary units of the bureaucracy are the 14 departments—collectively the largest part—most of whose heads carry the title *secretary* and who make up most of the cabinet. Also included are the *independent regulatory commissions*, the *government corporations*, the *unaffiliated agencies*, and a host of *boards* and *administrations*.

The secretaries are appointed by the president and approved by the Senate.[12] Most of the departments have more than one *undersecretary* who functions as the personal assistant to the secretary. Below the undersecretaries are the assistant secretaries, each of whom is responsible for a major division within the department. Each division is made up of bureaus. Each bureau is headed by a director or an administrator who functions as a bureau chief and manages the administrative programs of the departments.

Independent regulatory commissions are other major components of the federal bureaucracy. They are intended to make and administer regulatory policies in the public interest. The commissions, such as the Federal Trade Commission (FTC), the Civil Aeronautics Board (CAB), and the Federal Aviation Agency (FAA), are independent in the sense that, unlike the conventional departments, they are not in the chain of command leading to the president: the commissioners cannot be dismissed by the president at will. The commissions are quasi-legislative: they are empowered by Congress to make many supplementary laws of their own. They are quasi-judicial: they hold court-like hearings to make decisions affecting industry, commercial services, and private citizens. Most regulatory commissions deal with industries that are natural monopolies (such as electric power companies) or with business activities in which unrestrained competition damages the industry or the public interest.

Congress also uses the government-owned corporation to pursue specified government policies. These specially chartered corporations, such as the Federal Deposit Insurance Corporation (FDIC), the Tennessee Valley Authority (TVA), and the United States Postal Service, are created by the government to do a particular job. The FDIC is generally responsible for insuring the deposits of the banking public; and the TVA makes and sells electric power to the vast region in the Tennessee Valley, operating in much the same way as any large business corporation.

A host of other unaffiliated agencies, boards, and administrations stand on their own, but are directly responsible to the president or Congress. Some of these agencies are very large, complex, and important. The Veterans Administration (VA) operates a national system of hospitals and administers veterans' programs, employing nearly 200 000 people. It is larger than any of the departments except Defense. Other important unaffiliated bodies are the National Aeronautics and Space Administration (NASA) and the Environmental Protection Agency (EPA). Such agencies are often established in order to pioneer a particular policy area, NASA being an obvious case in point with respect to space.

A *professional* civil service in the United States originated as the product of an act of political violence. In the latter part of the nineteenth century, the patronage system (in which federal jobs were given as rewards for service to one of the political parties) flourished. A new president could make patronage appointments to most of the administrative jobs in the federal government. "To the victor belong the spoils" was the caption of the **spoils system** in US federal politics.[13] Old office-holders were simply turned out after a new president was inaugurated.

FACTFILE It was US President Andrew Jackson (1828–1836) who coined the term "spoils system," referring to his political right to appoint public personnel who were loyal to him and his party as one of the "spoils" of his election victories.

In 1881, an angered, unsuccessful spoils-seeker shot and killed President James Garfield. After a great deal of pressure from reform groups campaigning against the patronage system, Congress passed the *Pendleton Act* (1883), establishing the Civil Service Commission (now called the Office of Personnel Management); as a result, a merit system based on competitive examinations was created for hiring and promoting federal employees.

Today, over 75 percent of all civil servants in the United States are under the central merit system administered by the Office of Personnel Management. Most of the remaining federal employees are recruited by the separate merit systems of individual agencies such as the Federal Bureau of Investigation (FBI). There are over 1000 jobs not covered by civil service regulation that go mainly to people within the president's party (a downscaled spoils system). Many of these appointees are close friends and supporters of the president.

The Office of Personnel Management is the central employment agency for the national government. It advertises positions, receives applications and, most importantly, establishes, administers, and evaluates a system of competitive recruitment. When a government department or agency wants to hire someone, the Office of Personnel Management is notified. It then supplies the names of the three top achievers on the appropriate exam to the recruiting agency. The administrator must select one of the three successful candidates.

Unlike in Canada, in the United States both the executive and legislative branches of government have the power to create their own separate bureaucracy under the Constitution. The bureaucracy serves both executive and law-making functions of the president and the Congress. However, as in Canada, the American federal bureaucracy is involved in every stage of the policy-making process. It drafts the bills that eventually become laws, administers the execution of them, and interprets the patterns of detailed applications that determine what those laws eventually mean in practice. The more routine a policy decision, the larger part the bureaucracy is likely to play in it.

Presidents must give the bureaucracy executive direction because they represent the entire country and must see to it that administrators follow that direction. The Congress, which represents the many regional interests of Americans, must be ever watchful of the bureaucracy, too. Through its powers of appropriation and investigation, the Congress has to check possible abuses of bureaucratic authority from the perspective of constituents and constituencies.

However, the US federal bureaucracy has evolved into a power with an independent life of its own.[14] It is at least partially independent of the president, the Congress, and the courts. The federal bureaucracy is primarily directed by a relatively small group of experienced career-executive administrators with permanent civil-service status. These people occupy the "super grade" positions of the administration, and they remain in their positions despite changes in the White House or Congress. Career executives are protected from the perils of partisan politics and are expected to serve the "national interest" even through changes in the political fortunes of the two major political parties. For political scientists in the United States, the bureaucracy is viewed as the fourth branch of government.

Chapter Summary

Today, the administration of government is a vital part of all advanced societies and, some would argue, the largest and most powerful branch of government in many political systems. All governments create bureaucracies, whatever the character of the political regime. Bureaucracy gives government organizations their memory, their capacity to gather, store, and disseminate information, and the professional skills and practices to deliver public services.

But bureaucracy is not just a phenomenon of government. The twentieth century witnessed the *bureaucratization* of every area of human activity, in business, recreation, and all non-governmental international interaction.

This chapter demonstrates that in all modern political systems, bureaucracy comprises departments, regulatory agencies, commissions, bureaus, public corporations, and national industries; and it employs a sizable segment of the labour force.

Contrary to the general view that policy-making is the function of elected officials and that bureaucrats only implement and execute policy, bureaucracy is shown to be an integral actor in the processes of making policy and recommending legislation. Bureaucrats now directly influence policy in all modern societies, not only because of the information and advice they provide but also because public servants have, over time, empowered themselves to make policy. Thus, the role of bureaucracy overlaps with the legislative, executive, and judicial branches of government in the processes of formulating, interpreting, and implementing the laws.

Max Weber observed that bureaucracy tends to produce common attributes: division of labour, hierarchy of authority, written rules and regulation, impersonal delivery of services, and job security.

Government administrations in democratic states perform similar functions: they implement, formulate, and regulate policy; provide services; administer licences; gather and disseminate information; and redistribute wealth.

Canada's public service consists of all federal government departments, federal government agencies, central control agencies, and Crown corporations.

The public service operates on the merit principle, which takes politics out of the hiring and promoting of public employees.

Discussion Questions

1. Explain the origin and meaning of the term *bureaucracy*. Discuss Max Weber's characteristics of bureaucracy. Are they still relevant today? Is bureaucracy an inevitable part of the modern age? Could we survive with less of it?

2. Discuss why the "expert knowledge" of the professional administrator is needed for the formulation of sound public policy. Should the public be concerned that unelected government employees have such a powerful position in formulating public policy? Do you believe that only elected politicians should formulate the laws that govern us?

3. The average citizen is likely to think of the public service primarily in terms of the regulation of individual and group conduct, overlooking the vast and varied forms of protection, assistance, and services that government provides. List as many of these latter activities as you can and discuss the role they play in your life.

4. Do government bureaucracies form their own political constituencies that compete for power and benefits from government? How do bureaucrats protect their interests in the public system? How did the sponsorship scandal, which came to light in 2004, reflect on the accountability of the federal bureaucracy in Canada?

5. What are the formal and informal controls of bureaucracy, and why must this branch of government be so closely watched? Should Canada have a federal ombuds office?

6. Have you ever considered becoming a civil servant? What are some of the attractions of such a career?

8

Law and the Courts

After reading this chapter, you will be able to:

- distinguish between the concepts of *law* and *custom* and think about their role in Canada
- identify the four essential elements of law and consider their application in the laws we obey every day
- define *positive law* and gives examples
- outline the sources of law in Canada and other states
- explain the origin and meaning of *common law*
- differentiate between common law and civil law
- explain why Quebec uses civil law codes in private law
- describe the unique character of other legal systems
- conceptualize what the judiciary is and distinguish between the legal and judicial systems
- explain Canada's court system
- outline the functions of the judicial system
- understand the job of a Supreme Court Justice
- compare the Canadian and US judicial systems

• • • •

DEFINING LAW

Years ago a legal expert wrote: "Those of us who have learned humility have given up on defining law."[1] There are many definitions of law because there is no universal agreement about what law is and what it should do. Some definitions include the role played by administrators, journalists, legislators, and pressure groups in forming and changing law. In their definitions, Canadians place high value on the **rule of law** and the establishment of official legal services, such as the role of prosecutors, defence lawyers, and judges. Most societies see law as a powerful means of maintaining social order, by upholding the rule-of-law principle that no individual or group is ever above the rules governments legislate.

One of the difficulties in arriving at a definition of law is that it pervades culture without any clear-cut limits. Law is not sharply separable from all other forms of human action. That is why, for example, the laws of Russia are different from the laws of Canada. In every society, moral and ethical principles are often the basis of law.

But **custom** and **usage** may also gain legal importance if a people regard them as culturally significant. When it becomes necessary for a society to protect what it deems socially important, rules and regulations are established for that purpose.

> **FACTFILE** In Saudi Arabia, women are not allowed to socialize with men in public; for example, banks have branches with only female tellers and customers.

Laws codify certain norms, mores, and folkways present in every society. Norms tell us how we *should* and *should not* behave—how we should conduct ourselves in business, marriage, interpersonal relationships, and so on. *Folkways* are informal customs and etiquette (such as ways of eating and dress) that do not require severe sanctions when they are violated. *Mores* are customs that a society considers to be right, obligatory, and even necessary for group survival. Because we consider mores so important, they often form the basis of our laws, such as laws that deal with sexual assault, incest, murder, and child abuse. Laws are the final social parameters that set down prescribed and **proscribed behaviour** in precise terms, usually including guidelines for the kind and length of punishment to be given to violators.

A law differs from a custom in the quality of its obligation. A person who violates a custom may be regarded as eccentric but cannot be legally punished for an infraction. For example, a person may not approve of the dress and mannerisms of a rock star, but the star is not doing anything against the law. However, if someone rides a motorcycle beyond the prescribed speed limit or decides to undress in front of a police officer, that person may be liable to be arrested.

Laws that govern abortion, death, and dying, and certain kinds of human conduct, such as the use of marijuana, are subject to change as political and legal systems reflect transformations in the social perceptions of these rules. But laws are customs that persons must abide by or be prepared to accept the consequences. This means that laws must somehow be enforced; they are enforced by a legitimate agency that is recognized as having political and legal authority to do so.

> **FACTFILE** The prevalence of lawyers in politics and government is now a Canadian tradition: lawyers have filled more seats in Canada's House of Commons and Senate than any other profession.

According to E. Adamson Hoebel, "law is merely one aspect of our culture—the aspect which employs the force of organized society to regulate individual and group conduct and to prevent redress or punish deviations from prescribed social norms."[2] A number of leading legal experts have defined law in terms of the judicial process.

American Justice Oliver Wendell Holmes puts it this way: "The prophecies of what the courts will do in fact, and nothing more pretentious, are what I mean by law."[3] B.N. Cardozo emphasizes that law is a basis for *prediction* rather than a mere guess: "A principle or rule of conduct so established as to justify a prediction with reasonable certainty that it will be enforced by the courts if its authority is challenged is . . . a principle or rule of law."[4]

Taken together, these definitions contain the four essential elements of law as Canadians would understand it:

- The first is a *normative* element—a standard or model of conduct that may improve human behaviour and achieve some public good.

- The second is *regularity*—that laws are made by a recognized political authority, are predictable, and are applied universally. The practical advantage of this element is that it emphasizes law as a "process," not just a series of particular commands by governments. Law is a body of principles that is regularly enforceable on all persons and groups within a legal jurisdiction.

- The third essential element is that the courts will objectively *apply* and *administer* the law. The task of a court in actual litigation is to determine the facts of a case, to declare the rule that is applicable, and then to make a specific order that is the result of the application of the law to those facts that are considered relevant.

- Finally, for the law to have teeth there must be legitimate *enforcement* by a recognized legal authority.

FACTFILE   A trial jury in a criminal case is usually composed of twelve jurors, but juries of six have been used in the Yukon and Northwest Territories.

The lawmaking process and its enforcement by a system of courts are the primary means of peacefully resolving disputes in most societies. Modern industrialized states have formal institutions and offices, such as legislatures, the police, lawyers, courts, and penal systems, to deal with conflicts that arise in society. All these institutions generally operate according to codified laws—a set of written or explicit rules stipulating what is permissible and what is not. Transgression of the law by people gives the state the right to take actions against them.

The state has a *monopoly* on the legitimate use of ultimate force in any society because it alone can coerce its subjects into compliance with its legislation, regulation, customs, and procedures. Sometimes the state will use *deadly force*—killing civilians in the name of the law. This may take the form of capital punishment, as in 38 states of the United States. But it can also result in prejudicial and racist conduct on the part of a state. In Canada, shootings of Aboriginal people and people of colour by police have been linked to systemic racist-policing policy in many cities.[5] In 2008, Craig MacDougall, an Aboriginal youth, was shot to death by Winnipeg police who had been called to a disturbance at his house. Other shootings of Aboriginal men have been under investigation in Saskatchewan and Ontario.

FACTFILE   Under Canada's *Indian Act* (1876), Indians were bound to their reserves as legal minors and were made subservient to the Department of Indian Affairs, which had the mandate to "civilize" Indians.

The Rule of Law

Legal experts tell us that for the law to be effective, it must state clearly what will happen to lawbreakers, and penalties must be enforced. They also tell us that laws must apply equally and predictably to everyone, no matter what their status is in society. No individual, group, or institution shall be above the law, and no one ought to be exempt from it. The rule of law guarantees that society is stable, ordered, and predictable. It provides protection for individuals from arbitrary state action.

In Canada, the so-called rule of law requires that each individual accused of a crime be treated equally under the law, receive a fair trial with established procedures, and be accorded due process in all official actions taken against that individual. Such was the case of Colin Thatcher, a former Saskatchewan politician who was convicted of murder. In 2005, Jean Chrétien appeared before the Gomery Commission, which was investigating the facts of the "sponsorship scandal." It was the first time a former Canadian prime minister had testified before a judicial body in public. In 2008, another former prime minister, Brian Mulroney, appeared before a parliamentary committee investigating his questionable financial relationship with businessman Karlheinz Schreiber.

The rule-of-law principle applies as well to governments, which decide on, pass, and interpret the laws. It provides a guarantee of impartiality and fairness for citizens living in a democracy, no matter who they are. It is therefore crucial that the courts be independent of the political arena, and that the decisions made by the courts are not the result of pressure or interference by any individuals or groups.

There is one significant exception to the rule of law: it can differ in various situations involving the military. For example, the unique needs of the military as a specialized society separate from civilian society are used as a justification for policies that, in civilian life, would be a violation of individual rights. In most military forces, a soldier can be tried and imprisoned for not showing up at work. This penalty far exceeds that which most of us would expect to receive if we missed a day at work, and it reflects the perceived need for discipline during times of combat.

SOURCES OF LAW

The laws that human beings abide by are drawn from many sources.[6] Throughout history, legalists have struggled to identify the formal sources of law as derived from a deity, morality, nature, or human political and legal institutions. Ethical, moral, and natural principles have always been important guides to human behaviour, and many of these principles have been given legal sanction. But the principal source of legal practice within nation-states and for the international community has been positive law. *Positive law* is human-made law, derived from the will of the state. Its main sources are custom, legislation, statutes, treaties, and the decisions of courts.

Custom is a source of positive law because certain practices and usages are enforced by governments. For example, in many states the custom that the chief wage-earners (usually men) continue to provide support to spouses and children during marriage breakdown and after divorce was legislated as law by governments. Custom provides the raw material from which many laws are enacted or adjudicated. **Judicial rulings** are another source of positive law because the decisions of judges add to the total body of law.

Canadian judges not only adjudicate the law; they also interpret it and thus, in part, make it. Judicial interpretation is consequently seen as a source of law in most states. Constitutional laws are primary laws that give legitimacy to all other law-making bodies in society, including legislatures, the division of legislative powers, and the rights and duties of governments and citizens. Legislation in the form of constitutional amendment, decrees,

Perspectives   The Politics behind the Law

Political scientists know that law and politics are closely linked. They know that often politics precedes the making of law. In democratic societies, political debates that regularly occur can eventually become a source of the law or a force to change existing law. We know for example that the politics behind same-sex marriage, gun control, tax reduction, foreign policy and war swirl though the political system as issues that are debated to the point of government action. Politicians are the ones who make or change law.

But politics finds its way into the judicial system—the system we think is so neutral, so independent, so beyond political influence. Because laws are made by politicians, there is a tendency to think that the judicial system merely administers and adjudicates the law as it is made in legislatures.

When asked, many judges will deny that they make law. They say law is there already and that they merely discover it and on occasion "interpret" it, using their legal education and experience. They imply that they use a judicial process that is immutable. But, in fact, judges exercise discretion. They *do* make laws—when they interpret statutes, when they interpret the Constitution and when they determine which precedents to follow or disregard.

In so doing they reflect their own political preferences. Judges are human beings with their own perceptions and attitudes, even prejudices. They do not and cannot shed these the moment they put on their robes.

However, judges do not make law in the same way that legislators make law. Judges make law less directly, by telling governments what they cannot do, rather than what they must do. And judges make law less freely. They do not start with clean slates but with principles established in statutes, the Constitution, and precedents.

---

statutes, and treaties is another source of law. The sovereign authority of the state and its institutions are the sources of the validity of law in most legal systems. Many states regard law as valid because it is the expression of divine, moral, or natural justice; however, in the modern world it is clear that the legal validity of a system of law depends on its **enactment** and **enforcement**.

FACTFILE   In Canada, women are far more likely to be victimized in private—at home, by members of their families or people they know—than in public, on the streets.

The dynamics of social, political, and technological change also contribute to the formation of new law. In Canada, laws now forbid sexual harassment, interpersonal violence, smoking in certain areas, and discrimination on the basis of sexual orientation. Also, new technologies alter the ways we interact, often producing the need for laws to protect us from their abusive use. Technologies to help people commit suicide and the use of communications technologies for illegal gain or mischief are examples of additional needs for new law in society.

Focus On Types of Law

Administrative Law

Law that reflects the authority and procedures of government bureaucracies as well as the rules and regulations issued by these bureaucracies.

Admiralty Law

Law that applies to shipping and waterway commerce on the high seas and on the navigable internal waters of Canada.

Civil Law

As practised in Quebec, civil law is the codified law that governs private relations between and among individuals. It is designed to provide clear and precise solutions to practical legal problems in understandable language.

Common Law

Judge-made law that originated in England in the twelfth century to create a "common" national legal system, adopted in Canada, as well as many other states, and bases decisions on general principles of law, former judicial decisions, and flexible interpretations of statutory law.

Constitutional Law

The law derived from the words of both the written and unwritten elements of the Constitution, which can be interpreted by the Federal Court and Supreme Court of Canada as well as from cases decided in provincial Supreme Courts.

Criminal Law

Law that defines offenses against the public order and provides for punishment in the Criminal Code, provincial statutes, and municipal law.

Equity Law

Law that is used whenever common law remedies are inadequate in order to achieve justice and fairness for the parties involved.

International Law

Law that is established between and among nation-states, supported by treaties and international conventions and adjudicated in national and international courts.

Statutory Law

Law that is created by legislatures, executive orders, and harmonized from international treaties.

LAW AND LEGAL SYSTEMS

History reveals that *every* civilization has developed a recognizable legal system—a body of laws, rules, and regulations enacted by a lawmaking authority that delegates judicial powers to special groups of people. Western civilization developed two complete and influential legal systems, one from English *common law* and one from Roman *civil law*.

English Common Law

Although the Romans had evolved a formidable legal system well over 1000 years before the appearance of what we now call "Anglo-American law," it collapsed in Great Britain when Rome was forced to relinquish its frontiers in the face of barbarian onslaughts. The complete withdrawal of Rome's military presence from England in AD 410 meant the eventual disappearance of Roman culture on the island. On the European continent, civil-law systems are directly traceable to the Roman influence.

After Rome recalled its armies from Britain in the fifth century, tides of invaders crossed the English Channel for the next 500 years. Each of these groups of arriving Angles, Saxons, Jutes, and Danes brought their own rules for settling legal disputes. Over the centuries, they carved out petty kingdoms where legal customs became fixed. Even the final successful invasion of 1066, led by the Norman conqueror William, did not affect the different customary legal practices of these little enclaves, although it transformed the political life of England.

It remained for Henry II (1154–1189) to implant the unique legal practices of common law. King Henry trained representatives called "justices" to travel throughout England and administer his land law (the basis of taxation and property rights), breaches of the "King's Peace" (criminal law), and the supervision of local officials. In this way, judicial administration was made the same in all parts of the country, and differing customs were united into a body of law, "common" to the whole kingdom.

Perspectives   The Difference between Legal Rights and Human Rights

A *legal right* is a right derived from the law, the interpretation of the law, and/or sometimes even from the violation of the law. Legal rights are normally quite clear expressions of law in statutes, public policies, and judicial decisions. They can flow directly from the constitution, administrative law, and international law.

Human rights are not always backed by legal instruments. They are the rights we can claim simply because we are human beings. But they do not necessarily come out of our legal system as we might expect. For example, we have a right to food to sustain our lives, but the state does not give us a legal right to food. We have a right to decent housing, but the state may not give us a national legal right to a place to live.

We have a right to acquire knowledge, but the state may not provide us with affordable post-secondary education.

Some human rights are in fact protected by the law. The freedoms of speech, of religion, and of mobility are protected by civil law and the legal and judicial systems in most democratic states. But these same states do not guarantee the full breadth of rights we should derive because we are human creatures. Gradually, the expectations we have about human rights can be encoded into our laws and legal system. For example, rights of due process were gradually included in most democratic states, transforming from the original status of a human right ultimately to the full protection of a legal right.

In time, these justices began keeping records of their decisions in legal disputes. Thus, a body of **precedents** was built up. Justices developed the practice of following the precedent called *stare decisis et non quieta movere* (let the decision stand and not to move what has been settled), which added the element of predictability to regularity in the evolving legal system. By referring to past situations, they could make the same decisions in identical cases and arrive at judgments in legal disputes that were similar, but not the same. The system of relying on precedent made the law very conservative but also elastic and flexible. In short, it fulfilled the minimum requirements of justice in that it was predictable, regular, and evenly applied.

> **FACTFILE** Japan and the United States are the only two developed states to retain the death penalty.

Alongside laws administered by justices grew the rules of **equity**. Because the king was believed to be the fountain of justice, the keepers of his conscience were empowered to dispense justice and fairness, or equity, in ruling on legal disputes. In deciding a case *ex aequo et bono* (out of justice and fairness), the justices were authorized by the king to apply equity by overruling other rules that stood in the way of a remedy. Thus, if someone maliciously killed the productive animal of a farmer, not only would the animal have to be replaced, but compensation would have to be paid by the culprit for any losses the owner incurred while the matter was being remedied.

> **FACTFILE** The jury system allows for ordinary citizens to take part in the judicial process without being litigants or legal professionals.

Henry II recognized the potential advantages of swearing twelve men from the local area and four from surrounding towns as a jury to inform justices of persons suspected of grave infractions against the King's Peace. The use of a jury in civil cases grew from Henry's idea of using a group of neighbours to determine ownership and possession of disputed land. Once made available to the people, trial by jury established its superiority over trials by combat, ordeal (an experience that tests one's character and endurance), and swearing oaths that had been practised in England for half a millennium.

Gradually, the consolidation of English law into a complete corpus by absorbing independent systems of law (merchant law, **admiralty law**, **probate law**, etc.) gave England a body of law common to all in the realm. A later strand in the development of English common law came from the statutes or legislation enacted by Parliament. Today, in Canada, *stare decisis* is still followed in matters about which Parliament has not enacted legislation.

> **FACTFILE** Louisiana is the only one of the 50 US states that does not base its legal system entirely on common law. Quebec is the only Canadian province to use both civil and common law traditions.

Common law has been a major influence in the legal systems of India, Israel, and Pakistan, the Scandinavian countries, and the newer states in Africa and Asia. In all of these states, many acts of the national assembly have displaced much of the traditional character of common law. But still, their judges and attorneys bring the heritage of a thousand years of British legal development to the bench and to the bar.

While common law has evolved as a system that is flexible and adaptive, it has also remained firm on fundamental principles of law, such as rule of law, presumption of innocence, and judicial independence.

Roman Civil Law

The most impressive intellectual achievements of the Romans were in law, and the sharpest minds of the empire developed a comprehensive legal system. Roman law developed over many centuries, creating voluminous legal records of generations of lawyers and government officials. The emperor Justinian (527–565) attacked the problem of codifying the law in his *Digest, Corpus Juris*, and the *Code*. Justinian's Code became an essential part of Western legal tradition and affected every Western European state, as well as many legal systems in the New World.[7]

After Rome collapsed, Justinian's Code was challenged by the more primitive Germanic legal system, canon law, and disparate commercial and maritime legal practices. But Roman law was rediscovered in the twelfth century, after which it gradually reasserted its influence from the teachings and practices of European jurists and professors of law.

European states **codify** law in their legal systems. France's Napoleonic Code, beginning with the *Civil Code* of 1804, was the first great modern contribution to the civil-law system. It was widely copied in Belgium, Italy, the Netherlands, Portugal, Spain, and Latin American Republics. The legal systems of Germany, Japan, and Turkey have also relied heavily upon a codified law. In the French and Swiss codes, as well as others, law is developed not by the courts through definition and interpretation, but rather by legislatures, ministries of justice, and academic institutions. Reason, logic, and legal expertise are accorded high value in the civil-law system. The *letter*, rather than the *spirit*, of the law is the dynamic force behind legal systems based on civil law.

Quebec's Civil Codes

When the Seven Years' War ended, culminating in the Treaty of Paris of 1763, Quebec was brought under British rule. The British government moved to guarantee the private law of French Canada under the French-Canadian civil law, which is based on the French civil code. So today, the civil law codes remain the private law of Quebec. In August 1866, Quebec's private law was codified by legislative enactment as the *Civil Code of Lower Canada*. The only official revisions of the code came in 1981 and in 1994, when it was called the *Code Civil du Québec*.

The private law of Quebec deals mainly with persons, corporations, civil status, marriage, property, ownership, co-ownership, gifts, wills, trusts, contracts, loans, rentals, and pledges. Unlike the common law, civil law applies abstract principles or doctrines of law to the settlement of disputes. The facts of each dispute are analyzed on principle, not from prior judicial decisions that interpret the law. The civil law contains no formal notion of *stare decisis* or any other technique of binding case precedent. Instead, the writings of legal scholars and professors are given pre-eminent attention in the interpretation of civil-law doctrines.

FACTFILE   In 1763, under the terms of the Treaty of Paris, which ended the Seven Years' War, the British guaranteed Quebecers that the private law of French Canada would be protected as the civil law of Quebec.

Today in Quebec, the widespread use of the case approach in federal and public law has diluted the purity of the civil law. The Quebec system is sometimes described as "mixed" or "hybrid" because of the powerful influences of the common law. It must be remembered that the Quebec *Civil Code* predates the *Constitution Act, 1867*, and like the use of the French language, clearly illustrates the distinct character of Quebec society in the legal and linguistic landscape of Canada.

OTHER LEGAL SYSTEMS
Islamic Legal Systems

The Islamic system of law governs about 900 million Muslims, who live in many of the countries of Africa, Asia, and the Middle East.[8] Islamic law originated in the seventh century, based on rules regulating all areas of human conduct in traditional pastoral societies that possessed very few social and government institutions. Islam was the last of the three great world religions to emerge, and for many centuries it was more vigorous than either of its rivals—Christianity in the West and

Buddhism in the East. Today, it is the second largest of the world's religions.

Sometime about AD 610, a merchant's son named Mohammed began to preach to the people of the Arabian town of Mecca. Gradually, he delivered his teachings in the form of a new system of religion called Islam. The spread of this religion became one of the most extraordinary events of world history.

Believing himself instructed by the angel Gabriel, Mohammed passed the prophecies of Allah (God) to his many followers. The collection of prophecies known as the *Koran*, written from AD 651 to AD 652, calls upon followers to submit to the will of Allah. Those who submit are Muslims. Those who transgress his will are infidels.

Mohammed was little concerned with the subtleties of theology; he was interested in defining for the Muslims the ethical and legal requirements for an upright life. Islam retains this practical emphasis; jurisprudence remains the great intellectual interest of scholarship. In contrast to Christianity, Islam does not recognize a separate clergy and church: Allah is the direct ruler of the faithful on earth.

The message of Islam exerts a powerful appeal not only to the Arabs but to the global community. Compared with Christianity and Judaism, Islam is a starkly simple belief, easily explained and easily grasped. Islamic law centres on obligations—to God and to other people—rather than on any sort of individual rights or entitlements. Islam appeals strongly to the intense cultural, racial, and traditional pride of Arabs. The Koran is written in Arabic, and only in Arabic can Allah be addressed. According to the Koran, Allah instructs believers to convert or conquer non-believers.

The revelations in the Koran—at once a religious, an ethical, and a legal system—forbid wine drinking, usury, and gambling, and ban certain foods, especially pork. There was also a rudimentary sacred code of law, the Sharia, designed to check the selfishness and violence that had prevailed among the Arabs. Arbitration was advocated

to take the place of the blood feud, infanticide was condemned, and elaborate rules of inheritance safeguarded the rights of orphans and widows. Mohammed also made an effort to limit **polygamy** by ruling that no man might have more than four wives simultaneously. Divorce remained easy, but the divorced wife could not be sent away penniless. These and other provisions were enough to furnish the framework for a judicial system.

Because the Koran was immutable law, it proved incomplete as the Muslim states began to modernize, have more contact with the West, and establish sovereign national governments. In the nineteenth century, European legal codes were adopted to supplement Islamic law in Egypt and Turkey. In the twentieth century, Turkey abolished Islamic law altogether, as did Egypt as recently as 1956. However, in 1980, Egypt amended its constitution to make Islamic revelations the main source of its legislation. At present, 20 Muslim states combine some elements of Islamic law with European civil-law codes in commercial, criminal, and public law. These include Afghanistan, Iraq, Morocco, and Indonesia.

Some states, such as Bahrain, Saudi Arabia, and the United Arab Emirates, have attempted to retain the complete Islamic traditions. Pakistan's Constitution of 1973 forbids the enactment of laws that are contrary to the injunctions of Islam. As a consequence of renewed Islamic fundamentalism in that state, the traditional punishments of flogging, amputation, and stoning have been reinstituted as they were practised according to the Sharia. Libya, under Colonel Qaddafi, followed a similar path. Finally, Iran, under its supreme religious leader Ayatollah Khomeini, combines Islamic fundamentalism with fierce nationalism. Strong reactions against secular law have also surfaced in Malaysia, Syria, and Turkey.

Communist Legal Systems

What distinguishes communist legal systems from others is the effective control by a single agency, the Communist Party. The party influences judicial practices through the doctrine of social legal consciousness, which requires that lawyers and judges be guided by party policy when deciding cases. The fate of a defendant is decided on the basis of the regime's ideology.

> **FACTFILE** China's Mao Tse Tung stressed that women "hold up half the sky" and proclaimed the legal equality of women by outlawing a series of laws and traditional practices, including foot binding.

Under the principles of socialist legality, the range of activities defined as criminal is extensive. Crimes such as murder and theft are treated as in most states. But the severest punishments and widest interpretations of the law are crimes against the state, such as failure to meet production plans, inefficiency, and poor-quality production. Even harsher penalties are applied for political crimes, such as anti-state agitation, of which dissidents are frequently accused.

In all cases, the legal profession is controlled by the party. Judges are civil servants who are usually members of the Communist Party. Rarely can they conduct their courts independent of party influence. Lawyers are also tied to the Communist Party. At times they can exercise some independence in their defensive strategies, but they are legally bound to uphold the interests of the state. In China, people's courts and comrades' courts educate citizens in loyalty and compliance with party principles.

Combined Legal Systems

Many of the authoritarian states of Africa, Asia, and Latin America blend the customs, procedures, and codes found in other systems of jurisprudence into their own. Most of Africa was colonized by European powers that transplanted their legal traditions to each country. African legal systems reflect the civil-law codes of France, Germany, and the Netherlands, as well as British common-law

practices, Islamic legal prescriptions, and customary tribal law. Particularly in states influenced by British jurisprudence, judges often exhibit remarkable dedication to the integrity of the legal process. In states such as Kenya and Tanzania, judges have displayed great personal courage when their verdicts are counter to the political sentiments of the authoritarian ruler.

The legal systems of Latin America are also good examples of a blend of many influences. By far the major influence on the legal systems of Latin America has been Roman civil law. Bolivia adopted verbatim the French civil code. And Argentina, Colombia, Ecuador, and Paraguay modelled their codes after the French, German, and Swiss codes. The civil law as practised by Spain and Portugal was transplanted to the New World by the conquistadors. The constitutional and common law practice of the United States has also had considerable influence in Latin America, especially in the federal republics of Argentina, Brazil, Mexico, and Venezuela.

Finally, in Southeast Asia, Western powers have exerted considerable influence on the legal practices and institutions of the region. Many states refer to case precedents established under colonial rule. In the Philippines, courts cite legal precedents in the English and American courts, as well as legal decisions made before their independence.

THE JUDICIARY

The administration of justice has been one of the most important functions of government since the dawn of recorded history. Courts first appeared in Egypt in 2900 BC. At that time, Egyptian kings began to delegate a large part of their judicial powers to a chief judge who heard and ruled on cases at the royal residence. Somewhat later, courts in Mesopotamia applied the *Code of Babylon* and the *Code of Hammurabi*. The Hebrews, Hindus,

Arabs, Chinese, Greeks, and Romans had elaborate court systems to administer justice as a function of government.

Modern courts can be classified in two broad categories: courts of original jurisdiction (also called courts of first instance) and courts of appeal. A **court of first instance** has primary jurisdiction and hears prosecutions and actions in criminal and civil cases. A court of appeal hears a case and rules to confirm or reverse a decision made by a lower court. In some states, **appellate courts** review the decisions of lower courts to determine whether judicial errors have been made and a uniform interpretation of law is occurring. Thus, courts of appellate jurisdiction serve as a check upon errors of law that arise in the course of trials in lower courts. They also serve to give a losing party another chance to win a case. In all states, the scope of appellate jurisdiction—that is, the type of cases and legal questions that may be appealed—is determined by rules of procedure established by the courts themselves or by a legislative body.

FACTFILE   In Canada, international law is automatically incorporated into Canadian public law and is adjudicated as such in Canadian courts, which sometimes give judicial notice to international law decisions that are made in the courts of other states.

The Functions of the Judiciary

The primary purpose of the courts in democracies is to uphold the constitution as the first law of the land. What distinguishes the courts in democratic states from courts in authoritarian and totalitarian states is the relative neutrality and impartiality of judges when their own government is one of the parties before them. The degree of independence of the courts from the political and governmental system is an important measure of the ability of courts to act in justice and fairness to the litigants.

FACTFILE   In Canada, judges usually come from a wealthier, better-educated, more socially prominent stratum of society than do most other government officials.

In every state, judges are government officials, the laws they apply are made by the government, and from time to time the government may be one of the litigants. But while politics can never be excluded from the appointment process of judicial officials, it is important to know to what extent a judicial system remains detached from the political system that appoints and funds it. *Judicial independence* protects the courts from outside interference and gives judges legal immunity from the consequences of their decisions. This principle of judicial independence is not a component of every judicial system, although most common-law states outwardly proclaim it to be.

Adjudication

The judiciary differs from the executive and legislative branch of government by the way it conducts itself with respect to the lawmaking process. Courts are passive and do not initiate action; rather they wait until a case is brought before them. A case becomes an occasion for the courts to *adjudicate*—to settle disputes or to proclaim a general rule of law. The process of adjudication involves elaborate procedures for gathering evidence and establishing the facts in a case. Adjudication permits those actually affected by a law to bring forward the particulars of their case and to ask for a reasonable interpretation of the law in the light of the evidence revealed. To win in court, it is necessary to show that a claim is just, or that an indictment or settlement is just.

FACTFILE   The Canadian Judicial Council, created in 1971, consists of all the chief justices and associate chief justices of courts staffed by federally appointed judges, and it deals with complaints raised against individual judges.

Focus On Lawyers as Officers of the Judiciary

To better understand the role of judges in Canadian courts, we need to understand lawyers and the nature of their craft. As the officers of the courts in Canada, lawyers impact the way our country is governed. By stating the claims of their clients, they resolve social conflict within the terms of the law, especially statutory, criminal, and constitutional law.

Practising lawyers are called "the bar" because they are admitted past the low rail, or "bar" in the courtroom, while the general public remains outside the bar. Lawyers are bound by professional codes, which they must adhere to or face being "disbarred."

As members of the legal profession and advocates in the judicial system, lawyers perform important functions related to how the country is governed. First, they counsel people about the law that is passed by legislators and adjudicated by judges. Lawyers give advice about the law to governments as well as ordinary citizens. They assist in the peaceful settlement of disputes, often outside the judicial system because most civil cases are settled outside of court.

Second, lawyers are mediators who reconcile disputed claims that involve economic and social matters of justice. They provide a stabilizing role for government to maintain order in a rapidly changing society. Lawyers enhance the legitimacy of social rules enacted by the various levels of government. They uphold the importance of contractual obligations as an underlying democratic value.

Third, lawyers draft legal documents, and when they work for governments, write the language of legislation. Lawyers often have a great deal of knowledge and expertise that is useful in drafting legislations or constitutional amendments. In Canada, they are the second largest profession, after business, represented in the House of Commons.

Ultimately, lawyers are the architects of the judicial system by building and repairing the shortcomings that inevitably occur in a profession dedicated to justice. They provide relief for thousands of people seeking redress for grievances that they could not obtain elsewhere in the governing system.

A final commentary concerning adjudication relates to the effectiveness of the courts to generate social reform. It is sometimes argued that a single, decisive ruling by the courts may initiate reform far quicker than years of lobbying and legislation. Judicial rulings enjoy a decisive authority and legitimacy not often accorded to the prescriptions of political institutions. Courts that interpret the law in a sense also create it.

Constitutional Interpretation

Probably the single greatest influence a court can have on the destiny of a particular nation-state is **judicial review**. The practice, borrowed from the United States, where it has worked so well, is used in some form by the courts in most states today. Judicial review means that some courts may declare unconstitutional an executive, legislative, or judicial act that is judged in violation of the spirit and letter of the constitution. In the United States, any court may examine the **constitutionality** of an act when deciding a case before it. However, the United States Supreme Court enjoys full judicial review and can interpret what the clauses of the Constitution mean and set aside acts of the Congress or of state assemblies, as unconstitutional.

In Canada, the practice of judicial review has been *limited*, because it involved only questions of provincial and federal government jurisdiction from the 1867 Constitution. But this has changed significantly since the entrenchment of the Charter of Rights and Freedoms in 1982. The Supreme Court of Canada is now responsible for interpreting and enforcing the Canadian Constitution and the Charter of Rights and Freedoms. Prior to 1982, the role of the Supreme Court of Canada was limited to the application of law, as defined by statute or legal precedent, to cases brought before it. Since the proclamation of Canada's patriated Constitution, all law, the legislatures—even the federal Parliament itself— are *subordinate* to the Constitution. With that change came a dramatic increase in the power of judicial review in Canada, giving the Supreme Court the ultimate responsibility for interpreting the Constitution and for striking down laws that conflict with it. Thus, the adoption in 1982 of the entrenched Canadian Charter of Rights and Freedoms recast the Canadian judicial role to one more akin to that of the United States.

In other states, the power of judicial review exists, but usually in a more limited form. Parliament in the British tradition best represents the national will. Any law British Parliament passes is therefore nullified or **rescinded** only by another act of Parliament.

In Latin America about three-quarters of the states confer a limited power of review on the courts. A unique form of judicial review is Mexico's **writ of amparo**. Any citizen may apply to one of the federal courts to redress a law or act of government that impairs the rights guaranteed to a citizen in the Constitution. The writ applies to each case and does not declare as unconstitutional any act of Congress or of the President. Rather, it provides a remedy for a violation of individual rights in the instance to which *amparo* is applied. But in the process, a judicial review of the articles in the Constitution does take place because others could have their rights impaired by the same provision under similar circumstances.

Law Enforcement and Administration

Judicial institutions perform the important function of upholding the law in a society. The imposition of fines and other punishments is a credible component of law enforcement as administered by the courts. Courts enforce compulsory adjudication by the issuance of writs and orders that force parties to appear before a court to defend their actions. Court orders also enable and direct police officials to execute the law.

Courts authorize **warrants** of arrest, **summons** to appear in court, **subpoenas** to summon witnesses, **writs of mandamus** to order a party to perform an act required by law, **writs of habeas corpus** to remove the illegal restraint of personal liberty, **writs of prohibition** to stop a court or other government body from proceeding beyond its jurisdiction, and injunctions to order a stop of certain actions.

In civil-law states such as France, Italy, and Portugal, administrative courts issue writs and orders on the executive branch of government. In Greece and Japan, courts can interfere with executive actions if they clearly violate the constitution.

In many states, courts are assigned administrative responsibilities. In Canada and the United States, courts probate wills, manage the estates of deceased persons, grant and revoke licenses, grant admission to the bar and announce disbarments, administer bankruptcy proceedings, grant divorces, and naturalize aliens. In many states, when elections are disputed, courts conduct recounts to verify the results.

CANADA'S JUDICIARY

Federalism determines the structure of the Canadian judiciary. There are separate federal and provincial courts, with the Supreme Court of Canada being a general court of appeal— Canada's highest appeal court in all areas of law— as well as a court of first instance for certain types of cases. But the system of courts is essentially hierarchical and unified (Figure 8.1).

Provincial Courts

The following levels of court are found in every province, although actual functions, structures, and nomenclature vary among the provinces.

Within the hierarchy of the provincial judiciary are magistrates' courts, small-claims courts, and family courts. These courts hear criminal offences, small claims, and juvenile litigation, respectively. They adjudicate **summary offences**, bail hearings, preliminary criminal hearings, offences under the *Young Offenders Act*, and civil cases. Federal as well as provincial law may be decided in civil or criminal matters in all courts. Jurisdictional limitations are established according to the types of proceedings, the value of claims, and the nature of offences. Each province exercises sole jurisdiction over the creation and staffing of these courts at this level. Consequently, the administration and procedure of provincial courts will vary from province to province. But in all cases, judges are appointed by the lieutenant governor in council and paid by provincial appropriation.

Finally, provincial *superior courts* or *Supreme Courts*, the Cour superieure in Quebec or Courts of **Queen's Bench** elsewhere, are the high courts of justice established by provincial statute. Supreme Courts hear appeals from lower courts within the province and exercise unlimited jurisdiction in civil and criminal matters. At the top, there is a *superior appellate court*, ordinarily sitting with three judges, with the general jurisdiction to determine appeals from lower courts in the province. In some provinces, there is one superior court divided into trial and appellate divisions.

The appointment of all Supreme Court judges is by the federal government, with remuneration set by federal statute. Supreme courts exercise *concurrent jurisdiction* with lower courts for most indictable crimes and *exclusive jurisdiction* concerning the most serious **indictable crimes** such as murder. Apart from the processes of appointment and removal of judges, and of establishing rules of criminal procedure, the provinces are given jurisdiction to administer justice in the province, which includes determining the number of judges and the structure, organization, and administration of the courts.

Federal Courts

A federal court system, separate and independent of the provincial courts, has existed in Canada since 1875, when the **Exchequer Court** was created. Federal courts now consist of the Supreme Court of Canada, the Federal Court, the Tax Court, the Court Martial Appeal Court, and the territorial courts in the Northwest Territories, Nunavut, and the Yukon. The Federal Court, which replaced the Exchequer Court, was established by the *Federal Court Act* of 1970 with a trial

Figure 8.1   **The judiciary of Canada**

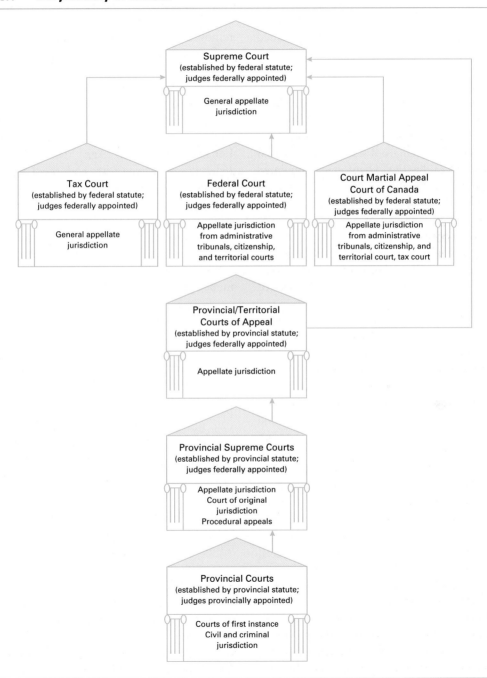

division and an appeal division. Sometimes called the "unknown Court," the Federal Court of Appeal is located in Ottawa, but both divisions will sit in other parts of the country when justified by demand and convenience. It rarely deals with high-profile legislation.

The Federal Court consists of a Chief Justice, an Associate Chief Justice, 10 judges of the Court of Appeal, and 19 judges of the Trial Division. Judges of each division are *ex officio* members of the other division. Five judges of the Court of Appeal and two judges of the Trial Division are appointed directly from the provincial superior courts. In order to qualify for appointment, a candidate must have been a judge of a superior court in Canada, or a barrister or advocate of at least 10 years' standing at the bar of a province. At least 10 of the judges must be persons who have been judges of the Court of Appeal or the Superior Court of Quebec, or have been members of the Quebec bar.

The Federal Court exercises original jurisdiction in matters involving suits against the federal government, inter-provincial and federal/provincial legal disputes, citizenship appeals, and matters formerly under the jurisdiction of the Exchequer Court, relating to the *Excise Act, Customs Act, Income Tax Act, National Defence Act, Patent Act*, and *Shipping Act*. The principal areas of litigation are revenue and taxation; trademarks and patents; immigration and citizenship; maritime and aeronautical matters; customs and excise; aspects of banking law; penal and correctional service matters; food and drug control; and administrative law. The Federal Court eases the load of appeals flowing to the Supreme Court, especially those of special national character, arising from federal boards, commissions, and tribunals.

Federal Court judges are sometimes called upon to determine if an administrative body, such as a *board* or *tribunal*, has violated the Charter of Rights and Freedoms. The Court now deals with a wide range of Charter issues, including those of equality, life, liberty, security of the person, and the

freedoms of association, expression, conscience, and religion, as they can often apply to administrative law. A recent judgment of the Federal Court removed the disqualification of judges from voting in federal and provincial elections.

In 1983, Parliament instituted the Tax Court of Canada to hear cases that arise from federal tax laws. This court has jurisdiction in matters arising from the *Income Tax Act*, Customs and Excise, unemployment insurance, the Canada Pension Plan, Old Age Security, the *War Veterans' Allowances Act*, and the *Civilian War Pensioners and Allowances Act*. It is also assisted by four **supernumerary** judges. These justices have been re-appointed beyond their retirement age for a specific period on the recommendation of the chief judge or judicial council, or have opted for semi-retirement before reaching retirement age.

The Supreme Court of Canada

The *Constitution Act, 1867*, made no mention of a Supreme Court of Canada. The Fathers of Confederation granted statutory authority to Parliament, which succeeded in passing the *Supreme Court Act, 1875*. But over the years many constitutional, legal, and political experts expressed concern that because the Supreme Court had been instituted by Parliament it could also be removed by ordinary legislation. Accordingly, in 1982 the Supreme Court of Canada was entrenched in the Constitution through sections 41(d) and 42(1)(d) of the *Constitution Act, 1982*.

FACTFILE   In 2004, Liberal Prime Minister Paul Martin announced that nominees to the Supreme Court would be reviewed by a special parliamentary committee that would report their findings to Parliament.

At first the Court had only six justices, and its first sittings were held in the Railway Committee Room of the House of Commons; thereafter, the

Court sat in the old Supreme Court building at the foot of Parliament Hill until 1946, when it took possession of its present building. But until 1949, the **Judicial Committee of the Privy Council** in London was the highest court of final appeal for Canadian civil cases, and until 1931 for criminal cases.

In 1949, the Supreme Court assumed that role. It sits only in Ottawa. Since 1949, the composition of the Court's bench has followed the pattern of appointing three justices from Ontario, three from Quebec, two from the western provinces, and one from the Atlantic region. This pattern had only one temporary deviation from 1979 to 1982, when there were two judges from Ontario and three from the West. All nine judges are appointed until age 75 by the governor general-in-council.

> **FACTFILE**   In 2006, Conservative Prime Minister Stephen Harper announced that future committees to review judicial selection would have greater access to the candidates after which he allowed an ad hoc parliamentary committee to question the candidacy of Justice Marshall Rothstein prior to his appointment.

Candidates must have at least 10 years' experience in law practice. Normally, Supreme Court judges are selected from provincial courts of appeal; for example, Beverley McLachlin was appointed in March 1989 from the British Columbia Court of Appeal. But from time to time, practising lawyers are elevated directly to the Supreme Court, as exemplified by the appointment, in 1988, of John Sopinka, who replaced Justice Willard Estey as one of Ontario's representatives on the bench. Judges are removable from the Supreme Court by the governor general-in-council (on the advice of the Cabinet), accompanied by a joint address to the Senate and the House of Commons.

> **FACTFILE**   Canadian judicial history was made on January 7, 2000, when Honourable Beverley McLachlin became the first woman to be appointed Chief Justice of the Supreme Court of Canada.

The chief justice presides over and directs the work of the Court, and serves as its principal administrator. The chief justice has only one vote, as do the other judges, in deciding cases. The other eight *puisne* (junior rank) justices unavoidably bring their own personal values and political philosophies to the bench. These men and women, ranging in age from their fifties to mid-seventies, have usually left more lucrative careers in law and teaching to accept prestigious judicial appointments—often initially to the courts of their home provinces.

The Supreme Court, notorious for its lengthy deliberations, has the capacity to hear only about 100 cases of the several hundred filed each year. As one justice told an interviewer, "We're like an oversold airline; we have an airplane with a hundred seats and a thousand passengers trying to get in." There are two classes of people who have the automatic right to appeal: those whose acquittals of crimes were reversed by provincial appellate courts on appeals from the Crowns, and those whose conviction were upheld by appellate courts with one of the judges dissenting on a question of law. An appeal is accompanied by a lawyer's written arguments, called **factums**, which, together with the appeal books containing all of the trial transcripts and judgments from the lower courts, frequently reach several thousand pages in length. One case involving Quebec's Bill 101, which legislated French as the only official language in that province, contained 55 volumes of complex legal arguments.

In response to a 1987 report by the Canadian Bar Association, the Court instituted reforms to streamline its operations for faster, more efficient service. The Court now limits most submissions to 40 pages and permits lawyers to beam their arguments (by video conferencing) to the Supreme Court's television screens via satellite. The Court has adopted the latest technologies to deal with its ever-increasing workload. Several years ago, all of the Court's record keeping was computerized so that every document filed with the Court could be tracked electronically. The Court uses satellite TV links for many of its routine hearings that are conducted to determine whether a full appeal will be heard. Such "applications for leave to appeal" do not require lawyers to come all the way to Ottawa for a 15-minute session with the judges. Most appeals are turned down.

In recent times, the Supreme Court has not hesitated to pass judgment on basic political and moral questions. For example, it ruled that television cameras can be barred from federal and provincial legislatures because the assemblies of Canada have "inherent privileges" that are a cut above constitutional rights to a free media. It ruled that those found not guilty of a crime by reason of insanity cannot be automatically committed to mental institutions and ruled that evidence obtained illegally by the police was admissible in court. In another decision, it ruled that the police cannot recruit informers to try to get confessions from accused persons. It concluded that the results of a polygraph test used to determine who is telling the truth has no place in Canada's legal system. And in 2007, the Supreme Court ruled that the police are not immune from civil liability by innocent people for negligence in their investigations.

Indeed, over the past two decades, these nine judges have made important rulings on the guarantees of equality and individual freedom in Canadian society. In this regard, the Supreme Court ruled that if police get authorization to wiretap private premises, they also have the right to enter these premises secretly to plant the wiretaps. In its ruling, the Supreme Court decided that even though Parliament does not say police can trespass, it undoubtedly meant to do so.

Crosscurrents   Wrongful Conviction: One Is One Too Many

Even if the Canadian system of criminal justice proved 99.5 percent accurate, it would still generate almost a thousand wrongful convictions a year—and those would reflect only some of the crimes under the *Criminal Code* for which innocent people are accused and convicted. All of these wrongful convictions let the culprits go free.

Wrongful conviction is almost always the result of wrongful criminal investigation. This can occur when prosecutors or the police bend or break laws in order to win convictions. In almost every public commission inquiry, misconduct by prosecutors and police is identified as what leads to the wrongful conviction of innocent individuals.

There are some outstanding examples of wrongful convictions in Canada: Steven Truscott, William Mullins-Johnson, Donald Marshall, James Driskell, Thomas Sophonow, Guy Paul Morin, Gary Staples. Many others could be added to this list.

That being the case, where are the weaknesses in our criminal justice system? One is conspiring with unreliable witnesses. Should we permit prosecutors to make immunity deals with witnesses who are in conflict of interest with the accused? It has been demonstrated in most cases that people with immunity will lie to protect themselves at the expense of those charged with a crime. In-custody informers can quickly corrupt the integrity of a case for both prosecution and defence, thus producing a wrongful conviction.

Another weakness is failing to regularly audit the methods used to examine blood and

DNA samples in various labs across the country. Forensic evidence and expert testimony are essential to a fair trial in a criminal case. When it is corrupted, it has disastrous consequences for innocent people. The conduct of disgraced forensic pathologist Dr. Charles Smith, who was the head of pathology at Toronto's Sick Children's Hospital, demonstrated how an unaudited scientist could directly contribute to the miscarriage of justice in hundreds of cases.

If crucial evidence is withheld by police or prosecutors in order to gain conviction, a defendant's constitutional rights are severely violated. For this reason, transparency of evidence and witnesses is essential at all stages of most criminal cases. When some prosecutors suppress or withhold evidence that could exonerate a defendant, they fail to meet the disclosure rights of the accused. In so doing, they also break the law. This has contributed to some of the most outstanding wrongful convictions in Canadian history.

Tunnel vision is another contributing factor during criminal investigations. Under the guise of *professional expertise*, once investigators have reached a conclusion in a criminal investigation, they stick to it, ignoring contradictory evidence and overlooking other possible suspects. This happens more frequently than honest, mistaken eyewitness identification or testimony, which can lead to a false conviction. Criminologists refer to this as "noble cause corruption"—when investigators deliberately overlook inconsistent evidence because they think they have the "right person," notwithstanding some factual contradictions.

The majority of criminal investigations follow appropriate procedures. But what structures do we have in place at all levels of a criminal investigation to prevent future wrongful convictions?

A focus on preventable errors can substantially reduce the number of wrongful convictions. But independent review is also an essential legal instrument to prevent wrongful consequences. Independent review uses people who were not involved in the original investigation to analyze a case that may have gone bad.

An example is Great Britain's independent Criminal Cases Review Commission, which reviews cases of alleged wrongful conviction. The mere presence of such an agency sharpens the criminal investigation in every stage throughout the country.

Canadians have had to pay millions of dollars in compensation to persons wrongfully convicted. Numerous commissions of inquiry have pointed almost unanimously to the negligence of prosecutors and police as significant factors in the investigations of innocent people.

Yet the system continues to inflict injustice by not declaring innocence once the facts of a corrupted investigation are known. Official apologies and compensation are not enough. Members of Parliament need to consider a third verdict in Canada's justice system—that of factual innocence in addition to guilty and not guilty.

In early October, the Supreme Court of Canada ruled that police can now be sued by innocent people harmed by negligent and shoddy investigations. This possibility may sharpen investigations and may provide sober consideration to investigators of the legal consequences for wrongful investigations.

Justice need not continue to be a cruel instrument when the abuse of rights has occurred against an individual. It should provide a remedy for those found innocent.

Focus On The Supreme Court

Profile of a Supreme Court Justice

Professionally, the present justices of the Supreme Court of Canada have a collective reputation for intensity on the bench. They often work 80-hour weeks, including weekends, and with an average age of 63, they make up one of the youngest benches in the history of the Court. But as private citizens, they do what most people do: raise their families, relax in sports such as swimming, tennis, and fishing, and go through the daily routines of managing their personal affairs.

An unwritten rule of the Court is that justices should lead restrained social lives and close their lives to public scrutiny so that their judicial impartiality is preserved for cases pending their decisions. Other restrictions affect judges' lives as well. They may not hold any other remunerative positions with the federal or provincial governments, nor can they engage in business. They must live in the National Capital Region or within 40 kilometres of it. For reasons such as these, a judge's life is a complicated one.

Before they are appointed to the Supreme Court of Canada, justices have earned solid reputations in the legal profession. Such is the case of Justice Rosalie Abella, who was appointed to the Supreme Court of Canada in 2004, after serving 12 years on the Ontario Court of Appeal.

Justice Abella, who is the first Jewish woman ever appointed to the Supreme Court, was born on July 1, 1946 in a Displaced Persons Camp in Germany. She came to Canada when she was four years old.

After graduating from the University of Toronto in 1970, she practiced civil and criminal law until at 29. She was appointed to the Ontario Family Court in 1976. This made her Canada's youngest person to be appointed to the Bench. She served on Ontario's Labour Relations Board, and its Law Reform Commission. She also provided advice on Access to Legal Services by the Disabled, academic discipline at the University of Toronto, and the Canadian Judicial Council's Inquiry on Donald Marshall, Jr.

Rosalie Silberman Abella has achieved great academic distinction, receiving 24 honourary degrees and publishing numerous articles in the areas of constitutional law, administrative law, and human rights. She created the term "employment equity" in a strategy to reduce barriers in employment faced by women, Aboriginal peoples, non-whites, and persons with disabilities. Her work has strengthened the concept of equality rights under the Charter of Rights and Freedoms.

Justice Abella begins most thought-filled weekdays the same way: by 8:00 A.M., she passes through the bronze doors at the entrance hall of the Supreme Court building, rides the elevator to the second floor, and enters her small book-lined chamber. There, she begins to read and answer correspondence that might include memorandums to and from members of the Court on current opinions circulated. All of these engagements must be conducted around the schedule of the Supreme Court, which holds three sessions during the year and sits about 16 or 17 weeks from the end of September to the end of June.

Most of her office time is spent reading and writing. She must read carefully the factums that are filed in application to the Supreme Court because they contain the lawyers' presentations of the facts on which the legal contests are based, as well as their refutations of the means of the adverse parties. She must interpret these in conference with her colleagues. Thus, the job demands a cautious, professional approach, tactfulness, diplomacy, and most of all, patience. **Law clerks** are assigned various tasks. Sometimes she will direct them in the research to be done, while in other circumstances she will request specific answers; and when the research is completed, the law clerks and the justice discuss the findings. Law clerks are lawyers recruited from all provinces, who share the invaluable experience of working closely with federal judges.

Usually, the Supreme Court convenes from 10:30 A.M. to 12:30 P.M., followed by a one-and-a-half-hour lunch at the Court House. The afternoon session runs from 2:00 P.M. to 4:30 P.M., followed by a half-hour Conference of the Court to discuss the cases of the day. The justices enter the Court through the door directly behind the long, elevated bench, wearing black silk gowns with white-collar vests. But usually at the formal opening and closing of each session, they will wear their bright scarlet robes trimmed with Canadian white mink, which they also wear at the opening of each new session of Parliament. The most junior justices sit on the far flanks and the others range closer to the chief justice, who occupies the centre position. A quorum consists of five members, but the full Court of nine sits for most of the cases, unless the illness of any of the justices prevents a full Court.

One day a month is devoted to motion hearings (motion day). Motion days start at 9:30 A.M. and the Court convenes at 10:30 A.M. and ends at about 4:30 P.M., with a one and a half hour break for lunch. Court motions are requests by parties to have their cases heard by the Supreme Court. The Court receives 20 to 30 motions a day. Justice Abella, like her other colleagues, must consider the merits of each request before giving an opinion. Each motion requires a judge to spend valuable time reading and doing research. Some motions are accepted; others are rejected. Those that are accepted have their day in court.

Unless by special leave of the Court, the only people who may argue before it, apart from the litigants themselves, are lawyers from any Canadian province or territory. When the arguments are being presented to the Court, any justice may ask questions of the lawyers retained. Sometimes a decision will be rendered at the conclusion of the arguments, but usually decisions are reserved for further deliberation or to enable judges to write their reasons. Decisions are made by the majority and need not be unanimous; dissenting reasons are frequently given. On adjourning, the justices file out the back door of the Court to their conference rooms directly across the corridor. At this time, Justice Abella sits by a circular oak table and begins the ritual of discussing the case she just heard. Each judge speaks to the points and issues raised in the case. The proceedings in this room are more confidential than federal Cabinet meetings.

The decisions of the Court are published on the internet and in the *Supreme Court Reports* and lodged in the Registry (scc.lexum.umontreal.ca), managed by the registrar, who holds the status of deputy minister responsible for the administration of the Supreme Court.

Dismissing an appeal from Alberta's attorney general, a unanimous Supreme Court struck down the federal *Lord's Day Act* because it compelled all residents to observe the Christian Sabbath, thereby violating the right of individuals to determine their religious preferences. And in a 5–0 decision, the Court ruled that the provision banning the use of languages other than French on public signs (Bill 101) was invalid because it violated the *Quebec Charter of Rights*.

Until the election of 2004, appointments to the Supreme Court were never a campaign issue in Canada. These highest judicial appointments have received little public scrutiny throughout Canadian history. Almost the only thing to appear in the newspapers is the name of the appointee, a few sentences about the person, and all sorts of quotes from professors and lawyers affirming that "this person has the best legal mind in Canada." Senior lawyers are reluctant to comment critically because they may wish to maintain good will in the judicial community in case they have to appear before the Supreme Court. In fact, the Canadian legal establishment very much opposes public hearings or some sort of ratification by a parliamentary body as in the United States. There, the US Senate hears evidence and testimony on the competence and appropriateness of presidential nominees and ratifies or does not ratify the appointment.[9]

Appointments follow strict protocol. The government decides from which region the appointee should come. As already noted, by law, three judges must come from Quebec; but by tradition, the rest of the provinces get their share (although some critics would strongly disagree). Ottawa asks the legal community to point out top candidates. Some applicants make the first contact, either by mentioning their interest to the province's chief justice or by writing directly to the federal justice minister or prime minister. Most Supreme Court members are appointed from appellate courts.

In 1999, a University of Toronto professor of law, Jacob S. Ziegel, made his case for greater scrutiny of Supreme Court judges before they are appointed. He proposed a nominating committee to supply the prime minister with a short list of Supreme Court candidates, rather than the mostly secretive practice followed in the past. And Ziegel advocated a procedure for Parliament to confirm the appointees made by the prime minister. This idea took hold in 2004 and 2006 through the use of a special parliamentary committee to question candidates and report their evaluations to Parliament.

Ideally, the Supreme Court should have a mix of talents, ages, ethnicities and backgrounds—men and women, academics, practicing lawyers, and judges with trial and appeals-court experience. This means appointing judges who are honest, unbiased, non-racist, non-sexist, industrious, empathetic, intelligent, and knowledgeable about the law.[10]

THE US JUDICIARY

State Courts

The laws that prevail in the United States facilitate the peaceful remedy of personal and group conflicts in a system of courts. At the state level, the legal machinery is complicated because the court systems of the 50 states operate within a variety of organizational patterns of jurisdictional and appellate arrangements. This diversity reflects the decentralization of the US legal system that has evolved in a large federal country (Figure 8.2).[11]

> **FACTFILE**   In the US, state courts interpret and apply their state constitutions and laws; their rulings may not be appealed to or reviewed by federal courts, except those decisions that raise a federal question of law or constitutional rights under the Bill of Rights.

At the lowest level are the local courts, whose jurisdiction is limited to minor civil and criminal matters. They are called *municipal courts* in 26 states and *county courts* in the remaining states. In addition, many cities have magistrate or police courts that deal with traffic violations and misdemeanors punishable by small fines and imprisonment for periods of up to six months. It is at this level that one finds the *rural justice courts*, staffed by justices of the peace who are often untrained at law and largely uncontrolled. These courts had their origin in feudal England, where justices of the peace enforced the King's Peace.[12] Today, in the United States, they are gradually disappearing and being replaced by special courts that deal solely with one kind of legal problem. Thus, many states have domestic-relations courts, juvenile courts, and probate courts (to examine the wills of deceased persons).

In all states, however, there is a distinction between the courts of general jurisdiction and those of special jurisdiction. The courts of general jurisdiction are responsible for major civil and criminal cases. These include trial courts, usually called *superior courts*, or circuit courts, and *appellate courts* of various kinds. Every state has an appellate judicial structure that culminates in a Supreme Court.

State court judges are selected in a variety of ways. In general, most states elect their judges.

Some states use executive appointment, subject to the approval of the state legislature.

> **FACTFILE**   Judicial review is an American contribution to modern government in that when courts declare a law or action unconstitutional, they not only void the matter, they also put it back on the public agenda, to be reconsidered by the executive or legislative branch of government.

Compared to the judicial machinery of the states, the federal court system is less complicated. There are specialized courts to deal with matters relating to customs and patents. But apart from these tribunals, US federal courts are organized in a three-layered pyramid. Most cases that fall under United States law are settled in federal district courts, with at least one in each state, the District of Columbia, and the Commonwealth of Puerto Rico. Their basic authority flows from Article III of the US Constitution, which extends the "judicial power [to] all cases, in law and equity, arising under this Constitution, the laws of the United States, and treaties made . . . under their authority and to the controversies between citizens of different states." At the second layer of the pyramid, 11 courts of appeal (plus one in the District of Columbia) review the conclusions (decisions) of district courts.

The US Supreme Court

At the apex of the pyramid, the highest federal court, the Supreme Court of the United States, hears cases from two separate avenues.[13] The Supreme Court hears cases on appeal from the circuit courts of appeal and, in special circumstances, from the district courts. Because the Court operates under a broad constitutional grant of power, it can take appeals from state judicial systems. But in matters of purely state law, the Supreme Court has no authority.

Figure 8.2   **The judiciary of the United States**

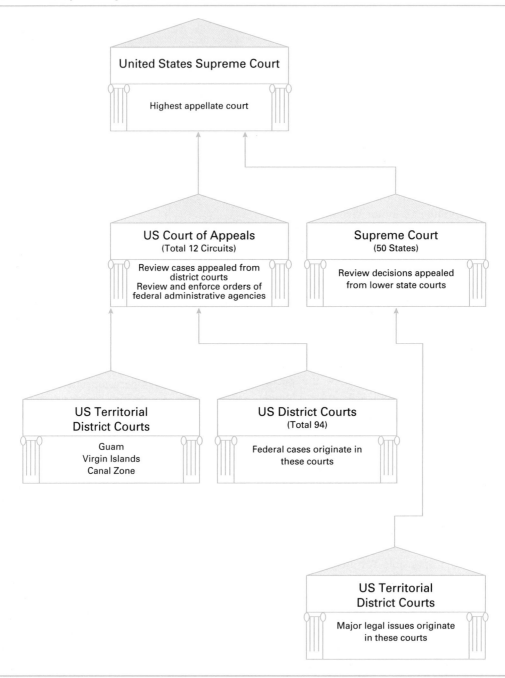

Crosscurrents   Should Canada Elect Judges?

In the United States, the appointment of judges is similar to the Canadian system at the federal level, but there are some important differences at other levels. In many states, voters are called upon to elect judges for various courts. Popular elections are used to choose judges, justices, and even the chief justice in some states. In California, for example, justices of the Supreme Court are elected for 12-year terms. Each county in the state has a superior court, with judges elected for 6-year terms.

Many states use partisan ballots for judicial elections, but some have begun to choose judges on non-partisan ballots. Unlike federal judges, who are appointed to serve for life, most state judges serve a limited term of office that is followed by a new election.

The reasoning behind the election of judges is that elected officials are more responsive to democratic pressures, such as popular demands on crime and punishment, than are appointed officials. Many Canadians criticize the Canadian system of justice because judges often hand down light or inconsistent sentences for crimes of sexual assault against women, molestation and abuse of children, general assault, and vandalism. They feel that judges are not in touch with popular opinion on the seriousness of certain crimes.

It is felt that judges who are elected would be more likely to perform their duties diligently, because they could be replaced if more responsive candidates ran against them. In addition, the election of judges means that it is more difficult for a political party, a governor, or, in Canada, a prime minister or premier, to control the judicial branch because partisan appointment is avoided. But some say that the political qualities that a person running for judicial office would need to win an election may not be the best qualities that make for a good judge. What do you think? Is Canada right to empower Cabinet to appoint all of its judges? Or should we elect our judges?

FACTFILE   At the United States Supreme Court the chief justice is only "first among equals" even though periods in court history are often named after the chief justice, for example, the Warren Court, the Burger Court, the Rehnquist Court.

The Supreme Court is a single tribunal of nine judges who hand down full opinions in no more than 100 to 150 cases a year. The Supreme Court, however, disposes of more than 9000 cases each year; in most instances this means that, after some examination, the Court concludes that the appeals lack merit.

All federal judges are appointed by the president, subject to the approval of the Senate. Senatorial approval means that senators, especially those from the state where a judge is selected, have veto power over the president's choice. Consequently, the appointment of federal judges leads to complicated political bargaining between the Justice Department, the senators of the state concerned, and local party leaders.

Unlike in Canada, where prime ministers show less concern for the political philosophies of potential Supreme Court candidates, US presidents consider political philosophies very significant. President George H.W. Bush Sr. ignited a political battle when he nominated Clarence Thomas to the Supreme Court. The day before the Senate was to vote on his confirmation, opponents of his nomination revealed that a University of Oklahoma law professor, Anita Hill, claimed that Thomas had sexually harassed her while she worked for him on the Equal Employment Opportunity Commission and, prior to that, at the Department of Education.

The dramatic Senate hearings that were televised around the world addressed charges of sexual misconduct, racism, and perjury from the testimonies of Thomas and Hill. Thomas denied the allegations and charged the Senate with racial prejudice and what he called a "high-tech lynching." No definitive conclusions were ever reached regarding Hill's allegations. In the end, Thomas was confirmed by the Senate, allowing the president to further solidify the Court's conservative majority.

FACTFILE   The rule of four is used to determine whether a case comes before the Supreme Court on petition. If four justices approve the petition, it will be granted and brought up for review.

Judges serve for life but can be removed for "cause" if impeached by the House and convicted by the Senate, following a special trial. The Supreme Court is a **gerontocracy** because most of its members are older than the general population. The inevitability of death or retirement on the highest court offers a historic opportunity for many presidents to fill several vacancies. Assuming that the appointees are relatively young, a US president can set the course of the Supreme Court for decades.

The US Supreme Court is primarily a public tribunal. Almost all of its cases are of two general types. First, the Court tests state actions against federal law, including the Constitution, laws, and treaties of the United States. Second, it interprets the meaning and decides the constitutionality of the work of Congress, the President, and the administrative agencies. Because of these functions, the Supreme Court is almost always controversial. It is the primary arbiter of political conflicts in legal dress, and its decisions that interpret laws—and ultimately the Constitution—are inescapably *political*,

even though Americans generally regard it as an apolitical institution.

In more than 200 years, the United States Supreme Court has often aroused ambivalent emotions among the American people. Viewed as a politically neutral government body, the Supreme Court elicits more deference from Americans than does the office of the presidency. In recent years, more than ever before, the Supreme Court has been regarded as the exemplar of democratic values, a role thrust upon it by the reluctance of other branches to act impartially on matters of political (or national) importance. But it has rarely stimulated a dispassionate response towards its judicial/political decisions, and the reason is plain. The Supreme Court addresses the conflicting forces that contend in US society, with decisions that mix law and politics. By so doing, it contributes to the formation of national policy and influences the direction of political change.

Chapter Summary

It is difficult to envision any modern society operating without the presence of law—that is, without a judicial system, a legal system, or a lawmaking system that prescribes and proscribes certain kinds of behaviour.

Law is the set of rules of conduct established by custom or laid down and enforced by a governing authority. The law has a number of important tasks: to make the operations of government and society predictable, precise, and consistent as social commands, passed by legitimate authority. There are thus four essential elements of law, as most definitions observe: the law is normative; the law is predictable; the law must be objectively applied by a legitimate authority; and the law must be enforced. Law is not only the means of achieving economic, social, and political order; it is also a fundamental ingredient of peaceful civilization.

All national and international law is positive law if it is regarded as human-made, derived from the will of the state. Custom has been the traditional source of positive law by providing the raw material from which laws are legislated, enacted, and adjudicated. Legislation, executive decree, administrative decisions, and constitutions are other sources of positive law. Court decisions are yet another source of positive law because judges, in certain rulings, make new law. In all of this can be found the dynamics of politics.

One institution the Normans created to unite England, which they conquered in 1066, was the King's Court, or *Curia Regis*. Before the conquest, disputes were settled according to local custom. The King's Court endeavoured to establish a "common," or unified, set of rules for the whole country.

Because of its English and French colonial heritage, a great portion of Canadian law is based on the English common-law system and, in the province of Quebec, on French-Canadian civil law. The civil-law tradition in Quebec follows general abstract legal principles that have been substantially codified. The Supreme Court of Canada is required by law to provide three judges from Quebec because it functions as a civil-law court for private-law appeals from Quebec and as a common-law court for public matters across the country.

Many of the states in Africa, Asia, and Latin America blend the customs, procedures, and codes found in other systems of jurisprudence into their own.

Discussion Questions

1. Think about the concepts of custom, ethics, justice, and law. Why are they related and why must they be distinguished?

2. Discuss on what grounds it is possible to justify the view that law is not, and cannot be, a matter of defining a simple concept with one simple meaning. What are some of the reasons why law is not easily equated with principles of universal justice? Why is it that law defies definition except in terms of culture?

3. What is a legal system? Discuss the contributions English common law has made to our legal system. Discuss the essential differences between common law and civil law.

4. Discuss why the Islamic legal system is indistinguishable from the social and political system. How effective is this kind of legal system in maintaining social order compared with other systems?

5. Review the functions of the judicial branch of government. Do we need more or fewer courts? How remote should the courts be from public scrutiny? Design the perfect Supreme Court. Discuss the size, the age of the justices, the number of cases, and the general workload of the ideal Court.

9

Understanding Constitutions

After reading this chapter, you will be able to:

- define constitution and constitutionalism

- contrast the elements of a written and an unwritten constitution

- apply these concepts to the character of Canada's Constitution

- outline the features of democratic constitutions and compare them

- trace the development of Canada's Constitution

- describe how the Constitution determined the framework of Canadian federalism

- understand the formulae for, and relate the challenges of, changing Canada's Constitution

- define the Charter of Rights and Freedoms

- discuss the impact of the Charter on our Constitution

- review the development and content of the Meech Lake and Charlottetown accords

- characterize the US Constitution

- discuss why Canada and the United States—two democracies with intimate histories—have developed such different constitutional traditions

● ● ● ●

WHAT IS A CONSTITUTION?

The word *constitution* carries an ancient, broad usage and a modern, narrow usage. The Greek word for constitution, *politeia*, refers to any form of government or regime as it functions in its entirety. The Greek *politeia* was the spirit (*ethos*) that animated the institutions of a government. The ancient Greeks saw the constitution as a cultural phenomenon—a formal expression of the way people conduct politics and the appropriate public attitudes that support a particular form of government.[1] Thus, to them a constitution was a product of culture, what modern political scientists call a "political culture." Hence, aristocracy,

monarchy, and democracy are embodiments of the attitudes, customs, usages, and values of a people—an ideal summation of their collective behaviour. In the ancient view, constitutions evolve as the political needs of people change in society.

Today, in most of the nation-states of the world, the word *constitution* is understood in a much narrower sense. The modern format for a constitution as exemplified by many but not all democratic states, e.g., Great Britain, is that it be a written document adopted at a given point in time by a sovereign authority. The British Constitution is really made up of a collection of documents spanning centuries. It consists of diverse major

Crosscurrents   If Constitutions Are So Important, Why Doesn't the World Have One?

There are some who say that the Charter of the United Nations and the Declaration of Human Rights already comprise a world constitution and its bill of rights. But in reality the United Nations Charter governs the goals of an international organization that functions to promote co-operation among states. The Charter is a founding document of the United Nations and does not claim to be the first law of the world. The Charter does not produce a government with executive and legislative institutions. It was written before the Cold War to give concrete expression for an enduring world peace.

The Declaration of Human Rights comes closer to a document that can have constitutional import for the world as it is written. It has legal standing in national and international courts and is the most qualified instrument we have to speak for global rights.

In a world of independent nation-states with powerful alliances, the idea of establishing a political authority over them that is both sovereign and universal is still only an idea that may come to fruition some time in the future.

As such, the need to prepare a document that will act as the *constitutional law* of such a world government is not a pressing one at this time.

Such a document would have to address the nature of world democracy. Who would draft the constitution? How would representatives be chosen and how would binding decisions be made? Where would the laws be made? What institutions would be created to make them? What would be the legal tradition behind the law? Would it be Islamic, Anglo-American, or some new amalgam of legal thinking? What about enforcement of the law? Who would do that?

The world doesn't have a constitution because it would be a daunting challenge to create one. Each government would bring its own political agenda to the negotiating table, would want to protect its politics against external intervention, and would not want to surrender much of its sovereign decision-making power and accountability to global institutions. But there is no doubt that if a world government is inevitable, a constitution outlining its scope and limitations is also inevitable.

acts of Parliament that time and custom have endowed with paramount authority.

> **FACTFILE**   The Royal Proclamation of 1763 was the first distinctively Canadian constitutional document. It created the colony of Quebec, giving it a governor general and an elected assembly.

Many modern constitutions are merely showcases for the international community and provide some governments with a rhetorical opportunity to appear "democratic." The ancients stressed the evolution of a constitution; modern governments stress the authoritative **enactment** of a constitution as a single event. But most contemporary students of constitutional law recognize the unwritten as well as the written dimensions of modern constitutions. No constitution can be properly understood solely as a written document. Judicial interpretations as well as modern political customs, **constitutional conventions**, and usages modify and sometimes nullify the written assertions of all constitutions in operation today.

Perspectives   Democracy without a Written Constitution

Sometimes it is difficult for Canadians to understand that constitutions can be both written and unwritten. They are surprised when they learn that Great Britain—often called the "cradle of democracy"—has no **written constitution** at all. The Constitution of Britain is said to be unwritten because there is no one document describing the institutions of government for the country. The British Constitution is a mixture of acts of Parliament, judicial pronouncements, customs, and conventions about the rules of the political game.

A large number of documents are British constitutional landmarks, including the Magna Carta (1215), which limits the powers of the monarch. Many acts of Parliament, such as the *Tallage Act* (1297), the *Habeas Corpus Act* (1679), the *Bill of Rights* (1689), and the *Welsh Language Act* (1993), fall under the constitutional law of Great Britain. None of these documents outlines Britain's entire system of government, as the Canadian and US constitutions do.

In Canada, the **unwritten constitution** includes such areas as the role and prerogatives of the prime minister, Cabinet solidarity, and the bureaucracy. But the bulk of Canada's constitutional framework is written on matters pertaining to the Queen, the governor general, the House of Commons, the Senate, and federalism, and now includes the Charter of Rights and Freedoms.

In Great Britain, acts of Parliament are supreme, subject only to the provisions of the great charters passed throughout British history. Nevertheless, Britain is undeniably a democracy with its unwritten constitution. Various acts of Parliament allow for free speech, open and free elections, competing political parties, and all the other characteristics associated with a democracy. If Parliament passes a law, it remains a law unless an act of Parliament is rescinded or overridden by another act.

As long as there is a basic consensus on how governing should take place, the British system has worked well. When such a consensus is lacking, however, no government, whether it has a written or unwritten constitution, can endure.

Some scholars avoid the distinction between the written and the unwritten features of a constitution and focus on the *formal* and the *effective* elements of constitutions.[2] The formal constitution is the original documents, statutes, charters, and other authoritative sources that explicitly outline the structures and goals of a government. The effective constitution is the actual **modus operandi** of a political system, which includes those customs and practices that in time evolve according to the spirit of the constitution, but are not specifically mentioned in the constitution. For example, Canada's formal constitution does not mention the federal Cabinet, political parties, or the federal civil service. There is no mention that the prime minister and the Cabinet must always have the support of, or even have seats in, the House of Commons. Effectively, these important institutions of Canadian government have constitutional *legitimacy* by legislation, custom, and judicial interpretation. Similarly, according to its constitutional documents, Great Britain is a monarchy, but effectively it is a parliamentary democracy, as is Canada. In the United States, members of the electoral college may elect any eligible person to the presidency. However, electors are effectively pledged to elect the same president that the American people select in a national election.

For analytical purposes, political scientists define *constitution* in the widest possible context. As we shall use the term, a constitution is a body of formal and effective rules and practices, written and unwritten, according to which the people and the political institutions of a society are governed. This broad definition enables the political scientist to recognize the functional constitution operating in each political system. Because in most states many fundamental constitutional principles remain largely informal and unwritten, the political analyst must include the accumulated traditions, political mores, and practices of a people as constituent parts of all constitutions.

The Meaning of Constitutionalism

Constitutionalism may be thought of as the superego of a democratic constitution. It is to a constitution what character is to an individual. The essence of constitutionalism is its belief system, which asserts the need for formal limitations on political power: that is, that power is curtailed and procedures of government are defined in a constitution.

Constitutionalism demands that states be faithful to their constitutions because the rules so provided are all that can protect people from arbitrary government policies and actions. In its purest form, constitutionalism treats government as a necessary evil: humans accept limited government to escape the chaos of anarchy. The term and its related concepts revolve around the idea that individual inalienable rights should be entrenched in a formal constitution. There is also the notion that constitutions should reflect fairness in that no undue advantage is to be given to one particular group.

At the turn of the twentieth century, constitutionalism almost disappeared from the standard vocabulary of students of politics, due to shifting academic fashions and a changing international system. The rapid growth in the number of nation-states adopting authoritarian regimes, as well as the emergence of totalitarian dictatorships after World War I, challenged the ideal of *limited government* protected by a constitution. Even among the democratic states, social, economic, political, and military *demands* encouraged the rapid expansion of government in all of the traditional private preserves of society. The legal ability of governments to ignore constitutional standards became insurmountable, and the practice of simply changing a constitution to meet the needs of autocratic executives became a common practice.

Examples abound showing that when constitutions become political liabilities to autocratic rulers, they simply replace them. For example, more than 200 constitutions have been in force in all the republics of Latin America since their independence in the period between 1810 and 1830. No constitution now in force in any Latin American state dates from its independence. The average number of constitutions for all of Latin America is about 10 for each state. The reality of constitutionalism in Latin America is that many constitutional provisions are ignored, suspended, or rewritten at the whim of the government in power.

FACTFILE   Just over a dozen constitutions date from the nineteenth century or earlier. Most of the constitutions in operation today were written and enacted following World War II.

It is important to note that just because a constitution exists, this is no guarantee that it really works. All independent nation-states, whether democratic or non-democratic, consider the promulgation of a constitution a necessary step towards attaining full recognition as a legal entity in the international system.

FACTFILE   The United States (1787) and France (1789) were the first modern states to use a formal written, codified constitution as the supreme law in the country, which was followed by most other states by the twenty-first century.

The practice of constitutionalism, which asserts the supremacy of the first law, is the only measure we have of determining whether a nation-state has a working constitution. A verifiable democratic constitution is more than pieces of paper. It is a living document that embodies much more than mere words can convey—it embodies principles that enable it to work and to survive.

THE FEATURES OF DEMOCRATIC CONSTITUTIONS

All democratic constitutions actually *restrict* government power. Those states that limit the powers of government by a written constitution or by statute and custom are called **constitutional regimes**. In order to evaluate the democratic character of a constitution, many political objectives, features, and procedures must be taken into account, including the extent to which the constitution

- promotes the public good;
- has procedures to make amendments;
- places limitations on the various branches of government; and
- enumerates individual rights and freedoms.

FACTFILE   In 1215, a weak King John was forced by a small number of English barons to place his seal on the *Magna Carta*. After it was signed, British monarchs were subject to the law and thus limited by it.

The Public Good

Constitutions provide the framework for achieving the goal of the public good. Working by the letter and spirit of a constitution, most democratic governments provide tangible goods and services that individuals cannot or will not provide for themselves. These goods and services, taken together, comprise the public good because any person can use or benefit from them, whether or not that person has actually contributed to them. The goods and services that comprise the public good cannot be provided to any one citizen without also being provided to other citizens.

> FACTFILE In order to enhance the public good, the *Constitution Act, 1940*, transferred jurisdiction over unemployment insurance from the provincial governments to the federal government, giving the program greater financial security and standard application across Canada.

The notion of constitutional government as the provider of the public good is tied to the age-old theory of the social contract, which, as we have seen, is hypothesized as the original agreement among people to create the state and its government. One important aspect of social contract theory is that the proper role of government is to provide goods and services that are not normally available from a private source.

What constitutes the "public good" at any particular time and place also depends upon the fundamental values and demands of citizens, and to a very large extent, on their scale of affordable priorities—their beliefs about what should come first. In the twenty-first century, governments set their public-policy priorities not only according to public demand, but also according to their capacity to financially meet those demands. Under pressure from taxpayers, governments must increasingly meet high public expectations regarding what is the public good in a changing political and economic environment.

The public good is grounded in democratic ideals, where political equality requires consideration of everyone's opinion, and a seeking of consensus, concessions, and public participation. These democratic constitutional ideals influence administration in the public sector by requiring governments to implement their public policies according to high social standards such as accountability, equal opportunity, majority rule, minority rights, and **political neutrality**.

Constitutions establish broad and positive purposes to enhance the public good and to achieve general public goals. They are not documents written primarily for governments; rather, they are legal instruments outlining the relationship of people to the governmental institutions of society. Constitutions establish the context within which people co-exist with government.

Amending Procedures

Most constitutions have certain procedures by which they can be formally changed. Constitutions vary with respect to flexibility and rigidity.[3] Only a few constitutions (e.g., those of Great Britain and New Zealand) are **flexible constitutions**, to the extent that they can be amended by the same procedures used to pass ordinary laws. But many constitutions, including Canada's, are **rigid constitutions** in the sense that they can be formally amended only by special procedures that are more difficult to enact than ordinary legislation.

Every special amending procedure is intended to ensure that constitutional reform is the result of serious deliberation. Amendments to the constitutions of many European states, including Denmark, Ireland, and Switzerland, must be approved by the electorate in a referendum. In Belgium, the Netherlands, and Sweden, an amendment must be approved by the national legislature, which is subsequently dissolved, followed by a general election to return a new legislature, which must pass the amendment in its identical form.

Almost all amendment formulas are intended to prevent arbitrary constitutional changes. In the United States, most amendments are proposed by a two-thirds majority of Congress, but the states have the power to ratify them, requiring the approval of three-quarters of the states. In Canada, provincial legislatures must give their approval for amendments on the use of the English and French languages, the composition of the Supreme Court, and the alteration of provincial boundaries. And in Australia and Switzerland, a majority of national voters must also be accompanied by a majority of state and canton voters before the amendment is passed.

Crosscurrents   Should Canada's Constitution Be Easy to Change?

Canada's Constitution has not been easy to change. As you will read in this chapter, passing an amendment to the Constitution requires great effort on the part of those who wish to do so. Canadians have struggled to reach agreement on a universally acceptable formula for constitutional change since the *Statute of Westminster* in 1931, tripping many times along the way. We failed—with Fulton–Favreau (1964), the Victoria Charter (1971), the Meech Lake Accord (1987), and the Charlottetown Accord (1992)—to bring all provinces and the federal government on the side of national constitutional harmony.

But what if it were easy to amend the Constitution? What if we could change it by simply passing an ordinary piece of legislation? Would the consequences be all that good? Would we be a more progressive society? Would it increase our chances of national survival and make us a more united people? One thing is certain: if changing the Constitution were easy, there would be more amendments. How many and what kind are unknown, of course.

Clearly, the easier it is for a constitution to be changed, the more likely the political process—which encourages organized interests to obtain special legislation—will be used. When a constitution can be amended easily, constitutional amendments may not even have to meet the level of scrutiny that an ordinary act of Parliament would meet. If our Constitution was easy to change, amendments could be proposed and entrenched in an attempt just to override unpopular court decisions or acts of Parliament.

Likewise, if the Canadian Constitution could be more easily amended, organized special interest groups would lobby Parliament or provincial governments to amend the Constitution rather than simply to pass new laws. The Charter of Rights and Freedoms would lose much of its effect if subject to frequent change. Social whims would replace the historical continuity and traditions of Canada.

The legacy of the failed Meech Lake and the Charlottetown accords gave many the impression that unless we make our Constitution more changeable, Canada will be in a state of permanent social stalemate. Some even argued that Canadians will be unable to develop as a sovereign people and that, without some quick constitutional agreement, we will lose Quebec—and ultimately all of Canada.

Not everyone believes that we should tinker with the Constitution to make it more amendable. Many feel that the Constitution, left as it is for the time being, still gives us the best option we have. They hold the opinion that we should use our collective energies to try to make it work.

One well-known Canadian academic who thinks this way is the historian Michael Bliss. Bliss believes Canadians should not have opened up their country's constitution so easily and so often. He feels we lived well for more than 100 years with the *British North America Act*, changing it very few times before presenting it for patriation and adding a Charter of Rights and Freedoms in 1982. It took more than 50 years to implement changes that were debated periodically since the 1920s. The achievements of 1981–1982 took place only after agonizing social and political debate.

Perhaps, as Bliss asserts, the status quo is the best option we have. According to him, we should stop knocking it, start defending it, and get on with making it work. Ottawa should back away and announce a moratorium on schemes for general constitutional reform.

Finally, some amendment formulae are designed to protect the rights of linguistic, religious, and cultural minorities. The Swiss constitution stipulates that Switzerland is a trilingual country, where French, German, and Italian have equal status under constitutional law. Canada's *Constitution Act, 1982,* specifies that "English and French are the official languages of Canada and have equality of status and equal rights and privileges as to their use in all institutions of the Parliament and Government of Canada."

Limitations on Government

Constitutions operating in the democratic model adhere to the fundamental principle that proclaims the supremacy of law, establishing limits on public officials in the exercise of their powers.[4] Limitations on government are established through a number of constitutional devices, including a blueprint of the formal structures of government, sometimes a system of checks and balances, judicial controls, and, in federal states, the distribution of powers among the various levels of government. By limiting the powers of government, its institutions, and personnel, a democratic constitution prevents the accumulation of power within the political system and is an instrument for protecting the rights of individuals from arbitrary interference by officials.

Federal constitutions can create even more limitations on government. Federal states have more than one sphere of government: a national system for the entire country and a subnational system of governments with specific powers over limited jurisdictions. In most federal systems, both levels of government can derive their legitimacy only from the powers enumerated in the constitution and from the various judicial reviews and

interpretations directed at resolving intergovernmental disputes. Federal constitutions vary considerably in their limitations of power among the different levels of government. In the United States, each state can legislate in any area not constitutionally reserved to the federal government or to the people. This strong national bias in the US Constitution has given the federal government the power to expand its activities into the areas of state jurisdiction. The Australian form is similar. In Canada, powers are separately delegated to the federal government (section 91) and the provinces (section 92), but Ottawa retains extensive residual powers. Areas of concurrent powers are specified in the Canadian Constitution.

Enumeration and Protection of Rights

Most constitutions establish and outline fundamental rights and freedoms for citizens. The safeguard of the rights of the individual has been the testimony of democratic constitutions since the American and French revolutions. In states such as Australia, Austria, Belgium, Canada, Iceland, Sweden, and the United States, the protection of civil rights enjoys widespread constitutional and community support. However, in the most repressive regimes of Cuba, North Korea, Libya, and Vietnam, individual rights are flagrantly violated by government policy, notwithstanding constitutional guarantees that formally promise to protect them.

> **FACTFILE** The preamble to France's Constitution states that country's adherence to the Declaration of the Rights of Man of 1789, giving it a powerful attachment to the history of the human and civil rights movement in the world.

In spite of the entrenchment of individual rights in the majority of constitutions around the world, the power to violate enumerated freedoms exists in all states. In the United States, for example, the constitutional rights of African Americans—such as the right to due process or the right to vote—have often been violated by law enforcement or elections authorities with little or no legal repercussions. Great Britain stands condemned by the international community for torturing suspected terrorists in the interrogation centres of Northern Ireland, and the United States has been likewise condemned for its treatment of prisoners at Guantanemo Bay. Public outcry is particularly passionate because these infringements of individual rights take place in the most genuinely democratic states.

Many other states have constitutions that are "democratic" in name only, whose governments routinely violate both civil rights and human rights. The government of Rwanda, for example, cooperated with vigilante groups to participate in the genocide of about two million Rwandans between 1994 and 1997. And despite constitutional protections, the government of President Slobodan Milosevic engaged in acts of genocide against the ethnic Albanian majority in the Yugoslav province of Kosovo from 1997 to 1999.

> **FACTFILE** The US-based Freedom House (www.freedomhouse.org) reported in 2006 that less than half of the 6.5 billion people on the planet enjoy the constitutional freedoms that Canadians take for granted, namely: freedom of speech, freedom of the press, freedom of religion, even the freedom of mobility in their own countries.

At the heart of democratic constitutionalism is the right to personal liberty. In Canada's Charter of Rights and Freedoms, this guarantee appears as the "right to life, liberty and security of person and the right not to be deprived thereof except in accordance with the principles of fundamental justice."[5]

> **FACTFILE** Section 7 of Canada's Charter gives everyone the right to life, liberty, and security of the person, and was used to throw out the abortion provision of the Criminal Code in the 1988 Dr. Henry Morgentaler case.

Closely associated with individual liberty is *freedom of speech* and *the press*. All states limit this freedom to some extent. In Great Britain and Canada, **slander** and **libel** can be committed against individuals only, who then can seek legal redress.[6] However, in Italy, institutions such as the army, the police, and the church can regard statements made about them as slanderous and libellous, with due legal recourse. In Great Britain, an editor was convicted of blasphemous libel for publishing a poem depicting Christ as a homosexual.

Freedom of speech and the press exists in most states, at least according to their constitutions. In some, this freedom is quite genuine and comparable to that of the most democratic states. In 2006, Chile's first woman president, Michelle Bachelet, reversed most of the harsh security laws that had been decreed by General Augusto Pinochet and were still on the books. By contrast, however, under Libya's sweeping press law, the government has virtual control over all news media in the country, and the president is immune from criticism.

There are numerous constitutional provisions and laws aimed to guarantee the *freedom of association and assembly*. But these and many other rights, which look so impressive on paper, are frequently limited with impunity, even in those nation-states that have a democratic commitment to free associations. Many governments retain the power to determine when a peaceful assembly becomes a threat to the order of the state. In some states, the formation of communist and fascist parties is illegal. Italy's constitution prohibits the Fascist Party, but the government has tolerated the formation of neo-fascist groups. In Latin America, five states—Brazil, Chile, Guatemala, Haiti, and Uruguay—not only have made the Communist Party illegal, but they also actively persecute party militants with torture and harassment.

In totalitarian states, the only legal party effectively controls the organization of groups such as labour unions, students, and women, by extending auxiliary party organizations into all levels of society and mobilizing popular participation in them. Many people participate in such groups only because the organization has a monopoly on some activity they want to engage in, not because it can effectively influence party policies.

Compared with the highly controversial freedom of association, *freedom of religion*, which most constitutions profess, has been a sporadic issue that makes headlines from time to time. In the United States, laws restrict the Mormon practice of polygamy. And Canadian authorities have prosecuted the Sons of Freedom, a small but distinct subgroup of the Doukhobors, for acts of violence and public nudity.

The majority of modern constitutions mention the rights to *privacy* and *private property*. The constitutions of France, Germany, Italy, Japan, and Turkey, for example, entrench the right to own private property, provided that such ownership does not conflict with the public interest. Canada's Constitution fails to include the protection of property rights except under the "security of the person" provision, section 7, which to some degree protects the right to acquire property. The US *Bill of Rights*, adopted in 1791, is long on states' rights and property guarantees. But it took an extensive period of judicial interpretation to resolve the competing demands of property rights in the United States. The US Supreme Court has come a long way from its notorious **Dred Scott decision**, in which it upheld the property rights of slave owners.

CANADA'S CONSTITUTION

The Constitutional Framework

There have been two major influences on Canada's constitutional history. Like the British tradition of constitutionalism, more than one document has constitutional significance in Canada. And like the US Constitution, the most substantive aspects of our Constitution are written. In fact, much of what is described as the Constitution of Canada is found in a number of documents and unwritten practices. Thus, Canada's Constitution includes the *Constitution Act, 1867*; the *Constitution Act, 1982*; the *Supreme Court Act, 1875*; the *Statute of Westminster*, 1931, and the *Letters Patent* of 1947; the *Emergencies Act*, 1988 (which replaced the repealed *War Measures Act*, 1917); the federal acts' that admitted new provinces since 1867 such as the *Alberta Act* and *Saskatchewan Act* of 1905; and the various customs, conventions, judicial decisions, and statutes that are considered permanent components of Canada's political system.

FACTFILE   The People's Republic of China has remained constitutionally stable with a totalitarian form of government ruling a capitalist economy under its fourth constitution since 1949.

Some experts believe that we must also include certain pre-1867 instruments that retain their constitutional significance, such as the Royal Proclamation of 1763, the *Quebec Act* of 1774, the *Constitution Act* of 1791, and the *Union Act* of 1840.[7] Some of the unwritten practices in Canada's Constitution include Cabinet solidarity, the dominance of the political executive over the formal executive, the role of the prime minister and Cabinet in Parliament, and the function of political parties in the parliamentary system.

The *Constitution Act, 1867*, is the heart of the overall Canadian constitutional framework. Despite the political, social, and economic changes that have taken place in the country since the nineteenth century, Canadians still hearken back to the *Constitution Act, 1867*, as the prominent source of all political and legal authority. Even though the original document is in part ambiguous and omits much (no reference to the Cabinet or political parties, for example), it has acquired layers of precedent and tradition. The *Constitution Act, 1867*, is the symbol of Canada's legal and political diversities. For Canadians, it is their first and highest secular law, containing the important principles of federalism and parliamentary democracy.

Focus On   Canada's Main Constitutional Principles

Monarchy: Canada is a constitutional monarchy, retaining the monarch as the head of state and the royal powers of appointment and legislative approval and proclamation.

Responsible Government: First applied in Nova Scotia, this principle asserts that the formal institutions of government, i.e., the monarchy, its representatives, and the executive branch of government, are responsible to elected representatives chosen by the people.

Constitutionalism: This principle proclaims the supremacy of the constitution as the first law of the land to which all other laws must conform and that all domestic governments are limited by constitutional rules and procedures.

Federalism: The division of powers and governing jurisdictions between the federal government and the provinces—each of which enforces its own laws directly on the people.

Democratic Values: While the Fathers of Confederation adopted institutions of government that are clearly undemocratic (e.g., the Crown and the Senate) the underlying principle that elections and political succession are popular choices embodies the ethos of the constitution.

Egalitarianism and the Charter: The Charter extends the benefits of rights that it guarantees to everyone, regardless of social background.

The Constitution and Federalism

The *Constitution Act, 1867*, made Canada the third state in history, after the United States and Switzerland, to adopt a federal system of government, and the first state in the world to combine parliamentary institutions with federalism. The essential legal characteristic of Canadian federalism is that both the federal and provincial governments enjoy exclusive and concurrent powers derived directly from the Constitution.

FACTFILE In 1867, Canada was referred to as a "Confederation," even though its Constitution crafted an authentic federal state.

Without understanding Canada's federal system, as outlined in the *Constitution Act, 1867*, it would be impossible to understand such factors as the distribution of popular support among the national political parties, voting behaviour in the House of Commons, the striking of a national budget, the pattern of policy outcomes, and the many other features of national politics. To a great extent, the provinces are the building blocks from which the national parties are organized and the operating agencies through which a large share of federal programs are carried out.

The *Constitution Act, 1867*, allocates and delineates the **exclusive powers** of the federal government under section 91, and those of the provinces under section 92 (see Figure 9.1). Under section 91, the federal government enjoys 29 classes of political functions in addition to jurisdiction over public property and public debt, banking, credit, navigation

Figure 9.1   Federal principle: Canada

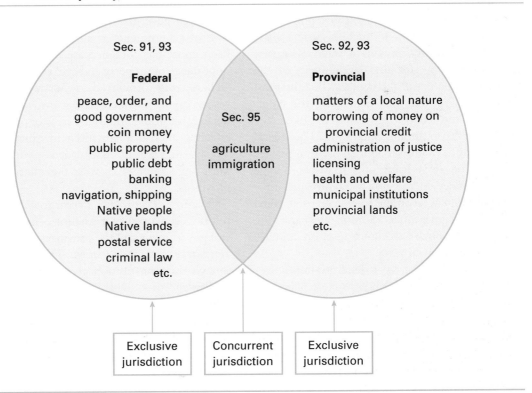

Sec. 91, 93

Federal

peace, order, and
good government
coin money
public property
public debt
banking
navigation, shipping
Native people
Native lands
postal service
criminal law
etc.

Sec. 95

agriculture
immigration

Sec. 92, 93

Provincial

matters of a local nature
borrowing of money on
provincial credit
administration of justice
licensing
health and welfare
municipal institutions
provincial lands
etc.

Exclusive jurisdiction

Concurrent jurisdiction

Exclusive jurisdiction

and shipping, Native people and their lands, postal services, and the criminal law. To the provinces, section 92 allocated exclusive powers stated as "generally all matters of a merely local or private Nature in the Province." These powers included the borrowing of money based on the credit of the province; prisons in the province and the administration of justice; licensing to raise provincial revenues; health and welfare; municipal institutions; and the control of provincial lands. Section 93 gives the provinces control over the education rights of religious minorities. But it also gives the federal Cabinet and Parliament the right to scrutinize provincial laws and to pass remedial legislation should provincial action in the area of education run contrary to section 93.

Federalism provided the provinces with an enormous number of opportunities for small victories in local affairs. But the intent of the Fathers of Confederation was that there indeed ought to be a central government with effective powers and institutions.[8] For them, nothing else would guarantee political unity, provide a stable monetary system, and allow for the development of the economic resources of the country. But the most distinguishing powers that established the dominance of the central government over the provinces were in the area of taxation. The federal government has almost unlimited taxation powers under section 91(3). It can offer to dispense huge sums of money to the provinces provided they spend the money according to policies established by the federal government. Section 92(2) gives the provinces the power of direct taxation to raise revenues for their purposes.

The superiority of the federal taxation power has enabled Ottawa to expand its sphere of activity into many areas of provincial jurisdiction to the point where most of the provinces have become dependent on the national treasury. In addition, the *Constitution Act, 1867*, granted the Parliament of Canada the power to make laws for "Peace, Order and Good Government." The courts have interpreted these words as a **residual power** to the federal government, so that when a particular matter cannot be distinguished from the specific categories of powers enumerated in the *Constitution Act, 1867*, it moves under the authority of Parliament. On the surface, residual powers that favour the federal government would seem to permit Ottawa the potential, at least, to govern Canada as if it was a unitary state. But this has not happened.

FACTFILE   The residual power enables the federal government to legislate in any area of jurisdiction that is not specifically assigned to the provincial governments in the Canadian Constitution.

The *Constitution Act, 1867*, does not tell us how Canadian federalism has actually evolved or how it currently works. Indeed, much of the transformation of Canada's federal system points in the direction of increased power and prestige for the provincial governments.[9] Since 1867, the expansion of governments at all levels in Canada has been enormous. But because of the present-day importance of property and civil rights, health and welfare, and provincial ownership of natural resources, the provinces have gained striking powers in most of the important areas of public policy affecting all Canadians, even in external affairs. Today, all areas of federal actions and policies must align themselves with the interests of the provinces.

Section 95 of the *Constitution Act, 1867*, refers to concurrent jurisdictions among the federal government and the provinces in the areas of *agriculture* and *immigration*. Here again, even though the Constitution gives supremacy to the Parliament of Canada, when conflicts arise on matters of concurrent jurisdiction, the federal government has been willing to negotiate its policies in these areas with the provinces.

In many other areas where exclusive federal jurisdiction is provided by the Constitution, the provinces have successfully challenged and penetrated the powers granted to Ottawa. For example, yielding to provincial preserves, the federal government gave control of family allowances to the provinces and withdrew its direct involvement in post-secondary education.

The *Constitution Act, 1867*, creates the need for the provinces and the federal government to frequently negotiate any unresolved constitutional jurisdictions. It sets the context and establishes definite outer limits within which each level of government may choose to operate. A less formal way to put this is to say that the written constitution does not tell us how intergovernmental relations work in Canada.

Backgrounder to the *Constitution Act, 1982*

For much of Canada's history as an independent nation-state from 1867 to 1982, the *Constitution Act, 1867*, lacked a Canadian **amendment procedure**.[10] Until 1949, the British Parliament amended the Constitution on all substantive matters by request from Canada, through a joint address to the House of Commons and the Senate. From 1949 to 1982, amendment of the *Constitution Act, 1867*, could be passed by Canada to increase the number of senators by two, one each from the Yukon and the Northwest Territories. But Parliament still could not amend the Constitution on a wide range of matters, including provincial jurisdictions, the English and French languages, and provisions on the tenure of Parliament. In fact, Canada was the only democracy that could not reform its Constitution in its entirety without the parliamentary approval of a foreign state.

FACTFILE   Constitutions, including Canada's, can also be changed by court decisions, amendment procedures that interpret the meaning of words, phrases, and clauses in the original and subsequent documents, as well as through constitutional conventions.

In 1980, Pierre Elliott Trudeau pledged that his majority government would **patriate** the Constitution, giving it a Charter of Rights and Freedoms and an amendment formula. Trudeau moved unilaterally to patriate the Constitution by introducing the Patriation Resolution in Parliament. The opposition parties resisted his plan, as did most provincial governments: only two provinces, Ontario and New Brunswick, supported it. This state of affairs culminated in a number of court battles to determine the legality of unilateral patriation. In February 1981, the Manitoba Court of Appeals, in a close decision of 3 to 2, ruled that the Patriation Resolution was legal. Two months later, the Newfoundland Court of Appeals ruled unanimously against unilateral patriation. In April of 1981, the Quebec Court of Appeal ruled in favour of the federal proposal in a 4 to 1 decision. Finally, on September 28, 1981, the Supreme Court, in a 7 to 2 decision, ruled that the federal government had the legal right to ask the Parliament of the United Kingdom to amend the *British North America (BNA) Act*, and to implement a Charter of Rights and Freedoms, without the unanimous consent of the provinces.

In the ensuing weeks, the Trudeau government bargained intensely with the provinces and reached agreement with all except Quebec on the final concessions of the Constitutional Accord. In December 1981, Parliament passed the *Canada Act* by a vote of 246 to 24 in the House and a vote of 59 to 23 in the Senate. In the same month the Act was delivered to the British Parliament by the secretary to the governor general and the Minister of Justice, Jean Chrétien. The British Parliament finally approved the *Canada Act* in March 1982, and on April 17 of that year the Queen proclaimed it as the *Constitution Act, 1982*, completing the process of patriation. It was the British Parliament's last bill binding on Canada. However, without Quebec's official acceptance of the accord, Canada would remain constitutionally impaired.

Canada's Amendment Procedures

The procedures for amending the Constitution are listed in Part V, section 38-49, of the *Canada Act, 1982*. Some procedures require the approval of the House of Commons and the Senate and the legislative assemblies of at least two-thirds (seven) of the provinces with at least 50 percent of the population of all provinces. This is referred to as the 7/50 formula.[11]

1. Only Parliament's approval is necessary for changes to its own structures.

2. Only a provincial legislature's approval is necessary for changes to its structure, such as whether to establish a provincial Senate.

3. Changes that apply to some but not all provinces can be made by passing resolutions in just those legislatures and the federal Parliament (such as resolutions that affect immigration and culture).

4. Changes to the monarchy, the amending formula itself, the composition of the Supreme Court of Canada, or the status of official languages require the *unanimous* consent of all eleven governments, through resolutions of their respective legislatures.

5. The majority of amendments apply the 7/50 rule, which requires resolutions for a change from Parliament and the legislatures from seven provinces representing 50 percent of the national population. Resolutions require three years to pass the required number of legislatures. This section provides that as many as three provinces can *opt out* of the amendments, and the federal government will provide reasonable compensation to them.

6. Amendments that apply the 7/50 rule with no opting out by provinces involve resolutions for changing: the way provinces are represented in the House of Commons; the selection, powers, and representation of senators; the Supreme Court of Canada (other than its composition); the extension of provincial boundaries into northern territories; and the establishment of new provinces.

Constitutional Rights and Freedoms

At the time of Confederation, Canadians felt secure in adopting the British guarantees of individual rights and freedoms embedded in the traditions of common law. The *Magna Carta* (1215), the *Habeas Corpus Act* (1679), and the *Bill of Rights* (1689) seemed quite enough to protect Canadians for most of the century after 1867.[12] In 1960, however, the John Diefenbaker government was determined to give legislative protection for these assumed guarantees by passing its Canadian *Bill of Rights*. This measure suffered from an inherent weakness: because it was a legislative rather than a constitutional enactment, it could be repealed by a simple act of Parliament. But by entrenching these rights in a new constitution in 1982, Canadians could feel more secure in the knowledge that the rigid amendment formulae would work to prevent any rapid erosion of basic freedoms.

Thus, with the proclamation of the *Canada Act, 1982*, which contains the 34-clause Canadian Charter of Rights and Freedoms, two important guarantees were branded on Canada's political culture. One was **substantive rights** that specify a condition of freedom and advantage that can be enjoyed for its own sake. Another was procedural rights that provided political and legal devices through which governments are controlled and the people protected from arbitrary action.

Section 1 of the Canadian Charter states that rights are subject "to such reasonable limits prescribed by law as can be demonstrably justified in a free and democratic society." On the surface, at least, rights are guaranteed in the Constitution, but they may be limited by Parliament and provincial legislatures. Enactment of the Charter has also placed the Supreme Court of Canada in the difficult position of arbitrating disputes to adjudicate on whether they are "reasonable" or have been "demonstrably justified."

FACTFILE In 1989, Quebec used the "notwithstanding" clause of the Canadian Charter of Rights and Freedoms to override the freedom of expression and equality rights guaranteed in that Charter. It did so in order to continue to regulate the use of commercial signs in languages other than French.

Similarly, section 33 states that "Parliament or the Legislature of a province may expressly declare in an Act of Parliament or of the Legislature, as the case may be, that the act or provision thereof shall operate notwithstanding . . . this charter." In effect, the Constitution allows the enactment of bills that say they operate *notwithstanding* the Charter of Rights and Freedoms. In other words, laws that infringe on the most fundamental rights of individuals may be passed, even though they contravene the spirit and letter of the Charter. The danger in such clauses is that legislators can simply specify that their legislation is operative despite certain provisions in the Charter. Canadians receive no more assurance from a legislated **bill of rights** than from an enacted charter of rights, if their rights can be pre-empted by a "notwithstanding" clause.

But the Canadian Charter does contain two major provisions that have received much praise from constitutional scholars. One is a clear statement of the *equality of men and women* (section 15(1)). The second is section 15(2), which is an affirmative-action provision. It permits the adoption of laws, programs, and activities to advance the cause of groups that are disadvantaged because of race, national or ethnic origin, colour, religion, sex, age, and mental or physical disability.

All the other provisions in the Charter resemble those of most democratic constitutions in the world today. Like many other democratic documents, the Charter affirms that "Canada is founded upon principles that recognize the supremacy of God and the rule of law." Under sections 2 to 5, it lists the basic *civil* and *political liberties* to which Canadians are entitled. Sections 7 through 14 outline the legal rights of Canadian citizens that also fall in line with other democracies, such as Germany, Great Britain, Sweden, and the United States.

The Meech Lake Accord, 1987

With the defeat of the *Parti Québécois* government by Robert Bourassa and his Liberal candidates in December 1985, the way was cleared for a new set of negotiations to gain Quebec's official acceptance of the 1982 Constitutional amendment.[13] In May 1986, at Mont-Gabriel, the new Quebec government laid out five conditions for its acceptance of the *Constitution Act, 1982*, in a manifesto entitled *Maitriser l'avenir* (*Mastering Our Future*). They were:

1. Recognition of Quebec as a distinct society.
2. A larger provincial role in immigration.
3. Provincial input into appointments to the Supreme Court of Canada.
4. Limitations on the federal spending power.
5. A veto for Quebec on constitutional amendments.

At the federal government's retreat at Meech Lake, Quebec, on April 30, 1987, Canada's first ministers agreed in principle to Quebec's five proposals. This was followed in June by an all-night negotiating session at the Langevin Block in Ottawa that resulted in the drafting of the 1987 Constitutional Accord.

The unanimous Accord reached at Meech Lake, Quebec by all the first ministers (the prime minister and all provincial premiers) was concluded after only one day of negotiations. The

Accord was approved in Ottawa by all the first ministers on June 3, 1987. Its provisions were contained in a bill that would have been enacted as the *Constitution Act, 1987*. It failed to be ratified by resolutions of the legislatures of Manitoba and Newfoundland.

FACTFILE In 2007, Prime Minister Stephen Harper appointed Bert Brown as Senator, after Brown was elected to the upper chamber in one of Alberta's Senate elections. He is the second Albertan after Stan Waters, appointed by Brian Mulroney in 1990, to receive appointment to the Senate after an election in the province.

The Charlottetown Accord, 1992

By 1992, another Accord was reached at the Charlottetown Constitutional Conference. In this constitutional agreement, the prime minister, 10 provincial premiers, leaders of the territories, and the Chief of the Assembly of First Nations developed a Consensus Report on the Constitution. This report completed a long process of constitutional negotiations, which included political representatives from the federal, provincial, and territorial governments. It also drew on numerous royal commissions and public meetings held over a two-year period.[14] The document that was produced reached an agreement to get Quebec's official acceptance of all constitutional provisions: to include a Canada Clause in the Constitution, to amend Canada's Constitution, to reform the Senate and modify the House of Commons, to entrench the Supreme Court, and to open the way for Aboriginal peoples to exercise their own governments.

To build a national consensus for the Consensus Report, the federal government decided to hold a referendum. For the first time in their history, Canadians were asked to give their approval to a sweeping set of constitutional proposals in a national referendum. The referendum was held on October 26, 1992, and attracted a large voter turnout. The result was that 54 percent of Canada's voters rejected the Accord. Only Newfoundland,

Prince Edward Island, New Brunswick, and the Northwest Territories gave significant margins to the "yes" side of the referendum question.

FACTFILE The British government passed acts to amend Canada's Constitution at Canada's request seventeen times before patriation and domestic procedures for amendment were installed in 1982.

THE CONSTITUTION OF THE UNITED STATES

The first organic superlaw of the United States was the **Articles of Confederation**. In 1777, these articles had been proposed to the states by the Continental Congress—the body of delegates representing the colonies that met to protest British treatment of the colonies and that eventually became the government of the United States. The proposed articles were finally ratified in 1781, and they provided for annual meetings of the states "in Congress assembled" to conduct the business of the United States, each state entitled to one vote. Soon after, the Articles of Confederation were widely viewed as unsatisfactory because the Government of the United States could not raise revenues on its own and the states were slow and often delinquent in submitting their appropriations so that the "confederate" government could operate. The perceived powerlessness of the US Congress led it to call for a constitutional convention that would create "a more perfect Union."

FACTFILE Many of the ideas in the US Declaration of Independence in 1776 came from English constitutional practice in the *Magna Carta* (1215), the *Habeas Corpus Act* (1679), and the *Bill of Rights* (1689).

This constitutional convention met in Philadelphia in 1787 to produce a relatively short but eloquent document, whose chief draftsman was James Madison. When this document was finally ratified by enough states in 1788, it became the Constitution of the United States. This same basic document, amended only 27 times in 217 years as of 2007, governs one of the most dynamic societies in the world today.[15]

The US Constitution is clearly organized and provides a straightforward declaration of the supremacy of the rule of law, as well as an outline of the institutions of government. Structurally, the Constitution deals with the following:

- Article 1: the legislative powers of the US government;
- Article 2: the powers of the executive;
- Article 3: judicial powers;
- Article 4: general provisions relating to the states;
- Article 5: the amendment formula;
- Article 6: the supremacy of federal law; and
- Article 7: **ratification** of constitutional amendments.

In all, four aspects of the American Constitution have contributed to its adaptability:

1. the amendment process;
2. broad grants of institutional power and authority;
3. the growth of extra-constitutional practices permitted by the silence of the Constitution on key matters; and
4. the judicial interpretation of constitutional generalities.

The Formal Amendment Procedures

The formal amendment of the US Constitution has been infrequent, and some of the amendments have been used for minor changes in the functions of government.[16] But most of the amendments have been significant in *how governments adapt* to new social circumstances. The original Constitution did not include a bill of rights, so the founders promised to adopt amendments to provide such rights. The first 10 amendments were proposed and ratified together, addressing vital issues of human rights. The famous "Civil War Amendments" (thirteenth, fourteenth, and fifteenth) outlawed slavery, defined the privileges and immunities of citizenship, and provided the right to vote regardless of race, colour, or prior servitude. Other amendments have given new meaning to the Constitution and expanded some democratic rights, such as the direct election of senators, women's suffrage, repeal of the poll tax, and the lowering of the voting age to 18. One of the most consequential amendments, the sixteenth, ratified in 1913, authorized the income tax. This tax has been the largest source of federal revenue.

Amending the US Constitution is not an easy process: the Constitution specifies *two* different tracks for its own amendment. The first is that amendments can be proposed by a two-thirds majority of both houses (357 of 535 members). Amendments are ratified when three-fourths of the states (38 of 50) approve them. The second (which has never been used) is by a national convention convened by Congress upon petition by two-thirds of the states. The same ratification process would apply to these proposals.

Broad Grants of Power and Authority

In some parts, the US Constitution seems to be deliberately ambiguous. Undoubtedly, the founding fathers used ambiguity as a strategy for winning the approval of the diverse factions that disputed the document. The vague phraseology contributed to the flexibility and accommodation the document provided for later generations to interpret some sections as giving broad grants of power and authority to key institutions. For example, the power of the Supreme Court to declare acts of Congress unconstitutional is neither explicitly stated nor denied in the Constitution. However, in 1803, the Supreme Court ruled that it did have the power of judicial review, an interpretation of the words in the Constitution that greatly enhances its political significance. The executive powers of the president are not distinctly spelled out in the Constitution, either. But the words "the President shall take care that the laws be faithfully executed" have justified the creation of a huge bureaucracy to administer and execute the laws of the land. They were also significant in 1999 for the impeachment proceedings against Bill Clinton.

The Silence of the Constitution

Flexibility and adaptability also flow from what is *not* written in the US Constitution. As with the Canadian Constitution, political parties are not mentioned in the original document and the party system is extra-constitutional. Every major elected official, and most appointed ones, takes office under the banner of a political party. All of this takes place outside the framework of the Constitution. Because of the absence of precise terminology, political institutions have been able to adapt to the requirements of contemporary politics. To say that a constitution is flexible is another way of saying that it does not provide ready-made answers for new political questions and social issues. The capacity of American politics to redefine its institutions has been facilitated by this silence in the Constitution.

FACTFILE   The US Constitution does not provide for direct voting by the people on national questions; it does not provide for national referenda.

Constitutional Generalities

The US Constitution is a document of general formulations that have been amenable to modern interpretation. In the modern world of American politics, this means that old words have been given new meanings and old institutions have acquired new functions. The original words of the Constitution have acquired modern-day application. The framers of the US Constitution opposed the manner in which colonial officials arbitrarily searched private residences. The Fourth Amendment, ratified in 1791, declared that "the right of the people to be secure in their persons, houses, papers, and effects, against unreasonable searches and seizures, shall not be violated." Today, despite technology that permits electronic surveillance, wiretaps, hidden microphones, and telescopic cameras, the principle inherent in the Fourth Amendment is sustained. The old argument that places individual rights above the government's right to know has been given credence in the American legal system.

Similarly, the electoral college is an example of new functions being assigned to old institutions. The electoral college, as laid down in the Constitution, was a method of choosing a president and a vice-president by a small group of respected citizens. This small group of people comprising the electoral college was to be chosen by the state legislatures. The electoral college continues to play a major role in selecting the president, but it does so by performing a function not at all envisioned by the framers of the Constitution. It has become an institution of popular democratic control, but it blatantly distorts the electoral percentages of a candidate's support. Because all of a state's electoral votes go to the winner of that state, it is possible for a candidate to be elected without winning a majority of the popular vote. Indeed, this was the case in 2000, when Al Gore won a majority of the popular vote, but George W. Bush won the most electoral votes and thus the election.

The Federal Principle

One of the primary objectives of the framers of the US Constitution was to allocate powers between the national and state governments within a federal structure, which at the time was a radically new idea in its application on a continental scale. The basic constitutional outline permits the federal government and the government in each state to be separate in *scope*—in which areas of jurisdiction each may govern. But the federal structure unites the national and state governments in *domain*—the people for whom they govern. In other words, the federal government and the government in each state operate directly on the individual, within their respective spheres of power.[17] The so-called residual powers, not explicitly granted by the Constitution to either the federal government or the states, are now held to belong to the federal government.

FACTFILE   Neither the federal government nor the states can dissolve or negotiate the breakup of the Union of the United States, unlike in Canada where the federal government under certain rules can negotiate the breakup of the country with a separatist province or provinces.

Under the Constitution, some powers are forbidden to the national government while others are granted exclusively to it. Many powers are forbidden to the states, but several are shared by both the national and state governments (Figure 9.2). The Constitution is rather hazy on state powers, in that they can do what has not been specifically granted to the federal government or forbidden to the states. Since 1787, conflicts over what is **exclusive**

Figure 9.2   **Federal principle: United States**

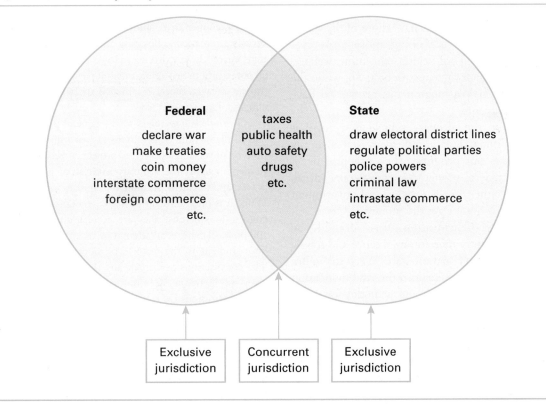

and **concurrent** jurisdiction between the states and the federal government have often been adjudicated by the Supreme Court, sometimes ruling in favour of national institutions and sometimes ruling for the states. By means of Supreme Court decisions and federal and state legislation, the whole concept of federalism, as originally conceived by the framers of the Constitution, has been reinterpreted under the pressures of a changing society that frequently makes new and different demands on government.

In recent years, the federal government has placed itself in the position of providing funds for the development of state-oriented programs over highways, schools, and public housing. Federal-guaranteed loans, grants-in-aid to states, and outright grants of money to federally designated areas have all brought the federal government more into the private lives of Americans than ever before. The powers of the national government have also increased significantly through Congressional legislative enactments, but so have those of the states. State governments are doing more than ever before in the fields of health, education, welfare, housing, and highway construction. So, while the government in Washington has grown, so have state governments.

However, the ultimate vehicle of control is money. Without federal aid, many states simply cannot carry out programs they urgently need. And with federal money comes federal control. The states either do what the central government wants or they do not get the money.

The US Constitution was drafted by eighteenth-century men for an obscure and fragile eighteenth-century nation-state. Yet, for more than 200 years it has remained the vital foundation of American government and a model for many other political systems. The Constitution of the United States has also continued to evolve and change: first, it has been amended only 27 times (even though more than 11 000 amendments have been introduced in Congress); and second, the power of judicial review has imposed important

changes on the meanings of the original document. Through the interpretations of the Supreme Court, the Constitution has been elaborated, enlarged, and updated to meet new conditions in a rapidly changing society.

Chapter Summary

All nation-states have constitutions of one type or another. A constitution delineates the organization, structures, and procedures for the operation of government, describing its powers, limitations, and tenure, and sometimes specifying certain inalienable rights and freedoms of citizens. Most constitutions are *written* documents that claim to embody the first legal principles that underpin the political and social fabric of society. But many constitutions have *unwritten* aspects, consisting of customs, conventions, or statutes that are followed with the same standard as written aspects.

Any comparative study of national constitutions reveals a remarkable diversity among the political systems currently in existence. However diverse, though, all constitutions represent integral parts of the political orders that are there to enhance security, prosperity, equality, liberty, and justice.

Constitutionalism refers to the general philosophical bias of democratic constitutions to place formal limitations on government power, to protect citizens and other residents against the arbitrary exercise of government power, and to permit accountable constitutional change. While it is often difficult to make generalizations about constitutions because they are peculiar to each regime and political culture, an attempt has been made to introduce students to the features of modern constitutions. The constitutions of Canada and the United States are given special treatment in this analysis.

Constitutions try to define what the public good is in the context of a fundamental law, from which all other laws derive their legitimacy.

A constitutional amendment procedure is the formula used to change the content of a constitution. Each state has its own formulae with varying degrees of rigidity and flexibility.

Democratic constitutions limit governments by defining the powers of each branch of government, distributing powers between and among levels of government, including bills of rights and charters of rights, and identifying where the sovereign power exists.

The *Constitution Act, 1867*, made Canada the third state in history, after the United States and Switzerland, to adopt the federal system of government and the first state in the world to combine federalism with parliamentary institutions.

Discussion Questions

1. Define *constitution*. What relationship does a constitution have with other laws in society—those that are legislated, implemented, and adjudicated? To what extent can a constitution be considered a "flexible" or a "rigid" document?

2. What are the underlying tenets of modern constitutionalism? How are these tenets reflected in the Canadian Constitution? What have been some of the major implications of these doctrines for changing the Canadian Constitution?

3. Discuss the doctrine of limited government. What provisions in Canada's Constitution limit the powers of government against individual citizens? Are these limitations meaningful?

4. List and discuss the rights and freedoms Canadians enjoy. What protections are missing in our Constitution and how could these omissions affect you as an individual? What additional rights would make the ideal constitution?

5. Is the federal principle incorporated in the *Constitution Act, 1867*, destined to undergo major amendment by Canadians in the near future? Which areas are likely to be most controversial?

Political Parties, Interests, and Pressure Groups

After reading this chapter, you will be able to:

- define political parties in different political systems

- recount how political parties evolved

- outline the types of political parties and classify different political parties under these prototypes

- describe the functions of political parties and explain why our system of government depends on how they perform

- list and describe the various political party systems that develop in different states

- explain how Canada's political party system developed and how it is sustained in our parliamentary system

- reveal how parties can be organized and how this affects their performance

- describe the evolution of primary political parties out of ideologies such as liberalism, conservatism, socialism, and communism

- classify Canada's various political parties according to the ideologies they portray

- distinguish political parties from pressure groups

- explain how the different functions of parties and pressure groups affect the operation of the political system

- classify pressure groups and evaluate their tactics

● ● ● ●

HOW POLITICAL PARTIES EVOLVED

In ancient Rome, representatives sought their re-election and the election of their friends by identifying with a prominent group.[1] Because Roman suffrage was very limited, there was little need for a group to use a label to attract voters. Their status in Roman society was often enough to win elections for members.

The first formal parties in England evolved from legislative factions that consisted of friendly groups of notables that were more like political clubs. The first modern party organization in Britain was established in the city of Birmingham as the Liberal Party in 1867. Groups were organizing in Canada around the time of Confederation. To some degree, parties organized for elections and maintained an ongoing structure that worked to unite them between elections. They formed electoral committees made up of prominent citizens who sponsored candidates by raising funds necessary for the election campaign.

FACTFILE   As institutions existing between elections, political parties initially appeared in the early nineteenth century in the United States, where the first political parties in the world were organized.

Initially, parties were divergent groups—almost totally without ideologies or programs—that formed within an expanding electorate, and they took opposite sides in the battle demanding recognition of voting **franchise** and dismantling property and class qualifications as impediments to political participation.

By the end of the nineteenth century, the growth of democracy and the rise of industrial societies spawned a new kind of political organization, the *mass political party*, which continues to serve as an institution designed to mobilize public participation on a grand scale in support of candidates and political programs. Today, most political parties appeal to the widest possible interests in their respective societies. Almost all contemporary parties are mass parties.

Some states, such as Chad, Ghana, Niger, Rwanda, and Uganda, outlaw political parties. In other states, such as Bahrain, Kuwait, Oman, and the United Arab Emirates, political-party systems have either not developed or are tied to the executive branch of government. In these states, a surviving traditional kingship has prevented the evolution of a **pluralistic** and competitive political-party system. The concentration of political power clusters around the monarch by custom and tradition.

WHAT IS A POLITICAL PARTY?

One of the most general and flexible definitions of a political party was provided by a Bahamian party leader, Sir Randol Fawkes: "A political party consists of a group of persons united in opinion or action, more or less permanently organized, which attempts to bring about the election of its candidates to public offices and by this means to control or influence the actions and policy of government."[2]

A political group can be defined in terms of the purpose for which it was organized, the size and character of its membership, its structure, and the functions it performs. Leon Epstein points to the distinguishing characteristic of the party "label" because, in his opinion, size and membership are less significant components. He defines a party as "any group, however loosely organized, seeking to elect governmental office-holders under a given label."[3] The French scholar Maurice Duverger, in contrast to Epstein, focuses on "ideologies, social foundations, structure, organization, participation, strategy—all these aspects must be taken into account in making a complete analysis of any political party."[4]

Crosscurrents   Is the Development of Green Parties a Global Event?

Unlike some traditional parties, which must struggle to retain their popular support, Greens are spreading their messages and gaining respect in most parts of the planet. Traditional parties that represent the ideas of liberalism, conservatism, socialism, and communism must include aspects of green ideology if they are to succeed in a competitive political system.

The Greens now have an international network of parties and movements. Since 2000, federations of green parties have been organized in Africa, the Americas, the Asia Pacific, and Europe. They hold or have held the balance of power in nine European states and are competitive in more than 100 countries. The Greens have control of five cities in Mexico and are expanding their presence in many urban centres around the planet.

The Global Green Network was established in 2001 and represents national green parties around the world. What is behind this global expansion? The organization of political parties that are dedicated to the preservation of the earth began with the emergence of the green revolution, which was started in the 1920s and led by Henry Wallace, who became a candidate for the US presidency in 1948.

In 2004 for the first time, the Green Party of Canada moved from the status of a **fringe party** to a competitive political contender against the four larger parliamentary parties at the federal level. In 2004 and 2008, the Greens ran candidates in 308 federal ridings and garnered about 4 percent and 7.5 percent of the popular vote, respectively. In 2008, they attracted support in every region and increased their federal political-party funding under Canada's new party finance laws.

Green ideology has gained credibility not just within the context of green parties but across party lines and within the circles of intellectuals and government bureaucracies around the world. Green is truly a global ideology that can only gallop to dominance in the years ahead and ultimately become an essential part of how we govern ourselves, our economies, and our cultures. It remains to be seen whether the Greens themselves will carry the banner of green political ideology or whether other political parties will succeed in incorporating their ideas, to the detriment of autonomous green parties.

In competitive party systems, all political parties have as their primary goal the conquest of power or at least some influence in the distribution of it. Political parties try to win seats in elections so as to take control of the offices of government. When this is not possible, they assume the strategy of an opposition that scrutinizes government action and offers alternatives to the electorate. In most cases, political parties seek support from a broad social base so as to claim representation and legitimacy in articulating the interests of the people. They are particularly adept at **aggregating** as many interests as possible under a common organizational structure and assuming some ideological identification, such as liberalism, conservatism, nationalism, socialism, or communism.

In authoritarian systems, one party or a small number of parties try to mobilize the backing of interest groups and voters. Where political competition is controlled or non-existent, the aggregation of many interests still takes place within parties, but the groups that are aggregated (such as unions, business organizations, and consumers) are mobilized to accept the party platform whether they support it wholeheartedly or not. In totalitarian states, a single party controls group demands and tries to create a single world view among the various groups in society.

TYPES OF PARTIES

Some parties, including the Liberal and Conservative parties in Canada and the Republican and Democratic parties in the United States, are basically of a pragmatic/brokerage type.[5] They are generally found in the well-developed party systems of traditional democracies. These parties are mass-appeal parties with no strong ideological commitments and no well-defined or differentiated party programs. Some analysts refer to these characteristics amusingly as "Tweedledum and Tweedledee," suggesting that brokerage parties sacrifice identity for electoral "market" success. Their chief goal is to elect their candidates to public office and to attract special-interest groups, giving them preferential legislative treatment in exchange for electoral and financial support

The fact that pragmatic parties can embrace the original ideas and platforms popularized by other parties, even though the same policies may have been previously attacked or ignored, indicates something important about them. On close examination, one observes that mass parties are **party coalitions**, composed of many dissimilar groups that, at times, seem only to share a common party label. Pragmatic parties are much more concerned with political success than with political philosophy, opting usually to put together a winning coalition of candidates rather than attempting to reconcile the doctrinal persuasion of the party label with the voters.

In contrast to the brokerage-type parties are the *ideological* parties, many of which were formed in the nineteenth century and early part of the twentieth century.[6] Operating within democratic as well as non-democratic party systems, these parties are doctrinal in that they pursue a set of prescribed principles in a political system. Ideological parties based on socialism and communism are almost universal among those states that permit political parties. Under the socialist label, they appear in the Netherlands and Norway as labour parties. Those based on Marxist-Leninist ideologies operate in numerous states, including Britain, Canada, France, Mexico, and the United States. Some ideological parties are organized around religious doctrines, such as the Swiss Evangelical Party, Pakistan's Islamic party, and Israel's United Torah Front.

Since World War II, many doctrinal parties have become less ideological and more pragmatic. The communist parties of Vietnam and Cuba are good examples of this post-war trend. The present Chinese Communist Party (CCP) moved sharply away from Maoism by stressing the importance of material economic considerations (as opposed to subjective human factors under Mao) in the development and basic unity of Chinese society.

One type of ideological party that deserves special mention is the *indigenous* or *nation-building* party.[7] Indigenous parties gear their platforms to the political systems in which they are found. They build their ideologies from *different* political doctrines that are relevant to the national problems in their particular social and economic environments. Increasingly, they have come to represent the peasant or tribal masses, the new proletariat, and the middle sectors. Many indigenous parties adopt a platform of land reform, nationalization of industry, a full range of economic and social reforms, and an opposition to communism. These parties operate in Latin America, in Venezuela, Peru, Costa Rica, and Mexico.

Another meaningful classification of ideological parties focuses on party objectives. *Revolutionary* parties are dedicated to the fundamental change of the political, economic, and social system in a society. The formation of revolutionary parties has been encouraged by population explosion, growing urbanization, the concentration of land ownership, and rigid class structures. More direct and immediate factors explaining the growth of revolutionary parties include the proven success of similar groups in other countries, such as in Cuba following the ascendancy of Fidel Castro in 1959. Contentious *Fidelista* movements sprang up in many countries, such as Peru, Guatemala, Venezuela, Uruguay, Argentina, and Bolivia.

In contrast to pragmatic and ideological parties are *special-interest* parties. These parties organize around a particular issue or interest and usually attract the support of an intensely dedicated and well-organized segment of the electorate. By so doing, special-interest parties focus on a dominant issue that the major parties are unwilling to endorse, and sometimes can take enough votes away from the larger parties to change the outcome of elections. When special-interest parties form a government, they are under pressure to implement their political goals as soon as possible. If this is not done, political support may decline within the party as well as in the electorate. Sometimes a special-interest party becomes the Official Opposition, as when the Bloc Québécois won the second largest number of seats in the 1993 Canadian federal election.

Another special-interest party is Quebec's Parti Québécois (PQ), a party that fights for independence within the confines of Quebec's political and governmental system. However, in 1984, René Lévesque announced his decision to jettison the goal of independence, the very raison d'être of

Gilles Duceppe leads the Bloc Québécois, registered as a national party that runs 75 candidates only in Quebec.

his party's existence for more than 16 years. But Levesque's successor, Jacques Parizeau, reaffirmed the secessionist aspirations of the party, returning to its special-interest character and restoring sovereignty as the number-one goal of its followers. After him, the goal of separation was substituted for good and efficient government by Lucien Bouchard until the "winning conditions" for a successful referendum were present in Quebec. His successor, Bernard Landry, failed to maintain the momentum of support for independence that thrived under previous PQ leaders, and his government was defeated in April 2003. Andre Boisclair served as leader from 2005 to 2007. Pauline Marois became the party's new leader in 2007.

In some states, women's parties have joined the political competition of the party system. Referring to themselves ideologically as the "third dimension," the Women's Alliance in Iceland rejects the pyramid structure of other political parties. In Belgium, the Women's Unity Party was organized in 1972, and similar parties have formed in Canada, France, and Norway. The Feminist Party of Canada has not been competitive electorally in the provinces or at the national level and is said to be dormant.

THE FUNCTIONS OF POLITICAL PARTIES

Political parties are institutions in most states and so are considered primary political units. They vary a great deal in their structure, goals, and the actual functions they perform in the political system. Parties often differ in political ideas and values. Thus, their legislative platforms differ from one another's. Parties draw support from many groups and usually seek to expand their membership across the country. They nurture different degrees of partisanship and different degrees of popular participation.

> FACTFILE   When political parties in Canada began in the 1860s, they were widely regarded as factious and not very likely to become the primary instruments for forming governments in the future.

Teaching Us about Politics and Government

All political parties are agents of political learning. They interpret political events, initiate new political philosophies, or combine old ones to form new policies and **platforms** and transmit political messages to the people through their candidates and the media.

In Canada, all political parties have a political socialization function in competition with other parties, groups, and the media. Canadian political parties are just one kind of institution among many competing institutions (e.g., the media) that openly and legitimately transmit political information. Some of the socializing activities of Canada's political parties take place in the riding associations and local clubs and societies affiliated with them. Riding associations seek to recruit and initiate new members. They canvass voters, distribute literature, and invite candidates to make speeches. At the leadership level of the parties, clubs, caucus meetings, and parliamentary committees are constantly training and indoctrinating party members as well as the general public.

Choosing Our Leaders

Parties differ in how they recruit members, candidates, and leaders. The techniques of recruitment include appointment, election, and party conventions, where political leadership is formally slated. In most party systems, the government party has access to a large number of patronage appointments that enhance executive leadership. In Canada, the recruitment of leaders is directly affected by how political parties nominate members. Political parties are the main vehicles of presenting and selecting Canada's representatives and their leaders. But people can enter the political system as *independents* without formal ties to any of the competing political parties. The success rate of independent candidates who run in many Canadian ridings is marginal.

> FACTFILE   In Canada, it is not necessary to belong to a political party to run in an election, and there is no constitutional requirement that a government be formed by a political party.

Vocalizing Our Interests

Another important function of political parties is to convert opinions, attitudes, beliefs, and preferences into coherent policies. Many interests requiring political expression exist in all societies. They can call for the legalization of abortion, legislation to institute capital punishment, the control of interest rates, the adjustment of tax laws to favour certain groups, or any other interest, such as giving military support to the US when it goes to war. Political parties vary in the intensity and extent to which they make and articulate interests. And the style of *interest articulation* varies among the different political-party systems.

In Canada, a wide range of social and economic interests is organized. Within a highly competitive political system, political parties seek to attract the support of many of these interest groups by articulating their demands as either government policies or as opposition strategies. But most of Canada's interest groups prefer to remain non-partisan, avoiding the politically hazardous tactic of affiliating with one of the parties competing in the political system. To win the support of the various interests, political parties invite interest groups to make their claims and influence party policy through the activities of the riding associations, annual party conferences, and in the party committees in Parliament.

In most non-democratic states, people have learned that they cannot effectively make demands on the government without fear of severe reprisals. Interest-group activity and interest articulation exists, but only on a relatively small scale and under controlled circumstances.

Bringing Many Interests under One Group

Interest articulation is the expression of group demands by means of campaigns, the mass media, direct action, petition, and lobbying of political elites. *Interest aggregation* is the joining of interests in such a way that they are related to the selection of government and party leaders and to the making and administering of policy.

The aggregative function of Canadian parties cuts across a wide variety of organized economic interests as well as professional and non-professional groups. But interest groups are aware that the structure of government and the political party in power are the two political realities that can bring about the materialization of their demands. Thus, the Cabinet, which itself usually is a microcosmic representation of many organized interests, is the target of concentrated group pressures.

Organizations such as the Canadian Chamber of Commerce, the Canadian Federation of Agriculture, and the Canadian Labour Congress make annual submissions to the Cabinet. When government is unresponsive, pressure groups will usually turn to opposition parties to carry their banners. In all cases where parties wish to aggregate the interests of groups, a process of bargaining takes place in which inducements are offered to these groups to gain their electoral support.

Making and Implementing Policy

In democratic political systems, parties may play a crucial role in making and implementing public policy. However, because of the competitive nature of democratic political systems, organizations other than political parties also shape the policy process. Besides political parties, interest groups and the civil service participate in policy-making. Sometimes the party system itself makes it difficult for political parties to make policies that are true to their ideology and their base of popular support. In some states, few parties ever gain a majority in the legislature at either the national or local level. In these states, parties need to participate in coalitions to form governments; this procedure usually requires a compromise of policy positions.

In democratic party systems, membership in a political party usually produces a high degree of cohesion when legislators vote for bills. Generally,

left-wing parties demonstrate a stronger party cohesion in legislative voting than do **right-wing** parties, partly because they take their ideology more seriously. This has also been true in Canada, where the New Democratic Party demonstrates stronger legislative and caucus loyalty than do the larger Conservative and Liberal parties, where political factions tend to form. In the United States, Republicans and Democrats show weaker legislative cohesion than do Canadian or European parties. This is because the parliamentary system requires greater **party discipline** to sustain the government in office.

In Canada, the policy-making and policy-implementing process is highly complex. It is true that parties generate and compete in the making of public policy. But it is hard to convert party platforms into government policy because of parliamentary procedures. The bureaucracy follows strict rules for converting party policy to law. Upper-echelon civil servants (deputy ministers and assistant deputy ministers) greatly influence the adaptation of party policy to public policy.[8] In addition, before any policy decision is implemented, such as the decriminalization of marijuana, many consultations take place among Cabinet ministers, advisory committees in Parliament, and provincial premiers.

POLITICAL-PARTY SYSTEMS

FACTFILE In Canada and the United States, political parties are not mentioned in either constitution. The founders of both nation-states regarded parties as dangerous and mischievous.

There are many ways to classify political parties. Numerous typologies have been designed; all are largely impressionistic: for example, personalistic parties, revolutionary parties. One type of classification involves the number of parties in the political-party system. The classification of party systems adopted in this study distinguishes single-party systems from multi-party systems.

One-Party States

The concept of a *party system* implies competition between two or more political parties. States without political parties or that have only one political party are therefore not systemic in terms of party competition. Before World War II, one-party systems appeared for the first time under communist and fascist regimes. They were unique because they outlawed all political competition and served as instruments of social control. They adhered to one all-encompassing orthodox ideology that outlined the conditions of political recruitment and determined the economic, military, and social strategies of the state.

Today, this type of party continues to flourish in non-democratic socialist states. In states such as China and Vietnam, the party functions as a permanent institution for which the government serves as an administrative agency. In these states, the party has established itself as a sort of supragovernment, a supreme decision-making and policy-making authority. This peculiar and historically novel scheme has merited the label *party state*.[9] Single-party systems are usually more **elitist** than mass parties, and more likely to attract personalistic leaders. Once in power, the governing party tends to surrender its policy-making and implementation functions to the state apparatus. Ideologically, these types of parties combine nationalism with an eclectic philosophy of modernization. They advance the need for dictatorship in order to overcome problems of corruption, disunity, or separatism, and counter them with enforced political integration, socialization, and repression.

Many one-party states are civilian regimes, most of them in Africa, the Caribbean, and the Middle East, such as Guinea-Bissau, Guyana, and South Yemen. African military regimes with one-party systems include Angola and Ethiopia.

Two-Party Competitive Systems

A two-party political system is one in which political power and government offices tend to alternate between two major political parties. This does not eliminate the presence of minor parties in electoral competition. In all political systems where it has evolved, the two-party system has never remained pure. Numerous minor parties have formed to challenge one or both of the dominant parties. And although these parties may disappear with time, their presence is seldom without influence. The chief function of minor parties in a two-party competitive system has been to raise new issues, or new ways of looking at old issues, to the political agenda. As they succeed in forcing new policies on the older, established parties, these minor parties tend to disappear. This is one of the ways that the party system stays alive and remains responsive to changing conditions and issues.

Some analysts have attempted to quantify the system, not so much for precision as to locate the parameters in which two dominant political parties compete: for political scientist Ronald McDonald, a two-party competitive system reveals two dominant parties each receiving approximately 40 percent of the seats but not more than 60 percent of the total number of seats in the legislature.[10]

The two-party competitive system exists only in some English-speaking democracies, and appears in some 20 states. The British party system is frequently cited as the classic example. Even so, more than a dozen minor parties also compete with the Conservative and Labour parties. The bipolar character of the British party system appears in other states that have at one time or another come under direct British influence, including the United States and the Commonwealth, in countries such as Barbados, Jamaica, and Malta. In the Republic of Ireland, the United Ireland party (*Fine Gael*: party of the Irish) and the Republican party (*Fianna Fail*) have been the two dominant parties.

As for the United States, it is not difficult to imagine a multiparty system in a country so diverse. There could feasibly be a party of labour, of southern whites, of blacks, Chicanos, of western agriculture, and so on. In fact, the contrast between the galaxy of American interest groups and the presence throughout America's political history of only two major parties is striking, notwithstanding the fact that at different times the United States has had more than two parties competing in its federal elections. The two-party competitive system has an extraordinary heritage: the Democrats descending from the party Thomas Jefferson founded for the election of 1800; and the Republican party, with its roots in the time of Abraham Lincoln.

Three factors set the United States on the road to biparty politics. First, since the War of Independence, two main political groupings (initially known as the Federalists and the Jeffersonian Democrats) organized around conflicting economic interests and built coalitions of support within the country. Second, the adoption of the single-member legislative district electoral rule has worked to discourage lasting third-party movements.[11] Finally, a major institutional incentive for preserving the two-party system has been the presidency. Because only *one* party can win the presidency in any given election, there is little point in voting for the presidential candidate of a party that has no chance of winning.

Many Minor Parties

Canada's party system retains its biparty character in spite of the persistent representation of minor parties in the House of Commons over the past seven decades (Table 10.1).[12] It is still a fact that the Liberals and the former Progressive Conservatives are the only two parties that have ever governed at the federal level. However, if we look at Canada's party system from the perspective of party

Figure 10.1   Two-party dominance in Canada's national government, 1867–2008

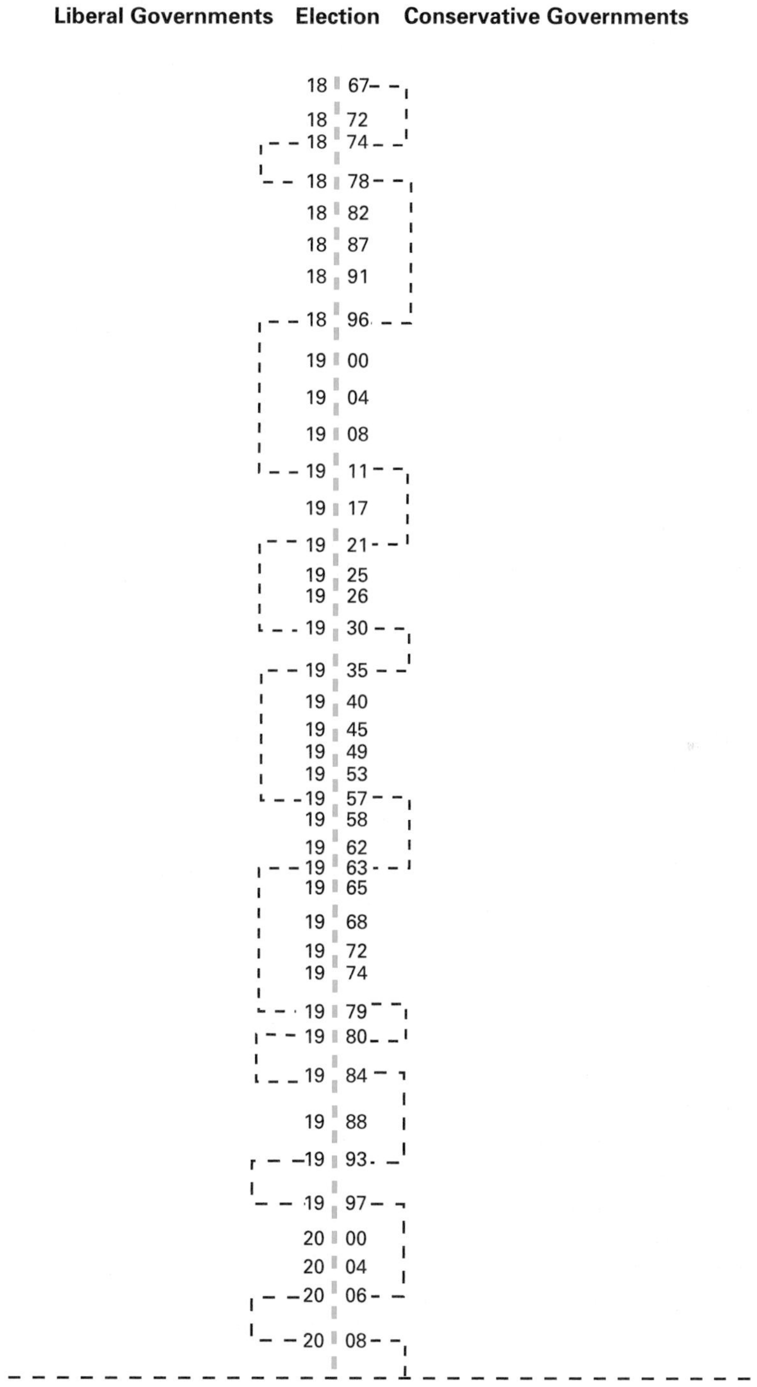

Liberal Governments   Election   Conservative Governments

```
                    18 ▌ 67– –
                    18 ▌ 72
        – – 18 ▌ 74 – –
        – – 18 ▌ 78 – –
                    18 ▌ 82
                    18 ▌ 87
                    18 ▌ 91
        – – 18 ▌ 96 – –
                    19 ▌ 00
                    19 ▌ 04
                    19 ▌ 08
        – – 19 ▌ 11 – –
                    19 ▌ 17
        – – 19 ▌ 21 – –
                    19 ▌ 25
                    19 ▌ 26
        – – 19 ▌ 30 – –
        – – 19 ▌ 35 – –
                    19 ▌ 40
                    19 ▌ 45
                    19 ▌ 49
                    19 ▌ 53
        – –19 ▌ 57 – –
                    19 ▌ 58
                    19 ▌ 62
        – –19 ▌ 63 – –
                    19 ▌ 65
                    19 ▌ 68
                    19 ▌ 72
                    19 ▌ 74
        – – 19 ▌ 79 – –
        – – 19 ▌ 80 – –
        – – 19 ▌ 84 – –
                    19 ▌ 88
        – –19 ▌ 93. – –
        – – 19 ▌ 97 – –
                    20 ▌ 00
                    20 ▌ 04
        – –20 ▌ 06 – –
        – – 20 ▌ 08 – –
```

Table 10.1 Party standings in the Canadian House of Commons, 1900–2008

Date of Election	Liberal	Conservative/ Unionist*/	Progressive	CCF – NDP	Social Credit	Reform/ Alliance	BQ	Independent	Total seats
Nov 7, 1900	133	80							213
Nov 3, 1904	138	75						1	214
Oct 26, 1908	135	85						1	221
Sept 21, 1911	87	134						1	222
Dec 17, 1917	82	*153							235
Dec 6, 1921	116	50	64					5	235
Oct 29, 1925	99	116	24					6	245
Sept 14, 1926	128	91	20					6	245
July 28, 1930	91	137	12					5	245
Oct 14, 1935	173	40		7	17			8	245
Mar 26, 1940	181	40		8	10			6	245
June 11, 1945	125	67		28	13			12	245
June 27, 1949	193	41		13	10			5	262
Aug 10, 1953	171	51		23	15			5	265
June 10, 1957	105	112		25	19			4	265
Mar 31, 1958	49	208		8					265
June 18, 1962	100	116		19	30				265
Apr 8, 1963	129	95		17	24				265
Nov 8, 1965	131	97		21	5			2	265
June 25, 1968	155	72		22				1	264
Oct 30, 1972	109	107		31	15			2	264
July 8, 1974	141	95		16	11			1	264
May 22, 1979	114	136		26	6				282
Feb 18, 1980	147	103		32					282
Sept 14, 1984	40	211		30				1	282
Nov 21, 1988	83	169		43					295
Oct 25, 1993	177	2		9		52	54	1	295
June 2, 1997	155	20		21		60	44	1	301
Nov 27, 2000	172	12		13		66	38		301
June 28, 2004	135	99		19			54	1	308
Jan 23, 2006	103	124		29			51	1	308
Oct 14, 2008	77	143		37			49	2	308

*Unionist: The conscriptionist Conservative government of Robert Borden, formed from a coalition of English Liberals and Conservatives.

Sources: Adapted from Politics Canada, 7th edition by Paul Fox and Graham White (Toronto: McGraw-Hill Ryerson Ltd, 1991), p.342 & Elections Canada, 2000, 2004 (www.elections.ca) © Paul Fox & Graham White. Reprinted by permission of Graham White and The Estate of Paul Fox. Calculations and adaptations rest solely with the author.

Table 10.2	Registered political parties sponsoring candidates, 2008

Registered Parties	Number of Candidates
New Democratic Party	308
Conservative Party of Canada	307
Liberal Party of Canada	307
Green Party of Canada	303
Bloc Québécois	75
Independent	67
Marxist-Leninist Party of Canada	59
Christian Heritage Party of Canada	59
Libertarian Party of Canada	26
Communist Party of Canada	24
Canadian Action Party	20
Progressive Canadian Party	10
Marijuana Party	8
neorhino.ca	7
First Peoples National Party of Canada	6
No affiliation	4
Animal Alliance Environment Voters Party of Canada	4
Newfoundland and Labrador First Party	3
People's Political Power Party of Canada	2
Western Block Party	1
Work Less Party	1

Source: Elections Canada, 2008 (www.elections.ca). Calculations and adaptations rest solely with the author.

competition, a multiparty system is discernible. For example, in the 2008 federal election, 14 *registered* parties competed for seats in the 308-seat House of Commons, but only 4 were successful at electing candidates (Table 10.2). The single-member-district (plurality) electoral system almost eliminates the representation of smaller parties in Canada's parliamentary institutions. Minor parties, also called "small" or "fringe" parties, run substantially fewer candidates and consequently reduce their chances of winning seats.[13]

Many of the small parties are driven by a cause; for example, the Libertarians' goal is to dramatically cut the size of government and to reduce taxes and social services. The Green Party of Canada is committed to cleaning up the environment and to making it a mainstream issue in the Canadian political system. A coalition of many groups is the Canadian Action Party, which wants to use the Bank of Canada to stimulate the economy to create jobs, eliminate the GST, reduce payroll taxes, and make major investments in education, health care, the arts, culture, and the CBC. The Communist Party calls for curbing the powers of big business and for the nationalization of key economic sectors, that is, energy, natural resources, the banks, and the media.

As registered political parties, none of these significantly affected the outcome of the 2008 election because most ran fewer than 308 candidates and Canadians knew very little about their platforms.

On the provincial level, one encounters a variety of party systems, not all of which are examples of the classic two-party type.[14] In Nova Scotia and Manitoba, the electoral struggle is between the Liberals, the Progressive Conservatives, and the NDP. In Alberta, the Progressive Conservatives, the Liberals, and the NDP compete with a new party, formed in 2004 as the Alberta Alliance party, which changed its name to the Wildrose Alliance Party of Alberta.

In Quebec, three parties have governed the province in the post-war period: the Liberals, Parti Québécois, and Union Nationale. The case of the Parti Québécois serves to illustrate how a provincial minor third party can surprise itself, as well as the country, by springing to power, weathering political storms, and staging impressive recoveries. And in Ontario before 1987, the Liberals had last won a provincial election in 1937; the Conservatives ("the Big Blue Machine") had governed continuously from 1943 to 1985. Until June 1985, when the Liberals, with assistance from the NDP, gained power on a vote of no confidence, Ontario was a singular provincial example of a dominant one-party system. In its 1987 election, Ontario gave the Liberals a strong majority with 95 of the 130 provincial seats and realigned the province in the direction of three-party competition. And in 1990, the NDP formed a government for the first time in Ontario, taking 74 of the 130 seats. But in 1994, the Progressive Conservatives were returned to power after nearly 10 years in opposition. In 1999, Mike Harris once again led his PC party to victory, winning 59 of Ontario's 103 legislative seats. But in 2007, the Ontario Liberals, led by Dalton McGuinty, won a majority for the Liberals for the third time in 65 years, taking 71 of the 106 seats.

On examination, Canadian politics deviates from a pure two-party model not only because of the presence of third parties, but also because one party—the Liberal Party—has dominated federal government in Canada throughout most of last century (Figure 10.1). Of the 32 federal governments since 1900, the Liberals formed 23. If we think that the two most successful parties should be roughly equal in the two-party system, that they should alternate frequently in power, and that almost every federal election is "up for grabs," the Canadian experience is not a strong example. Instead of being a relationship of two roughly equal competitors, the relationship between Canada's two government parties has been that of dominant to dominated. That is, one party has repeatedly formed a government, controlled the Senate, selected most of the Supreme Court justices, and elaborated public policy during its dominance with relatively few interruptions of power by the other party.

Nevertheless, the two-party system, as it persists in Canada, has been extolled as a model of political stability. As in its British and American versions, the Canadian system has been characterized by continuity and compromise. However, there are ideological differences detectable among the successful competing parties, especially the NDP and the Conservatives. There are disagreements on fundamentals, about social policy, the role of Parliament, and the nature of the federal system.

Multiparty Systems

A multiparty system exists where three or more parties contest elections, gain representation, and form coalitions with the governing party. Such a system may include a variety of major parties as well as minor parties that vie for political power and government offices. It is often necessary for a coalition of interests to work together in order to carry out a program of government. The number of organized political parties varies in multiparty systems. In Israeli elections, more than 25 parties compete because parties need to gain only 1.5 percent of the electoral vote to win a seat in the 120-member *Knesset*. Spain has up to 55 organized parties running candidates when elections are held.

Many factors work together to generate a multiparty system. The adoption of proportional representation and the expansion of the suffrage usually encourage its development. A lack of political consensus also contributes to the formation of a multiparty system. The widespread presence of conflicting political values and philosophies usually fosters the emergence of opposing groups that seek to change the structure of institutions or the formal policy-making process itself. Socio-economic factors such as ethnicity, language, or religion, contribute to the development of a pluralistic-party system. Multiparty systems basically reflect the ideological differences that evolve in a given society, as witnessed by the presence of anarchist groups, communist parties, nationalist parties, revolutionary parties, and socialist parties in many democratic states.

Multiparty systems can be *one-party dominant* and *multiparty competitive*. In a one-party-dominant system, a single party wins approximately 60 percent or more of the seats in a legislature and two or more other parties usually win less than approximately 40 percent of the seats.[15] Mexico has been a good example of a state with a one-party-dominant multiparty system. Until the election of 2000, the *Partido Revolucionario Institucional* (PRI) never had one of its nominees for president or governor defeated in elections since the party's founding in 1929. In 2003, the PRI regained its legislative dominance, winning 44 percent of the seats in the Chamber of Deputies. During the last decade, other parties have been able to win appreciable numbers of seats at municipal levels and in the Chamber of Deputies. Other examples of single-party dominance are India, with its Indian National Congress Party, and the Bahamas, with its Progressive Liberal Party.

Sometimes, however, even though one party may dominate in attracting popular votes, **coalition governments** are formed, often with great difficulty, and may vary in their composition from government to government. For example, in 2006, Ehud Olmert's Kadima party formed a coalition government primarily with the Labour party, giving it seven cabinet posts to form the new 27-member government in Israel's 120-seat *Knesset*.

As the case of Israel points out, multiparty-competitive systems can demonstrate great fragmentation when no single party dominates the system. In this looser expression of party competition, no single party wins more than 40 percent of the legislative seats. In cases like Israel's, parties enter and exit the electoral system with relative ease. Party formation and cohesion are often based on personalities, transient issues, or economic and political events that encourage ephemeral party organizations. Within these multiparty systems, coalitions are formed with ease. Opportunism, pragmatism, and mutual self-interest are the primary forces that encourage coalitions which, however, easily come apart, resulting in frequent general elections or in the interference and dominance of a strong overriding executive.

The most extreme cases of fragmentation have been Denmark, France, and Italy. Because of the large number of weak parties in these states, most parties represent only a small segment of the electorate. Many parties simply cannot claim to represent the interests of the entire electorate.

Are multiparty systems unstable?

In most multiparty systems, the maintenance of coalitions between elections is exceedingly difficult. "Gentlemen's agreements" based on ideology, personalism, friendship, money, and patronage are frequently offered to induce post-election allegiance.

Parliamentary instability is often the by-product in competitive multiparty systems. If political stability is defined in terms of the constitutional tenure of governments and their ability to carry out their policies predictably, then states in this category tend to demonstrate more frequent changes of government than one-party, biparty, and dominant-multiparty systems. But among all systems, multiparty systems are neither the most stable nor the most unstable.

Is it instability when a political party system facilitates political change? If a multiparty system, operating by democratic rules, spawns frequent changes of government, does that mean the parliamentary or congressional system is not stable? In any multiparty system, political change is constant. The survival of a government in a competitive-party system depends on its capacity to adapt to political change. Instability results when a system of government is not perceived to provide fair or proportional representation. Political stability over a period of time does not reflect the absence of change but the existence of a systemic capability for non-violent change in goals and leadership. To what extent does a multiparty system satisfy the demands of many competitive groups? If it does, and yet governments change frequently, does this mean the system is inherently unstable?

PARTY ORGANIZATION AND STRUCTURE

Political parties represent three distinct groups: candidates and officeholders, citizens who are party members or identify with the party, and the *formal party organization*. These groups can range from just a few legislators who influence policies under a shared party label, to a decentralized party structure that is open to anyone interested in becoming a candidate. This range can also include a highly centralized and almost closed party organization, characteristic of single-party state systems.

Political parties reflect essentially two organizational arrangements—*hierarchy* or *stratarchy*. Hierarchically organized parties are structured so that the distribution of power, privilege, and authority is systemic and unequal, with control of the party organization in the hands of a few people at the top. Robert Michels was the first student of organizational behaviour to note the *iron law of oligarchy* in party structures.[16] He observed that a full-time professional staff dominates the party organization and that the perspectives of the leader may not necessarily be those of the members.

Stratarchy is characteristic of some democratic political parties in which power is shared by the leader with several layers of the party organization. In this kind of party organization, the leader needs grassroots support and the voluntary contribution of workers, especially the few who are dedicated to working for the party between elections. The leader depends on the policy input and support of the membership below, while those who work within the party organization need the special stewardship skills of the national leader. In Canada, the Reform Party reflected a stratarchy of party organization while the Liberal party and the reconstituted Conservative party still exemplify oligarchies.

The organization of political parties usually reflects the organization of the state where they operate, that is, unitary or federal. In most federal states, national parties are really confederations of subnational party organizations, held together by national committees. The extent to which the national party regards itself as "integrated" or "federated" with the subnational party organizations will vary from one electoral system to another.

In Canada, the co-ordination of political strategies between the federal and provincial wings of the same party tends to vary from province to province, but in general can be characterized as independent co-ordination. Parties of the same name may, from time to time, share workers and facilities, but they generally tend to keep their distance at the highest levels of party organization.[17]

Focus On The Iron Law of Oligarchy

In Canada, most political parties are oligarchies. Anyone who observes political parties will soon conclude that, over time, a small and elite group of devoted members will come to control the top structures of the organization. An oligarchy means "rule by the few," and political parties usually reflect an oligarchic character. Only those who are members of the party elite have access to greater information, influence, and decision-making powers. The mass party membership views participation in the organization as merely a part-time commitment and tends to defer to the decisions of the leadership. Once this has happened, the party leadership inevitably develops its own set of values and perspectives that is different from the original aims of the party.

This "iron law" was outlined by the German social scientist Robert Michels. As he noted, once in their position of power, the party elite becomes cautious about rocking the boat. This is because it is in the interest of the leaders to expand the party's membership at the grassroots level. The easiest way to accomplish this is to moderate the party's positions so as to bring in new groups who may not have been previously willing to support the party in its original cast. In short, a political party is caught in a dilemma: it can refuse to moderate its policies to keep the hard-core membership loyal to its platform, in which case it may not attain power because its membership will not expand; or it may compromise its ideological and policy positions for greater numbers of supporters, but at the cost of losing its soul.

In addition to political parties, the iron law applies to almost every organization in society—business corporations, schools and universities, interest groups, religious organizations, and international organizations. It is especially evident in the parliamentary system of government, which constricts the flow of power and decision making in a cabinet.

Inter-provincial party ties also tend to be weak, other than in the New Democratic Party, which maintains extensive organizational and financial links among provincial parties and between the provincial and the national party.

In the United States, there is generally little organizational connection between state and national party organizations. In a majority of states, party chairpersons are not frequently involved in national committee affairs. Of the two political parties, the Republicans at the state level tend to receive more staff assistance, financial help, research and polling data, and campaign instructions from the national party organization than do state Democrats from their national organization.

But in both parties, the national organization tends not to intervene in state activities, unless asked.

The organization of Canada's three parliamentary parties is quite similar. Each has a *parliamentary wing*, which consists of the leader and the party caucus who are front line in the legislative battles in the House of Commons and the Senate. There is also an *extra-parliamentary wing*, consisting of the national party headquarters, a national executive, and its committees, which are dominated as well by the party leader. His or her image and performance affects the party organization at all three levels. The first is the grassroots organization at the *constituency level*. From here, federal candidates are nominated, delegates to conventions are elected, volunteer personnel and members are recruited, and fundraising campaigns are initiated. The *provincial level* is next on the pyramid of the national party organization. At this level, the party faithful plan and co-ordinate the strategies that are employed at the constituency level. Members of the executive at this level are responsible for all the federal constituencies in the province. The apex of the extra-parliamentary party organization is the *national level*.

The national association normally organizes a biannual convention to stimulate debate, consider new policy directions, and elect party officials.[18] Conventions are also the occasions for electing party leaders. Because the main impact of contemporary parties comes through elections, the party organization is an apparatus oriented toward the convention and the selection or retention of a national leader.

Party Membership

From an organizational point of view, a political party in Canada is a small inner circle, composed of officeholders, candidates, a professional staff, and the party faithful. But we often hear that someone is a "member" of the Liberal Party of Canada or the New Democratic Party. Yet generations of political scientists, lawyers, judges, and politicians have been unable to agree on exactly what it means to be a member of a party. Some see membership as party identification—a voter's sense of psychological attachment to a party that goes beyond merely voting for the party. Although this concept is useful to political scientists, party identification has no legal significance. A second definition of membership has to do with the process of "joining" a political party by meeting a set of criteria such as registering, paying dues, and doing committee work. In some European states, people can "apply" for membership (as in the Christian Democratic Party and the Socialist Party), be "accepted," pay dues, and carry membership cards. In the United States, legal membership in some states involves registration as a Democrat or a Republican. The main purpose of registration in these states is to prevent adherents of one party from voting in another party's primary. Some parties, such as the Communist Party, have strict criteria so that they can exclude people who do not meet their ideological standards.

In general, a party consists of all those people who participate in any of the following activities:

A. running for office under the party label

B. seeking nomination for candidacy

C. contributing money, working for a candidate

D. attending meetings

E. voting as a delegate

F. voting regularly for the party

Party Finance

Party organizations, activities, and campaigns require huge amounts of money. Funds are needed to pay for office space or the purchase of land and buildings, staff salaries (administration and research), telephone bills, computers, postage, travel expenses, campaign literature, polling, and advertising in the mass media.

In most democratic states, there are four primary classes of contributors: individuals, corporations, interest groups (defined broadly to include trade unions and private organizations), and the public treasury. For political parties, the ability to attract money is related to the quality of candidates offered, especially the leader; the party organization between elections and the campaign organization during elections; performance in past elections and standing in the polls; the capacity to present issues and promises put forward by the leader and the candidates; and the ability to *win* elections.

Next to voting, financial contributions to political parties are the most common form of political activity. The reasons for drafting legislation to regulate party financing tend to be similar among governments. The first is public disclosure and **transparency**: the amount of money parties raise and spend is brought out in the open. Second, regulations place limitations on the amounts of money parties can spend on elections and other activities, thus reducing the influence of money on politicians. Third, it reduces the dependence of political parties on wealthy donors by partially subsidizing election costs with public funds. Fourth, it requires parties to record their financial activities and to audit their books. Fifth, it discourages corruption of party fundraising by means of internal and external auditing requirements.

In Canada, *An Act to Amend the Canada Elections Act and the Income Tax Act* (political financing) was introduced in the House of Commons in January 2003 and came into force on January 1, 2004.[19] The legislation improves transparency in election financing by increasing disclosure rules affecting electoral district associations and leadership party contests. Corporations, unions, and associations would be barred from making contributions to any registered party or leadership contestant. However, they would be allowed to contribute up to $1,000 in total per year to a party's candidates, as well as to registered electoral-district associations. An individual's contributions are limited to $10,000 per year. And individuals would be restricted to a maximum of $10,000 in donations to leadership contestants of a party during a leadership race. For all contributions of more than $200, the name and address of the person or organization have to be reported to the Chief Electoral Officer.[20]

To avoid some of the spending restrictions in the legislation, all three parliamentary parties have increased expenditures outside the designated campaign periods when expenditures are limited only by a party's ability to raise money. The growth of non-election spending indicates a higher level of inter-party competition and reflects the importance party leaders assign to maintaining strong party organizations between elections.

PRIMARY POLITICAL PARTIES
Communist Parties

Among all ideological parties that have ever won power or that compete with other political parties in competitive party systems, communist parties are ideologically the most rigid and organizationally the most structured.[21] The principles of communism are drawn from the philosophies and practices of Karl Marx (1818–1883), his collaborator Frederick Engels (1820–1895), V.I. Lenin (1870–1924), Joseph Stalin (1879–1953), and Mao Tse Tung (1893–1976).

No communist party is ideologically identical to any other, but in all communist parties the members are expected to master the principles of Marxism-Leninism as interpreted by national party elites. Thus, notwithstanding the post–World War II emergence of different national roads to communism, most communist ideologies accept Marx and Lenin as their philosophical forefathers. Regardless of which communist system one studies—for example, the Chinese, Cuban, or Vietnamese—all political leaders use Marxism-Leninism to justify their public policies.

The Communist Party of Canada, formed in 1921, is also a Marxist-Leninist organization. When it was under the leadership of Tim Buck, the party adapted its strategies and tactics from the prevailing Soviet line. Like its counterpart in the United States, the Communist Party of Canada has played a minor role in the Canadian electoral system. In the 1988, 1993, 1997, 2000, 2004, 2006, and 2008 federal elections, the party attracted less than 1 percent of the electoral vote.

Today, communist parties in Italy, France, Finland, Ireland, Spain, and Portugal receive electoral support from manual workers and intellectuals because they advocate such a command economy. In Europe and some Asian states, communist parties want to take full command of the economy. There may be variations in application, particularly in China, where peasants are the backbone of the Communist Party. In Latin America, all political systems include communist parties, which operate either openly when legal or clandestinely when outlawed.

Socialist Parties

In "communist" states, socialism is a historical phase that must be completed before communism emerges as the final political synthesis in human social development. China is officially "a socialist state of the dictatorship of the proletariat led by the working class and based on the alliance of workers and peasants." But the socialist parties that have been formed in democratic states view socialism as the highest stage of political and economic development. They attract the greatest support in the democratic states of Europe: Austria, Belgium, France, Great Britain, the Netherlands, Scandinavia, and Germany. They also enjoy varying degrees of political support in Australia, Canada, New Zealand, and many of the states of Africa, Asia, and Latin America.

In contrast to the communist parties, the democratic-socialist parties seek to secure greater economic equality without the violent overthrow of the capitalist system. When forming a government, alone or in coalition with other political parties, socialist parties generally enact comprehensive social-service programs: old-age pensions, family allowance, health care, income supplements, and unemployment compensation. They also believe that economic growth should be stimulated largely through government investment in a modified market economy made up of public and private enterprises.

All socialist parties adopt one of three approaches to the economic order: *corporate socialism*, *welfare-state socialism*, or *market socialism*. Parties that promote corporate socialism, such as the Partido Socialista de Ecuador (PSE), assume that

experts and professionals—economists, engineers, managers, and scientists—can best plan the economy to serve the public good. They think the role of a socialist government is to co-ordinate public and private corporations to achieve full employment, low inflation, and the provision of social programs for the disadvantaged.

Welfare-state socialists, as in Canada, Sweden, and Germany, reject the state-planning corporate brand of socialism. For them, government should act as a *referee* in the economy, balancing the goals of public and private enterprises in a mixed economy.

Socialist parties that advocate market socialism, such as the Socialist Party of Peru and the Argentine Socialist Party, want an economy in which the government owns the means of production but yields control of production decisions to decentralized workers' councils. Workers decide on investment and production goals in the marketplace, and the role of the government is to rectify market inequalities.

Socialism in Canada

In Canada, democratic socialism maintains a low ideological profile.[22] When it first appeared in Canada, socialism was a movement that became a party. The Co-operative Commonwealth Federation (CCF) was formed in 1932, and in 1933 drafted its Regina Manifesto, which declared the party's ideological positions, founded on the principles of democratic socialism.

Led by J.S. Woodsworth, the party attracted the support of farmers and workers and contested federal and provincial elections from 1935 until 1960, when it reconstituted itself. Its first major success was in Saskatchewan, where it took power in 1944. The following year, the party captured an impressive 28 seats in the federal election. After World War II, economic prosperity and the tensions of the Cold War gradually eroded the pre-war electoral support for the party. The Winnipeg

Declaration of 1956, with its support for a mixed economy made up of private and public corporate units, indicated the party's abandonment of the dream of a North American socialist common-wealth.

In 1961, after one year of calling itself the New Party, the New Democratic Party (NDP) was founded.[23] In order to expand its popularity, the NDP united with major labour unions in the Canadian Labour Congress, taking on a more industrial image and departing somewhat from its rural and agrarian base of support. In effect, the NDP took action to become a mass party in Canadian politics, presenting itself as an alterna-tive to the Liberals and Conservatives.

Ideologically, the NDP never fully embraced socialism.[24] During the late 1960s and the early 1970s, a number of academics and intellectuals (the Waffle Movement) challenged the pragmatic and centrist tendencies of the party leadership to return to fundamental socialist principles with an emphasis on Canadian nationalism. The Waffle Movement was rejected in 1973 because its demands to nation-alize key industries were regarded as extreme. Today, ideological moderation seems to prevail in the party. What might be described as a pragmatic *centrist* platform characterizes the ideological focus of the NDP.

The party has been only marginally successful at the federal level. In the 1979, 1980, 1984, 1988, 1993, 1997, 2000, 2004, 2006, and 2008 federal elections, the NDP captured 26, 32, 30, 43, 9, 21, 13, 19, 29, and 37 seats, respectively. The party's caucus, following the 2008 election, constituted only about 10 percent of the membership of the House of Commons and has rarely exceeded 20 percent of the popular vote in federal elections. Provincially, the NDP has formed governments in Ontario, Manitoba, British Columbia, and Saskatchewan. And with the exception of the Opposition NDP in Nova Scotia, no major inroads have been made by the party in the Atlantic provinces or Quebec.

During its history, the CCF/NDP has had nine party leaders: J.S. Woodsworth, M.G. Coldwell, Hazen Argue, T.C. Douglas, David Lewis, Ed Broadbent, Audrey McLaughlin, Alexa McDonough, and Jack Layton, who was elected in 2003. The average tenure of the party's leader is 7.5 years, compared with 12.8 years for Liberal leaders and 5.7 years for Conservative leaders. Ed Broadbent, who served as leader for more than 14 years, led his party to its best showing in terms of seats and popular vote since 1961, but his cam-paign stumbled and stalled as the issue of free trade commanded the 1988 election, ultimately prompting him to step down as leader in 1989. Under MacLaughlin's leadership, the party's tra-ditional union and intellectual support eroded substantially. The 1993 federal election battered and bruised the NDP across the political land-scape, reducing its electoral support from 43 to 9, its lowest since 1961, and causing it to lose its status as a recognized party in the House of Commons. Under Alexa McDonough, the party gained seats in the 1997 and 2000 elections but was unable to regain credible levels in the House of Commons.

FACTFILE   Alexa McDonough, who retired from politics in 2008, is the first woman to lead a federal and provincial political party in Canada.

The new leader of the NDP, Jack Layton, has been active as an anti-poverty advocate. He worked to advance transportation and affordable housing in the 1970s. He was elected to Toronto City Council in 1982 and served on various utility and health boards. Layton also served as president of the Federation of Canadian Municipalities. He was elected leader of the New Democratic Party of Canada in January of 2003. Since that time, Layton has tried to reunite the party with a modernized platform and a revamped party organization. Under his leadership, the party standing rose from 19 seats in 2004, to 29 in 2006, and to 37 in 2008.

Liberal Parties

The origin of liberal political parties in the modern sense—those groups organized for the purpose of electioneering and controlling government through a representative assembly—lies in the chaotic years of European history between 1700 and 1800. In Great Britain, **Whigs** and **Tories** were the ancestors of the Liberals and Conservatives, the Democrats and Republicans, of two centuries later.

By the end of the nineteenth century, liberal parties were formed in many European political systems and in those of the western hemisphere. They reflected positive assumptions about human nature, asserting faith in the basic goodness and reasonableness of people, and in their perfectibility. Liberal parties promoted liberty itself, maximizing individual freedom and advocating laissez-faire to achieve the greatest social good.

The first liberal parties opposed any state intervention in the economy and emphasized free enterprise, individual initiative, and free trade. In the twentieth century, as governments became more democratized, liberal parties shifted this position to a more optimistic role for the state to regulate, administer, and promote society's affairs for the public good. Modern liberal parties advance economic and social reform through government regulation and stimulation of the economy and from positive social-welfare programs. They stand firm in their support for political and legal equality, by which the laws and political freedoms of a society should apply equally to all people.

In the contemporary world of liberal political parties, there are three ideological expressions: *libertarianism*, *corporate liberalism*, and *reformist liberalism*. Libertarians, as found in the Libertarian Party of Canada for example, adopt the classical laissez-faire position that accords people maximum individual liberty. They call for the resurrection of the "minimal state," in which government plays a passive role, operating only to protect individuals from force, fraud, and theft, to secure law and order, and to enforce binding contracts.

Corporate liberals, such as the Democratic party in the United States, recognize the importance of individual freedom but protect the role of large-scale institutions, such as government, business corporations, and trade unions, as important centres of decision making. The social good results from the interplay of all of these individual and corporate forces.

Reformist liberals, such as the Liberal Party of Canada and the Liberal Party of Australia, believe the government should represent the interests of the disadvantaged: the unemployed, the disabled, low-income senior citizens, consumers, and minorities. The role of the government is to redistribute wealth, and to develop programs directed at those economically deprived through monetary and tax policies. Through such policies as public health care and education, income maintenance, family allowance, and old-age pensions, the government can foster the freedom and equality of individuals in a social context.

The Liberal Party of Canada

In the election of 1874, Alexander Mackenzie led his Grits to electoral victory over John A. Macdonald's Tories with the support of rural and small-town Canadians, especially moderate-reform groups in Ontario and anti-business, anti-clerical reform elements in Quebec. The Liberals were defeated in 1878 and in the next three national elections. A new flock of voters, brought into the electorate by the accession of Manitoba and British Columbia to the federation, had different economic and social demands from the rest of the country.

The Liberals worked vigorously to broaden their base of support, building on urban and rural grassroots strengths in most of the provinces. By the time they came to power under the leadership of Wilfrid Laurier in 1896, the Liberal Party governed every province except Quebec. The new western provinces of Alberta and Saskatchewan contributed to the tenure of Liberal success until 1911. However, the party suffered deep divisions over the issue of conscription for overseas service, splitting support from English-speaking and French-speaking party members in Quebec and Ontario. Laurier retired and, at its leadership convention in 1919, the party chose William Lyon Mackenzie King as leader. King set the Liberal Party on its pragmatic reformist path, constructing an industrial-relations and welfare-state platform. King viewed the party primarily as a machine for winning elections and only secondarily as an instrument to advance the principles of liberalism.

> **FACTFILE** Mackenzie King is Canada's longest serving prime minister, having held that title for 21 years, 5 months, and 1 day.

His successor, Louis St. Laurent, strengthened the support of the party in Quebec and Ontario and greatly expanded the industrial and economic base of the Canadian economy. Liberals had come to accept the role of government as a major actor in the Canadian economy and, under St. Laurent's stewardship, projected the idea that their party was the governing party of Canada.

St. Laurent retired in 1958 and was succeeded by Lester B. Pearson, who, during his tenure as prime minister, never commanded a Liberal majority in the House of Commons. As a result, he was not in a strong position as a party leader to influence the direction of Liberal policies. In a minority government, Pearson and his ministers did not venture to develop a system of policy priorities. His avoidance of political controversy and the reluctance to create and debate during his tenure as leader of the party weakened the ideological appeal of the Liberal Party. Unable to win a majority of seats, Pearson gave way to new leadership.

His successor, Pierre Elliott Trudeau, was the first Liberal leader to assume that position with a previously articulated philosophy of policy making. Trudeau introduced what he called "rational" liberalism, which meant creating and expanding the role of bureaucracy to develop rational policies and decisions in all areas of the economic and social environment. It also meant enlarging and strengthening the chief advisory bodies around the prime minister—namely, the Privy Council Office and the Prime Minister's Office. During his tenure as leader of the Liberal Party, the size of Canada's public service grew enormously. Under successive Trudeau governments, Canada took on many of the characteristics of an administrative state by expanding the sphere of government into areas traditionally under private control, increasing government involvement and regulation of the economy, and increasing bureaucratic specialization and professionalization.[25]

Under Trudeau's stewardship, the Liberals remained faithful to the party's traditional tenets: defending the universality of social programs by keeping family allowances and old-age security payments free of means tests; advancing Canadian economic and cultural nationalism; protecting French language rights; and mapping out the constitutional destiny of the country.

Liberal fortunes fluctuated under Trudeau's leadership. An astounding victory in 1968 was followed by near defeat in 1972 and the struggle to maintain a minority government in the House of Commons. The Liberals enjoyed another substantial victory in 1974 but suffered electoral defeat in 1979. Trudeau announced his resignation, but in December 1979 the controversial Conservative austerity budget introduced by John Crosbie was defeated. Trudeau was persuaded to stay on as party leader and subsequently led the Liberals to a majority victory in the 1980 election. In his last three years as prime minister, the Liberal Party slipped to its lowest levels of popularity, stigmatized by budgets that failed to reduce unemployment, an uncontrollable deficit, and by a public increasingly cynical of its leader. Many believed that Trudeau's successor, whoever he or she might be, could—by tinkering with party re-organization, some policy renewal, and procedural reform—return the party to power.

Such was the bravura of the party elite at the Liberal leadership convention in June 1984 when John Turner was chosen as the Liberals' glittering political star. Turner, who had served in the Commons for 14 years, 10 of them in the Cabinet, had broken with Trudeau in 1975 and brilliantly divorced himself from the legacy of the tarnished Liberal record. From a distance, the star glistened with looks, personality, and intelligence. But on the hustings, he sparkled nervously, appearing awkward and dull to the merciless eyes of the TV camera. Turner served as prime minister for only 80 days, from June to September 1984. His uncertain ideological direction, coupled with lack of leadership moxy, led to the stunning electoral defeat that traumatized the Liberal Party in every part of the country.

Turner and the remnants of his parliamentary caucus embarked upon a comprehensive reconstruction of Liberal policies and finances from the grassroots to the party elite. Turner's inability to unite the party around him resulted from his controversial positions on issues such as the Meech Lake Accord and the Canada–US Free Trade Agreement. Lingering doubts about Turner's leadership skills persisted well into the 1988 election campaign and, in 1989, he resigned after much speculation.

His successor was Jean Chrétien, who won the Liberal leadership in 1990. After running a strong campaign, Chrétien won his first government in the 1993 federal election by holding out the promise of a kinder, more prosperous Canada, more strategies to meet the needs of unemployed Canadians, and a less obsessive focus on the market-driven economics embraced by former Progressive Conservative governments.

After the 1997 election, Chrétien implemented a multi-billion-dollar program to be cost-shared with provinces and municipalities to rebuild roads, bridges, and transit systems. But while the Chrétien government vocally supported universal health care and education, it cut billions of dollars in transfer payments to the provinces in order to reduce its large annual deficit. In response, provincial governments were forced to slash their budgets and downsized government services to the point that spending on education, health care, and welfare greatly declined.

Polls consistently showed Chrétien to be the most popular prime minister in the last half of the twentieth century, notwithstanding major changes to Canada's social safety net, his government's close call in the Quebec referendum of October 1995, and the failure of the government to fulfill its 1993 election promise to scrap the Goods and Services Tax (GST). The greatest success of the Liberals was the deficit-reduction program, which by 1999 had produced budgets with the largest surpluses in Canadian history.

In December 2003, Paul Martin, lawyer, corporate tycoon, and former federal finance minister, succeeded Jean Chrétien as Canada's twenty-first prime minister. Upon taking his position, Martin enjoyed high levels of popular support across the country. But in February 2004, the Auditor General's Report disclosed what came to be called the "sponsorship scandal," which involved the questionable allocation and spending of public money by the Liberals during the 1995 Quebec referendum and beyond. Martin had been the federal minister of finance when the sponsorship funding was allocated to fight the forces of separation during the 1990s in Quebec.

As Martin prepared to call an election, the unanswered questions surrounding the scandal caused serious public doubt about his leadership and his prior knowledge of how monies were spent while he was minister of finance. In the final analysis, many Canadians held misgivings about the political integrity of the Liberal Party. After attempting to re-establish public confidence about how his government would manage public monies in the future, Martin decided to call an election for June 28, 2004. Canadians gave him a lukewarm reception at the polls, reducing the Liberals to a minority government with 135 seats, down from 172, in the Commons.

Stephane Dion became the eleventh leader of the Liberal Party of Canada in December of 2006. He had been elected MP for Saint-Laurent-Cartierville since 1996. He served as Minister of Inter-Governmental Affairs, President of the Canadian Privy Council and Minister of the Environment under successive Liberal governments.

At the Liberal Party Leadership Convention in 2006, he won the party's leadership position on the fourth ballot, narrowly winning over his closest rivals Michael Ignatieff and Bob Rae. Such a close victory left doubts in the minds of many in his party that he could successfully lead the party or win an election to form a minority or majority government.

As Leader of the Opposition, Dion had an uphill battle gaining the confidence of Canadian voters to give him the opportunity to become prime minister. In the summer of 2008, Dion released his "green shift" plan to cut the general tax rate, including personal income tax, and to levy a $15.5 billion tax on carbon so as to reduce greenhouse gases in Canada. The plan had the effect of increasing popular support for the party before an election would take place.

But this proved to be short-lived throughout the election campaign in the fall of 2008. Stephane Dion's Liberals lost ground in Ontario and British Columbia. The party was also weakened financially by the end of the election. As a result of the magnitude of Liberal misfortunes under his leadership, Dion soon announced his intention to resign as party leader, setting the stage for a new leadership convention in 2009.

Michael Ignatieff became 12th leader of the Liberal Party in December 2008. The Toronto-born academic and prize-winning author returned to Canada from teaching at Harvard and Oxford to accept an appointment at the University of Toronto. The trilingual Ignatieff (who speaks English, French, and Russian) was first elected to the House of Commons in 2006. He was re-elected in the riding of Etobicoke-Lakeshore in 2008.

Ignatieff was quick to disconnect from the carbon tax and the Green Shift, two campaign policies that led to the crushing defeat of the Liberals under Stephane Dion in 2008. He also indicated his reservations about sustaining the Liberal–NDP coalition which had threatened to defeat the Harper government.

Michael Ignatieff is a formidable intellectual and political opponent for Stephen Harper in Parliament and on the campaign trail. He has shown a capacity to fundraise successfully for the Liberals and build a powerful party organization across Canada, particularly in Quebec.

Dealing with his first challenge in his role as leader of the Liberal Party, Michael Ignatieff—after much deliberation—chose to support Stephen Harper's budget in 2009, thus keeping the minority Conservative government in power and ending the life of the Coalition.

Small-*l* liberalism runs deep in the Canadian political psyche.[26] The Liberal penchant for pragmatism over doctrinaire solutions has made philosophical liberalism an ambiguous yet popular creed. What is certain is that liberalism in the post-Trudeau era is still a powerful political force in Canada.

Conservative Parties

During the nineteenth century, the first conservative parties were preoccupied almost exclusively with the defence of the monarchy and hereditary ruling classes against the demands of popularly elected assemblies.[27] But conservative parties shared other, more formal, ideological positions, possessing both political and historical depth that liberals could not match.

FACTFILE   In Canada, Conservative parties have won the greatest electoral victories, taking the largest percentage of popular votes over 50 percent, resulting in majority governments in the following federal elections: 1878, 1882, 1904, 1917, 1958, and 1984.

Early conservative parties emphasized the existence of natural human distinctions in wealth, opportunity, ability, intelligence, and privilege in the economic order of society. Their chief concern was the defence of traditional wealth against the onslaught of the Industrial Revolution. Conservative parties were deeply committed to the concept of private property as the fundamental dynamic of the economic order. For them, the economy was the interaction of government, institutions, landed aristocracy, and different classes of people as they related to the pursuit and ownership of private property. Property was the basis of a financial elite who provided economic order for generations of citizens. Both time and survival were the principal tests for the endurance of conservative economic principles.

The first conservative parties tended to see social justice achieved in a society that permitted social, economic, and political inequality, if only because these were the characteristics of all societies throughout recorded history. But in Europe, conservatives defended their elite social status as *noblesse oblige*—the responsibility of the dominant classes for the welfare of the whole society. Conservatism had not been so presumptuous as to identify the well-being of all citizens with the conservatives' own self-interest. But, from earlier times, upper classes carried an obligation to those of less fortunate status.

Many modern conservative parties—**neoconservatives**—advocate small government and the laissez-faire values of classical liberalism. Some conservative parties continue to be pessimistic about human nature and dubious about the effectiveness of government expenditures for domestic welfare programs. They believe that people are better off being left alone from the restrictions of government power and regulation. Conservative parties rate the private sector of society much more highly than do liberals and assert that social benefit will more likely come from the work of voluntary associations and private business than from government ventures. At a more abstract level, conservatives tend to resist fundamental changes in social or governmental arrangements, believing that meaningful improvement in the human condition will come only slowly and naturally in the form of evolution. They believe that the future must be built on the past and, therefore, they believe in maintaining traditions.

In Canada, conservatives see the role of political parties as "conciliators," building coalitions of interests to achieve a national consensus, harmonizing regional conflicts, and strengthening the fabric of society within the traditional framework of government institutions.[28] They stress social and legal order based on fundamental principles of conservation and preservation to protect the national interest. The conservative penchant for order requires the presence of a strong and effective government but with a limited or restricted role so as not to undermine self-reliance and individual freedom. As a balance to highly centralized government authority, conservative-party policies encourage the vitality of countervailing forces of power such as the provinces, trade unions, farm organizations, trade associations, and the media, to check the arbitrary tendencies of federal institutions.

Canadian conservatives remind people of the institutional prerequisites of social order. David Crombie summed up his feelings on what it means to be a conservative: "I am a Tory. I glory in the individual. I cherish community. I seek liberty. I neither trim nor tack to every social whim. I honour tradition and experience. I exalt faith, hope, and fairness. I want a peaceful ordered, well-governed Canada. I am a Tory."[29]

Most Canadians have a very low level of ideological consciousness.[30] People who call themselves

Conservatives often do not take the conservative position on specific issues, just as many self-declared Liberals stray from the liberal side of many issues. "Conservative" and "Liberal" are handy labels that many people apply when talking about politics. These terms are used far beyond our ability to define them. For most Canadians, political ideology is a series of assumptions and vaguely held beliefs.

The Progressive Conservative Party of Canada

In 1854, a coalition comprising business, professional, and church leaders in Ontario and French Catholic and business elites in Quebec was constructed by John A. Macdonald to unite the British North American colonies into a single political unit. Under his leadership, this amorphous partnership of business and church elites was the genesis of the Conservative Party (first called the Liberal-Conservative Party). Macdonald, who became the first prime minister of the Dominion of Canada, won six of the eight federal elections held in the later part of the nineteenth century. Canadian conservatism took shape as a powerful pragmatic political force, the result of a series of modernization measures that Macdonald called the "National Policy."[31] The chief component of the policy was the construction of the transcontinental railroad, completed in 1885. Other components included an industrialization plan nurtured by protective tariffs, primary-resource development in the Maritimes and the West, and the encouragement of interprovincial trade.

At first, Macdonald succeeded in maintaining the tenuous coalition of political loyalties in Quebec and Ontario. But in 1885, Macdonald's decision to execute Louis Riel, a francophone Catholic Métis who had led an armed rebellion in Manitoba and Saskatchewan, placed bitter strains on the Quebec segment of the Conservative coalition. The support of the Conservatives in Quebec was further eroded by the party's hedging on its commitment to provide financial support to Catholic schools. After Macdonald's death and a succession of new leaders between 1891 and 1896 (John Abbott, John Thompson, Mackenzie Bowell, and Charles Tupper), the Conservatives failed to appeal to voters.

The party remained out of power until 1911, when its leader, Sir Robert Borden, defeated the Liberal government of Wilfrid Laurier. Support for the Conservatives was drawn from an alliance of anti-American and protectionist forces in Ontario, combined with isolationist Quebec Conservatives who had come to an understanding with Borden that some from their ranks would be selected as cabinet ministers in the new government. This alliance disintegrated over the conscription crisis of 1917, which embittered many French Canadians because of Borden's insistence on conscripting men for overseas service in World War I. It soon became apparent to Quebecers that none of the French Canadians in Borden's Cabinet had much influence over his decisions. The party subsequently lost its support base in Quebec.

Arthur Meighen, Borden's successor as prime minister, carried on the legacy of Quebec's abandonment. Like Borden, Meighen failed to understand the sentiments of French Canadians. The Conservatives were quickly stigmatized as an English-speaking Protestant party by the Quebec electorate, and Conservatives would not see a revival of French-Canadian support until John Diefenbaker's landslide victory in 1958.

Lacking substantial support in Quebec, the Conservatives were defeated in 1921 and, except for a brief period between 1925 and 1926, were to remain out of office until 1930. The party's new leader and prime minister, R.B. Bennett, like Arthur Meighen, did little to expand the support base of the Conservative Party. He continued to antagonize Quebec by failing to keep the lines of political communication open to that province, and he divided his own party when, without consulting his Cabinet colleagues, he brought forward his New Deal program, based on Roosevelt's American package. Under Bennett, these two weaknesses—the inability to nurture support in Quebec and a proclivity to generate internal divisions and factionalism—became symptomatic of what was later called "the Tory syndrome."[32]

Bennett was soundly defeated in 1935, and three years later he turned over the leadership of the party to R.J. Manion and his successors. Arthur Meighen, John Bracken, and George Drew were unsuccessful in broadening the support base of the party, especially in Quebec, and could not defeat the Liberals in the period between 1940 and 1957. The name of the Conservative Party was changed to the Progressive Conservative Party in 1942. This newer party label helped Drew's successor, John Diefenbaker, defeat the Liberals by giving the party a more centrist position on the political spectrum.

In the election of 1957, Diefenbaker led the Progressive Conservatives to a minority-government victory. The following year, Diefenbaker led them to the greatest electoral victory in Canadian history. Perhaps the most ideological of any Canadian prime minister, Diefenbaker resuscitated conservatism in Canada and gave it a most discernible North American character. His "vision" of Canada, his devotion to the monarchy and the Commonwealth, his penchant for strong national government, the National Development Policy, the Bill of Rights, and his pro-Canadianism, all were hallmarks of Diefenbaker's toryism. But by 1962, Diefenbaker's personal charisma and strong electoral support had suffered a sharp reversal. He antagonized his party colleagues in Quebec because of his reluctance to appoint them to important Cabinet positions and by his indecisiveness in handling the **Munsinger scandal**. It was not long before serious intraparty divisions surfaced over the quality of Diefenbaker's leadership, resulting in his replacement by Robert Stanfield in 1967.

Stanfield took the reins of a deeply divided party, which was unable to rally its forces to oust the Liberals in 1968, 1972, and 1974. His style of party leadership was much less exciting and more subdued than his predecessor's. But Stanfield held a deep regard for conservative ideology, espousing the honest ideals of national purpose, order, and a reverence for Canada's institutions and symbols. Stanfield lacked the popular appeal necessary to convert his political philosophy into electoral support, and he retired under pressure in 1976.

Of the 11 candidates at the hotly contested leadership convention in 1976, Joe Clark emerged the winner at age 36, and with only four years of parliamentary experience under his belt. But nearly three years later, Clark led the party to a narrow victory in the May 1979 election. He resisted ideological pigeonholing, preferring to be judged as a pragmatic Tory rather than a party leader acting in accordance with preconceived conservative philosophy.

Although his tenure as prime minister and party leader was short-lived, it is possible to discern both conservative and liberal tenets in Clark's political thinking. He held that big government was much more of a detriment to Canada than were big business and big labour. Clark expressed confidence in the private sector to create jobs and to stimulate the recovery of the Canadian economy. But his expressed desire to privatize Petro-Canada, sell other Crown corporations, relocate the Canadian embassy in Israel, and support a tax policy governed by the principle of "short-term pain for long-term gain" generated serious doubts about the new Tory minority government. In December 1979, the Clark government's austerity budget and his government were defeated.

After two successive biennial meetings of the party in 1981 and 1983, where about one-third of the delegates voted to call a leadership convention, Clark, recognizing the growing dissension, announced his resignation and at the same time declared his candidacy in the upcoming leadership race.

It was billed as the largest political convention in Canadian history. As many as one-third of the voting delegates were undecided when they arrived at the convention, which fielded eight candidates. Clark led the other candidates on the first three ballots but was defeated by Brian Mulroney on the fourth ballot.

From the outset of his successful leadership campaign, Mulroney's personality and style changed the image of the Progressive Conservative Party. The party had selected its first leader from Quebec since Sir John Abbott. But unlike other Conservative leaders, Mulroney promised to bring Quebec in, not merely as a stronghold, but as an ongoing constituency of support for the Progressive Conservative Party.

During the 1984 election campaign, Mulroney's reputation as a competent conciliator, based on his career as a labour lawyer, boosted the stolid image of the party and had an enormous political payoff in his bid for Quebec support. Because of his adept conciliatory skills, not only did legions of Lévesque supporters work for Mulroney, but also the former premier complimented him for choosing so many "authentic Québécois candidates." In the process of political conciliation within Quebec, the Tories were able to crush the once impregnable Liberal stronghold, claiming 58 of the province's 75 seats in 1984 and 63 of its seats in 1988. Ideologically, Mulroney was a pragmatic centrist. When he first ran for the leadership of the party in 1976, some members of the party prematurely identified him as a **red Tory**.

But once in power, Mulroney entered the twilight zone of Canadian pragmatism, adopting a political strategy to solve Canada's problems that defies ideological identification. Mulroney saw the only way out as sustained economic growth: by creating new wealth, by unfettering the private sector in an atmosphere of deregulation, by encouraging federal/provincial co-operation, and by generating jobs out of the newly implemented Free Trade Agreement. After scandal hounded his

government, he stepped down as party leader, believing he could pass government on to a new leader who could win a third conservative term.

> **FACTFILE** Controversy followed Brian Mulroney even after leaving politics, forcing him to testify before Parliament as a former prime minister regarding his associations and money dealings with German businessman Karlheinz Schreiber.

The Conservative leadership campaign generated compelling media coverage of the convention, where two candidates seemed to dominate the events, Kim Campbell and Jean Charest. After a close and tough campaign, Campbell led the delegate support and held it into the convention, becoming the first woman leader of the Progressive Conservative Party and Canada's first female prime minister.

As a political leader, Kim Campbell had politically desirable attributes: her intelligence, gender, age, and her region of representation—western Canada. In her short tenure as prime minister, she adopted a smaller Cabinet, initiated an extensive government re-organization, and promised to develop a new kind of politics in the governing of Canada. She attended the G-7 (now G-8) meeting in Tokyo, playing her role carefully and using excellent photo opportunities with US President Clinton.

Campbell's policy package included a multibillion-dollar program for job training and adjustment, but regarded the reduction of the federal deficit as the only sure method of creating long-term economically "meaningful" jobs. She promised to eliminate the deficit within five years. She remained committed to the large transfer payments to the provinces but promised to seek cost-cutting efficiencies for programs such as medicare.

But Campbell ran into trouble early in the 1993 election campaign. She distanced herself from Mulroney and his best campaign advisers, refused to reach out to Jean Charest and his Quebec base, and headed into the election with only her personality as the party's major card. She was running neither on the Tory record, which many campaign advisers believed to be still saleable, nor on a distinctively new platform of her own.

Her performance in the televised debates inspired derision and disappointment among many of the Progressive Conservative candidates. Then, in the middle of the campaign, she made critical comments about Mulroney, Don Mazankowski, and Jean Charest in a press interview, which led to serious tensions within the election team. By election day, party organizers were in despair. Campbell lost the election to Jean Chrétien in 1993.

With the election lost, the party gave the awesome task of reconstruction to Jean Charest, one of only two Progressive Conservative survivors in the House of Commons who represented a party that did not have enough seats to be recognized as an official parliamentary party. As leader of the Progressive Conservatives, Charest sought broad approval for moderate policies to appeal to mainstream Canada. But his political career was challenged much more in 1998, when, after considerable pressure from across the country, he gave up leading the federal Progressive Conservatives to take on the leadership of Quebec's beleaguered Liberal Party in order to fight the sovereignist government of Lucien Bouchard. His victory against the PQ finally came in April 2003, when he soundly defeated the government of Bernard Landry.

In November of 1998, Joe Clark re-emerged as the leader of the federal Tories. He led the Progressive Conservatives from 1998 to 2003, attempting to build the party from the ground up across Canada and to distinguish it from the Alliance Party of Canada (formerly the Reform Party). He became a champion of Parliament, but the Progressive Conservatives did not rekindle their historic capacity to unite Canadian conservatives and rise to power in government.

The Alliance Party of Canada

In 1987, the Reform Association of Canada organized a western assembly on Canada's economic and political future. At the founding assembly in Winnipeg, a new political party called the Reform Party of Canada was born, with Preston Manning acclaimed as leader.[33] The Reform Party ran candidates in the 1988 federal election but did not win any seats. But in a by-election in 1989, Deborah Grey became Canada's first Reform MP. In the June 1997 federal election, Reform swept the western provinces, electing 60 MPs and becoming Her Majesty's Loyal Opposition.

The Canadian Alliance Party emerged after two United Alternative Conventions sought to lay the groundwork for a new political entity.[34] On March 25, 2000, 92 percent of Reform Party members voted to adopt the constitution of the Canadian Alliance. Its first leader was Stockwell Day, who became Leader of the Opposition in the House of Commons.

By March 2002, after much negative coverage, the party was on the verge of internal collapse and desperately sought to find a new leader. Stephen Harper was elected leader of the Canadian Alliance on the first ballot, receiving 55.04 percent of the votes. He took the reins of leadership in the Official Opposition.

The Conservative Party of Canada

The Conservative Party was formed by the merger of the Progressive Conservative Party of Canada and the Canadian Alliance Party in December 2003. The merger was announced in October 2003, by the two party leaders, Stephen Harper of the Alliance and Peter MacKay, who had succeeded Joe Clark as the leader of the Progressive Conservative Party in 2002.

The merger was the culmination of the "Unite the Right" movement in Canada, fuelled by the desire to create an effective and united opposition to the Liberal Party, which had been positioning itself for the 2004 federal election. The Conservative Party of Canada was registered with Elections Canada in December 2003, and its new party leader, Stephen Harper, was elected in March 2004, defeating former Ontario provincial Tory cabinet minister Tony Clement and former Magna International CEO Belinda Stronach.

Between March and the election campaign that began in late May, Harper had very little time to build a strategy for winning the election in late June. The party was unable to hold a policy convention and was forced to develop its policy framework on the hustings during the campaign.

Harper appeared to have most of the momentum in the election but was not able to translate it into a minority or majority win for the Conservative Party. The party won 99 seats by performing strongly in the West and by breaking into the Liberal stronghold in Ontario.

On November 28, 2005, a motion of no confidence introduced by Stephen Harper was passed by the House of Commons, which began an eight-week federal election campaign. Harper's Conservatives sprinted from the starting line, quickly taking the lead in the opinion polls and holding that lead throughout the rest of the campaign. The 39th General Election was held on January 23, 2006. The Conservative party won a plurality of seats, giving Harper 124 out of 308 or 40.3 percent of the seats in the House of

Commons. These results enabled Stephen Harper to form a minority government, becoming the 22nd Prime Minister of Canada. In 2008, Harper was able to win a second conservative minority government by winning 143 seats in the House of Commons with 37 percent of the popular vote.

The most serious challenge to his government came after the opposition learned that the minority government was cutting public subsidies to political parties and would address the economic crisis facing Canadians with a weak budget update. The immediate and unforeseen response of the Opposition was the creation of the Liberal-NDP coalition with Bloc support. The Coalition threatened to defeat the government in the new parliament. Harper's strategy was to avoid certain defeat by asking the Governor General to prorogue Parliament until his government could produce a more acceptable budget. His request was granted, and the government survived.

The Conservative Party of Canada is part of the evolution of Canadian conservatism.[35] The party is still referred to as "Tory" by the media and retains its ties to the historical Conservative Party, founded in 1854 by Sir John A. Macdonald and Sir George-Étienne Cartier, by virtue of the fact that the merged party assumed all the assets and liabilities of the Progressive Conservative Party.

PRESSURE GROUPS

What Are Pressure and Interest Groups?

Political parties are not the only decisive forces in shaping policy outcomes. In perhaps less obvious ways than political parties, pressure groups articulate the **interests** of people who want to influence decisions about public policy.[36] This kind of popular

---

Crosscurrents   Do Interest Groups Trump Political Parties on Representation?

Although not mentioned in the Constitution, and held in low esteem by most of the Fathers of Confederation, interest groups have proved both durable and effective instruments of representation in all political arenas. Joining together as teams of common interests works well to get demands heard in Ottawa, in the provinces, or at the municipal level of government.

Some believe that interest groups are much better at representation than are political parties because political parties are highly focused on the demands of their patrons. Instead of trying to please everyone to gain support, interest groups concentrate their efforts on getting things done.

The most successful groups represent their members on single issues. Many interest groups focus their attention on a single issue or a single cause. They attract the powerful support of individuals and other groups that have money and a strong commitment to their cause.

Single-issue groups have little incentive to compromise their position. They exist for a single cause, and no other issues really matter to them. They are passionate and effective in representing those most affected by their cause. They share the same intensity as their clients regarding their beliefs.

Among the most vocal single-issue groups have been the organizations on both sides of the abortion issue, anti-abortion and pro-choice groups. Other prominent single-issue groups include Mothers Against Drunk Driving (MADD), the gun lobby, and environmental groups.

participation in the political process is less familiar and apparent—and certainly less official—than voting, but it is nonetheless just as real and important. When a group of neighbours becomes concerned about the need for a stop sign on the corner of their street and circulates a petition to present at City Hall, they are a pressure group taking political action. Moreover, their efforts to influence the municipal government are considerably more direct, and likely to be more effective in achieving their goal, than reliance on a *political party* would be.

During the past century, the scope of group activity has widened and the quantity and variety of pressure groups has grown proportionally. Individuals the world over are more conscious of themselves as belonging to groups that can potentially exercise political influence.

To some degree, everyone is a member of a culture, race, religion, age, and gender group, and perhaps a professional, occupational, or labour group. Even if one professes to no religion, one is part of a group of atheists or agnostics. If one disavows membership in a political party, one is a member of a group that thinks the same way.

By definition, a *pressure group* or *interest group* is any collection of people organized to promote a goal they share or to resist some objective of government or other groups that somehow relates to the political process. A women's club is not, therefore, a pressure group unless its membership decides, for example, to demand (among other possibilities) equal rights with men in such things as property law, education, employment, and promotion.

The Canadian Medical Association (CMA) is a pressure group by our definition, even though its members are ostensibly organized for professional reasons. However, the association frequently concerns itself with public matters. The CMA was involved in the political process that led to the establishment of medicare, and it continues to press for influence in administering such programs. In the United States, the National Rifle Association (NRA), a powerful group of more than one million

members, seeks to advance the safe use of firearms and vehemently opposes gun-control legislation with an elaborate network of offices.

Numerous pressure groups of this kind—business, labour, professions, trade, religious, and other types—exist in order to promote their own objectives in the political process.[37] Pressure groups constitute an extra-institutional aspect of politics. They are intimately related to the daily functioning of legislatures, executives, courts, and political parties. One cannot understand the dynamics of any democratic political system without understanding the deep involvement of pressure groups at all levels of society.

> **FACTFILE** In 2004, the Supreme Court of Canada upheld the limits on spending during election campaigns by lobbyists to $150,000 nationally and $3,000 in any one riding.

Canadians are joiners; we belong to a variety of groups reflecting countless interests and political demands.[38] The essential problem in Canada's highly competitive democratic system is to balance all these various group demands within an ordered, yet free, society.

Types of Pressure Groups

Most democratic states are pluralistic societies, in which many different groups freely express their interests and demands on government. In non-democratic states, where the free expression of interests is closely monitored and controlled by a governing elite or a party apparatus, pressure-group formation may be difficult, if not officially considered subversive and illegal.

In democracies, hundreds, sometimes thousands, of pressure groups with some stake in the political and economic system stand up and are heard. The great advances in industry, communications, science, and technology have brought more organized groups into the process of decision making.

Gabriel Almond has developed a classification of pressure groups that applies to both democratic and non-democratic societies. These are anomic, non-associational, associational, institutional, and international pressure groups.[39]

Anomic pressure groups

Anomic groups are spontaneous gatherings of people whose behaviour demonstrates public concern and a demand for political action. Such anomic groups (*anomie* means being separated from social norms) do not feel bound by any need of organizing beyond the immediate expression of frustration, disappointment, or anger about a government policy or lack of government response to a question of public policy. Without previous organization or planning, anomic pressure groups vent their emotions as the news of government action or inaction sweeps a community and triggers a public reaction. These groups rise as flashes of support or non-support and, just as suddenly, subside.

In Canada, pro-choice crusaders and right-to-lifers react strongly to Dr. Henry Morgentaler's arrests and acquittals. Advocates on both sides of the issue have gained a great deal of public visibility and, as a result, have attracted anomic support in those provinces where abortion clinics have been opened or were about to open. For these people, the opportunity to demonstrate their political positions on abortion to the provincial and federal governments may come only once, and they may not attempt to extend their involvement any further. Their actions do not lead to violence, but there have been frequent incidents of civil disobedience.

In other political systems, anomic pressure-group behaviour occurs because parties, governments, and organized pressure groups have failed to provide adequate representation of their interest. Suicide bombers have become a growing example of anomic group activity. Some states, including Israel, Palestine, Iran, India, and the United States, have been marked by spontaneous group behaviour.

The pressures of anomic political activity flow from its spontaneity and the ultimate threat that it could result in widespread anti-government behaviour.

Non-associational pressure groups

Non-associational groups, like anomic groups, are not formally organized. But these groups are more aware of themselves as distinctive from other groups because they possess a common activity, characteristic, or interest. Members of non-associational groups share a feeling of identification without the cohesive interplay of leadership and organization. Examples are the unorganized unemployed; prisoners and former inmates; people who retain their ethnicity, such as Polish Canadians; consumer groups, such as vegetarians; and normative groups, such as non-smokers and non-drinkers.

These groups can be important in politics. For example, an increasing number of governments at all levels in Canada have moved to protect the rights of non-smokers by means of legislation, municipal bylaws, and agency regulations. These groups derive their political influence from their mere existence and from widespread support for their pressure on government and within the general population. But also, non-associational groups, poised in society as reference groups, can be rapidly transformed into well-organized associational ones. Groups may organize around ethnic interests, such as the National Congress of Italian-Canadians Foundation and the Italian-American Foundation in the United States, or around a common interest, such as the Non-Smokers' Rights Association in Toronto.

The potential supporters of an organized interest group are frequently dispersed throughout society, living in different areas and occupying different roles. Non-smokers' rights groups have been organized in almost every city in Canada—yet, just a few years ago, such groups were essentially people who were aware only that other non-smokers existed.

Associational pressure groups

Associational pressure groups include business, industrial, and trade associations, labour groups, agricultural groups, professional associations, and public-interest groups. These pressure groups represent the expressed interests of a particular group, maintain a full-time professional staff, and use effective procedures for formulating and processing interests and demands.

Despite their very real political interests, it is important to remember that most pressure groups do not exist exclusively, and often not much at all, for *political* purposes. A labour union is not organized primarily to bring political pressure; neither is the Canadian Food Processors' Association, the Canadian Federation of Independent Business, or the Canadian Manufacturers' Association. The importance these groups attribute to political pressure does vary a great deal, but to all of them it is essentially a by-product of their central concerns, not their basic reason for being. Moreover, the first requirement for interest-group leaders is to keep their members happy. A union leader who fails to produce a good contract may be defeated at the next election.

In Canada and the United States, professional groups of teachers, lawyers, physicians, and others are as numerous as business, consumers', women's and senior-citizens' groups; they actively pressure governments in promoting their interests. In fact, the list of associational pressure groups grows longer and more varied each year, reflecting the pluralistic and open character of these societies. These numerous pressure groups are active participants in the political process and are instrumental in implementing changes of policy or initiating new ones. For example, the Technical Committee of the Canadian Food Processors' Association educates as well as pressures the government to harmonize its regulations so that the industry functions in the public interest.

In other political systems, associational pressure groups tend to be less likely to protect their narrower interests, such as the rights of renters, taxpayers, bankers, and peasants. In many states, associational pressure groups are not nationally organized and play only a limited role in national politics. They lack autonomy and independence because they are controlled by other groups, such as political parties or the church. For example, in France and Italy, many trade unions and peasant organizations are controlled by the Communist Party or the Roman Catholic Church. The subordination of these pressure groups to other organizations restrains their capacity to operate in the wider national interest.

Institutional pressure groups

Institutional pressure groups are well-established social structures such as bureaucracies, churches, and universities. These highly self-conscious groups can and do make a stream of specific demands on government.

Most people do not perceive the institutional character of businesses. But they make up the largest number of institutions in our society. Business firms, acting independently or in concert, are probably the most important and active of all pressure groups operating for their economic interests in the body politic. Businesses tend to pressure all facets of the political system, sometimes concentrating on the regulatory agencies of government administration and at other times acting directly on the politicians who draft the laws that affect commercial practices.

Businesses as institutional entities have a number of advantages in dealing with governments in Canada. They are usually well organized and generally have an ample supply of money. This enables them to purchase advertising and retain professional lobbyists to press their interests on government. The business community generates the largest amount of money for lobbying tactics, as well as the largest number of active pressure groups operating on the federal, provincial, and municipal governments in Canada.

International pressure groups

Not all pressure groups work to change the policy perspectives of the national government. The newest type of pressure group has an international or a global mission. These groups operate within the confines of nation-states, yet are organized to articulate what in their view are issues of global and near-global significance. International pressure groups are the product of globalization and the power of organizations to extend their influence against governments everywhere.

> FACTFILE Doctors Without Borders/Médecins Sans Frontiéres (MSF) was founded in 1971 by France's Dr. Bernard Kouchner, whose international vision has made MSF the world's largest medical pressure group, helping victims of epidemics and natural and human-made disasters.

This type of pressure group includes such organizations as Amnesty International (AI), Doctors Without Borders/Médecins Sans Frontiéres (MSF), Greenpeace, and terrorist groups such as Al Qaeda. Amnesty International was instrumental in generating international efforts behind the establishment of an International Criminal Court. In the wake of human-rights violations in Kosovo, Rwanda, the Sudan, Sierra Leone, and in the US terrorist detention camp in Cuba, Amnesty International has lobbied national governments and international organizations to take action for humanitarian relief.

Pressure-Group Tactics

All pressure groups try to influence key decision makers. Groups may use both formal (lobbying) and informal methods (demonstration) to articulate their interests to policy makers. Pressure groups

Focus On Greenpeace: A Global Pressure Group

Originally known in 1970 as the "Don't Make A Wave Committee" from Vancouver, BC, Greenpeace was organized in 1971 to make a greener and more peaceful world. Greenpeace is a grassroots activist group with active organizational membership in more than 30 countries and more than three million individual memberships from around the world.

Basing its global strategy on the non-violent philosophy of Mahatma Ghandi and Quaker tradition, Greenpeace uses civil disobedience, peaceful demonstration, and international education programs to change the world. The "green" in its name highlights environmental protection, and "peace" refers to non-violent resolutions of

disputes. These tactics have been used to block deforestation, nuclear testing, whaling, sealing, the killing of endangered species, and pollution. The organization's overall goals are global peace, disarmament, and non-violence.

The power of Greenpeace flows from its existence as a global pressure group. Greenpeace does not restrict its lobbying tactics to national governments only; the scope of its activities is worldwide. The organization is able to attract media attention across the globe whenever it targets a particular issue for advocacy. Greenpeace sends its members around the world in an attempt to protest unacceptable circumstances, both to governments and international organizations.

vary in the tactics they employ and in the ways they organize and direct their influence. Thus, the strategies and techniques used by pressure groups are determined by the character of the governments they seek to influence, as well as by the nature of their goals and means.

Quite often in democratic states, pressure-group activity is conducted by **lobbying**. The term *lobbyist* developed in the United States from the practice of speaking to legislators in the lobby just outside the congressional chamber about pending matters. A regular occupant of the lobby, whose function was to influence legislators, came to be known as a lobbyist. Standard lobbying tactics, including appearances and testimony before legislative committees, are common practices in many political systems.

FACTFILE In the United States, the largest and most powerful interest group is the American Association of Retired Persons, with more than 43 million members who are 50 years of age and older.

Pressure groups lobby to induce legislators to introduce, modify, pass, or kill legislation. Professional lobbyists are sometimes hired on a part-time or full-time basis by interest groups that are preoccupied with the professional representation of their membership.

In Canada, the *Lobbyists Registration Act*, proclaimed in 1998, requires lobbyists to register with the federal government so that there is public knowledge about who is trying to influence policy makers. Under the Act, individuals who communicate for payment with federal public-officeholders for the purpose of influencing the development, introduction, passage, defeat, or amendment of legislation are considered lobbyists. Two types of lobbyists are recognized: *professionals*, who are in the business of lobbying for clients; and "*others*," who lobby on behalf of an employer. There is another group of lobbyists who do not have to register because they work on a voluntary basis, usually for a cause. The Act, as amended, requires lobbyists to register with the new Office of the Commissioner of Lobbying. The new rules for lobbyists, which came into effect in 2008, require lobbyists to be more transparent and accountable. Under the rules Canadians will have access to lobbying activities through the internet.

FACTFILE The new rules that regulate lobbying carry penalties for contravening Canada's *Lobbyists Registration Act* and the *Financial Administration Act* with fines up to $200,000 and/or from six months to two years imprisonment.

Most of the lobbyists who work to influence policy in Ottawa gained their professional credentials in private industry, inside government, or by espousing special-interest causes. Many lobbyists have worked closely with their governments and some are former politicians and cabinet ministers. Often, they are on a first-name basis with hundreds of politicians and reporters and are major spokespersons for the interests they represent. Hiring a lobbyist (sometimes a prestigious law firm, public-relations firm, or a legislative consultant) helps ensure that the group's interests are professionally made known to the decision makers in government.

FACTFILE A Montreal student, Heidi Rathjen, and a Toronto Ryerson University professor, Wendy Cukier, both with little money, no immediate political clout, or even much political savvy, successfully lobbied the federal government to pass Canada's gun control law in 1995 against a well-organized, politically connected gun lobby.

Numerous organizations maintain offices in the national capital, and many of them employ more than a dozen people to co-ordinate the political relations of the group. The lobbying staff may include, in addition to a director and assistants, a number of liaison officers, researchers, copywriters, an editorial staff, and specialists with contacts in the various branches of government.

The larger the interest represented, the more sophisticated its lobbying operation can be.

In recent years, changes have taken place in Canadian practices regarding pressure-group tactics, some of which involve *direct action*. They include demonstrations, organized boycotts and strikes, advertising, writing books, and staging various events to attract the media's attention and to inform the general public. Pressure groups will sometimes penetrate political parties to get closer to decision makers. Associations of campers, conservationists, environmentalists, bird watchers, and naturalists have used these methods, which have proved very successful in their communications with government agencies.

Mass demonstrations, providing information, and disseminating propaganda are becoming standard tactics for some pressure groups such as peace organizations. Dramatic but direct pressure on government was staged by Greenpeace protestors when, in an attempt to abort a military operation, they lofted balloons carrying nets toward the flight path of a cruise missile. With respect to the peace movement in Canada, it is evident that the public is taking notice.

Any survey of pressure-group tactics and techniques must also include illegitimate and coercive ones, like violence and terrorism. No society has escaped the use of violence and vandalism by pressure groups. The consequences of continued physical violence are alarming. But violence is, nevertheless, always a possibility with pressure-group activity. Terrorism has taken the form of deliberate assassination of diplomatic representatives, suicide bombings, armed attacks on other groups or government officials, the provocation of bloodshed, and the threat of bombing. Terrorists are often successful in drawing world attention to their cause, but at the same time they can lose public support by their violent actions.[40]

Chapter Summary

In many states, political parties are the most important functional vehicles of political participation and representation. In democratic as well as non-democratic states, they mobilize people, represent their interests, provide for compromise among competing groups, and are the vehicles that recruit the leaders of most contemporary nation-states.

The study of individual parties focuses on their origins, their organization, and their ideological bases. Political scientists are interested in the relations that parties have among themselves in what is called a party system, as well as the functions they perform both inside and outside the electoral system. Parties are identified and defined according to specific characteristics such as labels, membership, leadership, discipline, structure, finance, and ideological perspective.

In Canada and the United States, political parties are not mentioned in the constitution, but few observers can imagine how the electoral or government system could function without them. In both states, political parties have become part of the unwritten constitution, and they are vital to the formation of governments and to the operations of Congress and Parliament.

Pressure and interest groups also play a major role in the power structure of modern political systems. They differ in purpose and function from political parties. The growing number of interest groups, their size, and their character are changing the dynamics of representation and articulation in democratic political and governmental systems.

A political party is a group of persons united in opinion or action, more or less permanently organized, that wants to elect its candidates to public office so as to influence or control the actions of government.

Political parties can be categorized according to different types: pragmatic/brokerage parties are mass-appeal organizations with no strong ideological platforms; ideological parties are based on socialism, communism, Nazism, and feminism; nation-building parties draw from national ideologies to create programs of development; revolutionary parties want to fundamentally change the social, economic, and political system; and special-interest parties focus on dominant issues.

Political parties perform important functions: political socialization, leadership recruitment, interest articulation, interest aggregation, policy-making, and opposition.

Political-party systems emerge because of the kind of electoral system used, and they range from one-party to competitive two-party and multiparty systems.

Pressure groups are voluntary associations often organized to promote a goal their members share or to resist some objectives of government. Pressure groups appear as anomic groups, non-associational groups, associational groups, institutional groups, and international groups.

Discussion Questions

1. It is sometimes argued that democracy would not be possible in contemporary societies without political parties. Discuss what these institutions are and how, through them, the public is able to gain access to the governing elite, hold them accountable, and influence public policies.

2. Compare the roles of political parties in democratic and non-democratic states. Identify and discuss the various functions of political parties with particular reference to how they recruit political leaders, socialize the masses, and aggregate political interests in a society.

3. Discuss how party systems evolve. What type of system has evolved in Canada, the United States, Germany, Spain, and Italy? What factors have contributed to the development of multiparty systems in former communist states after the collapse of communism?

4. Discuss the differences in the functions of political parties and pressure groups. Give Canadian examples of the various types of pressure groups discussed in the text. How effective are they in Canada's parliamentary system of government? Why are many democratic governments moving to register the groups that pressure them?

5. In recent years, some pressure groups claiming to represent the "public interest" have emerged on the issues of abortion, the environment, gun control, and capital punishment. Identify and discuss the activities of some of these groups. How effective do you believe these groups are likely to be? Why?

11

Elections and Electoral Systems

After reading this chapter, you will be able to:

- define *psephology*

- differentiate among the concepts of voluntary and compulsory voting and suffrage

- describe what an electoral system is and how it can affect the results of elections

- list what the major electoral systems are and understand how they work

- discuss the advantages and disadvantages of proportional representation and simple plurality systems

- apply this knowledge to Canadian elections at the federal and provincial levels

- recount the results of the Canadian federal election of 2008

- discuss the campaign strategies used by the various political parties in the 2008 Canadian federal election

- explain the role of primaries as used in the United States

- compare the role of national conventions in Canada and the United States

- review the results of the 2004 and 2008 presidential elections in the United States

● ● ● ●

VOTING

Elections are one of humankind's oldest social institutions. Anthropologists have traced the practice to ancient Sumeria nearly 6000 years ago, when people living along the Tigris and Euphrates rivers elected leaders to bring them through emergencies and natural disasters.[1] Elections first took a formal central role in politics much later, during the fifth and sixth centuries BC, in the Greek city-states of the eastern Mediterranean. The Greeks elected people in popular assemblies to fill offices of political authority. They voted sometimes by a show of hands, sometimes with written **ballots** in the form of pebbles (*psephite*). Hence, the modern term *psephology*—the study of voting, elections, and electoral systems.

FACTFILE   The secret ballot was adopted in New Brunswick in 1855, for federal elections in post-Confederation Canada in 1874, and in all the then-existing provinces by 1877.

Today, elections may or may not be conducted democratically, but even the most authoritarian and totalitarian states are hard pressed to stage them. Although the frequency of elections varies among political systems, states that hold no elections are the exception to the rule. In the modern world, elections are omnipresent political practices, even among the most repressive regimes.

Many authoritarian as well as democratic states make voting obligatory: Belgium pioneered **compulsory voting** in 1893, followed by the Netherlands in 1917, and Australia in 1924. Other states that have adopted compulsory voting are Argentina, Brazil, Italy, Liechtenstein, Nauru, Paraguay, Peru, and Spain. In Italy, voting is not "legally" compulsory but is regarded by the state as a civic duty: failure to vote is recorded for five years on an elector's identity card. Italy also provides its citizens living abroad with free transportation home to vote. Some states, such as

Uruguay, have compulsory voting laws but do not enforce them. Even though voting is one of the simplest political activities, the percentage of electoral turnout varies from state to state (Table 11.1).

In most states today, the electorate is 21 years of age and older, an age qualification that usually permits the majority of citizens to vote. Table 11.1 illustrates a wide range in the percentage of voter turnout among the states selected: between 41 and 95 percent. In many states, the high proportion of eligible non-voters is a persistent concern to government leaders because, despite the simplicity of the voting process, the implications of the vote are profound.

FACTFILE   Twenty-five to forty percent of the electorate regularly do not vote in Canada's federal elections; this sector of qualified voters is primarily made up of the unemployed, as well as people with low incomes who identify themselves as working class.

When people withdraw from an election or feel no political anchorage in the political system, the resulting **voter apathy** can lead to voter discontent. Studies cannot really pinpoint all the causes of non-voting, but indifference is certainly among the most influential.[2] The groups usually cited as apathetic and alienated are women, the young, the uneducated, the poor, and those generally disfranchised from the political system. In Canada, where voter turnout has been, until recently, historically higher than in other democratic states, political alienation expressed as non-voting is often related to a region's economic weakness. In these areas, many non-voters feel that one government is as helpless as another to make any difference in reversing economic insecurities. Many non-voting Canadians feel alienated even while possessing an advanced education, working in high-status occupations, and enjoying comfortable incomes.[3]

In the advanced industrialized nation-states, non-voting often results from other factors related

Table 11.1	Voter turnout in national elections, selected states		
State	*Compulsory Voting*		*Average Turnout since 1945*
Australia	yes		95.1
Belgium	yes		92.5
Canada	no		70.1
Denmark	no		85.5
France	no		78.7
Israel	no		81.1
Italy	yes		92.4
Japan	no		73.0
Luxembourg	yes		91.0
Nigeria	no		41.0
United Kingdom	no		77.3
United States	no		48.9

Sources: For comparative data, see United Nations, Demographic Yearbook *(New York: UN, 2006); Elections* Canada, Serving Democracy: A Strategic Plan, 1999–2002, *and for 2008 http://www.elections.ca. All calculations and adaptations rest solely with the author.*

to the complications of living in a highly mobile society. Common reasons given by eligible non-voters for failing to go to the polls include a recent change of job or residence, not knowing where the polling places are, conflicting hours of work and family obligations, or sickness and disability.

In totalitarian states such as China and Vietnam, where voter turnout at national elections has traditionally been "directed," non-voting is penalized by fines, the publication of names at places of employment or recreation, and even the exclusion of public-service benefits. In such states, elections are considered a mechanism for demonstrating citizen support of the political system, as well as support for the slate of leaders running for government and party positions.

FACTFILE   The greatest voter turnout in Canadian federal elections took place on March 31, 1958, when 79.4 percent of qualified voters participated in the election that gave John Diefenbaker's government the largest majority (151 seats) in Canadian history.

Suffrage

Most states, whether democratic or non-democratic, apply the principle of **universal suffrage**, whereby every qualified person in the community, rather than everybody who happens to be in the community on election day, has the right to vote. The history of suffrage has been similar in many states: gradually, restrictions on voting have been removed with respect to sex, property requirements, and race. As a result, ever-larger proportions of the population have been included in the electorate.

FACTFILE   Nova Scotia was the first colony to adopt universal male suffrage in 1854, although it did not include Aboriginal males or any male receiving financial assistance from the government.

In the first Canadian election in 1867, only about 1 in every 30 adults was eligible to vote. Women were the largest single ineligible group. Through succeeding decades, restrictions on

Crosscurrents   What if They Called an Election and Nobody Came?

Political scientists know that voter turnout among all eligible Canadians is at an all-time low. Voters are losing interest in our elections. We know that voter apathy has been steadily increasing since the 1980s, when voter turnout began to slip from the post-war average of 75 percent. In the 1990s, a significant erosion of voter turnout became apparent, forcing a trend of declining participation through the remainder of that decade. In the 1993 federal election, voter turnout was 70.9 percent. In 1997, it dropped to 67 percent and continued to decline in the current century.

In the 2000, 2004, and 2006 federal elections, voter turnout had fallen even lower, to a level in the range of only 60 percent. And in 2008, the rate drifted even further downward to 59.4 percent. This trend is now seen as problematic by politicians and analysts.

Provincial elections are also experiencing lower voter turnout. In Nova Scotia, for example, voter turnout in the 2003 election dropped to 65.78 percent, the lowest since 1960 and down significantly from the 68.1 percent who participated in the election of 1999. In the 2006 provincial election, a new record was set for the lowest voter turnout, with just 61.65 percent of registered voters turning up to cast ballots.

At the current rate of increase in voter apathy, will Canada have a government *of* half the people, *by* half the people, *for* half the people in just another decade? And based on the downward projections, it is feasible to predict (with tongue in cheek) that at some point in the future no one at all will bother to vote when elections are called.

But just as disturbing are the low rates among young voters. In the four federal elections since 2000, less than 25 percent of those young Canadian voters eligible to vote showed up to vote. In other words, three out of four Canadians aged 18 to 24 did not bother to vote.

However, there is no shortage of initiatives designed to get young people interested in the democratic process. Elections Canada, the nonpartisan agency responsible for conducting federal elections, by-elections, and referendums, has taken initiatives to connect with younger voters. Special emphasis is placed on visiting campuses, sending out information targeted at them via voters' list mail-outs and through the internet.

Should we be worried about declining participation rates within the Canadian electorate? Among the young eligible voters in Canada, research shows that they are cynical, apathetic, feel alienated, and tend to withdraw from opportunities to get involved in politics.

Many younger Canadians don't feel they have any political anchorage in the parliamentary system. They also feel that their participation will not positively affect policy outcomes in their interests. In this case, they are right. Given the way our election rules are set up, even if people under 30 had voted in high numbers during recent federal elections, the policy mandate of the government would not be any different than it is without their votes. As yet, no one political party has become the voice of youth in Canada.

This all contributes to what political scientists see as youth disengagement. What this means is that if young people do not vote, they are also less likely to learn about or participate in the world of politics. In turn, they are not likely to get involved in community issues and are very unlikely to run for political positions.

Should Elections Canada give serious consideration to installing polling booths on voting day in places where young people hang out—schools, gyms, malls, and coffee shops? We need to change the electoral rules to meet the standards of proportional representation, so that people of all voting ages believe and see that their votes count. Finally, to reduce voter cynicism and apathy, politicians need to be held accountable for the promises they make in order to get elected.

---

suffrage were removed one by one. Women gained the right to vote in 1918; and in 1960, legislation amended the *Canada Elections Act* and the *Indian Act* to grant federal voting rights to Aboriginals.

> **FACTFILE** Since Confederation, only 23 self-identified First Nations and Métis have been elected to the House of Commons.

All political systems have established certain suffrage qualifications for people who want to vote in elections. One is *citizenship*. Most states permit only native-born and naturalized citizens to vote.

> **FACTFILE** In Canadian provincial elections, any citizen of Canada who has resided for six months in a province where the writ of election is dropped may vote in that election.

People with dual citizenship or multiple citizenship are usually allowed to vote in the country where they have taken up permanent residence and have demonstrated some loyalty toward the political system in which they wish to participate. Several Latin American states permit foreigners to vote in municipal elections after a five-year period of residence. Venezuela has permitted foreigners to vote in a number of its presidential elections.

> **FACTFILE** In 1970, a revised *Canada Elections Act* lowered the voting age and the age of candidacy from 21 to 18.

A certain minimum *age* is another requirement in all states extending the right or privilege of voting in government elections. The most common age limit is 21 years. But many states have lower limits. The Cuban Constitution permits persons aged 16 or older to vote for municipal councils, which are the only popularly elected bodies. Eighteen years of age is the limit in Canada, Great Britain, Israel, the United States, and Uruguay. Some Latin American states that use 21 as the voting age for most people will allow married persons to vote at age 18. Denmark has the highest limit, at age 25. Italy permits persons who are 21 and older to elect deputies to the Chamber of Deputies, but permits only citizens over 25 to vote for senators.

Another important qualification for voting in elections is *registration*. Most states compile voters' lists against which the names of people asking for ballots can be verified. There are basically two registration systems practised by states: one places the responsibility of registration on the voter; the other uses state-appointed officials to enrol eligible voters. In the United States, each voter must take the initiative by going to a registration office and applying.

> **FACTFILE** The National Register of Electors is a computerized database of Canadians who are qualified to vote. It contains the voter's name, address, electoral district, polling division, gender, and date of birth.

In Canada, the preparation of voters' lists is the responsibility of the **Chief Electoral Officer**, an independent, non-partisan civil servant and officer of Parliament, chosen by the House of Commons to administer the Canada Elections Act, and who issues writs of election to the **returning officer** in each **riding**.[4] The final federal door-to-door enumeration was held in 1997. The results of this final enumeration became the basis for the National Register of Electors implemented in 1998.

Finally, *literacy* continues to be a requirement in some states. Literacy requirements can disfranchise many persons. For example, Brazil and Ecuador disfranchise large numbers of illiterate Indians and peasants by literacy testing.

> FACTFILE   The position of Chief Electoral Officer (the person responsible for conducting federal elections) was created in 1920 by the *Dominion Elections Act*, the forerunner of the *Canada Elections Act*.

Besides these four qualifications, many states exclude certain people for various reasons. In many states, electoral laws exclude people in prisons, jails, mental institutions, judges, and the Chief Electoral Officer. In Canada, a judgment of the Federal Court in 1988 reversed the disqualification of federal judges from voting. In the same year, the Federal Court struck down as unconstitutional the section of the *Canada Elections Act* that denied the vote to the mentally ill. At one time, returning officers were permitted to vote *only* in the case of a tie vote in a riding; however, now all returning officers are permitted to vote.

One Canadian inmate challenged the *Elections Act* on the grounds that the Charter of Rights and Freedoms gives every citizen—including prisoners—the right to vote. Prisoners voted in the 1997 federal election when court decisions invalidated the prohibitions against inmates. The Liberal government appealed to once again remove or limit prisoners' voting rights.

> FACTFILE   The Commissioner of Canada Elections is responsible for investigating and enforcing electoral fraud; a fine, rather than imprisonment, may be issued upon conviction for an offence.

Women and Political Participation in Canada

Canadian women have always been involved in politics, but their participation has traditionally been "behind the scenes": organizing meetings, raising money, administering election campaigns, and canvassing voters. During the twentieth century, suffragists, prison reformers, daycare workers, social workers, nurses, unionists, and managers of women's centres were successful in lobbying for changes in government policy.

In Canada, women were not considered "people" entitled to the same political rights as men in the early years of the country's independent political life. In fact, no women were present in the debates leading to Confederation. At that time, women who wanted to take an active role in public affairs were considered "unwomanly," if not worse. It took until 1884 for the federal government to introduce the *Married Women's Property Act*, recognizing the rights of married women to hold property. Prior to that time, a man who was married to a woman who owned property could vote, but she could not, even though she paid the property taxes.

> FACTFILE   In 2007, during a by-election in Quebec, Stephen Harper asked the Chief Electoral Officer (CEO) to bar Muslim women from wearing veils when they voted, so that they would reveal their faces publicly while voting. The CEO refused on the grounds that such a restriction would violate the Charter of Rights and Freedoms.

The first municipal franchise was granted to "widows" and "spinsters" in Nova Scotia in 1893.

Table 11.2	Chronology of key Canadian voting rights
1867	The first federal election is held. Only men who own a certain amount of property are allowed to vote.
1885	The *Electoral Franchise Act* defines a "person" as a male, excluding a person of Mongolian or Chinese race.
1917	The *Wartime Elections Act* disfranchises Canadian citizens born in an enemy state and naturalized after March 31, 1902, as well as those whose "mother tongue" is the language of an enemy state, regardless of country of birth.
1917	Wives, sisters, and mothers of servicemen receive the right to vote.
1918	All adult women win the right to vote.
1948	The franchise is extended to Canadians of Japanese ancestry. The property qualification to vote is abolished.
1950	The Inuit, explicitly excluded in the *Dominion Franchise Act* of 1934, become eligible to vote.
1960	The *Indian Act* is amended to extend the franchise to Native Canadians living on reserves.
1982	The Charter of Rights and Freedoms is enacted.
1987	Judges become eligible to vote.
1988	People with mental disabilities are granted the franchise.
1992	Voting rights are extended to prison inmates, and the *Canada Elections Act* is formally amended to reflect the reversal of disqualifications of mentally challenged people, judges, and prisoners.
1993	Parliament passes legislation permitting Canadians to vote by special ballot if they cannot use their regular or advanced polls.
1996	The National Register of Electors is established, eliminating door-to-door enumeration. Amendments to the *Canada Elections Act* (Bill C-63) introduce longer and staggered voting hours.
1999	The Federal Court of Appeal rules that inmates serving a sentence of two years or more may no longer vote in federal elections.
2000	A new *Canada Elections Act* is passed, which among other things gives the Chief Electoral Officer the ability to develop and test electronic-voting procedures.
2002	The Supreme Court struck down the federal restrictions on voting rights for prisoners serving two years or more, so now *all* prisoners have a constitutional right to vote.

Source: Electoral Insights *1(2) (November 1999), and* Canada's Electoral System *(Ottawa: Elections Canada, 2001).*
See also The Evolution of the Federal Franchise *(www.elections.ca).*

Crosscurrents — Should Federal Prison Inmates Be Allowed to Vote?

In October 2002, the Supreme Court of Canada decided to allow inmates at federal penitentiaries to vote in federal elections, by-elections, and referendums. Canadians serving a term of less than two years in a correctional institution in Canada already had the right to vote.

But a section of the *Canada Elections Act, 1993*, denied voting rights to prisoners who were serving terms of two or more years. Yet a series of lower court rulings had effectively allowed all inmates to vote in the 1993 and 1997 federal elections. However, in 1999, the Federal Court of Appeal upheld the prohibition against those serving terms of more than two years.

The Supreme Court of Canada held that the section of the *Canada Elections Act* restricting the right to vote violated the Charter of Rights and Freedoms. The court argued that the voting ban was an additional punishment to a prison term, and that inmates who voted would not demean the electoral system.

Some 12 000 inmates are affected by the latest court ruling. The first opportunity for inmates to vote after the court ruling was in December 2002, when by-elections were held in Lac-Saint-Jean-Saguenay and Bertier-Montcalm, in Quebec.

Votes are counted and applied in the electoral district of the address the inmate has identified (such as residence before incarceration), rather than the electoral district that includes the institution.

But a number of federal bills for partial and equal franchise were defeated in the last decade of the nineteenth century. In 1929, Canadian women were declared "persons" under the *British North America Act* after five Alberta women took their case to the British Privy Council in London, England, which at that time was the final court of appeal after the Supreme Court of Canada. No longer would Canadian women be classed with lunatics and children as people who could not be viewed as responsible for their actions. After the famous "Persons Case" was decided, Canadian women were granted full political freedom. In 1931, Carine Wilson from Ontario became the first woman appointed to the Senate.

In the early twentieth century, **enfranchisement** of women was seen as a prerequisite for the eventual acquisition of political power. Most Canadian women gained the formal right to vote and to hold office at the federal level in 1918, while in the provinces access to the same right varied.

Before that, under the *Military Voters Act*, nurses were given the federal vote in 1917. The battle for the right to vote was most successful in the western provinces. Women there won the right to contest in provincial elections long before they could run in federal elections. Manitoba was the first province to give women the vote, in 1916. In eastern Canada, however, women could not vote and hold office until much later: in New Brunswick not until 1934, and in Quebec not until 1940.

For women, the first steps toward political equality led through the ballot box. However, winning the right to vote and holding public office did not win equal status for women.

Even today, only a minority of women seek positions of political and governmental power and fewer are successful at it. While some women hold high political office, they are much more likely to hold honorific posts, such as that of governor general or lieutenant governor, than to stand a chance of being elected prime minister or provincial premier. Women are most likely to run as candidates and win elections at the municipal level, and least likely to run and be elected at the provincial and federal levels. Yet the absolute turnout of women voters nationally is higher than that of male voters.

Women, who continue to bear the major responsibility for raising children and managing Canadian households, still face a great deal of societal pressure to keep this their first priority.

The social and psychological barriers that have prevented women from their rightful representation in Canada's male-dominated federal institutions appear to be crumbling slowly. The fact remains that women, who constitute over 50 percent of the population, have never held even 25 percent of the seats in the House of Commons. Recent elections have demonstrated that the Canadian electorate is beginning to love its daughters as much as its sons.

In the 2006 federal election, 64 women were elected to the House of Commons, one less than in 2004. But in 2008, 68 women won seats in the House of Commons, representing about 22 percent of elected MPs.

FUNCTIONS OF ELECTIONS

Elections in Democracies

Elections perform a variety of political and social functions in all states. In democratic electoral systems, elections are the primary mechanisms for recruiting political leaders and representatives. As the special democratic events that link the institutions of government with people who aspire to political careers, elections are the vehicle of **political succession**, a peaceful process that transfers power from one set of political leaders to another. Therefore, elections have a **homeostatic** function in a political system; they provide a process for orderly political change while preserving the basic continuity of political and government institutions.

Another function of elections is to **aggregate** individual choices into a *collective decision*. In all societies there is a continuous, often intense, political struggle to influence what collective goods will be provided, who will mostly pay for them, and who will benefit from them. In democracies, elections determine which majority will hold the reins of power to authoritatively allocate these collective goods. And, because no society stands still, new social challenges constantly provoke the need for the widest possible consensus on social problems. On the public agenda today are the issues of abortion, crime, drug abuse, defence, environmental protection, unemployment, and many others. Elections provide the channel for expressing new social concerns about these issues.

Still another function of elections is *political socialization*. Elections provide one of the few opportunities in most societies for all citizens to learn about the issues and personalities in the political system.

The 2008 Canadian federal election campaign gave voters a glimpse of some significant issues such as the economy and the environment. It failed, however, to address issues reportedly regarded by Canadians as very important—for example, health care, post-secondary education, the war in Afghanistan, and Aboriginal issues such as poverty and reconciliation.

While it is true that elections offer citizens only the minimum amount of voting participation with some impact on policy making, they are an important opportunity to educate the public about what must be done to survive in a complex world.

Election campaigns offer politicians an opportunity—and an obligation—to educate the public and to justify their political views. It becomes increasingly important for the citizenry, with access to both domestic and international sources of information, to learn and judge the quality of a regime's activities at home and abroad. Elections are one of the few genuine learning experiences that people, as a community, go through together.

The public is continuously exposed to political information conveyed by newspapers, television, radio, and the internet during election campaigns, usually followed by a substantial amount of media analysis after the election is over.[5]

In most states, this constitutes a political learning experience for the citizenry. The learning process provided by elections may also reinforce positive attitudes towards authority and political obligation. In most dictatorships, voting plays an important role in political socialization, serving as the symbolic input of citizen support for the undisputed authority and legitimacy of the party and the government.

Focus On   The Media and Campaigning

For the media, election campaigns have all of the elements of a good story: conflict and competition, drama, and well-known personalities. That is why most of the media cover election campaigns from the beginning to the end—from the rumours of an impending election, the selection of candidates at the local level, and the choice of party leaders at conventions to the final tally of votes.

Don Newman, CBC News: Politics

For Canadian voters, election campaigns have little reality apart from their media versions. Just a small number of reporters and commentators who follow the campaign trail can be very persuasive about the performance of the political competitors. The judgment of these journalists can make or break a political party, its leader and candidates across the country. They are recognized as the "experts" in their field, work for the most prestigious publishers and networks, and have developed the trust of the Canadian public through the stories they have reported in the past.

During Canadian elections the relationship between politicians and the media is said to be *symbiotic*, because the candidates and the media need each other. Those running for Parliament need the media to get their messages across to Canadian voters, and journalists need the campaigns to build their careers. It is also said to be *adversarial* because journalists see their role as not just conduits for party platforms but as political and professional critics, analysts, and reporters.

The media's powerful influence in Canadian elections has changed the types of candidates who enter the political and governing arena. Increasingly, media-savvy candidates can get elected if the media shine their spotlight on them soon enough. The idea is to get the attention of the media.

What voters actually see and hear of a candidate is mainly determined by what is called the "free media" (newspaper, radio, and television coverage) and the "paid" media (such as television advertising) accompanying an election campaign. The paid media are completely under the control of campaign organizers, whereas the free media are totally independent.

In the final analysis, the media exercise enormous power. They can make or break reputations, help to launch or destroy political careers, and build support for or rally opposition party platforms during election campaigns.

All things considered, the free media are so critically important to the maintenance of a democratic society that we must be prepared to take the risk that the media will occasionally abuse their power.

Finally, elections can foster a sense of *personal efficacy*, a feeling of psychological satisfaction derived from the belief that the political system is affected by and is working on your behalf. For those who vote in elections, personal efficacy means a perception that no matter how insignificant a single vote is, it may actually be part of a groundswell of messages to political leaders or aspiring political recruits. Much national research has shown that political participation is closely related to feelings of personal efficacy.[6]

Elections in Dictatorships

In many authoritarian states, elections are confused, hectic, and often negative learning experiences for citizens. In these kinds of political systems, the coup d'état is still a widespread method of government change. Elections are viewed as undesirable events that can result in political violence and corruption. People are exposed to electoral manipulation and fraud, unscrupulous campaigning, military intervention, suspicious candidacies, and last-minute political fiascos. Candidates try to magnify their own personal popularity and appeal by viciously attacking their political rivals, by slanderous name calling, or by identifying them as enemies of the regime.

In many African states, people are exposed to flagrant corruption of the electoral process.[7] The media are particularly vulnerable to official interference because they are subsidized by the government.

In dictatorships, registration procedures are often used to manipulate the electoral process and to discourage all but the most dedicated voters. Poor people, who are less interested in politics to begin with, because they have so many other immediate problems to worry about, must face the costs of required documents and photographs. In nation-states with large peasant populations, the long journey from the countryside to urban polling stations is a strong deterrent to voting. In addition, there are also the well-known practices of buying votes, threatening voters, and fraudulently tallying the votes cast.

Nevertheless, millions of people in authoritarian states turn out at the polls whenever elections are held. This occurs, at least in part, because they need to keep jobs, to maintain the support of superiors, or to avoid fines imposed in states with compulsory-voting regulations. In these political systems, people are voting in ever-increasing numbers despite what they have learned about fraudulent electoral practices.

MAJOR ELECTORAL SYSTEMS

An electoral system consists of all the customs, laws, procedures, and institutions used to elect representatives in a political system. A comprehensive description of an electoral system would include the customs and practices of campaigning and voting, the rules regulating the behaviour and funding of candidates, the methods of calculating and representing the popular vote, and the institutions (political parties, conventions, electoral colleges, and government agencies) that administer, recruit, and compete when elections are held.[8]

Most states have created an electoral system of their own to choose a government and its representatives. The size of the electoral district, the number of political parties that compete, and the timing of elections are all variables affecting the performance of any electoral system. For purposes of analysis and classification, political scientists divide electoral systems into two main types: **majority systems** and **proportional-representation** (PR) systems. Majority systems are designed to produce either a simple **plurality** or an **absolute majority** for one candidate representing a single constituency. Where more than one candidate is elected from multi-member constituencies, the candidates with the largest pluralities are declared elected. Majority systems appear as single-member constituencies,

Focus On Calculating Provincial Representation in the House of Commons

Commencing with 282 seats (the number the House of Commons had in 1985), each territory—Nunavut, Northwest Territories, and Yukon—is allocated one seat, leaving 279 seats. The total population of the 10 provinces is divided by the number of seats in the House of Commons for each province. The total population of each province is then divided by 279 (the number obtained after allocating seats to the territories) to obtain the national quota or quotient, which is then used to determine the number of seats for each province. The number of seats to be allocated to each province in the House of Commons is calculated by dividing the total population of each province by the national quotient. The *Representation Act*, 1985, guarantees that each province has no fewer seats than it had in 1976 or during the thirty-third Parliament.

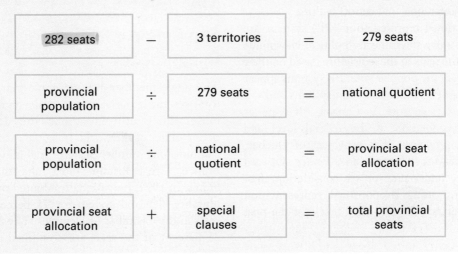

Table 11.3	Provincial and territorial seats in the House of Commons	
Province	**Number of Seats**	
Newfoundland	7	
Prince Edward Island	4	
Nova Scotia	11	
New Brunswick	10	
Quebec	75	
Ontario	106	
Manitoba	14	
Saskatchewan	14	
Alberta	28	
British Columbia	36	
Territories		
Northwest Territories	1	
Yukon	1	
Nunavut	1	
Canada	**308 (total)**	

Source: Electoral Insight *4(2) (October 2002); www.elections.ca and click on Federal Representation, 2004; and see* Elections Canada, "Representation in the House of Commons of Canada," *2002. All calculations and adaptations rest solely with the author.*

multi-member constituencies, and constituencies using the preferential and **runoff ballots**.

Proportional representation (PR) systems are designed to give the minority political viewpoints a share of the seats in the legislature based on their proportion of the popular vote. PR systems appear in constituencies using party-list systems and the single-transferable vote. In Canada, PR is under serious consideration at the federal level and within the provinces. The provinces of Quebec, New Brunswick, Ontario and Prince Edward Island have undertaken or are considering electoral reform using proportional representation (PR) and **mixed systems**, using first-past-the-post and PR.

MAJORITY SYSTEMS

The Single-Member Constituency

The single-member district/simple-plurality electoral system is the easiest to understand and the most widely utilized among the democratic nation-states of the world. It is used extensively in a diminishing number of states, including Canada, France, Great Britain, India, and the United States. In 1994, Italy partially adopted the simple-plurality electoral system for 75 percent of the seats in the Chamber of Deputies. The remaining 25 percent of the seats are now filled using PR.

Focus On First-Past-the-Post (FPTP)

By 2008, 68 of the world's 211 states, comprising nearly 50 percent of the world's population, chose their legislative representatives by means of FPTP. Canada is one of these states. The phrase *first-past-the-post* is misleading because technically there is no "post" for candidates to get by; simply put, the person who gains the most votes wins. In a two-member contest, one candidate will gain a clear majority of the valid votes cast. But when there are three or more candidates, there is no certainty that anyone will gain a majority, and whoever wins takes the seat with only a plurality of valid votes cast, i.e., one or more votes than the other contenders.

FPTP is one of the easiest electoral systems to use, although most Canadians do not understand how election results can often be so disproportional for both government and opposition parties. But in general, the FPTP system produces single-party majority governments. In 39 general elections since 1867, all but 10 have brought one party to power with a majority of seats.

But charges of unfairness in converting votes into seats have been levelled at Canada's FTPT electoral system. In only 3 of 25 elections since 1921 has a party won a majority of the seats, supported by a majority of voters.

In three elections since Confederation (1957, 1962, and 1979), the party that formed the government received a smaller share of the popular vote yet won more seats than the principal competing party. FPTP can also produce the situation in which one party wins at least as much, if not more, of the popular vote as another party but still ends up with fewer seats.

This is an effort to reduce the number of parties that compete and to produce a strong national government capable of handling widespread corruption.

The single-member district is based on a geopolitical principle that divides a state or its sub-national units into relatively equal constituencies, with one representative elected from each district. Almost always, the candidate who gains a plurality of popular votes wins the election. This *winner-take-all* (first-past-the-post) system usually means that the candidate who wins a plurality of support does not necessarily command the majority of votes cast in the constituency. In fact, a minority win almost always occurs in a single-member district when a candidate merely wins more votes than his or her opponents and does not get more than 50 percent of the total.

In the riding of Beaches-East York, Liberal candidate Maria Minna won the seat with a plurality victory (18 298 votes) over her nearest rival, NDP candidate Marilyn Churley (14 893). Minna took 40.9 percent of the votes cast. The other four competing candidates earned a majority of 59.1 percent. These results show the disproportionate effects of plurality in Canada's electoral system.[9]

In the 2008 federal election, the Conservatives formed a minority government with 143 seats and 37.6 percent of the popular vote. The Liberals won 77 seats from 26.2 percent of the popular vote; the NDP took 37 seats with 18.2 percent; the Bloc Québécois won 49 seats and 10 percent of the popular vote; the Green Party won 0 seats yet attracted 6.8 percent of the popular vote; and two independents gained seats from 0.7 percent of the popular vote.

Canadians elected three minority governments in succession in 2004, 2006, and 2008. These governments did not attract a majority of popular support, but majority governments have not usually attracted majority popular support either. For example, even with the return of a majority in the House of Commons after the 1993, 1997, and 2000 federal elections, the Liberals still represented less than half of the voters. When the percentage of votes given to opposition and other parties is taken together, over 50 percent of the electorate voted against the government. Because plurality is the rule of success in single-member constituencies, only on rare occasions will a majority of popular support be achieved.[10]

Multi-Member Constituencies

Another type of constituency used in majority electoral systems is the multi-member district. In these circumstances, two or more representatives are elected from the same riding. The multi-member constituency is used to elect members to Turkey's National Assembly, as well as to a number of provincial local legislatures in Canada, Great Britain, and the United States. Most people are unaware of the fact that US senators represent multi-member districts because two senators are elected from each state. Because one-third of the Senate is elected every two years, US citizens rarely have the opportunity to vote for two senators simultaneously. This produces the popular misconception that senators are elected from single-member constituencies.

In Canada, many of the provinces that had multi-member constituencies abolished them. For example, Newfoundland in 1972, Nova Scotia in 1981, Saskatchewan in 1965, Manitoba in 1958, British Columbia in 1991, and Prince Edward Island in 1996 all abolished multi-member districts. In multi-member constituencies, the electorate is permitted to vote for as many candidates as there are posts to be filled. As in the single-member district, the candidates with the highest pluralities are declared elected.

Preferential and Runoff Ballots

Some states—concerned that the plurality principle rarely achieves an absolute majority of support for successful election candidates—use a number of ballot techniques to guarantee that every elected representative wins with the approval of more than half the electorate.

One of these techniques is the **preferential ballot**, which is currently used to elect representatives to the Australian House of Representatives and to four of its eight states and territories. On the preferential ballot, the voter ranks the candidates contesting a constituency in order of preference, by placing numbers rather than Xs beside their names. In order to be declared elected, a candidate must obtain a majority of first-choice votes on the ballot. If no candidate gains a majority on the first count, the candidate with the fewest first-choice preferences is dropped and his or her ballots are redistributed based on the second-choice preferences on each. This time-consuming process is continued until an absolute majority of support is obtained by a candidate. He or she is then declared elected.

Another technique is to use a *runoff* or second ballot to facilitate an absolute majority victory for successful candidates. In France, for example, unless candidates for legislative and executive posts receive a majority on the first ballot, they compete in runoff elections that continue until a candidate polls a majority.

Runoff elections are held in 10 southern US states between the two top candidates when no candidate in the first primary gains a majority vote. In these states, where the Democratic Party tends to be dominant, winning the primary is tantamount to winning the general election. The runoff election guarantees that the candidate who wins the primary will have the majority support of the voters, rather than determining a victory by a mere plurality when three or more candidates are contesting an election.

PROPORTIONAL SYSTEMS

In a system of proportional representation (PR), the votes that would remain underrepresented or wasted in other electoral systems are given legislative representation in proportion to the total popular vote.[11] Hypothetically, had the principle of proportional representation been employed in Canada's federal election of 2008, the results would not have been as disproportional. The Conservatives would have won only 116 seats instead of 143; the Liberals would have fared better with 80 seats instead of 77; the Bloc Québécois would have earned only 31 seats instead of 49; the NDP could have received 56 seats instead of 37; and the Green Party would have earned 21 seats instead of none at all.

FACTFILE Because proportional representation tends to equate popular vote with legislative seat share as a 1:1 ratio, a multi-party system and coalition government are often a natural consequence.

PR is an attempt to give legislative expression to the dispersion of votes (majority and minority) as they accrue in a democratic electoral system.[12] The proponents of PR believe that a truly *democratic* assembly should reflect every representative point of view in a polity. PR is designed to preserve the electoral results of political parties according to their relative strengths in the electorate.

Many states employ a PR system: Denmark, Republic of Ireland, Germany (for half the seats in the *Bundestag*), Israel, and Sweden. New Zealand adopted proportional representation for its 1996 election to elect 120 members to its Parliament. Basically, these states allot seats in their legislatures in direct proportion to the distribution of votes. In fact, it can be argued that all PR systems now operative in modern democracies are variations of two basic types, the party-list system and single-transferable-vote system.

Party-List Systems

Party-list systems operate on the principle that all qualifying political parties are awarded seats in the legislature in proportion to the percentage of popular votes they attract in an election. Party lists are prepared by the leaders or executive committees of various parties and submitted to the electorate in multi-member constituencies. The size of the constituencies and the methods of counting and distributing seats vary from one state to another. But three distinct variations of the party-list system are detectable.

One variation gives the voter no choice among the candidates once the list is prepared. Israel is the best example of this "take it or leave it" **party-list system**. There is only one multi-member constituency in Israel—the *entire country*, which elects 120 members to the unicameral *Knesset* (parliament). All contending political parties must get 750 signatures from eligible voters before they can submit their lists, numbering up to 120 candidates. Once the list has been made, no independent candidates are able to get on the ballot as they can in some other states, including Denmark and Finland. Even the order in which the candidates appear on the list cannot be changed. At the polling station, the voter selects the ballot of his or her party as is, and deposits it in the ballot box. Each party is entitled to a number of seats in the *Knesset* according to its percentage of total popular vote. In Israel's system it is the party, rather than individual candidates, that is the primary attraction of voter support. The voter knows what the ideological position of each party is and that only the most experienced and influential candidates of those on the party list will occupy the seats the party is awarded on the basis of proportional representation.

> FACTFILE   In Ontario's proposed mixed-member proportional system, which was ultimately defeated in 2007, political parties would have nominated candidates as "List Members" before the election, and if they received more than 3 percent of the votes, they would have been elected to the provincial legislature.

Another variation of the party-list system is to give the voter some choice among the party's candidates. The voter may decide not to alter the party list and to vote for it in its entirety, or may move preferred candidates to the top of the party list. When a majority of voters indicates preference for certain candidates other than those originally listed by the party, the seats won by the party are allocated according to popular preference. Belgium, Denmark, and the Netherlands permit voters to indicate their preferences for only one candidate; Norway and Sweden permit voters to choose up to four candidates.

The final variation in the party-list system gives voters complete freedom to choose among candidates running in a multi-member constituency. The voter has as many votes as there are seats to be filled in the constituency. He or she may choose to expend all those votes on one particular candidate, or place one vote for several different candidates. The voter may also vote for candidates from different party lists. When the votes are totalled, each party is allocated seats in proportion to the total votes for all lists. This system is used in Switzerland and Finland.

The Single Transferable Vote

> FACTFILE   In 2007, federal legislation was passed to fix election dates for the House of Commons every four years in October, but the Prime Minister can still ask for a dissolution of Parliament and opposition parties can still defeat a government at their discretion.

The **single transferable vote** is a system of balloting that combines the principle that voters should have maximum choice of the candidates with a formula that guarantees all votes will be used to select representatives. Voters in multi-member constituencies indicate their preferences by writing numbers in the boxes beside the names of the candidates. A quota is established for each constituency to determine the minimum number of votes a candidate must have to be declared elected. The *Droop quota* is often employed. This quota (Q) is derived by dividing the total number of votes cast (V) by the number of seats to be filled (S) plus one, and adding one to the result:

$$Q = \frac{V}{S+1} + 1$$

Thus, in a three-member constituency with 100 000 votes cast, the quota would be 25 001. Initially, the ballots are sorted according to the first choices among voters. If no candidate obtains enough first-place votes to meet the quota, the candidate with the fewest first-place votes is eliminated. His or her ballots are then *transferred* to the candidates who received the largest number of first-, second-, and third-choice votes, but who may not have had enough votes to satisfy the quota. Eventually, the quota is satisfied by the single transfer of votes from eliminated candidates. This system is used in the Australian Senate, in the Northern Ireland Senate of Ulster, in Malta, and in other states.

Another commonly used quota is the *Hare quota*, named after Thomas Hare, a Victorian lawyer and associate of John Stuart Mill. This quota (Q) is derived by simply dividing the total number of votes cast (V) by the number of seats to be filled (S):

$$Q = \frac{V}{S}$$

Seats are allocated on the basis of a system that uses the largest remainder from the votes cast for a party. For example, in a four-member constituency where 20 000 votes have been cast, the quota would be 5000 (Table 11.4). Only two of the four parties (A&B) succeeded in surpassing the quota of 5000; thus, each are directly entitled to receive one seat. But under the largest remainder system, the third seat also goes to party A and the fourth seat to party C.

A nineteenth century Belgian lawyer, Victor D'Hondt, devised a system that divides each party's votes by successive divisors, and then allocates the seats in descending order of quotients (Table 11.5). The first seat will go to party A, the second to party B, the third to party A, and the fourth to party B.

CANADA'S ELECTORAL PROCESS

After the governor general dissolves a parliament on the request of the prime minister, the machinery for administering a federal election in Canada is put in motion. The Cabinet (Governor-in-Council) instructs the Chief Electoral Officer to issue writs of election to the returning officer in every federal riding in Canada. Returning officers are responsible for appointing deputy returning officers to the subdivisions in every riding, for receiving the nomination of the candidates, and for authorizing the printing of ballots.

To fill a vacant seat in a by-election, the Speaker of the House of Commons issues a Speaker's warrant. Within 180 days the governor-in-council sets the date of the by-election and the Chief Electoral Officer issues a writ directing the

Table 11.4	Four-member constituency, 20 000 votes cast Hare Quota: 5000					
Party	*Votes*	*Quota*	*Seats*	*Remainder*	*Seats*	*Total Seats*
A	8200	5000	1	3200	1	2
B	6100	5000	1	1100	0	1
C	3000	—	0	3000	1	1
D	2700	—	0	2700	0	0
Total	20 000		2		2	4

Table 11.5	Four-member constituency, 20 000 votes cast Division by D'Hondt divisors				
Party	*Votes*	*Divisor: 1*	*Divisor: 2*	*Divisor: 3*	*Total Seats*
A	8200	8200(1)	4100(3)	2733	2
B	6100	6100(2)	3050(4)	2033	2
C	3000	3000	1500	1000	0
D	2700	2700	1350	900	0
Total	**20 000**				**4**

returning officer in the designated electoral district to hold a by-election.

The 1997 federal election was the first to feature a *permanent voters list*—a national Register of Electors. The automated register holds data on Canadian citizens 18 or older who are eligible to vote. The register is used to produce preliminary lists for every federal election, reducing the election period by 23 percent, from 47 to 36 days. The provinces, territories, and municipalities can sign data-sharing agreements with Elections Canada to use the register's permanent list of electors for elections they hold at considerable cost-savings, because it eliminates the need for enumeration every time an election is called. The Register is updated with data from Canada Revenue Agency, Citizenship and Immigration Canada, provincial and territorial registrars of motor-vehicle and vital statistics, and provincial electoral agencies.

FACTFILE   Returning officers organize the election in each electoral district and are appointed by Governor-in-Council to report to the Chief Electoral Officer, who, in turn, reports directly to Parliament.

The returning officer designates the location of polling stations (divisions) each containing at least 350 voters in each riding. At these stations,

a deputy returning officer and a poll clerk watch over the polling process under the scrutiny of two agents representing each candidate. The voter is given a ballot on which are the names of the candidates running for office, two detachable serial numbers on the back, and the initials of the deputy returning officer (see Figure 11.1). For purposes of verification, the deputy returning officer tears off the first identical serial number.

After the voter has marked an "X" beside the name of the preferred candidate (in the voting booth), he or she folds the ballot paper so that the initials and the remaining serial number on the back can be read without unfolding it. The ballot is then handed back to the deputy returning officer, who confirms, by verifying the initials and the remaining serial number, that it is the same ballot paper given to the voter. If it is the same, the deputy returning officer then detaches the other identical serial number and deposits the ballot in the box. When the polls are closed, the ballots are counted by each returning officer in front of a poll clerk and the party scrutineers. The ballots are locked in the ballot box and given to the returning officer, who issues a declaration of election in favour of the winner. If there is a tie, the returning officer may cast the deciding vote after a judicial recount in favour of one of the candidates.

All candidates for election to the House of Commons must be Canadian citizens, 18 years of age or older. In order to file nomination papers, a candidate must be endorsed by 100 other electors (50 signatures suffice in certain sparsely populated electoral districts) and must provide a $1,000 deposit to the returning officer for the constituency. The deposit is refunded if expense returns are filed within the prescribed time limit and if the candidate obtains at least 15 percent of the ballots cast in the electoral district. Otherwise, the deposit is forfeited to the Crown.

General elections appear to be expensive political theatre in Canada. The Chief Electoral Officer's requirements for staff and supplies amounted to an estimated $291 million for the 2008 election. About 30 percent of the cost of the election is spent on the operation of polling stations and the printing of ballots. Then there are the fees and allowances paid to returning officers and election clerks. Added to these are headquarters expenses, cost of postage, wages, and extra staff, and special voting for the Armed Forces and the public-service electors (such as embassy staffs) overseas.

Figure 11.1   **Sample ballot**

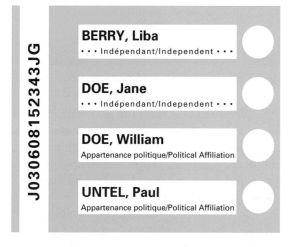

The final report of the Royal Commission on Electoral Reform and Party Financing was published in 1992, and contained many important recommendations to improve the operation of Canada's electoral system.[13] The implementation of some of these recommendations increased the general cost of staging a federal election. For example, the institution of the *special ballot* was introduced to replace **proxy voting** and voting in the office of the returning officer. The special ballot serves electors in the Canadian Forces; electors, their dependants, and spouses absent from Canada; federal or provincial public-service electors posted outside Canada; electors posted to an international organization; inmates serving sentences of less than two years; and electors residing in Canada who are unable to vote in their electoral districts.

> **FACTFILE**   During the nineteenth century, the polls stayed open for days, sometimes weeks, where candidates delivered their speeches from what are even today called hustings—high platforms erected near polling places.

Do Canadian elections really cost too much? We can compare the cost of Canada's federal elections to the cost of national elections held in other electoral systems. Actually, compared with the United States, Ireland, Israel, and Germany, the cost to each elector of a Canadian federal election is quite high.

Canada's electoral system is one of the largest in the world and carries a relatively high per-voter cost (about $11.43) as a result. However, there is always the possibility of improving a system that works well most of the time. Some shortcomings, such as human error, are unavoidable but others are correctable.

Referendums in Canada

In Canada, federal referendums are held under the *Referendum Act*. According to the Act, the government submits the text of the question (or questions) to each party that has 12 or more members in the House of Commons. A cabinet minister gives notice of a motion to approve the referendum question in the House of Commons within three days. Provinces may also stage referendums according to rules they establish in their provincial legislatures.

During this time, the motion is considered by the House for a maximum of three days and, if adopted, is sent to the Senate, which has three days to vote on it.

> **FACTFILE** In 2005, British Columbia and Prince Edward Island held referendums on whether to adopt an alternative voting system, involving proportional representation (PR). Neither passed, but BC promised another such vote on the same topic in 2009. Ontario held a similar referendum in October of 2007.

If the motion is approved by Parliament, the Governor-in-Council has 45 days to proclaim the referendum. As soon as the proclamation is issued, the Chief Electoral Officer issues writs to the appropriate returning officers, instructing them to conduct a referendum.

The question must be issued in both official languages and in selected Aboriginal languages. Polling day for a referendum is no earlier than the thirty-sixth day after the writs are issued. Electors vote by making a clear mark in the circle beside the word "yes" or "no" on the ballot.

CANADA'S ELECTION 2008

Campaign 2008

As in previous election campaigns, most of the party leaders tried to put forward newer, more refined images of their leadership styles. Prime Minister Harper portrayed himself as a less aloof, family-oriented politician who would stay the course on policy and leadership strategy; Jack Layton jumped ahead and boldly asked Canadians to make him

prime minister; Stephane Dion tried to inject more visual energy into his somber professorial image; and the newest contender, Elizabeth May, projected herself as an informed political competitor with a fighting spirit that is essential in Parliament. Gilles Duceppe kept his former image as a strong debater and a defender of Quebec interests.

In recent years, campaigning has become an increasingly sophisticated art. Politicians enhance their fortunes by engaging **spin doctors**, using consultants, photo-ops, computer-generated mailings, and carefully crafted image-making exercises that rely on tracking polls and interviews with focus groups. Party campaign strategists spend millions of dollars to shoot TV commercials, hire marketing gurus, and conduct exhaustive coaching sessions for leaders' debates.

Election campaigns are complex events. They are filled with party blunders, negative ads, voter cynicism, and the confusion of a five-way political party race. Under these circumstances, a large portion of the electorate can remain undecided and unwilling to commit their support until they enter the voting booth.

> **FACTFILE** An important case in 2003, *Figueroa v. Canada* (Attorney General), struck down the previous requirement that parties must field 50 candidates before they can officially register with Elections Canada.

The Debates

Now a standard feature of federal and provincial elections, debates receive mixed reviews by analysts and have mixed effects on the electorate.[14] From the media's perspective, the debates have all the elements of a good political story: high emotion, conflict, competition, drama, well-known personalities, and the possibility of a "defining moment" during the election campaign.

It is a mistake to believe that election debates will produce a discussion of issues in the spirit of open-mindedness. Debates are not organized to convey

knowledge but rather to evoke emotion and conflict among participants. Debates affirm public support for a particular leader among decided voters. However, they can persuade undecided voters who want to support an apparent "winner" within the context of a debate on issues and policies.

When all is said and done, debating is not a prime ministerial skill that is essential for making executive decisions. Prime ministers are usually not hampered by the same time constraints they face in a structured debate. They have the advantage of time and expert advice as well as party support in the House of Commons to do their job.

Debates 2008

Both Liberal leader Stephane Dion and Green Party leader Elizabeth May did very well in the televised French- and English-language debates.

Dion went into the French debate needing to gain momentum lost at the beginning of his campaign. He wanted the voting public to give him a second look as a leader and potential prime minister. He forcefully attacked Stephen Harper on most issues of the campaign, especially the economy. Elizabeth May had to show that she and her Green Party were not just included in the debates as a democratic courtesy. She proved to be a formidable debater against Harper and Layton, chastising the Prime Minister for not yet releasing his platform and for inertia on the financial crisis.

NDP Leader Jack Layton mounted a persistent attack against Harper's economic policies, which he claimed, are out of touch with ordinary Canadians. He taunted Harper for wearing a sweater to change his image as a cold leader. Bloc Leader Gilles Duceppe scored some bull's-eyes

Crosscurrents   What's Wrong with Minority Governments, Anyway?

Is having a minority government at the federal level necessarily a bad thing? What can we expect from a political executive that is constantly threatened by sudden death? Is death row a good place from which to govern a complex country like Canada? Should we be concerned about the capabilities of a government that does not hold either a majority of popular support or a majority of seats in the House of Commons?

Political scientists are concerned about any government that is not able to attract a "popular majority." However, they are not as concerned about minority governments, which are formed with fewer than a majority of seats in the House of Commons or in a provincial legislature. The key question to ask is, does the popular vote coincide with legislative representation?

Very few governments in Canadian history have been formed with a majority of the electorate's support (exceptions are Diefenbaker in 1958 and Mulroney in 1984). All other federal governments have governed us with legislative majorities where most Canadians didn't vote for the governing party, their candidates, or their policies. That happened for 67 years in the twentieth century and longer than 4 years in this century. We have been governed by what journalist Jeffrey Simpson calls a "friendly dictatorship."

Between 1867 (Confederation) and 2008, there have been 11 minority governments at the federal level in Canada: 1921–1925 (King); 1925–1926 (King); 1926 (Meighen); 1957–1958 (Diefenbaker); 1962–1963 (Diefenbaker); 1963–1965 (Pearson); 1965–1968 (Pearson); 1972–1974 (Trudeau); 1979–1980 (Clark); 2004 (Martin); and 2006 and 2008 (Harper).

Six of these governments were Liberal minority governments. Five of these governments proved to be relatively stable, lasting more than two years, with the prime minister, not the opposition, deciding when the next election would be called. These minority governments sought and found partners among the opposition parties for support to sustain them with the "confidence" of the House of Commons. They gave us good public policy: for example, the Canada Pension Plan, medicare, and other benefits befitting Canada as one of the best places in the world to live.

Historically, minority governments have tilted to the left to resuscitate their weakened legislative position. Their willingness to "dance with the one what brought ya" has given Canadians consultative, fair, and predictable government throughout the tenure of many minority governments in the past. In most of the previous Liberal minority governments, agreement between the government and the willing partner(s) was reached before any bill was introduced. This same strategy continued throughout the Harper minority governments of 2006 and 2008.

So, what are the advantages of a minority government? First, the government must be more compromising and considerate of the opposition-party platforms, or it will fall. Second, the apparent arrogance and righteousness of government is replaced by a healthy survival instinct. Politicians are nervous every day the House sits. Attendance improves, as does the need to listen to the electorate between elections. Politicians are more accessible to those who voted for them. Third, the voters get another chance to reaffirm their demands.

on Harper for calling the election when his fixed election law had another year of governing in store. He also got Harper to admit that he was wrong to support the invasion of Iraq before he became prime minister. Duceppe's strategy was to reach undecided Quebec voters and to stem the possibility that the Conservatives could increase their support base in that province.

As the frontrunner in the election campaign, Harper had the disadvantage of being attacked from all sides in the debates. The opposition leaders wanted to show that Harper sounded complacent about the economy and job losses. They succeeded in making Harper look less engaged and aloof.

The leaders' debates touched on many issues considered important to Canadians. But the war in Afghanistan received little attention, although Canadian soldiers are engaged in their biggest combat mission since the Korean War. Health care and post-secondary education were also generally overlooked. Instead, the economy overtook much of the debates as the leaders grappled with the impending consequences of a global economic meltdown. The environment was also a significant issue, with the Green Party's platform and the "greenshift" policy of the Liberals attracting much debate.

The quality of the 2008 debates was improved over previous debates because shouting matches (which had erupted in previous debates) were prevented by the moderators. And as in the debates of recent years, no leader was able to fire the magic bullet to fatally wound any of the other contenders' campaigns.

The Results

Election 2008 ended with a predictable result: another Conservative minority government. Even though the Conservatives gained 19 seats, the party attracted 168 000 fewer votes than it did in the 2006 election. The Conservatives benefited from a lower voter turnout among Liberal supporters. In some ridings, the Green Party split the opposition to the Conservatives by attracting defecting Liberal and NDP voters. The Conservatives won 11 new seats in Ontario and increased their portion of the popular vote by 13 percent. But in Quebec, the Conservatives were unable to benefit from the drop in support for the Bloc Québécois. In British Columbia, however, the Conservatives made gains in popular support and the number of seats.

The Liberal vote softened significantly across the country except in Quebec, where Stephane Dion gained seats. The party's overall performance was disappointing. Because most Canadian elections are leadership-driven, much was riding on how Dion would connect with voters. As a party leader, he struggled to project himself as a future prime minister. Stephane Dion and John Turner share the dubious distinction of attracting the lowest Liberal vote; they were the only party leaders whose total number of seats was reduced. But the main difficulty faced by the Liberals in the campaign was selling the idea of the greenshift as both a tax reduction and a green policy. In competition with the Green Party, the Liberals lost votes and in the crossfire, the Conservatives gained support on the issue of taxation.

> FACTFILE   Even though there have been some exceptions, as with Harper's government of 33 months, minority governments in Canada are usually short-lived—surviving an average of about 18 months between elections—compared with an average of 4 years for majority governments.

Stephen Harper handed Gilles Duceppe the issues he needed to retain the strength of the Bloc Québécois when so many were predicting the demise of Duceppe's party. Harper's cuts to the arts were portrayed as an attack on Quebec's culture by an Anglo government. It was the policy wedge that Duceppe injected into his argument that only the Bloc can defend Quebec's cultural interests. Harper's get-tough approach to young offenders ran against the ground-level civility in Quebec communities and suggested that a Conservative government is a right-of-centre threat to Quebec social values.

Under Jack Layton's leadership, the NDP set high standards for itself—to win enough new seats for an NDP prime minister to lead the country. The party earned its success in Ontario, winning 5 additional seats for a provincial total of 17. But the anticipated victories in Quebec did not materialize. In Atlantic Canada, the NDP not only held their pre-election seats, they took a first-time, one-seat victory in Newfoundland. Even though the NDP was not able to match its historic high point of 43 seats in the 1980s, it increased its party standing to 37 seats from 29 in 2006.

The only party to increase its vote share in the face of declining voter turnout was the Green Party. Elizabeth May's campaign succeeded in growing the support base of the party by more than 270 000 votes. As party leader, May did not win her bid to unseat defence Minister Peter MacKay in her riding. But along the campaign trail, she raised the Green Party's profile to bring it national status. She nearly doubled her party's popular vote and drew many of her candidates into second place results against Conservatives and Liberals in various ridings across Canada.

ELECTIONS IN THE UNITED STATES

Like Canadian elections, American elections are dramatic events in national political life. With the possible exceptions of assassinations and public scandal, they command more attention from more people than any other political phenomenon. Thousands of candidates take part in the numerous elections that characterize the American political scene.

The excitement of elections and electioneering is not limited to campaigns for the Presidency. It is also experienced in the elections of governors. In addition, all members of the US House of Representatives and about one-third of senators are up for re-election every two years. Many state and local officials are elected in the years between federal elections. There are also numerous referendums held on school taxes, bond issues, state constitutional amendments, and other municipal questions.

Elections in the United States are controversial events, as the Presidential elections of 2000, 2004, and 2008 demonstrated. Candidates and their supporters put a lot of energy and money into a wide range of campaign activities. Presidential campaigns can begin a few months after a presidential election.[15] Many aspiring candidates posture to test the political waters before they declare their intentions for party nominations.

These nominations are won only after arduous and expensive presidential primary campaigns during which the candidates try to lure the delegates. In 2008, Barack Obama raised more than $400 million for his primary and Presidential campaigns; by contrast, John McCain raised around $100 million.

Throughout the campaign, speeches are made, issues are debated, images are projected, personalities are revealed, and voters finally choose their government decision makers. The electoral process is, therefore, critical for the recruitment of candidates and for the operation of the political system. Even though elections by no means determine what the US government does, they can have an enormous impact on public policy.

One very important aspect of US elections is that they occur regularly. Federal elections take place on the exact dates specified in the Constitution, regardless of convenience or partisan advantage. They have never been postponed. State and local elections, though governed by different constitutional calendars, are also held regularly, as are primary elections held by states to nominate candidates. The regularity of elections

Table 11.6	**Canadian election results by province**						

2008	*Number of seats*						
Province	*C*	*L*	*NDP*	*BQ*	*I*	*G*	*Total*
Nfld	0	6	1	0	0	0	7
PEI	1	3	0	0	0	0	4
NS	3	5	2	0	1	0	11
NB	6	3	1	0	0	0	10
Que	10	14	1	49	1	0	75
Ont	51	38	17	0	0	0	106
Man	9	1	4	0	0	0	14
Sask	13	1	0	0	0	0	14
Alta	27	0	1	0	0	0	28
BC	22	5	9	0	0	0	36
Yukon	0	1	0	0	0	0	1
NWT	0	0	1	0	0	0	1
Nunavut	1	0	0	0	0	0	1
							(308)

C:	Conservative	BQ:	Bloc Québécois
L:	Liberal	NDP:	New Democratic Party
I:	Independent	G:	Green

Source: Canada, Elections Canada, "Results by Provinces," 2008. For raw data, see www.elections.ca/scripts/resval. All calculations and adaptations rest solely with the author.

guarantees that public officeholders are accountable to their constituents.

Elections in the US are structured in another important way. Most election activities—filing for candidacy, selection of nominees, raising and spending money, and a host of campaign activities—are shaped and regulated by law. Many of these laws are state regulations; they vary somewhat from one state to another. The patterns that emerge provide a basis for the study of US electioneering practices.

Primaries

In the early years of the American republic, party nominees were chosen by the caucus, an informal meeting of leaders who selected a candidate to carry the party banner in the election. Presidential candidates were selected by caucuses of party senators and congresspersons. As the electorate expanded, so did the complexity of party organizations at the grassroots level.

FACTFILE   Barack Obama won 27 of the state Democratic primaries and caucuses held in the 2008 primary season. Hillary Clinton won 23 and tied Obama in Guam, a US territory.

The method of caucus selection gradually became inadequate, and **party conventions**, made up of delegates elected by local party organizations, were established to choose party nominees for president, vice-president, and other elected offices. The conventions greatly democratized the nominating process, but **party bosses** tended to control the conventions, especially between 1850 and 1900. Conventions of this period often were rigged and controlled by certain party factions. The reformers of the progressive era at the turn of the twentieth century demanded that nominations be made directly by the people, not by politicians or party organizers.

The mechanism for so doing was the *direct primary*. The primary, taken from the Latin word for "first," is the first election to take place within the party. Primary elections are the means of involving party followers in the nominating process. They are followed by a general election in which parties compete. The primaries held in about 40 states are *closed*, requiring voters to declare in advance that they are registered members of a particular party. Other primaries are *open*, and do not force partisan declarations; people can decide when they enter the voting booth on election day in which party's primary they will participate. Voters are given each party's primary ballot; they vote on one. Idaho, Michigan, Minnesota, Montana, North Dakota, Utah, Vermont, and Wisconsin have open primaries. Some states have a *runoff primary*: when no candidate gets a majority of the primary votes, there is a runoff between the two candidates with the most votes. Two states, Alaska and Washington, provide a variant of the open primary called a *blanket primary*, which permits a voter to mark a ballot that lists the candidates for nomination of all the parties. Thus, the voter could help select the Democratic candidate for one office and the Republican candidate for another.

> FACTFILE   Only 17 US states held presidential primaries in 1968, compared with 32 in 1992, 42 in 1996, 44 in 2004, and 50 in 2008.

The South was the first region of the United States to institute the direct primary. However, its purpose was to prevent a coalition of poor blacks and poor whites from presenting their candidates for public office. By appealing to racism, dominant economic groups aligned with rural whites to sustain one-party domination in the region. In contrast, the political structure of the urban northeast was characterized by sharp competition between the parties.

The primary system has greatly influenced the structure of party competition and the outcome of presidential elections in the United States.[16] When they were first used in many states, it was widely believed the primaries would be a more democratic way to nominate candidates because they involve many more people than the handful who participate in conventions or caucuses. Later, primary elections were formed to involve party followers in the nomination process. But today the voters in primary elections are far from a simple cross-section of the population. Usually older, wealthier, and better educated, they tend to be more politically aware and ideologically conscious than people who vote only in general elections. Therefore, primaries retain an elitist character and so defy the democratic assumptions of most Americans.

The primary system today is confusing because each state has its own rules for presidential primaries. The variations are considerable and can have extraordinary consequences for the fortunes of presidential candidates. Because of the many issues in each state, candidates find it difficult to enunciate national policies. In New England, candidates usually must talk about the price of heating oil or the fishery. In New York, candidates must cultivate the support of Jews, African-Americans, and Italians in their concentrated urban constituencies, to the exclusion of other groups, such as farmers. In Texas and California, they court Hispanic voters and those involved in the oil industry. In the farm and industrial states, candidates must woo farmers whose needs conflict with those of steelworkers in Ohio and Pennsylvania.

Unquestionably, the primary permits voter participation in the selection of candidates for parties and independents. It permits unknowns to compete for office, and it gives candidates opposed to the party leadership a chance to win. Also, the primary greatly emphasizes image and personality and enhances the power of money and the media. In these ways, it has contributed both to democracy and to demagogy in American party politics.

National Conventions

Conventions are the next step in the process of selecting a presidential candidate. Unlike in Canada, where conventions actually choose the party's candidate, most conventions in the US tend to ratify the choice of the candidate who has succeeded in gaining the most committed delegates during the primaries. Even before the convention meets, the leading candidate usually has enough delegate votes to remove any doubt about the outcome.

Delegates to the presidential nominating convention are selected in a variety of ways. In some states, delegates are bound to the candidate winning the primary election, while in other states delegates can exercise their own discretion about voting at the national convention for the winner of the state primary. In yet other states, delegates are selected by state party committees. Few would argue that making sense of the bewildering array of primaries and caucuses to determine candidates for presidential conventions in the United States is easy.

Conventions perform other important functions in addition to the glamorous selection of a presidential candidate. They are the supreme governing bodies of their respective parties. They formulate rules for the parties and write the platforms. All of this is done in less than a week by several thousand people, most of whom do not know each other and, in all likelihood, will never meet again.

The Committee on Credentials works out conflicts that arise between rival groups of delegates from the same state or between rival groups pledged to different candidates. The Platform Committee works hard to placate all factions in the party and attempts to put together a statement of national party policies.

Conventions are also forums for keynote speakers. These orations are stylized political spectacles in which the speaker points to his or her party's achievements, views with alarm the sinister plans of the rival party, and attempts to excite the delegates to a state of high emotion.

When all the candidates have been nominated, balloting begins. The roll of the states is called and the world watches to see where the delegates' support will go. Party politicians prefer to decide the contest on the first ballot, minimizing the danger of exposing party divisions and reducing the risk of the convention's choosing a dark horse nominee. At a crucial time, a switch in an important state can start a bandwagon effect. California is always an important state to watch because it combines the advantages of many votes with being called to the roll near the top of the alphabet. As soon as the nominee has received enough votes to win, it is customary for rivals to move that the nomination be unanimous.

The nomination for the vice-presidency is usually an anticlimax because it is left to the determination of the party leaders. The considerations marking the choice are the personal preferences of the presidential candidates, the number of political IOUs resulting from the campaign, and the observance of the political maxim to "balance the ticket."

By the end of September in a presidential election year, the campaign is in full swing, and the candidates spend 15 to 20 hours a day making speeches, shaking hands, travelling, and meeting with the media until the election in November.

Elections are won and lost by forces such as party identification and short-term forces such as the issues and the personal appeal of the candidates. The mass media have become a crucial factor in influencing major shifts in electoral support of the candidates. Party identification seems to have lost much of its power. Even though the characteristics of people identifying themselves as strong Democrats and strong Republicans have remained stable since the early 1950s, Americans are voting in more widely diverse ways for the president and for the people they choose to send to their bicameral Congress.

Election 2008

The eight years between the 2000 and 2008 presidential elections not only changed the presidency but also changed the world. The events of 9/11 tested President George W. Bush's judgment about global terrorism, national security, and the American economy in ways that perhaps no other single event since World War II had tested a US president. It also deeply divided the country, leading to one of the most negative election campaigns in American history.

The election of Barack Obama as the 44th president of the United States created many significant firsts in US electoral history. Having an African-American president and first lady in the White House changed the image of the American presidency in the United States and around the world.

The election campaign between Barack Obama and John McCain was competitive. During the campaign, Republican support softened in states that had strongly supported George W. Bush in the 2000 and 2004 elections. While he was able to hold onto many of the states that had supported Bush, McCain was unable to hold other states such as Florida, Virginia, Indiana, Colorado, and New Mexico. Although Obama lacked the experience of his opponent, he promised to exercise diplomacy first instead of hard power and to address America's economic problems from the ground up, not from the top down.

Obama's election fulfilled a dream not only of Barack Obama, but also of Martin Luther King Jr. and many involved in the civil rights movement. Race has been the most visible scar of the American republic, and the lingering presence of racism has existed throughout US history. Obama's election brings the idea that all are created equal closer to reality at the highest levels of government.

> **FACTFILE**   The US Constitution says only that presidential powers and duties shall devolve on the vice president if the president dies, resigns, or cannot execute them.

No other officeholder in the United States has the same visibility, global recognition, prestige, and opportunity to speak to American voters on the issues. Most experts agree that the strongest presidents have ruled in difficult times. They have acted decisively and expanded presidential power to perform certain functions.

Presidential greatness is often discussed but is hard to define. All of the "greats," such as Washington, Lincoln, and Franklin Roosevelt, brought about desirable progress and guided the United States successfully through crises. Both George W. Bush and Barack Obama will be judged by these standards.

Chapter Summary

Elections are the events by which qualified citizens cast votes for candidates to make public decisions and enact laws on their behalf. Today, elections may or may not be conducted in democratic environments. In constitutional democracies, elections are the primary vehicles through which citizens can choose leaders and influence policies. Regular elections ensure that Canadians continue to be represented by candidates of their choice.

In dictatorial states, elections are staged as a political ritual whereby rulers seek to certify their political powers. Most states, however, whether democracies or dictatorships, stage elections. Some states make voting compulsory, as in Belgium, the Netherlands, and

Australia. All states place certain voting restrictions on age, residence, and registration.

In a democracy, elections perform certain social and political functions: they recruit political leadership; they enable us to change political leaders or retain the ones we have (political succession); they provide us with a self-adjusting mechanism (homeostasis) for social change, whereby society can correct its direction and vision; and they teach us about politics and government (political socialization).

One key question political scientists ask is whether our electoral system is capable of producing effective government and effective opposition. Do our election rules give all of the various voices in our political system a point of access to the decision-making institutions of government?

Political scientists divide electoral systems into *majority systems* and systems of *proportional representation* (PR). Majority systems are designed to produce either a plurality (one or more votes than any other opponent) or an absolute majority, whereby the winner needs at least 50 percent plus one of all the popular votes cast in a particular constituency.

In Canada, the plurality rule rarely produces a government that has the support of the majority of popular votes cast by the electorate.

The application of the rule of proportional representation is an attempt to give legislative expression to the dispersion of votes (majority and minority) as they are cast in a democratic electoral system.

In the United States, primary elections are preliminary contests in which a party picks delegates to a party convention or its candidates for public office.

Discussion Questions

1. Exercising the vote is one of the most basic rights of political participation. Is the vote of a single individual a powerful political tool? What can be said about the percentage of voter turnout in national elections for Canada and the United States?

2. What is an electoral system? Discuss the role of an electoral system in determining the outcome of an election. How does the single-member district with plurality affect Canada's party system? How would the use of proportional representation change the electoral performance of Canada's political parties? Should Canadians change their electoral system for a more representative and proportional one?

3. Outline the process unleashed when an election is staged in Canada. If a federal election were called today, who do you think would win and why? What about a provincial election?

4. Identify and discuss the advantages and disadvantages of the US primary system as a means of nominating candidates to elective office. Do you believe the advantages outweigh the disadvantages? Why or why not?

5. Do you believe televised debates between and among leadership candidates sway election outcomes in Canada and the United States? Which group of voters is most likely to be persuaded by debates? Are you a voter who observes debates before deciding which party or leader to support?

12

Analyzing the Global System

After reading this chapter, you will be able to:

- understand the scope of the global community and define the international system

- distinguish the international system from the global system

- identify the components of these systems and discuss how they are interrelated

- classify international organizations by purpose and function

- recount the development of the United Nations and outline what each of the major organs does

- describe the role and purpose of other international organizations, such as NATO, the WTO, and the Organization of American States

- define and describe the role of multinational corporations and non-governmental organizations on the development of the international system

- explain the presence and operation of transnational groups on the dynamics of the international system

- discuss the directions towards which the international community appears to be moving

- describe the role of Canada in global affairs

- identify the advantages and disadvantages of the North American Free Trade Agreement

• • • •

WHAT IS THE GLOBAL SYSTEM?

Think of the world as an economic and political community made up of state and non-state actors.[1] Today, this global community is complex and interdependent. The actions of one actor on any number of participants can touch and affect the lives of people anywhere.

Consider the following information:

- About $75 trillion is annually contributed to the world's economy by 212 independent nation-states.

- The United Nations, which is the only international organization (IO) with a global mandate, has predicted a food crisis of unprecedented proportion as 100 million additional people around the world are unable to buy enough food to avoid malnutrition and starvation.

- By 2008, non-governmental organizations (NGOs) operating in Canada were supporting 5000 development projects in more than 100 countries.

- About 300 multinational corporations (MNCs) control over 30 percent of the financial resources of the planet.

- Al Qaeda, the terrorist organization responsible for 9/11, includes Canada on its list of countries targeted for future attack.

- Individuals and organizations continue to work tirelessly to stop terrorism and global violence. For example, Peter Lown and Yevgeny Chazov, co-founders of International Physicians for the Prevention of Nuclear War, have affected the international system by their will and energies to work for peace.

The above examples serve to identify the *six* types of actors in the contemporary global system: states, international organizations, non-governmental organizations, multinational corporations, transnational groups, and individuals. The global system embraces all those forces (natural and human-made) that have an impact on the survivability of humankind. The international system comprises all those decisions, institutions, laws, and events that occur within the context of the nation-state and associations of nation-states.

Most present-day students of global politics are aware that, in addition to nation-states, the global political system consists of many autonomous actors interacting in patterned ways to influence the character of the system.[2] While still accepting the principal role played by states, it is no longer possible to ignore the presence of non-state actors and the growing influence they have on global events. Governments are aware they cannot solve the world's problems alone, and they recognize the need for a higher level of international co-operation, involving many different kinds of organizations.

Nation-States

The predominant actors of the international system are sovereign and independent states. On close examination, the international system reflects their behaviour and decisions. Nation-states create the rules of the system: they trade, aid, and invest with each other; they form international organizations; they host multinational corporations; they exchange diplomats; their citizens interact with foreign nationals; and they sign treaties and go to war.

FACTFILE   159 of the world's 212 nation-states are classified as younger nation-states because they were established during the twentieth century. Only 16, including the United States, were founded before the nineteenth century.

In this century, the viability of the nation-state has been challenged by many factors. The destructive power of contemporary weapons, the spectre of terrorism, the interdependence of the global economy, the international character of environmental pollution, energy conservation and climate change, the globalization of the mass media—all of these challenge the capacity of individual sovereign states to survive as independent autonomous members in the international system.

The nation-state, as it first evolved, was a response to challenges that were beyond the problem-solving capacity of small principalities and kingdoms. The state is not likely to wither away in the face of these challenges, but it may have to surrender more of its autonomous decision-making capacities to supranational institutions.

The 27-member *European Union* (EU) is a regional approach to trade and political and economic integration. With a 626-member, directly elected European Parliament, a system of courts, an EU Ombuds, a Common Agricultural Policy (CAP), and a European Monetary System (EMS), the EU is committed to completing the integration of goods and services. Other supranational efforts have begun in Central and South America, as well as in the Caribbean. Likewise, the proliferation of multinational corporations such as Exxon Corporation, ITT Corporation, and International Business Machines (IBM) has created new international approaches to trade, employment, and finance.

The predominance of the state is also threatened internally by decentralizing tendencies. As large centralized bureaucracies, modern states are domestically pressured to respond to the special needs of certain regions and groups. The need to efficiently manage national resources and to respond to language, religious, and minority rights can weaken the traditional sovereign preserves of national governments and their state bureaucracies. For people to accomplish their purposes, they have had to form even larger political and economic associations. The modern nation-state as we know it, with its strong tendency toward autonomy and

nationalism, is required to accommodate these new demands for international co-operation.

International Organizations

International organizations are unique constructs within the world community. They are formed solely on the consent of states, groups of non-governmental organizations (NGOs), and the private associations of individuals with transnational goals. Once formed, international organizations take on a life of their own, establishing a global presence greater than the sum of their parts. They perform a multiplicity of functions that give the international system rules, structures, and interdependence. These functions involve so many things: **collective security**, conferences, global and regional research, cultural ties, diplomacy, international administration, international economic co-operation, international law, international social co-operation, international trade, peaceful settlement of disputes, scientific exchanges, world business, world communications, and world travel.

All international organizations establish permanent organizations staffed by international civil servants whose ideas and attitudes transcend national interests. The frequent interactions of these people gradually build attitudes and customs that foster an ideology of internationalism.

International Governmental Organizations (IGOs)

International governmental organizations are voluntary associations of two or more sovereign states that meet regularly and have full-time staffs. IGOs may be described according to their size of membership or the scope of their goals. Only one organization, the United Nations, approaches global membership, with 192 states. Regional organizations, such as the Organization

Table 12.1	**Principal multi-purpose IGOs**	
Name	*Date Formed*	*Membership 2008*
African Union	2002	53
Organization of American States (OAS)	1948	35
Commonwealth	1926	53
Council of Europe	1949	47
The Andean Community	1969	4
Association of Southeast Asian Nations (ASEAN)	1967	10
League of Arab States	1945	22

Source: Barry Turner, The Statesman's Yearbook *(New York: Palgrave Macmillan, 2008).*

of American States (OAS), the African Union (established in 2002), and the Association of Southeast Asian Nations (ASEAN), are multi-purpose IGOs of limited memberships based on the geographical proximity of states sharing common interests (Table 12.1).

Many IGOs are formed as voluntary associations of independent states from various regions of the world that have some common purpose for co-operating with one another. For example, as of 2003, the 53 members of the Commonwealth of Nations are drawn from Africa, Asia, Europe, Oceania, and the western hemisphere. Once part of the British Empire, they freely co-operate and assist each other without formal agreements. Another example is the Organization of Petroleum Exporting Countries (OPEC), which is a functional IGO consisting of a group of 12 oil-exporting countries that formed an inter-governmental cartel to regulate the production, distribution, and pricing of oil (Table 12.2). A number of IGOs have a security orientation and collectively form a military alliance system for defence (Table 12.3).

At the turn of the twentieth century, fewer than 10 IGOs existed. By World War I, there were 50 IGOs. The rapid expansion of IGOs has taken place in the post–World War II era: from 1945 to the present, the number of IGOs grew from 90 to more than 400.[3] This represents the birth of an enormous number of international organizations in a very brief period of human history. The international system has become highly interactive and bureaucratized. What Marshall McLuhan described as the "global village" is under construction at the international level.

Why IGOs Multiply

There are several reasons for the continuous proliferation of international bodies at this time in human history. One is the realization in the minds of most national policy makers that no state acting alone can prevent war. Another is that a world composed of autonomous and nationalistic actors greatly enhances the possibility of violent conflict. The mass destructive powers of modern conventional and nuclear weapons have made war between any two states a global concern. No longer is it possible to isolate the destructive effects of contemporary warfare from all of humankind or from all living things on this planet.

FACTFILE In 1909, there were 37 IGOs and 176 NGOs. Today, the number of international organizations has ballooned to more than 400 IGOs and 5000 NGOs.

Table 12.2	Principal functional-regional IGOs		
Name		*Date Formed*	*Membership*
Asia-Pacific Economic Co-operation (APEC)		1989	21
Caribbean Community (CARICOM)		1973	20
Central American Common Market (CACM)		1960	6
Council for Technical Co-operation in South and Southeast Asia (Colombo Plan)		1950	25
European Atomic Energy Community (Euratum)		1958	15
European Free Trade Association (EFTA)		1960	4
European Union (EU)		1967	27
Mercado Comun del Sur (Mercosur)		1991	4
Organisation for Economic Co-operation and Development (OECD)		1961	31
Organization of Petroleum Exporting Countries (OPEC)		1960	12

Source: Barry Turner, The Stateman's Yearbook *(New York: Palgrave Macmillan, 2008).*

Yet another reason for the rapid growth of IGOs has been the great advances made in the technology of human communication. Instantaneous global telecommunications informs and alerts people about events in every corner of the world. Today, governments have immediate access to one another. The ability of diplomats and policy makers to travel long distances in short periods of time has been an impetus for governments to participate in international organizations

Table 12.3	Principal collective-security IGOs		
Name		*Date Formed*	*Membership*
North Atlantic Treaty Organization (NATO)		1949	26
Pacific Islands Forum		1971	17
Western European Union (WEU)		1954	10

Source: Barry Turner, The Statesman's Yearbook *(New York: Palgrave Macmillan, 2008).*

and to co-operate on solutions to international problems.

Other reasons for increasing the number of IGOs as actors in the international arena are global problems of poverty, starvation, underdevelopment, and disease. Governments have involved themselves in controlling these problems on a co-operative global level through the vehicles of international organizations. While **humanitarianism** may appear to be the main thrust behind the inclinations of governments to use international instruments to attack these problems, many governments are also motivated by practical expediency, as when developed economies apply their aid programs to developing economies to create new markets for their manufacturing and service sectors.

Yet another factor contributing to the widespread recognition that multinational organizations are needed to address complex human problems of great magnitude, is the expansion of the international civil service. By 2008, more than 83 000 people worldwide were employed on a full-time basis by IGOs. They administer the resolutions and international policies of global and regional institutions. International civil servants tackle the world's pressing problems with solutions that rise above national perspectives. They are much less inclined to accept the narrow nationalistic approaches to international difficulties than are the bureaucrats of autonomous governments.

THE UNITED NATIONS

The United Nations (UN) is the world's first IGO to gain the membership of nearly 90 percent of the states in the international community.[4] Membership is open to all independent nation-states on recommendation of the Security Council. By 2008, there were 192 member states, with most new members entering as former republics of the Soviet Union. It is the most representative intergovernmental forum ever organized by humankind. No other public institution in history has been mandated to accumulate and correlate information about every kind of global concern. The United Nations and its related agencies (see Figure 12.1) gather data on the frequency of international co-operation and **conflict**; on human rights; on variations in the key indicators of the international economic system (such as trade, investment, and development assistance); on world population trends; on the global demography of disease; on global ecology; and on food, energy, and development. In short, the world is a United Nations study.

> FACTFILE   Switzerland, which maintains strict neutrality in world affairs, voted in 2002 to join the United Nations.

The United Nations owns 20 acres of land donated by John Rockefeller for use as international territory. As an organization, the United Nations makes its own rules, has its own flag, and operates its own police force. It also owns a multilingual radio station, a post office, and a stamp mint. It uses six official languages: Arabic, Chinese (Standard Mandarin), English, French, Russian, and Spanish. The United Nations is not a **supranational organization**, nor is it a **world government**. There are no citizens, taxes, or regular army. It is a voluntary association of sovereign independent states for the purpose of dialogue to keep peace in the world. It serves as the only IGO capable of global decision making. Through its organizations, it attempts to foster peaceful relations among states and to promote economic equality and human rights for all people.

Security Council

The *Security Council* has the primary responsibility, under the Charter, for the maintenance of international peace and security. In general,

Figure 12.1   **Flow chart of the United Nations**

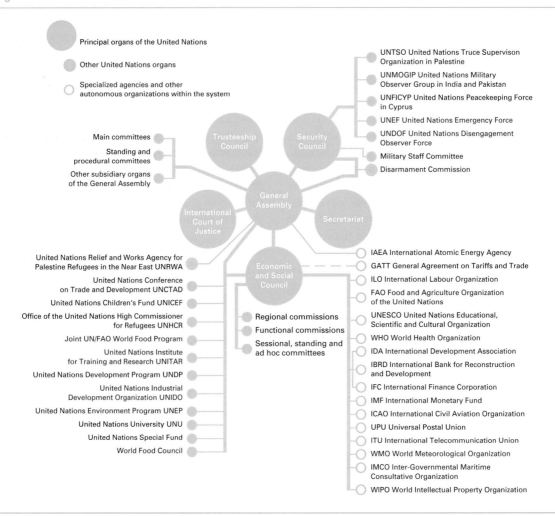

Principal organs of the United Nations

Other United Nations organs

Specialized agencies and other autonomous organizations within the system

Main committees

Standing and procedural committees

Other subsidiary organs of the General Assembly

Trusteeship Council

Security Council

UNTSO United Nations Truce Supervison Organization in Palestine

UNMOGIP United Nations Military Observer Group in India and Pakistan

UNFICYP United Nations Peacekeeping Force in Cyprus

UNEF United Nations Emergency Force

UNDOF United Nations Disengagement Observer Force

Military Staff Committee

Disarmament Commission

International Court of Justice

General Assembly

Secretariat

United Nations Relief and Works Agency for Palestine Refugees in the Near East UNRWA

United Nations Conference on Trade and Development UNCTAD

United Nations Children's Fund UNICEF

Office of the United Nations High Commissioner for Refugees UNHCR

Joint UN/FAO World Food Program

United Nations Institute for Training and Research UNITAR

United Nations Development Program UNDP

United Nations Industrial Development Organization UNIDO

United Nations Environment Program UNEP

United Nations University UNU

United Nations Special Fund

World Food Council

Economic and Social Council

Regional commissions

Functional commissions

Sessional, standing and ad hoc committees

IAEA International Atomic Energy Agency

GATT General Agreement on Tariffs and Trade

ILO International Labour Organization

FAO Food and Agriculture Organization of the United Nations

UNESCO United Nations Educational, Scientific and Cultural Organization

WHO World Health Organization

IDA International Development Association

IBRD International Bank for Reconstruction and Development

IFC International Finance Corporation

IMF International Monetary Fund

ICAO International Civil Aviation Organization

UPU Universal Postal Union

ITU International Telecommunication Union

WMO World Meteorological Organization

IMCO Inter-Governmental Maritime Consultative Organization

WIPO World Intellectual Property Organization

Source: United Nations flowchart © United Nations Secretariat. Reprinted by permission.

the council is charged with implementing the **peaceful settlement of disputes** and may consider any action viewed by its members as a threat to peace, a breach of peace, or an act of aggression subject to investigation. After investigating a dispute, the council is empowered to make recommendations for the peaceful resolution of conflict.

The Security Council consists of five permanent members (China,[5] France, Great Britain, Russia, and the United States) and 10 non-permanent members elected by the General Assembly for two-year terms. Each of the five permanent members can veto an action deliberated by the council. In order for the council to take an action against a violator of the charter, the five permanent members must agree on that action. In addition, a minimum of four non-permanent members must concur with the same action. Since 1945, Canada has been on the Security Council six times for two-year periods: 1948–1949; 1958–1959; 1967–1968; 1977–1978; 1988–1990; and 1998–2000.

General Assembly

The second principal organ of the United Nations is the *General Assembly*. This is the only body of the United Nations in which all member states are represented. Each of the 192 members has one vote. The General Assembly may discuss any question that falls within the scope of the United Nations Charter or that relates to the powers and functions of any other organ of the world forum. It may make recommendations to member states, as well as to the Security Council.

Decisions of the assembly have no binding legal force on governments, but they have a **quasi-legal** character because these decisions carry the weight of international opinion as expressed by its members. Three instruments are used by the General Assembly to formulate a consensus of world opinion.

The first is a General Assembly *declaration*: a broad statement of general principle on an important global concern. The Universal Declaration of Human Rights, passed in 1948, and the Political Declaration on HIV/AIDS (2006) are examples of such an instrument demonstrating world expectations.

A General Assembly *resolution* is another quasi-legal instrument of world opinion. Resolutions recommend that member-states follow a particular policy action, as when the body acknowledged the proclamation of the Palestinian state (1989). In the first 50 years of assembly business, the General Assembly has adopted countless resolutions and

declarations establishing the norms of international conduct.

Finally, a General Assembly *convention*, such as the Convention on the Rights of the Child (1990), is a legally binding instrument because it is a treaty requiring the ratification of signatory states that are then bound by its terms. Two types of conventions are used: multilateral treaties passed by the General Assembly and ratified by member states, and a United Nations treaty with a state, as when Egypt in 1956 signed a treaty with the UN to allow multinational peacekeeping forces to enter Egyptian territory.

The assembly also has assumed the power to conciliate international disputes and to make recommendations for collective measures against an aggressor. The **Uniting for Peace Resolution** of 1950 gives the assembly a backup role to the Security Council when that body is prevented from taking action by a permanent member's veto. A series of stalemates in the Security Council led to special emergency sessions of the General Assembly to deal with Afghanistan (1980), Palestine (1980 and 1982), Namibia (1981), the Occupied Arab Territories (1982), and Apartheid in South Africa (1989).

FACTFILE From 1955 to 2008 the United Nations targeted 65 resolutions at Israel to end the conflict with the Palestinians.

Canada is the only state in the world that has participated in some way in every peacekeeping operation of the United Nations system. Canada has participated in such operations in the Middle East, India/Pakistan, West New Guinea, Yemen, the Congo, Cyprus, and with UN peacekeeping forces in Haiti, Bosnia, Somalia, Rwanda, the Democratic Republic of the Congo, Kosovo, East Timor, Iraq, and Afghanistan. Canada also participated in non-UN peacekeeping activities in Indochina and Nigeria. Canada's major involvement in peacekeeping began with the establishment of the United Nations Emergency Force (UNEF), which was established after the Suez crisis in 1956. By 2008, Canada had contributed personnel to 26 peacekeeping missions since 1945, 14 of which are still in operation.

What Are Peacekeeping, Peacebuilding, and Peacemaking?

In its Charter role as a global institution dedicated to the peace and security of the planet, the United Nations has developed special instruments for securing international peace. They fall under the terms *peacekeeping*, *peacebuilding*, and *peacemaking*. The principal instrument used by the United Nations and some regional organizations in trying to control and prevent conflict is *peacekeeping* forces.

Ironically, peacekeeping is not mentioned in the United Nations Charter but has evolved as a major function of the global organization. Peacekeeping forces serve at the invitation of a host government and must leave if that government orders them out. Identified as UN *blue-helmet troops*, they are invited to mediate in conflict between or among states that have become destabilized.

In the past, peacekeeping forces have generally not been able to make peace—only to keep it. "Peacekeepers" actually perform two different roles: observing and keeping the peace. Observers are unarmed and are sent to a conflict area in small numbers simply to watch what happens and report back to the United Nations about what they observe. Because the UN is watching, the parties in conflict are less likely to break a ceasefire.

In 1992, UN Secretary General Boutros Boutros Ghali proposed to create the instrument of *peacemaking*, which he called "peace enforcement" units that would not only monitor a ceasefire but would enforce it if it broke down. These forces are more heavily armed because they may be required to weigh into battle on a rapid deployment basis. They are more able to respond within a few days on this basis, rather than within a few months as with some peacekeeping operations. Peacemaking has become more common since the 1990s, and is designed to impose peace usually to resolve internal domestic conflicts.

Peacebuilding is a term used to describe peacekeeping plus additional UN efforts to oversee the development of democratic activities. Prior to its military operations in 2003, the United States wanted the United Nations to play the role of peacebuilder in Iraq by supervising the writing of a democratic constitution, holding elections, and creating democratic decision-making institutions shortly thereafter. Peacebuilding encourages the use of democratic instruments that ultimately keep governments accountable to the will of the majority, who normally choose peaceful options in conflict resolution.

The Secretariat

The third major organ of the United Nations is the *Secretariat*. This is a body of international civil servants under the United Nations, numbering more than 50 000 people. In addition to the thousands who work in New York, the rest are dispersed in the Geneva office, as well as in the regional commissions operating in more than 130 states. The Secretariat organizes conferences, such as the United Nations Convention against Torture and Other Cruel, Inhuman or Degrading Treatment or Punishment (1999). The Secretariat is headed by a secretary general (Table 12.4), sometimes called the "president of the world." He or she (as yet, no woman has been secretary general) is nominated by the Security Council and approved by the General Assembly for a five-year (renewable) term.

The job of the secretary general is a complicated one that verges on the impossible. The

Table 12.4	Secretaries General of the United Nations, 1946–2008	
	Secretary General	*Years Served*
1st	Trygve Lie (Norway)	1946–53
2nd	Dag Hammarskjöld (Sweden)	1953–61
3rd	U Thant (Burma)	1961–71
4th	Kurt Waldheim (Austria)	1972–81
5th	Javier Pérez de Cuellar (Peru)	1982–91
6th	Boutros Boutros Ghali (Egypt)	1991–96
7th	Kofi Annan (Ghana)	1997–2007
8th	Ban Ki-Moon (South Korea)	2007–

Source: Table from www.un.org/sg/formersgs.stml. Secretaries General of the United Nations, 1946-2007.
© United Nations Secretariat. Reprinted by permission.

secretary presides over a budget of more than $3 billion; is the chief administrator for the United Nations and for all its specialized agencies; and is also accredited as a diplomat **plenipotentiary** (full powers) to the world in that the secretary is expected to bring parties in dispute to a peaceful settlement by means of the mediating and conciliating instruments at the disposal of the United Nations. The secretary general is held responsible for the professional actions of thousands of international civil servants and must work to keep their loyalties in the face of mounting criticism that the United Nations is an ineffective IGO. The personality and political style of the secretary general are crucial to the success of the United Nations as a credible world forum.

The Economic and Social Council

The fourth principal organ of the UN is the *Economic and Social Council* (ECOSOC). It was established at the insistence of the developing states that participated in the drafting of the United Nations Charter in San Francisco. They justifiably saw the Security Council as dominated by the great post-war powers and considered the General Assembly too unwieldy to promote the welfare of the smaller powers. The present-day importance of ECOSOC is seen in the dramatic enlargement of that body from 18 members to 27 after 1965, and to 54 members after the Charter amendment of 1971. All members are elected by a two-thirds vote of the General Assembly for three-year terms, with 18 elected each year.

ECOSOC conducts research on economic, educational, social, and cultural problems. It drafts conventions that, when adopted by the General Assembly and ratified by member-states, become international law. It co-ordinates the activities of most United Nations agencies. To assist in its operations, the council established six functional commissions (Human Rights, Narcotic Drugs, Population, Statistics, Status of Women, and Social Development). The council also administers five regional economic commissions: Economic Commission for Africa (ECA), Economic Commission for Europe (ECE), Economic Commission for

Latin America (ECLA), Economic and Social Commission for Asia and the Pacific (ESCAP), and the Economic Commission for Western Asia (ECWA).

Of the principal organs of the United Nations, ECOSOC is the most linked with all levels of the international community. By 2008, 753—or about 22 percent—of the NGOs operating in the United Nations member-states were listed on the ECOSOC roster, sending observers to its meetings, submitting written and oral statements to the council's commissions, and influencing the direction of its programs around the world.

Finally, an appreciation of the importance and complexity of ECOSOC's global influence is seen in its consultative role to a number of other United Nations bodies offering programs in the economic and social fields. These bodies include:

1. the United Nations Development Program (UNDP),
2. the United Nations Children's Fund (UNICEF),
3. the United Nations High Commissioner for Refugees (UNHCR),
4. the United Nations Conference on Trade and Development (UNCTAD),
5. the World Food Program, and
6. the United Nations University (UNU), which began operations in 1975 at its headquarters in Tokyo.

The Trusteeship Council

Another of the six principal organs is the United Nations *Trusteeship Council*. This body is also charged with the international supervision of trust territories. The membership of the council is composed of all trust-administering states, non-administering permanent members of the Security Council, and elective members drawn from the General Assembly. All the original trust territories had become independent or joined independent states by 1994; since 1994, it meets only on an extraordinary basis when its services are needed. This council suspended its operations following the independence of the Palau territory in the Pacific.

International Court of Justice

The sixth organ of the United Nations is the *International Court of Justice* (ICJ). The functions of this court are also discussed in Chapter 13.

The ICJ was founded in 1945 as the judicial arm of the United Nations to rule on disputes arising between states and to advise the UN on matters of international law. The ICJ has judged cases whose issues have ranged from fisheries to border disputes to nuclear testing. However, the ICJ has been the least productive organ of the United Nations: in four decades of existence, it has reviewed only about 100 cases (excluding advisory opinions), most of them concerning minor disputes, such as establishing boundaries or determining fishing rights. Less than a third of the members of the United Nations have accepted the compulsory jurisdiction of the court, demonstrating a lack of confidence on the part of most states in conflict to seek a legal remedy from such a highly visible and respected body. A number of cases are dropped from the ICJ by the parties. Some are settled out of court; the rest are removed because one party refuses to accept the ICJ's jurisdiction in the dispute.

As an international organization, the United Nations is more than the sum of its parts. Since its inception during World War II, the United Nations has come to be regarded as an autonomous international actor. Its members speak and react to a common theme as if the UN were an independent entity, expressing itself authoritatively through its various organizations. Not one of its members has the capacity, or even the will, to eradicate world problems. But as a global forum, each is made aware of the need to do so. The UN is an effort on the part of the community of states to concur on norms of international conduct to outlaw war and to reduce conflict. It provides for global **detente** through the peaceful settlement of international disputes.

So much has been expected of the United Nations. Many of these expectations were conceived when the UN was founded in 1945—to beat swords into plowshares, to change the ways its members behave, and to make the lions lie down with the lambs so there would be no more war.

In response to the daily human tragedy around the world, the United Nations must constantly reinvent itself. It has to learn how to move boldly and at the same time cautiously across the uncertain frontiers of the new world order.[6] There are bound to be disappointing moments along the way, in a world of risks and opportunities. Yet every day, the members of the United Nations get another chance to create the world of their Charter: a world of justice, human rights, peace and security, and a better life for all. It's a tall order. Many have said the United Nations is fragile, but it has been remarkably durable. Unlike its predecessor, the League of Nations, the United Nations is an international organization from which almost no state has departed.

OTHER INTERNATIONAL ORGANIZATIONS

The United Nations is the singular example of a broad-purpose world organization. All other IGOs neither approach global membership nor take the world perspective of the United Nations. Public international organizations with varying degrees of integration exist for collective security, economic advancement, and multi-purpose regional alliances. The United Nations Charter supports the formation of regional IGOs as institutions complementary to the goals of the UN.

NATO

Since 1949, the North Atlantic Treaty Organization (NATO) has functioned as a collective-security alliance of Western states against the perceived threat of communist aggression in the North Atlantic area.[7] Its 26 members form the largest and most highly organized international-defence system in the world.

All the **signatories** of the North Atlantic Treaty agree that "an armed attack against one or more of the parties to the treaty in Europe or North America shall be considered an attack against them all." This collective-security provision legally requires member-states to honour their commitments to take military action if aggression occurs against the **alliance**.

Collective security is supported by an extensive network of political and military structures designed to co-ordinate communications and decisions among members. The supreme governing organ of NATO is the *North Atlantic Council*, chaired by the secretary general of NATO in Brussels. The council consists of ministers of foreign affairs or defence and an ambassador from each of the NATO members. It meets at the ministerial level at least twice a year and at the ambassadorial level on a weekly basis. Its discussions and decisions flow from political/military matters, as well as from the financial and scientific aspects of defence planning.

Through the United Nations and other international organizations, the world has agreed to use the assets and experience of NATO to support international **peacekeeping operations**. It was NATO that provided the practical support for

UN peacekeeping efforts in Bosnia and Croatia, 1992–1995. With the signing of the Bosnian peace agreement in December 1995, NATO was charged with implementing peace through the NATO-led multinational Implementation Force. Since that time, NATO has also spearheaded the Partnership for Peace (PFP), a co-operative program of 27 members that agree to co-operate in defence budgeting, joint planning, joint military exercises, peacekeeping, search and rescue, and humanitarian operations.

FACTFILE In 2003, NATO assumed control of the International Security Force in Afghanistan (ISAF), marking the first time NATO led a mission outside of Europe.

In more than 50 years of existence, NATO has undergone stresses and strains in addition to a continuing consensus of support from its members. From time to time, European members have pushed to gain more control of the command structures of NATO, owing to the primacy of the United States and the often difficult defence relationships that member-states have with this nuclear superpower.

In the past, a number of members have asserted their independence: France, for example, withdrew in 1966. Canada reduced its NATO forces in Europe from 10 000 to 5000 in the early 1970s, but by the year 2007 had increased these numbers to 15 000. Greece withdrew its forces from NATO after Turkey's invasion of Cyprus in 1974, resuming full participation in 1980.

When the Warsaw Pact ceased to exist in 1991, NATO initiated a major review of its strategies on **nuclear deterrence**. Budget pressures and a changed geopolitical climate in Europe lessened the urgency to maintain such a formidable nuclear fortress in Europe. By the fall of 1991, NATO announced that all tactical nuclear weapons fired by artillery or short-range rockets would be removed from Europe. Despite disagreement on its future role, NATO still enjoys widespread support in Europe, as well as in North America, as an IGO essential for the collective security of its members.

Perspectives   The Globalization of Trade

Trade and trade issues predate the modern nation-state. The global economy actually began thousands of years ago when groups of people began to barter with other groups outside of their localities. This seemingly simple act of exchanging goods and services between and among societies created an economy greater than the sum of its parts. It was destined to become global.

From the start, trade engendered both cooperation and conflict among societies. Goods, services and currencies were exchanged, wealth was transferred, and labour was rewarded or threatened by competition. The ancient and medieval worlds faced trade issues requiring treaties to be signed, envoys to be exchanged, trade routes to be opened and leaders to negotiate solutions.

Significant trade across continents began in the sixteenth century during the so-called mercantilist period. Monarchs knew that trade made them wealthy and enhanced national power for them. They attempted to achieve "favourable" trade balances, whereby they would export more than they would import. In a world of little regulation, some states engaged in "predatory" practices, trying to create monopolies in foreign markets and establish colonies that could provide a wealth of natural and human resources.

The influential writings of Adam Smith (1723–1790) and David Ricardo (1772–1823) became popular among the emerging class of merchants. Smith called on governments to take a laissez-faire approach to their economies and trade. Ricardo stated his theory of **comparative advantage** and advocated that there should be free international market forces rather than **mercantilism**.

These liberal economic thinkers formed the ideological foundation for the rules of nineteenth-century trade. The industrial revolution greatly increased the amount and diversity of traded goods. But trade was not always voluntary or conducted for peaceful purposes. European states had colonies in Africa, Asia, India and Latin America. They often used force and violence to gain great advantage at the expense of colonies and weaker states. China and Japan were coerced into agreements that greatly benefited Europe and the United States well into the twentieth century.

World War I disrupted trade and spurred aggressive competition between and among economies. Later, the **Great Depression** fostered protectionist policies in the United States, Canada, and Europe to shield domestic industries from international competition. World War II ravaged the economies of Europe and Asia and distorted the growth of international trade.

The international response to the crisis of trade was met by creating the Bretton Woods System, named after the New Hampshire town where the planning took place. British economist John Maynard Keynes (1883–1946) called for a compromise on growing protectionism. He asked governments to liberalize their trade policies and to be open to multilateral negotiation in order to foster international economic stability. The Bretton Woods System created a new international monetary regime based on fixed exchange rates, which led to the General Agreement on Tariffs and Trade (GATT).

GATT would jumpstart a new approach to international trade in the twentieth century. It called on governments to reduce their tariffs on imports, to open their economies more to foreign competition, and to avoid discriminating against foreign producers and suppliers. Governments were urged to grant most-favored-nation status (MFN), whereby trade agreements would extend the same concessions to all members. GATT organized a series of "rounds": notably, the Kennedy Round (1962–1967); the Tokyo Round (1973–1979); and the Uruguay Round (1986–1993).

These rounds have led to agreements on reducing protectionist practices, eliminating non-tariff barriers and encouraging the free flow of goods and services across national orders. While many changes have occurred since World War II, the global economy is still evolving as a worldwide free-trade area. We are still far from a worldwide free-trade area.

The World Trade Organization (WTO)

Discussions to liberalize world trade policy began in 1943 among the Allies, leading to a new international trading order under a treaty called the

General Agreement on Tariffs and Trade (GATT) in 1947. The GATT was a provisional and limited agreement that established an international organization to promote freer world trade from its headquarters in Geneva, Switzerland.[8] The signatories of the GATT agreed to the **most-favoured-nation principle**, meaning that any favourable condition or privilege on trade given to one economy would automatically be extended to others.

> FACTFILE   In 1948, after a charter to create the International Trade Organization (ITO) was drafted in Havana to establish wide-ranging rules on trade, the US Congress rejected the charter because it believed the ITO would interfere in the formation of US internal economic policy.

In 1948, the GATT was institutionalized as an IGO, with a secretariat, a director general, and an administration to handle the work related to trade negotiations. By the early 1950s, the GATT had become the central international organization in the non-communist world committed to implementing a world-trading regime, and dedicated to the removal of trade barriers among members. On January 1, 1995, the GATT became the World Trade Organization (WTO). The previous GATT Secretariat now serves the WTO.

China and Taiwan are the most recent of the 144 members. The WTO's principal functions are dispute settlement and conference diplomacy. It uses expert panels to handle complaints about violations of its trade rules that cannot be resolved through more routine consultation procedures. Conference diplomacy is the instrument used to organize *rounds* of multilateral trade negotiations that look for ways to cut trade barriers and liberalize international trade. For example, the high point of trade co-operation in the GATT was the *Kennedy Round* of negotiations (named after US President John F. Kennedy), carried out from 1963 to 1967, which culminated in the removal of many tariffs that had become serious obstacles to trade among the major trading economies.

From 1967 on, pressures for trade **protectionism** and discrimination increased in North America, Europe, and Japan. Canada and the United States demanded changes in European and Japanese trade restrictions. By 1973, it was becoming clear that a new international economic order was emerging.

The *Tokyo Round*, which introduced the concept of a North–South dialogue in the GATT, took place from 1973 to 1979, resulting in some reduction of tariff and non-tariff barriers. These trade talks continued into the 1990s as the *Uruguay Round*, which negotiated the elimination of many technical barriers to trade. When the current GATT round was launched in Punta del Este, Uruguay, all members knew what was at issue. Either the GATT would dramatically expand its reach, or it would very probably fade into irrelevance. The most important new issues included in the Uruguay Round were services—a vast sector that embraces banking, insurance, telecommunications, construction, aviation, shipping, tourism, advertising, consultancy, and broadcasting.

> FACTFILE   The UN-affiliated International Labor Organization (ILO) estimates that more than 250 million children worldwide under the age of 14 work in "sweatshop" conditions, enduring low wages, dangerous duties, and abuse by employers.

Each round of GATT negotiations since World War II has cut tariffs worldwide from 40 percent to just 5 percent in the 2000s. Nevertheless, in place of tariffs, member states have found newer, less explicit ways to block trade under euphemisms such as "voluntary export restraints" and "orderly marketing arrangements." Many member states continue to subsidize agriculture, exempting farm trade from international trade law. Other economic sectors continue to be nurtured by the older instincts of protecting national economies from global influences and competition. But most of the world's trading economies are likely to continue to maintain a major stake in GATT if only because the WTO is the only global rules-based regime for trade.

The Organization of American States (OAS)

In many respects, the OAS, established in 1948, is the classic example of the type of multi-purpose regional organization endorsed by the Charter of the United Nations. The OAS is the most important IGO within the **inter-American system**. This hemispheric system now incorporates more than 100 permanent and ad hoc bodies, which include committees, institutes, academies, congresses, conventions, courts, economic associations, and treaties. In effect, a system of regional international relationships has developed since the early nineteenth century, based on the regular interaction and interdependence of the states of the western hemisphere.

Today, the OAS headquarters is in Washington, DC, where 35 regional states in the Americas meet to discuss regional economic, political, and military matters. Despite many invitations since the nineteenth century, Canada only joined the OAS in 1989, and now participates as a full member of the inter-American system.[9] In 1991, the OAS achieved universal regional membership of the 35 sovereign American states.

The largest decision-making body of the OAS is the *General Assembly*. It sits annually as a general conference of all members and has jurisdiction to consider any regional problem that a majority of its members wish to debate. The Permanent Council carries out directives of the assembly and performs pacific settlement functions when disputes among members are considered by the OAS. The *Inter-American Council for Integral Development* sponsors conferences, drafts treaties, and co-ordinates inter-American programs on culture, economic affairs, and education. When regional international disputes arise, the *Meeting of Consultation of Ministers of Foreign Affairs* is summoned at the request of a majority of members. The *Inter-American Juridical Committee* is a judicial advisory body of the OAS that promotes the codification and development of international law in the western hemisphere. The *General Secretariat* of the OAS, headed by a secretary general elected for five years, employs nearly 1400 staff and is the administrative arm of the OAS.

While the OAS functions as a general regional multi-purpose IGO, it also operates as a collective-security defence organization. All signatories to the Charter of the OAS are automatically parties to the **Inter-American Treaty of Reciprocal Assistance** of 1947 (Rio Pact). This pact, in which the US has played a dominant military role, was originally drafted to deal with the threat of communism in the western hemisphere. The collective-security provisions of the treaty have been invoked on a number of occasions since it was adopted at Bogotá in 1948: concerning Cuba in 1961–1962, and the intervention of an OAS peace force in the Dominican Republic in 1965.

> **FACTFILE**   Cuba, although a member of the OAS, has been barred from participating in the organization by a resolution passed in 1962.

In the area of the *peaceful settlement of disputes*, the OAS has played an important role, with the Permanent Council, the Meeting of Consultation of Ministers of Foreign Affairs, and the Inter-American Peace Commission serving as instruments through which **mediation** and **conciliation** are attempted. Among the many disputes considered by the OAS have been Costa Rica and Nicaragua (1948–1949, 1955–1956, 1959), Panama and the United States (1964 and 1989), and Haiti (1991).

The OAS was instrumental in resolving the "soccer war" between El Salvador and Honduras in 1969–1970, and in 1980 a peace treaty between these states was deposited with the OAS. Argentina and Chile requested that the **Holy See** mediate their disputes over the future of various island territories and maritime areas. And in 1981, the **good offices** of the OAS were used to restore peaceful relations between Ecuador and Peru. In 1982, the

OAS adopted resolutions in support of Argentina during the Argentine–British war over the Falkland Islands. But the United States supported Great Britain during the dispute and persuaded the Latin American members of the OAS to issue mild denunciations of British military action in the General Assembly.

In September 2001, an inter-American Democratic Charter was adopted, declaring the right of people in the Americas to enjoy democratic government. The new Charter permits members to intervene in hemispheric states that deny or destroy domestic democratic institutions.

But the OAS has also been used as a regional forum for the expression of US **hegemony**. The United States has used it to provide a **multilateral** legitimacy to the implementation of its **foreign policy** goals in the western hemisphere. The United States has often succeeded in converting its **unilateral** actions to the status of regional international "peacekeeping" many times without consulting the OAS.

Multinational Corporations (MNCs)

Since World War II, multinational corporations (MNCs) have become major international actors.[10] More than any other actors in the international community, MNCs have transformed the global economy through their increased influence of four resources in the world economic system: the technology of production and distribution, capital, finance, and marketing. As corporations with a world focus, MNCs are the first institutions in human history, with the exception of the Vatican, dedicated to central planning on a global basis.[11]

FACTFILE Of all of the multinational corporations in the annual *Fortune* 500 list of top companies in 2008, only 21 were headed by women.

Multinational corporations are international because they conduct business activities and own assets beyond the jurisdiction of one state. They have political as well as economic impact on the international system because they move and control goods, services, money, personnel, and technology across national boundaries. As actors in the international economy, MNCs have tremendous bargaining powers with governments and international organizations.

If we think of these two types of international actors (MNCs and nation-states) as economic units competing for dominance in a global economic system, we can make some interesting observations (Table 12.5). The annual sales of MNCs are comparable to the gross domestic product (GDP) of national economies. *ExxonMobil*, for example, is bigger than the combined GDPs of Israel, New Zealand, and Kuwait; *Wal-Mart* is bigger than Belgium.

By 2008, the world's 500 largest MNCs controlled more than $9 trillion in assets, and employed more than 29 million people; 40 of the world's 100 principal economic actors were MNCs; and out of more than 200 nation-states, approximately 100 had less economic strength than did these 40 global enterprises. Today, more than 7500 MNCs control and operate more than 27 000 subsidiaries that employ 3 percent of the world's labour force.[12] Even socialist states host MNCs or their subsidiaries.

Because of their enormous sales figures and profits, MNCs collectively aggregate large amounts of international currencies and are in the position to influence exchange rates. By the mid-1970s, MNCs controlled more than twice the total of all the international reserves held by all the central banks and international monetary institutions. By 2008, MNCs accounted for over a third of the activity in the world's market economies. They initiate 85 to 90 percent of the exports in advanced economies such as Britain, Canada, and the United States.[13]

Table 12.5	The 100 primary economic actors in the world, comparing select MNC sales with GDP of selected nation-states, 2008 (in billions of US dollars)

1. United States	$13 001	35. Daimler-Chrysler	190.1	69. Caterpillar	44.9
2. China	10 002	36. Venezuela	186.3	70. Oman	44.5
3. Japan	4200	37. Ireland	180.7	71. Congo (DR)	44.4
4. India	4200	38. Israel	170.3	72. Cameroon	42.5
5. Germany	2600	39. General Electric	168.3	73. North Korea	40.0
6. France	1900	40. Ford Motor	160.1	74. PepsiCo	39.4
7. United Kingdom	1897	41. Morocco	152.2	75. Cambodia	37.7
8. Italy	1805	42. Volkswagen	142.2	76. Supervalu	37.4
9. Brazil	1728	43. Singapore	141.2	77. Latvia	36.5
10. Russia	1755	44. New Zealand	106.9	78. Walt Disney	35.8
11. Canada	1300	45. Slovakia	99.2	79. Jordan	30.0
12. Korea (Rep)	1200	46. Sri Lanka	95.6	80. Coca-Cola	28.8
13. Mexico	1100	47. Honda Motor	94.7	81. Bolivia	27.9
14. Indonesia	948.3	48. IBM	91.4	82. 3M	24.4
15. Taiwan	680.5	49. Home Depot	90.8	83. Panama	24.3
16. South Africa	587.5	50. Bulgaria	78.7	84. Apple	24.0
17. Poland	552.4	51. Dominican Republic	77.1	85. Qatar	23.6
18. The Netherlands	521.1	52. United Arab Emirates	75.6	86. GAP	21.3
19. Pakistan	437.5	53. Libya	72.3	87. Trinidad and Tobago	21.1
20. Saudi Arabia	366.2	54. Sony	70.9	88. Staples	19
21. Wal-Mart	351.1	55. Proctor & Gamble	68.2	89. Georgia	18.0
22. Exxon Mobil	347.2	56. Hyundai Motor	66.6	90. Goodyear Tire	17.1
23. Belgium	342.8	57. Fiat	65.1	91. Chad	15.0
24. Royal Dutch Shell	318.8	58. Ecuador	61.5	92. Whirlpool	14.9
25. Sweden	290.6	59. BMW	61.4	93. Haiti	14.8
26. Austria	283.8	60. Toshiba	60.8	94. Sara Lee	13
27. BP	274.3	61. Croatia	60.3	95. Jamaica	12.8
28. Greece	256.3	62. Costco Wholesale	60.1	96. General Mills	12.4
29. Algeria	250	63. Target	59.4	97. Kyrgyzstan	10.7
30. Toyota	208	64. Kuwait	55.9	98. Starbucks	9.4
31. General Motors	207	65. Angola	53.1	99. Malawi	8.3
32. Denmark	201.5	66. Microsoft	51.1	100. Campbell Soup	7.8
33. Chevron	200.5	67. United Parcel Service	49.6		
34. Nigeria	191.4	68. Cuba	45.5		

Source: FORTUNE Global 500 © 2007 Time Inc. All rights reserved.

The economic power of MNCs often translates into political and social power. Politically, MNCs promise investment, jobs, the raising of living standards, and the introduction of technology to assist developing countries to modernize and industrialize. In return, they demand political stability, and concessions on taxation and government regulations. When national and corporate interests conflict, MNCs challenge the political decisions of governments from every possible vantage point.

In the social sphere, the global marketing strategies of MNCs homogenize consumer tastes the world over. Because MNCs have created the "global shopping centre," there is a resulting tendency for people all over the world to adopt the same tastes and the same consumption habits. The rise of the global corporation has become a significant cultural integrating force within the world community.

Non-governmental Organizations (NGOs)

We have identified the three dominant classes of actors in the contemporary international system: states, international organizations, and multinational corporations. But there are other actors, not always recognized by states and IGOs, which stimulate international co-operation on all levels of human interaction. NGOs are specialized organizations that work to develop national interest and involvement in world affairs, by organizing workshops, seminars, and conferences. These types of international organizations are created from every conceivable field of human endeavour, from agriculture to science and technology.

Non-governmental organizations perform an educational function in the countries where they operate: they contribute to the gathering and dissemination of information about international problems. At the same time, they generate an internal domestic interest in world affairs. In the process of mobilizing public and private support for global concerns, NGOs create a flow of ideas, materials, money, and people across national boundaries to promote co-operation and development in the international system.

By 2008, there were more than 5000 NGOs of diverse size, composition, and purpose functioning in the world. Many of these organizations have high visibility and are widely known in all countries: for example, Doctors Without Borders/Médecins Sans Frontières (MSF); the International Red Cross; and the International Chamber of Commerce. But others are not so prominent, such as the International Council for Philosophy and Humanistic Studies or the Council for International Organizations of Medical Sciences.

In Canada, more than 200 NGOs encourage and provide domestic links with all world areas. Organizations such as World Vision of Canada, Foster Parents Plan of Canada, and the Salvation Army are among them. Some NGOs are organized as professional associations that seek to protect the interests of their members but exercise an important role in the international community. For example, the Association of Canadian Medical Colleges (ACMC), with headquarters in Ottawa, has international affiliations with the Pan American Federation of Associations of Medical Schools and with the Pan American Health Organization.

Still other NGOs undertake humanitarian efforts. In the field of human rights, Amnesty International is the best known. Its Canadian office (in Ottawa) has been operating since 1973. Founded in England in 1961, it has devoted its major efforts in more than 160 nation-states to protect prisoners of conscience, and it collects information on the incidence of torture, arbitrary arrest, and capital punishment around the world. For example, Amnesty International found reasonable grounds to believe that cruel and inhuman treatment occurred at Archambault Prison in Quebec. The allegations, supported by the sworn statements of 17 prisoners, referred to beatings, spraying tear gas into prisoners' mouths, keeping inmates naked for weeks, depriving them of sleep, and adulterating their food. Amnesty International asserted that Canada had an international obligation under the United Nations Declaration on Torture to undertake a full, impartial inquiry.

Transnational Groups and Movements

Religious movements, transnational political organizations, and terrorist groups must also be included in a composite of the contemporary international system. In the twenty-first century, transnational actors have already added a new dimension of complexity to that system because they participate in a web of global interactions

Focus On   What Is Meant by "Islamic Fundamentalism"?

Islam is one of the world's major religions. It claims the allegiance of about one-fifth of humankind. Westerners widely assume that Islam is an Arab religion (since it was born in the Middle East) but most contemporary Muslims are not Arabs. In fact, the largest Muslim populations are in Indonesia and India. There are even large concentrations of Muslims in China and in many of the republics of the former Soviet Union.

Islam is the second-largest religion in Europe after Christianity, and it rivals Christianity in many African states. Growth trends in Islamic societies have global consequence.

Over the past decade, religious fervour has erupted in the Islamic world, and in the Middle East in particular. It has led to revolution in Iran, the assassination of president Anwar Sadat in Egypt, fierce conflict in Afghanistan, and political destabilization in Iraq. Much of this fervour has been inspired by fundamentalism, which is a commitment to the basics of Islamic religious doctrine.

The very word *Islam* means submission to the will of Allah (the Islamic God), who demands

personal integrity, social justice, and brotherhood among believers.

The principal foreign enemy of Islamic fundamentalists is the "Great Satan," the United States. Fundamentalists fear the invasion of American culture and political and military interference in their societies. A second reason for their hostility is the US support of Israel. The fundamentalists regard Americans essentially as barbarians whose economic, technological, and military influence threatens the integrity of Muslim societies and traditions.

Along with many Christian fundamentalists, some Muslims look with disapproval at sexual permissiveness in America; at the freedom of American women; at out-of-wedlock pregnancy, abortion, and divorce; at a preoccupation with pleasure, drugs, pornography, material possessions, and individualism at the expense of community.

Radical Islam has emerged as a powerful political force in the international system. The strength of Islamic fundamentalism reflects the continuing importance of the historic Arab empire.

that affect the behaviour of governments, international organizations, individuals, and corporations. They can play a major role in international relations.

Organized Religion

Christianity, Judaism, Islam, Hinduism, and Buddhism all have an international and global presence. Religion can be deeply involved in international conflict, particularly when a religion is closely allied to a state or reflects the beliefs of a majority of citizens.

Religious extremism has become a major ideological factor in world politics. The use of religion to rationalize extreme actions, such as terrorism or militancy against a recognized government, has a significant impact on efforts to maintain international peace. Religious nationalism (the convergence of religious belief with state policy) is now a basic fact of contemporary international politics, as witnessed in Afghanistan, Bangladesh, Northern Ireland, Israel, Lebanon, the Sudan, Sri Lanka, Iraq, and Iran.

We see religious nationalism in the Taliban in Afghanistan, a militant Islamic movement of Pashtun Islamic students. But religious nationalism is also felt in Jewish extremism, as when Israeli extremists killed more than 30 Muslims in the Shrine of the Patriarch. Violent actions of the Islamic Hamas, which wages war against Israel, provides another illustration.

Religious nationalism and fundamentalism have created numerous problems in the international system—among them questions of human rights, new separatist movements, increased transnational violence, and civil war.

Perhaps the most apparent example of an organized religion that has taken a leading role in world affairs is the Catholic Church. The Holy See is the government of the Catholic Church and represents the pope's authority. The pope is the religious leader of one-sixth of the world's population and is the world's most visible leader. The Dalai Lama is another prominent spiritual leader who has been influential in world affairs. Archbishop Desmond Tutu also fills this role, especially in his advocacy of human rights and anti-racism on a global scale.

International Political Movements

Many political groups and movements transcend national boundaries, appeal to an international clientele, and thus influence the global political system. Anarchism, communism, and socialism are international movements that have influenced most national political systems. Contemporary communists, in states where they are still organized, disagree on many fundamental issues but share the goal of building an international camaraderie.

In Latin America, *aprista*-type parties share the international goals of **aprismo**, which include land reform, nationalization of key industries, the solidarity of oppressed classes, the political representation of Indians, peasants, students, and intellectuals, and opposition to communism. This international dimension of aprismo makes it a noteworthy regional transnational political movement.

All ideologically kindred parties and movements of this kind seek to build links in the international community. The founding session of a worldwide organization of conservative parties took place in London in 1983; the International Democratic Union has 48 members, including the Conservative Party of Canada. The Socialist International is a similar organization of 89 full members, including Canada's NDP. For liberal parties, there is the Liberal International, with 56 members.

Terrorists

Terrorists are significant actors in the international system. The events of 9/11 changed the way most governments regard the phenomenon of terrorism.

In a world where many different groups and organizations are prepared to use violence to achieve political ends, terrorism almost eludes definition. Diverse groups—armies, insurgents, mercenaries, freedom fighters, religious and national liberation, and even individuals—are frequently identified with terrorism as users of violence and psychological weapons in global affairs.

State terrorism consists of the use of violence or the threat of violence by governments against their own populations as an instrument of political and social control. Almost always, state terrorism has international consequences due to the mass exodus of refugees or the intervention of other governments, as with Nazi Germany in the 1940s and in Cambodia in the 1970s. Amnesty International reports that many states continue to practise torture on suspected dissidents. In some of these nation-states, such as Syria, Uganda, Rwanda, Slovenia, and Slovakia, hundreds of thousands of civilians

Perspectives   Can Terrorism Be Defined?

Terrorism is premeditated, politically motivated violence. Terrorist acts are carried out against certain targets. They are usually noncombatant targets—as were the women and children killed in Beslan, Russia, in 2004—and sometimes just physical targets, but military personnel are targeted as well. Terrorist activities may be state-sponsored or conducted by subnational groups or clandestine agents who intend to influence a particular audience.

As a special form of political violence, terrorism does not appear to derive from a philosophy. Rather, it emerges out of various ideologies that believe in creating fear from violence for political gain. As an ideology, terrorism breaches widely held international norms of peaceful dispute settlement and of negotiation.

The use of the label "terrorists" seems to be a matter of perception of the objectives of political violence. For example, the Palestinian Liberation Organization (PLO) is variously perceived as a national liberation movement, a state, and a terrorist group.

---

have died in massacres perpetrated by their governments' military forces.

Revolutionary terrorism is seen as extreme social and political movements that resort to violence across national boundaries to achieve their goals. Revolutionary terrorism tends to attract much more international attention because it targets prominent citizens, airlines, airports, and embassies, and is usually reported globally in the media.

> FACTFILE   Hezbollah (Party of God), a terrorist organization also known as Islamic Jihad, is strongly anti-West, anti-Israel, and anti-American. With cells worldwide, the organization uses suicide bombing, kidnapping, and other forms of terrorist attacks.

Terrorist organizations exist all over the world, and today number more than 3000. The most enduring terrorist organizations tend to have religious, ethnic, and nationalist aspirations. The Bosnians, Croatians, and Kosovars in the former Yugoslavia, the Basques in Spain, and the Kurds in Iraq and Iran have organized as ethnic extremist groups. The growing power of Islamic fundamentalism is reflected in the presence of Hezbollah (Party of God) and a multitude of Shi'ite Muslim movements in Lebanon, Kuwait, and elsewhere.

> FACTFILE   The International Atomic Energy Agency reports that the availability of enriched uranium, the essential ingredient in nuclear weapons produced by the world's 430 fission reactors, increases the likelihood that small nuclear weapons will be created by terrorists.

Intimidation and random violence are unique features of these non-state actors: assassination, abduction, hijacking, hostage taking, and murder seriously defy the structures and routine interactions of international relations. Some governments have responded to the threat of terrorism by training anti-terrorist combat units.[14] The **Canadian Security Intelligence Service** (CSIS) and the emergency response teams of the Royal Canadian Mounted Police (RCMP), Great Britain's Special Air Services, Israel's 269 Headquarters Reconnaissance Regiment, and the US Delta Team are examples of counter-terrorist and intelligence-gathering groups.

Individuals as International Actors

The role that private individuals play outside government in the international system often goes unnoticed. But individuals have an impact on international affairs, and examples abound. Nobel Peace Prize–winner Joseph Rotblat helped invent the atomic bomb, but he also founded Nova Scotia's Pugwash Conference in 1957, which has sponsored many disarmament conferences since that time. American actor Ed Asner, star of television's *Lou Grant*, has raised millions for medical aid, food, and clothing to be sent to the people in Latin America. In 1985 at Live Aid, and at the Live 8 concerts in 2005, the near-global music extravaganzas raised millions for African famine relief, and were the brainchild and organizational achievement of one man, rock musician Bob Geldof.

In Canada, Terry Fox raised over $25 million from all over the world in his unique fight against cancer, and many millions of dollars more have been raised since he died. Another Canadian, Steve Fonyo, took up the same challenge and successfully completed Terry Fox's dream of running across Canada, attracting financial support from people and governments in Canada and around the world. And Vancouver wheelchair athlete Rick Hansen completed a 40 000-kilometre world tour to raise money for spinal research in the international community.

Individuals in their private capacity as artists, business people, journalists, professionals, tourists, and writers, are independent actors able to behave autonomously in the global arena. In recent years, individuals—in addition to states and international organizations—have been given some recognition internationally as subjects of world law under certain circumstances. In short, individuals are an integral part of the contemporary international community.[15] They are not merely cogs in the large bureaucratic machinery of states and international organizations because they have a capacity, through their actions, to influence the character of world affairs.

THE FUTURE OF THE INTERNATIONAL/GLOBAL SYSTEM

Is the international system the same as the global system? On one level, the international system is the playground of nation-states and international organizations, but as such it has never really been a complete reflection of the global system. On another level, the international system is an essential precursor to the emergence of a global system and the underpinning of the new world order.

The new world order encompasses the global system, which comprises nation-states, multinational corporations (MNCs), international governmental organizations (IGOs), non-governmental organizations (NGOs), private transnational groups, and all the current technologies that enable instantaneous communications.

Four major developments have contributed to the evolution of the old world order to this so-called new order in the twenty-first century.

The *first* is the widespread belief that globalization is a force to contend with—one challenging the very pillars of the old world order. The globalization thesis posits that governments are no longer in control of the very things that in the past gave the sovereign nation-state its meaning and legitimacy. Instead, governments everywhere find themselves bowing to the dictates of a global dynamic in a global marketplace.

The *second* is the proliferation of state and non-state actors involved in the global community. Their presence has altered the structure of the international system and the distribution of power

Focus On — Terrorism and Canada–US Border Security

The terrorist attacks of 9/11 changed the so-called undefended border between Canada and the United States into one of the most security-conscious international boundaries in the world. This is a border Americans regard as an integral part of their Homeland Security policy, which administers to about 200 million travellers each year and where over $1.5 billion in cross-border trade is transacted each day.

Immigration and Customs officials have dramatically increased surveillance on both sides of the 7000-kilometre border, which is made up largely of formerly unguarded back roads and commercial crossings. Leaders in each country fear that these kinds of undefended conditions could be the Achilles' heel of North America's war against terrorism.

Following 9/11, the Canadian government moved quickly to improve security at airports, ocean ports, and the various weak points along the Canada–US border. Police and border officials now have greater powers to interrogate, search and seize, and arrest people coming into the country. Billions of dollars have been allocated for airline security, a beefed-up military and coast guard, and support for intelligence gathering in the country. Canadian and US courts also have greater powers to convict and punish terrorists.

Both states are implementing a common approach to screen international air travellers before they enter either country. Common standards are now in place for using identifiers. These involve fingerprints, facial recognition, and iris scanning to confirm people's identities. At all major border points, a joint program called the Free and Secure Trade Program (FAST) is a "fast lane" clearance process to protect the current levels of daily trade in both economies.

The efficient movement of people and goods requires the right bureaucratic infrastructure to support it, and the technology and intelligence to secure it. In place are explosive-detection systems, as well as air marshals and aircraft-protection officers who work to secure the air system. High-energy gamma- and X-ray machines are used to detect dangerous chemicals and biological agents.

For matters involving intelligence and law enforcement, Canada and the United States have the integrated Foreign Terrorist Tracking Task Force and Integrated Border Enforcement Teams to co-ordinate enforcement efforts across the shared border. Project NorthStar is a grassroots organization of law-enforcement professionals at the federal, state, provincial, and local levels on both sides of the border. They organize communications, intelligence, joint operations, and prosecutions to fight the war on terrorism.

---

within it. The **balance of power** within the global-state system is defined by the number of major actors or poles in that system. *Pole* is the term used to refer to a "great power," usually measured in terms of military and economic strength.

The disintegration of the Soviet Union into 21 competitive nation-states dramatically changed the global balance of power, setting in motion new alliances and a new world configuration of states. The bipolar system of rivalry between the Soviet

Union and the United States disappeared. But new polarizations are being formed.

The *third* development that signals a new world order has been the growth of economic interdependence among the states of the world as demonstrated by the dramatic increase in world trade. Since the 1980s, world trade has increased from $1.3 to $13.0 trillion in 2008. This means that the economies of all states are now more dependent than ever before on each other's economic productivity. They must react to global forces that spawn recession, depression, and inflation—and do so without ever being in full control of their economic policies.

The *fourth* development is related to the third, in that most states around the world have shifted their economies from fully protected national markets to more open and common markets. The economies of states have therefore grown similar to one another, requiring their governments to run comparable and co-ordinated fiscal and monetary policies.

The more numerous the actors, the more complex and flexible the balance-of-power system becomes. In addition to the United States and Europe, the present balance-of-power system must also include China, Brazil, India, and Japan as significant players in the contemporary game of international politics.

This multipolar-bloc model goes one step further and portrays the international system as divided into many spheres of influence, with many actors. It views the world as a composite of large, autonomous, integrating regions, such as North America, Central America, South America, Western Europe, Eastern Europe, the Middle East, and the various regions of Asia.

These emerging regional units may be the forces that will replace states as the primary actors in global affairs. Increasingly, political scientists have challenged the credibility of a model that does not include all the actors in the system. In short, the conditions that might have facilitated

the view that states are the only poles of power in the contemporary world of international relations have changed dramatically. The state as a pole of power will probably remain a central characteristic of the global community in the future, but its pre-eminence has eroded and will, in all probability, continue to lessen as other actors gain power and influence. From the perspective of 2009, MNCs, IGOs, transnational groups and organizations, and supranational organizations are all ascendant global players.

New National Awakenings

Some of the newer states are quite artificial political creations, like the states around the Sahara or the scattered islands of the Caribbean, the South Pacific, and the Indian Ocean, where a multitude of "statelets" find it nearly impossible to manage their own social and economic space or to function as autonomous members of international society. Many peoples who are denied an identity by existing states (Inuits, Lapps, Samoyeds, and the North, Central, and South American Aboriginals) are laying claim to historical rights of place that antedate present territorial divisions. They are demanding self-government and the return of their lands, and are resisting forcible assimilation.

FACTFILE   There are 38 microstates—almost one-quarter of the nation-states on the planet—with populations of fewer than one million, most with minimal defence capabilities and marginal economies.

Other nations, locked within the confines of modern communist nation-states, broke out violently. By the turn of the twentieth century, five of the previous republics of the former Yugoslavia (Slovenia, Croatia, Bosnia-Herzegovina, Macedonia, and Kosovo), all under the crisis of civil war, had sought international recognition of their contemporary independence as nation-states. However, their capacity to build their war-torn economies as new independent states is quite a challenge in an era of European economic integration and the creation of a supranational government.

These new awakenings have coincided with the rise of radical movements since the 1960s (feminism, ecology, counter-cultures, anti-militarism, and terrorism). These trans-state sociocultural currents are increasing resistance to the dominance of territorial structures and the state-centric model in the global system.

Creating Regional Actors

The power of nation-states is challenged by large global corporations. Global corporations advocate an ideology that justifies the same basic claim: nationalism and territoriality are out of date and belong to the past. To these corporations, the world is an integrated marketplace that is hindered by the economic nationalism and protectionism of individual states. International organizations (IGOs) argue that autonomous governments must transfer more sovereignty to supranational organizations if regional and global problems are to be successfully resolved. Similarly, non-governmental organizations (NGOs) advance the principles of international co-operation and development as an alternative to national self-sufficiency.

In the contemporary international system, only a few states are in a position to control their own destinies. The seven most developed economies—Britain, Canada, France, Italy, Japan, Germany, and the United States—are able (albeit under greater limitations than ever before) to convert their national wealth and economic growth into independent foreign policies in matters of aid, investment, and trade. But for the majority of the other states of the world, independence is both a political and legal fiction. They see their destinies as tied to the global economy.

Economic Integration

In the wider context of international relations, there is a growing tendency among people and their governments to seek a regional approach to problem solving. Canada, Mexico, and the United States provide a rich example of a hemispheric movement toward a regional system of international co-operation and integration. So do the states of Latin America and the Caribbean. In 1960, the Latin American Free Trade Association (since 1981 the Latin American Integration Association [LAIA]) was established in response to the European Common Market to reduce tariffs among member states until a regional **free trade zone** was created. That same year, the Central American Common Market (CACM) was founded to promote regional economic development in Central America through a **customs union** and industrial integration. In 1969, a six-member-nation economic group created a subregional market, known as the Andean Community, to establish a **common market**. In 1993, this Andean common market created the Andean Free Trade Area. In 1973, the Caribbean Community and Common Market (CARICOM) established a regional organization designed to achieve a higher level of economic and political integration among Caribbean economies, based on the European community model. And in 1991, Argentina, Brazil (the main founder), Paraguay, and Uruguay founded the Southern Cone Common Market (Mercosur), culminating in a common market by 1995.

Canada and the United States entered a free-trade arrangement in the late 1980s and moved to expand their regional association to include Mexico in a North American Free Trade Agreement (NAFTA). When all these organizations are seen in the context of the entire inter-American system, a pattern of regional international integration is observable

Focus On **La Francophonie**

In October of 2008, 55 heads of state and government met in Quebec City for the twelfth summit of La Francophonie. Since the first summit, held in Paris in 1986, La Francophonie has grown to include 55 states and governments from five continents, representing 200 million French-speaking people.

As an international organization, La Francophonie has a summit meeting every two years, at which decisions are made covering five major areas: democracy and development; culture and communications; knowledge and progress; economic relations; and international relations. The Conference ministerielle and the Agence de la Francophonie are the two bureaucratic bodies that carry out the decisions taken at the summit. The administration of La Francophonie is headed by a secretary general, who is elected for a five-year term. Boutros Boutros Ghali was the first person to serve as the head of the Secretariat.

Past Francophonie Summits

Paris (1986)
Quebec City (1987)
Dakar (1989)
Paris (1991)
Mauritius (1993)
Cotonou (1995)
Hanoi (1997)
Moncton (1999)
Beirut (2002)
Ouagadougou (2004)
Ottawa (2006)
Quebec City (2008)

Canada has played a major role in the international promotion of the French language. The Montreal-based Agence universitaire de la Francophonie co-ordinates about 400 institutions of higher learning, fostering research, education, and training of the French language and its many cultures. TV5, the international French-language network, is a partnership among Belgium, Canada, France, Switzerland, and several African states, reaching about 100 million households in more than 100 countries. This huge network beams programs on business, culture, entertainment, and sports to a vast global audience, celebrating the French language.

La Francophonie is an important foreign-policy focus for Canada. It enables Canada's large francophone communities to direct Canadian foreign policy at issues affecting the spread of democracy, the developing economies, human rights, and international peace. Two Canadian provinces, Quebec and New Brunswick, have been conferred participating government status, especially in the areas of education and culture. Both have **"observer status"** on foreign policy and international questions.

Canada wants to diversify its trade through La Francophonie and sees itself as an experienced diplomatic agent for the peaceful resolution of disputes, when conflict occurs among francophone states. Canada also offers itself as an adviser on matters of economic integration, based on its involvement in NAFTA.

as a gradual approach to the building of political and economic communities in the Americas beyond that of the state.

CANADA IN THE INTERNATIONAL SYSTEM

John Holmes remarked that "Canada is an inescapably international country."[16] From a geographical perspective, Canada appears to be locked into the western hemisphere as a North American country. But while it is true that Canada is geopolitically consigned to interact with the United States, the network of Canada's international relations has never been contained in a geographically delimited hemisphere.[17]

Historically, the Commonwealth tie expanded Canada's international relations with Asia, Africa, the Caribbean, and Europe. These links introduced Canada to a network of global bilateral and multilateral interactions that earned Canada the widespread reputation of a good world citizen. As Barbara Ward has observed, Canada was the "first international nation," holding a global perspective.[18]

FACTFILE   La Francophonie is a term coined by the French geographer Onésime Reclus in 1880 to designate the community of people worldwide using French as their mother tongue.

Today, Canada continues to advance foreign policies with a global focus. Perhaps the most revealing component of Canada's reputation as an important international actor is its support and involvement in international organizations. In this regard, Canada's active participation in the creation of the United Nations, the Commonwealth, NATO, NORAD, the OAS, **L'Agence culturelle et technique de la langue française** (Agency for Cultural and Technical Co-operation), the World Trade Organization (WTO), the **International Monetary Fund** (IMF), and the **Organisation for Economic Co-operation and Development** (OECD) is an insight into the enormous scope of Canada's global presence. Internationalist engagement marked by a commitment to international institutions has continued under successive Canadian governments since 1945. By 2008, the number of international institutions that Canada has joined grew to more than 250.

Canada's openness to the world community is driven by its need to trade. Judged as a percentage of gross domestic product (GDP), Canada is the world's largest international trader. By 2008, 39 percent of its GDP was aggregated in trade, compared with 26 percent for Germany and the United Kingdom, 20 percent for France and the United States, and (surprisingly) only about 20 percent for Japan. Approximately four-fifths of Canada's world trade is with only one other economy—the United States. The economic exchange between these two states is the largest bilateral-trade relationship in the world, and was so even before the implementation of the Free Trade Agreement in 1989.

At the annual WTO meetings, Canada has actively supported resolutions to liberalize international trade and has encouraged the reduction of protectionist measures. At the regular meetings of the International Monetary Fund (IMF) and the **International Bank for Reconstruction and Development** (IBRD) (also known as the **World Bank**), Canada has supported the provisions of credits, loans, and subsidies to international importers in the developing countries.

It remains Canada's view that *multilateral efforts* can be of major importance in addressing national problems and in resolving many international problems of global significance—for example, the creation of a New International Economic Order (NIEO), international environmental issues, the food crisis, and human rights. Canada did not support the US war initiative in Iraq in 2003 because the United Nations Security Council had not approved such a military operation.

As a strong proponent of the NIEO, Canada supports the stabilization of international commodity markets, the expansion of development loans and assistance through the international banking system, and the preferential treatment of Third World products to enhance **balance of payments**. One major component of the global economy is the North–South dialogue. The dependence of the developing economies of the South on volatile commodity markets controlled by the developed economies is an ever-increasing source of world tension.

In 1981, 22 states met in Cancun, Mexico, to search for a solution to North–South economic disparities. There, the Canadian government promised to increase its aid program to 0.5 percent of GDP by the early years of the twenty-first century. This still falls well below Lester Pearson's suggestion in the 1960s that Canada and other developed economies dedicate 1 percent of their GDP to foreign aid. Only four countries (Denmark, Norway, Sweden, and the Netherlands) have given more than 0.7 percent of their respective GDP to assist developing economies. By 2008, Canada had still fallen short of its target of 0.5 percent of GDP for its aid program.

The most compelling arguments for narrowing the gap between the North and the South have been directed at financing the *international debt*. The IMF is usually the last resort for financially strapped developing economies. Through its efforts at the IMF, Canada has played a major role in the establishment of a special soft-loan fund (no interest except for a small annual service charge).

On *international environmental issues*, Canada was a major player in the negotiations that led to the signing of the United Nations Convention on the Law of the Sea in 1982. Canada, as the largest coastal state in the world, was successful in obtaining recognition of the need to manage offshore living and non-living resources, as well as for the provision of international legal measures to prevent marine pollution, particularly in Arctic waters. The creation of an International Seabed Authority to protect the resources of the deep seabed from indiscriminate exploitation and pollution was spearheaded by Canada.

> FACTFILE In 2008, the UN Climate Change Secretariat notified Ottawa that it launched an investigation into Canada's failure to meet the Kyoto Protocol's requirement for reporting emissions that harm the environment.

In pursuit of its environmental objectives, Canada has taken part in many international meetings, particularly those sponsored by the United Nations Environment Program (UNEP).

Canada was instrumental in the establishment of *EarthWatch*, UNEP's key program, which keeps an eye on all areas of the planet day and night. Canada initiated work on a convention for the protection of the stratospheric ozone layer that was signed by 45 states in March 1985. Canada also ratified a United Nations Convention on Long-Range Transboundary Air Pollution (LRTAP), which recognizes acid rain as a major international environmental problem. And, in 1989, Canada was one of 25 states to sign the Convention on Air Pollution to limit the emissions of carbon-dioxide gases. Canada also contributed to the establishment of the World Atmospheric Trust Fund. At the Earth Summit in Rio de Janeiro in 1992, Canada signed an "ecopact" on the preservation of biological diversity. The biodiversity treaty recognized the relationship between human poverty and the degradation of the environment, and the need to protect endangered species and the areas they inhabit by providing financial relief to developing economies. Canada's controversial initial support for the Kyoto Protocol, which was launched in March 1994, committed Canadians to reducing their carbon-dioxide emissions both privately and commercially by the first decade of the twenty-first century. But Stephen Harper's government rejected the protocol in 2007 after indicating that Canada could not meet the expected emission targets by 2012.

The *food crisis* in Africa jolted international attention to the spectre of a global food shortage in the late twentieth century. By 2001, the situation had actually worsened, even though the media were not focused on Africa's starving populations to the extent they had been in the mid-1980s. The food situation in Africa is a regional manifestation of a worldwide problem of massive food shortages and the need for thousands of tonnes of food aid and millions of dollars in development assistance. Emergency relief from Canada has been crucial in averting mass starvation not only in Africa, but also in Asia, Latin America, and the Caribbean. Canada endorsed the 1987 Beijing Declaration, which reaffirmed the international commitment to eradicate hunger and malnutrition through a world food strategy.

In the field of *human rights*, Canada has ratified all relevant international conventions: the International Covenant on Economic, Social and Cultural Rights (1976), the International Covenant on Civil and Political Rights and its Optional Protocol (1976), and the Helsinki Agreement of 1975. In January 1982, the International Convention on the Elimination of All Forms of Discrimination against Women came into force. Canada was instrumental in drafting and supporting this convention, and is a member of the committee that monitors the implementation of its provisions. Canada was also a member of the working group that drafted the Convention against Torture and Other Cruel, Inhuman or Degrading Treatment or Punishment, which came into force on June 26, 1987.

FACTFILE   Canada spearheaded the 1997 Land Mines Treaty, signed by nearly 100 states, which agreed not to use land mines, to stop their production, and to map and clear any mines that may have been laid.

CANADA, THE UNITED STATES, AND MEXICO IN THE INTERNATIONAL CONTEXT
The Free Trade Agreement

The complexity and constancy of Canada's relations with the United States are unique in international relations.[19] No other two states in the world share the intimacy of an undefended border 30 000 kilometres long, which more than 85 million people cross each year and across which more than $1.6 billion in international trade is exchanged every day. This two-way trade exceeds two-way trade between the US and Japan and between the US and any four of its European trading partners combined. Just one province—Ontario—buys more from the United States than Japan, the UK, France, or Germany.

Given the increasing intimacy of both economies, neither of the national governments on either side of the 49th parallel takes this sort of trading relationship for granted. Trade between Canada and the United States currently translates into about two million jobs in each economy. Prior to the implementation of the Canada–United States Free Trade Agreement (FTA) in 1989, both economies had already enjoyed a very large measure of free trade. Successive rounds of multilateral trade negotiations under GATT had eliminated tariffs on 75 percent of the goods and services flowing both ways across the border.

A great deal of this success had resulted from separate trade agreements involving agriculture, the fishery, and manufacturing. The historic Canada–US Automotive Products Agreement (Auto Pact) of 1965 brought tremendous economic benefits in increased production and employment in both countries. Since the implementation of the Auto Pact, two-way trade in automotive products skyrocketed from less than a billion dollars annually to over $56 billion by 2008.

At the Quebec Summit in March 1985, Canada and the United States committed themselves to reducing and eliminating the existing barriers on roughly 25 percent of trade that remained subject to tariffs. The gruelling negotiations that followed led to the signing of an historic 1407-page accord: the Canada–United States Free Trade Agreement, implemented January 1, 1989. This bilateral treaty eliminated all trade barriers (tariffs, duties, fees, quotas, or trade restrictions) between the two economies by 1999, thereby initiating the largest free-trade zone in the world.

The North American Free Trade Agreement (NAFTA)

In 1992, Canada, the United States, and Mexico signed the North American Free Trade Agreement. The NAFTA supplants the Canada–US Free Trade Agreement (FTA). The NAFTA creates the largest free-trade zone in the world, affecting about 400 million people and an economic output of nearly $9 trillion.

The trilateral negotiations culminating in signing the NAFTA at San Antonio, Texas, with 2000 pages of detailed trade conditions. More than 20 000 products are governed by this international treaty. Under the agreement, most tariff and non-tariff barriers would be eliminated by

2008. The treaty removes many restrictions on cross-border investments and other financial transactions. Advertising, banking, and insurance flow much more freely. Any trade disputes among the parties will be settled by an international commission with representation from all three signatories. There are provisions for other states in Central and South America and the Caribbean to eventually join the NAFTA, potentially creating a regional economic association like the EU.

Historically, Canada's trade with Mexico has been much smaller than with the United States, not exceeding 1 percent of Canadian imports and 2 percent of Canadian exports. By comparison, only 3 percent of Mexico's exports go to Canada, and 1 percent of Canada's imports come from there. Whether the overall economies of each state will be strengthened or weakened under the NAFTA is very controversial.

FACTFILE   By 2008, Mexico had become Canada's sixth-largest export destination and its fourth-largest source of imports.

Trade restrictions by each state are permissible under certain conditions according to the terms of the agreement: when there are critical domestic shortages of food or other essential products; when domestic cuts are required to prevent diminishing natural resources; to stabilize lower domestic prices on a commodity; and to secure other products in short supply. In the 2000s, Canada has fought political and legal battles over the issue of softwood lumber and over the containment of BSE ("mad cow" disease). Trade restrictions have had a significant affect on jobs and the industries involved on both sides of the border.

Under NAFTA, some barriers to agricultural trade disappear, stimulating a larger percentage of exchange over a 10-year period.[20] This inevitably triggers the need to reform North American farm policies so that Canada, Mexico, and the United States remain competitive in the global market for agricultural products.[21]

NAFTA ensures that Canada is the largest supplier of energy to the United States. In addition to petroleum products, Canada exports electricity, natural gas, and uranium. Before the NAFTA quotas, taxes and price restrictions were used to control the flow of energy trade and protect the domestic market and producers. NAFTA attempts to give greater freedom to banks, security and trust companies, and other lending institutions to penetrate the financial markets of the three member states.

Trade liberalization also affects government contracts. Cross-border bidding on government business expands trade opportunities for suppliers of goods and services subject to competitive tender. Certain restrictions will remain for contracts that fall into the area of national security.

Environmental Protection

Beyond NAFTA, *environmental protection* has appeared over recent years as a major question of international concern between Canada and the United States. **Acid rain** is at the forefront of the issues of bilateral concern between both states. Scientists and advocacy groups have provided much evidence to show that acid rain is formed from emissions of sulphur dioxide and oxides of nitrogen that mix in the atmosphere to produce acids that eventually fall to earth in rain, dew, snow, and dust.[22] Acid rain causes annual damages in the millions of dollars to Canadians; environmental groups such as the Canadian Coalition against Acid Rain say it threatens fishing, tourism, and farming in many parts of Canada and the United States. Two major sources of the problem are auto emissions and pollution from smelters. In

1991, Canada and the United States signed an acid-rain accord, binding their commitments to curb those emissions that cause acid rain.

Resource Management and Development

Resource management and development are two other areas high on the agenda of both states. Fresh water, taken for granted by North Americans as an inexhaustible and free natural endowment, is now considered a long-range resource issue on the continent. Given the growing awareness of the effects of acid rain, the quality of both surface water and ground water is already a great concern in some places.

Although water seems to be plentiful in North America, drinkable water is in much shorter supply. The long-range supply of water is not only threatened by increased consumption but also by pollution and spoilage. Other resources, such as nickel and zinc, as well as oil and natural gas, are all in finite supply and eventually will be exhausted. Long-term planning is recognized by all governments as essential to their national interest.

North American Defence

Defence is another cornerstone of Canada–US relations. Since the 1930s, Canadians have been aware that Canada is strategically *one* with the United States. After World War II, it became increasingly evident that Canada had a major military role to play in the defence of the North American continent. Thus, it was natural for Canada to enter into the NORAD (North American Air Defence) agreement with the United States in 1958. Cross-border collaboration between Canadian and American military forces intensified with the installations of the

Distant Early Warning (DEW) system. For nearly three decades, the DEW line served as Canada's main contribution to hemispheric defence and entwined Canadian military commitment with American strategic theory and practice.

Since 9/11, Canadian security policy has become more integrated with that of the United States. The strength of Canadian Regular Armed Forces was increased from 56 000 in 2001 to 67 000 in 2008. Under Operation Athena, Canadian soldiers were sent to Afghanistan in 2002 to fight terrorism and to keep order. Canadian soldiers have also been deployed to rebuild Iraq since 2004.

Chapter Summary

There is an international global society, consisting of numerous types of actors, more or less autonomous, that interact in patterned interdependent ways on a regular basis. The predominant actors of this world community are nation-states, international governmental organizations, multinational corporations (MNCs), non-governmental organizations (NGOs), transnational groups and movements, and individuals.

The competitive world in which nation-states must survive is draining the power and sovereignty of national governments. The laws of the global marketplace are displacing the capabilities of national governments to control their own economies and to provide their citizens with traditional government services. Internally, many states are experiencing divisive domestic tensions that threaten to break them up into smaller national units.

Many states are seeking membership in regional economic associations and supranational organizations in order to advance their economies. Regional economic integration in the form of free-trade zones and common markets is increasingly sought by contemporary states.

Canada's place in the global community should be examined from the perspective of Canada–US relations and the widening of the NAFTA, as well as from its role in the United Nations and other international organizations.

The United Nations and its six principal organizations (Security Council, General Assembly, Secretariat, Economic and Social Council, International Court of Justice, and Trusteeship Council) have never been more involved in charting the path of the international community. Since the end of the Cold War, the United Nations system has functioned closer to its original Charter goals, but not without serious budget problems.

The North Atlantic Treaty Organization (NATO), established in 1949, is undergoing transformation in size and goals, from its original mandate as a collective-security organization. Since the increase in terrorist activities after 2001, the framework for co-operation within NATO has strengthened its military and intelligence capabilities.

The World Trade Organization, known as one of a group of international organizations called "global governors," has played a significant role in reducing trade barriers and promoting freer trade among states.

The Organization of American States is a good example of a multi-purpose organization endorsed by the Charter of the United Nations. Established in 1948, the OAS provides a regional institutional framework for the peaceful resolution of disputes in the western hemisphere.

Canada is a member of all of the above international organizations and plays a leading role in global international affairs. Canada's openness in global affairs is demonstrated by its need to trade. With 40 percent of its GNP aggregated in trade, Canada is the world's largest international trader.

Discussion Questions

1. Identify the principal actors in the contemporary international system and discuss their roles in determining the stability and instability of that system.

2. Discuss how terrorism has changed the meaning of homeland security to governments and international organizations. If governments remain preoccupied looking inward with issues of homeland

security, will the threat of terrorism roll back or speed up the advance of globalization?

3. One hundred years from now, will nation-states still dominate international affairs? If not, what organizations will? In what ways do multinational corporations (MNCs) challenge the power of nation-states?

4. Unequal in size and unequal in power, Canada and the United States conduct a unique relationship in world politics. Why is it unique and how stable is it? List three issues that will unite our interests and three that will divide our interests in the next ten years.

5. Should Canada, the United States, and Mexico renegotiate the North American Free Trade Agreement (NAFTA)? List three areas that are negotiable and three that are not negotiable.

Law in the Global System

After reading this chapter, you will be able to:

- reflect on how international law has evolved

- understand why rules are necessary in the global system

- define international law

- consider the role of international custom in the making of international law

- compare the character of international law with the various qualities of national law

- consider how binding global laws can be made in the absence of an international legislature or a world executive governing body

- identify what global instruments make international law

- describe how international organizations make international law

- understand the nature of compliance and deviance in the global community

- describe the role of the International Court of Justice in resolving global and international disputes

- present the facts behind the creation of the International Criminal Court (ICC)

- comment on the role of national courts for adjudicating and creating international law

- consider the directions international law is likely to take in the future

LAW AND ORDER IN THE GLOBAL COMMUNITY

World order involves not just international power relationships, but also the rules and norms that make for the security of the global system. The rule of law has never been more important than in the age of globalization. States, international organizations, non-governmental organizations, and transnational actors increasingly need to be regulated in order to bring about world peace and prosperity. Globalization encompasses many aspects—including expanding world trade, telecommunications, monetary co-ordination, scientific co-operation, the growth of knowledge, and cultural exchange—but an especially important factor is law.

Other than political, economic, and military sanctions, there are no **compulsory enforcement** instruments for compelling a government or an international organization to answer for its conduct in the international system. There is no international legislature (no world parliament) for making laws; there is no regular international police force to counteract illegal behaviour and arrest violators; and there is no **compulsory adjudication** to force a law-violator to appear in court and respect the law.

On the surface, it would appear that international law is a deterrent against **deviant behaviour** in the international community. But is this a misconception? In reality, most states do not violate international law. The states that tend to violate the rules of the global system are the most powerful ones and the ones that claim allegiance to international law, such as Russia in Chechnya, the USA in Iraq, and China in Tibet. For most other states, **compliance** with the laws of the international community is often greater than the degree of compliance and enforcement found in centralized national legal systems, where institutions to legislate and enforce laws are present and developed.[1]

Compliance with international law tends to be greater than with **municipal law** because states comply with rules out of national interest. States are the architects of systems of law and order in international affairs, and so are willing to tolerate constraints on their own behaviour in the absence of strong legislative and enforcement mechanisms. In addition, in the international community (which is composed of about 200 members) there are enormous pressures on governments to comply with the expected rules of behaviour. By means of legal challenges, diplomatic manoeuvres, and political jabs, violators are made to face the judgments of their peers.

When a state violates international law, it is almost always detected by other states, which may take extra-legal as well as legal and judicial measures against the perpetrator. In 2004, the International Court of Justice (ICJ) ruled that the United States violated the rights of 51 Mexicans on death row because while in American custody they were not given the right to assistance from the Mexican government. Mexico, as well as some Latin American states, publicly criticized the US position. A long-time champion of the rule of law, the US was seen to be breaking it.

WHAT IS INTERNATIONAL LAW?

International law has been defined as "a *system* of law containing *principles*, *customs*, *standards* and *rules* by which relations among states and other international persons are governed."[2] As with most definitions, key terms demand elaboration. International law is "systematic" because it endeavours to establish persisting patterns of legal relationships among all members of the international community, which are interdependent and which need a peaceful and orderly environment to survive. The systematic nature of international law results from its universal design, intended to invite compliance from all members of the international community. The **legitimacy** of international law is based on the consent of states to regard its authority as binding on their behaviour. Because of this need for consent, the probability of compliance increases significantly when a great number of states accept a rule of conduct. Thus, a multilateral treaty ratified by 150 states may have greater legitimacy than one that only 25 states have ratified.

International law is made up of generally accepted principles of law governing the conduct of states. Principles are fundamental rules of conduct that guide the legal behaviour of states. One such principle is the *ius cogens* (law of pre-emptory norms), whereby a treaty becomes void if it is contrary to norms recognized by the international community as a whole.[3] For example, a treaty signed and ratified by some states to exterminate a racial or ethnic group runs contrary to the general principles of international law and thus is void. Another accepted principle is the **legal equality** of independent states. This principle is generally recognized and upheld as universal international law. For example, Bolivia's vote in the General Assembly of the United Nations carries the same legal weight as Canada's, despite the differences in the size and wealth of both states.

Customs form a substantial body of international law. In a landmark case of international law—*The Paquette Habana v. The Lola* (1900)—US Supreme Court Justice Horace Gray defined custom as "ancient usage ripening into law." The incorporation of customs into **codified law** occurred frequently in the twentieth century. Customs that are widely practised as binding on states will continue to surface in the twenty-first century, as humans develop new technologies and explore outer space. For example, outer space is being researched and tested for the use of defensive and offensive military technology in the early twenty-first century, despite the existence of twentieth-century treaties and conventions that have designated outer space as a non-military area.

Standards of conduct refer to the generally accepted procedures by which states reach agreements and apply solutions to resolve conflicts.

Rather than resort to the use of force to settle disputes, states are expected to negotiate, **adjudicate**, and **arbitrate** when conflicts arise. States are obliged to employ peaceful instruments and skills in their relations with the other members of the international community.

Until the twentieth century, only states were considered as "persons," entities with rights and obligations under international law. Today, **legal personality** is extended to international organizations and individuals. For example, diplomatic immunities are enjoyed by organizations such as the United Nations and the Organization of American States, and are protected by international convention. These organizations have rights and duties similar to those of states. Under international law, individuals have legal personality only in a limited set of circumstances. Because most individuals possess a **nationality**, their own states act as agents either to protect them or to prosecute them for behaviour that has international consequences.

> **FACTFILE** The Hague Conference for the Codification of International Law in 1930 asserted in its preamble to the Convention on Nationality that every person should have a nationality.

When individuals become refugees, or **stateless**, international law directs a limited measure of legal personality to them. The basis for the legal protection of refugees was established during the Convention Relating to the Status of Refugees in 1951. This convention determined the rights of refugees to work, to education, to social welfare, to religious freedom, and to legal processes. Article 15 of the Universal Declaration of Human Rights (1948) laid down standards for dealing with stateless persons. International law encourages states to adopt a flexible approach to granting nationality to stateless persons and to providing them with proper identity documents to enable their legal admission or travel to other states.

> **FACTFILE** A rare example of statelessness occurs when an individual is stripped of nationality by his or her own government, such was the case of Jews living in Germany and other Nazi-occupied states before and during World War II.

> **FACTFILE** One of the declared weaknesses of the Kyoto Protocol since its inception in 1997 has been the consensual nature of countries setting voluntary limits on their emissions of greenhouse gases to reduce climate change.

Finally, international law is a very special kind of law because of its consensual nature.[4] It is intimately tied to the decentralized international system that emerged in Europe in the sixteenth and seventeenth centuries. Since the Treaty of Westphalia in 1648, most states that compose this decentralized international community have shown a willingness to abide by the law of the majority and have developed habits of compliance with international norms. This international system has successfully developed an identifiable process for creating legally binding rules of conduct, even in the absence of a complete set of formal institutional law-making machinery. The sources of this process of law are officially recognized by the states of the world and have been documented as Article 38 of the Statute of the International Court of Justice, which is attached to the United Nations Charter.

SOURCES OF INTERNATIONAL LAW

The international legal system consists of a substantial body of law derived from five sources

1. widely recognized and practised customs of states
2. international treaties and conventions signed and ratified by states
3. general principles of law recognized by states
4. judicial decisions of national and international courts and tribunals
5. writings and teachings of qualified legal experts

These are fundamentally democratic instruments that help create and collect the legitimate laws of the international system.[5]

Some scholars have noted that the acts of international organizations, particularly the United Nations and its special agencies, develop international law.[6] Each of these five sources has contributed to international legal development by recognizing the historical compliance of states and international organizations with the rules of international conduct and by establishing new laws (Figure 13.1).

Ultimately, however, states themselves are the principal source of international law. They hold the power of consent to the norms and customs that have evolved over a long period of time, and they ultimately become parties to the treaties that bind them to the codified laws of international behaviour.

Custom

With the emergence of modern European states in the mid-seventeenth century, the vast majority of transactions among independent political units were governed by customs. This body of observable usages and practices in international conduct became widely accepted by states as obligatory and binding as law. Habitual, constant, and uniform conduct evolved in many areas of international behaviour. Rules of conduct in times of war,

Figure 13.1   **Sources of international law**

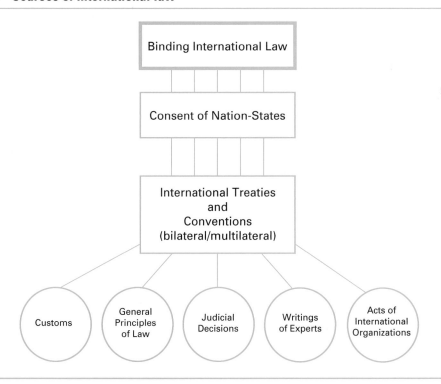

standard practices of navigation and maritime safety, diplomatic immunity, the observance of treaties, and the jurisdictions of states are examples of law built on the actual practices of states.

> **FACTFILE**   Starting with the Congress of Vienna (1815), governments saw the advantages of using international conferences to negotiate conventions that would convert custom into treaties and codified law.

Today, customs are transformed into legal rules because states recognized the expediency of order in a largely decentralized and lawless international community. The technical name for this psychological motivation to respect custom as law is *opinio iuris sive necessitatis* (*opinio iuris* for short), which means that legal forms of conduct are necessary if chaos is to be avoided.

Until the twentieth century, custom formed the bulk of international law among states. Difficulties were bound to ensue regarding customary international law because of inconsistencies in how states value and interpret custom.[7] For example, in the sixteenth and seventeenth centuries, states began to make conflicting claims about their jurisdictions within the territorial sea. Many states adopted the custom of regarding the border of the sea as three miles—the range of a cannonball fired seaward from the low-water mark on shore. Many states accepted this "cannon-shot" rule, but Scandinavian states claimed four miles of territorial sea and Spain and Portugal claimed six.

> **FACTFILE**   As early as 1370, the merchants and seafarers of Barcelona codified the customary law of the sea into a single code, which was published with the title Consulado del mar.

The codifying of international law has done much to clarify these types of inconsistencies in the practice of states. The Third United Nations Conference on the Law of the Sea (UNCLOS) (adopted on April 30, 1982) went a long way toward codifying these kinds of ambiguous practices of states. Article 3 of the convention reads

that "every state has the right to establish the breadth of its territorial sea up to a limit not exceeding twelve nautical miles." UNCLOS came into force in 1994 and to date has 154 state signatories and ratifications.

Today, even though customary law is still an important part of international law, treaties have displaced custom as its major source.[8] In a rapidly changing and more highly integrated international community, custom has come to be regarded as a scattered and imprecise source for determining rules of conduct. The confusion in locating the existence of, and determining the consent for, customary law has increasingly motivated states to negotiate law-making treaties.

International Conventions

Conventions are sometimes called treaties, covenants, accords, pacts, charters, declarations, statutes, or protocols.[9] Regardless of their name, all conventions are international law and have a binding effect on the parties that consent to them, based on the legal principle *pacta sunt servanda* (pacts are binding).

By definition, conventions are formal international agreements between two or more states. When they are entered into by only two states, the treaty is *bilateral*; when many states sign and ratify a treaty, it is said to be *multilateral*. As sources of international law, multilateral treaties perform two important functions: the codification of existing rules of customary international law (e.g., the Vienna Convention on Succession of States in Respect of Treaties, 1978) and the creation of new international law (e.g., the Kyoto Protocol, 1997).

Such treaties have global significance and are widely viewed to constitute world law because of their general and universal effect. Some international law experts have even identified multilateral conventions with the legislation of laws in municipal

Perspectives   Does International Law Protect Migratory Birds?

Birds know no national boundaries. When they migrate over borders they are not aware that they have entered the territory of another government, which may or may not be as vigilant about protecting them. For them, the planet is one place where they can survive if conditions remain viable for them.

In the nineteenth and twentieth centuries, hunters, farmers, and gun owners would often shoot birds for sport without any concern for whether their actions may have endangered a species of birds. In the United States, the Eagle, which is the national symbol of the country, was shot indiscriminately by hunters and poachers. It became necessary to protect species such as the Eagle with international laws, because they moved from one government jurisdiction to another.

We now know that birds are excellent barometers for natural systems that are threatened by human influences. Understanding the decline of Peregrine Falcons (the fastest animal in the world) and Bald Eagles in the late 1960s led to national bans on pesticides. Laws changed within the boundaries of Canada and the United States in order to protect these unique animals.

Many governments now recognize that it is in their national interest to protect birds while they live here through the various seasons. Canadian governments protect birds in the offshore Atlantic, the Gulf of Maine, the Georges Bank, the Bay of Fundy, and the Laurentian Channel.

Monitoring bird populations has become a vital exercise for national governments and international organizations. These institutions maintain major databases on bird populations and bird migrations. Such data enable us to analyze trends in our ecosystems and to evaluate the general health of the planet. The fate of bird species has provided global awareness about the need to protect the environment that sustains them, and us.

A large number of international treaties and domestic laws have been enacted to protect migratory birds on all continents. Some of these major international treaties include the Law of the Sea Treaty, the Convention on Wetlands, and the Bonn Convention on Migratory Species. The *Migratory Bird Act* of 1918 was passed by Canada, Mexico, Russia and the United States, and declares that all migratory birds and their parts (eggs, nests, feathers, etc.) were fully protected by international law.

legal systems. One noteworthy exception in this analogy is that conventions legally apply only to those states that consent to their provisions. Yet even under circumstances where a state does not ratify a treaty because it objects to some of its provisions, there are extra-legal pressures on non-consenting states to comply at least with the spirit of a law-making treaty, if not with the letter of the law in the treaty.

International law has been especially successful in protecting some well-known endangered species

frequently observed in Canada and the United States, such as the Whooping Crane, the Black Duck, and the Piping Plover. The US decision not to sign the 1982 Law of the Sea (UNCLOS) convention does not exempt that state from respecting most of the internationally agreed-upon provisions involving the laws of navigation, fishing rights, conservation, the continental shelf, and the proclaimed establishment off US shores of a 200-mile Exclusive Economic Zone (EEZ) that is compatible with many of the provisions of the convention. Because more than 150 states adopted the UNCLOS convention, the US is sensitive to the near-global consensus on this regime of maritime law and recognizes the rights of other states in the waters off its coasts, as outlined in the convention.

Article 102 of the United Nations Charter requires that all treaties be registered with the Secretariat of the United Nations so that they are known to the world. This requirement adds another important dimension of legitimacy to all treaties, bilateral as well as multilateral. Open publication of treaties is not only intended to discourage the practice of secret conventions; it also demonstrates the levels of consensus achieved concerning international norms and expectations.

FACTFILE   In 1817, the United States secured the demilitarization of its border with Canada through the Rush-Bagot agreement—an executive understanding between both governments that was the basis for describing the 49th parallel international boundary as the "longest undefended border."

The continuing development of international law has been greatly enhanced since 1947, when the General Assembly of the United Nations created the *International Law Commission* (ILC). The ILC is charged with the tasks of studying, recommending, and codifying international law. Its numerous international law experts—who represent most of the world's legal systems—research and codify customary law in the areas of recognition, state succession, diplomatic immunities,

Focus On **Canada and the Law of the Sea**

Canada has been a major player in the law of the sea, in particular as it has affected fishing in territorial waters and the high seas. Canadian leaders helped draft the Geneva conventions in the late 1950s and early 1960s, which codified many of the international customs on changing coastal jurisdiction. And Canada was at the forefront of the near-global negotiations that produced the 1982 Law of the Sea Treaty.

In 1995, Canada signed a United Nations treaty that promised to calm the troubled waters of high-seas fishing around Canadian territorial waters. The treaty gave Canada and the other signatories much more control over fishing for migratory stocks, such as cod, salmon, and turbot, by foreign fleets.

Canada's push for the treaty should end the likelihood of high seas showdowns like the so-called Turbot War in the spring of 1995 between Canada and Spain. The Spanish fishing vessels were targeted by Ottawa for gross violations of a number of international fishing agreements, which resulted in the seizure of a Spanish trawler. In the campaign to highlight Canada's case against the European Union for illegal turbot fishing in the international waters off the Grand Banks of Newfoundland, relations between Spain and Canada deteriorated.

About 25 states signed the UN agreement on straddling and migratory fish stocks, including Canada, the United States, Russia, and Norway. The UN agreement effectively overturns 500 years of international law in favour of conservation and management. States will no longer have the freedom to fish on the high seas as they did under the law of the sea. Instead, largely because of Canada's efforts in framing the agreement, foreign governments will be obliged to co-operate and regulate fishing to prevent the continued depletion of species and regenerate stocks for the future.

state jurisdictional immunities, law of the sea, nationality, statelessness, and arbitral procedures. They consolidate their legal research and prepare drafts that are reported to the General Assembly, which has often convened international conferences to adopt law-making treaties.

The ILC did the preparatory work for a convention on diplomatic relations at Vienna in 1961, a convention on consular relations at Vienna in 1963, a convention on the law of treaties at Vienna in 1969, the convention on state succession at Vienna in 1978, and conventions on the law of the sea at Geneva in 1958 and at the United Nations in 1982.

The writing of draft articles of agreement by the ILC has been instrumental in summarizing international laws that have evolved over a period of 2500 years. By gradually displacing the uncertainties of different customs practised by states, lawmaking treaties have injected a high degree of precision in the application of international law.

General Principles of Law

In cases where treaty law and customary law do not provide guidance in international disputes, the Statute of the International Court of Justice (ICJ) points to "the general principles of law recognized by civilized nations."[10] To avoid the possibility of a case remaining undecided and to ensure that justice is done when other sources of law provide no assistance, states in conflict will sometimes invoke generally recognized principles of national and international law to settle disputes.

Some of these general principles of international law revolve around the concepts of sovereignty, legal equality of states, territorial integrity, and non-interference in the internal affairs of other states. They have also been drawn from the principles of justice derived from natural law, which is increasingly relevant to the concept of globalization.[11] The concepts that each side in a

dispute is entitled to a fair hearing and that judicial decisions should be made *ex aequo et bono* (out of justice and fairness) when no exacting codes of law are applicable are examples of general principles of law applied in international tribunals.

> **FACTFILE**   In 1948, the General Assembly of the United Nations approved by acclamation the Universal Declaration of Human Rights, which is a statement of general principles of law such as due process, equal protection, good faith, and fairness.

The practice of incorporating international law into domestic legal systems is another general principle linking national and international law. Canada, the United States, Belgium, France, and Switzerland, to name but a few, have practised the adoption, incorporation, and harmonization of international law with domestic law-making processes.

This has important legal consequences for the nationals of one country contesting an international dispute in another domestic legal system. In the case of *The Paquette Habana v. The Lola*, Supreme Court of the United States (1900), the court reasoned that "international law is part of our law and must be ascertained and administered by courts of justice of appropriate jurisdictions." In *West Rand Central Gold Mining Co., Ltd. v. The King*, King's Bench Division, Great Britain (1905), the court ruled that "it is true that whatever has received the common consent of civilized nations must have received the consent of Great Britain, and that to which the latter has assented . . . could properly be called international law."

In Canada, over 20 percent of the Revised Statutes of Canada incorporate the rules of international customary and treaty law.[12] But Canadian courts have not ruled consistently on the relationship of international law to domestic law. In some early cases, such as *The Ship "North" v. The King* (1906), it appeared that Canada was following court practices in the United Kingdom to take "judicial notice" of the rules of international law and to interpret the rules of domestic law in a manner compatible with them. In 1943, however, in two cases (*Power of Municipalities to Levy Rates on Foreign Legations* and *High Comm'rs Residences and Reference re Exemption of U.S. Forces from Canadian Criminal Law*), a number of justices of the Supreme Court argued that even customary international law is part of Canadian law only if those customs are formally "incorporated" by Parliament or given judicial notice. In another case, *République Democratique du Congo v. Venne* (1971), the Supreme Court clearly supported the principle that customary international law is part of Canadian law. Similarly, in 1969, the Quebec Court of Appeal, in *Penthouse Studios Inc. v. Government of Venezuela*, recognized that even the changing character of custom is enforced in Canada.

> **FACTFILE** Natural law has been the starting point for international law because it sees law as derived from fundamental principles of justice that have universal and ongoing validity as general principles of law.

There is no question that different systems of national law try to conform to general principles of law as derived directly from the international community or from within themselves. The problems of seeking and interpreting general principles of law result from the isolated traditions of law throughout the world. The Anglo-American system, the **Napoleonic Code**, the Islamic system, and the system of law most communist states follow are based on different philosophical and cultural premises. But the disparity of fundamental legal systems does not take away the political need to foster legal uniformity. There exists a tacit understanding in the world community that international order is safeguarded by specific rules of common acceptance. The Statute of the International Court of Justice has recognized the imperative character of these rules as a primary source of international law. And among states, we can detect a conscious subordination of state activity to the general welfare of the international community.

Judicial Decisions

Judicial decisions are cited in Article 38(1) (d) of the statute "as subsidiary means for the determination of rules of law." The problem international law presents is twofold: in the absence of formal law-making institutions, it is always necessary to first establish agreement on the very idea of international law itself. This problem is significant for judicial decisions because they are viewed primarily as an indirect and subsidiary source of international law.

Yet upon close examination, the value of domestic and international court decisions as sources of international law can be discovered. If a court in a domestic legal system or an international tribunal interprets a contentious question of international law, its judicial opinion includes the rationale for the decision, the *ratio decidendi*. It indicates what the rule is held to mean at the time the decision is drafted. This provides the international community with a ruling on international law, a kind of precedent, to which analogous cases may conform.

Even though, in international law, there is no doctrine of *stare decisis et non quieta movere* (to stand by decisions and not to move what has been settled) to affirm the obligatory character of previous decisions as precedents, most court systems take **judicial notice** of them and usually take them into account. In time, as precedents are rendered by a series of similar judicial decisions, a body of legal opinions is formed. As early as 1815, Chief Justice John Marshall of the Supreme Court of the United States ruled in the case of *Thirty Hogsheads of Sugar v. Boyle* that "the decisions of the Courts of every country show how the law of nations, in the given case, is understood in that country, and will be considered in adopting the rule which is to prevail in this." In the *Barcelona Traction* case, the ICJ made reference to the rulings on nationality in an earlier *precedent* case (the *Nottebohm* case) in order to distinguish the nationality of a Canadian company that was controlled by Belgian shareholders and that incurred injuries inflicted by Spain.[13]

FACTFILE   Contrary to popular belief, most legal questions in international law are resolved in national courts, not in the International Court of Justice or the various other international tribunals that have been established.

The ICJ has not only taken judicial notice of previous cases in affirming the existence of customary and codified law but has, in some cases, created new law. In the *Reparation for Injuries Suffered in the Service of the United Nations* case (1949), the court certified the legal personality of the United Nations and affirmed the capacity of that international organization to assert claims against other entities in the international system for injuries suffered by its agents. Similarly, in the *Anglo-Norwegian Fisheries* case (1951), the ICJ stated new criteria for the delimitation of base lines from which to determine the width of the territorial sea. These criteria were adopted by the Geneva Convention on the Territorial Sea and Contiguous Zone (1958) and included in the Law of the Sea Convention in 1982.

FACTFILE   The main use of the World Court is to arbitrate issues of secondary importance between and among friendly states. States have used the court infrequently over the years (from 1946 to 2006, only 66 judgments and 27 advisory opinions were handed down).

There is no question that international law is both summarized and created by judicial decisions rendered by domestic and international tribunals. Each decision made by these courts carries its own prestige, which—when combined with the traditional and legal authority of the courts in question—creates a subsidiary but nonetheless important source of international law. In effect, all national judicial decisions of international consequence contribute to the substance of international law.

Writings of Learned Experts

In addition to being a legal system, international law is also a formal academic field of study, drawing expertise from the disciplines of history, law, philosophy, and political science. The academic study of international law developed concurrently with the modern nation-state system in the sixteenth and seventeenth centuries. Learned writers, or "publicists," as they were once called, began to analyze and interpret the evolution of international law.

Hugo Grotius (1583–1645), widely acclaimed as the founder of international law, published his *De jure belli ac pacis Libri Tris* (Three Books on the Law of War and Peace) in 1625. It was the first modern study of the law of states. Other noteworthy publicists to follow Grotius were Richard Zouche (1590–1660), Samuel Pufendorf (1632–1694), Emmerich de Vattel (1714–1769), and John Austin (1790–1859). In 1790, Jeremy Bentham invented the term "international law" to designate what had previously been called "the law of nations" (**jus gentium**, *droit des gens*) in his book *An Introduction to the Principles of Morals and Legislation*, which was published in 1789. In more recent times, names such as Hans Kelsen, Josef Kunz, James Brierly, Richard Falk, and Michael Akehurst are widely regarded as modern legal publicists.

Contemporary writers conduct comparative research into the behavioural aspects of international law. They plot trends in the legal expectations of states and monitor the international system for new sources of law in codified form, for any legal or academic reference is a major unofficial contribution to the body of scholarly materials on international law. Today, almost every state has a pool of international legal experts who publish work on a regular basis for use by justices who deliberate upon international cases.

ACTS OF INTERNATIONAL INSTITUTIONS

The Statute of the International Court of Justice does not list the acts of international organizations as a source of international law. However, a growing number of scholars now detect a substantial body of international law directly emerging from the work of numerous international institutions.[14] Most international organizations are institutional forums in which legal norms are debated, generated, and promoted by member states. Some well-known international organizations that promote world law are Amnesty International (London), the International Court of Justice (Hague), and the World Health organization (Geneva). Many of these organizations pass resolutions and declarations that carry **quasi-legal** authority and promote world law. It is true that these resolutions and declarations are not as binding as ratified treaties. But they represent a consensus of membership expectations on important matters of international behaviour.

FACTFILE   The UN Charter proclaims that states are equal under international law; have full sovereignty, independence, and territorial integrity; and should carry out their international obligations under international law.

In the **inter-American system**, resolutions and declarations adopted at conferences are regarded as binding by Latin American states, and thus create legal obligations among them. For example, the 1948 Charter of Bogotá established the Organization of American States (OAS), which obligates all signatory states to use peaceful settlement procedures, including diplomacy, good offices, mediation, investigation, conciliation, arbitration, and adjudication.

In the General Assembly of the United Nations, resolutions are not necessarily binding on member states, but often they call for the creation of an international conference to draft a multilateral treaty that would bind signatories. The consensus expressed through resolutions and declarations in the United Nations can lead to the creation of a new rule in conventional law or may reflect the presence of a new principle of international custom. For example, in 1963, the General Assembly passed its Declaration of Legal Principles Governing Activities in Outer Space and Celestial Bodies. Under the law, these bodies are free for exploration and use by all states in conformity with international law.

Another international organization that has played a pioneering role in creating new international law has been the International Labour Organization (ILO). Since its establishment in 1919, it has built a body of law known as the International Labour Code. At present, the code consists of the work of nearly 160 conventions that have dealt with a wide range of ratified recommendations in the areas of workers' rights, wages, insurance benefits, and the protection of women, young people, miners, and sailors. In a similar way, the World Health Organization (WHO) created the Code of International Health Regulations, adopted in 1969, to establish legal controls on hundreds of drugs used throughout the states of the world.

One other specialized agency of the United Nations, the International Civil Aviation Organization (ICAO), headquartered in Montreal, has been one of the most active bodies in the development of international law of air transportation. The ICAO has established regulations governing information and safety standards, airport facilities, and services in world air transportation.

The International Court of Justice

The International Court of Justice, sometimes called the World Court, is one of the six principal organs of the United Nations, with headquarters at The Hague, Netherlands. The court is attended

Crosscurrents — Did NATO Violate International Law by Its Actions in Afghanistan and the Former Yugoslavia?

Is the war in Afghanistan illegal? The US, assisted by Canada and Great Britain, has been bombing Afghanistan for the stated purpose of capturing or killing Osama bin Laden, other people associated with Al Qaeda, and hunting the Taliban.

The Charter of the United Nations clearly prohibits the use of force to topple foreign governments. It goes on to forbid the killing of non-combatants (that is, Afghani civilians). No member of NATO was attacked by Afghanistan. No resolutions of NATO provided collective legal authority to use armed force against Afghanistan or the Taliban. The United States put together its own group of allies within NATO, leaving the US in control of all aspects of the current military operations in Afghanistan. NATO may have placed itself in an illegal position of attacking a state in the Middle East to implement US foreign policy goals.

In 1999, 13 of NATO's member states conducted a massive military operation against Yugoslavia's president, Slobodan Milosevic. It led Canada into a war that set many precedents, not the least of which were the first air battles over European skies since 1945 and the first offensive assault by NATO on a sovereign nation-state. But NATO's decision to bomb Yugoslavia (which ceased to exist as a nation-state in 2006) raised fundamental questions of international law because it came without UN approval, against a state that created no immediate threat to the border of any NATO state.

Did NATO violate international law and the United Nations Charter? Was NATO acting in self-defence and therefore justified under international law in its act of military aggression? Based on the prescriptions of the 1948 United Nations Declaration of Human Rights, can an international organization wage a "humanitarian war" against a sovereign government that is reported to be abusing its citizens? If NATO conducts such a war in one circumstance, is it obligated to engage in similar military action against other states that violate humanitarian law? All of these questions reflect the uncertain environment in which international law can be interpreted, calling into question the righteous actions of NATO.

Unlike many other kinds of law, international law is still developing the institutional instruments it needs to make universally binding rules in the international system. In the absence of a world government, what can national governments or international organizations do to protect the vulnerable citizens of a state experiencing a civil war?

by 15 judges serving nine-year terms, and elected by a concurrent vote of the General Assembly and the Security Council. In order to provide fair representation, no two judges of the same nationality may sit on the bench at the same time. And if parties to the dispute do not have national judges elected at the time the case is heard, they may appoint their own judge with full voting rights. Cases are decided by majority vote and, in the event of a tie, the president of the court casts the deciding vote. The expenses of the International Court of Justice are borne by the United Nations: No court fees are paid by parties to the ICJ statute.

According to ICJ statute, only states are entitled to appear as litigants before the court. When contesting states permit the court to make a judgment in a case, that judgment binds the parties. For this reason, many states have been reluctant to register their legal complaints with the court. And sometimes countries that submit to the court simply ignore the decision. Several states, including such outstanding international citizens as Iceland, India, and France, have refused to submit to the panel's rulings.

Because the ICJ lacks compulsory adjudication, whereby states would be compelled to appear before the world tribunal to defend their actions, the court can hear only those cases that states choose to bring before it. To strengthen the position of the court in this regard, Article 36 of the statute provides the *optional clause*. Under this clause, states agree in advance to accept the compulsory adjudication of the court in questions of treaty interpretation, international law, breaches of international obligations, and reparations.

FACTFILE   Judges who sit on the ICJ do not represent their respective governments; they sit as independent magistrates in the Court and must be jurists of recognized competence in international law.

Canada and the United States accepted the compulsory adjudication of the court to settle a question of jurisdiction on the North American east coast. In 1984, the World Court ruled on a boundary dispute that had been raging for seven years between Canada and the United States over the rich resources and fishing grounds on the Georges Bank off the coasts of Maine, Massachusetts, and Nova Scotia.

The disputed jurisdictions resulted when both states extended their territorial limits 200 nautical miles to sea. In its decision, the ICJ dismissed the arguments of both states and developed its own criteria for drawing a new boundary line between Massachusetts and Nova Scotia (see Figure 13.2), asserting that Canada and the United States had based some of their claims on false premises. The decision was binding in accordance with a 1981 Canada–US agreement that registered the dispute with the ICJ and accepted its jurisdiction to rule on the Georges Bank with no appeal.

In this dispute, Canada proposed a line based on the principle of **equidistance** and disregarded the existence of Cape Cod and Nantucket Islands, arguing that they constituted unusual geographic protrusions of the US coastline. Washington claimed all of the Georges Bank with a proposed line that came as close as 25 nautical miles to Yarmouth, Nova Scotia.

FACTFILE   An advisory legal opinion is rendered by an international court in response to a question submitted by some authorized body, and it differs from contentious court proceedings in that there are no parties before the court as complainants or defendants.

The World Court awarded Canada one-sixth of the bank—only half the territory it claimed—but it unexpectedly got the northeast edge, where there are concentrations of scallop beds, vital to Nova Scotia's $60-million-a-year scallop industry. The area awarded to the United States amounts to five-sixths of the Georges Bank, over which Washington claimed total jurisdiction. Despite the dislocation and economic hardship the decision generated for the people in the fishing industries of both states, the court's ruling was accepted as international law. The court's ruling was unexpected by both parties and, in effect, created new law that will likely affect five other maritime disputes in which Canada is involved—three with the United States, one with France over Saint-Pierre and Miquelon, and one with Greenland.

Of the 173 states that are parties to the Statute of the International Court of Justice, only about 60 adhere to the optional clause, most with **reservations** that effectively render its acceptance meaningless. Since its creation in 1946, the court has rendered judgments in just over 100 cases. Many cases are removed without judgment because the defendant states refuse to submit to the court's jurisdiction or because the plaintiffs removed the case to settle out of court. Besides hearing and deciding on this small number of cases since 1946, the ICJ has been utilized for numerous advisory opinions, most of them

Figure 13.2 **Disputed fishing grounds (Canada/United States) adjudicated by the ICJ**

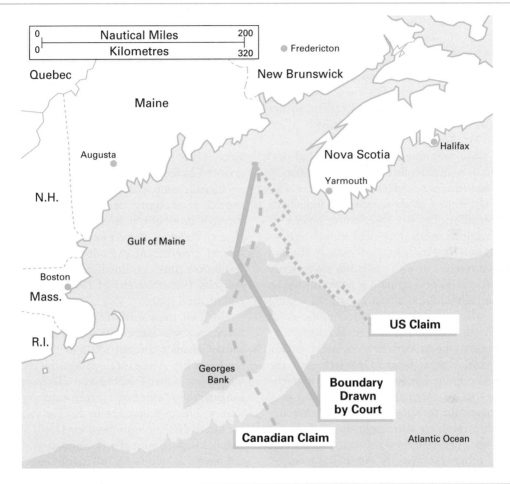

As witnessed by the short docket of cases since the 1950s, states are reluctant to submit to the jurisdiction of the World Court. There are *three* major reasons why states appear to distrust the court as a legal instrument for resolving conflict. First, powerful states tend to avoid the embarrassment of a legal judgment on their behaviour. They are unwilling to entrust matters of national importance to a non-national legal body with high international visibility. Second, states are more inclined to resort to political instruments such as negotiation, conciliation, and mediation to settle disputes peacefully. Third, many states (in the Islamic world) sense that international law is dominated by Western legal traditions that are alien to legal principles in their domestic systems; consequently they distrust the judicial process of the World Court.

> **FACTFILE** Genocide is defined as a list of prohibited acts committed with the intent to destroy in whole or in part a national, ethnical, racial, or religious group.

Focus On

Will Canada Be Able to Maintain Its Sovereignty over the Arctic?

Canadians are increasingly concerned about sovereignty over the Arctic. But are we concerned enough? Canada stands to lose 1 million square kilometres of Arctic sovereignty, which it has claimed for about 140 years.

As global warming melts the table land (ice) thought to be exclusively Canadian, the seafaring world and natural resources companies are willing to challenge Canada using international law and, sometimes, through sheer power politics.

Warming temperatures and longer navigation seasons have increased maritime traffic and renewed interest in who really has sovereignty in the Arctic. World opinion is powerful and so are the technological advancements of coastal states, which will use their technologies to enter Arctic waters and make their point.

Access to the Arctic is now coveted by many states: US, Russia, Japan, Denmark, and the entire European Union. They have the technologies to get there and stay there, and they also possess the military capability of enforcing what they think are their rights under international law. These states want access to the vast oil and other resources the Arctic has to offer. They also want the same rights of innocent passage they enjoy on the high seas in most other oceans of the world.

Since 1969, when the US icebreaker *Manhattan* entered our Arctic waters without Canada's permission, the US has ignored our historic claim. The Americans cruised through the Northwest Passage as if it was international waters, picked up a single symbolic barrel of oil from Prudhoe Bay, and then headed home in defiance of Canada's claim. The world took notice. For this and other reasons, successive US Administrations have not taken Canada's claim to Arctic sovereignty very seriously.

Canada immediately objected to the US incursion, holding that since 1880 the waters of the Arctic Archipelago have been Canadian internal waters by virtue of decreed historic title. The Inuit of Canada have used the waters since time immemorial. Canada has never doubted its sovereign ownership until recently.

Canada exercised unqualified and uninterrupted sovereignty over the Arctic mostly through its public policies, such as the *Arctic Waters Pollution Prevention Act*. In 2008, the federal government extended the enforceable "pollution zone" outlined in the *Arctic Waters Pollution Prevention Act* of 1970, from 100 to 200 nautical miles.

In 1988, the *Canada-US Agreement on Arctic Sovereignty* was signed to ensure that the US gains Canada's consent while in the waters of the Canadian Arctic Archipelago. In 2000, the US Coast Guard icebreaker *Healy* met all Canadian legal standards before entering Arctic waters. Things seemed to be resolvable.

But in 2007, US Ambassador David Wilkins stated his government's position that Canada can have the Arctic's 36 500 islands but that the water is international territory.

Only three Canadian Prime Ministers have taken Canada's sovereignty in the north as a matter of urgency. They led Conservative governments: John Diefenbaker, Brian Mulroney, and Stephen Harper. Unfortunately despite their concerns, there has been much less of a government presence and not much of a permanent population to show undisputed sovereign possession.

The Harper government announced its northern strategy, which entails building two new military facilities to bolster Canada's sovereign claim over the Northwest Passage. There will also be a new army training centre and a deepwater port to extend the range of Canadian ships in the Arctic at the eastern entrance of the Northwest Passage. Ships entering Arctic waters are now required to notify Canadians authorities.

The Harper government promised to refurbish existing federal buildings at Resolute Bay. The 60-year old Inuit Rangers program will be expanded with more funding and personnel over the next ten years. But will it be enough?

The doctrine of *freedom of the seas* runs contrary to Canada's Arctic claims. Opening the Arctic to international exploitation will certainly further erode the delicate Arctic environment. It will threaten the way of life of indigenous people and affect our status as a middle power.

The US might temper its demands now that terrorists would also gain unconstrained access to the Arctic as international waters. The US interest would be much better served by an ally, such as Canada, holding full sovereignty over these waters.

This issue is not going away soon for Canada. The world will continue to challenge the federal government on its sovereign position under international law.

For reasons such as these, the court has not **remedied** major international disputes. In their long-running boundary dispute over the waters surrounding the islands of Saint-Pierre and Miquelon, both Canada and France avoided the use of the ICJ in 1988, and opted instead to have a mediator help settle their differences over fishing quotas while negotiators continued to seek agreement on geographical boundaries. (France claimed 320-kilometre territorial waters and Canada recognized only a 19-kilometre boundary.)

Mediation, rather than adjudication, was more acceptable to the authorities in both countries, even after Canada arrested 17 French island fishermen and four politicians for illegally fishing in Canadian waters. The French retaliated shortly thereafter by seizing a Newfoundland trawler for fishing in the disputed waters off the islands of Saint-Pierre and Miquelon. However, in 1989, Canada and France agreed to resolve their 12-year territorial dispute by sending it to binding international arbitration. The international tribunal is composed of five judges—one from Canada, one from France, one from Uruguay, one from Italy, and one from the United States. In 1992, the **International Court of Arbitration** gave France exclusive economic jurisdiction over a sea corridor of 10.5 nautical miles, running south of the tiny French islands of Saint-Pierre and Miquelon for a distance of 200 miles. However, the corridor juts deeply into Canadian waters, where many fish stocks, including endangered species of cod, swim freely and through scallop beds that traditionally have been fished by Newfoundland fishers. The ruling forced France and Canada to open negotiations on the management of these important fish stocks.

FACTFILE   The Nuremberg and Tokyo trials in 1947–1948 recognized the need for a permanent international criminal court, the idea for which was revived by A.N.R. Robinson, the former Prime Minister of Trinidad and Tobago, who made the proposal for such a court before the General Assembly of the United Nations in 1989.

FACTFILE   Canada's *Crimes Against Humanity and War Crimes Act* (2000) criminalizes acts of genocide, war crimes, crimes against humanity, and breach of military responsibility, making them indictable in Canada regardless of where the crimes are committed.

Focus On   Creating the International Criminal Court

The twentieth century witnessed the greatest number of people ever killed in wars and acts of state aggression. Nine million people (mostly military combatants) perished during World War I. In that war, more soldiers were killed than civilians. But 64 million (mostly civilians) perished during World War II. Many more civilians and non-combatants died than soldiers.

It is estimated that more than 170 million people (mostly civilians) perished as a result of brutal foreign and civil wars during the twentieth century. Many of these people died largely because of criminal acts that fall outside the legal definition of acts of war. Such acts came to be regarded as crimes against humanity: genocide, ethnic cleansing, sexual slavery and maiming, amputation of limbs, and other crimes of war.

By the end of the twentieth century, the international community saw the need to create the world's first independent and permanent International Criminal Court (ICC). The United Nations Security Council was responding to injustice by creating ad hoc tribunals bound by their mandates to specific times and places. A permanent court with a mandate to bring to justice individuals responsible for the world's most serious crimes was deemed more effective and efficient.

On July 17, 1998, at an international conference held in Rome, 120 states voted to adopt a treaty to create the ICC. Only seven states voted against the idea, including China, Israel, Iraq, and the United States. Twenty-one states abstained for one reason or another. By April 2002, more than 60 states, the number required to establish the court, had ratified the treaty. By 2007, 105 states had ratified or acceded to the court, including nearly all the countries of Europe and South America, and roughly half of Africa. A further 41 states have signed but not ratified.

The jurisdiction of the court began when the required ratifications were submitted. In 2004, the governing body of the ICC, the Assembly of States Parties, elected the court's first bench of 18 judges, which include seven women and which represent all of the regions of the world.

In 2008, the president of Sudan, Omar Hassan al-Bashir, was charged with crimes against humanity committed between 2003 and 2008 by perpetuating genocide against 300 000 people, primarily in Darfur.

In 2009, the court will review the list of crimes under its jurisdiction. The expectation is that terrorism and drug trafficking will be added to the list at that time.

Since 1945, international bodies other than the ICJ have been used to address serious international questions. Political and military power has been the primary method employed by states in major conflicts such as Vietnam, Biafra, the Cuba, Northern Ireland, the Middle East, Yugoslavia, Iraq, and Afghanistan. Generally, international confidence in the court remains weak, and this diminishes the legitimacy of the highest tribunal in the world.

FACTFILE The first charges under Canada's *Crimes Against Humanities and War Crimes Act* were laid by the RCMP who arrested a thirty-year-old Rwandan, Desire Munyaneza, on charges of genocide, crimes against humanity, and war crimes.

Acts of the International Law Commission

The International Law Commission (ILC) is a principal instrument for codifying and developing international law. The procedures the ILC employs clarify and standardize existing international law, as well as help to draft the results of research for consideration as new law. The commission uses the following steps to execute its mandate in all areas of codifying modern international law:

- Researches and selects a relevant *international law* topic.
- Submits this topic to the General Assembly for approval.
- Appoints a commission rapporteur as liaison with the General Assembly.
- Reports preliminary drafts to the General Assembly.
- Meets to discuss and revise the submission.
- Receives feedback from governments.
- Incorporates suggestions into the draft.
- Submits the revised draft to the General Assembly.

The General Assembly then decides whether to convene an international conference to consider the commission's draft. If a conference is held, the participating delegates may make further revisions before the document is prepared for consenting governments to sign. It then follows the slow process of state ratifications before the new convention comes into force. Such were the procedures used by the commission for the Convention on the Reduction of Statelessness (1961) and the Convention on Liability for Damage Caused by Objects Launched into Outer Space (1971).

In spite of what appear to be enormous obstacles, the track record of the ILC is impressive. Most of the multilateral treaties signed and ratified since 1950 have been drafted by the ILC. Its main achievements are in the codification of international customary law; but because of its direct link to world legal opinion, it has great potential to make major breakthroughs in the creation of new laws. The codification and accompanying globalization of international law—a phenomenon witnessed for the first time in the twentieth century—has provided more opportunities and incentives for states to resolve international conflict peacefully rather than violently.

International law continues to evolve. Notwithstanding its many imperfections, the international legal system has come a long way. No legal system, regardless of its enforcement capabilities, can completely deter violations of the law. International law **proscribes** genocide, yet Idi Amin of Uganda, Pol Pot of Kampuchea, Iraq's Saddam Hussein, and Yugoslavia's Slobodan Milosevic ignored that proscription, killing thousands of their own citizens.

States believe it is of paramount importance that they appear not to be in violation of international law so that they can appeal to international morality and world public opinion in support of their actions. Every world leader is aware that the international system is a fishbowl into which all states can look to observe and judge the behaviour of their legal peers.

Slobodan Milosevic was the first sitting leader to be charged with war crimes while those criminal activities were still ongoing. The International Criminal Tribunal indicted him and four other Yugoslav officials for gross violations of humanitarian law.

Milosevic maintained his innocence, refused to recognize the jurisdiction of the International Criminal Tribunal, and accused NATO of committing war crimes because it had openly targeted the civilian infrastructure of Serbia and used cluster bombs that caused thousands of civilian deaths.

In March 2006, Milosevic was found dead in his cell at The Hague. His trial for war crimes and crimes against humanity therefore ended without a verdict.

In past centuries, international law merely served as a normative constraint on the exercise of certain types of power practised by states. But during the twentieth century, there existed the largest number of legally binding bilateral and multilateral treaties governing the behaviour of states in human history. We also saw more international organizations dedicated to the promotion and codification of world law than in any previous period. As the twenty-first century begins, a comprehensive set of binding rules, rights, obligations, and **principles** now can have immediate global impact upon the national interest of states.

THE FUTURE GLOBALIZATION OF LAW

Until recent decades, law in the international community has been the exclusive jurisdiction of the nation-state. The existence of law in a competitive state system requires the consent of governments. But with the advent of globalization, law now can bypass the nation-state to interface directly with individuals, corporations, and other non-state actors. The most serious challenge of international law has been universal acceptance and compliance with its dictates.

The globalization of law refers to the degree to which the whole world lives under a single set of legal rules. It is the process whereby regulations, rules, and legal standards are becoming universal. Such a set of rules might be imposed by individual nation-states or an international body.

In a world of international trade, tourism, and the interdependence of human communication, the need for transnational law has increased many times over. Because more and more states have opened their economies and their societies to outside influences, there is a growing recognition that we need a uniform system of law.

Already there has been movement toward uniform global contract law, commercial law, and foreign investment. People who engage in these activities in one part of the world will come under the same rules as people involved in them in other parts of the world.

The globalization of protective rights has exploded around the planet, prompting governments of all persuasions to respect the dictates of this branch of law. The law of human rights, consumer rights, commercial rights, product standards, and occupational health and safety has come closest to universal application.

FACTFILE   The United Nations has censured Canada on more than one occasion on its treatment of Aboriginal peoples.

Globalization imposes pressures on states and international organizations to create law responsively and with universal global application. The present array of international law-making institutions is functional, but it is imperfect. There is no world legislature or executive decision-making institution to make law in direct response to global need. The ground seems ready to accelerate the process of international lawmaking and implementation.

Globalization has also produced its own powerful momentum, generating rules and expectations in the absence of a fully developed legal institutional system. Scholars refer to this as **soft law**.[15]

The future effectiveness of world law depends on the willingness of national governments and their legal systems to comply with and enforce global norms. The most significant challenges to international law concern the use of force, intervention, and arms control.

The danger is always that powerful governments acting alone will intervene to protect their interests and values only, without approval of international bodies. The interventions by Russia in Georgia and by the United States in Iraq are cases in point. International law exists in part to prevent states possessing capable military power from intervening in the affairs of other countries unilaterally. But, as yet, international bodies do not have the authority to effectively stop unilateral interventions by superpowers and other nation states.

Will international law meet the challenges of the twenty-first century as a universal expression of human law and order? That will depend on how well states can respond to contemporary global demands and how they can create new rules to cope with a rapidly changing world. The twentieth century confirmed that international law does exist and can be made within an imperfect system. But how law will look in the twenty-first century and what kind of shape it will take as we approach the next decade are matters of profound importance.

Chapter Summary

For centuries, laws were made in a decentralized political environment requiring the consent of nation-states to build a body of rules for the safety of humankind. However, globalization is now placing new demands on the law-making capacity of the international community.

International law is a system of law containing principles, customs, standards, and rules by which relations among states and other international "persons" are governed. The sources of international law are state customs, international treaties and conventions ratified by states, general principles of law recognized by states, judicial decisions of national and international courts, and the writing and teachings of qualified legal experts.

As we begin the twenty-first century, international law is a significant force in the world of international relations. Never before have so many laws been codified to govern the behaviour of international actors. Never before have so many institutions been established to foster formal acceptance of international norms. Indeed, the twenty-first century will be remembered as the period of human history that saw the globalization of law.

There is as yet no international legislature for making international laws; there is no regular international police force to implement laws; and there is no compulsory adjudication to force a violator of the law to appear in court and respect the law. Most nation-states comply with international law simply because it is in their national interests to do so.

The International Court of Justice is a principal organ of the United Nations, with its headquarters at The Hague, the Netherlands. It comprises 15 judges, elected by the General Assembly and Security Council. They serve nine-year terms. The ICJ lacks compulsory jurisdiction, but Article 36 of the statute of the ICJ (optional clause) declares that states can agree in advance to accept the court's decisions as binding.

The International Law Commission (ILC) is the principal international body created under the United Nations for codifying and developing international law.

Most international law is adjudicated in national courts, which are recognized under Article 38(1)(d) of the statute of the ICJ as subsidiary means for determining the rules of international law.

Multilateral treaties make international law because they codify new general rules of international conduct and because, usually, they are binding on many states. Resolutions and declarations made by the decision-making bodies of international organizations have a legal character because they represent a consensus of membership expectations on important matters of international behaviour.

Discussion Questions

1. In the absence of a world legislature, where laws would be introduced, debated, and proclaimed, can it be said that international law is *real* law? How has globalization influenced the creation of international law?

2. Why do most states voluntarily observe international law most of the time? Why do some states violate international law? Give examples.

3. Discuss how the International Criminal Tribunals have influenced the development of international law.

4. Describe the role of the International Law Commission in the codification of international law.

5. What is the role of the United Nations in the creation of world law? How do regional international organizations like the OAS promote principles of international law and order?

CHAPTER 14

Foreign Policy and Diplomacy in International Affairs

After reading this chapter, you will be able to:

- explain the special role foreign policy plays in governing a country

- define foreign policy as an expression of national interest and global need

- understand how national interests are increasingly related to global issues

- identify some global issues that foreign policies must address

- describe the instruments of foreign policy-making

- outline the significance of diplomacy to resolve foreign policy issues

- see why diplomacy is a privileged profession

- state the factors that most influence twenty-first-century diplomacy

- describe the job of Canada's ambassador to the United States

- distinguish what diplomats do from what consuls do

- comment on the future of diplomacy in the modern world of telecommunications and computer technologies

• • • •

FOREIGN POLICY IN THE GLOBAL AGE

John F. Kennedy once observed that "domestic policy can only defeat us; **foreign policy** can kill us."[1] Canadians would gain first-hand awareness of this sentiment when a Liberal government set Canada's foreign policy goals in Afghanistan. Almost every week after Canadian combat forces landed there, soldiers died battling Taliban fighters and other so-called **insurgents**.

By foreign policy, we mean the **core objectives** a government wants to implement in the world by using certain techniques and strategies to achieve them. Sometimes foreign policies are restricted to statements of goals and ideas, such as how Canada would embrace global climate change; whereas at other times, foreign policies are national efforts to achieve particular objectives, such as free trade in the Western hemisphere or international security in North America.

> **FACTFILE**   Because Canada was a British colony prior to 1867, Prime Minister John A. Macdonald had no authority to make foreign policy for his new country: that power lay with the bureaucrats and the foreign minister at the British Foreign Office in Whitehall until the early twentieth century.

We might also say that foreign policy consists of what a government says and does in regards to other countries. The basic purpose of any government's foreign policy, of course, is its survival—to preserve its existence and security as a nation-state. As the world changes, so must our attempts to survive with policies that anticipate global trends in the **national interest**.

Canada's foreign policies are established through a process that usually originates with the prime minister, the Department of Foreign Affairs and International Trade (DFAIT), and sometimes other departments. Central agencies, such as the Treasury Board and the Department of Finance have a role to play in providing advice on the financial obligations Canada encounters for its military operations and foreign aid abroad. This advice is crucial for keeping Canadian foreign policies within the realistic realm of the federal budget.

Provinces may also exercise an influence on the direction that Canadian foreign policy takes. For example, Quebec as well as francophone communities in Manitoba, Ontario, New Brunswick, and Nova Scotia have been instrumental in Canada's participation in **La Francophonie**. This international organization has 53 member states that participate at regular annual meetings to promote the French language and its many cultures around the world, which affects all of Canada's francophone communities.

The principle of federalism is another influence on Canada's foreign policy. Because Canada depends so much on trade with the world, each province has a stake in what the prime minister and the Cabinet do in matters of foreign policy. An initiative to expand trade in the Middle East, for example, can have consequences for Canadian companies in various provinces doing business with Israel.

Foreign policy often is affected by parliamentary action and national public debate. Like other policy matters, foreign policy issues get on the legislative agenda for debate by governments and opposition parties, not only in the House of Commons but also in the Senate.

The making of foreign policy in a democracy such as Canada is often controversial. Many believe that foreign policy, which concerns dealings with people who live outside Canada, requires a degree of unity rarely found in domestic politics. Although vigorous debate is usually thought to show vitality in a democracy, such energies can lead to problems in foreign policy. Because foreign policy often involves high stakes—matters of security or putting men and women in harm's way—international politics seems to reflect the highest levels of urgency.

Focus On **The Case of Maher Arar**

Every day, the governments of the United States and Canada cooperate in the exchange of intelligence as part of their foreign policy strategy to fight terrorism.

On September 26, 2002, Maher Arar, a Canadian software engineer, was travelling from Tunis to Montreal via New York. He was arrested by US authorities, fingerprinted, and imprisoned, accused of having ties to Al Qaeda. After 12 days of being held in the US he was deported, not to his home in Canada even though he had his Canadian passport, but to Syria, his country of birth. There, he was imprisoned and severely tortured in order to force a confession that he was co-operating with terrorist groups.

This was an allegation made by the US Central Intelligence Agency and corroborated by the RCMP. It was later learned that the RCMP had fed the US misinformation about Arar, knowing that he would likely be tortured in Jordan or Syria.

In 2003, Arar was released without any explanation and he returned to his family in Canada. To the chagrin of Canadian diplomats and politicians, US officials did not apologize, nor did they provide any explanation for the "extra-legal" action they had taken against him and his family. Arar was a victim of the new security policies of the US and Canada designed to fight terrorism around the world.

An official Inquiry conducted in Canada and headed by Judge Dennis O'Connor recommended among other things that Arar be compensated for his ordeal. He was awarded $12.5 million, $10.5 million for pain and suffering and $2 million for legal fees. Even though Canada exonerated Arar of these suspicions and accusations, US officials continued to refuse him entry into the US. At the time of writing, Arar was still on the US list of suspected terrorists and believed by them to have connections with Al Qaeda.

In Canada, the RCMP was investigated for its role in how Arar had been sent to Syria even though he was a Canadian citizen protected by the Charter of Rights and Freedoms. Former RCMP Commissioner Giuliano Zacardelli admitted he had made a mistake in his judgment during Arar's detention in the US. He disclosed he had passed US authorities "incorrect information" about Mr. Arar, even though the RCMP knew that the information transmitted to the Americans was false and would eventually bring harm to Arar. Zacardelli was forced to resign his position as the leader of the Mounties.

In effect, the RCMP had participated in the unlawful arrest, imprisonment, and torture of an innocent Canadian in compliance with a foreign policy created by the United States and Canada to fight terrorism. This is one of the important cases that has forced the governments of Canada and the US to reconsider their practices regarding **extraordinary rendition**, which involves sending prisoners to countries known to torture detainees.

Foreign Policy in a Global Environment

In his classic book *Understanding Media*, Marshall McLuhan described the world as a "global village" because communications technology is connecting people everywhere, closely and instantaneously.

The global milieu is constantly connecting people, organizations, and governments as part of a new localized universe. This challenges the assumption that some policies can continue to be called "foreign." The new dynamic in the international system forces all domestic policies to take a global perspective. Because of this, we must think about foreign policies as direct extensions of domestic policies in the age of globalization.

Since 1992, "Earth Summits" have signalled a growing worldwide acknowledgement of a new group of foreign policy issues that connect domestic policies with global politics. Governments have become increasingly aware that human activities—the activities of their citizens—threaten and degrade or even destroy the earth's environment.

But reaching international agreement on how to deal with these challenges and crafting foreign policies to meet them at the national level has proved difficult. The Kyoto Protocol is an example of an agreement that has had difficulty getting many governments on board in order to make the legislative changes necessary to meet the standards of the treaty.

Canada signed the Protocol in 1998 and ratified it in 2002. A Liberal government agreed to meet the standards of the Protocol, but after its defeat in 2006 a minority Conservative government took power. The Harper government backed down from a foreign policy commitment made by the Liberals to meet long-term environmental goals in the Kyoto agreement. The minority Conservative government opted instead for a "made-in-Canada" solution to reduce greenhouse gases and carbon emissions.

Foreign Policies Must Address Terrorism

Perhaps the most troubling issue in the global arena is the spread of terrorism—the use of violence to demoralize civilians, foreign military, and governments. Most governments have developed foreign policy strategies for dealing with the external threat of terrorism as well as for providing national security against it.[2]

It is difficult to defend against terrorism from a policy perspective, especially in an open society that has constitutional protections for its citizens. Terrorists have the advantage of stealth and surprise. Each government concerned with the threat of terrorism must merge domestic security policy with foreign policy goals. This must also meet the standards of criminal and constitutional law.

> FACTFILE Canada's foreign policy addresses terrorism with security measures by enacting legislation that bans terrorist organizations, detains suspects, and contains a no-fly policy that prevents over two thousand individuals from boarding airplanes on Canadian soil.

Canada and the United States have vastly improved their domestic security and intelligence gathering capabilities. But these have been at the expense of civil and constitutional rights. Both governments have confronted terrorism directly as military operations against terrorist cells, domestically for Canada with the FLQ in the 1970s and operations in the Middle East, especially Afghanistan, and for the US in both Afghanistan and Iraq.

Terrorism can be a weapon of choice in domestic or foreign strife. For Canada, the 1985 Air India *Flight 182* bombing was declared in an inquiry to be an act of terrorism against Canadians, even though the plane crashed off the coast of Ireland, killing 329 passengers.

Domestic acts of terrorism have been predominant between Israelis and Palestinians. Domestic terrorist acts have disrupted civilians in Spain and Great Britain since 2004. Terrorist acts by rebels occur in Sri Lanka (the Tamils), Armenia (the extremist group PRIS), Russia (Chechen rebels), and Japan (secret cults).

Governments have applied much of their prevention and retaliation strategies to fight terrorism through their foreign policies.

Foreign Policies Must Address the International Economy

No country's economy is excluded from the global marketplace. Thus all foreign policy bureaucracies must include a strategy for surviving in the global economy.

Since the beginning of the twentieth century, trade among countries has grown rapidly (see Chapter 3, Fig. 3.2). Canada derives nearly 50 percent of its GDP from exports of goods and services. Imports of goods and services make up nearly 42 percent of its GDP of 1.178 trillion (2006).[3]

FACTFILE China has become Canada's second largest trading partner in a very short period of time, enabling the Canadian economy to diversify its flow of trade significantly outside of the western hemisphere and to lessen its dependence on the United States.

The global economy has fuelled international travel. The spending of foreign tourists bolsters the Canadian travel, hotel, and recreation industries. Canadian colleges and universities derive a significant portion of their revenues from educating foreign students.

The globalization of finances has been even more dramatic than world trade. Worldwide computer and communications networks link financial markets in all parts of the globe instantaneously, making it easier to move capital across national boundaries. That is why a steep decline in the American or Japanese stock markets can send prices plummeting on the Toronto Stock Exchange (TSX).

Coping with foreign economic issues has become just as difficult and, increasingly, just as important as coping with domestic issues. In a simpler time, the main foreign policy instrument was the **tariff**, a special tax added to the cost of imported goods to make them less competitive with locally made goods. In a world of free trade, this foreign policy instrument has become less desirable. Non-tariff barriers, such as quotas, subsidies, and quality specifications remain common means for limiting imports.

FACTFILE At present, much of Canadian foreign policy deals with the peaceful settlement of disputes that arise with the United States on matters of softwood lumber, steel, cattle, wheat, and other trade issues under the NAFTA and other treaties.

Substantial progress in foreign policy initiatives was made in lowering barriers in the North American Free Trade Agreement (NAFTA) among Canada, Mexico, and the US. The General Agreement on Tariffs and Trade (GATT) is the mechanism by which most of the world's governments negotiate their foreign policy positions on trade. The GATT included a Charter to create the World Trade Organization (WTO) to arbitrate international trade disputes.

A persistent issue for the prime minister and Cabinet is to open up foreign markets for Canadian goods and services. Ministerial missions have been sent for this reason to Europe, Asia, and Latin America. These foreign policy initiatives have succeeded in greatly expanding trade and investment with these regions. The federal government is especially eager to open lucrative markets in China in the areas of natural resources, telecommunications, and medical equipment.

THE INSTRUMENTS OF MODERN FOREIGN POLICY

There are a number of important determinants of foreign policy for Canada and other countries in the global age. Like other policy matters, foreign policy issues get on the official agenda primarily because of the influence of events and the actions of policymakers, both global and domestic.

No events have had greater impact on Canada's foreign policy than technological developments in global communications and the foreign policy actions of the United States. Communications technology makes it virtually possible to do business instantaneously anywhere in the world. And the powerful influence of the United States in the Canadian economy and in its society creates enormous pressure to support American actions abroad when they involve issues of war and national security.

FACTFILE   Prime Minister Trudeau ordered the first comprehensive review of Canadian foreign policy in 1968, which was published as a series of booklets entitled *Foreign Policy for Canadians*; the booklets were prepared by the Department of External Affairs and completed in 1970.

Against this background we must ask: Who makes foreign policy? What role does a political executive play? What role does Parliament or Congress play? What do our diplomats do? How important is diplomacy for settling global issues? And how in a democratic society can ordinary citizens make their views felt, so as to influence global policy?

What should Canada's objectives be in its relations with the rest of the world? Should Canada be a peacemaker, a peace enforcer, a better provider of foreign aid, or an intervening force in the internal affairs of other states? How many of Canada's resources should go into military operations around the world?

The Political Executive and Foreign Policy

In Canada there is no constitutional direction on the role of a prime minister in matters of government and of foreign policy. In fact, the prime minister is not even mentioned in the Constitution. All of the powers currently enjoyed by a Canadian prime minister and the Cabinet have evolved from tradition and from the specific actions taken by each PM that have been accepted as legitimate throughout Canadian history.

A prime minister's conduct of foreign policy depends in large measure on whether he or she is able to carry the public along on big decisions. For example, in July 2007, Prime Minister Harper drew Canada closer to Latin America and the Caribbean by visiting several heads of government there to discuss issues of free trade expansion and human rights. Harper declared that reviving and expanding Canada's political and economic engagement in the Americas is a major foreign policy goal of his new government. The Canadian public was generally supportive of this initiative. But Canadians were far less supportive of Stephen Harper's move to draw closer to President George W. Bush's positions on the Middle East and terrorism.

In the United States, the president's role in foreign and military affairs is rooted in the American Constitution. Article II, Section 2, designates the president as "Commander in Chief of the Army and Navy of the United States." In foreign policy matters, all presidents have interpreted this authority broadly and decisively. The president has the power to make treaties (provided that two-thirds of the senators concur), appoint ambassadors, and receive diplomats from other countries.

Canada's Department of Foreign Affairs and International Trade (DFAIT)

DFAIT is headquartered in the Lester B. Pearson Building on the banks of the Rideau River in Ottawa. This department is relatively large, with about 4000 employees in Ottawa and abroad. Diplomatic documents are constantly delivered there from the over 80 embassies abroad. High-speed coded communications link the Minister to Canadian embassies overseas almost instantly.[4]

FACTFILE In 1909, Prime Minister Laurier established the Department of External Affairs, the first federal government department dedicated to the formation of Canadian foreign policy as distinct from the British Foreign Office.

In principle, this department is the most directly connected with Canada's external relations. It supervises Canada's relations with nearly 200 independent states around the world and with the United Nations and other multinational organizations, such as the Organization of American States. It staffs embassies and consulates throughout the world.

Under Prime Minister Laurier, Charles Murphy was appointed Canadian Secretary of State for External Affairs. But in 1912, Prime Minister Robert Borden ran the External Affairs portfolio himself, as would all other prime ministers until after World War II.

The role of the minister of Foreign Affairs varies greatly according to the minister's relationship with the prime minister. A separate department named Foreign Affairs Canada (FAC) was created in 2003, distinguishing it from International Trade with its own minister. And a

Minister of International Cooperation provides the third major leadership component of Canadian foreign policy under the department acronym DFAIT.

FACTFILE National Defence and Canadian Forces has nearly 70 000 personnel and is the largest department by staff in the Canadian federal government.

Working closely with DFAIT in the exercise of foreign policy is the Department of National Defence and Canadian Forces (DND/CF). This department was created to bring all of the various activities of the Canadian military establishment under the jurisdiction of a single minister. At the same time, high-ranking military personnel consist of the commanding officers of each branch of the armed forces, created to formulate a unified military strategy.

National Defence and Canadian Forces keeps close contact with its counterparts in other countries, especially its NATO allies, coordinating exercises with them, comparing defence strategies, and developing Canadian military training.

The Role of the Public

Students of public opinion often note that the Canadian public may not show a deep or enduring interest in foreign policies. But there is significant public awareness of highly publicized issues like terrorism, the war in Afghanistan, and Canada's relations with the United States. When a foreign policy question becomes so big that it involves a society's major resources such as money and people, it can quickly turn into a domestic political issue.

The Canadian public is considerably engaged compared to Americans who are much less interested in foreign policy matters.[5] For most Americans, domestic policy concerns and personal affairs overshadow their interest in world affairs. As a rule, the American public is more interested in local political issues than foreign and military affairs. Nevertheless, public opinion is on the president's mind when foreign or military policy is formulated and implemented.

In Canada, the National Forum on International Relations has been successful through its annual conference in getting a wide spectrum of Canadians interested in foreign affairs. The Canadian Institute of International Affairs (CIIA) provides a nonpartisan forum of analysis and debate for Canadians.

While members of the public may develop well-defined views on domestic questions, on questions of foreign policy they tend to react in changeable moods. This is sometimes referred to as **mood theory**.[6] According to mood theory, the general public has very little influence on specific foreign or defence policy matters. But its perceived willingness by government to accept certain views, tactics, and programs carries considerable weight in making policy.

Historically, the public's mood has fluctuated between a willingness to accept greater Canadian involvement in world affairs and the contrary

Crosscurrents   Is Canada Waging an Illegal War in Afghanistan?

The Canadian public is divided on whether Canada's military presence in Afghanistan should remain as that of an "occupying state." While the majority of Canadians criticize the military combat mission, the strongest opposition to Canada's role in Afghanistan has been in Quebec.

In the election campaign of 2008, the Harper government stated that its exit strategy for Afghanistan was to leave in 2011. But some Canadians believe that Canada is there because of pressure from the United States and are calling for an earlier withdrawal. Canada's more traditional roles as peacekeeper and humanitarian aid provider in troubled areas of the world are widely regarded as preferable to its combat mission in Afghanistan.

A growing number of Canadians believe that Afghanis are in need of humanitarian missions, a role that Canada has historically played worldwide. They point to rural poverty caused by the eradication of the poppy crop, and criticize Canada's role in helping to enforce a counter-narcotics program that was developed by the US, not Canada.

Some international law experts and analysts also argue that the war in Afghanistan is illegal. They say the United States, assisted by Canada and Great Britain, is bombing Afghanistan in violation of international law. Experts say the war in Afghanistan also violates the Charter of the United Nations, the Geneva Conventions, which codified the rules of warfare, and the Rome Statute, approved by 120 states in 1998, which defines war crimes. The UN Charter specifically prohibits the use of force to topple foreign governments and the killing of noncombatants.

As Canada remains in Afghanistan in a combat capacity, Canadian troops risk being accused of war crimes or even crimes against humanity under the International Criminal Court, whose prosecutor can investigate accusations of criminal conduct at any time in any war.

Canada's presence in Afghanistan has raised significant public debate about whether its current involvement in combat missions with the US threatens Canada's reputation as an international peacemaker—and what Canada's future role should be in international conflicts.

urge to withdraw from the international scene, especially where the US dominates in policy matters.

> **FACTFILE** Contrary to the belief by Canadians that their country is generous, the United Nations annually reports that Canada is one of the world's least generous states, with foreign aid accounting for only 0.28 percent of its GDP, while Norway, Sweden, and Denmark top the list of assisting countries, each donating 1 percent of their GDP.

Relatively small leadership groups play a significant role in recommending most foreign policy decisions. Elites in Canadian business, education, communications, labour, and religion try to influence cabinet foreign decision-making. The members of Canada's foreign policy establishment, sometimes called the **attentive public**, exert influence by encouraging debate, by publicizing issues and using the media to project their positions. This portion of the general public is more interested in foreign affairs than most Canadians.

Although public opinion changes more frequently on foreign policy issues than on domestic ones, the public's underlying attitudes about these issues remain remarkably stable. Opposition to Canada's military role in Afghanistan was a reaction to the long-held public belief that Canada's primary foreign policy role is that of a peacekeeper.

Interest Groups Make Foreign Policy Demands

As with domestic policy, foreign policy is not neutral. It is not decided upon in a neutral way. The results of foreign policies can hurt some groups and help others. Thus, it is not surprising that interest groups try to make demands on government to follow a particular policy goal.

Many people take an interest in foreign policy when they think those issues affect them directly.

These individuals often join organizations that represent their positions to policymakers.

In many countries, there is a foreign policy establishment made up of powerful interest groups that helps to shape the global visions of a particular government. Depending on their reputation, financing, and social standing, they possess varying degrees of influence.

In Canada, organized labour groups are opposed to foreign imports because such imports compete with Canadian industries and reduce the number of available domestic jobs. The Canadian Chamber of Commerce and the Canadian Manufacturers Association influence Canadian foreign policy in matters of trade and currency.

Agricultural groups such as the Ontario Federation of Agriculture and the Canadian Cattlemen's Association are powerful lobbies for foreign policy issues that can arise involving the United States, Europe, and Japan. The issues of "mad cow" disease and softwood lumber often surface from Members of Parliament and push the Cabinet to develop a national policy framework to resolve these kinds of international disputes.

Veterans' groups such as the Canadian Association of Veterans and the National Council of Veterans Associations in Canada are active in foreign policy lobbying. They usually support a strong military capability for Canadian soldiers in Afghanistan and other missions undertaken by Canadian governments.

Ethnic groups are also involved in seeking to influence Canadian foreign policy. For example, in the Middle East, Canada's policies reflect the lobbying influence and activities of Canadian Jews, many of whom identify with Israel, and organizations such as the Muslim Association of Canada and the Canadian Islamic Association provide powerful influence about Canada's policies towards Iraq, Iran, and the Arab states of the Gulf.

DIPLOMACY AND FOREIGN POLICY

Diplomacy as an Instrument of Foreign Policy

Diplomacy is a major aspect of foreign policy and an expression of **soft power**. The profession includes all of a government's external relationships, from routine day-to-day diplomatic communications to summit meetings held between and among heads of government. On a daily basis, diplomacy is the representation of a government to other governments and international organizations. But at another level, diplomacy acts out the foreign policy objectives of a government.

Diplomacy is all about negotiating with other states in the national interest. It is as much about settling disputes and conflicts as it is about making things go smoothly by peaceful methods between states.

In order to do this, governments exchange ambassadors, establish consulates, negotiate treaties and attend international conventions to discuss common and global problems. Much of the conduct of diplomacy is enshrined in international law to protect diplomats and consuls from harm when doing their jobs.

Diplomacy is a set of negotiating skills used to carry out foreign policy. It may or may not be successful, depending on the willingness of the parties to negotiate. For Canadian diplomats, issues can range from softwood lumber to special problems arising out of health care and free trade. The prime concern of an ambassador is to keep international relations as efficient as possible.

Perspectives   Diplomatic Skills Are an Essential Aspect of National Power

Professor Huang Shoufeng (Chinese Academy of Social Sciences) defines Comprehensive National Power (CNP) as the "combined conditions of strength a country can use to compete in the international system." Intrinsic to the expression of national power are the obvious factors of a country's location, economy, and military strength. But Dr. Shoufeng also identifies the diplomatic skills of a government as an essential component of soft power, which is necessary to compete in the world of international relations.

Professor Shoufeng tells us that what constitutes legitimate power in international relations is changing. Greater legitimacy in the exercise of international affairs is assigned to diplomacy rather than power as military force. With the exception of a minority of states, there is near global rejection of military coercion as a means of satisfying national interests.

Because of the widespread destructive power of modern weapons, Dr. Shoufeng believes we are at a turning point in human history.

In the contemporary world of international politics, power is a multidimensional concept that is relative, not absolute. It is fluid and situational, not categorical or static. Power can be expressed through diplomacy; in this regard, it is the "power to" rather than the "power over."

Both China and Canada recognize that what constitutes power is changing across the global community. Greater legitimacy is assigned to power as *influence* rather than power as the use of *military force*. There is a groundswell of opinion in the international community that rejects power expressed as military coercion. Reliance on military solutions (**hard power**) is dangerous not just to states in conflict, but also to global security, environmental health, and human survival.

Perspectives   Sovereign Immunity Begets Diplomatic Immunity

Historically, diplomats have enjoyed immunity because they are the messengers of the sovereign or head of state. They represent the sovereign in a foreign place as if he or she were actually in that place. Thus, sovereign immunity is the legal underpinning of diplomatic immunities.

Sovereign immunity is based on recognized customary international law. Whatever the sovereign may do is immune from all prosecution—civil and criminal.

But in 2004, the Supreme Court of Chile did something rarely done to a former president who had enjoyed the benefits of both sovereign and diplomatic immunity since he was head of state.

Augusto Pinochet, who was president of Chile from 1973 to 1990, had seized power by toppling democratically elected Salvador Allende in a military coup. While Pinochet was president of Chile, it is widely believed that under his "Operation Condor" he violated the human rights of his political opponents. Operation Condor was the military code name for an intelligence network among South American dictators that Pinochet led in the 1970s. This operation was aimed at eliminating dissidents throughout the Latin American region.

Using Chile's secret police, Pinochet authorized the abuse, torture, and murder of thousands of Chileans and foreign nationals during his 17-year regime. But successive Chilean governments protected his sovereign immunity under international law. By doing this, they prevented his surrender to the authorities of France and Spain, who charged that he was responsible for the disappearances and deaths of a huge number of people, including French and Spanish nationals. These foreign governments believed Pinochet should be brought to justice.

Pinochet had been out of office since 1990, but remained untouchable under the laws of sovereign immunity in the courts until 2004. In that year, the Supreme Court of Chile upheld a lower court decision in May that removed the sovereign immunity granted to Pinochet under international law as a former head of state. Removing sovereign immunity is a rare occurrence in the international community because it is such an entrenched legal principle of international law. Foreign sovereigns or heads of state not only enjoy personal immunity from suit, but they also are not named as defendant parties to suits brought against them in their official capacity as the representatives of their states.

Evolution of Diplomatic Privilege

From the beginning, envoys demanded immunity from harm, having taken the risk that their presence before the enemy could result in their own demise. Because they were foreigners, they were considered impure. They submitted to the rituals of purification to assure their doubtful hosts that they could be trusted and were worthy of credibility. Once their

messages were delivered and accepted, the earliest envoys left to report the sentiments of their hosts to their superiors. But there were no embassies or standard diplomatic practices accepted by the governments of ancient peoples. There was simply the recognized need to contact and communicate with both friends and enemies in order to survive.

Although all civilizations have conducted diplomatic activities, it is generally believed that modern diplomacy has been influenced primarily by ancient Greece. The Greeks made passports, called *diplomas*, from double metal plates folded and sewn together. Diplomas granted the bearer travel privileges and special treatment when presented to officials in foreign places.

The Greeks chose exceptional people to represent them in foreign places. Their envoys were the finest orators, well versed in the knowledge of theatre, the arts, literature, philosophy, and the general principles of law. They were drawn from the highest levels of polite society, usually from an aristocratic background. Because the *polis* was a republic, controlled by an assembly, they were appointed with popular approval to negotiate the affairs of state with other city-states, as well as foreign places such as Sparta and Rome.

The Greeks believed that envoys enjoyed the immunities of the gods to protect them from the harmful impact of human disputes. But they also developed the secular political practice of respecting the dignity and integrity of visiting envoys and expecting reciprocal treatment for their diplomatic representatives travelling abroad.

For example, the Greeks had the idea that an ambassador represented the person of the sovereign, being entitled to the same respect that the sovereign would receive if he or she were personally present. Because sovereigns were so sensitive to embarrassment when visiting foreign places, the practice grew to accord diplomatic representatives the highest courtesy—that of personal **inviolability**. If a diplomatic delegation was in the unfortunate circumstance of being in a place where war was declared, they would be accorded **safe conduct** from hostilities, as when Sparta voted for war against Athens while the Athenian delegation was present negotiating a trade treaty. Gradually, the Greeks established a routine and institutional style of diplomacy that spread far beyond the Aegean corner of the Mediterranean Sea. Greek diplomatic practices influenced and shaped the diplomacy of the high Middle Ages, when the newly formed state system adopted

them as customary international law. They recognized **neutrality**, used **arbitration**, and empowered their envoys to further commercial relations with foreign governments.

> **FACTFILE** The Greeks called their messengers *angelos*, or angels, and accorded them the patronage of Zeus, the father of the gods, and Hermes, the messenger and herald of the gods, who was, as well, the god of cunning ruses and pretenses.

Unlike the Greeks, the Romans had very little respect for the principle of equality in negotiation. The goals of the Roman Empire were not usually open to compromise. Roman ambassadors, called *nuntii*, travelled abroad as quasi-governors who treated their foreign colleagues more like colonists than equal negotiators. However, the Romans, with their penchant for laws, stressed the importance of binding contracts, and elevated them to the sanctity of treaties.

Because of the dominance of the empire, the Romans were highly selective of the foreign envoys they received. When a representative from a foreign land came to Rome, authorities kept the envoy outside the city gates until diplomatic credentials were carefully scrutinized and the diplomatic status of the visitor was verified. Nowadays, this humiliating system of receiving and accepting emissaries has been replaced and refined by the practice of requesting *agrément* (agreement): that is, the sending state does not announce the appointment of its ambassador until the receiving state signifies its acceptance of the individual chosen. When followed by the two states, this procedure is called *agréation*.

In the early Middle Ages, after Rome's collapse, Byzantium rose as a world power. Chicanery, sharp dealing, and suspicion characterized Byzantine diplomacy. The Byzantines used diplomacy to weaken their adversaries by fomenting rivalry among them. Envoys acted as a **fifth column** in the lands where they were sent, engaging in **sabotage** and buying support by bribery and flattery. The

Byzantines used their envoys to spy wherever they were sent, a practice not uncommon today in many capitals of the world. History confirms that Byzantine practices had a corrupting influence on the evolution of diplomacy.

FACTFILE   What we would recognize as modern diplomacy—that is, an independent profession with qualified practitioners and resident missions—originated in Italy in the fourteenth and fifteenth centuries.

Medieval ambassadors functioned as permanent representatives of the state, gathering information, advising, and negotiating on behalf of the home government. The profession and practice of diplomacy was seen as an ongoing process rather than an expedience. Permanent diplomatic missions improved opportunities to sign treaties and facilitated the organization of summit meetings as a diplomatic practice. Of course, treachery, deceit, and intrigue continued to characterize medieval diplomacy. In France, Louis XI advised his ambassadors, "If they lie to you, see to it you lie much more than they."

Diplomats quickly learned that corruption and deceit were condoned but impractical because negotiations could not be conducted in good faith. Pragmatism and reason dictated honesty in diplomatic affairs.

The first resident embassy was opened at Genoa in 1455. Permanent embassies soon became acknowledged as inviolable sanctuaries for the records and files of diplomats, and they became the depositories for treaties and for the diplomatic reports. Custom dictated that the *host state* respect the sovereign integrity of the embassy. As permanent embassies began to replace travelling diplomatic missions, the practice of stealing or seizing diplomatic records from envoys grew less acceptable. Italian diplomats were the first to write periodic summaries of events taking place in the states to which they were accredited. They expected these reports to remain confidential within the security of their embassies.

By the seventeenth century, the professional status of diplomacy was well established. In 1626, under Louis XIII, Cardinal Richelieu opened the first ministry of external affairs to exercise French diplomatic leadership in European affairs through one government agency. Richelieu insisted that honouring treaties was an ethical as well as a pragmatic responsibility. Under his influence, the French recognized diplomacy as a permanent part of state policy. French became the leading language in diplomatic communication, with most of its nomenclature still used today.

FACTFILE   In 1945, Canada had diplomatic missions in just 22 states, mostly in the Commonwealth. By 2007, this number had grown to more than 170, of which 93 are embassies.

At the Congress of Vienna (1815) and Aix-la-Chapelle (1818), attending states ratified a *règlement* governing diplomatic titles and order of rank:

1. ambassador extraordinary and plenipotentiary and, from the Vatican, *papal legate and nuncio*,

2. envoy extraordinary, minister plenipotentiary, and, from the Vatican, *papal internuncio*,

3. minister resident, and

4. chargé d'affaires and chargé d'affaires *ad interim*.

The Congress of Vienna determined that the rank of *ambassador* was the highest that a diplomat can hold. From that time on, ambassadors or ministers were recognized internationally as chiefs of diplomatic missions. Official diplomatic quarters were designated an **embassy** when headed by an ambassador, and a **legation** when headed by a minister. The Congress was the first multilateral statement on the rules of diplomacy that codified the status and functions of diplomats. It gave diplomacy an international stamp of approval as a profession distinct from that of a statesman and legitimized the widely accepted immunities enjoyed by diplomats in the European world of politics.

Focus On Canada's Largest Embassy

By the standards of most other states, the Canadian embassy at 501 Pennsylvania Avenue, NW, Washington, DC, is huge. Located at the intersection of Pennsylvania and Constitution avenues, it is a few hundred yards from the US Capitol grounds, across from the buildings of the National Gallery of Art, and adjacent to John Marshall Park, a public garden.

The six-storey building, designed by Canadian architect Arthur Erickson, consumes 6.5 acres. The first and most prominent building American congresspersons see when they walk out on Capitol Hill is the Canadian embassy.

As one of largest embassies in Washington, Canada's includes a 175-seat theatre, an art gallery, a 20 000-volume library, a large general-purpose room called the Canada Room, a cafeteria, and an underground garage. The Rotunda of the Provinces is located in a spacious court that features lofty columns, one for each province and two of the territories. The Coat of Arms for the newest territory of Nunavut has been erected along with that of the Northwest Territories.

The embassy houses the roomy offices of the ambassador, as well as the economic, political, public affairs, defence liaison, administrative, and consular divisions. About 300 staff members administer the diplomatic work of the embassy 24 hours a day. A great amount of effort in designing the embassy was devoted to the electronic security systems, which enable the diplomatic staff to work in a safe and secure environment.

The embassy regularly displays works of leading Canadian visual and performing artists. Canadian sculpture, paintings, prints, photographs, and fabrics are on permanent display.

All ranks of Canadian ambassadors are represented in Washington. They conduct the formal diplomacy between Canada and the United States and work to sign treaties and other agreements that cover transportation, fisheries, wildlife, pollution control, defence, and a great many other activities.

The period from 1825 to 1914 was marked by relative peace and stability in international affairs. The six great empires of Europe—Austria-Hungary, Czarist Russia, Ottoman Turkey, Germany, Britain, and France—entered a period of diplomatic grace. This concept of Europe gave diplomats a sense of achievement and elevated their profession to a distinguished and specialized vocation. Diplomats associated as a small privileged group, the *corps diplomatique*, insisting on immunities, practising discretion, and avoiding the political brush fires of domestic politics.

TWENTY-FIRST CENTURY DIPLOMACY

Many States

Four factors influence the character of diplomacy in this century. The first is the presence of many states, each sending and receiving diplomats and struggling for a place in the international arena. As well, states that have never had diplomatic ties, or for various reasons denied each other diplomatic representation, have opened diplomatic missions.

Experts from every field of government are now attached to embassy staffs in most states, and modern negotiation has become a complex process of internal consultation whereby diplomats rely on technical expertise before a decision can be made or a report submitted. One of the jobs of the ambassador is to co-ordinate the work of all these people so that they can represent the policies of the Canadian government to the United States.

The Media

A second factor that has had a far-reaching effect on the world's diplomatic system is the ever-present and intrusive *communications media*. In all democratic states, the media have claimed the right to inform the public about all levels of government decision making. Large press contingents, armed with microphones and television cameras and intent on discovering and revealing what is going on, frequently descend on diplomatic meetings. This makes political compromise very difficult, and diplomats often regard the media as an intrusion into the delicate balance of the negotiating process.

Those with a professional commitment to diplomacy say that press surveillance inhibits the strategy of the negotiator. Secrecy provides negotiators with opportunities for making concessions without the fear of creating unnecessary anxiety in the public domain.

In 1979, Israeli peace crusader Moshe Dayan, after travelling in disguise, met with Egyptian authorities in Morocco to lay the groundwork for negotiations at Camp David. President Jimmy Carter ensured the seclusion of the negotiating parties by withholding invitations to the media. If he had not, public indignation in Egypt and Israel at what was being compromised might have scuttled the agreement. The Camp David accords of 1979 showed how the intimacy of secluded summitry, out of the range of the media, could accomplish in just a few days what lower levels of negotiation had failed to do after years of effort.

In modern diplomacy, the presence of the media is not entirely unwelcome and is used by states to inform the world of their policy positions.

International Negotiation

The third major influence on the modern world of negotiation has been *multilateral conference diplomacy*, where negotiations take place among many states simultaneously. Until the latter part of the nineteenth century, most diplomatic communications were bilateral. Whenever multilateral conferences were held, they tended to conclude peace treaties to terminate major European wars. But during the twentieth century, governments started to send diplomats to multilateral conferences dealing with such subjects as agriculture, the codification of international law, liquor traffic, navigation, tariffs, and weights and measures.

Diplomats were expected not only to represent the interests of their own states, but also to contribute to the formation of international law. Under the League of Nations, ongoing conference machinery was established that gave international diplomacy a new institutional framework.

After World War II, the United Nations and its specialized agencies provided a permanent forum for multilateral diplomacy. Since that time, the advances in communications technology, the speed of travel, and the widespread recognition that world issues are everyone's problems have made multilateral diplomacy a powerful law-making tool. Thousands of conferences have been hosted by the United Nations and other international organizations, such as the Organization of American States (OAS) and the African Union (AU).

Today, Canada participates daily in global and regional conferencing, as an ever-increasing portion of diplomatic communications is conducted through multilateral organizations. This in no way reduces the importance of bilateral relations between states, but globalization has dramatically increased and complicated international ties. At the United Nations, press releases to delegations run up to 20 000 pages a year. In addition to the rushed routine of embassy business, today's diplomat is expected to be aware of the complicated trends in multilateral diplomacy.

Inside the United Nations and other international organizations around the world, diplomats are given the opportunity to communicate with representatives of states with whom they may not share bilateral diplomatic exchanges. A lot of bilateral negotiations occur within the walls of these organizations, providing an atmosphere as private and secret as that afforded by traditional diplomacy. But the multilateral diplomat is a different breed of negotiator. He or she is representing more than the narrow interests of a state; the diplomat is also participating as an architect of a new international society, concerned with the global issues of population, climate change, nuclear proliferation, and world peace.

Much of Canada's multilateral diplomacy is conducted through its ambassador to the United Nations. The UN post is considered paramount for Canada for a number of reasons, including the fact that Canada is a major financial contributor. As well, Canada has been a major participant in United Nations peacekeeping operations. Increasingly, international issues are being successfully addressed by the UN system, and sovereign states have reached a mature recognition of the crucial role for this global multilateral organization.

Notwithstanding this, Canada's UN ambassador works at an international organization facing severe financial and personnel problems.

From his office on the United Nations Plaza, the ambassador has almost instant access to diplomats representing nearly 200 nation-states. Because there are so many diplomats in one place, constantly passing each other in the corridors and lounges, eating together, and meeting in the debating chambers of the UN, important contacts can be made between an ambassador and other individuals and groups. Canada's ambassador must conduct representation involving a heavy diplomatic itinerary: communicating the Canadian government's views to the councils of the United Nations as well as to individual governments; reporting; public relations; and gathering information, analyzing it, and recommending policy options.

Summit Diplomacy

The fourth development of major significance in modern international politics is **summit diplomacy**, a phrase coined by Winston Churchill. Occasionally, summit meetings of great historic value took place before the twentieth century, such as the Congress of Vienna (1815) and the Congress of Berlin (1878). But diplomatic mythology has always held as undesirable direct communication between heads of state.

Today, in the Age of Summitry, many observers are critical of diplomacy at the highest levels because political executives are not often trained in the skills of negotiation. Many diplomats advise that compromise is difficult when the prestige of the negotiating parties is at stake. The main argument against summiteering is that face-to-face meetings among leaders are much too dramatic and politically charged to provide a rational environment for delicate negotiations.

Former US Secretary of State Dean Rusk warned that "summit diplomacy is to be approached with the wariness with which a prudent physician prescribes a habit-forming drug . . . the experienced diplomat will usually counsel against the direct confrontation of those with final authority."[7] Most students of international relations note that summit diplomacy has no greater possibility of success than the traditional avenues of diplomatic communication.

FACTFILE   The visits to China of US presidents Richard Nixon in 1972 and Ronald Reagan in 1984, after many years of isolation, established a US–Chinese rapprochement that was possible only because of contacts at the highest levels of power.

The idea that only heads of state can settle intractable disputes or negotiate complicated international instruments has not been supported by much evidence, although there have been some notable successes for summitry. One of the most successful in terms of positive international relations was the so-called Shamrock Summit between Ronald Reagan and Brian Mulroney at Quebec City in March 1985. Both leaders inaugurated the institution of annual summit meetings. The idea was to bring regular top-level management to Canada–US affairs. In 1999, at a summit meeting in Mont Tremblant, Quebec, involving leaders of federal states, US President Bill Clinton came to the defence of his federalist colleague, Jean Chrétien, by making a speech strongly supporting national unity in the presence of Quebec nationalist Lucien Bouchard. Both leaders succeeded at summit diplomacy because of their personal friendship and similar foreign-policy goals.

The spectacular increase in the frequency of summit meetings indicates the new importance political leaders attach to them. In these times of instant communications and rapid travel, many leaders have discovered the political advantages of

world exposure by bypassing traditional diplomatic machinery and maintaining direct contact among themselves.

THE PROTOCOL OF MODERN DIPLOMACY

Today, diplomatic relations between states are conducted according to a vast code of behavior embodied in the Vienna Convention on Diplomatic Relations.[8] This was a major international effort to codify international law in the area of diplomatic privileges and immunities. At Vienna, the attending states set forth the rules of diplomatic practice to conform to contemporary conditions and standards of diplomacy. The heads of diplomatic missions were divided into three general categories. The first two categories are ambassadors and ministers respectively. These diplomats are **accredited** to the head of the host state. The third category is comprised of chargés d'affaires. These lower-ranking diplomats are accredited to the foreign minister of the host state.

FACTFILE   The Vienna conference was attended by 81 states, which drafted a comprehensive agreement covering diplomatic activities; it came into force by 1964.

The Appointment of an Ambassador

Before an ambassador is appointed to a post, the sending state seeks the approval or *agrément* of the receiving state. Approval is usually granted when the discretionary authority of the receiving state determines a diplomat is *persona grata* (a person in good grace). A receiving state may also declare a diplomat of another state to be *persona non grata* when that diplomat is found to be unacceptable after initial investigation, or when a diplomat engages in criminal and antisocial behaviour or meddles in the internal affairs of the host state. But such a practice is exceptional and contrary to the spirit of international relations. This reciprocal procedure of confidential application and acceptance is an important instrument of **protocol** that builds trust and confidence in interstate relations. In the mid-1980s, one Canadian ambassadorial appointee was not accepted by Portugal because its government believed that the appointment of former Liberal cabinet minister Bryce Mackasey was made on the basis of patronage and would soon be reversed by a new federal government.

Once *agréation* is reached, an ambassador is given credentials to present to the head of state. In Commonwealth states where the sovereign is the head of more than one state (the Queen for Canada, New Zealand, and Australia), ambassadors are provided with letters of introduction from prime minister to prime minister. In accordance with diplomatic protocol, *letters of credence* (Figure 14.1) are provided for the exchange of ambassadors outside the Commonwealth.

On arrival, an ambassador will inform the minister of foreign affairs or secretary of state that he or she is ready to assume the duties of the embassy. In a letter referred to as the *copie d'usage*, the ambassador indicates a willingness to present the letters of credence to the head of state and includes the predecessor's *letter of recall* that terminated the mission. Once a diplomat presents credentials to the head of state, he or she is considered officially to represent the sending state.

Sometimes the ambassador and members of the diplomatic staff are assigned to more than one state. No state maintains a diplomatic mission in every capital of the world. For economic reasons, most states are selective, balancing national interests against the costs involved in maintaining a permanent presence in a country. Canada has embassies and **High Commissions** in 112 capitals but conducts diplomatic relations with more than 190 states.

Multi-accreditation or plural representation, sometimes called in Canada "concurrent accreditation," can cause difficulties between states. Those states where the ambassador does not reside may feel that the *sending state* considers them less important to states where embassies are permanently established.[9] Problems arise when two or more states covered by the same ambassador engage in hostilities or break diplomatic relations. Parties in dispute will usually doubt the objectivity of the multi-accredited ambassador. These situations are potentially embarrassing both for the ambassador and for the states involved.

Privileges, Exemptions, and Immunities

It is a well-established and widely accepted rule of international law that all categories of diplomatic personnel are *immune* from civil jurisdiction of the courts of the host state.[10] This has never meant that immunity should give diplomats a license to violate the laws of the state to which they are accredited. For example, in 2000, two Russian diplomats were sent home from Canada to face charges in Moscow after allegations of drunk driving. In one accident an Ottawa woman was killed, and the other drunk driving incident seriously injured a pedestrian.

Although every state's diplomatic corps can report cases of envoys who conspire to break local laws, the majority of the world's diplomats readily comply with these laws. In cases of flagrant criminal activity by a foreign diplomat, the host state will declare the individual *persona non grata*.

Sometimes diplomats are expelled from their posts, or embassies are closed, because of sudden strains between governments.[11] Such was the case when Canada closed its embassy in Baghdad, with the outbreak of the Persian Gulf War in 1991. Another diplomatic practice used when

Figure 14.1   **Letter of credence**

In the Name and on Behalf of	Aux Nom, Lieu et Place de

Elizabeth II

by the Grace of God of the United Kingdom, Canada and Her other Realms and Territories Queen, Head of the Commonwealth, Defender of the Faith	par la grâce de Dieu, Reine du Royaume-Uni, du Canada et de ses autres royaumes et territoires, Chef du Commonwealth, Défenseur de la Foi

Michäelle Jean

Governor General and Commander in Chief of Canada	Gouverneur général et Commandant en chef du Canada

Your Excellency,

Wishing to promote the relations of friendship and good understanding which happily exist between our two countries, I have decided to accredit to You

Excellence,

Désireux de poursuivre les relations d'amitié et de bonne entente qui existent entre nos deux pays, J'ai décidé d'accréditer auprès de Vous

(Ambassador's name)

in the character of Ambassador Extraordinary and Plenipotentiary of Canada.

The Experience which I have had of his talents and zeal assures Me that the selection I have made will be perfectly agreeable to You, and that he will discharge his important duties in such a manner as to merit Your approbation and esteem.

I, therefore, request that You will give entire credence to all that he shall say to You in My name, more especially when he shall convey to You the assurances of the lively interest which I take in everything that affects the welfare and prosperity of Your country.

en qualité d'Ambassador Extraordinaire et Plénipotentiaire du Canada.

La connaissance que J'ai de ses talents et de son dévoue-ment Me sont autant de garanties que Mon choix Vous sera agréable et qu'il s'aquittera de ses hautes fonctions de façon à mériter Votre estime et Votre bienveillance.

Je Vous prie donc de bien vouloir lui accorder entière créance en tout ce qu'il Vous transmettra de Ma part, surtout lorsqu'il Vous renouvellera l'assurance du vif intérêt que Je porte à tout ce qui concerne le bonheur et la prospérité de Votre pays.

Given at My Government House,

Your Good Friend,

En Mon Hôtel du Gouvernement,

Votre Grand Ami,

Source: Department of Foreign Affairs & International Trade. Used by permission of Government of Canada.

tension develops between states is **recall**, not to be confused with recalling an elected official as can occur in British Columbia and the United States. In 1989, Canada recalled its chargé d'affairs from Tehran to express outrage at Ayatollah Khomeini's death threats against Salman Rushdie, author of *The Satanic Verses*. Similarly, Britain recalled its entire embassy staff and simultaneously expelled the Iranian chargé d'affaires because of the death threat to at least one of its citizens, Mr. Rushdie.

After a period of time, when relations have improved, most states will restore their diplomatic ties with another state. In 1992, Mexico restored diplomatic relations with the Vatican that had been severed for 125 years because Mexico had expropriated Church property, expelled foreign priests, and forbidden local priests to wear their clerical garb in public.

Not all states recognize immunities and privileges as an absolute right. Many states, including Australia, Canada, France, Great Britain, Italy, and New Zealand have placed conditions and restrictions on the immunities extended to foreign diplomats to protect their diplomats.

The United States holds exceptions to the inviolability of a diplomat when an envoy's conduct threatens the safety and security of the republic. In such cases, a diplomat will be restrained, although in time he or she will normally be sent home. US Homeland Security law and the *Patriot Act* (2001) permit the State Department to give the government more control over foreign diplomats.

The United States can retaliate against diplomats from governments that mistreat US envoys or whose diplomats habitually violate US laws. The US is empowered to disconnect telephones in Washington embassies, hold up shipments of goods, and refuse to allow foreign diplomats to buy property. The federal government can levy income taxes on the diplomats of states that tax the incomes of US emissaries overseas. Diplomats

are now required to get red, white, and blue license plates for their automobiles, as well as titles (proof of ownership) and liability insurance. Canada follows its policy of reciprocity in diplomatic affairs, which applies or denies privileges and immunities when they are reciprocated in the sending state.

These kinds of actions reflect changes in the official attitudes of some states toward traditional diplomatic privileges and immunities. Even though most states adhere to diplomatic protocol as codified by the Vienna Convention, many governments are legislating limitations on diplomatic privileges and immunities.

One of the most impressive statements on the question of national security and diplomatic immunity was made by Justice Bissonette of Canada in the widely publicized case of *Rose v. The King*.[12] Justice Bissonette reasoned that diplomatic immunity is relative, not absolute, and that if a diplomat commits a crime against the security of a state, he or she renounces the privilege of inviolability. Even though the Rose case occurred long before the Vienna Convention, it is certainly possible that Justice Bissonette's legal arguments could again be cited in today's courts.

Canada amended the *Diplomatic and Consular Privileges and Immunities Act* in 2001; it was first proclaimed in 1977. This Act enabled Canada to ratify the 1961 Vienna Convention while imposing several limitations on its application within Canada. By section 2(4) the minister of foreign affairs can withdraw privileges and immunities from foreign diplomats if those privileges are not properly accorded to Canadian diplomats in their state. And, under section (5), when a question arises as to whether a person is entitled to **diplomatic immunities**, the matter is decided by the secretary of state for Foreign Affairs and International Trade.

Diplomats enjoy personal inviolability as well as inviolability of premises and property. Full diplomatic privileges and immunities apply to

Perspectives   What Is Diplomatic Asylum?

Sometimes diplomatic immunities can be extended to people who are not diplomats. Diplomatic asylum is political protection afforded by one state to persons seeking refuge within its boundaries. Asylum shields from arrest or extradition anyone who is regarded as a political refugee. For example, in 2004, 44 North Korean men, women, and children sought asylum at the Canadian Embassy in Beijing. Some were seeking refugee status in Canada.

During the Tiananmen Square uprising in 1989, the US granted asylum to China's top diplomat and his wife. China had ordered his arrest for treason, demanding that the US government surrender him to local authorities waiting outside the US embassy in Beijing. That same year, General Manuel Noriega received temporary asylum from the Vatican embassy in Panama City, after evading the US military seeking to return him to the US for trial on drug-trafficking charges. After Noriega negotiated an agreement with US authorities, the Vatican decided to surrender Noriega to US forces.

This was not the first time the Vatican granted asylum to someone wanted by US authorities. In 1866, Pope Pius XI granted diplomatic asylum to John Surratt Jr., who conspired with John Wilkes Booth to assassinate US President Abraham Lincoln. In the end, the Pope surrendered Surratt to the US for prosecution.

One milestone case of asylum lasted for 15 years. It was when Hungary's Cardinal József Mindszenty sought asylum in the premises of the US embassy in Budapest. First arrested for antigovernment activities in 1948, and jailed in 1949, Mindszenty sought refuge in the US embassy in 1956. He remained there under asylum until 1971, when Hungary finally agreed to allow his safe passage to the Vatican.

---

diplomats and members of their families and staff in all official as well as most private activities, provided they are not nationals or classed as permanent residents of the state to which the diplomat is accredited. This is the basis for the granting of **diplomatic asylum**.

In most circumstances, a diplomat can sue but cannot be sued. However, if legal proceedings are initiated by a diplomat, he or she is subject to counterclaims. Under the convention, a diplomat is subject to legal action on private immovable property and on any commercial transactions undertaken outside official diplomatic functions.

The host state is obligated to protect the persons and property of a diplomatic mission and is not permitted to seize, search, or confiscate documents, wherever they may be. Because the premises of the mission and the private residences of the head of the mission and staff are inviolable, they may not be searched by agents of the host state without special permission from the sending state. The **diplomatic bag** may not be opened or detained whether it is carried by an envoy, a diplomatic courier, or a designated national official who is making a special journey to the sending state. Diplomats and their families are also exempt from the inspection of personal luggage.

FACTFILE   After 9/11, the United States and Great Britain made exceptions to the rule on inviolability of the diplomatic bag by exposing the satchel to sniffer dogs trained to search for ammunition, drugs, and explosives.

In addition to inviolability, diplomats enjoy a wide range of exemptions from national, regional, and municipal taxes. Except for services such as electricity, gas, refuse collection, water, and sewage, the premises of diplomatic missions are tax exempt. Any articles that are imported for the official use of the mission are also exempt from customs and excise duties, provided they are not sold or otherwise disposed of for profit in the host state.

CONSULAR IMMUNITY

Like diplomats, **consuls** are specialized agents of one state in another state. Unlike diplomats, however, consuls do not conduct political relations or negotiations between states. They are not accredited by one head of state to another to represent the person of the sovereign in a foreign state.

The consul represents the sending state in a different way from diplomats. Consuls are concerned with assisting nationals of their state and furthering the commercial, economic, cultural, and scientific relations between the sending state and the host state. They issue passports, visas, and appropriate travel and judicial documents to nationals. Consuls safeguard the interests of their nationals as individuals and corporations in a foreign state, particularly by acting as notary, civil registrar, and administrative agent for the sending state. They also exercise certain rights of supervision and inspection over crews of vessels having the nationality of the sending state.

Unlike embassies, consulates are not necessarily located in the capital city of the host state. They are usually opened in cities and towns that have special commercial significance to the sending state. In the US, Canada has consular posts in 17 cities, and each consulate provides consular services to a designated territory that includes a number of US states.[13] For example, the Canadian

consulate in Boston serves a territory that includes the states of Massachusetts, Maine, New Hampshire, Rhode Island, and Vermont.

FACTFILE Vice-consuls and consular agents are furnished with a document similar to an exequatur, usually known as a brevet.

Consular officers are appointed by their governments through diplomatic channels in the host state. They are given a commission, which is a written document showing the consul's name, rank (for example, consul general, consul, or vice-consul), the consular district, and the post. The host government issues an **exequatur** that approves and authorizes the appointment. The exequatur entitles the consul to certain privileges and immunities in respect of acts performed in the exercise of consular duties.

Originally, Britain provided Canadians with consular service. Eventually, Canada appointed its own trade commissioners to secure Canadian commercial interests abroad, while the British maintained responsibility for consular work. Canada opened its first diplomatic mission in Washington, DC, in February 1927. During World War II, the Canadian foreign service was expanded and Canada established its first consulate in Godthaab, Greenland, in 1940.

FACTFILE By 2007, Canada had 109 consular missions abroad; their responsibilities include immigration, commercial and public affairs, and trade. These missions are a busy and vital component of Canada's international presence. At certain locations, emergency consular assistance is available.

The Vienna Convention on Consular Relations in 1963 codified most of the pre-existing rules of customary international law regarding consular immunities. Under the convention, the privileges and immunities enjoyed by a consular officer are similar to those enjoyed by members of a diplomatic staff. They apply, however, to a lesser degree. The host state is obliged to protect the consular

Table 14.1	What missions do and cannot do

What Missions Do

- contact relatives or friends at home to transfer emergency funds
- help you replace a stolen or lost passport
- notify and provide information to next of kin about accidents or deaths
- direct you to information about local laws and customs
- inform relatives or friends if you are arrested, and try to ensure that your hearing and imprisonment conform to the standards of the foreign state
- provide a list of local doctors and lawyers
- help you during emergencies, such as natural disasters and civil disturbances

What Missions Cannot Do

- pay your hospital, medical, legal, hotel, or transportation bills
- make travel arrangements, provide services, cash cheques, or provide loans
- provide legal advice, investigate thefts or losses, post bail, or pay fines
- find you a job or get you a work permit or a driver's licence
- intervene in the law-enforcement or judicial processes of a foreign state
- provide postal services or hold your personal items for safekeeping

officers, but personal inviolability and immunity from jurisdiction apply only to acts performed in the exercise of consular functions. A consul must respond to civil actions by third parties for damages arising from acts of personal negligence. Consuls must appear before proper authorities if criminal charges are brought against them. If found guilty of criminal acts, consuls are liable to imprisonment in the host state. In the event that a consular agent is charged with a "grave crime," the Vienna Convention states that a consul may even be detained pending trial. In Canada, the *Diplomatic and Consular Privileges and Immunities Act* of 1977 provides that a "grave crime" is any offence determined by an act of Parliament for which an offender may be sentenced to imprisonment for five or more years.

In the Canadian case *Maluquer v. The King*, it was ruled that a foreign consul is not entitled to the same degree of immunity enjoyed by a person who occupies a diplomatic position. When acting as a private person, a consul has the same legal rights as any other resident alien. This restrictive theory applied by Canadian courts in cases involving consular immunity has been widely shared throughout the international system. The Canadian position was clarified further in the Act of 1977, which firmly distinguishes between the application of civil and criminal jurisdictions on diplomats and consular officers.

FACTFILE A rare termination of consular services can occur when a given state strongly disapproves of the actions of another state and closes consular facilities, as between Russia and Afghanistan.

In spite of conventional and judicial restrictions of consular immunities, all governments want to ensure the effective fulfillment of consular functions.[14] Thus, consulates, their archives, and their documents are inviolable and may not be entered by local authorities without the permission of the head of the consular post. The consular premises, including the residence of the head of the post, are tax exempt. All career income is tax exempt to consuls and so are fees for consular services that generate income for the consulate. All consular personnel are exempt from local regulations concerning residence permits and the registration and employment of aliens.

The host state is obligated to give consuls access to sending-state nationals who are arrested or detained. Consuls also have the right of access to information in cases of death, guardianship, shipwrecks, and aircraft accidents. Finally, consuls have the right to communicate with appropriate authorities in the receiving state in order to perform their official duties.

> FACTFILE   As of 2007, over 80 percent of Canadian diplomats held two academic degrees or more.

PROFILE OF AN AMBASSADOR

In the complicated world of international relations, today's ambassador needs to possess the specialized talents of many professionals: the survival instinct of a business person, the organization of an administrator, the charm of an actor, and the intellectual curiosity and objectivity of a social scientist.

Foreign services in all states, therefore, seek to recruit people of unique character and high training. There is no question that the *corps diplomatique* has traditionally been elite.[15] But today it is an elite not of breeding, but of talent. The academic qualifications of most diplomats are very high. Almost invariably they are university educated, holding professional degrees to the level of PhD.

They have had extensive experience in government, usually in the public service, and have made a career of climbing to the rank of ambassador. Many diplomats are multilingual: Europeans excel in this qualification because of the geographical proximity of people speaking many different languages. Canada is officially bilingual, and many of its foreign representatives are as well. Education and language skills are, to a great extent, personal achievements. But most of the formal training a diplomat receives is usually provided by the diplomatic corps of the sending state.

Yet all the formal training a diplomat receives cannot surpass the innate qualities of character—moral integrity, flexibility, loyalty, courage, and political sense—required for the job. Most diplomatic observers seem to agree that the personal attributes of the envoy, rather than his or her formal qualifications, have a decisive influence on the outcome of diplomacy. The intellectual context in which an envoy is trained is often not relevant to many of the issues conducted among governments.

Today's practitioners require, in addition to these traditional skills, knowledge of the latest technologies of peace and war. They must be aware that their negotiations transcend the interests of the governments they represent and that nuclear-age decision making has global consequences. Above all, ambassadors need to have what Sir Harold Nicolson called "the main formative influence in diplomatic theory . . . common sense."[16] In diplomacy, common sense is as much a skill as it is a gift. While such a quality may only on rare occasions change history, it is a vital ingredient in the daily operation of any embassy, whether in London, England, or Kuala Lumpur, Malaysia.

The art of negotiation requires a person who is an empathetic communicator—one who listens and understands. After all, the purpose of diplomacy is communication; everything connected with diplomacy—representation, protocol, procedures—is designed to facilitate communication with people. Diplomats have to be observant, pragmatic, and intuitive with the people they meet. Diplomats will make accommodations not because they are impressed with political rhetoric and argumentation, but because they believe that making a concession will be more useful or less harmful than refusing it. Thus, the strategy of diplomats is to provide convincing incentives that foreign diplomats will perceive as concessions in their self-interest.[17] In effect, the force of logic is more desirable than the logic of force in the negotiating process.

An ambassador must also take responsibility for a large operating staff that depends on his or her leadership. This amounts to maintaining a complicated network of people above and beyond the important political relations with the officials of the host country. Every embassy maintains a mission staff made up of accountants, translators, chauffeurs, secretaries, cipher clerks, radio operators, gardeners, lawyers, and hospitality personnel. Today's ambassadors are no longer considered too high up the ladder to get involved in the organization of a smoothly running embassy. Indeed, those with large staffs of diplomats, experts, and locally employed workers now have to manage and supervise in addition to carrying out their negotiating functions.

In spite of the glamour the public is anxious to attach to diplomacy, in reality it is a profession much like other professions. It is filled with routine and protocol, and meeting people is the essence of the diplomat's craft. This usually means attending luncheons and receptions, giving speeches, hosting guests, giving interviews, and being present at celebrations of the host state's national holidays.

Almost everything an ambassador does is related to representation, but going to a party or a dinner is really going to work. Social gatherings provide an atmosphere of friendship and good public relations as well as opportunities to share vital information. Of a total annual operating budget of $21 million, the Canadian embassy in Washington spends over $500,000 on representation.

An ambassador and his or her spouse attend approximately 200 social functions and host more than 150 events a year, both at the embassy and at their residence. These functions include breakfast briefings, meetings, lunches, receptions, dinners, and groups that are invited to the residence for tea or drinks. This is an important part of the information-gathering function of the diplomatic mission. Most of the information upon which an embassy will act comes from open sources and conventional channels. Formal meetings, conversations, newspapers, and public statements by governing officials all form the main sources of information needed to make or adjust foreign policy.

Usually the functional division of the mission provides the organizational framework for the acquisition of information. At Canada's embassy in Washington, the political section (headed by a minister who answers to the ambassador) attempts to acquire information on subjects relating to the political trends and foreign-policy positions of the United States. The economic and commercial sections, each headed by a minister (also answerable to the ambassador), seek to gain information that might be of interest to Canadian government officials concerned with trade and economic policy. The Canadian embassy also has attachés concerned with military, scientific, cultural, and agricultural matters that affect both states.

The role of the ambassador is crucial in the process of receiving and transmitting information. It is the ambassador who usually reports to Ottawa any changes that may affect Canada's relations with the United States. Because information comes in a constant flow, what the ambassador chooses to send to the Department of Foreign Affairs, as well as the other departments of government, is important. His or her ability to give priority to certain trends and events and to press diplomatic views to Ottawa determines whether the Cabinet can adjust its policies to meet new conditions in the United States.

Ambassador Wilson has to identify those significant political and constitutional changes in the

Focus On   Canada's Ambassador to the United States

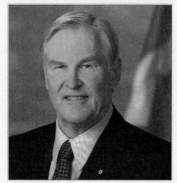

Michael Wilson assumed his responsibilities as Ambassador on March 13, 2006, becoming the twenty-second representative of Canada to the United States. He was Chair of UBS Canada, an operating division of UBS AG, one of the world's leading financial institutions. He oversaw all UBS operations in Canada, which included the investment bank, pension fund management, and wealth management businesses. Prior to joining UBS in July 2001, Wilson was responsible for RBC Financial Group's institutional asset management business. He also served as a Vice Chair of RBC Dominion Securities, responsible for senior client relationships and advice to both Canadian and international companies and governments.

In 1979, he was elected to the House of Commons. In September 1984, he was appointed Minister of Finance and remained in that role until May 1991. He then became Minister of Industry, Science and Technology and Minister for International Trade. During his tenure as member of the Cabinet, he represented Canada at the IMF, IBRD, OECD, GATT and the G-7 Ministers meetings.

Ambassador Wilson is active in a number of professional and community organizations including Neuro-Science Canada Partnership, the Centre for Addiction and Mental Health, the Canadian Council for Public-Private Partnerships, and the Canadian Coalition for Good Governance. Ambassador Wilson is an Officer of the Order of Canada, and has honorary degrees from the University of Toronto and York University.

United States that have taken place over the past 10 years and have far-reaching implications for Canadian interests. For example, the system of checks and balances in the US among the three branches of government has become increasingly complicated. There is usually a strong spirit of congressional independence from the presidency, demonstrated by the much greater involvement of the legislative branch of government in foreign affairs. The US Congress is much more ready to assert its prerogatives, is receptive to interest-group lobbying, and is less willing to follow the lead of the White House.

The Canadian ambassador to the United States no longer deals primarily with officials of the State Department. In the twenty-first century, diplomats must deal with a myriad of politically active individuals and groups that now have a dramatic effect on the political landscape in the United States. Washington is populated by an army of lawyers, public-relations experts, political-action committees, pressure groups, political strategists, tacticians, and fundraisers. Then there is the Congress, with more than 20 000 staff members working on politics and substance.

In addition to the traditional departments of government, the Canadian embassy staff must negotiate with many of the independent federal regulatory agencies and commissions established by Congress, such as the Federal Aviation Agency and the Federal Maritime Commission. Added to this is the complication of monitoring the tactics of nearly 20 000 lobbyists who, at any time, may pressure executive and congressional staff members and officials on matters related to Canadian interests.[18] These can range from acid rain to special problems arising out of health care or free trade. Special-interest groups can have a damaging effect on trade and employment for both economies.

The separation of powers in the US makes negotiating an especially complicated process. The executive branch of government may enthusiastically agree to a set of concessions in a negotiation, but the Senate, responding to an effective lobby, may not ratify the agreement or may add unanticipated provisions to it.

On matters of trade, the ambassador actively lobbies for Canadian interests. Trade between Canada and the United States creates enormous benefits to both states. On an annual basis, Canadians and Americans exchange over US$400 billion worth of goods and services.

Much of the success behind Canada–US agreements can be attributed to the behind-the-scenes efforts of the ambassador and his staff. In this connection, an important aspect of the ambassador's job in Washington is that of sensitizing Congress to the effects of trade actions on Canada. Canada's economy is easily sideswiped by US actions aimed at others. When this happens, the ambassador will attempt to inform members of Congress and their committees that trade restrictions hurt both economies.

In addition to representing Canadian interests in the American political system, the embassy staff also administers routine claims from Canadians who are visiting or who are involved in business in the United States. These run annually into the thousands. The Canadian embassy acts as a broker for its citizens, administering travel and business matters requiring official representation. The mission is required to protect those nationals who may have legal difficulties and to assist in ensuring their fair treatment according to the laws of the host state. An arrest or an affront to a Canadian in the United States, as in the case of Maher Arar, may put strains on embassy officials who desire to settle these matters in good faith; the embassy staff never knows what political factors might be involved in a given incident.

No matter how varied the duties of an embassy might be, the prime concern of an ambassador is to keep international relations as routine and as friendly as possible. The Canadian embassy in Washington must see that the large volume of transactions across the Canadian–US border is facilitated by the least amount of conflict between the two governments. For that reason, the Canadian government has assigned the largest single concentration of diplomatic talent it has to Washington to make sure the United States does take notice.

In the Ottawa headquarters of the Department of Foreign Affairs and International Trade, the United States has an entire branch of its own, headed by an assistant deputy ministry. This branch includes six divisions: general relations (political and legal matters); trade and economic relations; trans-boundary matters (environment, energy, security, and transportation); marketing; trade and investment; and programs. All these institutional representations reflect the large volume of international transactions that take place between Canada and the United States.

Chapter Summary

If all the world's a stage in the twenty-first century, there are more actors on it than ever. The world—its environment, economics, and politics—intrudes on us more each day.

Effective foreign policies have become paramount for the survival of modern societies. In the past, foreign relations were almost exclusively transactions between governments, using military, economic, and diplomatic methods to achieve foreign policy goals. Today's stage is global in size and the issues governments must face in their domestic environment increasingly affect the rest of the world.

Foreign policy is like domestic policy—it involves decision making—but it also involves decisions that go far beyond the borders of each state to affect the world commons. Global issues have emerged as paramount in all national policy agendas. The world—its environment, economics, and politics—has intruded in all governments. In this chapter we looked at Canada's global connection and the contours of foreign policy-making for all states.

Today, military power (hard power) does not automatically bring success in foreign policy. In an era of tight global connection, human rights issues, climate change, the economy, and energy do not merely parallel their domestic manifestations. The way foreign policy confronts the international face of these key issues shapes what we can do about them at home.

Diplomacy (soft power) plays a significant role in foreign policy. The skills and protocols of classical diplomacy throughout history prepared the way for the evolution of an internationally recognized profession of negotiators. They developed the widely used sets of procedures and practices for resolving conflicts between governments and for enhancing the political and economic ties among nation-states.

Diplomatic immunities flow from sovereign immunities, providing diplomats with *inviolability*, the principle of protecting diplomats and their property from harm, and a wide range of exemptions from domestic civil and criminal jurisdictions.

Because of the existence of more than 200 independent nation-states that exchange diplomats and host embassies, legations, and consulates, and the increasing number of multilateral international organizations that require diplomatic representation from member states, the world diplomatic corps has become sizable.

Until the end of the nineteenth century, most diplomatic communication and negotiation took place bilaterally, between two states. But in the twentieth century, states began to participate in multilateral conferences, enabling the diplomats of many states to negotiate new international law.

Summit diplomacy, a term coined by Winston Churchill, involves direct communication between and among heads of state or heads of government.

Diplomatic immunity evolved from customary law to provide the inviolability of diplomats and to protect them

from the application of certain civil and criminal actions that would interfere with their professional performance.

Consuls are specialized state agents, concerned with the representation of nationals and promoting the business, cultural, economic, and scientific interests of the sending state in a host state.

Discussion Questions

1. How can ordinary people influence their country's foreign policies?

2. Design a workable foreign policy for Canada and the United States in the areas of cross-border trade and tourism.

3. Can Canada develop an independent foreign policy when it is so closely linked geographically, economically, and diplomatically, to a superpower (the US)?

4. What impact do the media have on foreign policy?

5. What are three of the largest threats to Canada's security in this century?

6. What are some of the outstanding interests of Canada today in world affairs?

7. Identify three or four foreign policy goals that you believe should be pursued by Canadian diplomats and leaders. Which institutions of government must work to achieve those goals?

8. Discuss the evolution of diplomacy as a privileged profession with unique exemptions and immunities.

9. Discuss the privileges and immunities of ambassadors. Compare these with the exemptions that apply to consuls.

10. Discuss the four major contemporary influences on diplomacy. Has terrorism changed any dynamics in diplomacy? If so, how?

11. Outline what, in your opinion, would be the desirable personal and professional qualifications of a good diplomat.

12. How are embassies different from consulates? How can you use an embassy or consulate to help you when travelling or living abroad?

15

Global Challenges in the Twenty-First Century

After reading this chapter, you will be able to:

- incorporate information from previous chapters into a discussion of global challenges

- discuss how globalization has changed the problems we face and how we address them

- identify the challenges facing us in the twenty-first century

- understand peacekeeping and discuss issues arising from it

- clarify major global issues, such as arms control, arms proliferation, the population explosion, the global food crisis, HIV/AIDS, and climate change

- feel confident about taking upper-level courses in political science

THE CHALLENGES

The phenomenon of globalization has both positive and negative consequences for how we resolve the challenges we face in the 2000s.[1] For good or ill, the word *globalization* has entered the lexicon of all languages, and we cannot avoid its use. Globalization is *economic* in that goods, services, capital, and information flow freely around the world; globalization is *social* and *cultural* in that people and ideas can move around the world relatively unhindered; globalization is *military* in that war and terrorism are transportable everywhere; and globalization is *environmental* in that actions taken in one part of the world have the capacity to migrate to all parts of the world.

FACTFILE   By 2007, Third World debt had reached its highest level at nearly $6 trillion, threatening to cause landslide defaults among developing economies, recessions in developed economies, and political and economic instability around the world.

Scholars of globalization agree that, on the positive side, the world is much more connected than ever before. Some supporters wonder who could possibly be against globalization—particularly in an age when access to the world can provide so much opportunity. Corporate globalization demands "free trade" at all costs to enable the flow of capital and labour, to eradicate economic nationalism, and to grow the "global economy." Never before in human history have so many markets been accessible to business, institutions, and governments.

To its supporters, globalization has produced more organizations dedicated to resolving the complex problems we face beyond our national borders. Global reach, once the exclusive capability of great powers, is now available to many others. The world has never been more bureaucratized at levels above and below national governments. Each year the number of non-governmental organizations increases, creating a web of international connections around the world.

As for knowledge, the grand perspective of human awareness has risen to the level of protecting the planet, its various forms of life, and the delicate balance between how we live and how the earth is affected by us. The exchange of human knowledge about matters of global import has never been faster or greater. New academic, scientific, and technological knowledge spreads electronically and instantly to every corner of the earth.

In addition, general principles of global governance with strong democratic values are gaining legitimacy throughout the international community. The idea that the world can and should legislate the rules we need to survive is gaining wider acceptance. Global executive and legislative institutions are no longer impossible dreams. And the creation of judicial institutions with a global jurisdiction has already taken hold during the years since World War II.

On the negative side, globalization has made the world a more dangerous place.[2] Weapons can be marketed worldwide. The very same markets that provide opportunity globally are desirable targets for terrorists who can get their messages of fear and intimidation to the widest audiences. **Weapons of mass destruction** (WMDs) include three general types: biological, chemical, and nuclear. They have become miniaturized, portable, and available to any state, group, or individual who wants to use them. Globalization has furthermore dramatically increased the disparities in wealth and power between the *haves* and the vast numbers of *have-nots* around the world, as it allows for even more exploitation of the developing countries and their economies by developed states.

THE GLOBAL CHALLENGE OF PEACE

Philosopher George Santayana warned us of the dangers of not remembering the past. It is perhaps even more dangerous to remember the past incorrectly. Throughout history, every major military technology invented—including nuclear weapons—has been used in wars among groups and states. In the twenty-first century, the danger of nuclear war is part of a much older problem, which is that humans will use violence to settle disputes among themselves. Long before the existence of nuclear arsenals, societies could and did set out to destroy one another entirely.

It is ironic that the historic race to build the most destructive weapons should now lead government leaders to consider an option that has been available to them from the dawn of human history: peace. "Peace, which costs nothing, is attended with infinitely more advantage than any victory with all its expense."[3]

FACTFILE   Land mines are regarded as the world's most dangerous weapon, causing about 26 000 deaths and serious injuries, mostly to civilians, every year. Every 20 minutes, someone around the world is injured or killed by a land mine.

The term *peace* is often given many meanings. Some define peace narrowly as the absence of war. But to the majority of people in the world, peace is more than the mere absence of war. The word has positive connotations, implying rights to pursue human happiness through economic, social, and political opportunity. Religious and political thinking reinforce this positive view. Peace and good will are definitely linked to our conception of what is morally right and politically desirable. Peace is associated with trust, mutual respect, and with living free from the reality of war. On the international level, peace means the free collaboration and interaction of nation-states. At a personal level, peace is a state of mind.

The relative character of this highly prized human goal is subject to differing and at times contradictory interpretations between and among governments. Peace, like wealth or well-being, is a highly charged ideological concept. For **Al Qaeda**, for example, peace is possible only after the United States withdraws from the Saudi

Arabian peninsula and when the "infidels" have been punished or destroyed for their uninvited involvement in the Arab world.

Differing ideological perspectives on peace have generated barriers of distrust among states. The world of inter-state relations is viewed by many leaders as essentially predatory and anarchic. On this presumption, states spend resources on arms in order to engage or deter aggression, and thus to achieve greater security. In these circumstances, peace is equated with military preparedness, deterrence, and arms competition. Here the concept of **strategic superiority** plays a major role in announcing to the rest of the world that the military arsenal a state possesses is awesome and destructive. This has been a major component of US foreign policy since the 1990s.

The current challenge to peace focuses on the widespread possession and proliferation of weapons. After the atomic bomb was invented, the choices available to humankind became narrow and ominous. The subsequent development of **thermonuclear** weapons and sophisticated delivery systems of great range and accuracy severely limited our choices. Of course, the dismantling of these weapons is an option, by far the most lucid but least likely one. At a time when terrorism is on the rise, nuclear weapons can be dismantled, but they cannot be uninvented.

FACTFILE   During World War II, the so-called state-of-the-art blockbuster bombs exploded with a force of 10 tons of TNT (explosive material); today's nuclear bombs have an average explosive force of 6.49 million tons of TNT.

The immediate imperative is to use all available political and legal instruments to ensure that nuclear weapons are not used, and to survive international conflicts that involve conventional weapons as best we can. But although nuclear weapons are widely viewed as presenting the gravest threat to world peace, in fact the greatest threat to global security arises from conventional weapons used by governments and terrorists. Modernized conventional weapons are approaching the destructive scale of nuclear weapons without the residual radioactive effects. Even at the level of small-group terrorism, modern conventional technology has severe destructive potential.

Peacekeeping

With ever-increasing hopes and expectations, governments are looking to international organizations to supply solutions to the challenge of peace. In the area of **peacekeeping**, the United Nations has responded frequently.[4] Since 1988, the UN has conducted more peacekeeping missions than it did in its first 55 years of operation. Military men and women from more than 100 states have worn the blue beret and the blue helmet in the service of peace, security, and stability. By 2007, there were over 64 000 peacekeepers on duty in 18 missions. Peacekeepers have monitored and enforced ceasefires, verified security agreements, ensured the delivery of humanitarian aid, provided basic government structures and services, and assisted in transitions from colony to modern government.

Peacekeeping can be defined as actions designed to enhance international peace, security, and stability that are authorized by competent national and international organizations and undertaken by governments co-operatively with military, humanitarian, and civilian police, and other interested agencies and groups. The words *peacekeeping* and *peacemaking* are not mentioned in the United Nations Charter. The general subject falls under the "Peaceful Settlement of Disputes" and "Action with Respect to Threats to the Peace, Breaches of the Peace, and Acts of Aggression" clauses of the Charter. The UN Military Observer Group, established by the Security Council in April 1948 to supervise the ceasefire between India and Pakistan, is generally regarded as the first UN peacekeeping mission, although the word *peacekeeping* only came into use in 1956 at the time of the Suez crisis.

The great divide that once existed between military and humanitarian aid has been bridged. The peacekeeping umbrella continues to expand to encompass non-traditional activities—for example, the use of a civilian police force such as the RCMP and experts in the operations of elections, such as officials of Elections Canada. Peacekeeping also involves *peacemaking*, which entails the use of force by an international organization sanctioned by the United Nations.

When a nation-state considers its potential contribution to a peacekeeping mission, it decides the percentage of each of the following ingredients: personnel, financing, material and equipment, research, education, and training. Each of these must be considered against the backdrop of command, control, and communications. This involves the need for a central authority that can define and oversee the entire peacekeeping operation.

> **FACTFILE**   Peacekeeping does have casualties: Since 1948, more than 2300 UN peacekeepers have been killed in the line of duty.

Canada has always played a prominent role in peacekeeping. Since 1948, Canada has enjoyed a positive, international peacekeeping reputation that is second to none. More than 100 000 men and women of the Canadian Armed Forces and thousands of Canadian civilians have taken part in these missions—more than from any other nation-state. Even though its peacekeeping commissions have been in gradual decline, Canada has contributed personnel, material, and resources (such as the expertise to disarm and destroy land mines) to every UN peacekeeping endeavour—no other state has matched that record. The negative consequence has been that some Canadians have lost their lives in the service of peace, and in rare cases Canada has been discredited because of unlawful actions on the part of some soldiers.

Throughout the years, most military and civilian peacekeeping ground forces have been very successful. When they have been unable to carry out their mandates, the UN Security Council has insisted that they remain in place and function as best they can, as in the recent cases of Afghanistan, Bosnia, the Congo, East Timor, Golan Heights, Haiti, Rwanda, and Sierra Leone.

Global Peace Movements

The increasing integration of global values around ideas of non-violence and pacifism have encouraged the rapid spread of peace movements (see Table 15.1). Movements against specific wars, or against war and militarism in general, usually involve large numbers of people who are willing to take direct action against governments that wage war. People associated with most peace movements engage in many activities and often take to the streets to protest war and militarism.[5]

Peace activists are found in every country of the world. They advocate plans for nuclear and conventional-arms control ranging from **unilateral disarmament** to freezes, bans, and moratoriums. The idea that adding more weapons to existing arsenals will deter aggression is under fire in many states. The notion of **nuclear freeze** calls for an immediate halt to the development, production, transfer, and deployment of nuclear weapons. But while the idea is popular just about everywhere, there is disagreement as to whether the freeze should be "unilateral" or "mutual and verifiable."

Britain's Campaign for Nuclear Disarmament (CND) calls on all nuclear-weapons states to dismantle their nuclear arsenals. The CND is anti-military, anti-American, and anti-NATO. In Canada, groups such as the Canadian Peace Congress and Project Ploughshares want Canada to be a **nuclear-weapon-free zone** (NWFZ). This would include opting out of the North Warning System for continental defence and refusing to permit US Trident submarines to enter Canadian waters. The agenda of some peace activists (particularly after NATO's operation against Yugoslavia in 1999) also call on Canada to leave NATO and to proclaim its neutrality in international affairs. The Toronto Disarmament Network (TDN), formed in 1981, represents more than 60 peace groups that maintain a network of organization and communication with other disarmament groups around the world. Besides this group, nearly 1000 peace groups are operating in Canada.

Table 15.1   Peace groups in Canada

Act of Earth	Artists Against War	Canadian Arab Federation
Canadian Coalition for Nuclear Responsibility	Canadian Islamic Congress	Canadian Labour Congress
Canadian Muslim Civil Liberties Association	Canadian Network to Abolish Nuclear Weapons	Canadian Voice of Women for Peace
Greenpeace Canada	Operation Objection	Physicians for Global Survival
Writers Against the War	War Resisters Support Campaign	

Source: cpa@web.ca; www.peace.ca.

Focus On   A Canadian Professor of International Affairs

Profile of Dr. Lee-Anne Broadhead

Dr. Lee-Anne Broadhead is an associate professor of political science at Cape Breton University (CBU). She received her professional training in political science, library science, and history at four universities: Trent (BA), Queen's (MA), Toronto (MLS), and Leeds (PhD).

Before joining the faculty at CBU, Professor Broadhead taught in the Department of Peace Studies at the University of Bradford in England. There she developed her skills as a teacher, researcher, and writer, with a focus on the interdisciplinary subject area of peace research. Drawing from a wide range of academic perspectives—geography, history, library science, international relations, political science, and sociology—her work focused on the complex, multifaceted search for peace and justice in a turbulent, violent, and profoundly iniquitous global system. Her studies led to publications in numerous journals, including, among others, *Canadian Women Studies/Les cahiers de la femme*, *International Journal*, and the *British Journal of Canadian Studies*.

Since she joined CBU in 1999, Dr. Broadhead has become a powerful academic voice in the field of international relations, peace research, and student political awareness. She is the author of *International Environmental Politics: The Limits of Green Diplomacy* (Lynne Rienner Publishers, 2002) and collaborates with other professors on a wide range of publications aimed at academic and more general audiences.

Professor Broadhead is an active scholar and believes that teaching can benefit her students by encouraging them in the research they choose to do. As a professor of international relations, she believes that all learning begets research, teaching, and active involvement in the world around us. It is crucial, as she notes, to recognize "that the way we conceive of the world decisively shapes our methods of resolving problems within it." She asserts that we must use an accurate framework for understanding a complex global system.

Courses offered by Dr. Broadhead include "International Politics in a Changing World," "International Politics of the Environment, Terrorism and Security Policy," and "Revolution and Resistance." These courses are designed not simply to be topical. They give her students a world view that they can incorporate into their personal and professional lives, and they foster general intellectual development and critical skills.

Many students of Professor Broadhead note that her approach to international relations inspires in them a deep personal commitment to the state of the world, both human and natural. She believes that international politics affects us all, and that we can positively affect international affairs by acquiring professional knowledge and critical insights into the workings of the world around us.

Professor Broadhead practises what she teaches, by being deeply committed to the university's academic life, community organizations, and many other social and political groups, including Science for Peace, Peace Quest Cape Breton, and The Pugwash Conferences on Sciences and World Affairs (Canadian Group).

European Nuclear Disarmament (END) was organized to persuade nuclear-weapons states to renounce the possession and use of their arsenals. This group called for a zone free of nuclear weapons from Portugal to Poland. In Belarus, Kazakhstan, Russia, and the Ukraine, peace advocates call for a NWFZ in Europe.

FACTFILE   Since 1939, there has not been a single day when war was not being waged somewhere in the world.

Another zone proposal is the "zone of peace" (ZOP). The concept goes much further than the NWFZ. The ZOP is a regional approach to general disarmament and not merely a ban on one particular type of dangerous weapon. States that would compose the zone agree to resolve their disputes peacefully, without resorting to bacteriological, chemical, conventional, or nuclear arms. The concept was endorsed by the UN General Assembly in 1978, but rejected by superpowers because it would have deprived them of their military bases in virtually every region of the world. One option is to declare the Arctic a zone of peace. But Canada has not been proactive on the idea because of its treaty obligations in NORAD. The concept of the ZOP may be more acceptable now that the Cold War has ended and the extreme rivalry of the nuclear powers has subsided.

Peace in Space

Space has been assigned a strategic importance by a growing number of states. With space exploration has come the opportunity to infinitely expand human knowledge. But the conquest of this new frontier is accompanied by the danger that it will one day become an extension of territorial and military conflict. By the twenty-first century, the number of military satellites deployed by states is more than 100 a year. Early-warning satellites and other electronic-intelligence satellites comprise the greater number of these, making it virtually impossible for any state to now conceal its military operations.[6]

The Strategic Defense Initiative (SDI), announced by former US President Ronald Reagan, moved the world into a new era of military competition in space. SDI, or "Star Wars," aspired to replace the principle of Mutual Assured Destruction (MAD) with a theory of assured defence—by using space to build a high-tech shield to detect, track, and intercept missile attacks launched on the ground by enemy states. While SDI is not a reality, the concept is conceivable and, therefore, probable as an eventual military strategy for space. But space provides the world with many opportunities for non-military use as well.

Canada has been involved in outer space for about 50 years, since the launching of the *Alouette I* satellite in 1962. A Canadian Space Policy was adopted in 1974. It states that Canadian space technology will be used for peaceful purposes. The development of the Canadarm, which is used on US space shuttles and in the Canadian Astronaut Program, has captured much public attention.

The peaceful benefits of space exploration involve communications, remote sensing, industry science, and interplanetary travel. The International Telecommunications Satellite Organization (Intelsat) was created in 1964 to rapidly transfer information related to news, sports, and cultural events. In 1975, only Canada, the Soviet Union, and the United States had communications satellite systems. By the year 2008, Intelsat with its 15 systems had more than 100 member states, including Canada, and formed the nucleus of the global space-based telecommunications system. Canada owns and operates four Intelsat earth stations, which are the backbone of its ANIK satellite series.

Another non-military opportunity in space is **remote sensing**. In 1972, the United Nations Committee on the Peaceful Uses of Outer Space (COPUOS) gave global approval for the remote observation of the earth's surface, its weather patterns, environmental depletion, and other phenomena by means of air-borne and space-borne platforms. Two of the more commonly known uses of remote sensing are weather forecasting (to gather data on hurricanes, tornadoes, and other severe storms) and crop assessment (to gather data on crops, forests, grasslands, deserts, and fisheries).

FACTFILE The first ideas of using space weapons for earth wars are thousands of years old and are found in Chinese, Egyptian, and Greek mythologies.

Commercial satellites provide enormous opportunities for commercial development and experimentation. Weightlessness and airlessness in space make possible the production of certain goods that are not efficiently manufactured on earth. For example, the manufacture of homogeneous crystals, so important to the electronic industry, are much more efficiently produced in conditions present in space. New or better drugs can also be manufactured in the weightless environment of space. Almost every field of human enterprise can benefit from space exploration.

There is still no internationally agreed-upon definition of where the boundary is that divides national air space and outer space. Scientists of the Committee on Space Research (COSPAR)

have recommended the lower boundary of outer space be established at an altitude of 100 km. This is the altitude at which satellites can orbit freely beyond the earth's gravitational pull. Many states, including Canada, believe it is important to reach agreement on a space boundary because of the legal and practical risks in the application of a growing regime of space law.

In 1963, the Partial Test Ban Treaty (PTBT) prohibited the explosion of nuclear weapons above the atmosphere. In 1967, COPUOS drafted the Outer Space Treaty. Prohibiting the extension of sovereignty beyond national air space, signatories to this treaty agree not to orbit weapons of mass destruction, install such weapons on celestial bodies, or establish military bases in space. The ABM Treaty (1972) prohibits developing, testing, and deploying anti-ballistic missile (ABM) systems that are air-based or space-based. Another agreement that governs the activities of states on the moon and other celestial bodies is the Moon Treaty (1979). It prohibits placing nuclear weapons on or around the moon.

FACTFILE Space weapons include space stations firing re-entry missiles at earth targets, satellite killers, microwave- and laser-beam weapons, and orbital mines.

Peace is a human relationship towards which people and their governments must choose to work. It first requires the political will to eliminate the root causes of conflict. This involves trust, the opening of all possible lines of international communication, and the strengthening and reform of international institutions. It requires an increase in economic and social interaction: people doing business with each other and meeting each other through a vast network of social exchanges involving the arts, sciences, sports, and tourism. But just as arms control is essential, so is it necessary to address the global problems of population and hunger before a lasting peace can be achieved. These are some of the immediate challenges.

THE GLOBAL CHALLENGE OF ARMS CONTROL

Even before the first atomic bomb was tested, other weapons of mass destruction (chemical and biological) were being stockpiled for military use. As early as 1915, chemical weapons had made their appearance on the battlefields of Europe, and Canadians were among the first casualties. By the end of World War I, 1 300 000 people had been victims of chemical warfare.

FACTFILE The United States is the world's largest exporter of weapons and spends more than any other nation-state on the development of weapons technology.

The Hague International Peace conferences of 1899 and 1907 were the first proposals for international arms-control standards. The Geneva Protocol of 1925 (signed and ratified by more than 110 states) prohibits the use of asphyxiating, poisonous, or other gases and analogous liquids in warfare between states party to the agreement. But the protocol does not prohibit the development, production, and stockpiling of such weapons. In March 1988, one of 20 states possessing chemical weapons—Iraq—unleashed mustard and cyanide gas on its own Kurdish civilians in Halabja, resulting in thousands of deaths.

During the 1950s and 1960s, the world witnessed the development of new generations of more sophisticated and deadly weapons at an unprecedented pace.[7] In 1971, Canada and a small group of other concerned states proposed the Convention on the Prohibition of the Development, Production, and Stockpiling of Bacteriological (Biological) and Toxin Weapons and on Their Destruction, which was adopted by the General Assembly in 1972 and came into force in 1975. Under the provisions of this convention, the parties renounced the development, use, and transfer of these weapons and undertook to destroy them within nine months of ratification.

FACTFILE More Canadians were killed by conventional weapons during World War I (56 501) than during World War II (43 612).

In 1985, the General Assembly on recommendations by the Ad Hoc Committee on Chemical Weapons called for the speediest conclusion of a convention banning chemical weapons and providing for their destruction. Since that time, every superpower summit placed the issue of chemical weapons on its agenda. In 1989 in Paris, representatives from 149 states pledged to move the international community towards a treaty to ban the "use" of all chemical weapons. Finally, in 1990, a chemical-weapons treaty was signed by the United States and the former Soviet Union.

The acronym *SALT* represents the first round of Strategic Arms Limitations Talks between the United States and the former Soviet Union over a two-and-one-half-year period from 1970 to 1972. The SALT I Anti-Ballistic Missiles (ABM) Treaty prohibited the United States and the Soviet Union constructing ABM defence systems at more than two sites. Both parties further agreed to freeze the number of offensive ballistic-missile launches at their existing levels until 1977. The SALT II ABM Protocol, signed in Moscow in 1974, further limited the superpowers to one defensive site and committed both parties to limit the number of warheads they carry. SALT II was never ratified by the US Senate, even though both Presidents Jimmy Carter and Ronald Reagan were committed to arms limitations.

START was coined by the Reagan administration in 1980 to begin a new round of nuclear-arms negotiations as distinguished from SALT I and SALT II. The Strategic Arms Reduction Talks brought the Americans and the Soviets to the bargaining table in Geneva in 1982. They involved not only weapons deployed by the superpowers, but also the intermediate nuclear forces (INF) in Europe. After six years of intensive negotiations, the United States and the Soviet Union signed the intermediate-nuclear forces treaty in 1987, eliminating an entire class of nuclear weapons from Europe and the rest of the world. In 1991, after nine years of sporadic negotiations, START was finally signed in Moscow by Presidents Mikhail Gorbachev and Bush. With the ratification of the START II treaty by the Russian Duma in 2000, the US and Russian arsenals were reduced to about 3000 warheads, down from the 6000 agreed to under START I. Even though these treaties produced a reduction in the numbers of strategic nuclear arsenals, both states still retain a massive nuclear capability. In the former Soviet Union, most of these weapons are now located in Belarus, Kazakhstan, Russia, and the Ukraine. The US and the Russian Federation have been negotiating START III since the late 1990s with the goal of setting a ceiling of 2000–2500 strategic nuclear weapons for each of the parties, which will reduce the total number deployed warheads permitted under START II by about 40 percent.

The major offensive weapons subject to negotiations are the **intercontinental ballistic missiles** (ICBMs), bombers, and submarine-launched missiles, all of which are deadly accurate and capable of rendering nuclear devastation on an unimaginable scale. Thus, every word exchanged behind the closed doors of disarmament negotiations has a direct impact on every citizen of this planet.

In 1993, the US and Russia agreed to eliminate all multiple independently targetable re-entry vehicles (MIRVs)—MX and Minuteman missiles for the United States and SS-18, SS-19, and SS-24 missiles for Russia—by 2004, creating the smallest stockpiles since the Kennedy and Khrushchev administrations in the early 1960s. But the spread of nuclear and conventional military technologies to a growing number of states will make it impossible for the relative few that possess these weapons to reduce them to zero.

Compliance

Even though states are willing to sign **arms-control agreements**, they are not necessarily going to observe all of the provisions these treaties contain. The effective verification of the parties that sign such agreements is a fundamental process of arms control. **Verification** is an agreed set of procedures whereby the parties to an arms-control agreement inspect the compliance of other parties to the terms of the treaty. Most states advocate on-site inspections, but some states have resisted such instruments for verifying their compliance to an arms-control treaty. Surveillance from high altitudes or from space enables some states to verify the conduct of other states without their agreement to on-site inspections. *Intelligence* is another national instrument employed by states seeking to keep informed about the weapons capabilities of other parties to arms-control agreements. Thus, when verifiable agreements are in place, there are a number of alternative checks on the conduct of signing states.

Strategic Weapons

The doctrine of **mutually assured destruction** (MAD) holds that no aggressor state will launch a nuclear attack so long as it knows that the other side will be able to retaliate with an equally devastating nuclear blow. Even though the Cold War has ended, MAD is still the fundamental dynamic behind the concept of modern deterrence. But not all nuclear weapons provide the same deterrent value. For states such as the US, France, and Britain, nuclear submarines are a very credible deterrent because they are globally mobile and harder to detect and destroy at sea. They are usually not vulnerable to a first strike.

Today, the United States could eventually deploy nearly 15 000 **strategic nuclear weapons**. When **tactical nuclear weapons** are added to strategic ones, the total combined global arsenal if deployed would equal about 90 000 strategic weapons (see Figure 15.1).

Figure 15.1   **The nuclear club: Estimated active nuclear weapons, 2007**

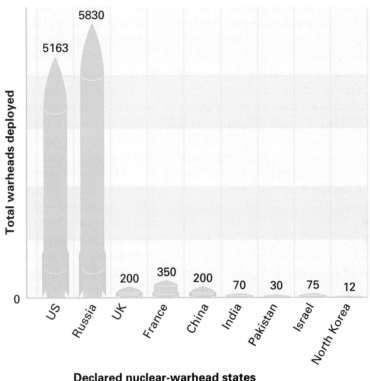

Source: *www.armscontrol.org/factsheets/nuclearweaponswhohaswhat.asp.*

THE GLOBAL CHALLENGE OF WEAPONS PROLIFERATION

Nuclear Weapons

As far back as the mid-1940s, when the first development of nuclear weapons was under way under the **Manhattan Project**, US scientists were arguing for the non-proliferation of nuclear-weapons technology. By the early 1950s, the US, UK, France, USSR, and China had begun to build and expand their nuclear programs almost solely to amass weapons, and designed and operated nuclear facilities for that purpose. By the 1980s,

Argentina, Brazil, India, Israel, North Korea, The Republic of Korea (South), Pakistan, South Africa, and Taiwan had all developed the capacity to assemble and stockpile nuclear weapons. These states, now numbering about 20, are the principal nuclear-weapons powers.

> FACTFILE   The atomic attack on Hiroshima in August 1945 killed 100 000 people. Sixty-five of the 150 doctors in the city died instantly, leaving 8 doctors for every 10 000 survivors; of the 1780 nurses in the Japanese city that day, 1654 were killed immediately.

The first efforts to contain **nuclear proliferation** concentrated on regulating the peaceful uses of nuclear power. By 1945, Canada, the US, and the UK had signed the Agreed Declaration on Atomic Energy, which resolved that nuclear proliferation was a threat to world peace. The following year at the United Nations Atomic Energy Commission, the US proposed that an international atomic-energy agency be established to regulate and control all aspects of the uses of nuclear energy. One of the first resolutions of the United Nations created the Atomic Energy Commission (AEC) with Canada, China, France, Britain, the US, and the USSR as members. The AEC was finally dismantled in 1955 because of disagreements among members over how to control the spread of nuclear weapons.

FACTFILE   Belarus, Kazakhstan, South Africa, and Ukraine are states that possessed nuclear weapons but disposed of them within their territories by the mid-1990s.

In 1957, the International Atomic Energy Agency (IAEA) was founded, with headquarters in Vienna. The major aim of the IAEA is to prevent the diversion of atomic materials to military uses and to disseminate information on the peaceful applications of nuclear technology. Canada was the first state in the world to renounce the possession and spread of nuclear weapons, and has been represented on the board of the IAEA since it was founded. *Safeguards* are applied by requiring member states to design their nuclear facilities according to international standards, to keep detailed records of nuclear operations, and to submit reports to the IAEA. *Inspections* are conducted on site to verify that states are not diverting peaceful nuclear-energy facilities or materials to build nuclear weapons. Still, highly enriched weapons-grade uranium manages to slip by the eyes and ears of the IAEA. By 2004, 529 facilities around the world were producing nuclear materials.

The United Nations drafted the Non-Proliferation Treaty (NPT) in 1968. Today, about 170 states adhere to its provisions. They agree not to transfer nuclear weapons or assist non-nuclear-weapon states to manufacture them. And, non-nuclear-weapon states agree to abide by IAEA safeguards on the peaceful application of nuclear technology. In 1999, the United Nations sponsored the Comprehensive Test Ban Treaty (CTBT), which was signed by 150 states to halt the spread of nuclear weapons globally.

Some nuclear and potentially nuclear-weapons states have not signed the NPT or the new CTBT, primarily because they see its provisions as discriminatory between states that have already manufactured nuclear devices and those that have not. They point out that nuclear-weapons states can keep—and even increase—their arsenals; also, while nuclear-weapons states are under no obligation to submit to IAEA safeguards and inspections, non-nuclear-weapon states must do so on signing. By 2000, most of the states that held reservations about signing the treaty did so. The US Senate did not ratify the CTBT because many Republicans in the Senate feared that a halt to testing would damage the United States' ability to maintain its nuclear arsenal. Nearly 160 states have ratified the global Comprehensive Test Ban Treaty. The underlying aim of the treaty is to get states to give up their right to test nuclear weapons, so that they will not try to develop them.

Many non-nuclear-weapons states assert that those states that have already stockpiled nuclear weapons have not lived up to their obligations to stop testing and spreading nuclear-weapons technology and ultimately to negotiate their way towards general and complete disarmament.

Canada's policy terminates the sale of nuclear materials and equipment to any state that does not apply safeguards in all its nuclear facilities. The United States has developed a similar policy under its *Nuclear Non-Proliferation Act*. And in Latin America, the Treaty of Tlatelolco, signed in 1967, prohibits the acquisition or production of nuclear weapons anywhere in Central and South America. This treaty effectively makes Latin America a nuclear-free zone.

But perhaps the most controversial unilateral action to control nuclear proliferation was initiated in 1981, when Israel bombed a nuclear reactor under construction in Iraq. Israel argued that its attack was a pre-emptive strike against Iraq to prevent its developing nuclear weapons. Iraq countered by charging that such an act was extreme, given that the reactor was being constructed according to IAEA standards and Iraq was a signatory of the NPT. During the Gulf War, coalition forces did extensive damage to Iraq's nuclear capabilities, and the US war and occupation of Iraq since 2003 further inhibited that state from building nuclear weapons.

Conventional and Other Weapons

One of the short-lived myths of the post–Cold War period is that the world would be a safer place. Events have challenged this dangerous assumption almost every week. For millions of Rwandans, Bosnians, Somalis, Albanians, Sudanis, and Iraqis, the world has never been less safe. They are the victims of the so-called conventional wars, fought with **conventional weapons**—bombs, rifles, tanks, and mortars.

FACTFILE   The United States is the largest exporter of conventional weapons around the world, followed by Russia, France, and the United Kingdom. In 2008, Canada ranked twelfth out of twenty-two states in the export of conventional weapons.

Even though the world is still ultimately threatened by nuclear weapons, we are no less threatened by the advances that have been made in conventional-weapons technology since World War II.

With the exception of the few atomic weapons used against Japan in the mid-1940s, all wars since that time have been fought with conventional weapons supplied by the major industrial powers. Since the end of World War II, nearly 60 million people, most of them in the developing states, have died as a result of the limited wars that have swept the planet. Nuclear bombs killed none; they were killed by conventional weapons. Conventional weapons have evolved to become highly destructive, even though these kinds of weapons are still regarded as "limited" because no residual destruction follows their use, unlike that of nuclear weapons.

Chemical and Biological Weapons

Chemical and biological warfare has been waged sporadically over the centuries. Historically, the prevailing belief about using such weapons was that they violate the most fundamental principles of warfare, namely **military necessity** and chivalry. **Chemical weapons** not only kill; they also maim and cause untold human and animal suffering and destroy forests.

FACTFILE   Athenians poisoned the water supplies of their enemies in 600 BC; and in the fourteenth century, the Tartars used biological warfare against their enemies.

During the last century, the horror of chemical warfare was first experienced at Ypres in Belgium in 1915, when German forces released chlorine gas on thousands of Allied troops. The Allies retaliated with similar gas attacks against the Germans, and in 1917 the Germans again used chemicals against the Allies, this time in the form of mustard gas. The world reacted strongly against the use of such weapons by the adoption of the Geneva Protocol, 1925, which forbids the use of chemical and biological weapons. But states were still allowed to produce and stockpile these weapons. Partly for this reason, the US did not ratify the protocol until 1975.

The 1972 United Nations Biological Weapons Convention prohibited the manufacture and stockpiling of biological and toxin weapons, at first by more than 100 states. But the growing threat of

the rapid spread of these two categories of deadly weapons led to more conferences on the subject. In 1989, a Conference on the Prohibition of Chemical Weapons was held in Paris. More than 100 states agreed not to use, produce, or stockpile such weapons, and drafted the Convention on the Prohibition of the Development, Production, Stockpiling and Use of Chemical Weapons and on Their Destruction in 2005.

The Sale of Arms

FACTFILE Ironically, almost all the conventional weapons that have killed so many millions since World War II were manufactured by the five permanent members of the United Nations Security Council, the body mandated to prevent the scourges of another world war.

Despite the near global concern about the extent of international violence, the trade in arms remains buoyant. This trade is dominated by the United States, which is the major supplier of all arms exports in Asia, Africa, and Latin America. Russia retains second position in global arms sales. France is the third-largest arms-exporting state in the world, accounting for about 11 percent of the market. France's conventional arms sales are targeted at states that want to avoid dealing with the superpowers. Behind France are the United Kingdom, Israel, Germany, China, and Italy, each with a share of the global arms market. Other states have established their own arms facilities for the production of conventional weapons and equipment; these include Brazil, India, Iran, Jordan, Libya, Singapore, South Africa, The Republic of Korea (South), and Taiwan.

About 80 percent of world military expenditures are made for conventional weapons and equipment. In the past decade, developing states have contributed significantly to the rapid expansion of these purchases. Poor states, such as Ethiopia and Somalia, spend a greater proportion of their gross domestic product (GDP) than do much wealthier ones such as Canada, Norway, Finland, and the Netherlands.

In 1978, the United Nations held a Special Session on Disarmament (UNSSOD I). The final document became the basis of the first international arms-control agreement negotiated through a special United Nations conference. The Convention on Prohibitions or Restrictions on the Use of Certain Conventional Weapons Which May Be Deemed to Be Excessively Injurious or to Have Indiscriminate Effects, as well as three protocols, were opened for signature in 1981. Nearly 60 states have signed the convention. A second Special Session on Disarmament (UNSSOD II) was held in 1982 to continue the development of international law in this area, but a consensus was not achieved on most agenda items and a multilateral convention was not forthcoming.

Canada controls the export of conventional weapons by the *Export and Import Permit Act*, which regulates the sale of military materials abroad. The departments of National Defence and Foreign Affairs and International Trade approve all military sales outside Canada.

Evidence on the predictors of war in history challenges the assumption among many world leaders that military strength prevents war and military weakness invites aggression. Some studies now conclude that when disputes are accompanied by arms competition, they are more likely to escalate into war than are disputes that transpire in the absence of arms competition. The present proliferation of arms is as unprecedented in magnitude as would be the wars that could result from it.

The Globalization of Terrorism

Just as there has been a proliferation of weapons, so terrorist activities have also spread worldwide.[8] Most terrorist attacks have been directed against developed states, but increasingly developing states have become targets.

The spread of nuclear, chemical, and **biological weapons** around the world is a dangerous development because governments that acquire these weapons are more dangerous. But these weapons can also get into the hands of terrorist groups. The problem with chemical and biological weapons is that they are easy to make and easy to hide. Such weapons can also be mounted on missiles with long-range capabilities, enabling groups to acquire them and use them against their enemies.

The ability of the international community to contain terrorist activities is limited. International institutions necessary to control terrorists are not well developed or are hampered by governments that do not want to share information or co-operate with each other. **Interpol** is an international police force that gathers information on criminal activity around the world. Headquartered in Lyon, France, Interpol operates in four official languages to share information among the police forces of member states.

Terrorists conduct a very special kind of human aggression by engaging in psychological warfare against their enemies.[9] Terrorist acts can be state-sponsored or *state terrorism*, whereby governments organize and conduct the violence. Or they can be group-sponsored, whereby aggrieved groups strike without warning at selected targets using stealthy technology. State terrorism consists of government repression of domestic or external opposition, and sometimes selective illegal violence directed at individuals or groups perceived as threats to the state. Sometimes state-sponsored terrorism can provide an incentive and assistance to terrorist groups in other countries. Usually,

Crosscurrents   The Strategic Logic of Suicide Terrorism

It is difficult to understand any ideology that rewards suicide for political gain. How can such a desperate act of self-destruction be carried out by the very people who will not be here to see the fruit of their political protests?

Remember, the suicide terrorist has no chance of surviving his or her attack. The terrorists who commandeered the three aircraft in the United States on September 11, 2001, knew when they were boarding that their lives would soon end violently. In some cases, the attacker fully expects to be killed by others during an attack. It is the ultimate act of terror against civilians or the military.

Suicide terrorism is the supreme giving of oneself for a perceived political good. It is directed by a fanatic act of human will that makes it the perfect conventional weapon. Before the 1980s, suicide terrorism was rare but not unknown. Since that time, the phenomenon has been increasing as a successful strategy for implementing political change. Suicide terrorists acted to compel US and French military forces to abandon Lebanon in 1983, to drive out Israeli forces in Lebanon in 1985, and to discourage Israeli forces in the Gaza Strip and the West Bank in 1994. They were strategically used by the Palestinians for attacks in Israel, have been employed in Sri Lanka by the Tamils since the 1990s, were vividly witnessed in the US on 9/11, and continue to be insurgent strategies in Iraq during the American occupation.

The ultimate goal of suicide terrorism is to create massive ground-level fear in whatever society is under attack. The attacks are usually well organized, well planned, violent, and highly publicized in the media. The purpose of this strategy is to change government policy, especially where states have armed forces in the homelands of terrorist groups. Terrorist attacks give pause to the society where they occur because people fear they may be vulnerable to more violence in the future unless their governments change the direction of their policies.

non-state terrorism is the weapon of groups that represent a cause rather than a government.

Conventional arms have been the weapons of choice for most terrorist groups and state terrorist activities. Advances in the technologies of small explosives have greatly benefited terrorists around the world. But chemical and biological weapons are much more insidious because they are relatively easy to produce, and the materials for them are more accessible and less expensive than many conventional and most nuclear weapons. Advanced biotechnology enables the manufacture of new weapons containing deadly viruses and toxins that can be harnessed easily and delivered by terrorists.

The *miniaturization* of nuclear weapons makes their acquisition more likely for transnational groups as well as for states that do not have the capacity to manufacture them. Present trends point to the acquisition of nuclear weapons by international actors that may be more inclined to resort to nuclear weapons to achieve their goals. Conflicts that are currently limited to the use of conventional weapons could more easily involve the use of nuclear weapons should they be in the possession of non-state actors.

Focus On   The Costs of Deterring Terrorist Attacks

Conventional wisdom has held that *deterrence* means to show an arsenal of force to a potential and powerful enemy—to show force by acquiring weapons of mass destruction without necessarily using them.

But terrorism has changed the direction of deterrence in states that feel threatened by the strategies of extremist groups. In addition to its traditional meaning, deterrence has come to mean doing whatever is necessary to prevent acts of terrorism on national soil or against nationals in other parts of the world.

Al Qaeda's 9/11 attacks on the United States forced governments in the West to invest billions of dollars on security matters so as to deter terrorist activities on their soil. The states that have invested the most to enhance their security are the United States, Great Britain, Spain, and Germany; together they have spent over a trillion dollars.

After the 9/11 attacks, former Prime Minister Jean Chrétien pledged $7.7 billion to strengthen Canada's defences against terrorism. This was just the first installment to deter a terrorist attack on Canadian territory. Two new agencies were created to deter terrorist attacks—the Canadian Air Transport Security Authority and the Canadian Border Services Agency.

By 2008, Ottawa had spent an estimated $24 billion on a range of strategies to deter terrorism such as high-tech detection scanners, airport security cameras, reinforced pilots' cabins doors on domestic commercial aircraft, and border personnel at Canadian ports and land-border crossings.

The strategy also includes an increase in the military budget of over $9 billion since 2002 to fight the Taliban in Afghanistan. The RCMP's annual budget was increased by $1 billion and the budget of Canada's domestic spy agency, CSIS, has been doubled since 2002.

The new deterrence is displayed as national security on the ground level and on the borders of states. It is less of a show of force by disclosing weapons between and among states and more of a domestic strategy to catch those deemed to be terrorists who infiltrate national societies.

For Canada and the United States, the main challenge with the threat of terrorism is to continue the protection of civil rights, and to address other problems that threaten the lives of citizens, such as disease, pollution, poverty, and the perils of living in an urbanized society.

THE GLOBAL CHALLENGE OF POPULATION

In the eighteenth century, the world's first great demographic transformation began in Europe, increasing the earth's total human population from about 800 million in 1750 to 3 billion in 1960 (Figure 15.2).[10] Today, with more than six billion people populating the earth, human beings number more than any other type of vertebrate, having recently pulled ahead of rats. At our current annual growth rate of 1.7 percent, there will be only one square foot of earth surface for every human being in 700 years. And in 1200 years, the human population will outweigh the earth.

Figure 15.2   **Growth of world population (in billions of people)**

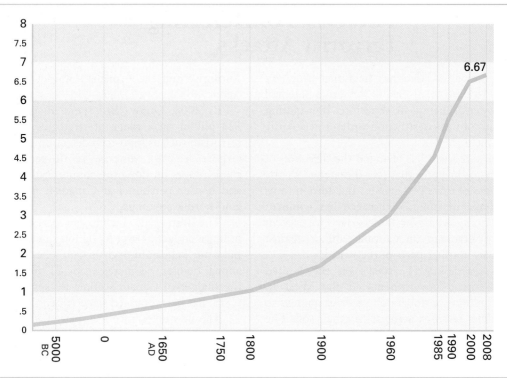

Source: Frederick Pearson and J. Martin Rochester, International Relations: The Global Condition in the Late Twentieth Century *(New York: McGraw-Hill, 1992), 57; Negative Population Growth,* Population Data *from www.npg.org.*

Now that this great demographic transformation is nearly complete, its impact can be analyzed. On the surface, the results have been generally positive: the fall in the **death rate** has increased **life expectancy** to an unprecedented level; most infectious diseases are now medically controllable; and the level of education has risen substantially.

However, a second great demographic transformation has been under way since World War II. Population growth in the developing world is far greater than in the developed countries, often more than 3 percent a year (doubling in about 20 years), as opposed to just over 1 percent (doubling in about 70 years). At current rates, world population growth approaches nearly 100 million per year. Between 1990 and 2008, about 90 percent of the global population increase occurred in developing countries. Of the 6.5 billion people who populate the world 5.2 billion live in developing countries. The best current estimates also suggest that the population of developing countries will likely double in the next century and thereafter remain stable (Figure 15.3).

In the industrialized states of Europe, as well as Australia, Canada, Japan, and the US, a low **mortality rate** has been accompanied by a low **fertility rate**. This circumstance is also well

Figure 15.3   **Where the human race is growing (in billions of people): Developed regions and developing regions**

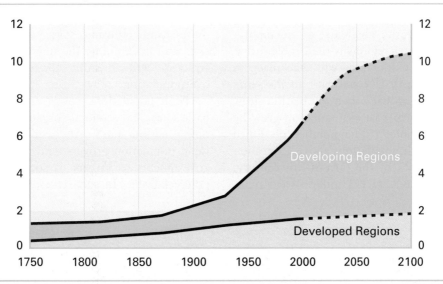

Sources: United Nations, World Population Prospects: The 2006 Revision and World Urbanization Prospects *(New York: UN, 2007). See also www.prb.org.*

under way in states such as Argentina, Hong Kong, Taiwan, and Singapore, where economic development has reached a fairly high level. However, in most of the developing states of Africa, Asia, and Latin America, this demographic transition has not proceeded far. The death rate has been falling rapidly over the past 40 years, but the fertility rate only began to decrease in the 1980s. It is because of this disparity in the rates that the population in developing countries is still growing rapidly.

We know that population growth has a built-in momentum that takes years to stabilize or reverse. At present, the total population of developing states, taken as a group, is over 5 billion. By 2025, this will have risen to more than 7 billion, and to 10 billion by 2100. In just 90 years, the world's population will be more than 11 billion.

Over the coming decades, the consequences of population growth will challenge the pace of national economic development and the political stability of the developing regions. In these states, rapid population growth will worsen employment opportunities, exacerbate urban growth, put pressure on food supplies, widen the gap between the rich and poor, and foster non-democratic regimes.

In the years between 1980 and 2008 alone, the total number of working-age people in developing economies increased by more than one billion. Only under the most optimal growth conditions in labour-intensive economies could these people secure employment.[11] In most developing economies, there are intensive pressures to create jobs in the public sector. In these states, government itself is the major employer. The most likely effects of this trend will be inflation and economic stagnation unless jobs can also be created at the same pace in the agricultural, manufacturing, and service sectors of developing economies.

Complicating the challenge of unemployment in developing regions is the problem that future population increases will take place in cities. According to UN statistics, in the years 1990–2008, the global urban population grew by 712 million while rural population grew by 224 million people.[12] The number of Third World cities with populations above 10 million grew from 3 to 21 by the turn of this century. By 2008, Mexico City (33 million) had more people than Canada; São Paulo (27 million), Shanghai (25 million), Mumbai, and Jakarta (each with 18 million) now experience unacceptable levels of congestion and municipal dysfunction. Housing, sewage, garbage collection, and maintaining the physical urban infrastructure will all suffer the consequences of overpopulation.

High population growth rates threaten the basic social and economic organization of developing nation-states. All problems related to rapid population growth tend to be viewed by governments as threats to social stability and political order. In such cases, an authoritarian

Focus On The Population Explosion

Every second that goes by, another five babies are born into the world. The annual numbers are so large that it is hard to imagine what they mean. So try to imagine shrinking the world's population to the size of a village of 100 people and keeping all the existing human ratios the same. In this global micro-village there would be 57 Asians, 21 Europeans, 14 from the Americas (which would include 1 Canadian) and 8 Africans.

Fifty-two would be female and 48 would be male. Fewer than half of the married women in the village would have access to birth control. One quarter of the women would have suffered rape or attempted rape.

Eighty-nine people would be heterosexual and 11 would be homosexual. Just six people would own 59 percent of the village's wealth and they would all be North Americans. Eighty of the 100 would live in substandard housing. Seventy would not be able to read and would have dropped out of school at an early age. Fifty would be suffering from malnutrition and would have an average life expectancy of 47 years. Only one person would have a university education. One person would own a computer.

What we would know from watching this microcosmic village is that world population growth is concentrated in poor countries. India and China are two such countries. India's population passed the one billion mark in 2000. But by 2012, India is expected to surpass China as the world's most populous country. The United Nations Population Fund notes that the world's population has doubled in only about 40 years. Yet most of this growth took place in the less-developed states. In 1960, 2.1 billion of the world's 3 billion—70 percent—lived in less developed regions. By 2008, over 5 billion of the world's 6.7 billion—80 percent—lived in less developed regions, producing major challenges for preventing starvation and providing adequate housing, education, and health care.

response to people by government is almost inevitable. Since 1970 in China, for example, the government has instituted a comprehensive birth-control policy involving forced sterilization, abortion, penalties, and fines to reach the goal of one-child families and **zero population growth** (ZPG).

A growing number of states—Bangladesh, India, Kenya, Nigeria, Pakistan, and the Democratic Republic of the Congo—have moved toward a more pervasive regulation of social life, particularly with respect to birth control. Some states, such as China and Cuba, restrict people's movement from rural to urban areas to control rapid population growth in certain areas of the country. And restraints on reproductive freedom may become more common where governments, through incapacity or lack of awareness, allow demographic pressures to build to extremes. Some governments have created policies to expand basic family education, to encourage small families, to ensure a more equitable distribution of income, and above all else to raise the status of women socially, economically, and politically. Brazil, Sri Lanka, The Republic of Korea (South), and Taiwan currently follow policy prescriptions along such lines.

The Problem of Small Population

While it is true that uncontrolled population can and does perpetuate poverty in a nation-state or region, it is also true that a small population can keep an economy poor.[13] A small population can compound and exacerbate national economic and social difficulties. Today, there are about 130 states with populations under 22 million, about one-half of these with populations under 10 million. Most states with fewer than 10 million are found in Africa (28) and in the Americas (16).

States with small populations face higher costs to administer social-development programs because their tax revenues are small. Their markets are not big enough to attract labour-intensive or capital-intensive industries, leading to a low level of domestic competition, a tendency to form monopolies, and generally sluggish economic growth. As a result, the economies of nation-states with small populations can nurture poor standards of performance, low productivity, and technological obsolescence. These states also reflect low levels of education and employment skills.

Global Population from the National Perspective

For the majority of independent states, including Canada, the increasing number of people in the world is a distant problem. For example, Canada's population of 33 million would shrink without the annual increases through immigration. Unless a state with a small population has high density (such as El Salvador and Taiwan), its rate of population growth tends not to concern its government. Low-population states point to the small number of states that are responsible for the alarming post–World War II global-population explosion. The obvious conclusion from their national perspective is that the world should pressure the few states with large populations to stabilize global population growth.

Few governments are willing or prepared to give serious consideration to controlling their populations. Canada, for example, offers its population a Child Tax Benefit Program and tax policies to encourage families to grow. While the US government promotes family planning, the Canadian government has not taken a position on this issue and financially supports fertility. Japan was the first state to pass fertility laws: abortion was legalized, and the population's fertility rate fell dramatically. Taiwan began one of the world's most successful contraceptive programs in 1964 and dropped its fertility rate from 5.4 in

1963 to 3.1 by 2006. But these are among the few exceptions.

Nationalists argue that population growth is a sovereign preserve in the national interest. Global institutions point to the nature of national population growth and call for international co-operation to control it. Part of the remedy is to stop thinking of population as a national problem only. The world is much greater than the sum of its national parts. To prevent the disastrous consequences of global overpopulation, governments and the international organizations representing them will have to co-ordinate massive education and information programs.

THE GLOBAL CHALLENGE OF HUNGER

More People than Food

About 200 years ago, Thomas Malthus (1766–1834) alarmed the world by pointing out that the global population increase would press more and more insistently on food supply.[14] If unchecked, a **geometric progression** of world population growth would result in widespread misery and starvation. Until recent times, the Malthusian prediction was widely discredited. But Malthus's theory may have been more premature than erroneous. Globalization has sharpened the inequality between population growth and food supply.

During the nineteenth and the early part of the twentieth centuries, with the opening up of new land and the introduction of better agricultural methods, food production increased more than the **arithmetic progression** predicted by Malthus. We now realize, however, that this growth will not continue indefinitely and that world population will soon outstrip global food production. At present, if all the food produced were divided equally among the world's people, no one would die of starvation.

But, according to the Club of Rome's "Project on the Predicament of Mankind," by the year 2010, if what food is produced were to be divided equally among the more than 7 billion people on earth, we would all gradually die of starvation. The prevailing distribution system is partly responsible for hunger and starvation. Even if the states of the world perfected their distribution systems, the growth of global population at current rates will severely strain the means of subsistence for all of humankind sometime during this century.[15]

Quite simply, there is not enough capital, skill, or time available to change the traditional habits and attitudes among the bulk of the world's people. Population is already catching up with and outstripping increases in food production. The fact is that an annual increase of more than 100 million mouths to feed requires more food than can possibly be added to production year after year.

There are also intervening factors that worsen the situation: **land-tenure systems** that leave large tracts of unproductive land in the hands of a few; a high proportion of non-productive persons in the agricultural sector; the high cost of fertilizer and agricultural technology; and adverse weather conditions resulting in drought and famine. Global food problems will continue to stem primarily from the production and distribution of food. And both of these elements will also continue to be affected by climate conditions, technology, farm-management practices, and government policies. Improving the global diet will be a complex and demanding challenge.

FACTFILE   As of 2007, according to the African Union, 24 of the 53 African states, with a population totalling 178 million, are in the grip of food shortages and mass starvation.

Not until there were pictures on television of the ghastly images of pain and suffering of Ethiopian and Sudanese families did the world take notice. In addition to famine, civil war, deforestation, and the overuse of Africa's land have destroyed food production on that continent. Undernourished, the land simply could not withstand the crisis or begin to feed an ever-growing population. The spreading drought is simply the latest event in a tragedy many years in the making.

In one sense, at least, the famine has been a turning point. So enormous is the disaster that its bitter lessons have alerted the aid-granting states of the world. Many African governments have finally started giving emergency priority to expanding food production and to saving the land. Aid agencies are beginning to drive home the message that horrors like Ethiopia and Sudan will be repeated time after time unless long-term development becomes a world priority.

If present trends continue, Africa, which already receives 60 percent of the world's food aid, will only be able to feed less than half its population during the twenty-first century. Ethiopia, Somalia, and the Sudan are a startling vision of what lies ahead in Africa unless the spread of the desert southward (currently at a pace of 10 kilometres each year) is halted. Each famine is worse than the last. Vast populations are being displaced. Their search for food becomes steadily more desperate.

FACTFILE In 2008, United Nations Secretary General Ban Ki-Moon declared that the world is indeed experiencing a "food crisis," owing to the increasing cost of food for many more millions of people, and caused by higher fuel costs and the conversion of thousands of acres of agricultural lands to the production of biofuels.

Apart from human extinction by war, the number of people on this planet will somehow have to adjust to the resources available for supporting them. The question is: by what means? Starvation is one means well under way. Production techniques, of course, could be improved; the yield per acre could be increased; unused lands in Asia, Africa, and Latin America, and on tropical islands could be developed; arid and semi-arid regions could be made productive when processes are economically feasible to convert sea water to fresh; and the seas could be farmed. But even if high-efficiency production were currently under way, at current rates of reproduction human societies would still outgrow the food supply early during this century.

Human beings do not grow and produce food in relation to population growth. Food production is essentially a response to a money-market mechanism that returns profit. If starving African children were lifted out of the desert and placed in a well-stocked Canadian supermarket, the children would still die from starvation. Why? Because they could not get past the cash register. All national economies, whether of capitalist or socialist organization, produce food in response to domestic and international market demands that are usually accompanied by some kind of economic reward. Otherwise, food supply is redirected to more profitable markets or the industries die and production ceases.

The problem of food production and distribution has not been addressed on a global scale. Extensive planning based on a future world outlook is essential if hunger is to be controlled. It is not difficult to predict with certainty what single desirable future we want. It is one that provides every human being with the basic dignity of enough to eat. Without a global food policy, we will reaffirm our sad destiny of witnessing more and more starvation.

Our future, if we choose to follow the same path, will see much of the population of the world increasingly debilitated, diseased, aberrant, and violent. As agriculture falters, states that are net exporters of food, like Canada and the United States, will have to apply triage in their food diplomacy. Beyond that, farming will be carried out only to the extent of supplying those who can afford to buy food. The world's labour force, increasingly malnourished and ailing, will become less productive, the **green revolution** will falter, and the commercial distribution of food will serve only those in affluent economies.

THE GLOBAL CHALLENGE OF AIDS

The AIDS Epidemic

Acquired immunodeficiency syndrome (AIDS) was first identified as such in 1981, even though some medical scientists had tracked the syndrome under different identifications since the 1940s.[16] It is brought on by the human immunodeficiency virus (HIV), which damages the immune system by selectively infecting certain cells called T-cells. Wherever it is diagnosed, this deficiency in the body's normal defences leaves the individual vulnerable to repeated viral, bacterial, and parasitical infections that can ordinarily be controlled or eliminated. Victims of AIDS worldwide typically die of rare forms of pneumonia and cancer.

AIDS is transmitted from person to person (Figure 15.4). The HIV virus is fragile, easily killed by bleach, alcohol, detergent, heat, or drying. It is thus transmitted though the intimate exchange of body fluids, specifically through blood transfusions, open sores, shared IV needles, and semen (sexual contact). High rates of AIDS are identified in various parts of the world among those who re-use medical syringes, those who abuse drugs, and those who engage in unprotected heterosexual and homosexual contact with multiple partners.[17]

As has been historically typical in cases of threatening epidemics, the world's reaction to AIDS and its victims has not been generally characterized by either rationality or empathy. The response of the international system has been deficient and disorganized. The international community has been uncoordinated in its efforts to deal with the spread of the HIV virus. National AIDS strategies are too narrowly implemented as government programs rather than by pooling the resources of many governments, non-governmental organizations, international organizations, and the private sector.

Figure 15.4   **How humans get AIDS: Proportion of infections by mode of transmission**

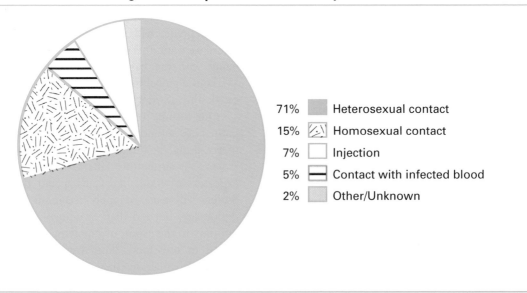

71%	Heterosexual contact
15%	Homosexual contact
7%	Injection
5%	Contact with infected blood
2%	Other/Unknown

Source: Division of HIV Epidemiology, Bureau of HIV/AIDS, STD and TB, Laboratory Centre for Disease Control, Public Health Agency of Canada, 2002. © Reproduced with the permission of the Minister of Public Works and Government Services Canada, 2009. (www.hcsc.gc.ca).

The Global Pandemic

AIDS challenges humanity because it is every-where. It is a *pandemic*, occurring on all inhabited continents. Every nation-state in the world today has officially reported cases of both carriers and fatalities. The virus appears globally. Everywhere in the world, HIV spreads through the same basic and narrow routes of transmission—by means of sex, through the blood (e.g., transfusions), and from mother to fetus. It is a virus that affects people directly, individually, and collectively. No insects, food, or water supply mediate the virus's threat to humanity.

> **FACTFILE** In 2007, the World Health Organization (WHO) reported that improved medical and drug research have been important factors for reducing the number of people living with HIV/AIDS from 42 to 32.7 million.

There have been 20 million deaths from AIDS since the beginning of the epidemic, and even with a reduction of the total number of cases world-wide, an estimated 15 000 people a day become infected with HIV. Most of those who are HIV positive develop full-blown AIDS within 12 years.

Globalization is related to the spread of AIDS. The so-called pandemic transfers internationally through business, migration, military operations, and tourism—reflecting the interdependence of the global environment.[18] Of the 32 million currently infected, most did not even know there was such a disease before they were infected. Each year, over five million people are newly infected with HIV and more than three million people worldwide die from AIDS. About 85 percent of the people with AIDS live in the global South (Figure 15.5).

AIDS in Canada

> **FACTFILE** The first case of AIDS in Canada was reported in 1982. By 2007, nearly 16 000 people with AIDS had died since Canadian governments began to record cases in the 1980s. By 2007, there were 60 000 people in Canada living with HIV—up from 50 000 in 2002. Over 20 000 AIDS cases had occurred in Canada since the epidemic began.

Figure 15.5 **Regional dispersions of AIDS**

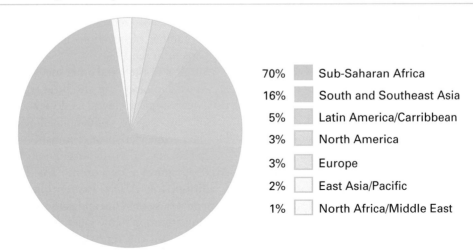

70% Sub-Saharan Africa
16% South and Southeast Asia
5%   Latin America/Carribbean
3%   North America
3%   Europe
2%   East Asia/Pacific
1%   North Africa/Middle East

Source: United Nations, World Health Report 2004 *(World Health Organization, 2004); www.unaids.org.*

More than one million have been infected with the HIV virus, which causes AIDS. Currently, nearly 5000 new cases are reported in Canada each year. The economic and social costs to Canada of the AIDS epidemic are large, but not as great as in many other parts of the world.

Although initially the outbreak of AIDS was concentrated in Canada's major cities, among intravenous–drug users and gay men, that pattern has been changing. As the epidemic matures, Canada's smallest cities are seeing an increase in the number of cases. According to Health Canada and the WHO, the transmission of AIDS is primarily through heterosexual activity in most developed countries.

FACTFILE Stephen Lewis, Canada's former Ambassador to the United Nations, was appointed by the Secretary General as Special Envoy for HIV/AIDS in Africa from 2002 to 2006. He established the Stephen Lewis Foundation to help HIV/AIDS victims and now serves as a Scholar-in Residence at McMaster University.

The initial response of the medical communities and governments to the problem of AIDS was not only slow but also political: gay men and Haitians are the two groups that were first targeted as high risk. Some conservatives and traditional religious groups even asserted that the disease was a punishment by God for immoral behaviour.

Outraged by the slowness and reluctance of federal and provincial governments in Canada to respond, the gay and lesbian community began to mobilize politically in the 1980s. Rallies, news conferences, and a strategy for inducing wider societal concern about the condition, as well as support for programs to find a cure, were launched. By the 1990s, a concerted effort was made to demonstrate that AIDS was a threat to all Canadians, not just to high-risk groups. This became dramatically clear when AIDS-contaminated blood was identified as the source of infection for persons falling outside the high-risk groups.

Massive demonstrations were organized in Ottawa and across the provinces. The media added its support to the pressure for AIDS research and treatment, while public-service television ads depicted white, middle-class, non-gay men and women with AIDS (the lowest-risk group). After much prodding, federal and provincial governments began to provide core funding for AIDS research, treatment, and education programs.

FACTFILE In 2005, the federal government launched its Federal Initiative to Address HIV/AIDS in Canada. This provides funding to educate people who do not practice safe sex in all communities, including gay men, injection drug users, Aboriginal communities, prison inmates, and people from countries where HIV is endemic.

In the 2000s, Canadian statistics indicate that AIDS is still most likely to be a major problem for intravenous drug users, persons who engage in anal sex, and people linked to these two groups. These would include bisexual men who can pass it on to other men and women, and pregnant women with AIDS who can infect their unborn children. Particularly disturbing is the discovery that many younger gay men (over 45 percent in one study) engage in unprotected sex—anal intercourse without condoms. Between 2001 and 2008, women made up about 25 percent of new HIV infections in Canada. This represents a dramatic increase in the number of infections in women—up from 8.9 percent in the 1980s.

Surgical workers and other medical professionals exposed to blood can also be at risk. Even dentists wear surgical gloves, as do law-enforcement persons exposed to contaminated needles or to bleeding crime victims or criminals.

In Canada, AIDS advocacy groups, such as the AIDS Committee of Toronto (ACT), the Black Coalition for AIDS Prevention, and AIDS Vancouver use marches and gatherings as a way of drawing attention to the killer virus. Other groups have bypassed the very slow government procedures for testing and licensing new drugs and are conducting independent testing of drugs and medication that can help reduce the symptoms or prolong the lives of AIDS sufferers.

Public policy on AIDS in Canada is affected by a variety of complicating factors, including federalism, our parliamentary system of government, and the public–private split in our political system as to who is responsible. As is usually the case with complex public issues, there is conflict about how important the issue is relative to other issues—a question of obvious importance in the case of AIDS because some groups in Canada fear that spending more money on AIDS will reduce spending on research linked to other health problems.

THE GLOBAL ENVIRONMENT
Pollution and Development

The idea of progress, beginning in the eighteenth century, eventually led us to the dangerous conclusion that industrialization and technological change result in manageable environmental consequences. Industrialization has been taken as a license to pollute the air and water with impunity. Most national economies are in the business of doing just that every day, with the encouragement of government policies. We think technology can liberate us from disease, hunger, ignorance, and premature death. We may recognize that modernization has advanced us, but often at incalculable environmental costs.

An intense concern about the environment and related matters is **environmentalism**. Global issues of the environment have only recently become a concern to the public as they and their governments begin to measure the deathly onslaught of pollution, which is causing climate change and environmental degradation.[19] Almost every state, regardless of wealth or ideology, now faces environmental problems at least as severe as the next. Developed and underdeveloped states almost always trade off ecological sensitivity for economic growth, often allowing foreign governments and multinationals to pour chemicals into their coasts, lakes, rivers, and soil.

In Canada and the United States, high levels of toxic waste are steadily discharged into the oceans, creating hazardously high concentrations of arsenic, cadmium, copper, lead, mercury, nickel, polychlorinated biphenyls (PCBs), and zinc in the delicate salt-water ecology. Plant and animal life absorb the toxins and die, or share these insidious contaminants with their human predators. Chronic land-based pollution—chemical spills, sewage, and garbage—mix with the agricultural runoff of fertilizers and pesticides to produce an anti-ecology, an independent toxic system that robs the environment of its benign life-sustaining forces.

One tragedy of international dimensions, first reported by Swedish authorities, was the explosion of a nuclear reactor at Chernobyl in the former Soviet Union in 1986, which contaminated a vast area on the European continent. Many years later, livestock in Northern Europe could still not be slaughtered for food because of their high radiation levels.[20]

Nothing has come to symbolize the vulnerability of the environment to the selfish national goals of an industrialized civilization more than massive ocean-going oil tankers crossing the high seas. Many supertankers are over 300 000 tonnes, and bigger ones are being built. When a supertanker spills its oil into the ocean, fisheries and beaches are despoiled. Thousands of species are threatened and the world's delicate ecological balance is imperilled.

The *Exxon Valdez* spill in 1989 was the largest in US history (more than 38 million litres), covering 2500 square kilometres, and damaging the fragile **ecology** of Alaska well into the twenty-first century. The Gulf War in the Middle East also caused tremendous environmental damage in the ocean waters in the Persian Gulf and the Gulf of Oman, as did the massive firestorms caused by the deliberate ignition of Kuwaiti oil wells. Having suffered staggering levels of damage to the environment and to human health from the war waged by the United States since 2003, economically strapped Iraq will require huge international investments to reverse these effects.

Changing the Earth's Ecology

During the summer of 1988, hundreds of climatologists, lawyers, biologists, engineers, and atmospheric chemists from six continents convened in Toronto to address an emergency: radical changes in the global atmosphere. This World Conference on the Changing Atmosphere focused on two phenomena: the destruction of the ozone layer and global warming. In both cases, conference participants called for individual, national, and international actions as we entered another century of industrial productivity. Since this meeting in 1988, a United Nations panel has reported on climate change every five years.

FACTFILE Hundreds of scientists, some sitting as the Intergovernmental Panel on Climate Change (IPCC), met in Paris in January 2007 and declared that the phenomenon of climate change currently being observed around the world is man-made.

Serious ozone depletion has been identified in the Antarctic: an ozone hole the same size over the North Pole would cover all of Canada. The ozone layer is very thin—about as thick as a pane of glass encircling the earth. Since the dawn of civilization, this rarefied protective layer of gas has prevented animal and plant life from frying in the direct rays of the sun.

Scientists blame the deterioration of the ozone in part on chlorine originating from the breakdown of **chlorofluorocarbons** (CFCs). These human-made chemicals, which are very useful (in aerosol cans, heat pumps, refrigerators, freezers, air conditioners) and rather benign at sea level, break down in the atmosphere into chlorine,

which combines with and destroys ozone. Canada contributes 2 percent of the global CFC problem. If all states legislated a stop to the production of CFCs today, it would still take another century for these toxins to be cleansed from the atmosphere.

FACTFILE The Kyoto Protocol contains measures to assess performance with penalties to signing states that fail to meet their emission targets by 2012.

Beginning in 1992, ozone damage prompted Environment Canada to provide the public with daily reports on the cancer-causing rays. The ultraviolet (UV) radiation report informs Canadians whether reduced levels of ozone produce a higher risk of dangerous radiation exposure. Canadians can then decide whether to take precautions such as wearing hats, applying sunscreen, or using sunglasses to protect themselves from the ultraviolet rays. Canada is one of a growing number of states that now provide their citizens with regular UV reports.

Global warming is also occurring rapidly, owing to large atmospheric accumulations of carbon dioxide from fossil fuel–burning and emissions of methane from agricultural and industrial practices. Scientists predict the earth is rushing toward a historically unprecedented average global warming of up to 4.5 degrees Celsius within the next 50 years. Over the past 150 years, 1987 was the warmest year globally, and the four hottest years in the last 130 years have been reported since 1980.

FACTFILE Scientists at the Ontario Science Centre believe that approximately 70 000 years ago climate change reduced the world's population to only about 2000 people who survived in the area of Africa known as Sumaria.

In 1992, 148 states agreed to a pact to fight rising world temperatures. Many scientists had warned that these temperature rises threaten to change the earth's climate in very destructive ways, such as raising ocean levels, which will cause flooding in some areas, and drying other areas of the globe to desert. The treaty was signed at the

Crosscurrents   The Politics of Global Warming

Global warming has resulted from two political occurrences: dramatic increases in human urban populations and the rapid industrialization of many economies during the twentieth century.

These two simultaneous phenomena relate significantly to progressive increases in the temperature of the earth's atmosphere because they are responsible for the buildup of greenhouse gases (carbon dioxide, CFCs, and methane) trapped in the atmosphere. Global warming has been further exacerbated by indiscriminate clear-cutting of forests, lack of reforestation, and ineffective government policies to lower greenhouse-gas emissions.

The 1997 Kyoto Conference established the first near-global protocol to reduce worldwide emissions of greenhouse gases to 5 percent below 1990 levels by the year 2012. One hundred and fifty-nine states agreed to set their own targets to achieve this goal; the EU, the US, and Canada agreed to reduce their emissions by 8, 7, and 6 percent, respectively. Two of the world's worst polluters—India and China—had signed on by 2007. Canada ratified the Kyoto treaty in December 2002. But the new Conservative minority government of Stephen Harper backslid on Canada's original commitment to the treaty. The government introduced its *Clean Air Act* with its "made-in-Canada" targets to reduce carbon emissions at rates that fall below the expectations of Kyoto.

If the environmental scientists are right, global warming is the result of our way of life, and that is a very difficult thing to change. In general, many observers believe that "free riding" on the global warming issue would be quite easy and quite likely. While many states are willing to co-operate in curbing the greenhouse emissions, some states—the free riders—can reap the rewards of a reversal of global warming without paying the price of committing significant amounts of their GDPs to reducing their own emissions. Free-riding states could then devote their unspent financial resources to other economic goals at the expense of the Kyoto agreement.

But free riding can nullify the general efforts to check global warming. If every state co-operates, the efforts to curb global warming are likely to be effective, producing the best outcome for everyone on the planet. However, states that co-operate with international efforts to check global warming and reduce carbon-dioxide emissions could suffer unemployment, increasing energy costs, and higher taxation. Some states, such as Canada and Russia, could even benefit from the effects of global warming, while states close to the equator would face negative consequences of climate change. And if one large emitter, such as the US or China, defects, or if a group of regional states defects, the efforts of the rest of the world may come to naught. The net result could be that each state, perceiving this possibility, decides that it would be better off not to co-operate under the Kyoto protocol, because the chances are high that at least someone is going to defect.

Earth Summit in Rio de Janeiro in June 1992. The United Nations Conference on Environment and Development, which met at Rio de Janeiro, reaffirmed the Declaration of the United Nations Conference on the Human Environment in 1972.

At the 1992 conference, wealthy states agreed to give financial and technological help to developing ones. The conference was designed to mitigate the so-called **greenhouse effect**, in which certain gases trap the world's heat.

Many states have become concerned about **acid rain**, which results from conditions that contribute to the greenhouse affect. About 150 000 Canadian lakes have already been seriously damaged by acid rain, and another 15 000 lakes are believed to be biologically dead as a result. While the measure of pH acidity is neutral at 7, some Canadian lakes consistently measure 5 (vinegar measures 3). In 1990, Canada and the United States signed the Clean Air Act, committing their industries to reducing sulphur-dioxide and nitrogen-oxide emissions by the year 2000.

FACTFILE   In Ontario, 400 lakes are considered biologically dead and life is threatened in an additional 4800 lakes.

One of the solutions to the problem of acid rain is that states regenerate their forests. Trees absorb environmental impurities and convert them to oxygen. The twentieth century witnessed the most extensive **deforestation** on most continents. Much of North America has suffered deforestation as human habitat has encroached and continues to encroach on the natural world. In the tropics, especially in Brazil and Indonesia, enormous areas of forest are being cleared for commercial farming, hydroelectric dams, and industrial development. These trees are usually burned, generating more carbon and killing the very trees that help keep the carbon dioxide in balance. By 1997, Brazil had lost a forest with an area larger than Denmark, Belgium, Switzerland, and Austria combined. Africa loses between 3 and 5 million hectares of forest each year, and at this rate will have no significant forests by 2060.

Deforestation usually happens when people want to use land for living purposes or for agriculture. As a result, not only are trees felled by the millions, but the biological heritage these trees support is also destroyed. All of the animals that rely on trees for their survival become threatened and eventually endangered. By 2008, Canada listed 552 species of plants and animals as endangered.

Included for the first time were well-known mammals, such as polar bears and grizzly bears. Other additions were birds, reptiles, and amphibians, as well as fish and certain caribou.

FACTFILE   Among the 552 species on Canada's endangered list are the beluga whale, the Vancouver Island marmot, the northern bobwhite, and the burrowing owl.

The changing atmospheric phenomena of warming and ozone depletion, from human-made chlorofluorocarbons (CFCs) and other gases, has dangerous consequences for agriculture. The major world food crops, wheat, rice, corn, and soybeans in particular, are very sensitive to ultraviolet radiation. They will respond by a drop in yield worldwide. In southern parts of Canada, scientists measure a 3 percent to 4 percent decrease in ozone levels. At 10 percent or 15 percent ozone depletion, food production in Canada, as well as worldwide, would be seriously decreased.

In 1988, the World Congress on Climate and Development met in Hamburg, Germany, and called upon all states, led by the industrial states, to take unilateral action, with the aim of reducing carbon dioxide emissions by 30 percent by the year 2000 and 50 percent by 2015. Environmentalists and scientists urged state participants to reduce their use of fossil fuels, reduce their rates of deforestation, and commence reforestation as soon as possible.

Solutions to global warming and ozone depletion are fundamentally political and international. Canada's actions on global climate change have met with criticism from experts within the country as well as from outside.[21] The idea that a remarkable technological fix is waiting in the wings is unrealistic.

In this era of tight global connection, problems of peace, arms control, hunger, population growth, and environmental deterioration require more than a domestic response. The international character of these problems requires solutions beyond national

Focus On The Energy We Consume Leaves a Footprint on the Earth

Every individual on the planet consumes energy in order to survive. Among the many predictors available to measure the energy we use are three indicators: per-capita energy consumption, per-capita electricity consumption, and per-capita carbon dioxide (CO_2) emissions. (Scientists have confirmed that CO_2 emissions from fossil and bio-fuels are the greatest cause of climate change.) They help us understand the individual footprint we make by living on earth. We can use these indicators to compare ourselves as energy consumers to individuals who use the same indicators in other countries.

To slow down or reverse climate change individuals must reduce energy consumption and CO_2 emissions. Energy consumption is a universal measure and is better for making comparisons about wealth and poverty than using currency and gross national product (GNP). It allows us to compare the energy footprint on the planet of one person living in Nepal or Kenya to that of someone living in Canada.

Individuals in Nepal barely consume energy when compared with Canadians. Someone in Nepal or Kenya would have to consume *more* energy in order to reach the developed levels of Canadians and the Americans.

If the developed world asks the developing world to reduce energy and electrical consumption (see the Kyoto Convention) so as to lower CO_2 emissions, individuals in Kenya would have to turn off light bulbs in hospitals and schools.

Country/ Continent	Energy Consumption (Kilograms Oil Equivalent per Person)	Electricity Consumption per Capita per Year (KWh)	CO_2 Emissions per Person per Year (Metric Tons per Person per Year)
Canada	7 999	16 787	16.9
Germany	4 263	6 852	10.2
Nepal	350	67	0.1
India	514	408	1
Kenya	495	118	0.3
Africa*	647	444	0.8
North America	7 929	13 416	19.9
World	1 631	2 326	3.9
UAE	11 332	12 279	25.6
Saudi Arabia	2 426	5 886	12.0

*Not all African states supplied data to World Resources Tables. Averages for Africa are based on data supplied from participating states.

Source: World Resources: The Wealth of the Poor (*Washington: World Resources Institute, 2007*); (*http://earthtrends.wri.org*).

Whereas, in Canada, the energy needed to take a bath, use your computer, have a car, build a house, and light a university cafeteria is taken for granted. In Nepal most people cannot afford to do any of these things. To ask them to turn off a light bulb so the world will emit less CO_2 is to ask them to become poorer than they already are.

But are Canadians willing to cut their energy consumption to the levels of individuals living in Nepal or Kenya? How much less would Canadians have to reduce energy consumption to meet, for example, the standards even of a German, who would be regarded as living in a highly developed country?

jurisdiction, to the level of a global will. But in the final analysis, we are individually and socially equipped to solve the problems we have brought upon ourselves. Hunger, overpopulation, and war are not extra-human forces acting upon us. They are engineered by our attitudes, ignorance, and actions. Our greatest threat is the way we think. As cartoonist Walt Kelly's Pogo observed, "We have met the ENEMY . . . an' HE IS US."

Chapter Summary

The international community is a global village in which economic, political, or military events in one part of the village are felt immediately in all parts of the village. The New World Order carries most of the challenges of the Old World Order, as well as some new ones. Globalization, nuclear- and conventional-weapons proliferation, uncontrolled population growth, the spread of depopulating diseases such as HIV/AIDS, the spectre of world hunger, and the widespread destruction of the ecology by unregulated industrialization and urbanization—all of these are the challenges we face in the twenty-first century. In the midst of these ominous realities, allies become enemies, world resources change in value, and the global economy surges and falters.

Because we are the architects of our own problems, such as war, arms competition, population growth, hunger and pollution, the solutions these problems

invite are essentially political in nature. Thus, how we deal with the arms race and the threat of nuclear war will test our political skills and our political wills. Similarly, these problems are amenable to political strategies. With respect to these, Thomas Malthus's contention nearly two centuries ago—that world population growth would eventually outstrip the capacity of producers to supply global food needs—is presented as a political forecast, avoidable and resolvable only by international political will.

The New World Order is characterized by the influence of globalization, the spread of democracy, collective security, and Pax Americana—peace as envisaged by American foreign-policy makers.

The challenge of peace involves peacekeeping, peace activism, disarmament, arms control, treaty compliance, and the creation of zones of peace and nuclear-weapons-free zones. Arms control focuses on control over the production, sale, and spread of nuclear and conventional weapons, verification of treaty provisions, and treaty compliance.

Terrorism and superpower intervention are other challenges in the New World Order. State terrorism is government sponsored. Group-sponsored terrorism threatens the security of the international system as well as that of the particular nation-states where the acts of terrorism take place.

The challenge of population growth requires international strategies and a global vision. The greatest increases in global population have taken place since 1985 and are taking place in the developing regions of the world, not the developed regions.

The challenge of hunger, now deemed by the United Nations to be a world crisis, is related to world population growth and environmental destruction. It is also very much affected by how and where food is produced and distributed. Food aid policies of wealthy countries are another part of the equation. And often, when food is delivered to poorer countries, political corruption leads to the misappropriation of food aid; people who should get the food do not.

HIV/AIDS is a transnational disease that requires not only international medical research efforts but also an international and global strategy for arresting the spread of the disease. AIDS can depopulate states in the same way that war and natural disasters do.

The destruction of the earth and its environment is a problem requiring immediate and ongoing planned international strategy. The solution involves the participation of all states, each creating public policies to regulate and control industrial, consumer, and state behaviour that harms the environment and its ecology.

Discussion Questions

1. Has the frequency of international acts of violence diminished in the twenty-first century, or are conditions for peace diminishing? Do you think the risk of annihilation posed by nuclear weapons has caused a reduction in the frequency of war since the end of World War II? In your opinion, has the US war in Iraq since 2003 made the world more dangerous or more stable? Has Canada's military presence in Afghanistan contributed to international peace?

2. Discuss the hypothesis that the best way for nation-states to preserve peace is to prepare for war. Does global interdependence promote peace? What kinds of foreign-policy strategies and tactics would you recommend to meet the challenge of peace? Why is peace such an ideologically charged concept?

3. Discuss whether negotiated arms-control agreements can achieve the goal of arms reduction and possible disarmament. Is total disarmament possible, or even desirable?

4. If the world has a population problem, does Canada have a population problem? Should Canada generate public policies to produce zero-population growth? Should Canada consider changing its immigration policies in order to reduce its population?

5. Can we say that a "sustainable environment" is a human right? Why? What can individuals do to reverse the destructive tide of industrialization? List five things Canadians can do to reduce their high energy consumption. Can we have a major positive impact on the environment at the municipal level? How? Should we declare pollution to be an act of *terricide* (murder of the earth) and consider it a crime against humanity?

Endnotes

Chapter 1

1. David Easton, *A Framework for Political Analysis* (Englewood Cliffs, NJ: Prentice-Hall, 1965), 50.

2. As Harold D. Lasswell so aptly put it in the title of his book, *Politics: Who Gets What, When, and How* (New York: McGraw-Hill, 1936).

3. V.I. Lenin, "Left Wing Communism: An Infantile Disorder," in *Selected Works* (New York: International Publishers, 1943).

4. Quoted in Stuart Schram, *The Political Thought of Mao Tse Tung* (New York: Frederick A. Praeger, 1969), 287.

5. Lewis Eigen and Jonathan Siegel, *The Macmillan Dictionary of Political Quotations* (New York: Macmillan, 1993).

6. John Redekop, "Canadian Political Institutions" in John Redekop, *Approaches to Canadian Politics* (Scarborough, ON: Prentice-Hall Canada Inc., 1983), 149.

7. Gregory Mahler and Donald MacInnis, *Comparative Politics: An Institutional and Cross-National Approach* (Toronto: Pearson Education Inc., 2002), 10–11.

8. Ronald Smith, *Psychology* (St. Paul, MN: West Publishing Company, 1993), 592–593.

9. Gabriel Almond, "Comparative Political Systems," *Journal of Politics* 18 (1965): 396; See Paul Sniderman et al., *The Clash of Rights: Liberty, Equality and Legitimacy in a Pluralist Democracy* (New Haven: Yale University Press, 1996).

10. Samuel Beer and Adam Ulam, *Patterns of Government* (New York: Random House, 1958), 12.

11. Sidney Verba, "Conclusion: Comparative Political Culture," in Lucian W. Pye and Sidney Verba, eds., *Political Culture and Political Development* (Princeton: Princeton University Press, 1965), 515.

12. Stephen Ullman, "Regional Political Cultures in Canada: A Theoretical and Conceptual Introduction," in Richard Schultz, Orest Kruhlak, and John Terry, eds., *The Canadian Political Process* (Toronto: Holt, Rinehart and Winston of Canada, Ltd. 1979), 7.

13. Richard Simeon and David Elkins, "Regional Political Cultures in Canada," *Canadian Journal of Political Science* 7 (3) (September 1974): 397; and Donald Savoie, "All Things Canadian Are Now Regional," *Journal of Canadian Studies* 35 (1) (2000): 203–217.

14. See Suzanne Peters, *Exploring Canadian Values: Foundations for Well-Being*, and *A Synthesis Report* (Canadian Policy Research Networks, Inc., 1995).

15. Seymour Martin Lipset, "Historical Traditions and National Characteristics: A Comparative Analysis of Canada and the United States," *Canadian Journal of Sociology* 11 (2) (1998): 133–155.

16. Robert Dahl, *Modern Political Analysis* (Englewood Cliffs, NJ: Prentice-Hall, Inc., 1965), 50.

17. Karl Deutsch, *Politics and Government: How People Decide Their Fate* (Boston: Houghton Mifflin Company, 1980), 26.

18. Mel Hurtig, *Pay the Rent or Feed the Kids* (Toronto: McClelland & Stewart Inc., 1999).

19. UNESCO, *Statistical Yearbook, 2000* (Paris: UNESCO, 2000).

20. Jack Layton, "City Politics in Canada," in Michael Whittington and Glen Williams, *Canadian Politics in the 1990s*, 3d ed. (Scarborough, ON: Nelson Canada, 1990), 401–422.

21. Canadian Federation of Mayors and Municipalities, *Puppets on a Shoestring: The Effects on Municipal Governments of Canada's System of Public Finance*, (Ottawa, April 28, 1976).

22. Quoted in K.G. Crawford, *Canadian Municipal Government* (Toronto: University of Toronto Press, 1954), 4.

23. Lucian Pye, *Politics, Personality and Nation-Building* (New Haven, CT: Yale University Press, 1963), 1–14; Donald Savoie, "All Things Canadian Are Now Regional," *Journal of Canadian Studies*, 35 (1) (2000): 635–664.

24. H. Richard Hird, *Working with Economics* (Toronto: Maxwell Macmillan Canada, Inc., 1992), 127–128.

25. Manfred Borchert and Rolf Schinke, eds. *International Indebtedness* (London: Routledge, 1990).

26. David Easton and Jack Dennis, *Children in the Political System* (New York: McGraw-Hill, 1969), 7. See also Robert Coles, *The Political Life of Children* (Boston: The Atlantic Monthly Press, 1986).

27. Roberta Sigel, "Assumptions about the Learning of Political Values," *Annals of the American Academy of Social and Political Science* 361 (1985): 1; M. Jennings and R. Niemi, *Generations and Politics* (Princeton, NJ: Princeton University Press, 1981).

28. See Charles Horton Cooley, *Human Nature and Social Order* (New York: Schocken, 1964). As applicable to Canadians, see David V.J. Bell, in Michael Whittington and Glen Williams, *Canadian Politics 2000*, 5th ed. (Scarborough, ON: ITP Nelson, 2000).

29. James Chowning Davies, "Political Socialization: From Womb to Children," in Stanley Renshon, ed., *Handbook of Political Socialization* (New York: Free Press, 1977), 142–147.

30. David Easton and Jack Dennis, "The Child's Image of Government," *The Annals of the American Academy of Political and Social Science* 361 (1965): 56.

31. The principals in the survey were T.G. Carroll of Brock University, Donald Higgins of St. Mary's University, and Michael Whittington of Carleton University. The findings of this study are summarized in Richard Van Loon and Michael Whittington, *The Canadian Political System: Environment, Structure, and Process* (Toronto: McGraw-Hill Ryerson Ltd., 1981), 120.

32. Ronald Landes, "The Use of Role Theory in Political Socialization Research: A Review, Critique and Modest Proposal," *International Journal of Comparative Sociology* 17 (1–2) (March–June 1976): 59–72.

33. Roberta Sigel and Marilyn Hoskin, "Perspectives on Adult Political Socialization—Areas of Research," in Allen Renshon, ed., *Handbook of Political Socialization: Theory and Research* (New York: Free Press, 1977) 267.

Chapter 2

1. See F. L. Baumer, *Main Currents of Western Thought*, 4th ed. (New Haven, CT: Yale University Press, 1978), 373–376; and Bernard Susser, *Political Ideology in the Modern World* (Boston: Allyn and Bacon, 1995), Chap. 1.

2. Karl Deutsch, *Politics and Government: How People Decide Their Fate* (Boston: Houghton Mifflin Company, 1980), 9.

3. Robert Dahl, *A Preface to Democratic Theory* (Chicago: University of Chicago Press, 1956), 132. And see Eric Wolf, *Envisioning Power: Ideologies of Dominance and Crisis* (Santa Clara, CA: University of California Press, 1999), Chap. 1.

4. Reo M. Christenson et al., *Ideologies and Modern Politics* (New York: Dodd, Mead & Company, 1971), 5.

5. Robert E. Lane, *Political Ideologies* (New York: Free Press of Glencoe, 1962), 14–15; and Ian Adams, *Political Ideology Today* (New York: Manchester University Press, 1993).

6. Andrew Hacker, *Political Theory: Philosophy, Ideology, Science* (New York: Macmillan, 1961), 5.

7. Carl Friedrich, *Man and His Government: An Ethical Theory of Politics* (New York: McGraw-Hill, 1963), 90.

8. Lyman Tower Sargent, *Contemporary Political Ideologies: A Contemporary Analysis* (Fort Worth, TX: Harcourt Brace College, 1998), Chap. 1.

9. See Edmund Morgan, *Inventing the People: The Rise of Popular Sovereignty in England and America* (New York: W.W. Norton, 1988), 12–19.

10. See Karl Mannheim, *Ideology and Utopia*, trans. L. Wirth and E. Shils (New York: Harcourt, Brace Jovanovich, 1936), 36.

11. Maurice Duverger: *Political Parties* (New York: John Wiley & Sons, Inc., 1954), 425.

12. See Thucydides, *The History of the Peloponnesian War*, ed. Sir Richard Livingston (New York: Oxford University Press, 1951), 111–113.

13. *Aristotle in Twenty-Three Volumes, XXI Politics*, trans. H. Rackham (London: Heinemann, 1977), Book III, 331.

14. Leonard T. Hobhouse, *Liberalism* (New York: Oxford University Press, 1911).

15. John Dewey, "The Future of Liberalism," *The Journal of Philosophy* (April 25, 1935): 225–230.

16. See Rod Preece, "The Political Economy of Edmund Burke," *Modern Age* 24 (1980): 266–273.

17. F.J.C. Hearnshaw, *Conservatism in England* (London: Macmillan and Co. Ltd., 1933), 22–23. For contrast see David Green, *The New Conservativism* (New York: St. Martin's Press, 1987).

18. Rodney Carlisle, ed., *Encyclopedia of Politics: The Left and the Right* (Newbury Park, CA: Sage, 2005) 2 vols.

19. Nancy Love, ed., *Dogmas and Dreams: A Reader in Modern Political Ideologies* (New York: Seven Bridges Press, 2006), Chap. 6.

20. Terence Ball and Richard Diggar, *Ideals and Ideologies* (New York: Pearson Education, Inc., 2006) 191–192.

21. Sydney Hook, *From Hegel to Marx: Studies in the Intellectual Development of Karl Marx* (New York: Columbia University Press, 1994).

22. Leon Baradat, *Political Ideologies: Their Origins and Impact*, 8th ed. (Upper Saddle River, NJ: Prentice-Hall, 2003), 45–63; and Anthony Marx, *Faith in Nation: Exclusionary Origins of Nationalism* (New York: Oxford University Press, 2003), 12–39.

23. For a short history of racism in Canada, see D.G. Hill and M. Schiff, *Human Rights in Canada: A Focus on Racism*, 2d ed. (Ottawa: Canadian Labour Congress and Human Rights Research and Education Centre, University of Ottawa, 1986); and B. Singh and Peter Li, *Racial Oppression in Canada* (Toronto: Garamond Press, 1988).

24. See Frank Harrison, *The Modern State: An Anarchist Analysis* (Montreal: Black Rose Books, 1983); Eric Wolf, *Envisioning Power: Ideologies of Dominance and Crisis* (Santa Clara, CA: University of California Press, 1999).

25. Stephen Chilton, *Defining Political Development* (Boulder, CO: Lynne Rienner Publishers, 1987), 1–135; see Magnus Blomstrom and Bjorn Hettne, *Development Theory in Transition* (London: Zed Books Limited, 1984), 8–26.

26. See Jack Gladstone, "The Comparative and Historical Study of Revolutions," *Annual Review of Sociology, 1982*, 200; Crane Brinton, *The Anatomy of Revolution* (Englewood Cliffs, NJ: Prentice-Hall, 1952); and A.S. Cohan, *Theories of Revolution* (London: Thomas Nelson and Sons, 1975), 162–175.

27. Ralph Turner and Lewis Killian, *Collective Behavior* (Englewood Cliffs, NJ: Prentice-Hall, 1972), Chaps. 16–19.

28. Francis Beer, *Meanings of War and Peace* (College Station, TX: Texas A&M University, 2001).

29. Jo Freeman, "The Origins of the Women's Liberation Movement," *American Journal of Sociology* 78 (4) (1973): 792–811; Nancy McGlen and Karen O'Connor, *Women, Politics, and American Society*, 2d ed., (Upper Saddle River, NJ: Prentice Hall, 1998).

30. See Nancy Anderson, Linda Briskin, and Margaret McPhail, *Feminist Organizing for Change: The Contemporary Women's Movement in Canada* (Toronto: Oxford University Press, 1988); Angela Miles, *Feminist Radicalism in the 1980s* (Montreal: Culture Texts, 1985), 1–39.

31. Bonnie Fox, "Conceptualizing 'Patriarchy,'" *Canadian Review of Sociology and Anthropology* 25 (2), (May): 163–182; and Monica Boyd, *Canadian Attitudes towards Women: Thirty Years of Change* (Ottawa: Supply and Services Canada for Labour Canada, 1984).

32. Arlene Tigar McLaren, ed., *Gender and Society* (Toronto: Copp Clark Pitman, 1989), 337–346.

Chapter 3

1. See T.V. Paul, John Ikenberry, John Hall, eds. *The Nation-State in Question* (Princeton, NJ: Princeton University Press, 2003). See also Francis Fukuyama, *State-Building: Governance and World Order in the 21st Century* (Ithaca, NY: Cornell University Press (2004).

2. Ted Gurr, *Peoples versus States: Minorities at Risk in the New Century* (Washington, DC: United States Institute of Peace Press, 2000); Joyce Mass, and George Wilson, *Peoples of the World* (Detroit MI: Gale Research Inc., 1992).

3. K.J. Holsti, *International Politics: A Framework for Analysis*, 7th ed. (Englewood Cliffs, NJ: Prentice Hall, 1995), 136.

4. Herman Bakvis and Grace Skogsad, *Canadian Federalism*, (Don Mills, ON: Oxford University Press, 2008), 3–20; and Robert Young, ed., *Stretching the Federation: The Art of State in Canada* (Montreal: McGill-Queens University Press, 1999).

5. Robert Dahl, "The Concept of Power," *Behavioural Science* 2 (July 1957): 201–215.

6. Ray S. Cline, *World Power Trends and U.S. Foreign Policy for the 1980s* (Boulder, CO: Westview Press, 1980), 113; and Ray S. Cline, *The Power of Nations in the 1990s: A Strategic Assessment* (Lantham, MD: University Press of America, 1993).

7. Quoted in Kim Richard Nossal, *The Politics of Canadian Foreign Policy* (Scarborough, ON: Prentice-Hall Canada Inc., 1985), 12.

8. Office of the PM, press release, May 29, 1968.

9. Herman Bakvis and Grace Skogstad, *Canadian Federalism: Performance, Effectiveness, and Legitimacy* (Toronto: Oxford University Press, 2002), 1–24, 197–199; Michael Whittington and Glen Williams, *Canadian Politics, 2000*, 5th ed. (Scarborough, ON: ITP Nelson, 2000).

10. See Gabriel Almond, G. Bingham Powell Jr., and Robert Mundt, *Comparative Politics* (New York: HarperCollins College Publishers, 1993), 135–137.

11. K.W. Robinson, "Sixty Years of Federation in Australia," *Georgia Review* 50 (January 1961): 2.

12. See D.V. Smiley, *The Federal Condition in Canada* (Toronto: McGraw-Hill Ryerson, 1987), 87–90; and Robert Young, ed., *Stretching the Federation: The Art of State in Canada* (Montreal: McGill-Queen's University Press, 1999).

13. See David Baldwin, *Economic Statecraft* (Princeton, NJ: Princeton University Press, 1985).

14. Raymond Duncan et al., *World Politics in the 21st Century* (New York: Longman, 2002), 64.

15. See Michael Byers, *The Role of Law in International Politics* (New York: Oxford University Press, 2001).

16. Paul Kennedy, *The Rise and Fall of the Great Powers* (New York: Random House, 1988); and John Mearshimer, *The Tragedy of Great Power Politics* (New York: W.W. Norton, 2001).

17. See Michael Sullivan, *Power in International Relations* (Columbia, SC: University of South Carolina Press, 1990); and Charles Kegley Jr. and Eugene Wittkopf, *World Politics: Trend and Transformation* (New York: Thompson Wadsworth, 2004).

18. Hans Morgenthau, *Politics among Nations*, brief ed., revised by Kenneth Thompson (New York: Knopf, 1993), 116.

Chapter 4

1. Karl W. Deutsch, Jorge Dominguez, and Hugh Heclo, *Comparative Government: Politics of Industrialized and Developing Nations* (Boston: Houghton Mifflin Company, 1981), 13. See also S.E. Finer, *The History of Government from the Earliest Time*, Vols. I–III (New York: Oxford University Press, 1999).

2. See James H. Meisel, *Pareto & Mosca* (Englewood Cliffs, NJ: Prentice Hall, 1965), 57–62, 141–160.

3. David Truman, *The Governmental Process* (New York: Knopf, 1951). See also Clark Power and Daniel Lapsley, eds., *The Challenge of Pluralism* (South Bend, IN: University of Notre Dame Press, 1993).

4. Gabriel Almond and Sidney Verba, *The Civic Culture Revisited* (Boston: Little, Brown, 1980).

5. Allan Kornberg, "Caucus and Cohesion in Canadian Parliamentary Parties," *American Political Science Review* 60 (March 1966): 83–92.

6. Bernard Crick, *In Defence of Politics* (London: Weidenfeld and Nicolson, 1964), 56.

7. See Patrick Watson and Benjamin Barber, *The Struggle for Democracy* (Toronto: Lester & Orpen Dennys Ltd., 1988), 79.

8. Richard Van Loon and Michael Whittington, *The Canadian Political System: Environment, Structure and Process* (Toronto: McGraw-Hill Ryerson Ltd. 1981), 630–636; and Gregory Inwood, *Understanding Canadian Public Administration* (Toronto: Pearson Education, 2004), Chap. 12.

9. Gregory Mahler and Donald MacInnis, *Comparative Politics* (Toronto: Prentice Hall, 2002), 94–97.

10. Benjamin Ginsberg, Theodore Lowi, Margaret Weir, *We the People: An Introduction to American Politics*, 6th ed. (New York: W.W. Norton & Company, 2007), 16–17.

11. See Alan Cafruny and Glenda Rosenthal, *The State of the European Community*, Vol. 2: *The Maastricht Debates and Beyond* (Boulder, CO: Lynne Rienner Publishers, 1993); and Kelly Kate Pease, *International Organizations* (Upper Saddle River, NJ: Prentice–Hall, 2000), 25–28.

12. See Gabriel Almond et al., *Comparative Politics Today: A World View*, 7th ed. (New York: Longman, 2000).

13. George Thomas Kurian, ed., *The Illustrated Book of World Rankings*, 5th ed. (Armonk, NY: M.E. Sharpe Inc., 2001), 77–91.

14. Carl J. Friedrich and Zbigniew Brzezinski, *Totalitarian Dictatorship and Autocracy* (New York: Praeger Publishers, 1956), 9–10; and Alan Ebenstein, et al., *Today's Isms*, 11th ed., (Upper Saddle River, NJ: Prentice-Hall, 2001).

15. Nancy Love, ed., *Dogmas and Dreams: A Reader in Modern Political Ideologies*, 3d ed. (New York: Seven Bridges Press, 2006).

Chapter 5

1. William Haviland et al., *Cultural Anthropology* (Toronto: Nelson, 2005), 318–351.

2. David Johnson, *Thinking Government*, 2d ed. (Peterborough, ON, 2006), 209–222.

3. Gary Wasserman, *The Basics of American Politics* (New York: Pearson Education, Inc. 2008), 72–76.

4. Donald Savoie, *Governing from the Centre* (Toronto: University of Toronto Press, 1999), 81–95; and David Smith, *The Invisible Crown: The First Principle of Canadian Government* (Toronto: University of Toronto Press, 1995).

5. Milton Cummings Jr. and David Wise, *Democracy under Pressure*, 9th ed. (Fort Worth, TX.: Harcourt College Publishers, 2001), 437–442.

6. Michael Curtis et al., *Introduction to Comparative Government* (New York: HarperCollins College Publishers, 1993), 1–26.

7. See Peter Aucoin, "Prime Minister and Cabinet" in James Bickerton and Alain Gagnon, eds., *Canadian Politics* (Peterborough, ON: Broadview Press, 1999).

8. "Canadians Think the Queen Is Just Fine," *Weekend Magazine*, October 2, 1977: 4. See also "The Queen's Eroding Role," *MacLean's* (June 15, 1992): 32; and David Smith, *The Republican Option in Canada, Past and Present* (Toronto: University of Toronto Press, 1999).

9. Stephen Brooks, *Canadian Politics* (Toronto: Oxford University Press, 2004), 218–259.

10. Leslie Pal and David Taras, eds., *Prime Ministers and Premiers: Political Leadership and Public Policy in Canada* (Scarborough, ON: Prentice-Hall Canada, 1988). See also Kim Campbell, *Time and Chance: The Political Memoirs of Canada's First Woman Prime Minister* (Toronto: Doubleday Canada, 1996).

11. Robert Jackson, Doreen Jackson, *Politics in Canada* (Toronto: Pearson Education Canada, 2009), 290–293; and Jeffrey Simpson, *The Friendly Dictatorship* (Toronto: McClelland & Stewart, 2001).

12. Privy Council Office, *Decision-Making Processes and Central Agencies in Canada: Federal, Provincial and Territorial Practices* (Ottawa, 1998).

13. Karen O'Connor and Larry Sabato, *American Government* (New York: Addison Wesley Longman, Inc., 2002), 480–488.

14. Richard Neustadt, *Presidential Power* (New York: New American Library, 1964), viii.

15. William Young, *Essentials of American Government* (New York: Appleton-Century-Crofts 1964), 251.

16. Gregory Mahler and Donald MacInnis, *Comparative Politics* (Toronto: Pearson Education, 2002), 51–53.

17. Jay Taylor, *The Rise and Fall of Totalitarianism in the Twentieth Century* (New York: Paragon, 1993), 3–21; and Juan Linz, *Totalitarian and Authoritarian Regimes* (Boulder, CO: Lynne Rienner Publishers, 2000).

Chapter 6

1. See Gregory Mahler and Donald MacInnis, *Comparative Politics: An Institutional and Cross-National Approach* (Toronto: Prentice-Hall, 2002), 77–82.

2. Based on comparisons of legislatures described in Brian Hunter, ed., *Stateman's Year Book, 2003* (London: Macmillan Press, 2003).

3. Hanna F. Pitkin, "The Concept of Representation," in Pitkin, ed., *Representation* (New York: Atherton Press, 1969), 16.

4. Paul Fox and Graham White, *Politics: Canada*, 6th ed. (Toronto: McGraw-Hill Ryerson, 1987), 453–500. See also *Parliamentary Names & Numbers* (Ottawa: Renouf Publishing Co., 2004), and www.sources.com.

5. Kenneth Kernaghan and David Siegel, *Public Administration in Canada* (Scarborough, ON: Nelson Canada, 1995), 640–655.

6. Martin Westmacott, "Whips and Party Cohesion," *Canadian Parliamentary Review* (Autumn 1983): 14–19.

7. Gordon Robertson, *A House Divided: Meech Lake, Senate Reform and the Canadian Union* (Halifax: Institute for Research on Public Policy, 1989); Roger Gibbins, *Senate Reform: Moving toward the Slippery Slope* (Kingston, ON: Institute of Intergovernmental Relations, Queen's University, 1983), 1–50; and Canada, *Report of the Special Joint Committee of the Senate and the House of Commons on Senate Reform* (Ottawa, January 1984).

8. Susan Welch, John Gruhl, et al., *Understanding American Government*, 6th ed. (Belmont, CA: Wadsworth/Thomson Learning, 2001), 282–319. See also Barbara Sinclair, *Legislators, Leaders, and Lawmaking: The US House of Representatives in the Post-Reform Era* (Baltimore, MD: Johns Hopkins Press, 1999).

9. Thomas Dye, *Politics in America* (Upper Saddle River, NJ: Prentice-Hall, 2001), 348–353.

10. Constantine Danopoulos, *From Military to Civilian Rule* (New York: Routledge, 1991), 200–288.

11. Robert Fatton Jr., *Predatory Rule: State and Civil Society in Africa* (Boulder, CO: Lynne Rienner Publishers, 1992), 60–185.

12. World Bank, *World Development Report, 1993* (New York: Oxford University Press, 1993).

13. See James Danziger, *Understanding the Political World* (New York: Pearson Education, 2005), 256–257.

14. Lucian Pye, *China: An Introduction*, 4th ed. (New York: HarperCollins, 1991), 35–57.

Chapter 7

1. Stanley Udy Jr., *Organization of Work: A Comparative Analysis of Production among Non-industrial Peoples* (New Haven: HRAF Press, 1959), 10–35; Max Weber, *Economy and Society* (New York: Bedminster Press, 1968).

2. Donald Kagan, Steven Ozment, et al., *The Western Heritage since 1300* (New York: Macmillan Publishing Co., Inc., 1983), 550–553.

3. See Joel Aberback and Robert Putman et al., *Bureaucrats and Politicians in Western Democracies* (Cambridge, MA: Harvard University Press, 1981); and see Gabriel Almond and G. Bingham Powell Jr. et al., eds., *Comparative Politics Today: A World View* (New York: Longman, 2000), 121–144.

4. Economic Council of Canada, *Responsible Regulation* (Ottawa: November 1979), 16; Hugh Segal, "The Accountability of Public Servants," *Policy Options 2* (5) (November–December, 1981): 11–13.

5. United Nations, *Yearbook of National Account Statistics, 2006* (New York: United Nations, 2006).

6. Guy S. Claire, *Administocracy* (New York: Crowell-Collier and Macmillan, Inc., 1934). See also James J. Guy, "Administocracy," in *International Encyclopedia of Public Policy and Administration* (New York: Westview Press, 1999), 27–29.

7. The Prime Minister's Office, press release (Ottawa, June 25, 1993).

8. J. Johnson, "The Role of the Deputy Minister," in Kenneth Kernaghan, ed., *Public Administration in Canada: Selected Readings*, 5th ed. (Toronto: Methuen, 1985), 293–297.

9. Flora MacDonald, "Cutting through the Chains," *Globe and Mail*, November 7, 1980: 7; and Treasury Board Secretariat, *Guidelines for Ministers' Offices* (Ottawa: Her Majesty the Queen in Right of Canada, 2006), Appendix A.

10. Donald Savoie, *Breaking the Bargain: Public Servants, Ministers and Parliament* (Toronto: University of Toronto Press, 2003), 136–147.

11. Gregory Inwood, *Understanding Canadian Public Administration: An Introduction to Theory and Practice* (Toronto: Pearson Education Canada, 2004), Chap. 5.

12. Paul Barker, *Public Administration in Canada* (Toronto: Nelson, 2008), Chap. 11.

13. Thomas Dye, *Politics in America* (Upper Saddle River, NJ: Prentice Hall, 2001), 451–460.

14. Milton Cummings and David Wise, *Democracy under Pressure* (Fort Worth, TX: Harcourt Brace Jovanovich College Publishers, 2001), 455–485.

Chapter 8

1. B.N. Cardozo, *The Growth of the Law* (New Haven: Yale University Press, 1924).

2. E. Adamson Hoebel, *The Law of Primitive Man* (New York: Athenaeum Press, 1968), 4.

3. Quoted in H.A.L. Fisher, *The Collected Papers of Frederic William Maitland* (Buffalo, NY: W.S. Hein, 1981), 173.

4. See Jerome Frank, *Law and the Modern Mind* (New York: Coward-McCann, 1949), 46; Beryl Levy, *Cardozo and Frontiers of Legal Thinking* (Cleveland, OH: Press of Case Western Reserve University, 1969), 31.

5. See C. Yerbury and C. Griffiths, "Minorities, Crime, and the Law," in M. Jackson and C. Griffiths, eds., *Canadian Criminology: Perspectives on Crime and Criminality* (Toronto: Harcourt Brace Jovanovich, 1991), 315–346.

6. Richard Yates and Ruth Yates, *Canada's Legal Environment* (Scarborough, ON: Prentice Hall Canada Inc., 1993), 56–82; and Janie Trembley, *Comparative Analysis: The Common Law and Civil Law Tradition in the Canadian Context* (Vancouver: University of British Columbia Press, 1998).

7. Donald Kagan et al., *The Western Heritage since 1300* (New York: Macmillan Publishing Co., 1983), (I-23)–(I-41).

8. See John Esposito, ed., *Islam and Development: Religion and Sociopolitical Change* (New York: Syracuse University Press, 1980), ix.

9. A. Wayne Mackay, "Judicial Free Speech and Accountability: Should Judges Be Seen but Not Heard?" *National Journal of Constitutional Law* 3(2) (October 1993): 159–242.

10. See P. McCormick and I. Greene, *Judges and Judging: Inside the Judicial System* (Toronto: Lorimer, 1990), Chap. 4; and see also James Snell and Frederick Vaughan, *The Supreme Court of Canada: History of the Institution* (Montreal: Institute for Research on Public Policy, 1999).

11. Milton Cummings Jr. and David Wise, *Democracy under Pressure*, 9th ed., (Fort Worth, TX: Harcourt Brace, 2001), 492–527.

12. Kermit Hall, ed., *Oxford Companion to the Supreme Court* (New York: Oxford University Press, 1992).

13. James MacGregor Burns et al., *Government by the People* (Upper Saddle River, NJ: Pearson Prentice Hall, 2004), 376–403.

Chapter 9

1. Mark Hagopian, *Regimes, Movements and Ideologies* (New York: Longman Inc., 1984), 38–39.

2. J.R. Pennock and David Smith, *Political Science* (London: Collier-Macmillan Limited, 1965), 241.

3. Robert Jackson and Doreen Jackson, *Contemporary Government and Politics* (Scarborough, ON: Prentice-Hall Canada, Inc., 2001), 167–201.

4. See Keith Banting and Richard Simeon, eds., *Redesigning the State: The Process of Constitutional Change in Industrialized Nations* (Toronto: University of Toronto Press, 1985), Chap. 1.

5. See Donald Abelson et al., *The Myth of the Sacred: The Charter, the Courts and the Politics of the Constitution in Canada* (Montreal: McGill-Queen's University Press, 2002).

6. David Schneiderman, *Freedom of Expression and the Charter* (Toronto: Thomson Professional Publishing Company Limited, 1991), Introduction. See also Christopher Manfredi, *Judicial Power and the Charter: Canada and the Paradox of Liberal Constitutionalism* (Toronto: Oxford University Press, 2001).

7. See Peter Hogg, *Constitutional Law of Canada* (Toronto: Carswell, 1999), 7–25.

8. Bayard Reesor, *The Canadian Constitution in Historical Perspective* (Scarborough, ON: Prentice-Hall Canada Inc., 1992), 45–50; and Robin Boardway, *The Constitutional Division of Powers* (Ottawa: Supply and Services, 1992).

9. Peter Russell, *Constitutional Odyssey* (Toronto: University of Toronto Press, 1993).

10. See Garth Stevenson, *Unfulfilled Union: Canadian Federalism and National Unity*, 4th ed. (Montreal: McGill-Queen's University Press, 2004), 17–38.

11. See Marc Kilgour, "A Formal Analysis of the Amending Formula of Canada's *Constitution Act, 1982*," *Canadian Journal of Political Science* 16 (4) (December 1983): 772–777.

12. F.L. Morton, *Law, Politics and the Judicial Process in Canada* (Calgary, AB: University of Calgary Press, 1984), 2.

13. See K.E. Swinton and C.J. Rogerson, *Competing Constitutional Visions* (Toronto: Carswell, 1988); and Christopher Moore, *1867: How the Fathers Made a Deal* (Toronto: McClelland & Stewart, 1997).

14. Patrick Monahan and Ken McRoberts, *The Charlottetown Accord* (Toronto: University of Toronto Press, 1993).

15. Thomas Dye, *Politics in America* (Upper Saddle River, NJ: Pearson Education, Inc., 2007), 79–80.

16. Lee Epstein and Thomas Walker, *Constitutional Law for a Changing America: Institutional Power and Constraints*, 4th ed. (Washington, DC: CQ Press, 2001), 61–77.

17. Karen O'Connor and Larry Sabato, *American Government Continuity and Change* (New York: Addison Wesley Longman, 2002), 34–68.

Chapter 10

1. Lily Ross Taylor, *Party Politics in the Age of Caesar* (Berkeley: University of California Press, 1961), 6–23.

2. Sir Randol Fawkes, *The Faith That Moved the Mountain* (Nassau, Bahamas: Nassau Guardian, 1979), 211.

3. Leon Epstein, *Political Parties in Western Democracies* (New York: Frederick A. Praeger, Inc., 1967), 9; and William Cross, *Political Parties* (Vancouver: UBC Press, 2004).

4. Maurice Duverger, *Political Politics and Pressure Groups* (New York: Thomas Nelson and Sons, 1972), 5.

5. See Janine Brodie and Jan Jenson, "Piercing the Smokescreen: Brokerage Parties and Class Politics," in Alain Gagnon and Brian Tanguay, eds., *Canadian Parties in Transition* (Scarborough, ON: Nelson Canada, 1989), 24–44.

6. Roy Macridis, *Modern Political Regimes Patterns and Institutions* (Boston: Little, Brown & Co., 1986), 64–70.

7. Gabriel Almond and G. Bingham Powell Jr., *Comparative Politics Today: A World View* (Glenview, IL: Scott, Foresman and Company, 1988), 82–88.

8. Kenneth Kernaghan and David Siegel, *Public Administration in Canada* (Scarborough, ON: Nelson Canada, 1999), 459–532.

9. Arend Lijphart, *Electoral Systems and Party Systems: A Study of Twenty-Seven Democracies, 1945–1990* (New York: Oxford University Press, 1994); Hugh Thorburn and Alan Whitehorn, eds., *Party Politics in Canada*, 8th ed. (Toronto: Prentice-Hall, 2001).

10. Ronald McDonald and J. Mark Ruhl, *Party Politics and Elections in Latin America* (Boulder, CO: Westview Press, 1989), 20–35.

11. John Green and Daniel Shea, eds., *The State of the Parties: The Changing Role of Contemporary American Parties* (Lanham, MD: Rowman and Littlefield, 1999), 102–134.

12. Janine Brodie and Jane Jenson, *Crisis, Challenge & Change: Party & Class in Canada* (Toronto: Methuen, 1988), passim; and R.K. Carty et al., *Rebuilding Canadian Party Politics* (Vancouver: University of British Columbia Press, 2000).

13. See Alain Gagnon and Brian Tanguay, "Minor Parties of Protest in Canada: Origins, Impact and Prospects," in Alain Gagnon and Brian Tanguay, eds., *Canadian Parties in Transition* (Peterborough, ON: Broadview Press, 2007), 225–253.

14. Rand Dyck, *Provincial Politics in Canada* (Scarborough, ON: Prentice-Hall Canada, 1991), 1–31, 626.

15. Ronald McDonald, *Party Systems and Elections in Latin America* (Boulder, CO: Westview Press 1971), 17.

16. See Oligarchy in Jack Plano and Milton Greenberg, *The American Political Dictionary*, 11th ed. (Belmont, California: Wadsworth, 2001).

17. See Robert Michels, *Political Parties* (New York: The Free Press, 1962).

18. See Rand Dyck, "Relations between Federal and Provincial Parties," in Alain Gagnon and Brian Tanguay, eds., *Canadian Parties in Transition* (Scarborough, ON: Nelson Canada, 1989), 186–219.

19. See *Electoral Insight*, 5 (1): March 2003), 36.

20. See www.elections.ca/ election contributions.

21. W. Philips Shively, *Power Choice* (New York: McGraw-Hill, 232-33.

22. Alan Whitehorn, *Canadian Socialism: Essays on the CCF-NDP* (Don Mills, ON: Oxford University Press, 1997).

23. William Cross, ed., *Political Parties, Representation, and Electoral Democracy in Canada* (Toronto: Oxford University Press, 2002).

24. See Hugh Thorburn, *Party Politics in Canada* (Scarborough ON: Prentice-Hall, 2001) 307-337.

25. O.P. Dwivedi, ed., *The Administrative State in Canada* (Toronto: University of Toronto Press, 1982) 233-250

26. See Christina McCall-Newman, *Grits: An Intimate Portrait of the Liberal Party* (Toronto: Macmillan of Canada, 1982).

27. See N.K. O'Sullivan, *Conservatism* (New York: St. Martin's Press, 1976).

28. See Robert Stanfield, "Conservative Principles and Philosophy," in Paul Fox, ed., *Politics Canada*, 7th ed. (Toronto: McGraw-Hill Ryerson Ltd., 1991), 297–300.

29. Quoted from the CBC Radio program "The House," aired June 11, 1983.

30. William Christian and Colin Campbell, "Political Parties and Ideologies in Canada," in Alain Gagnon and Brian Tanguay, eds., *Canadian Parties in Transition* (Toronto: Nelson Canada, 1996).

31. See Rod Preece, "The Political Wisdom of Sir John A. Macdonald," *Canadian Journal of Political Science* 7 (3) (September 1984): 459–486.

32. George Perlin, *The Tory Syndrome: Leadership Politics in the Progressive Conservative Party* (Montreal: McGill-Queen's University Press, 1980).

33. Reform Party of Canada, "Summary of Assembly Results," (Memorandum to Members), December 15, 1989.

34. See Hugh Thorburn and Alan Whitehorn, eds., *Party Politics in Canada*, 8th ed. (Toronto: Prentice-Hall, 2001); and Anthony Sayers, *Parties, Candidates,*

and Constituency Campaigns in Canadian Elections (Vancouver: UBC Press, 1999).

35. Kenneth Carty et al., *Canadian Party Politics for the 21st Century* (Vancouver: UBC Press, 2000).

36. See Paul Pross, "Pressure Groups: Talking Chameleons," in M.S. Whittington and G. Williams, eds., *Canadian Politics in the 1990s* (Scarborough, ON: Nelson Canada, 1990), 285–309; William Coleman and Grace Skogstad, eds., *Policy Communities and Public Policy in Canada* (Toronto: Copp Clark Pitman, 1990), Introduction.

37. Leslie Pal, *Interests of State* (Montreal: McGill-Queen's University Press, 1992), especially Chap. 6; and Joanna Everitt and Brenda O'Neill, eds., *Citizen Politics: Research and Theory in Canadian Political Behaviour* (Don Mills, ON: Oxford University Press, 2002), 16–44.

38. See Paul Pross, ed., *Pressure Group Behaviour in Canadian Politics* (Toronto: McGraw-Hill, 1975); Hugh Thorburn, *Interest Groups in the Canadian Federal System* (Toronto: University of Toronto Press, 1986), 69.

39. Gabriel Almond and G. Bingham Powell Jr., eds., *Comparative Politics Today: A World View*, 7th ed. (New York: Longman, 2000), 56–67; and Luigi Graziano, *Lobbying, Pluralism and Democracy* (London: St. Martin's Press, 2001), 22–51.

40. See Robert Pape, "The Strategic Logic of Suicide Terrorism," *American Political Science Review* 97 (3) (August 2003): 20–32.

Chapter 11

1. T.H. Jacobson, "Primitive Democracy in Ancient Mesopotamia," *Journal of New Eastern Studies* 11 (1943): 159–172.

2. Mark Franklin, *Voter Turnout and the Dynamics of Electoral Competition in Established Democracies since 1945* (Cambridge, UK: Cambridge University Press, 2004).

3. Jon Pammett and Lawrence LeDuc, "Evaluating the Turnout Decline in Canadian Federal Elections: A New Survey of Non-voters," (Ottawa: Elections Canada, 2003); Lawrence LeDuc and Jon Pammett, "Voter Turnout in 2006: More than Just the Weather," in Jon Pammett and Christopher Dornan, eds., *The Canadian Federal Election of 2006* (Toronto: Dundurn Press, 2006).

4. Paul Fox, "Electing a Canadian Government," in Paul Fox, ed., *Politics: Canada*, 5th ed. (Toronto: McGraw-Hill Ryerson Ltd., 1982), 368; Elections Canada, *A History of the Vote in Canada* (Ottawa: Minister of Public Works and Government Services Canada, 1997).

5. See David Taras, *Power and Betrayal in the Canadian Media* (Peterborough, ON: Broadview Press, 1999), Chap. 8; John Miller, *Yesterday's News: Why Canada's Daily Newspapers Are Failing Us* (Halifax: Fernwood Publishing, 1998), Chap. 1; James Winter, *Democracy's Oxygen: How Corporations Control the News* (Montreal: Black Rose, 1997).

6. See André Blais, *To Vote or Not to Vote? The Merits and Limits of Rational Choice Theory* (Pittsburgh: University of Pittsburgh Press, 2000); and Henry Milner, ed., *Making Every Vote Count: Reassessing Canada's Electoral System* (Peterborough, ON: Broadview Press, 1999).

7. Gregory Mahler and Donald MacInnis, *Comparative Politics: An Institutional and Cross-National Approach* (Toronto: Prentice-Hall, 2002), Chap. 15; Juan Linz, *Totalitarian and Authoritarian Regimes* (Boulder, CO: Lynne Rienner Publishers, 2000).

8. See Douglas Amy, *Behind the Ballot Box: A Citizen's Guide to Voting Systems* (Westport, CT: GPG-Greenwood Publishing Group, 2000); Neil Nevitte et al., *Uneasy Status Quo: The 1997 Canadian Federal Election* (Toronto: Oxford University Press, 1999).

9. Herman Bakvis and Laura MacPherson, "Quebec Bloc Voting and the Canadian Electoral System," *Canadian Journal of Political Science*, 28 (4) (1995): 659–692; Dennis Pilon, *Canada's Democratic Deficit: Is Proportional Representation the Answer?* (Toronto: CSL Foundation for Research and Education, 2000).

10. William Irvine, "The Electoral System: The Laws of Political Science as Applied to the 1988 Federal Election," in Hugh Thorburn, ed., *Party Politics in Canada*, 6th ed. (Scarborough, ON: Prentice-Hall Canada, 1991), 87–93.

11. See Paul Fox, "Should Canada Adopt Proportional Representation?" in Paul Fox and Graham White, *Politics: Canada*, 7th ed. (Toronto: McGraw-Hill Ryerson Limited, 1991), 343–350.

12. James John Guy, *Expanding Our Political Horizons: Readings in Canadian Politics and Government* (Toronto:

Harcourt Brace, 1997), 194–195; Daniel Pellern and Patrick Thomson, "Proportional Representation Is Likely to Create More Problems than It Would Solve: The Single Transferable Vote Offers a Better Choice," *Policy Options* (October 2004): 54–59.

13. Canada, *Royal Commission on Electoral Reform and Party Financing*. Reports, 4 vols. (Ottawa: The Canada Communication Group-Publishing, 1992); Law Commission of Canada, *Voting Counts: Electoral Reform of Canada* (Ottawa: Minister of Public Works, 2004).

14. Lawrence Leduc and Richard Price, "Campaign Debates and Party Leader Images: The 'Encounter 88 Case,'" *Canadian Political Science Association* (Victoria, 1990); David Lanoue, "Debates That Mattered: Voters' Reaction to the 1984 Canadian Leadership Debates," *Canadian Journal of Political Science* (March 1991): 51–65.

15. Thomas Dye, *Politics in America*, 7th ed. (Upper Saddle River, NJ: Prentice-Hall, 2007), 263–277.

16. Paul Beck and Marjorie Hershey, *Party Politics in America* (New York: Longman, 2005), 115–137; Gary Wasserman, *The Basics of American Politics* (New York: Pearson Education, 2008), 194–230.

Chapter 12

1. For comprehensive analyses of the "actors" in the international systems, see Raymond Duncan, Barbara Jancar-Webster, and Bob Switky, *World Politics in the 21st Century* (New York: Longman, 2002), 60–84.

2. Barry Buzan and Richard Little, *International Systems in World History* (Oxford: Oxford University Press, 2000).

3. John Rourke, *International Politics on the World Stage* (Guilford, CT: Dushkin Publishing Group, Inc., 2002), 60–61.

4. Lawrence Ziring, Robert Riggs, and Jack Plano, *The United Nations: International Organization and World Politics*, 3d ed. (Orlando, FL: Harcourt Brace & Company, 2000); and *Basic Facts about the United Nations* (New York: United Nations, 2002).

5. Until October 25, 1971, the Chinese seat on the Security Council was occupied by the Republic of China (Taiwan). After that date, the Chinese seat was occupied by the People's Republic of China.

6. Kofi Annan, *General Statement to the General Assembly*, Millennium of 2000 (New York: United Nations, September 6–8, 2000).

7. See Adrian Hyde-Price, *European Security beyond the Cold War: Four Scenarios for the Year 2010* (Beverly Hills, CA: Sage Publications, 1991); Jolyon Howorth and John Keeler, *Defending Europe: The EU, NATO, and the Quest for European Autonomy* (New York: Palgrave Macmillan, 2003).

8. Bernard Hoekman and Michael Kostecki, *The Political Economy of the World Trading System: From GATT to WTO* (New York: Oxford University Press, 1999).

9. James J. Guy, "Canada Joins the OAS: A New Dynamic in the OAS," *Inter-American Review of Bibliography* 39 (4) (1989): 500–511.

10. See Winifred Ruigrok, "International Corporate Strategies and Restructuring," in Richard Stubbs and Geoffrey Underhill, eds., *Political Economy and the Changing World Order* (Don Mills, ON: Oxford University Press, 2000).

11. Raymond Duncan, Barbara Jancar-Webster, and Bob Switky, *World Politics in the 21st Century* (New York: Longman, 2002), 254–286.

12. See Glen Hastedt and Kay Knickrehm, *International Politics in a Changing World* (New York: Longman, 2003), 110–113.

13. See David Saari, *Global Corporations and Sovereign Nations: Collision or Cooperation* (Westport, CT: Quorum/Greenwood, 1999).

14. *White House Statement on Domestic Preparedness against Weapons of Mass Destruction* (Released May 8, 2001).

15. James N. Rosenau and Michael Fagan, "A New Dynamism in World Politics: Increasingly Skillful Individuals," *International Studies Quarterly* 41 (1997): 655–686; Ronnie Lipschutz, *After Authority: War, Peace and Global Politics in the 21st Century* (Albany, NY: SUNY Press, 2000), 3.

16. John Holmes, *Canada: A Middle-Aged Power* (Toronto: McClelland and Stewart Ltd., 1976), 66.

17. James J. Guy, "The Growing Relationship of Canada and the Americas," *International Perspectives* (July–August 1977); and James Rochlin, *Discovering the Americas: The Evolution of Canadian Foreign Policy Towards Latin America* (Vancouver: University of British Columbia Press, 1994).

18. Barbara Ward, "The First International Nation," in William Kilbourn, ed., *Canada: A Guide to the Peaceful Kingdom* (Toronto: Macmillan, 1970), 45–48; and see Stephen Brooks, "Globalization and Its Consequences in Canada," in Kenneth Pyke and Walter Soderlund, *Profiles of Canada* (Toronto: Canadian Scholars' Press Inc., 2003), 223–248.

19. See Gregory Mahler and Donald MacInnis, *Comparative Politics* (Toronto: Prentice Hall, 2002), 255.

20. See John Rothgeb, *US Trade Policy: Balancing Economic Dreams and Political Realities* (Washington, DC: CQ Press, 2001).

21. See Duncan Cameron and Mel Watkins, *Canada under Free Trade* (Toronto: James Lorimer & Company Ltd., 1993); Tom Keating, *Canada and World Order*, 2d ed. (Toronto: McClelland & Stewart, 2002).

22. Gregory Hein, *Interest Group Litigation and Canadian Democracy* (Montreal: Institute for Research and Public Policy, 2000; Lisa Young and Joanna Everitt, *Advocacy Groups* (Vancouver: UBC Press, 2004); Al Gore, *An Inconvenient Truth* (New York: Melcher Media/Rodale, 2006).

Chapter 13

1. See Richard Falk, *Revitalizing International Law* (Ames, IA: Iowa State University Press, 1989); and John Rawls, *The Law of Peoples* (Cambridge, MA: Harvard University Press, 1999).

2. See Hugh Kindred et al., *International Law Chiefly as Interpreted and Applied in Canada*, 4th ed. (Toronto: Edmond Montgomery Publications, 1987), 1–10; Michael Byers, *Custom, Power and the Power of Rules* (Cambridge: Cambridge University Press, 2000).

3. Christos Rozakis, *The Concept of* Ius Cogens *in the Law of Treaties* (Amsterdam: North-Holland Publishing Company, 1976), 1–10.

4. See Lung-chu Chen, *An Introduction to Contemporary International Law: A Policy-Oriented Perspective* (New Haven, CT: Yale University Press, 1989), Chap. 1.

5. See Thomas Franck, *The Power of Legitimacy among Nations* (New York: Oxford University Press, 1990); and also Thomas Franck, "The Emerging Right to Democratic Governance," *The American Journal of International Law* 86 (1992): 46–91.

6. See Peter Toma and Robert Gorman, *International Relations: Understanding Global Issues* (Pacific Grove, CA: Brooks/Cole Publishing Company, 1991), Chap. 10; William Kaplan and Donald McRae, *Law, Policy, and International Justice* (Montreal: McGill-Queen's University Press, 1993).

7. See A. Watts, "The International Rule of Law," *German Yearbook of International Law* 15 (1993).

8. Gerhard von Glahn, *Law among Nations*, 6th ed. (New York: Maxwell Macmillan, 1996), 14–17.

9. Ibid., 12–13.

10. See Nagendra Singh, *The Role and Record of the International Court of Justice* (Dordrecht, The Netherlands: Martinus Nijhoff, 1989).

11. Wolfgang Friedmann, "The Uses of 'General Principles' in the Development of International Law," *American Journal of International Law* 57 (1963): 279–299; Josef L. Kunz, "Natural Law Thinking in the Modern Science of International Law," *American Journal of International Law* 55 (1961): 951–958.

12. S.A. Williams and A.L. de Mestral, *Introduction to International Law* (Toronto: Butterworths, 1979), 27.

13. See Barcelona Traction Case, *International Court of Justice Reports* (1970), 3, 42.

14. See M.S. McDougal and M. Reisman, eds., *International Law in Contemporary Perspective* (Mineola, NY: Foundation Press, 1981); Robert Turner, "International Law, the Use of Force, and Reciprocity: A Comment on Professor Higgins' Overview," *The Atlantic Community Quarterly* 25 (1987): 160–174.

15. Kenneth Abbott and Duncan Snidal, "Hard and Soft Law in International Governance," *International Organization* 54 (2000): 421–456.

Chapter 14

1. Lewis Eigen and Jonathan Seigel, eds., *The Macmillan Dictionary of Political Quotations* (Toronto: Maxwell Macmillan, 1993), 227.

2. Jessica Stern, *Terror in the Name of God: Why Religious Militants Kill* (New York: HarperCollins, 2003).

3. John Ravenhill, ed., *Global Political Economy* (New York: Oxford University Press, 2005).

4. David Johnson, *Thinking Government* (Peterborough, ON, 2006), 439.

5. Innovative Research Group, Inc. *Visions of Canadian Foreign Policy*, (Ottawa: The Dominion Institute, November 4, 2004).

6. The mood theory concept was originally conceived by Frank Klingberg. See Jack Holmes, *The Mood/Interest Theory of Foreign Policy* (Lexington: University of Kentucky, 1985).

7. Dean Rusk, "American Foreign Policy in the Eighties," (Washington, DC: LTV Washington Seminar, 1980).

8. See Peter Toma and Robert Gorman, *International Relations* (Pacific Cove, CA: Brooks/Cole Publishing Company, 1991), 289.

9. See Robert Hopkins Miller et al., *Inside an Embassy: The Political Role of Diplomats Abroad* (Washington, DC: Congressional Quarterly Press, 1992).

10. See Grant McClanahan, *Diplomatic Immunity: Principles, Practices and Problems* (New York: St. Martin's Press, 1989).

11. See Hans Tuch, *Communicating with the World* (New York: St. Martin's Press, 1990); and Dean Minix and Sandra Hawley, *Global Politics* (New York: Wadsworth Publishing, 1998).

12. *Rose v. The King* (1946), 88 C.C.C. 114 (Que. C.A.).

13. Foreign Affairs and International Trade Canada, *Canadian Embassies*. Online at: www.international.gc.ca/ciw-cdm/embassies-ambassades.aspx?lang=eng.

14. See Martin Herz, *The Consular Dimension of Diplomacy* (Washington, DC: Institute for the Study of Diplomacy, Georgetown University, 1983).

15. Gerhard von Glahn and James Taulbee, *Law among Nations: An Introduction to International Law*, 8th ed. (New York: Pearson Education, 2007), Chap. 15.

16. Sir Harold Nicolson, *Diplomacy*, 4th ed. (New York: Oxford University Press, 1988), 23.

17. Abba Solomon Eban, *Diplomacy for the Next Century* (New Haven, CT: Yale University Press, 1999), 17–28.

18. Gene Grossman and Elhanan Helpman, *Special Interest Politics* (Boston: MIT Press, 2001).

Chapter 15

1. Robert Keohane and Joseph Nye Jr., "Globalization: What's New? What's Not? (and So What?)" *Foreign Policy* 115 (Spring 2003): 1014–1119.

2. John Micklethwait and Adrian Wooldridge, "The Hidden Promise of Globalization: Liberty Renewed," in Terrence Ball and Richard Dagger, *Ideals and Ideologies* (New York: Pearson Education, 2006), 474–482.

3. Thomas Paine, *Rights of Man*, ed. Henry Collins (Middlesex, UK: Penguin Books, 1969), 238.

4. Joshua Goldstein, *International Relations* (New York: Longman, 2003), 273–278.

5. Peter Akerman and Jack Duvall, *A Force More Powerful: A Century of Non-violent Conflict* (New York: St. Martin's Press, 2001).

6. Bob Preston, ed., *Space Weapons: Earth Wars* 2d ed. (Santa Monica, CA: Rand, 2002).

7. Richard Kokoski, *Technology and the Proliferation of Nuclear Weapons* (London, UK: Oxford University Press, 1996).

8. Graham Allison, *Nuclear Terrorism: The Ultimate Preventable Catastrophe* (New York: Henry Holt, 2004); Dan Caldwell and Robert Williams Jr., *Seeking Security in an Insane World* (Lanham, MD: Rowman and Littlefield, 2006).

9. Andrew Kydd and Barbara Walter, "Sabotaging the Peace: The Politics of Extremist Violence," *International Organization* 56 (2) (2002): 263–296; and "The invisible enemy," *The Economist* (November 19, 2000).

10. Glenn Hastedt and Kay Knickrehm, *International Politics in a Changing World* (New York: Longman, 2003), 484.

11. Tatyana Soubbotina and Katherine Sheram, *Beyond Economic Growth: Meeting the Challenges of Global Development* (Washington, DC: World Bank, 2000).

12. United Nations, *World Population Prospects: The 2006 Revision and World Urbanization Prospects* (New York: United Nations, 2007).

13. See Allen Crosbie Walsh, "Special Problems in the Population Geography of Small Populations," in John Clarke, ed., *Geography and Population: Approaches and Applications* (Oxford: Pergamon Press, 1984), 69–76.

14. Thomas Malthus was a British professor of political economy whose major work, *An Essay on the Principle of Population* (1798), had a major impact on the social sciences and the development of demography.

15. Food and Agricultural Organization, *The State of Food Insecurity in the World, 1999* (Rome: FAO, 1999).

16. W.F. Batchelor, "AIDS 1988: The Science and Limits of Science," *American Psychologist* 45: 853–858.

17. *Report on the HIV/AIDS Epidemic* (Geneva: *UNAIDS*, June 2000) and Online at: www.unaids.org/epidemic_update/report/glo_estim.pdf.

18. Kofi Annan, "We Can Beat AIDS," *The New York Times*, June 25, 2001.

19. Urs Luterbacher and Detlef Sprinz, *International Relations and Global Climate Change* (Boston: MIT, 2001).

20. Murray Feshbach, *Ecological Disaster: Cleaning Up the Hidden Legacy of the Soviet Regime* (Washington, DC: Brookings, 1995).

21. Lee-Anne Broadhead, "Canada as a Rogue State: Its Shameful Performance on Climate Change," *International Journal* (Summer 2001): 461–480.

Index

Il Duce, 48
Il-sung, Kim, 155
ILC. *See* International Law
    Commission (ILC)
ILO. *See* International Labour
    Organization (ILO)
IMF. *See* International Monetary
    Fund (IMF)
immunity, 401
    history of, 401–402, 403, 404
impeachment, 116, 150, 170
imperialism, 60
*Imperialism: The Highest Stage of
    Capitalism*, 60
inalienable rights, 247
Indian Act, 43, 218
indictable crimes, 230
individual, role of, 45, 51
    global, 357
individualism, 108
indoctrination, 26
Industrial Revolution, 51
industrialization, 12
INF. *See* intermediate nuclear
    forces (INF)
infrastructure, 19, 94
initiatives, 107, 167
institutional pressure
    groups, 299
insurgencies, 25, 392
intelligence, 130
    military, 131
Intelsat. *See* International
    Telecommunications
    Satellite Organization
    (Intelsat)
Inter-American Council for
    Integral Development, 349
Inter-American Democratic
    Charter (2001), 350
inter-American system, 349, 380
Inter-American Treaty of
    Reciprocal Assistance
    (Rio Pact) (1947), 349
intercontinental ballistic missiles
    (ICBMs), 428
interest aggregation, 272

interest groups, 32, 296–297
    foreign policy and, 399
    representation, 296
intermediate nuclear forces
    (INF), 428
internalization, 25
International Atomic Energy
    Agency (IAEA), 430
International Bank for
    Reconstruction
    and Development
    (World Bank), 362
International Chamber of
    Commerce, 352
International Civil Aviation
    Organization (ICAO), 380
international co-operation, 51
International Congress Centre,
    Brussels, 119
international conventions, 374–375
International Court of
    Arbitration, 385
International Court of Justice (ICJ)
    (World Court), 344, 371,
    372, 378, 380–382, 383, 385
International Criminal Court
    (ICC), 385–386
International Democratic Union, 354
*International Environmental Politics:
    The Limits of Green
    Diplomacy*, 424
international governmental
    organizations (IGOs), 195,
    337, 339, 343
    multi-purpose, 337*t*
    proliferation of, 337, 339
international institutions, 380
International Journal, 424
International Labour Organization
    (ILO), 380
International Law Commission
    (ILC), 376–377
    codifying laws, 387–388
international law, 371
    conventions and, 374–375
    custom and, 374
    definitions of, 371, 372

endangered species and,
    375–376
international institutions and, 380
judicial decisions and, 378–379
legal principles and, 377, 378
migratory birds and, 375
NATO and, 381
sources, 372, 373, 373*f*
writings of learned experts
    and, 379
International Monetary Fund
    (IMF), 132–155, 362
international organization (IO),
    335, 336
    UN as, 344–345
International Physicians for the
    Prevention of Nuclear
    War, 335
international pressure groups, 300
International Red Cross, 352
International Seabed Authority, 363
International Telecommunications
    Satellite Organization
    (Intelsat), 425
internationalism, 41, 336
interpellation, 170
Interpol, 433
*Introduction to the Principles of Morals
    and Legislation, An*, 379
Investment Canada, 192
inviolability, 402
IO. *See* international
    organization (IO)
Ipsos-Reid, 27, 101
Irving, K. C., 10–11
Islam, 40, 353, 354
    fundamentalism, 353, 354
Islamic legal system, 225
ius cogens (law of pre-emptory
    norms), 371

J
James II, 50, 174
Janis, Irving, 48
Jean, Michaëlle, 142
Jefferson, Thomas, 50, 274
jihad, 68